The Political Life of Urban Streetscapes

Streetscapes are part of the taken-for-granted spaces of everyday urban life, yet they are also contested arenas in which struggles over identity, memory, and place shape the social production of urban space. This book examines the role that street naming has played in the political life of urban streetscapes in both historical and contemporary cities. The renaming of streets and remaking of urban commemorative landscapes have long been key strategies that different political regimes have employed to legitimize spatial assertions of sovereign authority, ideological hegemony, and symbolic power. Over the past few decades, a rich body of critical scholarship has explored the politics of urban toponymy, and the present collection brings together the works of geographers, anthropologists, historians, linguists, planners, and political scientists to examine the power of street naming as an urban place-making practice. Covering a wide range of case studies from cities in Europe, North America, Sub-Saharan Africa, and Asia, the contributions to this volume illustrate how the naming of streets has been instrumental to the reshaping of urban spatial imaginaries and the cultural politics of place.

Reuben Rose-Redwood is an Associate Professor of Geography and Chair of the Committee for Urban Studies at the University of Victoria in British Columbia, Canada. His research focuses on the cultural politics of place naming, geographies of urban memory, and the spatial history of the geo-coded world. He is the co-editor of *Performativity, Politics, and the Production of Social Space* (2014) and has published in a broad range of scholarly journals, including *Progress in Human Geography*, *Social & Cultural Geography*, *Urban History*, and the *Annals of the Association of American Geographers*. His work on the historical geography of New York's urban streetscape has also been featured in various popular media outlets, such as the Discovery Channel, the History Channel, and the *New York Times*.

Derek Alderman is a Professor in the Department of Geography at the University of Tennessee, USA. His research interests and published work focus on the role of place and street naming in the context of African American identity politics and civil rights struggles in the southeastern United States. He is co-author of *Civil*

Rights Memorials and the Geography of Memory (2008) and is perhaps best known for advancing scholarly and public understanding of the politics of naming streets after Martin Luther King, Jr. He is also frequently sought after by the news media to comment on this and other cultural issues.

Maoz Azaryahu is a Professor of Cultural Geography at the University of Haifa, Israel. His research focuses on urban and landscape semiotics as well as the cultural and historical geographies of national myths and public memory in Israel and Germany, landscapes of popular culture, the politics of street naming, and the cultural history of places and landscapes. He is the author of numerous books and articles, including *Von Wilhelmplatz zu Thälmannplatz: Politische Symbole im Öffentlicehn Leben der DDR* (1991), *State Cults: Celebrating Independence and Commemorating the Fallen in Israel 1948–1956* (1995, in Hebrew), *Tel Aviv: Mythography of a City* (2006), and *Namesakes: History and Politics of Street Naming in Israel* (2012, in Hebrew).

The Political Life of Urban Streetscapes
Naming, Politics, and Place

**Edited by Reuben Rose-Redwood,
Derek Alderman, and Maoz Azaryahu**

Routledge
Taylor & Francis Group

LONDON AND NEW YORK

First published 2018
by Routledge

2 Park Square, Milton Park, Abingdon, Oxfordshire OX14 4RN
52 Vanderbilt Avenue, New York, NY 10017

Routledge is an imprint of the Taylor & Francis Group, an informa business

First issued in paperback 2020

British Library Cataloguing-in-Publication Data
A catalogue record for this book is available from the British Library

Library of Congress Cataloging in Publication Data
Names: Rose-Redwood, Reuben, editor. | Alderman, Derek H., editor. |
Azaryahu, Maoz, editor.
Title: The political life of urban streetscapes : naming, politics, and place /
edited by Reuben Rose-Redwood, Derek Alderman, and Maoz Azaryahu.
Description: Abingdon, Oxon ; New York, NY : Routledge, 2017. |
Includes bibliographical references and index.
Identifiers: LCCN 2017004187| ISBN 9781472475091 (hardback) |
ISBN 9781315554464 (ebook)
Subjects: LCSH: Cities and towns--Political aspects. | Streetscapes (Urban
design)--Political aspects. | Public spaces--Political aspects. | Cultural
landscapes--Political aspects. | Sociology, Urban.
Classification: LCC HT113 .P64 2017 | DDC 307.76--dc23
LC record available at https://lccn.loc.gov/2017004187

ISBN: 978-1-4724-7509-1 (hbk)
ISBN: 978-0-367-66773-3 (pbk)

Typeset in Times New Roman
by Saxon Graphics Ltd, Derby

Reuben dedicates this book to Cindy, Sierra, and Riley

Derek dedicates this book to Donna

Maoz dedicates this book to his parents Yaffa and Pessach

Contents

List of figures   xi
List of tables   xiii
Notes on contributors   xv
Acknowledgments   xxi

1   The urban streetscape as political cosmos   1
REUBEN ROSE-REDWOOD, DEREK ALDERMAN, AND MAOZ AZARYAHU

2   Reading street names politically: a second reading   25
KARI PALONEN

3   Colonial urban order, cultural politics, and the naming of
streets in nineteenth- and early twentieth-century Singapore   41
BRENDA YEOH

4   Revisiting East Berlin and Haifa: a comparative perspective
on renaming the past   56
MAOZ AZARYAHU

5   "Armed with an encyclopedia and an axe":
the socialist and post-socialist street toponymy of
East Berlin revisited through Gramsci   74
JANI VUOLTEENAHO AND GUY PUZEY

6   Building a new city through a new discourse:
street naming revolutions in Budapest   98
EMILIA PALONEN

7   Locating the geopolitics of memory in the Polish streetscape   114
DANIELLE DROZDZEWSKI

8 Toponymic changes as temporal boundary-making:
   street renaming in Leningrad/St. Petersburg   132
   ANAÏS MARIN

9 The spatial codification of values in Zagreb's city-text   150
   LAURA ŠAKAJA AND JELENA STANIĆ

10 Nationalizing the streetscape: the case of street renaming
   in Mostar, Bosnia and Herzegovina   168
   MONIKA PALMBERGER

11 The politics of toponymic continuity: the limits of change
   and the ongoing lives of street names   185
   DUNCAN LIGHT AND CRAIG YOUNG

12 Toponymic complexities in Sub-Saharan African cities:
   informative and symbolic aspects from past to present   202
   LIORA BIGON AND AMBE J. NJOH

13 Coloring "Rainbow" streets: the struggle for toponymic
   multiracialism in urban post-apartheid South Africa   218
   WALE ADEBANWI

14 Street renaming, symbolic capital, and resistance in Durban,
   South Africa   240
   JAMES DUMINY

15 Street naming and the politics of belonging: spatial injustices
   in the toponymic commemoration of Martin Luther King, Jr.   259
   DEREK ALDERMAN AND JOSHUA INWOOD

16 From number to name: symbolic capital, places of memory,
   and the politics of street renaming in New York City   274
   REUBEN ROSE-REDWOOD

17 Toponymic checksum or flotsam? Recalculating Dubai's grid
   with Makani, "the smartest map in the world"   290
   MARAL SOTOUDEHNIA

18 Contemporary issues and future horizons of critical
    urban toponymy   309
    REUBEN ROSE-REDWOOD, DEREK ALDERMAN, AND MAOZ AZARYAHU

    Author name index   320
    Subject index   326

Figures

4.1 Borough boundaries in Berlin with the boundary between the
Soviet sector and the western sectors marked in solid black 60
4.2 Ha'atzma'ut Road (Independence Road), Haifa, Israel
(photograph by author) 68
7.1 Kraków's Old Town in 1943 121
7.2 Kraków's Old Town in 1964 125
10.1 The newly renamed House of Culture,
Croat House—Duke Stjepan Kosač 175
10.2 A street in West Mostar newly named after a Catholic priest
born in 1871 and "replacing" a street name honoring the
Yugoslav Partisans 176
11.1 Old and new street names in Timişoara, Romania (2015).
Strada Turgheniev commemorates Ivan Turgenev,
a nineteenth-century Russian writer. The street was renamed
in 1993 to commemorate a senior figure in the Romanian
Orthodox Church. 191
11.2 A street name sign in central Bucharest (2005). *Strada
Măndineşti* was renamed *Strada Sf* [Saint] *Dumitru* in 1993.
However, the signage gives the former name with the new
name in brackets. 193
11.3 Old and new street names on an apartment block in Bucharest
(2009). During the socialist era the street was named *Strada
Furnirului* (Street of the Wood Laminators). It was renamed
Strada Vintila Mihăilescu (after a Romanian geographer) in
1992. However, the old name remains on a number of the
apartment blocks along this street. 194
12.1 Clearly written, conspicuously posted, and well-positioned street
signs at an intersection in the formal area of Akwa, the erstwhile
colonial district, of Douala, Cameroon (photograph by
Ambe Njoh) 206
12.2 A house at the corner of Streets No. 5 and No. 8 in Dakar's
Médina. The resident has sign-posted it by hand, indicating his
occupation (photograph by Liora Bigon). 210

12.3 An example of the signage system of Mutengene, as inscribed
in white chalk by authorities of the Société Nationale
de l'Electricité du Cameroun (SONEL), the quasi-national
electricity corporation in Cameroon (photograph by
Liora Bigon)   213
13.1 Taking anti-apartheid activism to the streets in Durban,
South Africa (photograph reprinted with permission from
Kyle G. Brown)   227
14.1 Map of renamed streets in Durban, South Africa circa 2008
(cartography by James Duminy)   244
14.2 Renamed street sign in Glenwood, Durban, South Africa, 2014.
New signs had identical structures and the same "DIN A Text"
official typeface. Old signs were left atop the new, crossed out
with red tape (photograph by Andrew Duminy).   247
16.1 "Freedom from Shanties" (*Harper's New Monthly
Magazine* 1880)   281
17.1 Navigating the geo-coded world of Dubai with Makani   296
17.2 Miscalculating encoded orthography with Makani   297

Tables

6.1	"Populist" elements of Budapest's city-text in the 2010s	110
7.1	Street name changes within the Planty in Kraków, Poland	118
7.2	Street name changes on main roads outside the city center of Kraków, Poland	119
8.1	The fourth wave of street renamings in Leningrad/St. Petersburg (1991–onward)	140
8.2	The wave that was not: un-renamed places with imperial or religious connotations in Leningrad/St. Petersburg	141
16.1	The renaming of the West Side avenues, 1880–1890	279
16.2	A select list of commemorative place names in Harlem, 1925–2007	283

Contributors

Wale Adebanwi is a Professor in the Department of African American and African Studies at the University of California, Davis and Visiting Professor, Institute of Social and Economic Research, Rhodes University, Grahamstown, South Africa. He received his PhD in Social Anthropology as a Gates Scholar at Trinity Hall, University of Cambridge, UK, as well as in Political Science at the University of Ibadan, Nigeria. His research has focused on a range of topics addressing the question of the social mobilization of interest and power in contemporary Africa. He is also the author of *Authority Stealing: Anti-Corruption War and Democratic Politics in Post-Military Nigeria* (2012), *Yoruba Elites and Ethnic Politics in Nigeria: Obafemi Awolowo and Corporate Agency* (2014), and *Nation as Grand Narrative: The Nigerian Press and the Politics of Meaning* (2016). He is the editor or co-editor of six other books.

Derek Alderman is a Professor in the Department of Geography at the University of Tennessee, USA. His research interests and published work focus on the role of place and street naming in the context of African American identity politics and civil rights struggles in the southeastern United States. He is co-author of *Civil Rights Memorials and the Geography of Memory* (2008) and is perhaps best known for advancing scholarly and public understanding of the politics of naming streets after Martin Luther King, Jr. He is also frequently sought after by the news media to comment on this and other cultural issues.

Maoz Azaryahu is a Professor of Cultural Geography at the University of Haifa, Israel. His research focuses on urban and landscape semiotics as well as the cultural and historical geographies of national myths and public memory in Israel and Germany, landscapes of popular culture, the politics of street naming, and the cultural history of places and landscapes. He is the author of numerous books and articles, including *Von Wilhelmplatz zu Thälmannplatz: Politische Symbole im Öffentlicehn Leben der DDR* (1991), *State Cults: Celebrating Independence and Commemorating the Fallen in Israel 1948–1956* (1995, in Hebrew), *Tel Aviv: Mythography of a City* (2006), and *Namesakes: History and Politics of Street Naming in Israel* (2012, in Hebrew).

Liora Bigon is an Africanist urban historian at the Institute of Western Cultures, Hebrew University of Jerusalem, and the Holon Institute of Technology, Israel. She has published six books and edited collections including: *A History of Urban Planning in Two West African Colonial Capitals* (Mellen, 2009); *Garden Cities and Colonial Planning: Transnationality and Urban Ideas in Africa and Palestine* (Manchester University Press, 2014); *French Colonial Dakar: The Morphogenesis of an African Regional Capital* (Manchester University Press, 2016); and *Place Names in Africa: Colonial Urban Legacies, Entangled Histories* (Springer, 2016).

Danielle Drozdzewski is a Senior Lecturer in Human Geography at the University of New South Wales in Sydney, Australia. Her research draws upon ethnographic approaches to examine the geographies of remembrance and in particular the intersections of identity, cultural memory, and place. She is keenly interested in how memories of war are articulated in public spaces, through memorialization and commemorative vigilance, and also in private spaces through family narratives across generations. She has conducted research in Poland, Germany, Thailand, Singapore, Britain, and Australia. Her recent edited collection, *Memory, Place, Identity: Commemoration and Remembrance of War and Conflict*, was published by Routledge in 2016.

James Duminy is a Research Officer in the African Centre for Cities at the University of Cape Town in South Africa and General Secretary of the Association of African Planning Schools. He holds master's degrees in town and regional planning (University of KwaZulu-Natal, South Africa) and urban history (University of Leicester, United Kingdom). His research interests center on the interface between planning theory and history, with a focus on colonial and postcolonial Africa within the context of the wider global South.

Joshua Inwood is an Associate Professor at Pennsylvania State University where he holds a joint appointment with the Department of Geography and the Rock Ethics Institute. His research interests focus on understanding the social, political, and economic structures that make human lives vulnerable to all manner of exploitations, as well as how oppressed populations use social justice movements to change their material conditions.

Duncan Light is a Senior Lecturer in the Department of Tourism and Hospitality at Bournemouth University, UK. His research focuses on the cultural geographies of post-socialist change with particular reference to Romania, a country he has visited extensively. In particular, his work explores the relationships between urban space, political identities, and public memory. He has published on practices of renaming streets and urban places in Romania in journals such as *GeoJournal, Journal of Historical Geography*, and the *Annals of the Association of American Geographers*. His recent work has also examined the relationships between place naming and tourism practices.

Anaïs Marin is an Assistant Professor and Marie Curie Fellow with Collegium Civitas in Warsaw, Poland. A political scientist with expertise in post-Soviet and border studies, her doctoral thesis, defended in Sciences Po Paris in 2006, was dedicated to the "paradiplomacy" of St. Petersburg and the city's influence on Russian foreign policy-making in the 1990s. She has taken part in several research projects on Eastern European borderlands and served as a pro bono adviser for the Task Force on External Borders of the Association of European Border Regions (AEBR). In parallel to her academic career as a border and IR scholar, she has provided policy advocacy for the Finnish Institute of International Affairs (FIIA), a think tank based in Helsinki (2010–2014). As a Marie Curie Fellow, she is currently conducting comparative research on the "dictaplomacy" of authoritarian regimes in post-Soviet Eurasia (2015–2017).

Ambe J. Njoh is a Professor of Environmental Science and Policy in the School of Geosciences at the University of South Florida. He has written eleven books and published more than a hundred journal articles and book chapters. His most recent book, *French Urbanism in Foreign Lands* (Springer, 2016), examines the influence of France on the urban built environment in various countries. His latest work on toponymic inscription has focused on Nairobi, Kenya and Dakar, Senegal, and appears in the *Journal of Asian and African Studies* (2016).

Monika Palmberger earned her PhD at the University of Oxford and is currently a Visiting Professor at the Interculturalism, Migration and Minorities Research Centre, University of Leuven and a Hertha Firnberg Research Fellow at the Department of Social and Cultural Anthropology, University of Vienna. She has published widely in internationally renowned journals on questions of memory, generation, aging, and migration, and is the author of three books: *How Generations Remember: Conflicting Histories and Shared Memories in Post-War Bosnia and Herzegovina* (Palgrave, 2016), *Memories on the Move: Experiencing Mobility, Rethinking the Past* (with Jelena Tosic, Palgrave, 2016), and *Caring on the Move: Ethnographic Explorations of Aging and Migration Across Societies* (with Azra Hromadzic, Berghahn, forthcoming).

Emilia Palonen is a Senior Lecturer in Political Science at the University of Helsinki. She has published widely on populism and commemoration in Hungary and the history of Budapest as well as engaging with Fidesz politics of marking spaces in Budapest, architecture, and nationalism. She has worked on Academy of Finland projects focusing on transnational Hungarian left-wing intellectuals and on populism. Her background is in urban and area studies and poststructuralist theory, and she has worked as a Lecturer in Cultural Policy Studies and Political Science, specializing in Public Administration and Organization Studies.

Kari Palonen is a Professor of Political Science at the University of Jyväskylä, Finland. He has served two five-year terms as Academy of Finland Professor, directed the Finnish Centre of Excellence in Political Thought and Conceptual

Change, and he is currently the editor-in-chief of the journal *Redescriptions*. His recent books include *"Objektivität" als faires Spiel. Wissenschaft als Politik bei Max Weber* (2010), *Rhetorik des Unbeliebten. Lobreden auf Politiker im Zeitalter der Demokratie* (2012), *The Politics of Parliamentary Procedure: The Formation of Westminster Procedure as Parliamentary Ideal Type* (2014), *Politics and Conceptual Histories* (2014), and *From Oratory to Debate* (2016).

Guy Puzey is a Lecturer in Scandinavian Studies at the University of Edinburgh. His main research interests are in language policy, and his Arts & Humanities Research Council-funded doctoral thesis drew on the theories and metaphors of Antonio Gramsci to examine the political dimension of language activist campaigns in Norway and Italy. Puzey has carried out extensive research focusing on the relative visibility of languages in public spaces, while in critical toponomastic studies, he has incorporated the linguistic landscape approach into studies of power and place naming. In 2011, he edited a special section of *Onoma*, the journal of the International Council of Onomastic Sciences, on "Toponomastics and Linguistic Landscapes."

Reuben Rose-Redwood is an Associate Professor of Geography and Chair of the Committee for Urban Studies at the University of Victoria in British Columbia, Canada. His research focuses on the cultural politics of place naming, geographies of urban memory, and the spatial history of the geo-coded world. He is the co-editor of *Performativity, Politics, and the Production of Social Space* (2014) and has published in a broad range of scholarly journals, including *Progress in Human Geography*, *Social & Cultural Geography*, *Urban History*, and the *Annals of the Association of American Geographers*. His work on the historical geography of New York's urban streetscape has also been featured in various popular media outlets, such as the Discovery Channel, the History Channel, and the *New York Times*.

Laura Šakaja is a Professor of Cultural Geography at the University of Zagreb. She received her PhD in social and economic geography from the State University "M. V. Lomonosov" in Moscow and a PhD in geography from the University of Zagreb. Her publications include the books, *Culture and Space: Spatial Organization of Cultural Activities in Croatia* (*Kultura i prostor: prostorna organizacija kulturnih djelatnosti u Hrvatskoj*, Zagreb, 1999) and *Introduction to Cultural Geography* (*Uvod u kulturnu geografiju*, Zagreb, 2015). She has also published works on mental maps and imaginative geographies, daily environments, and the spatial aspects of ethnic relations. In recent years, her work has been focused on street toponymy and urban statuary as semiotic features of the city. She is currently involved in research on blind persons' images of urban space.

Maral Sotoudehnia is a doctoral student in the Department of Geography at the University of Victoria. Her research interests include the commodification of urban space, the spatial politics of smart geo-addressing applications, and the production of digitally mediated forms of value in disruptive computing applications. Her dissertation research investigates the intersections between cryptocurrencies such as Bitcoin, their underlying blockchains, and how both accelerate or resist the creation of financially inclusive and exclusive spaces.

Jelena Stanić has an undergraduate degree in geography from the University of Zagreb and an MSc in Environmental Sciences, Policy, and Management from the University of Manchester. Her undergraduate thesis examined the impact of different political regimes on the urban toponymy in the Croatian capital of Zagreb, from random space interventions to the mass encoding of the city with ideological values and landmarks. After receiving her MSc degree, Jelena has turned her career toward the environmental field in which she has been involved through research and consulting positions.

Jani Vuolteenaho is a Senior Lecturer in human geography at the University of Turku, Finland. His previous contributions to critical toponymic literature range from an award-winning article on the everyday uses of unofficial place names in early-twentieth century Helsinki (Dyos Prize in Urban History; co-authored with Heikki Paunonen and Terhi Ainiala) to topical case studies on spectacular naming as a place-making and branding tool. Vuolteenaho has edited several journals, anthologies, and theme issues, including *Terra*, the cultural magazine *Särö* (Rupture), *COLLeGIUM: Studies Across Disciplines in the Humanities and Social Sciences*, and *Critical Toponymies*, a groundbreaking collection of essays on the politics of place naming.

Brenda Yeoh is a Professor (Provost's Chair) in the Department of Geography and Vice-Provost (Graduate Education) at the National University of Singapore (NUS). She is also the Research Leader of the Asian Migration Cluster at the Asia Research Institute at NUS. Her research interests include the politics of space in colonial and postcolonial cities, along with a wide range of migration research themes in Asia, such as cosmopolitanism and talent migration; gender, social reproduction, and care migration; and international marriage migrants.

Craig Young is a Professor of Human Geography in the Division of Geography and Environmental Management at Manchester Metropolitan University, UK. His research interests include a focus on the cultural geographies and politics of identity (from the individual to the urban and the nation) in the context of post-socialist transformation, particularly in Eastern Europe, including street names. He is the co-editor of *Cosmopolitan Urbanism* (2006) and co-author of a number of articles on post-socialist identity formation in journals such as *Nationalities Papers, Europe-Asia Studies, Transactions of the Institute of British Geographers*, and the *Annals of the Association of American Geographers*.

Acknowledgments

We first discussed the idea of publishing an edited book on the politics of street naming at the Naming Places/Placing Names Workshop in Greenville, North Carolina, which the three of us organized in Fall 2007. The workshop brought together a band of scholars from North America, Europe, and Australia to discuss the political aspects of place naming, and we would like to thank all the participants for their camaraderie and ongoing contributions to the field of critical toponymy. Following the Greenville workshop, two of the participants, Lawrence Berg and Jani Vuolteenaho, published the first edited book on the "critical turn" in toponymic scholarship entitled, *Critical Toponymies: The Contested Politics of Place Naming* (2009), and a year later we published an article in *Progress in Human Geography* on new directions in critical place name studies (Rose-Redwood Alderman, and Azaryahu 2010). Over the past decade, the field of critical toponymy has grown considerably, and the present collection brings together classic and contemporary writings on one major thematic focus of this literature: the politics of street naming. By focusing on the political life of urban streetscapes, we hope that this edited volume demonstrates the relevance of critical toponymic scholarship to the field of urban studies more broadly. We are especially grateful to the authors who have contributed to this book, since, without their efforts, this collection would not have been possible.

We would also like to acknowledge the anonymous peer reviewers for their constructive feedback on the book proposal and initial drafts of the chapters as well as the editorial teams at Ashgate and Routledge. In particular, we are grateful to Commissioning Editor, Katy Crossan, and Editorial Assistant, Amanda Buxton, both formerly at Ashgate, who oversaw the first stage of this book project. Midway through the project, Ashgate was incorporated into Taylor & Francis, and we would therefore like to thank our new Editor, Faye Leerink, and Editorial Assistant, Priscilla Corbett, at Routledge for seeing this book manuscript through to completion.

Much of the editorial work on this project took place during the Summer and Fall of 2016 when the lead editor was on sabbatical, so we would like to acknowledge the institutional support of the University of Victoria for providing the time and resources that aided in the completion of this project. We are also grateful to family, friends, colleagues, and students for their moral support and encouragement, especially: Maleea Acker, Helena Andrade, Jen Bagelman, Julian Bakker,

Lawrence Berg, Liora Bigon, Nick Blomley, Spencer Bradbury, Jordan Brasher, Janna Caspersen, Lindsay Chase, Keith Cooper, Teresa Dawson, Terrence Dicks, Lisa Domae, Chris Fortney, Barry Fruchter, Michael Glass, Daniel Good, Marguerite Holloway, Alicia Hubka, Jolene Jackson, Lisa Kadonaga, Sun-Bae Kim, Sara Koopman, Bob Lamm, Jen Mateer, James McCarthy, Preston Mitchell, Matthew Mitchelson, Pamela Moss, Cam Owens, Alison Root, Amber Rose, CindyAnn Rose-Redwood, Sierra Rose-Redwood, Riley Rose-Redwood, Maral Sotoudehnia, Steve Spina, Simon Springer, Jordan Stanger-Ross, Jonathan Tilove, Eliot Tretter, Brian Tucker, Jani Vuolteenaho, and Melvin White.

A number of chapters included in this collection are reprinted with permission from previously published works. Chapter 2 is a revised reprint published with permission from the Finnish Political Science Association. The chapter originally appeared as Palonen, K. (1993), "Reading Street Names Politically," in K. Palonen and T. Parvikko (Eds.), *Reading the Political* (pp. 103–121), Helsinki: The Finnish Political Science Association. Chapter 3 is a revised reprint published with permission from Wiley. The original publication appeared as Yeoh, B. (1992), "Street Names in Colonial Singapore," *Geographical Review*, 82(3): 313–322. Chapter 7 is a revised reprint published with permission from Elsevier and originally appeared as Drozdzewski, D. (2014), "Using History in the Streetscape to Affirm Geopolitics of Memory," *Political Geography*, 42: 66–78. Chapters 8, 15, and 16 have been reprinted with permission from Taylor & Francis and were previously published as Marin, A. (2012), "Bordering Time in the Cityscape. Toponymic Changes as Temporal Boundary-Making: Street Renaming in Leningrad/St. Petersburg," *Geopolitics*, 17(1): 192–216; Alderman, D. and Inwood, J. (2013), "Street Naming and the Politics of Belonging: Spatial Injustices in the Toponymic Commemoration of Martin Luther King Jr.," *Social & Cultural Geography*, 14(2): 211–233; and Rose-Redwood, R. (2008), "From Number to Name: Symbolic Capital, Places of Memory, and the Politics of Street Renaming in New York City," *Social & Cultural Geography*, 9(4): 431–452. Lastly, Chapters 9, 12, and 14 are revised reprints published with permission from SAGE and originally appeared as Šakaja, L. and Stanić, J. (2011), "Other(ing), Self(portraying), Negotiating: The Spatial Codification of Values in Zagreb's City-Text," *Cultural Geographies*, 18(4): 495–516; Bigon, L. and Njoh, A. (2015), "The Toponymic Inscription Problematic in Urban Sub-Saharan Africa: From Colonial to Postcolonial Times," *Journal of Asian and African Studies*, 50(1): 25–40; and Duminy, J. (2014), "Street Renaming, Symbolic Capital, and Resistance in Durban," *Environment & Planning D*, 32(2): 310–328.

1 The urban streetscape as political cosmos

Reuben Rose-Redwood, Derek Alderman, and Maoz Azaryahu

Through its street names, the city is a linguistic cosmos.

—Walter Benjamin (1999, 522)

Introduction

There are few spaces as ordinary and mundane, yet politically charged, as a city's streets. A site of everyday routines and fleeting encounters, the "street" can also become a place of memory as well as a space of political protest, mass demonstration, and revolutionary action (Çelik, Favro, and Ingersoll 1994; Schechner 2003; Hebbert 2005; Butler 2015). The governing authorities of city and state, of course, have long viewed the urban streetscape as a political technology of infrastructural power, not only in terms of the regulation of circulatory flows of people, goods, and capital, but also as a space in which to inscribe the ideologies of the ruling regime, and its vision of history, into the landscapes of everyday life. One of the primary ways in which the latter has been achieved over the past few centuries is through the naming of city streets. Just as the statues and monuments of a fallen power are often demolished in the wake of revolution (Verdery 1999), so too are streets renamed to mark a temporal break with the past as the newly established regime seeks to reshape the spaces of the present in its own image (Azaryahu 1996). Yet no matter how forcefully a political regime may attempt to control the material and symbolic infrastructure of the streets, its power is never absolute nor is its ability to erase the imprint of former regimes complete or ever fully accepted by the public (Rose-Redwood 2008a; Light and Young 2014). Consequently, while the act of street naming contributes to the production of the urban streetscape as a *political cosmos*, such world-making practices are characterized by what geographer Doreen Massey (2005, 9) calls "contemporaneous plurality." Put simply, the urban streetscape is a space where different visions of the past collide in the present and competing spatial imaginaries are juxtaposed from one street corner to the next. It is precisely at the spatial intersections of different temporal worlds that the "political life" of urban streetscapes unfolds.

Over the past three decades, a rich body of scholarship has emerged that examines the politics of street naming as part of a broader shift toward developing theoretically informed approaches to the critical study of place naming, or critical toponymy (Azaryahu 1986, 1996; K. Palonen 1993; Alderman 2003; Berg and Vuolteenaho

2009; Rose-Redwood, Alderman, and Azaryahu 2010; Vuolteenaho et al. 2012; Light and Young 2014; Giraut and Houssay-Holzschuch 2016). This "critical" turn in toponymic studies has shifted attention from the traditional focus on the toponym-as-linguistic-object and instead highlighted the contested processes, and spatial politics, of naming places more generally (Berg and Vuolteenaho 2009). Critical scholarship on the politics of street naming has been at the forefront of these efforts, and such works have considerably enriched our understanding of the political life of urban spaces. Importantly, critical studies of street naming are not confined to a single discipline, but, like the very practice of place naming itself, represent a convergence of diverse perspectives from across the social sciences and humanities.

The aim of this book is to showcase critical scholarship on the contested politics of street naming in both historical and contemporary cities as well as to chart new directions for this emerging field of interdisciplinary inquiry. As the contributions to this edited collection illustrate, streetscapes are part of the taken-for-granted spaces of everyday urban life, yet they are also contested arenas in which struggles over identity, memory, and place shape the social production of urban space. The renaming of streets plays a key role in the remaking of urban commemorative landscapes, and, as such, political regimes of varying stripes have enlisted street naming as a strategy of asserting sovereign authority, ideological hegemony, and symbolic power.

To explore these issues and more, the present collection brings together the works of geographers, anthropologists, historians, linguists, planners, and political scientists to examine the ways in which the naming of streets intersects with more wide-ranging struggles over the spatial politics of urban memory, social justice, and political ideology. The primary goal of this book is therefore to assemble the writings of both leading and emerging scholars in the field of critical toponymy to demonstrate how conceptually and empirically rich analyses of the politics of street naming have much to offer to contemporary theorizations of space, place, and landscape. Drawing upon a wide range of case studies from Europe, North America, Sub-Saharan Africa, and Asia, the contributions in this volume provide detailed accounts of how the practices of street naming have been instrumental to the reshaping of urban spatial imaginaries, the cultural politics of place, and material struggles over the right to the city.

In the remainder of this introductory chapter, we provide an overview of critical scholarship on the politics of place naming generally, and street naming in particular, situating such works within the context of more general developments in cultural landscape studies. As part of this overview, we consider three primary frameworks that have informed critical approaches to examining the politics of street naming, which can broadly be conceived as viewing the urban streetscape as a "city-text," "cultural arena," and "performative space." Each of these perspectives offers a distinct, but not necessarily mutually exclusive, lens through which to interpret the political life of urban streetscapes.

The use of semiotics as an interpretive toolkit to analyze how political regime changes have transformed the *city-text* arose during the 1980s and 1990s as part of the movement among cultural geographers and other scholars to rethink the landscape-as-text (Azaryahu 1986, 1990, 1992, 1996, 1997; for a discussion of the landscape as a "text" more generally, see Duncan and Duncan 1988; Duncan

1990). This textual approach to the politics of toponymic inscription was largely responsible for the initial upsurge of interest in the political aspects of street naming as a contested spatial practice of commemoration, and the semiotic perspective continues to inform contemporary scholarship in this area (Light, Nicolae, and Suditu 2002; Pinchevski and Torgovnik 2002; Light 2004; E. Palonen 2008; Azaryahu 2011a, 2011b, 2012a, 2012b, 2012c; Šakaja and Stanić 2011).

From the mid-1990s onward, there has also been a growing interest in examining how street naming and related toponymic practices are implicated in the racialization and gendering of urban space, where the latter is viewed as a *cultural arena* in which the politics of recognition are played out across the fault lines of race, gender, and class (Alderman 1996, 2000, 2002a, 2002b, 2003; Berg and Kearns 1996; Dwyer and Alderman 2008; Rose-Redwood 2008c; Alderman and Inwood 2013). Such works have sought to cast the study of street naming as part of the geographies of social justice, focusing particular attention on the struggles of socially marginalized groups to claim their rightful "place" in the public sphere of the urban streetscape.

Both of these approaches have emphasized the contested politics of designating "official" street names—that is, the processes through which streets are named by governing authorities who claim a monopoly on the legitimate forms of toponymic inscription. However, a number of recent studies have demonstrated that the political liveliness of street names and other toponyms is not reducible to official naming processes and procedures alone (Rose-Redwood 2008a, 2016a; Light and Young 2014; Tucker and Rose-Redwood 2015; Crețan and Matthews 2016). Drawing upon theories of performativity, non-representational theory, and ethnographic methods, this third line of critical toponymic inquiry insists that we must also attend to the reception of street naming practices among urban residents in their everyday lives, which leads to a deeper consideration of naming-as-speech-act as well as both the unconscious habits and more overt forms of everyday resistance at work in the production of the urban streetscape as a *performative space*.

Each of the approaches outlined above, and discussed in more detail below, has much to offer to a critical analysis of what we might call "streetscape politics." Yet they by no means exhaust the possible interpretive frameworks that might be drawn upon to investigate the interrelations of naming, politics, and place in the urban context (in particular, see Berg and Vuolteenaho 2009). The contributors to the present collection find inspiration for their work in a diverse range of theoretical traditions, which we take as a positive sign of the vitality and conceptual experimentation that continues to characterize the field of critical urban toponymy.

From cultural indicator to technology of power: contextualizing the critical turn in urban toponymy

The current focus of critical toponymic scholarship on the political aspects of street naming is a significant departure from conventional approaches to urban toponymy, which have long been mired in local antiquarianism, largely reducing the study of street naming to the compilation of encyclopedic lists of street names for specific cities. Writing about the history of streets and their names has been a popular genre through which to narrate local history for over a century, and these works are often filled with amusing tales, folkloristic anecdotes, and urban legends as an entertaining way to inform the public about local traditions and urban heritage. Underlying the traditional study of toponymy is a linguistic approach that has sought to uncover the origin and meaning of individual place names, which are viewed as *cultural indicators* of settlement patterns, migratory flows, regional identification, and historical ecologies (Leighly 1978; Shortridge 1985; Jett 1997).

Although this traditional approach to toponymy can still be found in the pages of specialized journals, its heyday was during the first three-quarters of the twentieth century when many linguists, anthropologists, and geographers subscribed to what we might call the toponym-as-cultural-indicator paradigm. This perspective conceived of place names as a collection of objects, or artifacts, to be compiled and classified as cultural "specimens" that indicate the inherent characteristics of different cultures (Wright 1929, 140). In the field of geography, such an approach was closely associated with the Berkeley tradition of cultural landscape studies that Carl Sauer and his disciples, such as Wilbur Zelinsky (1967, 1988), developed. The Berkeley-based literary scholar George Stewart's landmark study, *Names on the Land* (1967 [1945]), was particularly influential, inspiring none other than H.L. Mencken (1948) to pen his own commentary on the street names of American cities. The Berkeley School dominated the field of cultural geography throughout much of the twentieth century until it was challenged by the so-called "new" cultural geography in the 1980s, which called into question the homogenization and reification of "culture" promulgated by the old guard (Duncan 1980).

By the 1980s, there was growing interest in the politics of landscape symbolism and representation as cultural geographers and other scholars engaged with a range of theoretical perspectives, including Marxism, humanism, and semiotics (Lowenthal 1975, 1985; Harvey 1979; Cosgrove 1984). With its emphasis on the textuality of the landscape as a "signifying system" (Duncan 1990, 17), this intellectual milieu paved the way for a re-examination of the discursive and ideological underpinnings of street naming as a political phenomenon. Yet, prior to the 1990s, studies of street names generally appeared in specialized onomastic journals with a limited audience in the more established disciplines of the social sciences and humanities (e.g., McCarthy 1975, Stump 1988, Bar-Gal 1988, 1989). In an academic universe where English is the predominant language of scholarship, the Anglophone hegemony has also led academic works on street naming written in languages other than English to be ignored (e.g., Bar-Gal 1988). This has had the effect of such works being largely consigned to the margins of scholarly research.

However, there were some notable exceptions. For instance, Daniel Milo's (1986) work on French street names was published in Pierre Nora's monumental project, *Lieux de Memoire* (1984–1992). Drawing upon the early-twentieth century sociologist Maurice Halbwachs's (1980 [1950], 1992 [1925]) classic works on collective memory, Nora's large-scale project had a significant influence on studies of social and cultural memory as well as public forms of commemoration. First appearing in French and later translated into English in the late-1990s, Milo's study examined French street names as "sites of memory" in multiple cities over a long time frame. Similarly, Priscilla Ferguson's (1988) reading of the street names of Paris also laid the foundation for theorizing urban streetscapes as spatial narratives and signifying systems where spatialities and temporalities intertwine.

One of the first scholarly works devoted explicitly to examining how commemorative street naming is embedded in the construction of official political identity was Maoz Azaryahu's (1986) study of the political history of East Berlin's street names. Azaryahu's (1988, 1990, 1991, 1992) subsequent writings during this early period focused on the political dimensions of toponymic commemoration as an aspect of municipal politics in Berlin during the 1920s. In particular, he provided a detailed history of commemorative street renaming during phases of major political transition and argued that toponymic changes, which served to inscribe historical narratives into urban space, were indicative of broader ideological reorientations in society. In the early-1990s, other scholars also began to develop theoretical frameworks for "reading street names politically" (K. Palonen 1993; also, see K. Palonen, this volume). Kari Palonen's (1993) study of the politics of street naming in Helsinki is especially noteworthy, because it was the first publication to attempt a comprehensive overview of the emerging literature of street name studies.

Most of the theoretically innovative research on street naming at this time was written by historians, political scientists, sociologists, and literary scholars. Initially, geographers were surprisingly not at the forefront of this area of scholarly inquiry despite its inherently geographical focus. An important exception was Brenda Yeoh's path-breaking work on the historical geography of street naming in colonial Singapore, which compared the official European-style street naming practices of the governing authorities with the "alternative systems of street names that originated among the immigrant Asian communities" (1992, 313; Yeoh, this volume; also, see Yeoh 1996). What set Yeoh's (1992) work apart from other early studies was that it moved beyond focusing solely on the official practices of street naming and called attention to the importance of competing ontologies of place that were enacted through informal, everyday speech acts (also, see Pred 1992). Moreover, she demonstrated that street nomenclature was more than a passive artifact but was rather a means of claiming a city's landscape, symbolically and materially, and using the power of urban space to legitimize or de-legitimize certain worldviews and identities.

Garth Myers was also an important geographical voice at this time in exploring how place names are "played with as tactics of power, or used as vehicles of derision" (1996, 238). Myers (1996) focused on the vernacular naming of neighborhoods in Zanzibar, and he convincingly argued that urban naming practices served as a means of social and spatial boundary-making as well as the othering of people and places. Like Yeoh, he noted that place naming was "exercised both by those having a great deal of social power and by those comparatively lacking it" (Myers 1996, 244). Myers encouraged the analysis of toponymic resistance, a point echoed specifically in the context of street renaming by anthropologists Faraco and Murphy (1997) in their analysis of political regime change in Spain. Uncovering the existence of this tension between using streetscapes as instruments of elite control versus their capacity to be used for counter-hegemonic purposes proved to be an early foundational idea in the development of critical toponymic studies (Alderman 2008).

Various other works published by geographers were seminal to the shift from the linguistic study of names as cultural indicators and artifacts to the critical analysis of naming as a technology of power. Azaryahu's (1996) landmark study on the "power of commemorative street names" was particularly influential and remains the most cited article in the field. His discussion proved consequential in elucidating how street names operated, simultaneously, as a system of locational orientation and as a socio-political text of historical commemoration. Given the practical importance of street names and "their recurrent and unreflected use in various contexts, both ordinary and extraordinary," Azaryahu illustrated the ways in which street naming inscribes political messages and commemorative meanings into many facets and settings of everyday urban life and thus makes the past "tangible and intimately familiar" (1996, 321). In contrast to traditional approaches that reified and failed to unpack the street naming process, Azaryahu's (1997) work was critical in characterizing street naming as directed not only by ideological considerations but also through decision-making procedures and the wider re-planning of the political geography and semiotic order of the city. A number of scholars have followed Azaryahu's lead in reconstructing the larger political decisions and identity-building work behind street name changes. Light's (2004) work on street renaming in postsocialist Romania is an early and noteworthy example of this vein of scholarship (also, see Light, Nicolae, and Suditu 2002).

Additionally, Lawrence Berg and Robin Kearns (1996) broke important conceptual ground in further defining and refining our understanding of the role of naming in the social construction and contestation of place (also, see Kearns and Berg 2002). Drawing from emotionally charged debates over the re-instatement of Maori names within Aotearoa/New Zealand, Berg and Kearns (1996) argued that place naming, as part of both the symbolic and material order, represents a way of "norming" or legitimating hegemonic power relations and therefore plays a significant role in the cultural politics of place. They set an important precedent in demonstrating how the contested politics of naming can become intertwined with the wider discourses of gender and racial identity as well as nationalism. Much of the scholarship on the politics of place naming has tended to focus on the use of toponymic inscription as a spatial strategy for promoting nationalistic histories and agendas; yet, since the mid-1990s, there has been a growing body of literature that examines the multiple axes of power and identity at play in the naming of streets and other places, thereby illustrating how the spatial struggles over race, gender, class, and nation are mutually constitutive.

Inspired by this focus on the interrelations of race, space, and place naming, Derek Alderman (2000) sought to make explicit the resistant and contested capacity of street renaming and its relationship to African American struggles for political and cultural recognition in the urban context. Examining the politics of naming roads for slain civil rights leader Martin Luther King, Jr. (MLK), he critically examined the role that a street's site and situation—its geography—plays in debates over remembering King. Stakeholders can and do advocate different ideas about where best to locate memories in urban public space, and, due to continuing racial inequalities, MLK streets are vulnerable to being segregated and marginalized. Alderman's contributions to the field have highlighted how traditional toponymic research, as well as more recent critical scholarship, has failed to realize that the mere occurrence of street names represents only half of the story. The specifics of a street name's intra-urban spatiality affect the negotiation of its meaning(s) and reception among different local populations. The larger cultural politics of MLK streets is only realized by examining how names fit into the broader geography of the city and how local political actors and groups struggle with each other in determining not just the existence but also the geographical scale of influence and visibility that the name is given (Alderman 2003). Alderman's early emphasis on the locational politics of street naming ushered in other studies of street naming in the context of center-versus-periphery spatial relations (Šakaja and Stanić 2011; Nada 2014) as well as broader political questions about how the emplacing of name and memory within the urban landscape affects the efficacy of social justice struggles (Alderman and Inwood, this volume).

The studies noted above from the late-1980s to the early-2000s, along with others cited in this volume, laid the foundations for the field of critical toponymy. By the end of the first decade of the twenty-first century, the field had matured to the point that the first anthology and progress report on critical toponymies had been published (Berg and Vuolteenaho 2009; Rose-Redwood, Alderman, and Azaryahu 2010). Lawrence Berg and Jani Vuolteenaho's book, *Critical Toponymies: The Contested Politics of Place Naming* (2009), was particularly influential in marking the "critical turn" in toponymic studies. We are now in a period of active theory construction in which scholars are expanding and problematizing conventional understandings of how toponymic inscriptions operate as technologies of power inside and outside the context of formal political regimes, resistance movements, and people's official and unofficial performances of identity (Light and Young 2014; Tucker and Rose-Redwood 2015; Giraut and Houssay-Holzschuch 2016). In the next section, we consider three of the main approaches to the critical study of street naming that continue to influence contemporary scholarship on the urban streetscape as city-text, cultural arena, and performative space, in order to highlight the evolving and dynamic nature of critical urban toponymy.

Street naming and the political life of urban streetscapes

Street naming, political regimes, and the commemorative politics of the city-text

One of the major themes to arise from the critical turn in toponymic scholarship has been a focus on the relation between political regime change and transformations to the symbolic infrastructure of the urban streetscape (Berg and Vuolteenaho 2009), where the latter is conceived as a "city-text" to be interpreted through the lens of semiotics, discourse analysis, and ideological critique. As discussed above, this general emphasis on the textuality of street naming coincided with the widespread interest in landscape symbolism, representation, and textuality that swept through the social sciences and humanities during the 1980s and 1990s. If the landscape was to be understood as a "text," as many cultural geographers and other scholars had argued at the time, then the act of street naming appeared to be a quintessential example of producing the city-as-text.

From a semiotic perspective, each signifier (street name) serves to represent a particular referent (street) within a system of signification (city-text). Viewed in this light, the city-text functions as a system of spatial orientation in which each street name acquires its meaning both intertextually and relationally. However, as numerous studies have shown, street naming is not a utilitarian aid to wayfinding alone but also plays a crucial role in embedding historical narratives into the spaces of everyday life (e.g., Ferguson 1988; Azaryahu 1996). If a commemorative street name is to be understood as a signifier, its referent is not only the street to which it refers but also the historical figure or event which is thereby brought into the sphere of public memory as part of a political regime of spatial inscription.

Along with monuments and other memorials, commemorative street names celebrate that which the governing authorities deem worthy of public remembrance and are thus employed in the semiotic construction of urban memory in the cityscape. The commemorative naming of streets generally entails the reproduction of the ethos and ideology underpinning the ruling socio-political order through officially mandated urban toponyms. Although historical narratives become "materialized" in urban space through the naming of streets (Rose-Redwood 2008a), the spatial configuration of the city-text is synchronic rather than chronological, since the traces of naming practices from different historical eras and political regimes often intermingle in the spaces of contemporaneous plurality that constitute the political cosmos of the urban streetscape. City-texts are thus composed of commemorative elements, yet they are largely devoid of a *narrative structure* and the clear sense of "before" and "after" that this entails (Azaryahu 1996).

As an officially authorized version of history inscribed into the cityscape, a city-text is an expression of changing power relations and shifting political priorities. The streetscape can therefore be viewed as a *palimpsest*, which is continuously being written and re-written by multiple "authors" as well as reinterpreted by different "readers." Moreover, this re-writing of urban space is never fully complete, since the city-text is always open to a layering of different historical narratives onto each other in a process that Foote (1997) has called "symbolic accretion" (also, see Dwyer 2004). The official authors of a city-text generally attempt to assert their claim to a monopoly over the designation and meaning of street names, yet over time these authorial intentions often fade from public memory since many urban residents do not pay attention to the deeper historical meaning of commemorative toponyms in the context of their daily routines. This process of *semantic displacement* takes place when there is a "change of referential framework that occurs when a historical name becomes a spatial designation" (Azaryahu 1996, 322). Consequently, all the commemorative posturing of the ruling elites may lose much of its force when we consider that street names often become empty signifiers to many urban residents who use them as spatial identifiers on a daily basis but may not know, or care, who or what has been commemorated in a street name (Light and Young 2014).

Nevertheless, this does not seem to have deterred those in power from using commemorative naming practices to naturalize and legitimize their authority. The use of street names for commemorative purposes is based on an ancient tradition of naming cities after their historical or mythical founders. Following the example of Alexander the Great, new cities in the Hellenistic and Roman Empire were named after kings and emperors, prominent examples being Alexandria, Antioch, and Caesarea. However, the administrative regulation of street naming as a political technology of modern government can be traced back to seventeenth-century France. In 1605, the centralized control of assigning street names was initiated in Paris during the reign of Henri IV. Under the aegis of the Duke de Sully, the king's right hand and the grand commissioner of public works, large-scale projects of urban development were initiated in France, including building new bridges and streets in Paris. In conjunction with the dean of the city guilds, standing at the head of the city council, and the city's aldermen, names were given to new streets in the city. These were royal names celebrating dynastic titles and commemorating members of the newly established royal family of the House of Bourbon such as *rue* and *place Royale*, *rue* and *place Dauphine*, and *rue Christine*, the latter of which was named after the second daughter of the French king (Cousin and Lacombe 1899).

Paris was also one of the first cities to systematically install official signage at street intersections. In 1728, the chief of police issued an order to inscribe the names of streets on the walls of buildings, thereby making street names both a matter of official record and a visual aspect of the urban streetscape (Cousin and Lacombe 1899). This new street regulation was later emulated in other countries as well. In 1763, a royal decree in Sweden required that street signs should be placed at the corners of important streets in Stockholm (Pred 1992), and a bill was passed in 1765 requiring local councils in England to number houses as well as to affix street signs at intersections (Miles 1973).

Since the eighteenth century, the numbering of houses and naming of streets has become one of the primary strategies of urban spatial ordering that governments have adopted to more efficiently tax, regulate, and control urban populations (Thale 2007; Rose-Redwood 2008b, 2012; Rose-Redwood and Tantner 2012; Tantner 2009, 2015). The use of numbers as street names has also been widely adopted in some countries, such as the United States, where the utilitarian logic of number is united with the symbolic value of commemorative naming (Rose-Redwood and Kadonaga 2016). During the nineteenth century, those promoting such spatial practices often viewed the urban streetscape in explicitly textual terms with street and house numbers being likened to the "page numbers" of a book with urban space conceived as a "great ledger of the community" (Rose-Redwood 2008b). Unlike the "new" cultural geography of the 1980s and 1990s, this earlier iteration of the city-as-text focused less on questions of spatial narrative and more on creating a legible *typography*, or "page layout," for the city-text. Yet even numerical street names can acquire symbolic value as part of the urban commemorative landscape (Rose-Redwood 2008a, 2008c; Zerubavel 2014).

Urban toponyms—whether they be numbers or names—have the potential to become constitutive elements of a commemorative system of nomenclature that inscribes an officially approved narrative of historical memory into the geography of the city. In particular, naming streets after persons and events interweaves "an authorized version of history into ordinary settings of everyday life" (Azaryahu

1996, 312). As an honorific measure, commemorative street naming is an act of civic canonization that aims to secure a place for that which is commemorated in an officially sanctioned "hall of fame" embedded in the rhetorical space of the cityscape.

As an expression of power, street naming often plays an important role in struggles over the symbolic control of public space. Such toponymic conflicts are especially acute in the context of bi-lingual or multi-lingual societies, where the very decision of which languages to use on street signs, as well as the placement of each in relation to the other, can itself be a politically charged issue (Jones and Merriman 2009; Azaryahu 2012a; Bigon and Dahamshe 2014). Yet, in both mono-lingual and multi-lingual contexts, street names play an important role in the geopolitics of public memory and are therefore susceptible to being replaced during periods of revolutionary change of the socio-political order. As an act that signifies control over history and public space, rewriting the city-text is a practice of historical revision that doubles as a "ritual of revolution." During periods of significant political change, street renaming generally involves both the *decommemoration* of the previous regime's pantheon of heroes and its replacement through processes of *recommemoration*, where the newly established regime typically views such changes as a legitimate form of "symbolic reparation" for past wrongs whereas the champions of the old order often see these very same developments as vengeful acts of "symbolic retribution" (Swart 2008; Azaryahu 2011a; Adebanwi, this volume).

One of the first instances of the commemorative renaming of streets as a result of revolutionary change occurred in Paris during the French Revolution, and such street name changes became routine during successive regime changes in France thereafter (Cousin and Lacombe 1899). In 1792, a decree was issued that required all royal and clerical denominations to be replaced by revolutionary national and republican names. The old Christian saints lost their titles, while the new "saints" of the revolution were inducted into the revolutionary hall of fame through engraving their names onto the walls at the street corners. Under Napoleon's rule, an official decree issued in 1800 stipulated a revision of street names in Paris, and, with the collapse of the imperial regime in 1815, some 50 Parisian streets were renamed, most of them regaining their pre-1789 designations (Cousin and Lacomb 1899). The susceptibility of commemorative street names to political changes shows that, from the perspective of the governing authorities, the ideological reorientation entailed in the rewriting of the city-text seems to trump the spatial disorientation and urban confusion that may result from the renaming of streets.

There is now an extensive body of critical scholarship that examines the politics of street renaming in the wake of major political transformations (Berg and Vuolteenaho 2009). In particular, the toponymic changes that accompanied the rise and fall of communism in the Soviet Union and its satellite states have garnered considerable attention (e.g., Light 2004; Gill 2005; E. Palonen 2008). Likewise, the struggles over street renaming associated with other geopolitical flashpoints, such as the Palestinian–Israeli conflict and the end of apartheid in South Africa, have been the focus of numerous studies (e.g., Peteet 2005; Swart 2008). Scholars have also considered the toponymic legacy of imperial conquest, colonialism, and the ongoing efforts to rewrite the city-text as a spatial strategy of nation-building in various postcolonial contexts (Bigon 2008, 2009; Nash 2009; Giraut and Houssay-Holzschuch 2016; Wanjiru and Matsubara 2017). Some recent studies, including several included in the present volume, emphasize the *limits* to toponymic changes that have occurred as a result of political shifts, highlighting the continuing presence of "left-over" street names that remain in place despite the fact that they do not align with the prevailing ideology (Light and Young 2014; Light and Young, this volume). Such works are significant because they call attention to the spatial unevenness of toponymic change, which complicates the narratives we tell about the political life of urban streetscapes.

Although other approaches to critical toponymy have emerged in recent years, the semiotic analysis of the city-text continues to offer new insights into the politics of street naming (E. Palonen 2008; Azaryahu 2011a, 2011b, 2012a, 2012b, 2012c; Šakaja and Stanić 2011). Yet semiotic approaches have never implied "a reduction of the city in its entirety to a mere text" (Azaryahu 1996, 324). On the contrary, they can help us appreciate "*not* that the world (space-time) is like a text but rather that a text … is just like the rest of the world" (Massey 2005, 54, italics in original). Only then can we avoid what Massey refers to as "the longstanding tendency to tame the spatial into the textual" (2005, 54). It is precisely this taming of space and place into "text" that critical toponymic scholarship has sought to call into question by de-naturalizing the regimes of spatial inscription that make up the taken-for-granted spaces of everyday life. While urban streetscapes are not reducible to the inscriptions of sovereign power alone, they most certainly are one of the most significant spaces in which the statist dream of rendering "representation" and "reality" equivalent— by transforming history into geography—intersects with the everyday lives of urban inhabitants whose geographical imaginations and lived experiences will forever exceed the sovereignty of signification.

Urban streetscapes as cultural arenas and the geographies of social justice

The urban streetscape is not merely a blank slate upon which sovereign powers inscribe their ideologies, it is also a "cultural arena" in which different social groups struggle over what histories and whose identities are to be recognized or ignored in and through the official city-text (Alderman 2002a; Rose-Redwood, Alderman, and Azaryahu 2010). Viewing the streetscape as a cultural arena—while just one of several possible analytical lenses—can help us understand the socio-political processes and conflicts that underlie the production and consumption of urban toponyms. It also leads to a deeper consideration of who has the power (or not) to name, who has a right to the city and to be visible within the streetscape, and whose visions of, and claims to, the urban past, present, and future will predominate (Dwyer and Alderman 2008). The geographies of street naming are therefore not solely the product *of* social power but also an important conduit for *achieving* power—making the political authority, ideological persuasions, and geographical imaginaries of aspiring sovereigns appear to be part of the "natural order" of the world. And, yet, such processes of naturalization are never complete and, in some cases, can become the subject of intense political controversy.

The stakes are high for defining and debating street naming because of the powerful role that place and landscape play in social life. As Peteet (2005, 153) observes, "[n]ames, and their meanings, form part of the cultural systems that structure and nuance the way we see, understand and imagine the world." Put simply, place naming has the potential to bring new worlds into being by calling forth particular socio-spatial actions—including violence, dispossession, and exclusion. Counter-naming practices can also be used to contest hegemonic national narratives (Zeidel 2006) and "unsettle" dominant territorial claims (Murphyao and Black 2015). The endowing of places with new oppositional names and meanings can be controversial since these narrative struggles frequently become weapons in broader debates over who and what should be remembered (and conversely forgotten).

Importantly, the social and political "life" of street names illustrates that a city's road network is not simply a set of abstract spaces and flows but also the vehicle for emotion, memory, and a sense of place (Alderman 2006; Caliendo 2011). These emotional geographies are not separate from the political, economic, and social struggles of urban populations; rather, they constitute and structure their experiences with, and perceptions of, being included or excluded from wider notions of urban citizenship. As a growing number of activists, academics, and public officials have recognized, the (re)construction of urban streetscapes through the renaming of streets is not simply a matter of semiotics and semantics alone but is also an important practice in achieving or denying broader geographies of social justice (Alderman and Inwood, this volume).

For historically marginalized groups across a wide range of national contexts, city streets have emerged as arenas in which to question the absence of their culture and heritage within traditional place-based narratives. Woodman (2015), along with a growing number of scholars, argues that absence is something actively created through naming practices and that it exerts a presence or influence in social life more generally. Moreover, Swart (2008) explores how the rewriting of street names in post-conflict societies can serve as a mechanism of transitional justice for formerly victimized and invisiblized groups, providing a form of symbolic reparation for reclaiming their identity and dignity while also being a legal instrument of change in advocating for basic civil rights.

Place renaming is now strategically employed by indigenous peoples, racialized minorities, and other marginalized groups to challenge their exclusion and misrepresentation within long-established framings of public space (Monmonier 2006; Koch and Hercus 2009; Rose-Redwood 2016). In the United States, this has been most clearly seen in the efforts of African Americans to cleanse the urban landscape of references that valorize white supremacy. In the immediate wake of the Charleston Massacre of 2015 and the ongoing Black Lives Matter movement, a number of American communities became embroiled in debates about why their schools, parks, and streets memorialize the names of southern Civil War generals, leaders of the Ku Klux Klan, and other historical defenders of slavery and racism (Sullivan 2015; Bryan 2016). Many of these communities have called for a renaming of such places as part of a restorative justice project that sees the killing of African Americans by white supremacists and trigger-happy police as an extension of a society that de-values the memories, experiences, and welfare of people of color. For some activists, the symbolic violence inflicted through racist street naming patterns is part of, rather than apart from, the wider physical violence, discrimination, and oppression faced by black America.

The cultural arena of the urban streetscape is therefore a site of socio-political struggle and resistance. This resistance can take the form of overt protest in the streets and official renaming campaigns at city hall, but it can also involve more informal yet no less important dissident performances, such as the refusal to use a particular street name in everyday speech or the layering of counter-meanings onto a name as a means of reappropriation and reclamation. For instance, the name Hayti—long used pejoratively by whites to refer to black settlements in the southern United States—was claimed and reimagined by African Americans in Durham, North Carolina, to mark and promote the urban district's proud history of black economic empowerment and cultural expression amid humiliating Jim Crow segregation and discrimination (Kellogg 1977).

While urban toponymic patterns are highly racialized, they are also deeply gendered. A recent study of seven world cities found that, on average, only 27.5 percent of the streets studied had female names (Poon 2015). The gender inequalities inscribed into many city-texts prompted a French feminist group, Osez le Féminisme, to protest the fact that only 2.6 percent of Parisian streets have female names. Unsurprisingly, the limited number of women honored are the wives or daughters of famous men. This massive gap in the recognition of men and women on street signs exists, ironically, at the same time that Paris is becoming known for its progressive street and transportation policies. Osez le Féminisme's protest for street equity involved covering the official street signs of 60 roads with the names of women, which attracted significant public attention but was only a temporary reversal of power (Jaffe 2015). Such media reports and acts of resistance notwithstanding, the study of the gender politics of street naming is still a woefully neglected theme in urban studies and critical toponymic scholarship.

It may be tempting to frame streetscape struggles over race and gender in the starkly black and white terms of a dominant/marginalized duality, yet it is also important to recognize that the political actors involved in the contested politics of street naming are not monolithic groups (Rose-Redwood 2008c). Giraut and Houssay-Holzschuch (2016) insist that critical toponymic studies should move beyond exclusive categories to explore the various combinations and nexuses that emerge between different contexts, actors, and technologies of toponymic inscription if we are to better understand the politics of place naming in comparative perspective. The complex range of interests that converge within the arena of street naming can complicate and even compromise the very definition of what a geography of social justice looks like and for whom, and on whose terms, the urban streetscape enacts justice. Indeed, toponymic resistance is not by any means restricted to those historically known to be excluded or discriminated against (Morin and Berg 2001). Amid the growing push for city street networks to foster multicultural inclusion, there has been significant push-back from those unwilling to relinquish their power and ideological position within the landscape. For example, while the call to remove street names that reference the slave-holding Confederate States of America is increasingly felt across the United States (Blinder 2016), it is striking how few cities have actually engaged in the place renaming that would topple these racist images. In fact, some states such as Tennessee have recently passed "heritage protection" laws that could clearly limit the rewriting of racialized street names as well as impede the removal of Confederate memorials and monuments (*The Denver Post* 2016).

Although urban streetscapes have undoubtedly been arenas of toponymic conflict, recent research has engaged in a productive critique of the commonplace framing of the politics of street naming through the analytic lens of resistance. Moving beyond an overly politicized and reductionist notion of contestation, Light and Young (2014) point to the role that habit plays in everyday practices to explain why people often do not use newly introduced street names. Other scholars have also argued that we must move away from seeing resistance, rather statically, as "a property deduced from a presupposed hegemony" and instead make room for a more performative conception of toponymic power that recognizes the diversity of modes, acts, and political subjectivities involved in the contestation of street naming (Duminy 2014, 325). It is to this third approach to the politics of street naming that we now turn.

Beyond representationalism: from the city-as-text to the urban streetscape as a performative space of everyday life

Given that the field of critical toponymy initially emerged as part of the cultural turn in the social sciences and humanities, much of the scholarship on the politics of street naming has conceptualized the urban streetscape in textual and representational terms. Indeed, whether we adopt a semiotic approach or view the landscape as a cultural arena, street naming is typically understood as a form of "representation" in a double sense. On the one hand, urban place names are commonly viewed as signifiers that *linguistically represent* that which is signified, and, on the other hand, the visibility of street signs is seen as an important way to *politically represent* different social groups in the public spaces of the city. In other words, despite all the nuances of its analyses, much of the critical scholarship on street naming, and place naming more generally, continues to be framed within the orbit of representationalist modes of thought.

As an epistemological and ontological project, representationalism is based upon the belief that the primary purpose of language is to represent the world. According to this viewpoint, language is representational and representation is linguistic. This chain of equivalence between language and representation has a long history and is deeply ingrained in both modern scientific thought and humanistic inquiry (Rose-Redwood and Glass 2014). Whether we view names as mere labels that are ascribed to pre-existing things in the world (à la positivism) or naming is understood as a reflection or representation of social power (à la critical social theory), we shall in both cases remain tethered to the chain of representationalist thought. The problem with this way of thinking is that language has many more uses in the world beyond its representational function *and* the act of representation can take many different forms beyond the medium of linguistic textuality. This is significant for critical toponymic scholarship because it means that it is possible to think about place naming and related forms of spatial inscription as *more-than-representational* practices. This de-coupling of language and representation is essential if we are to move beyond representational modes of analysis and towards a critical account of urban streetscapes as "performative spaces" of everyday life.

A number of scholars have begun to explore the implications that performative and non-representational theories have for rethinking the politics of place naming as a spatial practice. As early as the 1990s, Myers (1996) called attention to the performative aspects of place naming and the need to move beyond the map by considering the *uses* of toponyms in ordinary speech situations through ethnographic methods (also, see Entrikin 1991). Kearns and Berg (2002) extended this line of inquiry by examining place name pronunciation as a performative act, drawing upon Judith Butler's conception of performativity as "the reiterative and citational practice by which discourse produces the effects that it names" (1993, 2). This emphasis on the performativity of naming is grounded less in the textual analysis of semiotics or hermeneutics and more in the *pragmatics* of speech acts as embodied practices. Focusing on the contextual and relational uses of language in ordinary life, pragmatics has its roots in the theory of performative utterances, or speech acts, developed by J.L. Austin during the mid-twentieth century, which served as the basis of his classic study, *How To Do Things With Words* (1962). Austin insists that speech has the capacity not only to describe or represent pre-existing objects or events but can also perform an action in the world, since "to *say* something is to *do* something" (1962, 12, italics in original). For Austin, a speech act is only performative when it is uttered in the "appropriate circumstances" by an authorized spokesperson following established procedures. Subsequent theorists, such as Derrida (1988) and Butler (1993), have challenged this conventionalist reading of performativity by demonstrating how the very process of authorization is itself a performative practice that can never escape the contingency of its own self-validating logic and is thus always open to potential contestation (Rose-Redwood and Glass 2014; Butler 2015).

Since the act of naming is a primary example which Austin himself uses to illustrate the notion of the performative utterance, it should come as no surprise that one of the first accounts to critically examine street naming as a political practice took Austinian speech act theory as its point of departure (K. Palonen 1993, also, see K. Palonen, this volume). In hindsight, the performative approach to street naming seems to have been largely eclipsed for much of the 1990s by representational readings of the city-text. Over the past decade, however, there has been growing interest in reconsidering the performative and more-than-representational dimensions of street naming. For instance, Rose-Redwood (2008a) explores the "performative limits of the official city-text" in his study of the renaming of Sixth Avenue as the Avenue of the Americas in mid-twentieth century New York. In particular, he illustrates how the official act of street renaming is not guaranteed by governmental decree alone but very much depends upon its performative "uptake" in everyday urban life. Likewise, Adebanwi (2012) offers a comparative analysis of the geopolitics of street naming in New York and Lagos, Nigeria, from a performative perspective, while Duminy's (2014, 310) study of political conflicts over street renaming in Durban, South Africa, seeks to advance a "performative conception of symbolic capital and resistance [that] may aid our understanding of naming processes in contested memorial landscapes." These in-depth case studies have enriched our understanding of the performances and counter-performances associated with street naming and, in the process, have heightened our awareness of the performative limits of official naming practices, on the one hand, and the performative force of everyday speech acts, on the other.

One of the most significant methodological developments to arise from the performative turn in urban toponymic scholarship has been a renewed interest in studying how official and unofficial street names are used by urban residents in their everyday lives. As noted above, Light and Young (2014) provide a particularly compelling account of the importance of habit in shaping the use of urban place names in ordinary speech situations. Using a mixed-methods approach, they show how a market named in honor of a prominent Communist Party activist, Piaţa Moghioroş, in Bucharest, Romania, was officially renamed during the postsocialist era, yet the majority of urban residents continued to use the original name more than two decades after its official decommemoration. In this specific case, Light and Young (2014) contend that the ongoing usage of a socialist place name in a postsocialist context is not so much a form of conscious resistance to the current political-economic regime—as the notion of the urban streetscape as a "cultural arena" might suggest—but is rather a result of habitual practices among ordinary "users" of urban spaces.

While not explicitly drawing upon theories of performativity per se, several other recent studies have also explored the everyday uses of street names in different contexts (e.g., Shoval 2013; Creţan and Matthews 2016). This emphasis on the reception and use of urban toponyms has enlarged the scope of critical urban toponymy by moving beyond the archive and the map to consider the daily "life" of street names. As a result, such works have demonstrated that there is far more to the politics of street naming than a focus on the proclamations of political authorities alone would suggest. This emerging research trajectory, therefore, has the potential to broaden our conception of the relation between place naming and politics in a number of important ways. Specifically, it demonstrates that there are indeed limits to the sovereign assertion of a monopoly over naming practices, since, whether through unconscious habit or overt resistance, the users of urban space may undercut the legitimacy of officially sanctioned street names. This insight leads to a realization that the political life of urban streetscapes is not solely confined to the arena of formal politics, and thus our critical analyses of street naming must likewise extend beyond the sovereign declarations of officialdom. Finally, a performative approach to studying the everyday use of street names can help elucidate how naming is not a singular act of political will but rather depends upon a series of reiterative citational practices enacted by a diverse array of social and political actors. This shifts our attention from the production to the *re*production of urban space, because the performative force of a particular name is contingent upon its repetitious use in daily life.

Naming, politics, and place: key themes in the present collection

Although there is far more to the politics of the "street" than the issue of naming alone, the contributions to this edited collection illustrate how the social struggles over street naming have played a significant role in the political life of urban streetscapes. Each of the contributors to the present volume approaches the field of critical urban toponymy from a different vantage point—both theoretically and empirically—yet there are also a number of common themes across the chapters showcased in this book. One major focus is the relation between street naming and the "colonial urban order" from Southeast Asia (Yeoh, this volume) to Sub-Saharan Africa (Bigon and Njoh, this volume) as well as the contested politics of street name changes in postcolonial contexts, with the case of South Africa being a prime example (Adebanwi; Duminy, this volume). Another thematic area that features prominently in the present book is the use of street naming as a political technology of nationalism and the toponymic consequences of the political-economic transition from socialism to postsocialism in Europe (Azaryahu; Drozdzewski; Light and Young; Marin; Palmberger; E. Palonen; Šakaja and Stanić; Vuolteenaho and Puzey, this volume). In many respects, these two geopolitical transformations—the shift from the colonial-to-postcolonial and socialist-to-postsocialist—have framed much of the critical scholarship on urban toponymy over the past three decades, so it is to be expected that many of the chapters in this collection speak directly to these concerns.

However, as we outlined above, there are other important issues associated with the politics of street naming that deserve consideration as well. In particular, several chapters in this collection call attention to the ways in which street naming has contributed to the racialization of urban streetscapes (Adebanwi; Alderman and Inwood; Bigon and Njoh; Duminy; Rose-Redwood; Yeoh, this volume). As these studies illustrate, the naming of streets should not be seen in isolation from broader questions of social and spatial justice, especially in relation to the politics of racism, racial segregation, and the ongoing legacies of white supremacy. Street naming is also implicated in the gendering of urban space. More often than not, the street naming process has been dominated by masculinist policy agendas resulting in far fewer streets being named in honor of women than men in cities around the world, as a number of contributions in this volume attest (Duminy; K. Palonen; Rose-Redwood; Vuolteenaho and Puzey, this volume).

Additionally, class power and the privileges of property ownership have long influenced the practices of place naming, and the naming of streets is no exception. Street naming is often a strategy for generating "symbolic capital" by enhancing the prestige of particular individuals or groups (Duminy; Rose-Redwood, this volume). This form of "reputational politics" (Alderman 2002a) is, in large part, why the commemorative work that street naming performs is so important, because it not only naturalizes and legitimizes selective visions of the past but is also instrumental in *spatializing* the social boundaries of belonging and exclusion along the axes of race, gender, class, ethnicity, and citizenship (Alderman and Inwood, this volume). The commemorative politics of street naming is therefore a reoccurring theme in urban toponymic scholarship. Yet the commemorative value of street names sometimes conflicts with the governmental imperative of using street addresses as the basis of producing spaces of legibility, especially with the growing prevalence of digital geo-addressing technologies and the rise of the "smart city" (Sotoudehnia, this volume; also, see Rose-Redwood 2012).

Taken together, the contributions in this book explore a wide range of thematic concerns related to the politics of street naming in a diverse array of geographical locales. They also draw upon a variety of theoretical perspectives, including everything from semiotics and discourse analysis to theories of performativity, hegemony, and postcolonialism. In particular, Kari Palonen draws upon Austinian speech act theory and Weber's conception of politics to offer a "second reading" of his landmark study on "reading street names politically" (Chapter 2). Brenda Yeoh also revisits her classic study of official and vernacular street naming in colonial Singapore, illustrating how "daily use implied competing representations of the landscape, rather than a single, municipally imposed image" (Chapter 3). In Chapter 4, Maoz Azaryahu examines the interplay between decommemoration and recommemoration through a comparative analysis of street renaming campaigns in East Berlin and Haifa. Similarly, Jani Vuolteenaho and Guy Puzey also consider the case of street toponymy in East Berlin, yet they do so by way of an innovative engagement with Gramsci's theory of hegemony (Chapter 5). In Emilia Palonen's chapter, she turns her attention to "street naming revolutions" in Budapest and builds upon Laclau and Mouffe's theory of discourse to explore how the act of street naming produces a "discursive universe" (Chapter 6).

The next four chapters by Danielle Drozdzewski (Chapter 7), Anaïs Marin (Chapter 8), Laura Šakaja and Jelena Stanić (Chapter 9), and Monika Palmberger (Chapter 10) also trace the discursive effects of political regime changes on the "city-text" in Kraków (Poland), Leningrad/St. Petersburg (Russia), Zagreb (Croatia), and Mostar (Bosnia and Herzegovina), respectively. In doing so, these contributions examine how street naming practices are implicated in spatializing the geopolitics of memory, the socio-political processes of Othering, temporal boundary-making, the spatial codification of values, and the inscription of nationalist ideologies into the urban streetscape. Whereas most studies of the politics of street naming emphasize the transformations to the city-text that result from political regime changes, Duncan Light and Craig Young draw our attention to the performative limits of street naming, the "ongoing lives" of street names from past political regimes, and the "politics of toponymic continuity" (Chapter 11).

The regional focus of the book then shifts to the African context with Liora Bigon and Ambe Njoh offering a general account of the "toponymic complexities" in Sub-Saharan African cities (Chapter 12), while Wale Adebanwi (Chapter 13) and James Duminy (Chapter 14) both explore the toponymic politics of race and identity in post-apartheid South Africa. Similarly, Derek Alderman and Joshua Inwood consider how African Americans have historically been "written out" of cultural landscapes in U.S. cities and highlight the ways in which naming streets in honor of slain civil rights leader Martin Luther King, Jr., has been part of a broader movement for social and spatial justice (Chapter 15). Drawing upon Bourdieu's theory of symbolic capital and Massey's work on the relationality of place, Reuben Rose-Redwood then examines the spatial politics of race, gender, and class as they unfolded with the renaming of streets in nineteenth- and twentieth-century New York (Chapter 16). In the penultimate chapter, Maral Sotoudehnia brings together the field of critical urban toponymy with scholarship on digital geographies and critical software studies to consider recent efforts by Dubai's government to create a new digital geo-coding system to render the urban landscape into a space of calculability (Chapter 17). Lastly, we close the book by offering some concluding reflections on the future horizons of critical toponymic inquiry (Chapter 18).

In the varied accounts outlined above, the urban streetscape is presented as a city-text of historical commemoration, a cultural arena in which struggles over spatial justice unfold, and a performative space of everyday urban life. We view the diversity of theoretical approaches in the current volume as a positive indication that toponymic scholarship is no longer languishing in the "atheoretical caverns of geographical inquiry," as Myers (1996, 238) lamented two decades ago. On the contrary, the field of critical toponymy has blossomed, and by assembling classic and contemporary studies on the politics of street naming into a single collection, this book highlights the breadth, depth, and geographical scope of urban toponymic scholarship as well as its relevance to wider theoretical debates about space, place, and landscape.

Whether we view the urban streetscape as a text, cultural arena, or performative space, the practice of street naming is an act of *world-making*, whereby the naming of streets, and the establishment of a "street name regime" (K. Palonen, this volume), aims to bring new "worlds" into being by reshaping the geographical imaginaries and spatial coordinates of everyday life. This world-making capacity of street naming led the urbanist Walter Benjamin to envision the urban streetscape as a "linguistic cosmos" (1999, 522; also, see Ferguson 1994; Regier 2010). However, it should be recalled that the term "cosmos" generally implies a "world or universe as an ordered and harmonious system" (*Oxford English Dictionary* 2016). This dream of the streetscape as a well-ordered cosmos has seduced one political regime after the next. Yet, if this book seeks to convince the reader of anything, it is that the "order" and "system" which political authorities attempt to impose upon the urban streetscape is necessarily a contingent spatio-temporal order, which is always open to the possibility of contestation and transformation. If the streetscape is indeed a "cosmos," as Benjamin suggests, then it is most certainly a *political* cosmos—or a world of spatial politics—that is subject to the vicissitudes of changing political fortunes, social struggles, and habitual routines, which collectively constitute the political life of urban streetscapes.

References

Adebanwi, W. (2012). "Glocal Naming and Shaming: Toponymic (Inter)National Relations on Lagos and New York Streets." *African Affairs*, 111(445): 640–661.

Alderman, D. (1996). "Creating a New Geography of Memory in the South: (Re)naming of Streets in Honor of Martin Luther King, Jr." *Southeastern Geographer*, 36(1): 51–69.

Alderman, D. (2000). "A Street Fit for a King: Naming Places and Commemoration in the American South." *The Professional Geographer*, 52(4): 672–684.

Alderman, D. (2002a). "Street Names as Memorial Arenas: The Reputational Politics of Commemorating Martin Luther King in a Georgia County." *Historical Geography*, 30: 99–120.

Alderman, D. (2002b). "School Names as Cultural Arenas: The Naming of US Public Schools After Martin Luther King, Jr." *Urban Geography*, 23(7): 601–626.

Alderman, D. (2003). "Street Names and the Scaling of Memory: The Politics of Commemorating Martin Luther King, Jr. within the African American Community." *Area*, 35(2): 163–173.

Alderman, D. (2006). "Naming Streets for Martin Luther King, Jr.: No Easy Road." In R. Schein (Ed.), *Landscape and Race in the United States* (pp. 213–236). New York: Routledge.

Alderman, D. (2008). "Place, Naming, and the Interpretation of Cultural Landscapes." In B. Graham and P. Howard (Eds.), *The Ashgate Research Companion to Heritage and Identity* (pp. 195–213). Farnham: Ashgate.

Alderman, D. and Inwood, J. (2013). "Street Naming and the Politics of Belonging: Spatial Injustices in the Toponymic Commemoration of Martin Luther King Jr." *Social & Cultural Geography*, 14(2): 211–233.

Austin, J.L. (1962). *How To Do Things With Words*. Cambridge, MA: Harvard University Press.

Azaryahu, M. (1986). "Street Names and Political Identity." *Journal of Contemporary History*, 21(4): 581–604.

Azaryahu, M. (1988). "What is to be Remembered: The Struggle over Street Names, Berlin 1921–1930." *Tel Aviver Jahrbuch für deutsche Geschichte*, 17: 241–258.

Azaryahu, M. (1990). "Renaming the Past: Changes in 'City-Text' in Germany and Austria 1945–1947." *History & Memory*, 2(2): 32–53.

Azaryahu, M. (1991). *Vom Wilhelmplatz zu Thälmannplatz. Politische Symbole im öffentlichen Leben der DDR*. Gerlingen: Bleicher Verlag.

Azaryahu, M. (1992). "The Purge of Bismarck and Saladin: The Renaming of Streets in East Berlin and Haifa, a Comparative Study in Culture-Planning." *Poetics Today*, 13(2): 351–367.

Azaryahu, M. (1996). "The Power of Commemorative Street Names." *Environment and Planning D*, 14(3): 311–330.

Azaryahu, M. (1997). "German Reunification and the Politics of Street Names: The Case of East Berlin." *Political Geography*, 16(6): 479–493.

Azaryahu, M. (2011a). "The Critical Turn and Beyond: The Case of Commemorative Street Naming." *ACME: An International E-Journal for Critical Geographies*, 10(1): 28–33.

Azaryahu, M. (2011b). "The Politics of Commemorative Street Renaming: Berlin 1945–1948." *Journal of Historical Geography*, 37(4): 483–492.

Azaryahu, M. (2012a). "Hebrew, Arabic, English: The Politics of Multilingual Street Signs in Israeli Cities." *Social & Cultural Geography*, 13(5): 461–479.

Azaryahu, M. (2012b). "Renaming the Past in Post-Nazi Germany: Insights into the Politics of Street Naming in Mannheim and Potsdam." *Cultural Geographies*, 19(3): 385–400.

Azaryahu, M. (2012c). "Rabin's Road: The Politics of Toponymic Commemoration of Yitzhak Rabin in Israel." *Political Geography*, 31(2): 73–82.

Bar-Gal, Y. (1988). "The Street Names of Tel Aviv: Chapter in Cultural-Historical Geography of the City 1909–1934." *Cathedra*, 47: 188–131.

Bar-Gal, Y. (1989). "Cultural-Geographical Aspects of Street Names in the Towns of Israel." *Names: A Journal of Onomastics*, 37(4): 329–344.

Benjamin, W. (1999). *The Arcades Project*. Cambridge, MA: Belknap Press.

Berg, L., and Kearns, R. (1996). "Naming as Norming: 'Race', Gender, and the Identity Politics of Naming Places in Aotearoa/New Zealand." *Environment and Planning D: Society and Space*, 14(1): 99–122.

Berg, L. and Vuolteenaho, J. (Eds.) (2009). *Critical Toponymies: The Contested Politics of Place Naming*. Farnham: Ashgate.

Bigon, L. (2008). "Names, Norms and Forms: French and Indigenous Toponyms in Early Colonial Dakar, Senegal." *Planning Perspectives*, 23(4): 479–501.

Bigon, L. (2009). "Urban Planning, Colonial Doctrines and Street Naming in French Dakar and British Lagos, c. 1850–1930." *Urban History*, 36(3): 426–448.

Bigon, L. and Dahamshe, A. (2014). "An Anatomy of Symbolic Power: Israeli Road-Sign Policy and the Palestinian Minority." *Environment and Planning D*, 32(4): 606–621.

Blinder, A. (2016). "Drive Spurred by Church Killings to Ban Confederate Symbols Falters." *The New York Times*, March 14: A10.

Bryan, S. (2016). "Hollywood Considers Rechristening City Street Named for KKK Founder." *Sun-Sentinel*, May 19: www.sun-sentinel.com/local/broward/hollywood/fl-street-names-hollywood-kkk-update-20151118-story.html.

Butler, J. (1993). *Bodies That Matter: On the Discursive Limits of "Sex."* New York: Routledge.

Butler, J. (2015). *Notes Toward a Performative Theory of Assembly*. Cambridge, MA: Harvard University Press.

Caliendo, G. (2011). "MLK Boulevard: Material Forms of Memory and the Social Contestation of Racial Signification." *Journal of Black Studies*, 42(7): 1148–1170.

Çelik, Z., Favro, D., and Ingersoll, R. (Eds.) (1994). *Streets: Critical Perspectives on Public Space*. Berkeley: University of California Press.

Cosgrove, D. (1984). *Social Formation and Symbolic Landscape*. London: Croom Helm.

Cousin, J. and Lacombe, P. (1899). *De la nomenclature des rues de Paris. Mémoires de la société l'histoire de Paris et de l'ile-de-France*, 26: 1–24.

Creţan, R. and Matthews, P. (2016). "Popular Responses to City-Text Changes: Street Naming and the Politics of Practicality in a Post-Socialist Martyr City." *Area*, 48(1): 92–102.

Derrida, J. (1988). *Limited Inc.* Evanston, IL: Northwestern University Press.

Duminy, J. (2014). "Street Renaming, Symbolic Capital, and Resistance in Durban, South Africa." *Environment and Planning D: Society and Space*, 32(2): 310–328.

Duncan, J. (1980). "The Superorganic in American Cultural Geography." *Annals of the Association of American Geographers*, 70(2): 181–198.

Duncan, J. (1990). *The City as Text: The Politics of Landscape Interpretation in the Kandyan Kingdom*. Cambridge: Cambridge University Press.

Duncan, J., and Duncan, N. (1988). "(Re)Reading the Landscape." *Environment and Planning D: Society and Space*, 6(2): 117–126.

Dwyer, O. (2004). "Symbolic Accretion and Commemoration." *Social & Cultural Geography*, 5(3): 419–435.

Dwyer, O. and Alderman, D. (2008), "Memorial Landscapes: Analytic Questions and Metaphors." *GeoJournal*, 73(3): 165–178.

Entrikin, J.N. (1991). *The Betweenness of Place: Towards a Geography of Modernity*. Baltimore, MD: Johns Hopkins University Press.

Faraco, J. and Murphy, M. (1997). "Street Names and Political Regimes in an Andalusian Town." *Ethnology*, 36(2), 123–148.

Ferguson, P. (1988). "Reading City Streets." *The French Review*, 61(3): 386–397.

Ferguson, P. (1994). *Paris as Revolution: Writing the Nineteenth-Century City*. Berkeley: University of California Press.

Foote, K. (1997). *Shadowed Ground: America's Landscapes of Violence and Tragedy*. Austin: University of Texas Press.

Gill, G. (2005). "Changing Symbols: The Renovation of Moscow Place Names." *The Russian Review*, 64(3): 480–503.

Giraut, F. and Houssay-Holzschuch, M. (2016), "Place Naming as *Dispositif:* Towards a Theoretical Framework." *Geopolitics*, 21(1): 1–21.

Kellogg, J. (1977). "Negro Urban Clusters in the Postbellum South." *Geographical Review*, 67(4): 310–321.

Koch, H. and Hercus, L. (Eds.) (2009). *Aboriginal Placenames: Naming and Re-naming the Australian Landscape*. Canberra: Australian National University Press.

Jaffe, E. (2015). "The Streets of Paris, Renamed for Women." *CityLab*, August 27: www.citylab.com/design/2015/08/the-streets-of-paris-renamed-for-women/402526.

Jett, S.C. (1997). "Place-naming, Environment, and Perception among the Canyon de Chelly Navajo of Arizona." *The Professional Geographer*, 49(4): 481–493.

Halbwachs, M. (1980 [1950]). *The Collective Memory*. F. Ditter, Jr. and V. Ditter (Eds.). New York: Harper & Row.

Halbwachs, M. (1992 [1925]). "The Social Frameworks of Memory." In L. Coser (Ed.), *On Collective Memory* (pp. 35–189). Chicago: University of Chicago Press.

Harvey, D. (1979). "Monument and Myth: The Building of the Basilica of the Sacred Heart." *Annals of the Association of American Geographers*, 69(3): 362–381.

Hebbert, M. (2005). "The Street as Locus of Collective Memory." *Environment and Planning D*, 23(4): 581–596.

Jones, R. and Merriman, P. (2009). "Hot, Banal and Everyday Nationalism: Bilingual Road Signs in Wales." *Political Geography*, 28(3): 164–173.

Kearns, R. and Berg, L. (2002). "Proclaiming Place: Towards a Geography of Place Name Pronunciation." *Social & Cultural Geography*, 3(3): 283–302.

Leighly, J. (1978). "Town Names of Colonial New England in the West." *Annals of the Association of American Geographers*, 68(2): 233–248.

Light, D. (2004). "Street Names in Bucharest, 1990–1997: Exploring the Modern Historical Geographies of Post-Social Change." *Journal of Historical Geography*, 30(1): 154–172.

Light, D., Nicolae, I., and Suditu, B. (2002). "Toponymy and the Communist City: Street Names in Bucharest, 1948–1965." *GeoJournal*, 56(2): 135–144.

Light, D. and Young, C. (2014). "Habit, Memory and the Persistence of Socialist-Era Street Names in Post-Socialist Bucharest, Romania." *Annals of the Association of American Geographers*, 104(3): 668–685.

Lowenthal, D. (1975). "Past Time, Present Place: Landscape and Memory." *Geographical Review*, 65(1): 1–36.

Lowenthal, D. (1985). *The Past is a Foreign Country*. New York: Cambridge University Press.

Massey, D. (2005). *For Space*. London: Sage Publications.

McCarthy, K. (1975). "Street Names in Beirut, Lebanon." *Names: A Journal of Onomastics*, 23(2): 74–88.

Mencken, H.L. (1948). "American Street Names." *American Speech*, 23(2): 81–88.

Miles, J.C. (1973). *House Names Around the World*. Detroit, MI: Gale Research Co.

Milo, D. (1986). "Le Nom des Rues." In P. Nora (Ed.), *Les Lieux de Mémoire: Lan Nation*. Paris: Gallimard.

Monmonier, M. (2006). *From Squaw Tit to Whorehouse Meadow: How Maps Name, Claim, and Inflame*. Chicago, IL: University of Chicago Press.

Morin, K. and Berg, L. (2001). "Gendering Resistance: British Colonial Narratives of Wartime New Zealand." *Journal of Historical Geography*, 27(2): 196–222.

Murphyao, A. and Black, K. (2015). "Unsettling Settler Belonging: (Re)naming and Territory Making in the Pacific Northwest." *American Review of Canadian Studies*, 45(3): 315–331.

Myers, G. (1996). "Naming and Placing the Other: Power and the Urban Landscape in Zanzibar." *Tijdschrift voor Economische en Sociale Geografie*, 87(3): 237–246.

Oxford English Dictionary (2016). "Cosmos." Oxford: Oxford University Press.

Nada, S. (2014). "Gender Aspects of Public Urban Space: Analysis of the Names of Belgrade Streets." *Sociologija*, 56(2): 125–144.

Nash, C. (2009). "Irish Place Names: Post-colonial Locations." In L. Berg and J. Vuolteenaho (Eds.), *Critical Toponymies: The Contested Politics of Place Naming* (pp. 137–152). Farnham: Ashgate.

Nora, P. (Ed.) (1984–1992), *Les Lieux de Mémoire: Lan Nation*. Paris: Gallimard.

Palonen, E. (2008). "The City-Text in Post-Communist Budapest: Street Names, Memorials, and the Politics of Commemoration." *GeoJournal*, 73(3): 219–230.

Palonen, K. (1993). "Reading Street Names Politically." In K. Palonen and T. Parvikko (Eds.), *Reading the Political* (pp. 103–121). Helsinki: The Finnish Political Science Association.

Peteet, J. (2005). "Words as Interventions: Naming in the Palestine–Israel Conflict." *Third World Quarterly*, 26(1): 153–172.

Pinchevski, A. and Torgovnik, E. (2002). "Signifying Passages: The Signs of Change in Israeli Street Names." *Media, Culture and Society*, 24(3): 365–388.

Poon, L. (2015). "Mapping the Sexism of City Street Names." *CityLab*: www.citylab.com/politics/2015/11/mapping-the-sexism-of-city-street-names/414094.

Pred, A. (1992). "Languages of Everyday Practice and Resistance: Stockholm at the End of the Nineteenth Century." In A. Pred and M. Watts (Eds.), *Reworking Modernity: Capitalisms and Symbolic Discontent* (pp. 118–154). New Brunswick, NJ: Rutgers University Press.

Regier, A. (2010). "The Magic of the Corner: Walter Benjamin and Street Names." *The Germanic Review: Literature, Culture, Theory*, 85(3): 189–204.

Rose-Redwood, R. (2008a). "'Sixth Avenue is Now a Memory': Regimes of Spatial Inscription and the Performative Limits of the Official City-Text." *Political Geography*, 27(8): 875–894.

Rose-Redwood, R. (2008b). "Indexing the Great Ledger of the Community: Urban House Numbering, City Directories, and the Production of Spatial Legibility." *Journal of Historical Geography*, 34(2): 286–310.

Rose-Redwood, R. (2008c). "From Number to Name: Symbolic Capital, Places of Memory, and the Politics of Street Renaming in New York City." *Social & Cultural Geography*, 9(4): 431–452.

Rose-Redwood, R. (2012). "With Numbers in Place: Security, Territory, and the Production of Calculable Space." *Annals of the Association of American Geographers*, 102(2): 295–319.

Rose-Redwood, R. (2016). "'Reclaim, Rename, Reoccupy': Decolonizing Place and the Reclaiming of PKOLS." *ACME: An International E-Journal for Critical Geographies* 15(1): 187–206.

Rose-Redwood, R., Alderman, D., and Azaryahu, M. (2010). "Geographies of Toponymic Inscription: New Directions in Critical Place-Name Studies." *Progress in Human Geography*, 34(4): 453–470.

Rose-Redwood, R. and Glass, M. (2014). "Geographies of Performativity." In M. Glass and R. Rose-Redwood (Eds.), *Performativity, Politics, and the Production of Social Space* (pp. 1–34). New York: Routledge.

Rose-Redwood, R. and Kadonaga, L. (2016). "'The Corner of Avenue A and Twenty-Third Street': Geographies of Street Numbering in the United States." *The Professional Geographer*, 68(1): 39–52.

Rose-Redwood, R. and Tantner, A. (2012). "Introduction: Governmentality, House Numbering and the Spatial History of the Modern City." *Urban History*, 39(4): 607–613.

Šakaja, L. and Stanić, J. (2011). "Other(ing), Self(portraying), Negotiating: The Spatial Codification of Values in Zagreb's City-Text." *Cultural Geographies*, 18(4): 495–516.

Schechner, R. (2003). "The Street is the Stage." In E. Striff (Ed.), *Performance Studies* (pp. 110–123). New York: Palgrave Macmillan.

Shortridge, J.R. (1985). "The Vernacular Middle West." *Annals of the Association of American Geographers*, 75(1): 48–57.

Shoval, N. (2013). "Street-Naming, Tourism Development and Cultural Conflict: The Case of the Old City of Acre/Akko/Akka." *Transactions of the Institute of British Geographers*, 38(4): 612–626.

Stewart, G. (1967 [1945]). *Names on the Land: A Historical Account of Place-naming in the United States*. Boston, MA: Houghton Mifflin.

Stump, R. (1988). "Toponymic Commemoration of National Figures: The Cases of Kennedy and King." *Names: A Journal of Onomastics*, 36(3–4): 203–216.

Sullivan, P. (2015). "Alexandria Streets with Rebel Ties Could Change." *The Washington Post*, September 14, B1.

Swart, M. (2008). "Name Changes as Symbolic Reparation after Transition: The Examples of Germany and South Africa." *German Law Journal*, 9(2): 105–20.

Tantner, A. (2009). "Addressing the Houses: The Introduction of House Numbering in Europe." *Histoire & Mesure*, 24(2): 7–30.

Tantner, A. (2015). *House Numbers: Pictures of a Forgotten History*. London: Reaktion Books.

Thale, C. (2007). "Changing Addresses: Social Conflict, Civic Culture, and the Politics of House Numbering Reform in Milwaukee, 1913–1931." *Journal of Historical Geography*, 33(1): 125–143.

The Denver Post. (2016). "Tennessee House's Bill to Better Protect Historic Names OK'd." February 19, 14A.

Tucker, B. and Rose-Redwood, R. (2015). "Decolonizing the Map? Toponymic Politics and the Rescaling of the Salish Sea." *The Canadian Geographer*, 59(2): 194–206.

Verdery, K. (1999). *The Political Lives of Dead Bodies: Reburial and Postsocialist Change*. New York: Columbia University Press.

Vuolteenaho, J., Ameel, L., Newby, A., and Scott, M. (2012). "Language, Space, and Power: Reflections on Linguistic and Spatial Turns in Urban Research." *COLLeGIUM: Studies Across Disciplines in the Humanities and Social Sciences*, 13: 1–27.

Wanjiru, M.W. and Matsubara, K. (2017). "Street Toponymy and the Decolonisation of the Urban Landscape in Post-colonial Nairobi." *Journal of Cultural Geography*, 34(1): 1–23.

Woodman, P. (2015). "The Toponymy of Absence." *Review of Historical Geography and Toponomastics*, 10(19–20): 7–16.

Wright, J. (1929). "The Study of Place Names: Recent Work and Some Possibilities." *Geographical Review*, 19(1): 140–144.

Yeoh, B. (1992). "Street Names in Colonial Singapore." *Geographical Review*, 82(3): 313–322.

Yeoh, B. (1996). "Street-Naming and Nation-Building: Toponymic Inscriptions of Nationhood in Singapore." *Area*, 28(3): 298–307.

Zeidel, Ronen (2006). "Naming and Counter-naming: The Struggle between Society and State as Reflected by Street Names in Iraq and the Arab Sector in Israel." *Orient*, 47(2): 201–217.

Zelinsky, W. (1967). "Classical Town Names in the United States: The Historical Geography of an American Idea." *Geographical Review*, 57(4): 463–495.

Zelinsky, W. (1988). *Nation into State: The Shifting Symbolic Foundations of American Nationalism*. Chapel Hill: University of North Carolina Press.

Zerubavel, Y. (2014). "'Numerical Commemoration' and the Challenges of Collective Remembrance in Israel." *History and Memory*, 26(1): 5–38.

2 Reading street names politically

A second reading

Kari Palonen

Introduction

The politics of names and naming was among my main research interests in the first half of the 1990s, but it soon took a backseat to other research foci. I came to prefer studying texts for which the link with political theorizing was more obvious and the case of naming seemed to concern rather marginal issues. Perhaps what Quentin Skinner (1996, ch. 4) writes, specifically that renaming is only a rather marginal aspect in the study of conceptual changes, also cooled my interest in the topic. However, I would now like to revisit my earlier interest in the politics of naming in the present chapter by offering an updated account, or "second reading" in the parliamentary sense, of my essay, "Reading Street Names Politically" (Palonen 1993b). The main idea is to incorporate an abridged account of the politico-theoretical scheme sketched in the Introduction of the original book, *Reading the Political* (Palonen 1993a), and later revised on various occasions, particularly in "Four Times of Politics" (Palonen 2003). In this second reading of street names politically, I insist on the politico-theoretical perspective as well as emphasize the procedural aspects of politics.

Four aspects of politics

How is politics manifested in the naming of streets? This requires a specification of the constitutive aspects of politics. I will apply the Weber-inspired perspective on *politics as a contingent and controversial temporal activity*. From this perspective, space is only frozen time, stability a temporal absence of change. Regarding street naming as a political activity also introduces different temporal layers to the polity (for a discussion of historical times, see Koselleck 2000). In particular, I illustrate the practices and the possibilities of naming politics through a historical sketch of the politics of street naming in Helsinki, read in the broader European context.

Naming and nominating belong to J.L. Austin's classic list of performatives within the class of exercitives. This concept is defined by him as follows:

> An exercitive is the giving of a decision in favour of or against a certain course of action, or advocacy of it. It is a decision that something is to be so, as distinct from a judgement that is so: it is advocacy that it should be so, as

opposed to an estimate that it is so; it is an award as opposed to an assessment; it is a sentence as opposed to a verdict.

(Austin 1990 [1962], 155)

In other words, the choice aspect renders to the act of naming a political dimension: names could always be different and they are subject to potential conflicts, often of actual controversy. Naming is the contingent act *par excellence* and, as such, it can be understood to be a paradigmatic case for doing politics.

A comparison with voting is illustrative. In both cases an open question is posed, candidates for action are presented and the selection among them completes the act. In this sense, voting can be understood as a special case of naming in which the presentation and selection of the candidates is explicit. Voting subjects a question, or the choice of person, to a contingent decision instead of finding some extra-political "reasons" for a standpoint or an appointment of a person (cf. Weber 1971 [1917]). However, diverse attempts to "normalize" voting, to diminish, neutralize, or control the contingency, can also be used in studying the politics of naming.

Weber's thinking is shaped by concepts of chance, by horizons of the possible, by occasions or opportunities for action and their complex relationships. For example, Weber's concept of "the state" is based on the chances to become obeyed (*Gehorsamschance*), a term mentioned in his last 1920 lecture series (see Weber 2009 and my comment on it, Palonen 2011). For Weber, some chances to act otherwise are present in any kind of situation, but every chance is precious and limited in time. When some projects are "realized," this always means a loss of some chances available in previous situations.

For understanding politics in temporal terms, I split the first term in the conventional triad (politics, policy, polity) into two temporal activities, politicization and politicking (first in Palonen 1993a). In 2003, I presented the relationships between the four aspects of politics in these temporal and Weberian terms:

> *Politicization* names a share of power, opens up a specified horizon of chances in terms of this share, while *politicking* means performative operations in the struggle for power with the already existing shares and their redistribution. *Polity* refers to those power shares that have already been politicized but have also vested interests that also tacitly exclude other kinds of shares, while *policy* means a regulation and coordination of performative operations to specific ends and means.
>
> (Palonen 2003, 59)

Nothing is political in itself but must be politicized by someone. Politicization consists of marking something "political" or "politics" and thereby opening a horizon of contingency in dealing with this. In this sense, naming is inherent to politicization, either by marking something previously unnamed or challenging things previously named otherwise. Giving a distinct name is an act of politicking, which might be set in relationship to certain policies or initiate new ones. In the politics of naming, we can thus distinguish two dimensions—naming or not naming—connected to politicization and polity, and *this* naming vs. *that* naming, referring to politicking and policy.

A polity refers to a type of regime, which is historically a contingent result of specific past politicizations and the exclusion of others. The regimes do have a certain degree of flexibility and fluid borders, but similarly to speaking of constitutionalist, presidential, or parliamentary regimes, we can distinguish certain ideal types of street naming. For the analysis of specific cities, situating them to such regime types might be perhaps the most important point of departure.

The original politicizing aspect is barely visible in modern cities as streets are named even before they are built. Streets today don't exist without a name, although the "parliamentary" moment of naming might occur later. I speak of political actors regarding both those naming and those named.

My narrative departs from the minimal level of street naming policy, referring to the normative and teleological dimensions of naming. The next move connects this to the broader register of politicking moves. Similarly, I start by establishing the principles and limits of polity and then situate these to a broader perspective of politicization, including those contesting the current forms of the polity.

The final section on the use of rhetorical genres in the interpretation of Helsinki's street naming politics originally focused exclusively on the tempi of the three rhetorical genres. Quentin Skinner's rhetorical studies inspired me to take a more historical view on rhetoric and contributed to my studies on parliamentary procedures (Palonen 2014a, 2014b). I have understood parliamentary debates as the modern paradigm of the deliberative genre as speaking *pro et contra* and separated from it negotiation or diplomatic rhetoric (Palonen 2010). In contrast to the 1993 version of this chapter, I now insist that even the modest degree of parliamentary culture present in Helsinki city politics might have played a role in the rhetorical shift from forenames to surnames after 1900.

Street naming policy in the city

In contemporary urban politics, street naming policies regulate the contingency of naming. They contain procedures, authoritative agents, and criteria for the proposal and acceptance of street names. A definite procedure distinguishes the authoritative character of street naming from the slow and spontaneous practices in older cities (for the constitution of the naming monopoly in France, cf. Milo 1986, 287–289). The first inhabitants do not vote on the street names in the area, but rather the names are given without knowing who will be the inhabitants (for a critique, cf. Flierl 1991, 9). In the stage of actual naming, hardly anyone has a personal interest to be engaged with it. Still there have been attempts from below both to remove names from the city-text as well as to introduce new ones, but in what was then West Berlin, for example, they were hardly successful (cf. Sackgassen 1988, 46–55, 89–100).

The establishment of an authoritative, formal procedure excludes unofficial naming, which, however, sometimes has been an ingenious act of resistance (on the

"Jan Palach Square" in Prague, see Moníková 1987, 184–185). The authoritative act of street naming can also be a source of conflict, for example between career officials and naming experts, while the city council's parliamentary committees hardly have more than a veto power over decisions (for Helsinki, cf. Terho 1979, 19–20).

Among the normative criteria for street names, the most important is the *stability principle*: for unlike firm or product names, street names are intended to be "timeless" (Närhi 1979, 26) and the change of them is regarded as exceptional. Street renamings are a politically interesting type of policy change, not only when a regime changes (cf. Azaryahu 1990) but also in more prosaic situations such as municipal reforms. The common adoption of a one street-one name principle, which prohibits the plurality of used names, is typical of many other situations of naming as well.

Street names are supposed to be accepted as legitimate by the inhabitants, although they are seldom subjected to a referendum. Naming experts frequently prefer a colorless city-text to names which could provoke protests and quarrels. A provocative rhetoric has scarcely a chance of acceptance in street naming.

In particular, commemorative names referring to persons, events, and concepts are always controversial. With Benjamin we can speak of an act of "municipal immortality" (1983, 643), and with Arendt we can see in it a manifestation of having been somebody rather than nobody (1981 [1960], 169–171). Commemorations are subject to explicit policy regulations. As a general rule, for instance, the death of a person has often been a minimal criterion for conferring a street name, but even in western countries this criterion is not followed without exceptions.

Another criterion for street names is that the "greatness" of persons to be commemorated must be generally recognized. The French Ministry of the Interior categorically stated in 1946: "l'œuvre de ces personnalités doit être à l'abri de toute polémique" [the work of these personalities must be free of any controversy] (quoted in Toillon 1984, 11). A dilemma for naming policy is to balance the administrative criterion of incontestability with a political majority's claim to draw its own profile in street naming. Another dilemma concerns the political traditions of the city: should they be prolonged or can the actual majority impose its will, even at the cost of the requirement of a stable street name: in the Parisian suburbs the former communist majorities are still visible in street names.

Street names as a means of politicking

A street naming policy with its procedural, personal, and normative dimensions can only limit the acceptable and give paradigmatic example for "good" names. Conventional politics appeals to policy precedents, principles, and authorities, not actively using the range of freedom permitted by them. The autonomy of the decisions and the superiority of politics over administration (cf. Weber 1971 [1918]) tend to be absent and the significance of street names as a medium of politics remains disputed.

Street name politicking can be oriented towards proposing new names, changing the old ones, or reinterpreting the political in the existing names. Virtuosity may well be already manifested in single cases as well as in turning street names into a playground of one's own politicking in general. Politicking does not have an immediate interest in the general profile of street names.

A change of street names always needs special justification. Of course, street names have been changed even where no revolutions or other regime changes have occurred (for Berlin, see *Sackgassen* 1988, 282). Perhaps research has compromised the role of a person in history or an event does not appear any longer as glorious as it was once thought to be. Sometimes an old street name has become politically compromised into a pejorative metonymy, say *Braunauer Straße*. And conversely, the death of Dag Hammarskjöld or the murder of John F. Kennedy has spread the name to streets all over the world: in France in 1978, for example, Kennedy was present in 49 of 95 *préfectures* (Milo 1986, 307).

Because new names are always needed, a promising strategy to have a singular name introduced lies in the naming of new streets. In this soft way, the profile of the city-text could slowly be altered, for example, by increasing the number of streets named for women. This kind of "compensatory naming" has also been used as a means of preventing the return to the old names after the fall of pro-Soviet regimes (for East Berlin after 1989, cf. Flierl 1991). But it is difficult to imagine compensating military names—West Berlin, for example, had ca. 250 of them (cf. *Sackgassen* 1988, 21)—by introducing names such as *Pacifist's Square, Civil Disobedience's Avenue, Conscientious Objector's Street,* or *Deserter's Boulevard.*

Especially in France and Germany, the streets named after persons usually also give a presentation of the person. A way of politicking is to change only the reference person, not the street name itself. In West Berlin, the presentation of *Petersallee* was changed from the imperialist Carl Peters to the CDU local politician Hans Peters (*Sackgassen* 1988, 122–123). In Besançon, Pierre-Joseph Proudhon only got half of *rue Proudhon* named after him, while the other half remained named for an older, conservative relative of his (Touillon 1984, 143).

It is obviously more difficult to explicitly revise the policy principles of street naming than to add new ones to them. It is easy to refer to precedents, for example when living persons have got a street or an *ad hoc* suspension of a principle can also be accepted without controversies. In these cases, the city council can manifest its sovereignty and show the limits of guidance by policy principles.

Reinterpreting a principle and opposing the policy criteria together form the simplest means of politicking by street names. A paradigm is set by the famous but controversial "sons and daughters" of a city. By granting a street to them, an opposition of the inhabitants is to be expected but not doing so would show the city to be afraid of an original person: a Besançon without a street dedicated to P-J. Proudhon would manifest the narrow-mindedness of the local politicians. A consciously provocative rhetoric for introducing controversial figures into the city-text can be considered as a kind of proof in the mastery of politicking.

In politicking, the commitment to a definite name is instrumental to the manifestation of virtuosity in the naming situation. In this sense, alternatives to name changes are to be understood as tentative and liable to be altered if a suitable compromise name is found. Politicking transcends the interest in naming and in streets as a political space and is rather related to alternative media of politicking.

The naming polity

A naming polity constitutes a name regime for the city, shapes its profile and regiments its change. It is based on past politicizations that are recognized as legitimate: the naming polity preserves the existing modes of the politicized as well as regulates them to acceptable forms. It mediates between policy and politicking, between choosing street names and acting by means of them. The profile of the name regime in a city is shaped both by the content of these aspects and by the links which try to hold them together.

The maintenance of the naming polity consists, above all, in the defense of the city council's autonomy with respect to naming decisions over the attempts to universalize policy rules as if they were quasi-natural. A name polity exists only where at least some *Spielraum* for politicking is manifested over the claims of making the street naming a merely administrative or police question.

The power in a naming polity also relates directly to the right of the actual majorities in the city council to draw their own lines into the city-text, thereby contributing to the street naming profile of the city. Policy regulations that are too strict would leave the city without a singular profile in political imagination. But a naming polity would also temper sudden changes in street names, by the will of an actual majority, in the name of the political traditions of the city.

The street name regime also sets limits to politicking, for example by preventing an over-extended use of naming streets after persons, events, and concepts. The tendency towards the autonomization of street names from their original political references in the course of history leaves them only known to insiders, who could read out of them shifting temporal layers in the city's dominant political color and its tolerated nuances. The polity may also contain moves against the practice of using unauthorized names (on Lodz, see Enzensberger 1987, 372).

Paradigmatic name types can always be used, if occasionally new names or name changes are urgently needed, and they may give a specific profile to the city-text. The opposition between the politicizing moment and its slow withering away within the name regime can concern both the content and the character of paradigmatic names.

In the capitals of Europe, we can detect three old paradigms for street naming: clerical, monarchic, and military names (e.g., Ferguson 1988, 387). Their decline can be interpreted as a diminishing of politicking in so far as they are replaced by names from nature, local history, "culture," and other harmless areas. Those overtly "apolitical" names may be made to neglect the elective and controversial character of street naming and by granting it willingly to experts and specialists.

The dilemma of creating a singular profile of street names in modern Europe lies just here: should the clerical, monarchic, and military names be replaced by others even at the cost of lowering the possibility of politicking by street names or should the rudimentary and oppressive presence of names with strong partisan allusions be retained and only compensated by names with opposite connotations? The same dilemma was faced in Eastern Europe in relation to communist naming culture.

Politicization of street naming

The politicization of street names concerns the profile of a city's street names. In terms of my politics-typology, all naming of streets is politicizing, independently of the content of the names. It is therefore important to identify the initial moments of politicization as well as those that break with the limits of the existing polity and alter the naming situation in a manner which opens up new horizons for politicking by names. Politicization is a deconstructive move by reverting the naming situation from its submission to the current naming regime. But how the situation is used, and by whom the openness can be employed, is not a question of politicization but of politicking.

Except in cases of completely new cities and streets, the primary temporal dimension of politicization is the past. It is directed towards street names that canonize a certain selected past, which are also subject to change or reinterpretion. Politicization in terms of decanonization proceeds by compromising either the value or the significance of a canonized reference in a street name. Politicization disputes the inevitable partiality in favor of the history of the winners, so typical both to unreflective and consciously partisan acts of street naming.

The decanonization of street names is by no means necessarily replaced by rehabilitating persons *post mortem* through street naming—this is rather a move in politicking. In its formality, politicization merely renders naming into a controversial issue. Constitutive for a politicized reading of street names is rather an obstinate refusal of constructive alternatives: if they are presented, they are only instruments for getting rid of the compromised names. The politicization of street names may be strategically concentrated on eliminating some key canonized names, knowing well that the chances are normally minimal in such cases and therefore a concentration of efforts in selective campaigns may be wise.

A minimal decanonization does not even attempt to change the street names but aims at improving the competence and interest among citizens in reading the existing street names politically. Learning to give attention to the partisan and regulating character of the city-text (e.g., to the dominance of clerical, monarchic, and military names) may sometimes be an effective means for opening the situation to politicking. Even the replacement of the communist culture of naming in Eastern Europe by seemingly apolitical names may be a politicizing move as the deconstruction of a regime, which renders the naming both less ritualistic and more open to invention, as compared to a replacement by opposite "heroic" names.

The city's profile in commemorating persons, events, and concepts in its streets may be rendered more significant and thus the requirement for using street names as a means of politicking more central. By such means the presence of history, the actuality of past struggles and conflicts, and the invocation of the significance of past events and persons for the present, may be manifested. The problem with this variant lies both in the conventional view of politics and in the lack of understanding of the relative, situational, margin-oriented character of politicization.

A subversive politicizing strategy of street naming offers opportunities for diverse inversions and modifications of past naming by using nicknames or altering the content and compromising the original reference. The critique of the history of winners canonized by dates does not require much research and imagination in finding events from other years with opposite political significance. Opening the naming situation by politicization may also result in making the naming appear to be more playful than a canonical event. Besides inversions, playing with names through verbal jokes is always possible, such as through the use of ironic names (for both self-irony and the rehabilitation of commonly pejorative names by the German feminist naming culture, cf. Pusch 1990). It is possible to invent ingenious acronyms from the initials and in general using manufactured names, which only indirectly refer to words in common language or which attempt to create new words.

Politicization by these means may also introduce supplementary names for the streets, as is common practice in personal names. If a writer, for example, uses a pseudonym, why couldn't she also do the same thing for the address: it would require ingenuity also in the post office. This would deny the monopoly of one authorized name for streets and abandon the principle of one street-one name, by allowing streets to concur with each other in the number of nicknames. Related to the plural experience of the street itself by its inhabitants and users, this would be a simple means of politicization. Not only cities but also streets could have a name profile of their own, instead of a single name.

Still, a type of limit for politicizing street naming may be found both in the singularity and in the stability requirements. Without some definite singularity and rigidity in designating an object, it would hardly be possible to speak of proper names at all. But this does not necessarily mean that all streets should have only one authorized name, which always remains the same.

From forenames to surnames: street names in Helsinki[1]

A brief look at the map of the inner city of Helsinki is enough to show a predominance of forenames, which gives the city-text a singular profile. Of course, forenames are a common resource of street naming, particularly in relation to the calendars of the saints and the names of royalty. In Helsinki, however, key forenames are secular and non-dynastic. To read them politically requires recourse to the history of the country, city, and practices of street naming themselves as well as comparisons with other European capitals, especially Paris and Berlin.

Using street names for commemoration as a system of nomination, related to the idea, "d'adopter des noms qui n'eussent pas de rapport direct avec le lieu auquel ils étaient imposés" [to adopt names not directly related to the place in which they were imposed] (Milo 1986, 287), is of quite recent origin historically. It can be located in Paris and dated back to the construction of Place de l'Odéon in 1779; it was then radicalized during the Revolution, especially in the context of the project of Abbé Gregoire from 1794, and continued again by Napoleon Bonaparte (cf. Milo 1986, 286–301).

Helsinki was founded by King Gustaf Vasa of Sweden in 1550, but it remained a provincial town. In the war between Sweden and Russia, the city was largely burned down in 1808, and by the Peace Treaty of Hamina in 1809, Finland was transferred to Russia with the status of an autonomous Grand Duchy. Helsinki was made the capital of Finland in 1812—it was both closer to St. Petersburg and farther from Stockholm than Turku. Swedish was the official language of Finland. Finnish street names were introduced unofficially in the 1860s and officially after 1900, when Finnish became the majority language. I will call the city by the Finnish name Helsinki, but use the Swedish street names for the period until ca. 1900 and the Finnish names for the later period.

The city was rebuilt as a capital of Empire style, according to the city plan of J.A. Ehrenström with C.L. Engel as the architect. In the context of Ehrenström's city plan, the naming of all of the streets arose in response to public safety concerns, particularly in relation to fire. Ehrenström and the Governor General of Finland, Fabian Steinheil, formed the first committee for street naming in Helsinki, submitting their proposals to Alexander I who visited Helsinki in 1819. In the new Fire Order of 1820, only a few old local names referring to the context and in two cases—*Esplanaden* and *Bulevarden*—to the streets themselves were retained; otherwise new names were introduced. For them the new French system of using non-natural and non-local references was practiced consequently, as if as a mark of distinction for a capital. The new system marks an original politicization of the street name polity in Helsinki. Even today, the street names in the city are to be related to this politicizing and polity-creating act.

In a wider political context, creating a capital for the Grand Duchy of Finland was a measure of nation-building, balancing the Russian requirements and the attempt to create a specifically Finnish system of administration and "government." The key political figures were the Governor General, the trustee of the czar in Helsinki, and the Ministerial State Secretary, as a trustee of "the Finns" in St. Petersburg, while the Senate, "the internal government," only later gained a key place in politicking. After the transfer to Helsinki in 1828, the university became another place of politicking, and the factions in the Diet largely originated in student politics (cf. Klinge 1989).

The composition of the street naming committee and the procedure, with the veto-power of the czar himself, are indices of the key role of street naming in the capital's bureaucratic-diplomatic style of politicking. No normative rules or procedure for decisions on the naming polity were created: naming partly followed some general paradigms, but to a large extent required inventions, using the skills of politicking by the committee members which established the singularity of the nomenclature of street names in Helsinki.

An extraordinary space for politicking was created by the inapplicability of the common paradigms of street naming in Helsinki. In a Lutheran country, saints were not honored. However, the clerical element was represented by a few names of Russian, Greek Orthodox saints (St. Anna, Andreae, Georg, Helene, Vladimir), but there could not be too many. Some central streets were dedicated to the Romanov family, namely to Alexander I's wife Elizabeth, his mother Maria, along with her maiden name of princess Sophia (of Württemberg), and his brothers Konstantin and Mihail—all of them still alive in 1820. The czar himself was not honored with a street name until after his death (1833) with the naming of

Alexandersgatan. No recourse to Swedish monarchic names was made, and Finland did not have a nobility or a military of its own. Names such as *Kaserngatan* and *Manègegatan* referred to actual military establishments.

Republican or revolutionary conceptual names, as well as those glorifying Russia and the Empire, were not suitable in Finland, especially after the Vienna Congress. In the city center, *Unionsgatan*, proposed by the emperor himself, refers to the union of Finland with Russia in 1809 and *Fredsgatan* refers to the Peace Treaty of 1809. To them may be linked *Senatsgatan* (1820–1836), later changed to *Nikolaigatan*, acccording to the church—and the new czar—which ran north to the *Senatstorget* (1836), the key square of the city. *Regeringsgatan* (1836), referring to the government, runs to the west of the *Senatstorget.* All of these manifested a strong loyalist bias.

However, there still remained a need for new names. As a curious but ingenious act of politicking, the committee transferred the forenames of the leading bureaucrats of the Grand Duchy and of the capital to the streets of the city! It was a self-legitimizing measure commemorating the effects already done for the benefit of the country and the city, but doing so discretely, often only using the second forename, made them appear both as normal forenames for outsiders and as a subtle reference for insiders. This move corresponds to the bureaucratic style of politicking, which had no need for popular support, and it made all names look relatively harmless to the Russian authorities. Perhaps street names also functioned as an *Ersatz* for the proper Finnish nobility.

Only a few of those to whom streets were dedicated in Helsinki in 1820 or 1836 were already dead. Gustaf Mauritz Armfelt (1759–1814), the first Ministerial State Secretary, was commemorated with *Mauritzgatan* posthumously, yet the others who "got a street" in Helsinki in 1820 or 1836 were still alive. To Armfelt's follower Robert Henrik Rehbinder (1777–1841) was dedicated *Stora* and *Lilla Robertsgatan* (1820) and even *Henriksgatan* (1836), and the naming committee members Fabian Steinheil (1762–1831) and Johan Albrecht Ehrenström (1762–1847) themselves were commemorated in street names (*Fabiansgatan*, 1820, *Albertsgatan*, 1836), as well as Carl Ludwig Engel (1778–1840), who received *Ludwigsgatan* in 1820. Other streets named in 1820, 1836, or 1842 were also named for city or state officials, most of whom were still alive (*Abrahamsgatan, Bernhardsgatan, Eriksgatan, Fredriksgatan, Kristiansgatan, Rikhardsgatan, Simonsgatan,* and *Vilhelmsgatan*). Along with them a woman may be added: *Kajsaniemi* Park (1842) was named in honor of Kajsa Wahllund (d. 1843), who ran a restaurant there. The dedication of a street to these persons was both a sign of gratitude and recognition as being "somebody."

Most of these names are still used in the inner city of Helsinki. In the early years of the twentieth century, however, a transition from a forename regime to a surname regime occurred. Forenames were still used, but they were introduced into the city-text simply as forenames, using the Bible (women's names) and the national epic, the Kalevala, as the main sources. In some cases, the older style of using forenames of local and national heroes was still practiced, but the historian and story-teller Zachris Topelius (1818–1898), for example, got *Zachrisgatan—Sakarinkatu* only after his death (1901)—and *Topeliuksenkatu* (1906) already manifested the paradigm shift.

The shift in naming policy is intelligible in terms of changes in the Finnish polity at large. After 1809, the Swedish-model Estate Diet was called into its first session only in 1863, and only after that date was street naming subject to quasi-parliamentary control. Onni Pekonen (2014) has analyzed how a group of Liberals around the newspaper *Helsingfors Dagblad* managed to introduce remarkable features from the West European parliamentary culture into the procedures and practices of the Finnish estates. Thus, parliamentary aspects were present in the Finnish polity before the radical parliamentary reform of 1906. Even if the suffrage to the city council remained plutocratic until 1918, parliamentary practices were also well known in the city politics of Helsinki. A need for legitimizing the names before the city council and the electorate had become obvious, and with the surname-style of commemoration the politico-cultural role of past agents could be made more visible.

The latter half of the nineteenth century produced Finnish national heroes and appealed to popular support. By manifesting that the Finns could also create "somebodys," a "triad of great men" was canonized (cf. Klinge 1982): the folklorist and compiler of the Kalevala, Elias Lönnrot (1802–1884); the poet J.L. Runeberg (1804–1877); and the philosopher, Fennoman ideologist, and senator J.V. Snellman (1806–1881), with Topelius as the fourth wheel. Streets were dedicated to Lönnrot and Runeberg only in 1906. Even Snellman, the most political of them, had streets proposed for him outside the urban core, but only in 1928 did *Snellmaninkatu* replace the name of *Nikolainkatu* in the city center. The special canonization of these heroes is also manifested by supplementary dedications of small parks as well as a number of names relating to the Kalevala, several referring to Runeberg's epic of the 1808–1809 war (esp. *Vänrikki Ståhlinkatu*), thereby making the use of Swedish military names possible, and also to the title of Topelius's national stories (*Välskärinkatu*).

Additionally, a number of "smaller national heroes" of the nineteenth century obtained street names in the first years of the new century: the "national author" Aleksis Kivi (1906), as well as his critic, the linguist August Ahlqvist (1906); the jurist Mathias Calonius (1906); the fennougrist M.A. Castrén (1901); "the father of Finnish elementary school" Uno Cygnaeus (1906); the painter Albert Edelfelt (1906); the natural scientist J.J. Nervander (1906); the polar explorer A.E. Nordenskiöld (1906); the orientalist G.A. Wallin (1901), and the poet J.J. Wecksell (1908). The most obvious sign of the paradigm shift in commemoration is that in 1908 Armfelt, Engel, and Rehbinder had their surnames printed into the city map. A transition from a cabinet-style to a more public-style of politicking required more singularized heroes.

After the turn of the century, streets were also dedicated to heroes from the Swedish period, including both kings and queens (Carl, Gustaf, Kristina, Adolf), whereas Ulrika was present already in 1842, related to the Ulrikesborg's baths. Also included were the Sture family of Swedish regents in the fifteenth century, the Lutheran reformer Agricola, the governors Brahe and Fleming, the economist Chydenius, the admiral Ehrensvärd, the poet Franzén, and the historian Porthan. The practices of a nationalist historiography were transferred to the city map. This tradition spoke of Sweden-Finland and separating the Finns from others in the Swedish kingdom and, conversely, introduced continuity into "Finnish" history beyond the divide of 1809.

The paradigm shift, as well as the rehabilitation of the Swedish period, is remarkable when placed in the context of the russification policy, especially in the years from 1898 to 1904, when Governor General Bobrikov was assassinated—a park in the suburb of Kulosaari was named after the assassin Eugen Schauman in 1958—and again from 1908 to 1914. Street naming by surnames may be interpreted as a massive measure of commemorating "great Finns" from the past, not so easily to be eradicated by the simple administrative means of russification. Even the Russians Galizin and Speranski (the councillor of Alexander I, responsible for the autonomy of Finland), whose names were added to the streets of Helsinki during this period, were pro-Finnish, like the widow of Alexander III, who was honored with a street name as a Danish princess (*Dagmarinkatu* 1906).

The Russians did not intervene in the capital's internal affairs. In the context of a general strike during the Russian Revolution in Fall 1905, and of the subsequent introduction of the unicameral parliament *Edukunta* with universal suffrage in 1906, the abolition of "national" street names would not have been easy for them. However, the democratization and parlamentarization of Finnish politics did not result either in an introduction of conceptual street names from the republican or revolutionary tradition—the proposal concerning *Frihetsgatan* (Freedom Street) in 1900 was not accepted. Since this period, the paradigm of surnames has remained the normal measure of commemoration.

In the 1920s, an expert committee was established for the renaming of the city's streets. Russian names were moderately changed, removing Nikolai but not Alexander, and leaving out only the "too Russian" names of Konstantin, Vladimir, and the surnames Kulneff (a hero from Runeberg's epic), Galizin, and Speranski. Even *Unioninkatu* was not replaced by *Yliopistonkatu* (University Street), although the independence of Finland undid the union of 1809. Snellman, Lönnrot, and Aleksis Kivi were commemorated with "better" streets than earlier, the senator Leo Mechelin (1838–1914), viewed as suspect by the Russians, had obtained a street already in 1917, and otherwise the nationalist commemoration continued.

The independence of Finland as a republic did not bring republican street names to Helsinki. Freedom, equality, brotherhood, republic, democracy, and even independence are still absent from the capital's streets. Proposed names referring to Europe, England, and America were not introduced. Some names corresponding to this paradigm, however, have been adopted since 2000. This may be related to a procedural change: street naming has moved from national to municipal politics. The only conflict over names in the 1920s concerned the Finnish name of *Jägaregatan*: a Social Democrat opposed the change of *Metsästäjänkatu* (Hunter's Street) to *Jääkärinkatu*, referring to the Jäger, a conspiratory Finnish battalion trained in Germany during World War I.

Following World War II, new suburbs were built and many names were needed, but naming was increasingly left to expert committees and naming officials. As a tendency, commemorative naming has diminished, and those commemorated are poets, actors, musicians, businessmen, and suburban leaders rather than politicians. Notable exceptions are the streets dedicated to the presidents (Ståhlberg, Relander, Svinhufvud, Kallio, Ryti) in the upper class suburb, Kulosaari, in the late-1950s.

In three cases, a street name was given as a birthday present: the main street in the western part of the city was named after Field Marshall Mannerheim (1867–1951) during the war in 1942, replacing the second forename of Rehbinder (*Heikinkatu-Henriksgatan*) and another long street; the composer Jean Sibelius (1865–1956) was honored with a park name in 1945, but his former home street was named after him only after his death; President Urho Kekkonen's (1900–1986) former home street was dedicated to him in 1980, whereas the same was done with President J.K. Paasikivi (1870–1956) only posthumously (1959). The post-World War II presidents—Mannerheim was president from 1944 to 1946—were thus located in the city center. Paasikivi also obtained a square with a statue opposite to Mannerheim's mounted statue near the parliament.

But who are not commemorated by street names in Helsinki? As elsewhere (for West Berlin, cf. *Sackgassen* 1988, 56–57, 83–88), the history of winners written by street names has been a masculinist history. There are queens and princesses, daughters of former proprietors and biblical women, but dedications to women based on their own merits have been few: Kajsa Wahllund, the philanthropists Aurora Karamzin (*Aurorankatu* in 1906, *Karamzininkatu* in 1967) and Alli Trygg (who was honored by a park dedication in 1939), and the writer Minna Canth (1844–1897), who was commemorated with a street name in 1917, were the only ones before World War II. The early feminists, who contributed to the first women's suffrage in Europe, have hardly been commemorated by streets, *Lucina Hagmanintie* in Haaga being the only exception.

The city council in Helsinki has always had a "bourgeois" majority, and even moderate "leftists" have seldom been commemorated. The street of the Social Democratic Party office in Siltasaari was, however, named *Paasivuorenkatu* (1938) for the moderate Social Democrat trade union leader Matti Paasivuori (1860–1937) during the first coalition of Social Democrats and bourgeois parties. A leftist, female poet, Katri Vala (1901–1944), was commemorated by the naming of a park (1953); and even a former commissar of the Reds from 1918, Oskari Tokoi (1873–1963), who soon broke with the Bolsheviks and emigrated to the United States, posthumously obtained *Tokoinranta* in Siltasaari in 1968.

The exclusion of foreigners is an official policy of the city (cf. Terho 1979, 18; Närhi 1979, 28), allegedly due to the difficulty of writing and pronunciation. Still, proposals for such dedications have been accepted in some cases: Henry Ford on the basis of a factory in 1945; Dag Hammarskjöld on the basis of a UN recommendation (1963); V.I. Lenin on the occasion of his hundredth birthday in 1970 (behind the headquarters of the communist party), and for Copernicus in honor of his five hundredth birthday in 1973. *Lutherinkatu* was already given in 1906, without a mention that Martin Luther was a foreigner. A committee of the city in 1992 decided to remove *Lenininpuisto* from the city-text, but this was finally rejected by the city council.

Street naming in Helsinki during the period of Finnish independence has downplayed the politicizing idea of commemoration. When neither controversial persons nor republican concepts are used as new street names, the naming polity has become more like one of a provincial city rather than one of a capital in Europe.

All of this is probably connected to the growing power of naming experts and officials who mostly fear controversies and politicking. The policy aspect of street naming has only left space for politicking in exceptional circumstances. The politicizing profile of a capital created by Ehrenström's committee of street naming contained an element of representation, viewing the names from the perspective of visitors rather than of inhabitants, while the expert-based name policy is closely related to the interests of homes, cars, and post offices, holding flaneuring as suspect.

EU membership has reorganized political conflicts in Finland: the divide between the isolationists and the Europeans has become important across the traditional divisions. The name of Helsinki has, after 1975, been used as a political metonymy, like Yalta or Maastricht. Aspirations of becoming a European metropolis, connecting the east and the west, have arisen in Helsinki. One condition for doing this is to break with the low political profile of street naming, not necessarily by counter-commemorating but rather by appealing to the linguistic imagination by word playing of all kinds. A politicizing approach would make the inhabitants ask for the origins and the acceptability of the present street names as an integral part of both city politics as well as everyday life.

The rhetoric of street naming

Since Aristotle's *Rhetoric*, the distinction between the past-oriented forensic, the future-oriented deliberative, and the present-oriented epideictic genres of rhetoric (Aristotle 1980, 1358b–1359a), remains a valuable conceptual tool, which can also be applied to the politics of street naming. As oriented towards a future use, street naming is always deliberative, but it can have different links to forensic and epideictic rhetoric. Taking my suggestions on the temporality of the politicking and politicization aspects as starting points, my hypothesis is that politicking and policy are deliberative-epideictic, while politicization and polity are deliberative-forensic operations.

The introduction of a street name always contains a future-oriented dimension. Politicking with street names can be understood negatively, as opposed to the functionalization of singular acts of naming for policies and naming regimes. In this sense, it manifests the autonomy of the present by opposing pre-decided policies to become the future fate of street names in the city. But a policy also has an epideictic dimension in the requirement of "beautiful" or "pleasant" street names.

In a name polity, the rhetoric of names is functionalized to a combination of forensic and deliberative rhetoric. In this case, the forensic rhetoric bound with the formation of stable paradigms for the name polity has an obvious priority. But, like other regimes, the street name polity is open to change, mediated by singular, but functionalized, decisions on new street names. Additionally, the politicizing rhetoric of street naming is forensic in its politics of history and memory, regarding the chances of decanonizing the past, but it is also deliberative in opening new playfields for contingency, for politicking with names in general.

This triad of rhetorical genres can render intelligible the paradigm shifts and slow transformations in the politics of street naming in Helsinki. The politicizing move of creating a name polity around 1820 used both a specific forensic rhetoric oriented towards a very near past and combined it with an epideictic rhetoric of forenames, experienced as pleasant street names. The paradigm shift after 1900 to a regime of surnames uses forensic rhetoric oriented toward the past but also contains a deliberative dimension in connection with the new parliamentary elements of the polity.

The transition to a regime dominated by policy experts combines a change towards the epideictic rhetoric of pleasant names with a provincial turn in forensic commemoration. A break with this practice is, to some degree, possible by a politicizing counter-commemoration of women, foreigners, and so on. Reinterpreting the past, by rejecting the conventional and constructive rhetoric of naming experts, in favor of a more playful rhetoric of irony appears, in the present European political context, to be a more promising rhetorical strategy, both for Helsinki and for other cities. The shift after 1981 in Finnish politics from the semi-presidential towards a parliamentary political culture has the potential to provide the conditions for such a change.

Note

1 This discussion is based on a number of commentaries (Aminoff and Pesonen 1971; Pesonen 1971; Närhi 1979; Terho 1979) and the name directories, *Helsingin kadunnimet* (1971) and *Helsingin kadunnimet* 2 (1979).

References

Aminoff, B. and Pesonen, L. (1971). "Helsingin kadunnimistön synty ja kehitys vuoteen 1946 mennessä." In L.A. Pesonen (Ed.), *Helsingin kadunnimet* (pp. 31–64). Helsingin Kaupungin Julkaisuja 24: Helsinki: Valtion painatuskeskus.

Arendt, H. (1981 [1960]). *Vita activa*. München: Piper.

Aristotle (1980). *Rhetorik*. German trans., F. Sieveke (Ed.). Munich: Fink.

Austin, J.L. (1990 [1962]). *How to Do Things with Words*, J.O. Urmson and Marina Sbisà (Eds.). Oxford: Oxford University Press.

Azaryahu, M. (1990). "Renaming the Past: Changes in 'City Text' in Germany and Austria, 1945–1947." *History and Memory*, 2(2): 32–53.

Benjamin, W. (1983). *Das Passagen-Werk*, R. Tiedemann (Ed.). Frankfurt/M: Suhrkamp.

Enzensberger, H.M. (1987). *Ach Europa!* Frankfurt/M: Suhrkamp.

Ferguson, P. (1988). "Reading City Streets." *The French Review*, 61(3): 386–397.

Flierl, T. (1991). "Mit der Geschichte leben." In D. Guhr, T. Schneider, and G. Wehner (Eds.), *Berlin: Plenzlauer Berg. Straßen und Plätze* (pp. 6–13). Berlin: Hentrich.

Flierl, T. (1992). "Die Straßennamenumbenennungen in Prenzlauer Berg—der Diskussions— und Entscheidungsprozeß." Berlin: Aktives Museum Faschismus und Widerstand (mimeo).

Helsingin kadunnimet (1971). Helsingin kaupungin julkaisuja 24.

Helsingin kadunnimet 2 (1979). Helsingin kaupungin julkaisuja 32.

Klinge, M. (1982). *Kaksi Suomea*. Porvoo: WSOY.

Klinge, M. (1989). *Keisarillinen Aleksanterin yliopisto, 1808–1917*. Keuruu: Otava.

Koselleck, R. (2000). *Zeitschichten*. Frankfurt/M: Suhrkamp.

Milo, D. (1986). "Le nom des rues." In P. Nora (Ed.), *Les lieux de la mémoire II* (pp. 284–315). Paris: Gallimard.

Moníková, L. (1987). *Die Fassade*. München: Hanser.

Närhi, E.M. (1979). "Kaavanimistö kielen osana." In L.A. Pesonen (Ed.), *Helsingin Kadunnimet 2* (pp. 22–28). Helsinki: Helsingin kaupungin julkaisuja 32. Helsinki: Kauppakirjapaino.

Palonen, K. (1993a). "Introduction: From Policy and Polity to Politicking and Politicization." In K. Palonen and T. Parvikko (Eds.), *Reading the Political* (pp. 6–16). Helsinki: The Finnish Political Science Association.

Palonen, K. (1993b). "Reading Street Names Politically." In K. Palonen and T. Parvikko (Eds.), *Reading the Political* (pp. 103–121). Helsinki: The Finnish Political Science Association.

Palonen, K. (2003). "Four Times of Politics: Policy, Polity, Politicking and Politicization." *Alternatives*, 28(2): 171–186.

Palonen, K. (2007). *Re-thinking Politics: Essays from a Quarter-Century*. K. Lindroos (Ed.). Helsinki: The Finnish Political Science Association.

Palonen, K. (2010). *"Objektivität" als faires Spiel. Wissenschaft als Politik bei Max Weber*. Baden-Baden: Nomos.

Palonen, K. (2011). "The State as a Chance Concept: Max Weber's Desubstantialization and Neutralization of a Concept." *Max Weber Studies*, 11(1): 99–117.

Palonen, K. (2014a). *The Politics of Parliamentary Procedure*. Leverkusen: Budrich.

Palonen, K. (2014b). *Politics and Conceptual Histories*. Baden-Baden: Nomos.

Pekonen, O. (2014). "Debating 'the ABCs of Parliamentary Life': The Learning of Parliamentary Rules and Practices in the Late Nineteenth-Century Finnish Diet and the Early Eduskunta." PhD dissertation, University of Jyväskylä.

Pesonen, L.A. (1971). "Kadunnimistön tarkistus v. 1946 alueliitoksen johdosta ja nimistön laatiminen uusiin kaupunginosiin." In L.A. Pesonen (Ed.), *Helsingin kadunnimet* (pp. 69–86). Helsingin kaupungin julkaisuja 24.

Pusch, L.F. (1990). *Alle Menschen werden Schwestern*. Frankfurt/M. Suhrkamp.

Sackgassen. Keine Wendemöglichkeit für Berliner Straßennamen (1988). Berlin: Dirk Nischen.

Skinner, Q. (1996). *Reason and Rhetoric in the Philosophy of Hobbes*. Cambridge: Cambridge University Press.

Terho, O. (1979). "Nimistö kaavan osana." In *Helsingin kadunnimet 2* (pp. 15–21). Helsinki: Helsingin kaupungin julkaisuja 32.

Toillon, E. (1984). *Les rues de Besançon*. Besançon: Cêtre.

Weber, M. (1971 [1917]). "Wahlrecht und Demokratie in Deutschland." *Gesammelte politische Schriften* (pp. 245–291). Tübingen: Mohr.

Weber, M. (1971 [1918]). "Parlament und Regierung im neugeordneten Deutschland." *Gesammelte politische Schriften* (pp. 306–443). Tübingen: Mohr.

Weber, M. (2009). *Allgemeine Staatslehre und Politik. Mit- und Nachschriften 1920. Max-Weber-Gesamtausgabe III/7*, G. Hübinger (Ed.). Tübingen: Mohr.

3 Colonial urban order, cultural politics, and the naming of streets in nineteenth- and early twentieth-century Singapore

Brenda Yeoh

Introduction

The power of naming, according to Todorov (quoted in Robinson 1989, 160), is "often the first step in taking possession," and place names are among the first signifiers to commemorate new regimes and reflect the power of elite groups in shaping place-meanings. Thus, "the sudden rash" of Tlaxcalan place names in northern Mexico cannot be explained without understanding Aztec colonial policies of the fifteenth century, while making sense of the Germanic place names of southern Chile, Brazil, and Paraguay cannot be divorced from knowledge of the nineteenth-century streams of immigrants into the region (Robinson, 1989, 160). Todorov also reminds us that Columbus was:

> careful to name the sequence of the first five newly discovered places [in the Caribbean] in a rank order which tells us a great deal of the context of his historic enterprise: the Savior (San Salvador); the Virgin Mary (Santa Maria de la Concepciòn); the King (Fernandina); the Queen (Isabela); and finally the Royal Prince (Juana).
>
> (quoted in Robinson 1989, 160)

In a similar fashion but a different context, streets christened Victoria, Albert, Queen's, King's, Coronation, and Princess Elizabeth (after British royalty) ubiquitously found in major ex-colonial South and Southeast Asian cities were inscribed onto the landscape as part and parcel of the lexicon of British nineteenth-century colonialism. In the case of colonial Sub-Saharan Africa, "place- and street-names were drawn from a European spatial and environmental design lexicon" while toponymic inscription was treated as "an occasion to embellish the power of [European] countries in a foreign land" (Bigon and Njoh 2015, 29).

Moving into the twentieth century, Cohen and Kliot (1992) illustrate the way the Israeli nation-state has selected Biblical and Talmudic place names for the administered territories of the Golan, Gaza, and West Bank in order to reinforce national Zionist ideologies and project Israel as the rightful heir to the Holy Land. Similarly, Bigon and Dahamshe (2014, 619) demonstrate how the Israeli road-sign system in the Galilee region has become a means of "symbolic power" to "defamiliarise the Arabic toponymic repertoire" and advance the Hebraization of the landscape amidst heightened ethnolinguistic and sociopolitical tensions. As Byrnes (2002, 28) reminds us, the naming of places operates on at least three levels—identifying a place, owning it metaphorically, and codifying and categorizing space—and in doing so, place naming produces a "taxonomy of knowing: a way of seeing, ordering and recording the world in order to possess it."

In this vein, Emmerson (1984, 4) points out that names, following the so-called "Humpty Dumpty position," are "rooted neither in reality or custom, but express instead the power of the namer over the thing named." At the same time, the naming process did not only reflect the power of dominant others to assign place-meanings, but was contingent on the social relations of deference and defiance at work. As Rose-Redwood et al. (2010) have shown, toponymics as a field of study has moved in the course of the last two decades from a central focus on etymology and taxonomy, to one interested in the cultural politics of place naming and toponymic practices as a means of lending insight to sociocultural, political, environmental, and ideological struggles (also, see Berg and Vuolteenaho, 2009). The bulk of critical scholarship on toponymics in recent years has concentrated on postcolonial contexts (and other parallel times of major political change such as the post-war or post-apartheid periods) where (re)naming practices quickly become contested arenas in which the inscription of state or elite ideologies of nation-building is being recalibrated or challenged by "counter-hegemonic ideologies of subordinate groups" (Alderman 2008, 205). In the case of postcolonial and newly independent Singapore, Yeoh (1996, 305) argues that the "mapping of nationalist ideologies onto Singapore's street-names was an uneven process, reflecting the contradictions and swings in the policies of nation-building and at the same time incorporating to some extent the reactions and resistances of its citizens." Elsewhere, Berg and Kearns (1996, 99) contend that "the process of naming places involves a contested identity politics of people and place," and they go on to show how the debate over the reinstatement of Maori names in Aotearoa/ New Zealand traded explicitly in the rhetorics of "race," "culture," and "nation," while Duminy (2014, 324) draws on post-apartheid street naming in Durban to illustrate "the emergence and performance of diverse, competing claims surrounding historical memory, as well as contemporary political and symbolic legitimacy." Clearly, an energized cultural politics of naming—"how people control, negotiate, and contest the naming process as they engage in wider struggles for legitimacy and visibility" (Rose-Redwood et al. 2010, 457)—often accompanies a major change of regimes.

This chapter, however, gives attention not to the cultural politics of regime change but to the inner workings of colonial power at its heights in the late-nineteenth and early-twentieth centuries. Drawing on colonial Singapore as a case study, the chapter turns attention back to the colonial regime where the "power of the namer over the thing named" was magnified by colonial policies of dispossession and control operating under conditions characterized by highly asymmetrical power relations. A system of street names bearing the inscription of imperial personalities and racialized imagery, and based on European perceptions of urban order and functioning, was put in place in colonial Singapore as part and parcel of the lexicon of British nineteenth-century colonialism. In this context, opportunities to overtly contest or negotiate the naming process were highly circumscribed. Instead, as the chapter goes on to discuss, the emergence of alternative Asian systems of place signification in daily use served as competing representations of the colonial urban landscape. The juxtaposition of more than one system of street names testified to the syncretic character of the colonial city and belied the colonizers' vision of the urban landscape well-integrated by a single, overarching system of signification. Street names in the rapidly growing colonial city were hence part of an indefinable but interminable contest of Sisyphean proportions between colonizers, the colonized, and place. In this vein, the chapter moves on to reflect on the tensions between colonialism's schemes of power to remake the city in its own image, on the one hand, and the everyday strategies to evade control and continue with their own livelihoods, daily routines, and communal rituals on the part of colonized inhabitants, on the other.

Street naming and urban order in the colonial city

In colonial Singapore, the municipal authorities were empowered to establish a network of place and street names to facilitate the identification, demarcation, and differentiation of the urban built environment for the purposes of colonial rule. From the early days of the Settlement, Stamford Raffles decreed that "each street should receive some appropriate name" and that it was "the duty of the police to see [that they were] regularly numbered" (Buckley 1984, 84). Under section 28 of the Indian Act XIV (Conservancy) of 1856, the commissioners were empowered to affix in a "conspicuous ... place at each end, corner, or entrance of every street" in the town of Singapore a board on which was "the name by which such street is to be known" (Harwood 1886, 1263–1264). A clear and well-ordered system of street and place names was essential to the colonial and municipal authorities for a number of practical purposes. Accurate addresses and clearly signposted streets were necessary for levying house assessments and public utility rates as well as for efficient postal, firefighting, and transport services. Portions of streets in colonial Singapore were occasionally renumbered, reclassified, or renamed to accommodate the requirements of the municipal assessment office.

Street names that were phonetically similar were often changed in order to avoid confusion and delay in summoning the fire brigade to the correct location in the event of a fire. In 1858, it was noted in the municipal meetings that much confusion reigned among the streets of Singapore because not only were certain streets, canals, and squares nameless, there were others where the same name had been given to two or even three streets (Buckley 1984, 667). The municipal commissioners embarked on the process of removing some of the confusion by naming and renaming some of the streets but the duplication of names was not entirely remedied. Half a century later, during a fire in early 1908, the fire brigade was delayed as a result of the confusion of D'Almeida Street (a street in the European business quarter off Raffles Place) with Almeida Street (a street in Chinatown off South Bridge Road, later renamed "Temple Street"). Vigilance in ensuring urban order was hence a continual colonial endeavor, as exemplified by the renaming of Syed Ali Road to Newton Road (after Howard Newton, the assistant municipal engineer in the late-nineteenth century) to avoid confusion with Syed Alwi Road (*MPMCOM* October 16, 1914).

The legibility of the urban environment was also crucial to the surveillance functions of the state, functions which ranged from the taking of a population census, orthodox police work such as inspecting houses, instituting arrests, posting notices, and serving summons on occupiers, to public health concerns such as tracing the source and spread of "dangerous infectious diseases." A well-organized network of street names was necessary if clandestine activities, dangerous diseases, and the Asian population in general were to be rendered less amorphous, more visible to the observation and "gaze" of the authorities, and hence more accessible to control.

The official naming process

The naming of places, whether as a conscious, deliberate event or a more informal process of evolution, is in varying degrees a social activity. As Pirie (1984, 43) has argued, this is so "either by virtue of it involving joint decisionmaking and/or in respect of it occurring within a given social milieu in which there are formal or informal conventions of name selection, assignment and adoption." The naming process is hence not only of toponymic significance but also embodies some of the social struggle for control over the means of symbolic production within the urban built environment.

In colonial Singapore, official street and place names were assigned at municipal meetings on the approval of the commissioners.[1] Names for consideration were normally proposed by the municipal assessor, although suggestions sometimes originated with the municipal president, one of the commissioners, or the requests of property owners. Once decided, notice of new or changed street names was advertised in the press and the schedule circulated amongst various heads of government departments including the chief police officer, the commissioner of lands, and the secretary of the Fire Insurance Association. The official naming process was strongly dominated by the opinions of municipal and government officers, and occasionally, those of influential property owners, but it was relatively impervious to the views of people who lived on or used the streets, and was hence generally detached from the social milieu of the plebeian classes. Street nomenclature became a means by which the authorities were able to project onto the urban landscape their perceptions of what different areas within the city represented.

Rationales for colonial street names

Certain themes tended to predominate in the christening of streets in Singapore. A street name often commemorated prominent figures, especially persons who were considered to have contributed significantly to public works and urban development. Among the 225 municipal street names listed by H.W. Firmstone, an official with the Chinese Protectorate (Firmstone 1905), approximately 45 percent served a commemorative function; two-thirds of those honored Europeans, and the remainder paid tribute to Asians. Europeans included resident councillors and governors, commemorated in names such as Raffles Place, Crawfurd Street, and Jervois Road; royalty, in Alexandra Road, Victoria Street, and Connaught Drive; and war heroes, in Havelock Road, Jellicoe Road, and Nelson Road. Prominent citizens and civil servants might be honored: Still Road and Makepeace Road were named after journalists; Paterson Road and Palmer Road after leading members of the mercantile community; Pickering Street after the first Chinese Protector; Cook Street and Oldham Lane after missionaries; Hullet Road after a schoolmaster; and Everitt Road after a lawyer.

Municipal commissioners and officials were not reluctant to attach their names to streets. Between 1880 and 1930, more than forty streets in Singapore were dedicated to their memory. The selection of suitable streets to honor individuals was a carefully calculated process aimed at ensuring that the length, location, and importance of the chosen street were commensurate with the esteem due the person. For example, in choosing road names for the Tiong Bahru area, which was opened by the Singapore Improvement Trust in the early-1930s, it was suggested that the trust manager, Walter H. Collyer, would not object to having his name given to one of the streets, "although he would be quite entitled to object to a street named after him unless it [was] a really long one" (SIT 1930).

Landowners and property owners who contributed land for streets or who defrayed the cost of making, metalling, or draining them often requested that those streets be named after themselves or family members. Streets in Singapore thus acquired names such as Norris Road, Chin Nam Street, Cheng Yan Place, and Eu Tong Sen Road (Raja-Singam 1939). By perpetuating the names of ostensibly deserving citizens and eminent public servants, municipal street nomenclature represented the city as one dominated by enthusiastic public service and a whole gamut of civic talent. Commemorative street names inscribed on the city landscape a tangible record of persons who had contributed to its development.

As a city that prided itself for being the capital of the Straits Settlements and the Malay States—"the Clapham Junction of the Eastern Seas" (Shanghai Yuan Dong di li xue hui 1917)—colonial Singapore included numerous streets whose names recalled linkages with places on the Malay Peninsula and surrounding territories. These accounted for slightly more than 10 percent of the street names at the beginning of the twentieth century (Firmstone 1905); examples were Malacca Street, Ophir Road, Manila Street, and Rangoon Road. Municipal commissioners often favored the orderly progression of a naming pattern in a zone of the city. When a road near Rangoon, Mandalay, and Moulmein roads was named in 1929, a Burmese designation was considered most suitable. Martaban Road was chosen, followed in later years by additions of Pegu Road and Bhamo Road (SIT June 8, 1929). Such practices resulted in clusters of related street names based on a common theme.

Although residential segregation on racial lines was not legal in Singapore, colonial street names often indicated an unofficial dichotomy between European and Asian residential areas. Roads in certain parts of the built environment, specifically the European residential suburbs, received names that denoted the symbolic transfer of sentiment and the imagery of colonial hopes. In Tanglin and Claymore, the aristocratic European suburbs, the well-shaded, picturesque streets bore names such as Orchard Road and River Valley Road or conjured the idyllic imagery of the English countryside through names like Devonshire Road and Chatsworth Road. European suburban roads also often originated as plantation carriageways or estate boundaries and were thus named after properties of well-known inhabitants (Lee 1988).

During the late-1920s, some municipal commissioners commented on the choice of nonlocal street names. In October 1927, one Asian commissioner questioned why a new road from Orchard Road to Cairnhill Road had been christened Bideford Road. The explanation was that "Bideford was the town from which the owner of the land on one side of the road came," but it failed to satisfy the commissioner, who remarked that he had never heard of the place *(MPMCOM* October 7, 1927, October 29, 1927). In January 1929, another commissioner objected to the naming of new roads on the Lavender Road reclamation area after Cawnpore, Lucknow, Simla, Lahore, Benares, and Karachi, on the argument that there was no "natural connection between this Colony and these places." He asserted that there was "no need to go outside Malaya for names," as there were "plenty of people deserving recognition," a viewpoint supported by an Indian Muslim member of the municipal board (*MPMCOM* January 30, 1929).

Despite these differing opinions, official names derived from British places continued to abound. When Tanjong Katong was developed as a residential area and a seaside resort for Europeans in the 1920s, the roads there were named after British seaside resorts such as Bournemouth, Boscombe, Margate, and Wareham (Raja-Singam 1939). The names of British counties and urban centers inspired road names such as Dorset Road, Norfolk Road, Bristol Road, and Shrewsbury Road (Assessment Department 1921). The abundance of anglicized road names in premier suburbs for Europeans allowed the residents of the bungalows sequestered in park-like expanses to escape the impress of the tropics and native culture and symbolically to exist in British settings.

Place and race

Areas associated with different Asian communities were also reflected in street names assigned by the first town committee of Singapore, appointed in 1822 to "appropriate and mark out the quarters or departments of the several classes of the native population" to "prevent confusion and disputes" (Buckley 1984, 81). The committee designated separate divisions by racial group: the European area was dignified by the term town, but the Asian immigrants were relegated to separate *kampungs* (villages). Street names in each division were identified with the intended inhabitants, as evidenced by Arab Street in the Arab *kampung* and Chuliah Street in the Chuliah *kampung*. In the Chinese *kampung*, street names such as Canton Street, Chin Chew Street, Macao Street, and Nankin Street testified to the care taken by the committee "to advert to the provincial and other distinctions among this peculiar people" (Buckley 1984, 83).

Although some of the proposed street names did not materialize and although the principle of residential separation did not survive in its entirety after the nineteenth century, the plan provided the basis for a system of street names that associated racial identity with specific places. Even as the rapid influx of Chinese immigrants extended the perimeters of the original Chinese *kampung*, overflowed its bounds, and spread throughout the town, street names associated with the Chinese, such as Amoy Street, Tew Chew Street, Hong Kong Street, and Wayang Street, continued to be concentrated in the traditional heart of the Chinese *kampung*, later elevated to "Chinatown." Similarly, in the vicinity of Arab Street, names such as Haji Lane, Bussorah Street, and Shaik Madersah Lane identify the historical presence of the Arab *kampung*. Street names on the site of the original Bugis *kampung*, such as Java Road, Sumbawa Road, and Palembang Road, proclaimed the linkages with the Indonesian islands. The Chuliah *kampung* marked on the original plan apparently never emerged, but an early concentration of southern Indians on the western fringe of Commercial Square left its impress in the name Kling Street, which leads off the square. Kling Street was shown on the earliest comprehensive plan of the town, drawn from an actual survey (Tassin 1836), and reflected the name used for southern Indians in Singapore. "Kling" originated as a Malay-Javanese corruption of Kalinga, the name of an ancient empire in southern India that had trading connections with the Malay archipelago (Crawfurd 1856). By 1905, approximately 10 percent of municipal street names alluded to associations with various Asian communities (Firmstone 1905).

In later years, similar attempts were made to associate place with race, albeit with increasing complications. In 1925, it was proposed that a new road off Serangoon Road in the Indian district be named Bombay Road. However, it was learned that the name would be offensive to the Indian community, because of the association of the site, a former convict burial ground, with the phrase *orang kena buang Bombay* (Malay for "people thrown out of Bombay"), a pejorative term for Indian convicts transported to Singapore. To avoid that negative association, the proposal was abandoned and the road was named St. George's Road, by virtue of its proximity to St. Michael's Road (SIT April 9, 1925). Name selection in other racially demarcated areas sometimes encountered similar problems. On balance, however, by the end of the nineteenth century, the endurance of street names invested with racial and cultural connotations testified to the tendency in colonial consciousness to order society by separating the populace into recognizable racial units.

Another category of municipal street names, accounting for approximately 15 percent, included those originating in physical features, landmarks, or other material symbols. Only about one-quarter of these signaled the presence of non-European landmarks: Pagoda Street, Mosque Street, and Synagogue Street, for example, were named for religious buildings; Club Street and Wayang Street, for places of entertainment. The bulk of such names, however, referred to transportation features such as bridges and canals, military installations, and topographic features.

Some 6 percent of municipal street names offered information on early economic activities (Firmstone 1905). The most prominent was Commercial Square, the center for European business on the south bank of the Singapore River. Other examples were Carpenter Street, Merchant Street, Fish Street, Sago Lane, Garden Street, and Buffalo Road. These street names tended to persist even after the activity to which they alluded had ceased or been relocated.

Although municipal authorities attempted to choose street names recognizing Asian communities where that was deemed appropriate, and although Asian landowners succeeded in toponymically claiming several streets for themselves, most municipal street names honored the perceptions of power-holding Europeans rather than those of the residents of specific areas. Even when original names derived from the Malay vernacular were preserved, they often were transmogrified to suit English-speaking tongues. For example, the word Saranggong, apparently signifying an area named after the *ranggung*, a long-legged water bird, was eventually transmuted into "Serangoon," while kalang puding, which referred to the garden croton, evolved into "Kalang Pudding."

Asian street naming practices

Unlike the official municipal labels assigned and decreed by law, Asian street names came informally from community-defined conventions and parameters. Practices that gave names and meaning to the built environment and to areas of the city were likely to be part idiosyncratic and part socialized (Cohen 1985). Asian place names often differed not only from those assigned by the authorities but also among various ethnic and dialect groups; occasionally there could be more than one name within a group for a specific place. The 225 municipal street names cited in 1905 had the equivalent of 365 Hokkien and Cantonese names, which yields a ratio of 1.6 Chinese names for each municipal one (Firmstone 1905). As names that evolved spontaneously through usage, Asian street names tended to remain characteristic of the local patois. Some 65 percent of Chinese street names came from material symbols and landmarks that formed an integral part of daily life. Temples, theaters, markets, gambling dens, bridges, and wells lent their names to streets. Kwong Fuk Min, the Cantonese name for Lavender Street, means "Kwong Fuk Temple Street"; Sin Pa Sat Pin, the Hokkien name for Ellenborough Street, means "beside the new market"; Kiau Keng Khau, the Hokkien name for Church Street, means "the mouth of the gambling houses"; and Tai Cheng Keak, the Cantonese name for Kampong Glam beach, means "foot of the big well." Certain Chinese street names also provided clues to the hidden dimensions of everyday life, as they signified the territorial boundaries of different groups in the Chinese community. Streets such as Ghi Hok Koi (Carpenter Street), Ghi Hin Koi (China Street), and Siong Pek Koi (Nankin Street) were named after the headquarters of important secret societies, which might well imply that the streets were once the operational territories of each group (Mak 1981; Archive and Oral History Department 1983).

The close association between the identification of places and the local, everyday life of the non-European groups was also evident in the 7 percent of

Chinese place names that denoted specific trading, artisanal, and agricultural activities. These included certain streets that were well known for trade specializations, such as Tau Hu Koi, or Upper Chin Chew Street, which means "beancurd street." It was so named because of the number of beancurd manufacturers located there. Macabre, though equally essential, activities were identified in Kuan Chha Tiam Koi, or "coffin-shop street," and Sey Yun Kai, or "street of the dead," named for the preponderance of death houses where the dying waited out their days and for the shops selling funeral paraphernalia in the same area. Agricultural pursuits also featured in names such as Chhai Hng Lai, translated as "within the vegetable gardens," and Eng Chhai Ti, translated as "ground where [a vegetable called] *eng chhai* is planted."

Approximately 15 percent of Chinese street names were purely descriptive or directional in content. Some indicated location by specifying a general area or proximity to another street; others identified streets on the basis of the number of buildings originally erected along them. For example, Ji Chap Keng means "twenty buildings"; Chap San Kang means "thirteen shops"; Peh Keng A means "eight small buildings," a name not inappropriate for a very short street. The numerical mode of description figured in the names of main thoroughfares on both sides of the Singapore River: Tai Ma Lo, or "great horse-carriage way," and Ji Ma Lo, or "second horse-carriage way," were Cantonese names for South Bridge Road and New Bridge Road on the southern side as well as for North Bridge Road and Victoria Street on the northern side. Other descriptive street names owed their origins to the physical structure of the streets. Among these were names like Gu Kak Hang, meaning "ox-horn lane," an apt descriptor of a crescent-shaped street leading off and back to Tanjong Pagar Road; and Tan Pin Kai, meaning "one-sided street," as it had houses only on one side.

In contrast to municipally imposed names, naming in the Chinese community seldom was commemorative. Only 5 percent of Chinese street names, as opposed to 65 percent of municipal ones, honored eminent persons (Firmstone 1905), and none of the honorees were European. Furthermore, where a specific street was named for an Asian person, it was normally because of the proximity of the street to a material feature, such as a house or shop, belonging to the person rather than as a memorial of the person's contribution to Singapore society. Among the examples were Seng Po Toa Chhu Au, which means "behind Seng Poh's big house," and Heng Long Kai, which means "street where chop Heng Long is located."

There was little direct correlation between municipally imposed and Asian-derived street names. Albert Street, honoring Queen Victoria's consort, had Asian aliases. Among the Chinese it was called Bo Moan Koi, meaning "the street where sesamum oil is pressed," or Mang Ku Lu Seng Ong Kong, meaning "Bencoolen Street district joss-house." To Tamil speakers, it was Thimiri Thirdal, or "place where people tread fire," a reference to the firewalking ceremony held on the street during the Thaipusam festival (Haughton 1891). The Chinese knew less than 5 percent of municipal street names in their transliterated form. To the Cantonese, Cecil Street was Si Shu Kai and Robinson Road was Lo Man San Kai, attempts at transliteration that distorted pronunciations beyond recognition.

Firmstone (1905, 125) himself noted that whilst "Lo Man San" (Robinson) was "quite Chinese in sound," there was no guarantee that "the name [would be] intelligible to the ordinary Cantonesespeaking Chinaman" and that "a very long rigmarole" would be necessary to interpret "Robinson Road" clearly.

The contrast between municipal and Asian street names went beyond differences in etymological content and phonetics. The two systems also represented different ways of signifying the landscape. Whereas municipal street names primarily sought to identify the urban landscape with civic notions of appropriateness and ordering, Chinese nomenclature was strongly anchored to local features, symbols, and activities that formed a significant role in daily experience. Whereas Chinese names tended to match the use of streets to which they were attached, municipal street names attained a level of signification that conveyed meaning over and above the immediate material functions of the streets themselves. Another important difference lay in the precision with which the urban landscape was divided and defined. Municipal street names labeled exact, clearly bounded streets; Asian varieties tended to identify general locations relative to specific landmarks or distinguished by the presence of certain activities. For the authorities, clearly labeled and defined streets were crucial to the governing and policing of the city. For the Asian communities, street names served as signposts of daily activities. They were inseparable from the substance of everyday social practice but did not necessarily require the precision dictated by the colonial project or ordering the urban landscape.

Counter-toponymics in the colonial urban landscape

A dual (or more precisely, multiple) system of place identification existed in Singapore: the official network of street names and a range of alternative descriptors attached by indigenous and non-European immigrants. The two systems of place names had little common ground: the full English meaning and nuances of municipal street names was not comprehended in the Chinese (and other Asian) cultural repertory and vice versa. The language of place not only facilitates the interpretation of the mental images of various cultural groups, but where the naming process differs between groups it also provides a valuable tool in understanding contrasting representations and uses of the colonial landscape and its physical artifacts.

The capacity of Asian communities to develop and use their own names and signifiers to denote and differentiate parts of the landscape also implies that each community had a certain latitude in bringing a diversity of sociocultural influences to bear on the urban landscape. Practices that conferred names and meaning to the urban built environment were not entirely idiosyncratic but depended on Asian perceptions and uses of specific places in terms of their associations with various types of socioeconomic activities, religious or symbolic sites, and territorial gangs. The persistence of different systems of signification in the city showed that municipal representations of the landscape did not command an unchallenged hegemony. Instead, it pointed to a multiply differentiated, if vastly unequal, city rather than the colonial ideal of a unitary city ordered by a division into recognizably racial containers that functioned under a single, overarching system of authority.

In this context, street naming was a fraught process reflecting multiple concerns and many moving parts. To take an example, in selecting a name for a new road leading from Kreta Ayer to Anson Road over the site of a former Chinese (Cantonese-Khek) burial ground (SIT March 28, 1925), the collector of land revenue, J. Lornie, preferred one which would reflect the original association of the place with the Chinese community. One of the earlier suggestions—"Aljunied Road"—was hence rejected on the grounds that it "might more appropriately be given to an area in which Mohammedans had some interest." "Choon Guan Road," in memory of Lee Choon Guan, a well-known Straitsborn Hokkien shipping and real estate tycoon who had died recently (Song 1902, 111-12), was strongly favored. However, some of the municipal commissioners feared that as the former burial ground belonged to the Cantonese and Khek communities, objections might be raised against a street name commemorating a member of another dialect group. "Man Sau Road," after Leong Man Sau, a prominent member of the Cantonese community who died in 1916 (Song 1902, 432–433), was suggested instead, but it was turned down by the municipal assessor on the grounds that it was phonetically similar to "Mansoor Street," an existing road off North Bridge Road. It was ultimately decided to abandon the search for a Chinese name and to christen the road "Maxwell Road" in honor of "the eminent services to Malaya of three generations of public servants [who were] all members of one family" (Makepeace 1921, 431–442).

While the naming process was heavily skewed towards favoring British colonial imaginaries of what constituted apposite ways of naming the growing city's streets, this had little relation to (let alone power over) the messy realities in the sphere of everyday life. In colonial Singapore, municipal street names, even when selected for their ostensibly ethnic character or according to colonial racial templates, were seldom comprehended and were frequently ignored by the Asian communities. In the late-nineteenth century, Haughton (1891, 208) observed that "the names given by the municipality to the various streets [were] only used by the European portion of the population, and the Chinese, Tamils and Malays [had] names for the streets very different from their Municipal titles." Although successive town committees had selected what had been perceived as suitably "ethnic" names such as "Hongkong Street" and "Macao Street" (for Chinese areas) and "Jalan Sultan" (for Malay areas), "the fact remain[ed] that Municipal names [were] ignored by the natives, with the exception of the police, who [were], of course, compelled to learn them" (Haughton 1891, 208). Many residents of Chinatown, for example, continued to live in ignorance of the English name of the street in which they lived, largely because of the difficulties involved in phonetically translating English street names into the vernacular. Examples of such translations such as "'Nor Mee Chee' to mean North Bridge Road and 'Sow Mee Chee' to mean South Bridge Road [were] typical of the inability of the Chinese language to give sound to an 'r'" (RajaSingam 1939, 14–15).

From the perspective of the colonial authorities, they despaired at what they saw as the haphazard and imprecise manner in which Asians identified places and furnished addresses. Firmstone, for example, concluded his study of Chinese street and place names in Singapore and the Malay Peninsula as follows:

> It is characteristic of the Chinese that in identifying streets, accuracy is the last thing that strikes them as essential. If you ask a Chinaman—or better still a Chinese woman—newly arrived and resident in Singapore, where he lives, the inevitable answer will be "Singapore." A second query will perhaps elicit information as to the district of the town or island, but it will take many questions before the actual address can be ascertained, though it might have been given directly, if the person questioned had thought that it was of any importance.
>
> (1905, 206)

Not only did the Chinese have their own sets of street names, but also their "happy-go-lucky way of using one expression to describe any one of perhaps a dozen streets" was extremely frustrating from the European perspective (Firmstone 1905, 206). Tek Kah, or "foot of the bamboos," so named because part of the road was formerly bordered by thick bamboo groves, described an ambiguously defined territory at the town end of Bukit Timah Road and included Albert Street, Selegie Road, Short Street, and the numerous lanes in the neighborhood. The Malays were said to carry this tendency of ambiguous identification even further: they took "little notice of streets, and as a rule, only describe[d] places by *kampungs*" (Haughton 1891, 49).

Asian street names also tended to be incomplete and uneven in their coverage, abundant in areas occupied by or associated with their own communities but sparse elsewhere. Unlike municipal street names, which were literally invented at committee meetings and officially assigned to roadways at specific dates, Asian street names evolved through an informal process, as initially nameless corridors of movement grew in importance and function. Their multiplication was both unsystematic and uncharted, becoming known to members of the community who lived in or used the streets but often impervious to the authorities, including government interpreters who remained "lamentably ignorant" of Asian designations of place (Firmstone 1905, 206). Asian disregard for municipal street names and the corresponding ignorance of Asian naming practices on the part of authorities had practical significance for those involved in governing and policing the city. Often addresses could not be ascertained accurately for instituting arrests, serving court summons, or tracing the spread of infectious diseases. The latter, for example, was often frustrated by either the deliberate falsification of addresses where victims of infectious diseases had stayed on the part of relatives and friends, or the inability or reluctance of Asians to furnish accurate addresses. The non-comprehension and non-acceptance of municipally assigned street names and the use of alternative systems rendered the Asian population less open to the surveillance strategies of the colonial state (Yeoh 1996).

Municipal attempts to enhance the acceptability and the usage of official street names among the Asian communities had limited success. In 1912, a Chinese municipal commissioner proposed that Chinese and Malay characters corresponding phonetically to the existing English-language names should be added to the street signs to popularize the official designations (*MPMCOM* July 21, 1912). Although the municipal board unanimously endorsed the proposal, it ultimately was not implemented because of high cost and the difficulty of expressing many of the names phonetically (*MGCM* June 24, 1921; *MPMCOM* June 24, 1921; *MMSC3* July 8, 1921). When pressed further by Asian commissioners and the Mohammedan Advisory Board to add Asian characters to street name plates, the municipal president R.J. Farrer expressed his skepticism as to the usefulness of Asian name plates, arguing in the case of Malay names that the addition would only benefit "an infinitesimal section of the population" as there were "very few inhabitants of the town who [could] read Malay (Arabic) characters but [were] unable to read Roman characters" (*MPMCOM* December 29, 1922). This was refuted by one of the Malay commissioners, Che Yunus bin Abdullah, who argued that Malay characters would be extremely useful and would be of especially "great assistance to Malay policemen who [were] unable to read the Roman characters" (*MPMCOM* December 29, 1922).

What prompted Asian community leaders to press for the addition of Asian street names appeared to have been a desire to stake their communities' claims on the landscape. Dr H.S. Moonshi, for example, prefaced his arguments for the addition of Malay characters by reminding the Board of what he saw as the basic Malay character of Singapore. He argued, "as Singapore is a Malay country and the prevalent language is Malay, Municipal Commissioners should add Malay characters in the new streetname plates to be put up" (*MPMCOM* December 29, 1922). In the same way, for the Chinese municipal commissioners, the addition of Chinese names represented a means of impressing on the built environment the Chinese character of the city. Although the requests were rejected on financial grounds, they indicated that the contest for identification in the landscape was also expressed at the level of official discourse.

Conclusion

In Singapore, whilst colonialism established a network of official place and street names reflecting the mental images of the dominant culture, names given by non-European immigrant cultures continued to persist beneath the surface. As a process, the naming of places in Singapore was not the simple prerogative of the municipal authorities but was contingent on social dynamics, albeit under conditions of highly uneven power relations between colonizers and the colonized.

The authorities had the power to select what were considered appropriate names and to assign them formally to the streets of the city, but the Asian communities comprised the social milieu which retained the power over whether the names took on common usage or were ignored or substituted. Official street nomenclature and its representations of meaning did not automatically pass into local currency but instead encountered impermeable barriers. Instead, the existence of alternative Asian name systems in daily use implied competing representations of the landscape, rather than a single, municipally imposed image. The naming of places was also an important element of the colonial enterprise of governance and surveillance. Failure to impose and enforce the adoption of one uniform system of place names partly reflected the lack of absolute power for the colonial authorities and the cultural politics in the interstices of everyday life in the colonial city.

Note

1 In the 1920s, with the increasing complexity of municipal affairs and the necessity for a division of labor amongst commissioners, the task of deliberating on street names was assigned to a special committee. Minute papers, normally containing the municipal assessor's suggestions, were first circulated to the municipal president, committee members, and occasionally heads of various government departments for opinions to be registered before coming before the committee.

References

Alderman, D. (2008). "Place, Naming, and the Interpretation of Cultural Landscapes." In B. Graham and P. Howard (Eds.), *The Ashgate Research Companion to Heritage and Identity* (pp. 195–213). Aldershot: Ashgate.

Archive and Oral History Department (1983). *Chinatown: An Album of a Singapore Community*. Singapore: Times Books.

Assessment Department (1921). *Administrative Report of the Singapore Municipality*. Singapore.

Berg, L. and Kearns, R. (1996). "Naming as Norming: 'Race', Gender, and the Identity Politics of Naming Places in Aotearoa/New Zealand." *Environment and Planning D: Society and Space*, 14(1): 99–122.

Berg, L. and Voulteenaho, J. (Eds.) (2009). *Critical Toponymies: The Contested Politics of Place Naming*. Aldershot: Ashgate.

Bigon, L. and Dahamshe, A. (2014). "An Anatomy of Symbolic Power: Israeli Road-Sign Policy and the Palestinian Minority." *Environment and Planning D: Society and Space*, 32(4): 606–621.

Bigon, L. and Njoh, A. (2015). "The Toponymic Inscription Problematic in Urban Sub-Saharan Africa: From Colonial to Postcolonial Times." *Journal of Asian and African Studies*, 50(1): 25–40.

Buckley, C. (1984). *Anecdotal History of Old Times in Singapore*. Singapore: Oxford University Press.

Byrnes, G. (2002). "'A Dead Sheet Covered with Meaningless Words?' Place Names and the Cultural Colonization of Tauranga." *New Zealand Journal of History*, 36(1): 18–35.

Cohen, A. (1985). *The Symbolic Construction of Community*. London: Tavistock.

Cohen, B. and Kliot, N. (1992). "Place Names in Israel's Ideological Struggle over the Administered Territories." *Annals of the Association of American Geographers*, 82(4): 650–680.

Crawfurd, J. (1856). *Descriptive Dictionary of the Indian Islands and Adjacent Countries*. London: Bradbury and Evans.

Duminy, J. (2014). "Street Renaming, Symbolic Capital, and Resistance in Durban, South Africa." *Environment and Planning D: Society and Space*, 32(2): 310–328.

Emmerson, D. (1984). "'Southeast Asia': What's in a Name?" *Journal of Southeast Asian Studies*, 15(1): 1–21.

Firmstone, H. (1905). "Chinese Names of Streets and Places in Singapore and the Malay Peninsula." *Journal of the Straits Branch of the Royal Asiatic Society*, 42: 53–208.

Harwood, J. (1886). *The Acts and Ordinances of the Legislative Council of the Straits Settlements from 1st April 1867 to 1st June 1886*, Vols. 1 and 2. London: Eyre and Spottiswoode.

Haughton, H. (1891). "Native Names of Streets in Singapore." *Journal of the Straits Branch of the Royal Asiatic Society*, 23: 49–65.

Lee, K. (1988). *Singapore House, 1819–1942*. Singapore: Times Editions.

Mak, L. (1981). *Sociology of Secret Societies: A Study of Chinese Secret Societies in Singapore and Peninsula Malaysia*. Kuala Lumpur: Oxford University Press.

Makepeace, W. (1921). "Concerning Known Persons." In W. Makepeace, G. Brooke, and R. Braddell (Eds.), *One Hundred Years of Singapore, Vol. 2* (pp. 416–464). London: John Murray.

MGCM (*Minutes of General Committee Meeting [of the Municipal Commissioners]*). June 24, 1921. Deposited in the National Archives, Singapore.

MMSC3 (*Minutes of Meeting of Sub-committee 3 [of the Municipal Commissioners]*). July 8, 1921. Deposited in the National Archives, Singapore.

MPMCOM (*Minutes of the Proceedings of the Municipal Commissioners at an Ordinary Meeting*). February 28, 1908; October 1, 1909; July 21, 1912; October 16, 1914; June 24, 1921; December 29, 1922; February 25, 1927; October 7, 1927; October 29, 1927; January 30, 1929. Deposited in the National Archives, Singapore.

Pirie, G. (1984). "Letters, Words, Worlds: The Naming of Soweto." *African Studies*, 43(1): 43–51.

Shanghai Yuan Dong di li xue hui. (1917). *New Atlas and Commercial Gazetteer of the Straits Settlements and the Federated Malay States*. Singapore: Kelly & Walsh.

Raja-Singam, S. (1939). *Malayan Street Names: What They Mean and Whom They Commemorate*. Ipoh: Mercantile Press.

Robinson, D. (1989). "The Language and Significance of Place in Latin America." In J. Agnew and J. Duncan (Eds.), *The Power of Place* (pp. 157–184). Boston: Unwin Hyman.

Rose-Redwood, R., Alderman, D. and Azaryahu, M. (2010). "Geographies of Toponymic Inscription: New Directions in Critical Place-Name Studies." *Progress in Human Geography*, 34(4): 453–470.

SIT (Singapore Improvement Trust 266/25) (March 28, 1925). *Selection of a Name for a New Road from Kreta Ayer to Anson Road*. Deposited in the National Archives, Singapore.

SIT (Singapore Improvement Trust 222/25) (April 9, 1925). *New Road off Serangoon Road Leading to a Government Rehousing Site to be Named*. Deposited in the National Archives, Singapore.

SIT (Singapore Improvement Trust 892/29) (June 8, 1929). *Naming of Roads Running from Balestier Road to Mandalay Road*. Deposited in the National Archives, Singapore.

SIT (Singapore Improvement Trust 535/30) (1930). *Road Names for Tiong Bahru*. Deposited in the National Archives, Singapore.

Song, O. (1902). *One Hundred Years' History of the Chinese in Singapore*. Singapore: Oxford University Press.

Stump, R. (1988). "Toponymic Commemoration of National Figures: The Case of Kennedy and King." *Names*, 36(3–4): 203–216.

Tassin, J. (1836). *Map of the Town and Environs of Singapore Drawn from an Actual Survey by G. D. Coleman*. Calcutta: Lithographic Press.

Yeoh, B. (1996). "Street-Naming and Nation-Building: Toponymic Inscriptions of Nationhood in Singapore." *Area*, 28(3): 298–307.

4 Revisiting East Berlin and Haifa

A comparative perspective on renaming the past

Maoz Azaryahu

Introduction

Street naming has become a conventional feature of urban commemoration that expresses not only administrative control over, but also inscribes ideological agendas within, urban space. As already demonstrated during the French Revolution and addressed in a growing number of scholarly works since the mid-1980s, street names belong to the geopolitics of public commemoration, which makes them susceptible to replacement within the context of regime changes, postcolonial transitions, and population exchanges following wars. In such circumstances, a large-scale commemorative renaming of streets and the rewriting of the historical narrative inscribed on street signs, city maps, and in official registers signify a break with the recent past and the onset of a new era in political history. Such revisionist measures introduce the change of regime into the language of the cityscape and into the practices of everyday life.

Renaming the past is about asserting political control over both history and public space. Possibly a prolonged process punctuated by discontinuities evincing shifts in political priorities, renaming the past involves political and ideological incentives and constraints that direct the actual timing and scale of the commemorative renaming of streets. Notably, beyond demonstrating the new regime's prerogative to restructure the commemorative landscape of the city, renaming the past is a function of specific political interests, pressures, constraints, and priorities, one issue of which is the timing of politically motivated toponymic changes. The actual timing and extent of renaming the past is contingent on the dynamic relationships between various political actors involved in decision-making at state, city, and borough levels as well as on the pressures from below exerted on the street naming authorities by individuals and civic organizations.

Another issue is what constitutes the primary objective of a large-scale renaming of streets. In principle, renaming the past is about rewriting the history celebrated on street signs so as to make it ideologically congruent with the new regime's vision of history. In particular, renaming the past involves a twofold procedure. One is *damnatio memoriae* (damnation of memory) evident in the decommemoration of heroes and events associated with and representative of the old regime. Milan Kundera observed that "The streets that do not know their names are the ghosts of monuments torn down" (1996, 127). As is often the case in such circumstances, renaming streets is both a celebration of triumph and a mechanism for settling scores with the vanquished regime. The other is the commemoration of heroes and events representing the new regime and its vision of history. When regime change is construed in terms of restoration, commemoration may assume the form of recommemoration, namely, the reinstitution of names removed by the former regime, for renaming streets is about substituting one name for another. However, the actual pattern and dynamic of renaming the past, and specifically the interplay between decommemoration and commemoration, involves particular ideological emphases and political priorities that reflect specific interests and needs as well as power constellations that influence and direct the renaming process.

A revised version of an article originally published in 1992, this chapter employs a comparative perspective to explore the dynamic of renaming the past as a technique of historical revision. At the center of this historical investigation is the juxtaposition of patterns of renaming the past carried out in Spring 1951 in Haifa, Israel, and in East Berlin, the capital of communist East Germany. In both cities renaming the past followed a change of regime and the establishment of a new political order. The two renaming operations were contemporaneous but unrelated. The juxtaposition of the toponymic changes in these cities and the comparative perspective this affords provide insights into the political dynamics of renaming the past as a measure of historical revision in the context of regime change.

Historical background: Berlin's street names, 1813–1947

The German Empire (Kaiserreich)

Nationalized by the Prussian state in 1813, the names given to Berlin's streets and squares celebrated the Prussian dynasty and its military glory. After the unification of Germany in 1871 and the institution of Berlin as *de facto* capital of the German Reich, street names also commemorated German national figures such as Schiller and Lessing. As commemorations of the Prussian victory in the Franco-Prussian war of 1870 following which the German Empire was founded, streets were named after battlefields and victories. In Berlin and adjacent towns, streets were named after the members of the Hohenzollern dynasty, most notably kings and Emperors. Streets were named for Bismarck, the "founding father" of the Second Empire. Generally speaking, the history commemorated in Berlin's street names evinced the political hegemony of Prussia in the German Reich.

The Weimar Republic

In November 1918, the Kaiser abdicated and the short-lived first German republic was established. Notably, Greater Berlin was incorporated in October 1920 and, as a result, some street names appeared simultaneously in different boroughs. The transition from monarchy to republic was not articulated by a corresponding erasure of the dynastic heritage from the street signs of the German capital, even though this matter was continually raised by communists and Social Democrats in the city council (Azaryahu 1988). In practical terms, street naming in Berlin was a prerogative of the Prussian state and although the Social Democrats governed Prussia, the republican authorities undertook no comprehensive renaming of the dynastic past.

The Third Reich

The Nazis, aware of the propaganda value of street names and determined to erase all traces of the Weimar Republic, were swift in their actions to rename all those streets associated with the former regime and its history. In his memoirs Willy Brandt, the future German chancellor, wrote: "In Lübeck on 20 March (1933) a large number of people were taken into so-called protective custody. Soon thereafter the renaming of streets began" (Brandt 1982, 80). National-Socialist commemorations honored Nazi leaders and heroes.

Berlin, 1945–1948

The renaming of the Nazi past was high on the political agenda for reviving political life in Berlin following the collapse of the Third Reich (Azaryahu 1990, 2011). The city was divided into four sectors, each ruled by an allied military government. The unelected city government instituted by the Soviets in May 1945 was communist-led. Even though the need to "democratize" the street signs was a matter of consensus, two different approaches became apparent. The moderate approach advocated by conservative circles sought to undo Nazi commemorations and to re-institute the pre-Nazi names. The communists, at the other end of the political spectrum, supported a radical approach, according to which the democratization of political life should include the renaming of both Nazi and Prussian (namely military and monarchic) traditions. The communist-led municipal administration launched a large-scale renaming operation that went beyond the purge of Nazi commemorations to include Prussian commemorations as well, but the new Social Democratic administration that took office after the democratic elections held in Berlin in October 1946 scaled down the purge of the official register of street names. The renaming process was officially concluded in February 1947, with the official renaming of 151 streets in the 20 boroughs of Berlin.

Historical background: Haifa's street names, 1934–1948

Naming streets in Haifa began in the late-1920s with the rapid urban development of what had been in the Ottoman period a small settlement at the foot of Mt. Carmel, and its transformation into an industrial center of British mandate Palestine. Haifa was a mixed Arab-Jewish city, and during the 1940s the two communities were of similar magnitude: approximately 70,000 residents. From the early-1930s, the two communities lived in geographically separated areas of the city with the Arabs concentrated in the lower parts of the city and the Jews residing in Hadar Ha-Carmel, the new Jewish neighborhood built on the slopes of Mt. Carmel.

As an expression of the cooperation between Jews and Arabs at the municipal level, each community was autonomous with regard to naming streets in its respective neighborhoods (Goren 2006). In 1934, the municipality set up a Names Committee with both Jewish and Arab members, the role of which was largely limited to coordinating the naming of streets at the municipal level. The municipal council was involved in naming streets in the area near the new Imperial port built by the British government and these street names celebrated imperial rule. In 1934, the main thoroughfare along the port area was named *Kingsway*, and the following year a thoroughfare in downtown Haifa was named after King George V. Central streets were named after General Allenby, who had led the victorious military campaign against the Ottomans in the Near East in 1917, and Stanton, the first British governor of Haifa.

The commemorative naming of streets in Arab Haifa began in 1935. Streets were named after the Hashemite kings of Transjordan and Muslim Caliphs, warriors, and victories as well as philosophers and poets from the Golden Age of early Islam. In 1937, the Municipal Council approved the naming of streets after Saladin, who had defeated the Crusaders in 1187, conquering Jerusalem, and the Hijaz, the area of the holy Muslim cities of Mecca and Medina. In 1948, around 80 Arab street names were included in the official register of street names. The street names in the Jewish areas of the city—their number was around 300 in 1948—were regulated by the Hadar Ha-Carmel Committee and inscribed the Zionist narrative of Jewish history and national rebirth onto the local street signs. Central thoroughfares in Hadar Ha-Carmel were named after Herzl, the founding father of modern Zionism, and Max Nordau, the celebrated author who had supported Herzl.

Renaming the past: the necessary condition

Intended for posterity, the lifespan of commemorations is limited by the politics of commemoration. Any large-scale commemorative renaming of streets is a result and expression of a radical reshaping of power relations; renaming the past is a function of a discrepancy between the worldview of power-holders and the historical narrative inscribed on street signs. The renaming of streets in East Berlin and Haifa in 1951 were local variations on a national theme: the establishment of the communist East Germany in the Soviet zone of occupation in Germany and the establishment of the Jewish State of Israel in part of former British Mandate Palestine.

In November 1948, Berlin was divided in two (Figure 4.1). The communists, with the support of the Soviet military government, declared the eight boroughs of the Soviet sector (East Berlin) as "democratic" Berlin under communist municipal government, and East Berlin became the capital of the German Democratic Republic, which had been officially established as a state in the Soviet zone of occupation in Germany on October 7, 1949.

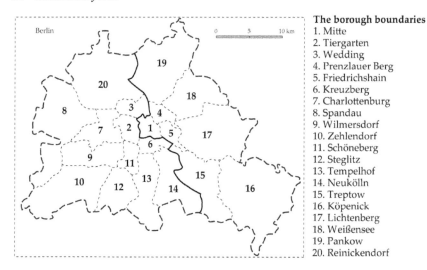

Figure 4.1 Borough boundaries in Berlin with the boundary between the Soviet sector and the western sectors marked in solid black

The 1947 partition plan of British Mandate Palestine assigned Haifa to the future Jewish state. In April 1948, the *Haganah*, the Jewish militia, defeated the local Arab militia and secured control of the entire city, following which most Arab residents and political leaders left the area with new Jewish immigrants settling in the abandoned Arab sections of the city. On May 15, 1948, the State of Israel was proclaimed and all of Haifa became part of the sovereign State of Israel.

Priorities, constraints, and prolonged delays

The immediate dismantling of street signs bearing the name of Adolf Hitler in German cities after the surrender to the Allies signaled the demise of the Nazi regime (Azaryahu 2011, 2012). Such symbolic acts are of great political resonance. Of particular interest are circumstances in which renaming the past is delayed for a prolonged period, creating a situation where the persistence of the old system of commemorative names is openly incongruent with the new regime and its vision of history.

East Berlin

As evinced by the failed attempt of the communist-led municipal government in May 1945–October 1946, Berlin communists were well aware of the need to align the municipal registry of commemorative street names with their vision of a new, democratic Germany. With the division of Berlin in November 1948, the communists were no longer constrained by the need to share power with other parties. In a speech delivered on the occasion of the tenth anniversary of the "democratic Berlin," East Berlin mayor Friedrich Ebert explained:

From these days on Berlin's working masses in the eight boroughs of the east could proceed without hindrance under the leadership of the parties of the working class in the way they had begun since 1945 in the whole of Berlin.

(Neues Deutschland 1958)

In regard to naming streets, the communist authorities had a free hand to mold the commemorative landscape in the section of the city under their control according to what was the ideologically correct version of historical heritage from their perspective. This was Marxist-Leninist in terms of doctrine and "progressive" and "democratic" according to official propaganda. Significantly, other cities in the Soviet Zone of Occupation in Germany had already achieved the radical "democratization" of the street signs prescribed by the communist party.

The first stage in reshaping the commemorative landscape of East Berlin was not about the decommemoration of "reactionary," mainly Prussian, traditions but rather about the commemoration of prominent communist leaders and heroes. According to a well-established convention, the naming of streets or squares after historic figures was occasioned by anniversaries, thereby emphasizing the symbolic honor entailed in the commemorative gesture. On August 18, 1949, on the occasion of the fifth anniversary of the execution by the Nazis of Ernst Thälmann, the leader of the communist party, in Buchenwald, the municipal government of East Berlin announced the forthcoming renaming of both *Wilhelmplatz* in Berlin-Mitte (the historical center of Berlin) and the nearby subway station *Kaiserhof* after Thälmann (*Neues Deutschland* 1949a). The slain communist leader of the KPD personified the legacy of communist anti-fascist martyrdom and was a distinguished member of the East German pantheon. The renaming ceremony was held on November 30 in the presence of the leaders of the communist state and the martyr's widow (*Neues Deutschland* 1949b). This renaming was emblematic in how it combined decommemoration and recommemoration into a powerful message about the demise of the old "reactionary" political order and the onset of a new "progressive" political order.

In honor of Lenin's eightieth birthday on April 22, 1950, Mayor Ebert initiated the renaming of a main thoroughfare and a square in Prenzlauer Berg and Friedrichshain *Leninallee* and *Leninplatz*, respectively (Minutes 1950a). In January 1951, the central committee of the ruling communist party requested the municipal government of East Berlin to rename the *Lustgarten*, a prestigious location in the city center, *Marx-Engels-Platz* (*Tägliche Rundschau* 1951a). The involvement of the central committee in this commemorative matter indicated the outstanding importance assigned to it by the communist authorities.

Naming main thoroughfares after Stalin, the Soviet leader, and Wilhelm Pieck, the president of the German Democratic Republic (GDR), celebrated the new political order in the Soviet sphere of influence. Naming streets after heads of state belonged to the cult of personality of communist leaders. In each member state of the Soviet Bloc, the dual cults of Stalin and of the local communist leader celebrated the new communist order and indicated subordination to the Soviet Union.

On December 22, 1949, on the occasion of Stalin's seventieth birthday, the *Frankfurter Allee* in Friedrichshain was renamed *Stalinallee*. The old street signs were removed in the morning and in the afternoon tens of thousands gathered in the street, which had been decorated with flags and slogans (*Berliner Zeitung* 1949). Wilhelm Pieck, the president of the GDR, was also celebrated by the regime as the founding father of the communist German state. A year later, on the occasion of Pieck's seventy-fifth birthday, the *Lothringer Straße* in Berlin-Mitte and Prenzlauer Berg was renamed *Wilhelm-Pieck-Straße* (*Neues Deutschland* 1951a).

Clearly the priority of the newly instituted communist government was to commemorate the prominent heroes of the Stalinist pantheon on the street signs. In their symbolic capacity as representations of the ruling regime, these new commemorative names asserted—through their placement in prestigious locations—the transformation of East Berlin into the capital of the communist state under construction in the Soviet zone of occupation in Germany.

Haifa

In April 1948 the former mixed, Jewish-Arab city became predominantly Jewish. The need to express the transformation of Haifa into an Israeli city with an overwhelming Jewish majority by means of renaming streets was on the municipal agenda. The national government was not involved. The pressure to rewrite the registry of street names in accord with political and demographic conditions largely came from below. "Concerned citizens" sent letters urging the municipal government to implement what they considered to be necessary changes. The first letter concerning the need to rename streets was discussed by the municipal council in October 1948 (Minutes 1948). Whereas some letters dealt with fundamental issues, others were concerned with specific names that should be replaced or given to streets.

A basic issue was the need to rename so-called "foreign" names—mainly British and Arab—in Haifa. In general terms, replacing "foreign" street names was construed as a statement about post-1948 Haifa as a mainly Jewish city in an independent State of Israel. The number of such "foreign" names was estimated to be around 100, approximately a quarter of the street names in the official register. The letters sent to the municipality differed in regard to the extent and scope of the toponymic changes needed. A maximalist approach maintained that the municipality should initiate a comprehensive purge of "foreign" commemorations from the municipal street name registry. Several letters requested renaming specific Arab street names after fallen soldiers (Letter 1950a). Remarkably, there were no specific demands to decommemorate King George V or General Allenby. However, the first letter to the municipal government regarding the need to rename streets specifically requested the decommemoration of Stanton, the first British governor of Haifa, in light of his openly anti-Zionist position. As the author of the letter explained, "there should be no objection to renaming Stanton St. ... No one will be sorry when this name will no longer adorn the walls of Haifa" (Letter 1949b).

In response to the letters urging renaming, the municipal government acknowledged the need to harmonize the street names with the new political and demographic conditions, but it deferred the task to the new municipal administration:

> The problem you raised—replacing Arab street names by Hebrew ones and giving names to new streets—has been on our mind for a few months already and we acknowledge the need to solve it once and for all. However, we cannot do it [prior to] new elections to the municipal council.
>
> The ... municipal council to be elected will address the issue and will formulate clear principles regarding both changing names and giving new names so that the new names will express in both content and sound the political transformation that has taken place in our country and our city.
>
> (Letter 1950b)

"Renamings, at long last"

Renaming the past is about taking measures directed at harmonizing the official register of street names with the ideological underpinnings of the ruling political order. A revolutionary transformation of the ruling order is a necessary condition only. As the cases of East Berlin and Haifa show, a prolonged delay in implementing ostensibly anticipated toponymic changes is a possibility. Such a delay is the result of a dynamic interplay of specific priorities and constraints. In the case of a delay, the question arises as to what prompts the municipal authorities to put an end to the impasse and vigorously engage in renaming the past.

Pressures and incentives: East Berlin

Despite the need to introduce Stalinist commemorations into the cityscape, the issue of decommemoration (i.e., renaming the ideologically incorrect past inscribed on East Berlin's street signs), was also on the municipal agenda. Pressure to proceed in this direction was exerted from above. On March 30, 1950, the East German government decreed that all cities and towns in the GDR should rename streets that did not comply with the ideological premises of the East German regime (Minutes 1950d). Unreported in the East German press, the decree stipulated that:

> [s]treets, roads and squares that carry militaristic, fascist and anti-democratic names or such named after people, places and other terms associated with military, fascist or anti-democratic acts, should be renamed by 31 July 1950.

Whereas in 1945 the purge of Nazi names was at the top of the renaming agenda, in 1950, after the most explicit Nazi names had already been purged, the emphasis was on the need to cleanse the official register of street names of the "reactionary" legacy of former political regimes, most notably "military" and "monarchic" commemorations. According to the second clause of the decree, street name changes were to be approved by elected local authorities. This lent a democratic aura to a procedure that in fact had been ordained by the communist state and executed by communist-controlled local governments. The third clause specified the criteria for selecting new names. These were to be names of people and places, terms or appellations "closely connected" with the "anti-fascist" and "democratic" regime of the GDR, or names rooted in vernacular traditions. Above all, persons after whom streets were to be named should be distinguished for their special accomplishments in the service of "progress."

The decree of March 30, 1950, made the purge of "reactionary" street names mandatory throughout the GDR. Following the declaration of this decree, the issue of purging "reactionary" public commemorations in East Berlin was raised on the official municipal agenda. At its meeting on May 4, 1950, the East Berlin municipal government stipulated the renaming of three streets in Niederschönhausen in Pankow (Minutes 1950b). The reason given was that Wilhelm Pieck, the President of the GDR, requested renaming streets with "military and monarchic" names in the area; remarkably, the three streets were in the vicinity of the *Schloss Niederschönhausen* (castle), the official residence of the President of the GDR. In actuality, three monarchic names were replaced: *Kronprinzenstraße* became *Majakowskistraße*, after the famed Soviet revolutionary poet, and *Kaiserin-Auguste-Straße* was renamed *Tchaikowskistraße*, after the renowned Russian composer. Replacing monarchic names by Soviet/Russian commemorations was a resonant statement about the ideological reorientation of the GDR. The third, *Friedrich-Wilhelm-Straße* was renamed *Stille Straße* (Quiet Street), "because of its character" (Minutes 1950b).

The renaming of the monarchic past in the vicinity of the presidential palace was laden with political meaning, but it had little actual impact on East Berlin as a whole. Of greater impact on the historical cityscape of the East German capital was the decision of the municipal government taken on May 11, 1950, one week later, to "exile" the famous equestrian statue of Friedrich II (the Great) to Sanssouci, the palace complex of the Hohenzollern dynasty in Potsdam (Minutes 1950c). Designed by Christian Rauch in 1851, the statue adorned *Unter den Linden*, the central boulevard of Prussian Berlin. The official reason given for the monument's removal was the alleged damage it had suffered during the war.

The decree issued by the East German government in March 1950 set a time limit for the comprehensive purge of all street names that did not accord with the ideological criteria specified. Notably, most other cities and towns in the Soviet Zone of Occupation had already expunged undesired commemorations from the official register. In these circumstances, the purge of "reactionary" commemorations in East Berlin seemed to be a question of time only.

Remarkably, despite preliminary signs to the contrary, East Berlin's municipal government failed to maintain the time limit set by the decree. It is unclear whether pressure was exerted on the municipal government from above to initiate extensive renaming of the past according to the criteria stipulated in the decree. However, there was a clear incentive for an extensive renaming operation in East Berlin: the third Festival of Youth and Students, which was due to be held from August 5 through 9, 1951, in East Berlin.

At its meeting on December 22, 1950, the city government announced its support for the first international event in Berlin since 1939:

> The municipal government of Greater Berlin greets with special joy the Council of the World Organization of the Democratic Youth for its decision to hold the World Youth Festival 1951 in Berlin. The municipal government considers the convening of this great peace meeting in Berlin to be a large award for the city. It is proof that in the eyes of democratic people in the whole world Berlin has remained not only the capital of Germany, but is also acknowledged as a center of power in the struggle for world peace.
>
> The youth of the world will find in Berlin in summer 1951 a different population than that of before 1945, a Berlin that no longer subscribes to hatred of peoples and races but a Berlin that expresses solidarity with the struggle of youth for peace.
>
> (Minutes 1950e)

As the announcement makes clear, the planned communist-oriented world festival was of the utmost importance to the East German regime. In his autobiography, Erich Honecker, then head of the state's Youth Movement, the *Freie Deutsche Jugend* (FDJ), which was the formal host and organizer of the festival, noted that the festival offered the opportunity "to demonstrate the change which had taken place in our country since the liberation from fascism" (Honecker 1980, 188). At its weekly meeting on March 8, 1951, the municipal government issued a decree about the realization of the world youth and students festival (Minutes 1951b). This paved the way for making the necessary preparations for the mega-event scheduled for the summer.

Early in April 1951, the prime minister of the GDR made a public appeal to the citizens to "support the world youth festival" (*Neues Deutschland* 1951b). On April 12, *Neues Deutschland*, the organ of the ruling communist party, announced, speaking for its readers: "We greet the students of the world" (*Neues Deutschland* 1951c). On the same day, the municipal government passed a resolution to rename 25 streets in East Berlin. The headline of the report about the resolution in the *Tägliche Rundschau*, a newspaper published by the Soviet Army in the Soviet zone of occupation in Germany, announced: "Renamings, at long last"; according to the newspaper, the resolution was "the first part of the renamings that have long been demanded by the population" (*Tägliche Rundschau* 1951b). The renaming procedure was top-down, and the reference to an alleged popular demand to rename streets indicated the need of the regime for democratic legitimacy.

Prospects and incentives: Haifa

The obstacle specified in the anticipated changes to the official registry of street names in Haifa was of a formal nature, namely, the understanding that the pre-1948 city government did not represent the electorate and therefore did not have the authority to initiate necessary changes. Elections for a new municipal council took place in November 1950 (*Al Hamishmar* 1950). Negotiating a coalition proved difficult, and a mayor was only elected in January 1951, with Abba Khoushy, the powerful leader of MAPAI (Labor) in Haifa, at the helm.

The election of a mayor put an end to two and half years of caretaker municipal government. In February 1951, the Municipal Council elected a municipal Names Committee that was entrusted with the task of proposing street names to the council, which was the sovereign body in this matter (Minutes 1951b). This was a stark break with the past, when neighborhoods were independent in this respect. The new Names Committee meant centralization at the municipal level.

The first meeting of the Street Names Committee was convened in March 1951. In its first session the chairman explained that the role of the committee was to institute new names and to replace "the street names which did not have Hebrew names, of which there are approximately one hundred" (Minutes 1951c). He noted that in his view the names selected should be commemorations of Jewish and Israeli history. On the agenda of the meeting were also Arab street names that were in neighborhoods resettled by Jews after 1948. As a committee member noted, the issue was "highly political." The consensus was that "foreign" street names should be changed, but the question was whether the change should be comprehensive or only partial, with most members supporting the latter approach. One maintained that the names were familiar and there should not be a "wholesale" purge of Arab names. Another suggested to check all names, but to consider each according to its merit, the aim being to delete "absurd" names such as *Stanton St.* A third member proposed retaining Arab street names pertaining to the history of Haifa. The chairman's view was that most Arab names should be deleted from the registry.

However, the renaming of streets in Haifa in May 1951 was not about a purge of "foreign" street names. The incentives were the third anniversary of the Jewish military victory in the battle for Haifa in April 1948 and Israel's third Independence Day celebrated a few weeks later. For the mayor, the anniversaries were both an obligation and an opportunity to celebrate Israel's Independence on the street signs.

Patterns of renaming

East Berlin: decommemoration and recommemoration

Aimed at decommemorating the Prussian-German monarchy and military tradition inscribed on street signs, the renaming operation in East Berlin in April–May 1951 was carried out in four successive rounds. At the weekly meeting of the municipal government on April 12, 1951, the director of the department for transportation and municipal enterprises presented a list with 25 streets to be renamed (Minutes 1951d). The responsibility of this department for street names was instituted in 1947 by the municipal government of a then still unified city (Azaryahu 2011). Further resolutions followed suit, with 26 renamings on May 10, 35 on May 24, and 69 on May 31 (Minutes 1951e; Minutes 1951f; Minutes 1951g). Altogether, 155 streets were renamed in the eight boroughs of East Berlin in the course of the toponymic cleansing decreed by the communist municipal government. In comparison, the purge of politically incorrect street names in the 20 boroughs of Greater Berlin in 1947 entailed 151 renamings in a city with almost 9,000 street names.

Each of the four renaming rounds had clear thematic characteristics. The first two were directed at erasing the memory of the ruling Prussian dynasty and included names such as *Kaiser-Wilhelm-Straße, Auguste-Viktoria-Straße, Prinz-Heinrich-Straße*, or *Prinz-Oskar-Straße*. The third round was directed at deleting street names expressing the monarchic idea such as *Kaiserstraße, Königstraße*, or *Kronprinzenstraße*. The most prominent "casualty" of the third round was Otto von Bismarck, the founding father of the German Empire, whose name was obliterated from the street signs of Lichtenberg, Weißensee, Köpenick, and Treptow.

The fourth round focused on decommemorating the Prussian-German military heritage, represented through the names of prominent generals and celebrated victories. Among the generals were heroes of the anti-Napoleonic "Wars of Liberation" at the beginning of the nineteenth century such as Gneisenau, Yorck, and Blücher, and Prussian generals involved in the wars against Denmark (1864), Habsburg Austria (1866), and France (1870) that led to the founding of the German Empire under Prussian leadership. In this round of renaming, commemorations of the Prussian-French war of 1870 also disappeared, most prominently streets named after significant battlefields, such as *Sedanstraße, Belfortstraße*, and *Metzstraße*.

The main thrust of the renaming operation was to "democratize" and "demilitarize" the street signs. The new street names, obviously indispensable, were a by-product of the purge of ideologically incongruent commemorations. The purge of "reactionary" street names was an opportunity to fill the vacancies with the names of heroes of the German revolutionary tradition and of communist activists as well as of martyrs of the anti-Nazi resistance movement, thereby enhancing the "progressive" tone of the version of history inscribed on the street signs. Street names in Treptow commemorated Thomas Münzer and Florian Geyer, the heroes of the Peasants' rebellion of 1525. Friedrich Engels and Ferdinand Lassalle were commemorated in Pankow and Köpenick, respectively. At the same time, "progressive" writers, artists, and scientists such as Kurt Tucholsky, Romain Rolland, Max Lieberman, and Marie Curie were commemorated as well.

In certain areas, efforts were made to replace disgraced "reactionary" thematic arrangements of names with others that were more ideologically and culturally congruent. In Karlshorst, where the Soviet military administration had its headquarters, streets that had been named after members of the Hohenzollern dynasty were renamed after lakes in Brandenburg, the region in which Berlin is situated (*Tägliche Rundschau* 1951b). The street names in the so-called "French neighborhood" in Weißensee commemorated battlefields of the Franco-Prussian war of 1870, and hence, according to official assessment, belonged to the "militaristic" and "imperialist" tradition. Following the renaming operation, the "French neighborhood" was transformed into a "composers' neighborhood," where street names commemorated famous European composers.

Haifa: commemoration and decommemoration

In April 1951, Haifa's newly elected mayor approached the recently established municipal Street Names Committee to offer "a few street names that should be given on Independence Day" (Minutes 1951h). In its session on April 16, a few days after the third anniversary of the battle for Haifa, the council discussed "giving national names to streets" to commemorate the victory (*Herut* 1951a). According to another newspaper, the new names were to celebrate Israel's third Independence Day (*Davar* 1951). In a festive session held some three weeks later, on the eve of Independence Day, the council formally approved five renamings that "symbolized Israel's War of Independence" (*Herut* 1951b). Later that month, the Municipal Council approved two more renamings (*Al Hamishmar* 1951). The commemorations combined local and national aspects of Israel's national narrative. The national aspect was evident in the names *Derekh Ha'atzmaut* (Independence Road), *Rehov Kibbutz Galuyot* (Ingathering of the Exiles St.), and *Rehov Shivat Zion* (Return to Zion St.). The latter two names were prominent themes of the Zionist narrative of the return of the Jewish people to their ancestral homeland. The name *Ma'ale Hashihrur* (Liberation Slope) commemorated a decisive battle waged there during the battle for Haifa. The names *Shderot HaHaganah* (Haganah Blvd.), *Rehov Hameginim* (Defenders St.), and *Rehov Hagiborim* (Heroes St.) conflated the local and national aspects of Israel's War of Independence. Notably, the new street names were generic commemorations, celebrating values such as independence or ingathering of the exiles or the heroes and defenders in general, befitting the collectivist ethos of the period (Figure 4.2). Despite specific requests from bereaved families, no individual fallen soldiers were commemorated.

Figure 4.2 Ha'atzma'ut Road (Independence Road), Haifa, Israel (photograph by author)

Though the renamings of streets in Haifa were few in number, their symbolic impact was substantial. The purge of "foreign" street names was not a priority, but rather a welcome by-product of the stated intention to commemorate Israel's independence on street signs. The importance assigned to the new commemorations was underlined through selecting central thoroughfares in downtown Haifa, the names of which were British and Arab commemorations. Three commemorations of the colonial past in downtown Haifa were purged: *Kingsway* became *Atzmaut (Independence) Road*, *King George V St.* became *HaMeginim (Defenders) St.*, and *Stanton St.*, named after the anti-Zionist British official, became *Shivat Zion (Return to Zion) St.* in what was a clear case of a symbolic retribution. These three renamings replaced the colonial past with Zionist history. Some Arab names were also replaced. *Iraq St.* became *Rehov Kibbutz Galyot (The Ingathering of Exiles St.)*, a symbolic message in its own right since it was instituted when Iraqi Jews were leaving Iraq, most of them for Israel. *Saladin St.*, a significant Arab-Muslim commemoration, was renamed *Rehov Hagiborim (Heroes St.).*

Aftermath

East Berlin

The purge of "reactionary" Prussian names from the street signs of East Berlin also included decommemorating the heroes of the anti-Napoleonic Wars of Liberation (1813–1815), prominent among them Prussian generals and field-marshals Gneisenau and Scharnhorst, Yorck and Blücher, Lützow and Körner. However, a year after these men had been consigned to oblivion a change in official doctrine reinstated their heroic stature in the East German pantheon. The transition to "national historiography" in East Germany was in tune with the need for a "progressive" military heritage to lend ideological support to the creation of the East German armed forces in 1952 (Azaryahu 1991, 135–141). As a result of this about-turn in official historiography, the Prussian generals of the Wars of Liberation became hailed as "Prussia's best men" (*Neues Deutschland* 1952).

In June 1952, the communist party prompted their commemorative "rehabilitation." According to this new official policy, monuments to the generals should be restored. Regarding streets that had been renamed "as the result of a false interpretation of socialist historiography" (*Der Spiegel* 1952), the official policy was that though the discarded street names should not be restored, they should be considered for use with new streets built in the course of the reconstruction of East German cities, as long as the local population was supportive, which was especially the case in former Prussian garrison towns.

Renaming the past in East Berlin was about purging the memories of the monarchy and military glory of Prussia from the street signs. However, such historical memories persisted in West Berlin, which was unaffected by the ideological zeal of the communist regime: as a result of the incorporation of Greater Berlin in 1920, many street names, prominent among them being commemorations of the Prussian dynasty and military history, recurred in different boroughs of the city. Such dynastic and militaristic commemorations were eliminated in 1951 in East Berlin, but persisted in West Berlin.

Haifa

Inscribing preeminent Zionist commemorations on Haifa's street signs in May 1951 was a symbolic celebration of triumph. The toponymic changes were clearly not about a comprehensive purge of "foreign" street names. However, this issue was writ large on the municipal agenda. In 1953, the mayor urged the Municipal Names Committee to accelerate the tempo of changing the 72 "foreign" street names still extant in the city (Letter 1953). Preliminary proposals included 39 Arab street names; however, the number of changes was reduced by July 1953 to 19 names, among them names of streets in an area in downtown Haifa that lay in ruins (Minutes 1953). The Municipal Council approved only one change: the name of Omar al-Mukhtar, an anti-colonial pan-Arab martyr, was replaced on the street signs by that of Naftali Herz Imber, the author of the lyrics of *Hatikvah*, the Zionist anthem that became Israel's national anthem.

Notwithstanding the mayor's frustration with the slow tempo of the purge of "foreign" names in 1953, it transpired that the policy of the city leaders in regard to "foreign," mostly Arab, street names was actually careful, measured, and selective. The names changed were those of pan-Arab heroes or geographical areas outside Israel. Early Caliphs and Arab philosophers were not decommemorated. In April 1958, the tenth anniversary of Israel's independence, the Municipal Council approved changing four Arab street names (List 1959), and this was the last change in the official registry of "foreign" street names in Haifa.

Conclusion

The comparative perspective employed in the study of renaming streets in East Berlin and Haifa in Spring 1951 offers insights into the dynamic and patterns of renaming the past as a political procedure aimed at harmonizing the names and commemorations inscribed on local street signs with the new political order and its ideological underpinnings. However, major power shifts are a necessary condition only. The actual tempo and patterns of renaming the past are the result of a particular interplay of pressures, constraints, incentives, and priorities.

A large-scale renaming operation entails a purge of the official registry of street names. A major issue is the relationship between commemoration and decommemoration as aspects of renaming the past. In East Berlin, the objective of renaming the past was to purge "reactionary" (i.e., "monarchic" and "militaristic") commemorations from the street signs of the communist-ruled sectors of Berlin and to abrogate the dissonance between the vision of history inscribed on the street signs and the ideology of the communist regime. In Haifa, on the other hand, the primary objective was to commemorate Israel's independence on the street signs, while decommemoration was a welcome by-product of this procedure.

As the cases of East Berlin and Haifa show, renaming the past is a process that can stretch over a prolonged period of time. Renaming the past in Haifa in Spring 1951 was the beginning of the process whereas in East Berlin it marked its end (Azaryahu 1986). Renaming the past in Haifa marked the start of realigning local street names with the narrative of Israel's independence. The purge of "foreign" street names in later years was partial only and ended in 1958. In East Berlin, renaming the past in April–May 1951 was the last stage of a process that began in May 1945, when, after the surrender of Nazi Germany, the purge of "reactionary" street names was a high priority.

Renaming the past in East Berlin in 1951 took place in the communist part of a divided Berlin. The commemorative traditions discarded in East Berlin were left intact in West Berlin, where streets further commemorated German and Prussian military and monarchic traditions. With the reunification of Germany and Berlin in 1990, renaming the communist past became a major political issue (Azaryahu 1997). However, the recommemoration of German emperors and Prussian generals whose names had been erased in 1951 in East Berlin was not on the public agenda: according to municipal regulations, duplicate street names were to be avoided, and therefore street names already in existence in West Berlin could not be introduced in East Berlin. Paradoxically, the ideologically oriented purge of "reactionary" traditions in East Berlin in 1951 proved in the long run to be a contribution to reducing the number of duplicate commemorations in the re-unified city.

References

Al Hamishmar (1950). November 16: 4 (Hebrew).

Al Hamishmar (1951). May 22: 1 (Hebrew).

Azaryahu, M. (1986). "Street Names and Political Identity: The Case of East Berlin." *Journal of Contemporary History*, 21(4): 581–604.

Azaryahu, M. (1988). "What is to be Remembered: The Struggle over Street Names, Berlin 1921–1930." *Tel Aviver Jahrbuch für deutsche Geschichte*, 17: 241–258.

Azaryahu, M. (1990). "Renaming the Past: Changes in 'City-Text' in Germany and Austria 1945–1947." *History & Memory*, 2(2): 32–53.

Azaryahu, M. (1991). *Vom Wilhelmplatz zu Thälmannplatz. Politische Symbole im öffentlichen Leben der DDR*. Gerlingen: Bleicher Verlag.

Azaryahu, M. (1992). "The Purge of Bismarck and Saladin: The Renaming of Streets in East Berlin and Haifa, a Comparative Study in Culture-Planning." *Poetics Today*, 13(2): 351–367.

Azaryahu, M. (1997). "German Reunification and the Politics of Street Naming: The Case of East Berlin." *Political Geography*, 16(6): 479–493.

Azaryahu, M. (2011). "The Politics of Commemorative Street Renaming: Berlin 1945–1948." *Journal of Historical Geography*, 37(4): 483–492.

Azaryahu, M. (2012). "Renaming the Past in post-Nazi Germany: Insights into the Politics of Street Naming in Mannheim and Potsdam." *Cultural Geographies*, 19(3): 387–400.

Berliner Zeitung (1949). December 22: 2.

Brandt, W. (1982). *Links und Frei: Mein Weg, 1930–1950*. Hamburg: Hofmann und Campe.

Davar (1951). April 17: 4 (Hebrew).

72   *Maoz Azaryahu*

Der Spiegel (1952). June 18: 9.

Goren, T. (2006). "Cooperation is the Guiding Principle: Jews and Arabs in the Haifa Municipality during the British Mandate." *Israel Studies*, 11(3): 108–141.

Herut (1951a). April 17: 4 (Hebrew).

Herut (1951b). May 9: 4 (Hebrew).

Honecker, E. (1980). *From My Life*. Oxford: Pergamon.

Kundera, M. (1996). *The Book of Laughter and Forgetting*, translated by A. Asher. New York: HarperPerennial.

Letter (1949a). S. Zilberfarb to the Municipality of Haifa, June 16. Haifa Historical Archive, file 3205 (Hebrew).

Letter (1949b). A Yaeli to the Mayor of Haifa, March 27, Haifa Historical Archive, file 3205 (Hebrew).

Letter (1950a). E. Epstein to the Mayor of Haifa, September 25, Haifa Historical Archive, file 3205 (Hebrew).

Letter (1950b). General Director of the Municipality of Haifa to M. Zelkind, July 27, Haifa Historical Archive, file 3205 (Hebrew).

Letter (1953). A. Khoushy to the Street Names Committee, November 3, Haifa Historical Archive, file 32579 (Hebrew).

List (1959). "A List with Changes Approved by the Municipal Council in 1958/9." Haifa Historical Archive, file 31802 (Hebrew).

Minutes (1948). Session on October 19 of Haifa's Municipal Council (Hebrew).

Minutes (1950a). Session on April 6 of Berlin's Municipal Government, Landesarchiv Berlin, C Rep. 100–105, No. 846.

Minutes (1950b). Session on May 4 of Berlin's Municipal Government, Landesarchiv Berlin, C Rep. 100–105, No. 847.

Minutes (1950c). Session on May 11 of Berlin's Municipal Government, Landesarchiv Berlin, C Rep. 100–105, No. 848.

Minutes (1950d). Session on July 25 of Potsdam's Municipal Council, Stadtarchiv Potsdam, Ratsprotokolle, film 271.

Minutes (1950e). Session on December 22 of Berlin's Municipal Government, Landesarchiv Berlin, C Rep. 100–105, No. 854.

Minutes (1951a). Session on February 5 of the Municipal council of Haifa (Hebrew).

Minutes (1951b). Session on March 8 of Berlin's Municipal Government, Landesarchiv Berlin, C Rep. 100–105, No. 855.

Minutes (1951c). Session on March 12 of Haifa's Street Names Committee, Haifa Historical Archive, file 32509 (Hebrew).

Minutes (1951d). Session on April 12 of Berlin's Municipal Government, Landesarchiv Berlin, C Rep. 100–105, No. 856.

Minutes (1951e). Session on May 10 of Berlin's Municipal Government, Landesarchiv Berlin, C Rep. 100–105, No. 857.

Minutes (1951f). Session on May 24 of Berlin's Municipal Government, Landesarchiv Berlin, C Rep. 100–105, No. 857.

Minutes (1951g). Session on May 30 of Berlin's Municipal Government, Landesarchiv Berlin, C Rep. 100–105, No. 858.

Minutes (1951h). Session on April 16 of Haifa's Municipal Council of Haifa (Hebrew).

Minutes (1953). Session on July 8 of the Street Names Committee, Haifa Historical Archive, file 5895 (Hebrew).

Neues Deutschland (1949a). August 19: 1.

Neues Deutschland (1949b). December 1: 1.

Neues Deutschland (1951a). January 10: 1.
Neues Deutschland (1951b). April 7: 1.
Neues Deutschland (1951c). April 12: 2.
Neues Deutschland (1952). June 2: 4.
Neues Deutschland (1958*)*. November 30: 2.
Tägliche Rundschau (1951a). January 20: 1.
Tägliche Rundschau (1951b). April 13: 2.

5 "Armed with an encyclopedia and an axe"

The socialist and post-socialist street toponymy of East Berlin revisited through Gramsci

Jani Vuolteenaho and Guy Puzey

Introduction

Writing about Berlin, Maoz Azaryahu once outlined a paradigmatic approach in contemporary research on the politics of honorific street naming:

> The selection of street names is a political procedure determined by ideological needs and political power relations. Even if it may be presented as a response to popular sentiments, it is always implemented by nominated agents of the ruling political order and the naming procedure is a manifest feature of authority. ... In democratic regimes, local government is legally in charge of naming streets, even though the state may have some rights as to the names of streets in specific areas of the national capital that are rendered nationally representative. Such differences matter less in authoritarian regimes, where local and central authorities are only formally differentiated.
>
> (1997, 481)

Whilst not denying the serviceability of the above generalizations in many research settings, in this chapter we will argue that focusing on the overtly political procedures and meanings of street naming is not the only avenue to the advancement of critical toponymic scholarship. One valuable contribution of "politicized" street naming research in recent decades has certainly been the accumulation of detailed mappings of local-scale and intra-state governmental and party-political processes and contingencies, especially in periods following radical or revolutionary political changes. In particular, research into socialist and post-socialist urban contexts across Eastern and Central Eastern Europe has revealed much about top-down processes and the political wrangling linked with odonymic de- and re-commemorations. It has also highlighted the honorific-pedagogic functions that street (re)naming serves for the legitimization of political systems and rendering as "natural" state-sanctioned ideological values and interpretations of the past (e.g., Azaryahu 1986, 1996, 1997, 2009; Light 2004; Gill 2005; Marin 2012; Palonen 2015). As a flipside, however, this research has tended to sideline less obviously political aspects of street naming. It is symptomatic, for instance, that many critical readings of street toponymy have revolved around explicitly honorific inscriptions of historical events and heroic individuals typical of high-prestige urban locations. As Rose-Redwood (2008), Vuolteenaho and Ainiala (2009), and Berg (2011) have all noted, critical toponymists have often turned a blind eye to other types of thematic, possessive, or otherwise deceptively "banal" street and place names that proliferate in the urban landscape.

We also argue that, more generally, a restricted analytical understanding of "the political" as a more or less autonomous sphere of power-holding elites has regularly taken place at the expense of the more elusive roles of "the cultural" and "the popular" in street naming practices (cf. Verdery 1991; De Soto 1996). Crucially, for our present purposes, criticism of this latter bias resonates with the conceptions of power developed by Antonio Gramsci (1891–1937), according to which power is not merely a one-directional, top-down process. In his elaboration of the notion of hegemony, Gramsci advocated for an understanding of the cultural roots of power and the co-existing processes of coercion and consent that shape relationships between rulers and the ruled in any given society. Equally intriguingly, although less widely known, Gramsci's approach to political theory was closely tied to his strong interest in language practices. As a young journalist in the late-1910s, as we will outline in the following section, Gramsci even specifically criticized the "evisceration of the old Turin" in honorific-odonymic terms, advocating instead for a street naming policy consistent with "solidarity through memory."

This chapter's approach is to explore Gramsci's specific writings about street naming and more general ideas on hegemony to guide and inspire the study of power and street naming. As a result, it is hoped to shed light on more covertly political dynamics in street naming practices. This Gramscian approach will be applied, in this instance, to the research setting of East Berlin, both during the period of the German Democratic Republic (GDR) and after its demise in the context of a unified Germany. After investigating relevant insights from Gramsci, we will tackle the multiple, and often paradoxical, manifestations of Marxist-Leninist state socialism as an allegedly "people-empowering" ideology in the street toponymy of East Berlin in 1945–1989. Analyzing both honorific and thematic street names, we trace how the (1) self-aggrandizement of the party-led political system (through so-called cult naming), (2) ideals of socialist internationalism, and (3) socio-cultural indigenization of a distinctively German socialism were manifested across East Berlin's inner-city and suburban districts. Next, we will apply a Gramscian lens to street name revisions as well as instances of resilience of the GDR's toponymic legacy in post-socialist urban development. In line with Gramsci's postulations, our methodological emphasis in both periods analyzed is simultaneously on blatantly top-down (coerced) and legitimacy-seeking (or otherwise reciprocal) relationships between name-giving elites and ordinary Berliners. Whilst acknowledging the historical, administrative, and socio-cultural particularities of Berlin as a stage of socialist and post-socialist toponymic transformations, we conclude by discussing the wider implications of Gramsci's work for the understanding of power in critical street naming studies.

Extrapolating odonymic lessons from Gramsci

Gramsci's international reputation is predominantly based on his *Quaderni del carcere* (*Prison Notebooks*), which he wrote while imprisoned by Mussolini's Fascist regime in 1926–1935. This work covers a range of historical, cultural, and political topics, including elaborations of classical treatments of political maneuvering and pre-existing hegemony theories, observations on civic revolts and legitimacy crises raging in many European states at that time, and commentaries on contemporary popular culture. Gramsci's influence as a theorist of power has been wide-ranging and enduring across political and cultural research, not least among subsequent hegemony theorists (e.g., Williams 1980, 1983; Laclau and Mouffe 1985; Laclau 2005; Johnson 2007; Thomas 2009; Coutinho 2012). His thoughts on matters such as the relationship between the state and civil society, different types of hegemony, the role of "organic intellectuals" as cultural mediators of hegemonic power, and the oppositional pairing of hegemony and subalternity have been applied to the study of many different societies and political systems.

A brief outline of Gramsci's discussion of hegemony

One of Gramsci's innovations was that he conceived dominant influences as not solely "limited to matters of direct political control" but also encompassing "a more general way of seeing the world and human nature and relationships" (Williams 1983, 145). In certain societal situations, the power of a hegemon can be so strong that aspects of the prevailing political-cultural system—including its founding ideologies and historical narratives—are widely internalized as "common sense." This notion resonates with critical toponymists' current insistence on the power of place naming to make political ideologies appear as the "natural order of things" in the eyes of ordinary citizens (e.g., Azaryahu 2009, 62). However, Gramsci also argued that any organized society is composed of both political society (the state, the official) and civil society (the popular, the cultural sphere). Furthermore, he made it plain that an effective hegemony can only be won and sustained through existing ideologies, traditions, and particularly what he termed a "national-popular collective will" (Gramsci 2007, 1559; translation in Gramsci 1971, 130). While the institutionalized practices of power by a hegemony-seeking regime are of necessity coerced, they simultaneously hinge on the cultural sphere and its everyday producers (intellectuals, teachers, journalists, artists, civic organizations, etc.) who may have an "organic" connection to the lay people and communities. The influence of cultural hegemony thus derives not only from coercion or force, but also from popular consent.

Significantly, Gramsci saw language-related practices as the fundamentals of an "educational relationship" between the rulers and the ruled. "Every relationship of 'hegemony,'" he argued, "is necessarily an educational relationship and occurs not only within a nation, between the various forces of which the nation is composed, but in the international and world-wide field, between complexes of national and continental civilisations" (Gramsci 2007, 1331; translation in Gramsci 1971, 350). In a fundamentally two-way relationship, the rulers mobilize intellectual labor to propagate their ideological worldview as unquestioned common sense. In this process, language practices—from language education proper to linguistic standardization and "lessons" about significant historical events disseminated through schoolbooks and other popular media—all play quintessential roles. In this way, Gramsci showed insight into occasions when the official and the popular were in a reciprocal dialogue. In Joseph Femia's (1981) formulation, Gramsci's utopian-Marxist conception of "integral hegemony" embraced political systems that are democratic and organically representative of society. Furthermore, Gramsci acknowledged that in seeking to guarantee popular consent, regimes of power often resort to a degree of self-criticism as "the cultural environment ... reacts back" (2007, 1331; translation in Gramsci 1971, 350). This bi-directionality, of course, is not always the case: a dominant ideology can also be merely coercive, monologic, and hence deemed a "minimal" hegemony (only catering for elites) or a "decadent" hegemony (a corroded integral hegemony no longer able to satisfy the masses) (Femia 1981).

The fact that Gramsci's political thought was heavily influenced by his interest in linguistics and his personal experience of power relations between languages has often escaped the attention of political and social scientists, although there are researchers who underscore the utility of this aspect of Gramsci's thinking (e.g., Lo Piparo 1979; Ives 2004; Thomas 2009; Puzey 2011, 2016; Carlucci 2013). A particularly intriguing discussion of coerced power in language practices was penned by Gramsci himself, as a young dissident intellectual and journalist, when he engaged in scathing criticism of ongoing street name changes in Turin. We will now turn to this early polemic.

Gramsci as a critical toponymist

On June 1, 1917, a newly announced list of projected renamings in Turin's city center by the municipal street naming committee was discussed in *Avanti!*, a left-wing newspaper co-edited by Gramsci. These proposals were the latest step in the ongoing gentrification or embourgeoisement of Turin's inherited street toponymy, a process that had begun after Italian Unification, with an initial focus on the memorialization of the House of Savoy and of Risorgimento heroes and symbols. The former *via Dora Grossa* (named after a river) had become *via Giuseppe Garibaldi*, while *via Gasometro* ("Gasometer Street") had been renamed *via Giovanni Camerana* (after a poet), among several other street name changes privileging nationally exalted heroes over the inherited odonymy. The newest proposals continued in this spirit of "progressive" eradication, aiming to change *via dell'Ospedale* ("Hospital Street") to *via Galileo Ferraris* (after an engineer and physicist, 1847–1897) and *via del Deposito* ("Warehouse Street") to *via Quinto Agricola* (after a Roman general), for instance.

In the very same issue of *Avanti!*, Gramsci's critical commentary was published. As a brief odonymic case study of Gramsci's own, this short article bore the sardonic title, "Il progresso nello stradario" (Progress on the Street Map). Gramsci complained about the decorative function of the proposed names, void of any organic meaning connected to the places in question. With more than a hint of nostalgia for the local working-class heritage, Gramsci wrote:

> Armed with an encyclopedia and an axe, [the street naming committee] is proceeding with the evisceration of the old Turin. Down come the old names, the traditional names of popular Turin that record the fervent life of the old medieval commune, the exuberant and original imagination of the Renaissance artisans, less encyclopedic but more practical and with better taste than the merchants of today. They are replaced with medal names. The street map is becoming a medal showcase. ... Every name [in the artisans' city] was a branch of life, it was the memory of a moment of collective life. The street map was like a common patrimony of memories, of affection, binding individuals together more strongly with the ties of solidarity through memory. The shop-keeping bourgeoisie has destroyed this heritage. ... All the princes, regents, ministers and generals of the House of Savoy have been given their niche. ... The encyclopedia has provided the rest. The bourgeois city is cosmopolitan, in other words a false international, a false universality. ... It is the triumph of the colourless and tasteless cosmopolis.
>
> (Gramsci 1982 [1917], 183–184; translation by Guy Puzey)

It is perhaps not surprising that a Marxist philosopher would criticize bourgeois naming practices, but Gramsci was also criticizing the "evisceration of the old Turin." This is entirely in keeping with his approach to organicity: the notion that there should be an organic link of ideas between political and intellectual power structures and the social groups they seek to represent. Here, Gramsci was calling for more sensitive, considered, and authentic naming, with a sense for the actual social history of a place and not only the history represented by elites and their heroes drawn from encyclopedias. In the terminology of the *Prison Notebooks*, the Turin street naming case was illustrative of a mismatch between political and civil societies, and of a coercive political culture from the viewpoint of local working people.

While Gramsci was not the only writer to recognize political tensions in the urban geography of street names prior to the recent critical turn in place name studies (Berg and Vuolteenaho 2009), his criticism of Turin's neotoponymy intriguingly anticipated subsequent writings on hegemony and recent critical toponymic literature. Indeed, a dominant streak in the latter field has been a premise that place names—and especially street names, with their immediate dependency on political regimes and ideologies—mirror hierarchies of social power and temporal disruptions in regimes of governance. Much of this research has analyzed odonymic de- and re-commemorations in the aftermath of regime changes in socialist and post-socialist cities.

Still, the implications of Gramsci's notion of hegemony go far beyond his time-specific journalistic criticism of Turin as a city where "the official" and "the elitist" did not communicate with the organic meanings of "the popular." As already insinuated, from a Gramscian perspective, it is somewhat problematic that critical toponymists have often treated commemorative street naming as a merely one-way (top-down) symbolic practice. In this regard, critical scholarship on street naming has tended to halt its analytical and theoretical curiosity on the same level that the young Gramsci concluded his commentary on Turin's street name changes, namely on the conception of the urban namescape as an elitist "medal showcase" with its functions of memorialization, commemoration, and aggrandizement. In other words, critical street name scholars have largely failed to address the complexities of toponymic power related to the reciprocal relationship between the rulers (elites) and the ruled (civil society). Consequently, socio-culturally attuned research questions on covert strategies to affect people's worldviews, or the name-givers' responsiveness to protests and popular sensibilities, have thus far mainly escaped their analytical and conceptual attention (for some partial exceptions and openings to dislodge this otherwise widespread trend, see Vuolteenaho and Berg 2009; Rose-Redwood, Alderman, and Azaryahu 2010; Alderman and Inwood, this volume).

Writing in 1930, in one of the *Prison Notebooks*, Gramsci returned briefly to the subject of street naming. Even though this was a fleeting mention, in this connection he framed the role of street names as part of the "ideological structure of a ruling class," due to their influence on public opinion. Hence Gramsci saw street naming as a component in the organization of ideological structures, and he went on to explain how important the study of these structures could be:

> The press is the most dynamic part of the ideological structure, but not the only one. Everything that directly or indirectly influences or could influence public opinion belongs to it: libraries, schools, associations and clubs of various kinds, even architecture, the layout of streets and their names. ... Such a study [of how the ideological structure of a ruling class is actually organized], conducted seriously, would be quite important: besides providing a living historical model of such a structure, it would inculcate the habit of assessing the forces of agency in society with greater caution and precision. What can an innovative class set against the formidable complex of trenches and fortifications of the ruling class?
>
> (Gramsci 2007, 333; translation in Gramsci 1996, 53)

Here Gramsci provides an engaging reminder of the potential significance of studies exploring the dynamics of such things as "the layout of streets and their names," suggesting both a framework and a socio-political imperative for critical odonymic studies, while also demonstrating that recognition of the political implications of naming—and of street naming specifically—date back considerably longer than much recent work has acknowledged.

Returning to the more recent wave of critical place- and street-naming studies, a fortunate new trend is that the scholarship on odonymic memory politics is showing increasing signs of rapprochement with the Gramscian emphasis on the civic sides of political and societal life. For instance, geographers interested in socialist and post-socialist street name reforms have stressed the importance of research into how name changes are perceived by ordinary people (e.g., Azaryahu 2011a; Light and Young 2014; Creţan and Matthews 2016). Also, in theoretical terms, it has been increasingly acknowledged that "the power of political elites to reshape urban space and public memory is not absolute" (Light and Young 2014, 682), and it is "important not to reduce the symbolic struggle over street naming to a binary opposition between the 'elite' and the 'marginalized'" (Rose-Redwood 2008, 447). Equally productive approaches have featured in studies that have sought explanations for "odonymic inertia" that apparently jars with a society's ruling ideology (e.g., Gill 2005; Light and Young 2014), or reflected on the relationship between revolutionary and restorative naming strategies (Giraut and Houssay-Holzschuch 2008, 2016). For this Gramscian-inspired study, aiming to take seriously both overt and covert political motivations in the street toponymy of East Berlin, these new research directions are promising points of departure.

Variations of medal naming and odonymic indigenization in socialist East Berlin

The establishment of state-socialist political systems in East-Central Europe after the Second World War was essentially a relationship between hegemonic and subaltern polities: a geopolitical situation in which one center (the Soviet Union with its Russian heartland) exerted its influence on different peripheries (the Sovietized territories and satellite states of Europe's Eastern Bloc). The early decades following the Bolshevik revolution saw the birth of distinctively socialist street naming discourses in the Soviet Union (e.g., Murray 2000; Marin 2012; Nikitenko n.d.; Puzey and Vuolteenaho 2016), which authorities across the "national democracies" of East-Central Europe and beyond recycled in decades to come. One of the archetypal street naming discourses was faithful to the classic "nationless" ideals of Marxism and working people's heroic role in world history, epitomized by "internationalist" commemorations of revolutionary thinkers and fallen dissidents, or ideals themselves, with street names such as *улица Розы Люксембург* ("Rosa Luxemburg Street") and *мост Равенства* ("Equality Bridge"). After Lenin's death in 1924, another influential discourse was that of the Stalinist "cult model" (Murray 2000, 17), representing the apex of the self-aggrandizement of the one-party state and its living and late leaders (e.g., *Кировский проспект*, "Kirov Avenue"). Thirdly, not all previous national heroes were expunged from the Soviet namescape. As writers such as Pushkin and Dostoevsky could be associated with anti-Tsarist attitudes or making a case for the "humiliated and insulted," they characteristically remained untouchable. In the otherwise subaltern non-Russian territories annexed to the Soviet Union in the inter-war period, a policy of "local rooting" or "indigenization" (*коренизация*) was also adopted to instill "a socialist consciousness in the non-Russian peoples of the Soviet Union in so far as possible rooted in their own linguistic and cultural media" (Murray 2000, 75–76). In this section, we will trace variations of these three street naming discourses in the eulogizing of socialism and the first communist state on German soil in the street toponymy of East Berlin.

The immediate post-war years

After the Second World War, Berlin was divided ideologically. The de-Nazification and democratization of social and political life was a vexed task, not least due to the relative autonomy of the city's twenty boroughs in local planning and naming matters (Azaryahu 1986, 2011b; Fuchshuber-Weiß 1994, 1473). Nonetheless, a fragile initial consensus existed among the city's new rulers on the urgency to rid the namescape of Nazi-era inscriptions, seen as incongruent with the founding ideals of the emergent democratic Germany. For instance, *Herman-Göring-Straße*, which had been named after the notorious Nazi Field Marshal, reverted to *Ebertstraße* in honor of the first President of the Weimar Republic, Friedrich Ebert. The borough *Horst-Wessel-Stadt*, which had been dedicated to a Nazi martyr and propaganda symbol, took back its monarchical name *Friedrichschain* ("Friedrich's grove"). It was, however, disputed whether it was sufficient to obliterate the legacy of the Third Reich by reinstating such earlier names, or whether a more thorough reform should be enacted. Right-wing politicians generally insisted on a return to the Weimar situation (Azaryahu 2011b, 486). In lieu of this limited purge, advocates of the KPD (*Kommunistische Partei Deutschlands*, Communist Party of Germany) and its successor, the SED (*Sozialistische Einheitspartei Deutschlands*, Socialist Unity Party of Germany) suggested a much more radical anti-Fascist, anti-militarist, and anti-monarchist approach. In the view of many communists, the task ahead was to "accomplish a 'true' democratization of public space" through a new array of progressive street names (Azaryahu 1997, 483).

Even before the city's official partition in November 1948, the Moscow-backed SED sought to take sway over political life in the eight boroughs of the city's Soviet occupation zone. Interestingly, however, the number of honorific inscriptions related to the victorious Soviet forces remained moderate. One explanation for why these names would be a delicate issue among Berliners was related to recent and all-too-well-recalled wartime atrocities by Soviet soldiers against civilians. In Berlin alone, approximately 100,000 women had been raped in the final days of the Third Reich (Beevor 2003, 410). Even so, the name *Platz der Befreiung* ("Liberation Square") was given, as a reminder in the suburban landscape of the encirclement of the Nazi capital by Soviet forces, as well as *Bersarinstraße* in Mitte and *Bersarinplatz* in Friedrichschain. In the case of Soviet Colonel General, Nikolai Berzarin (1904–1945), the first commander of occupied Berlin, responsiveness to local sentiments apparently mattered, as he "had become a surprisingly popular figure, credited with vigorous efforts to feed the starving Berliners" (Ladd 1997, 213; Beevor 2003, 409).

The commemorations of the former leaders of Germany's workers' movement and martyr communists appeared frequently in the Soviet sector. Among the exalted communists in key historical inner-city locations were Karl Liebknecht (1871–1919; *Horst-Wessel-Platz* reverted to *Liebknechtplatz* in 1945) and August Bebel (1840–1913; *Bebelplatz* replacing *Kaiser-Franz-Josef-Platz* in 1947). Of particular symbolic significance for the forthcoming, distinctively German "road to socialism" was the naming of *Rosa-Luxemburg-Platz*, swiftly replacing the aforementioned *Liebknechtplatz* in 1947. In contrast to Liebknecht, together with whom she was assassinated in Berlin in January 1919, Luxemburg was an "independent" Marxist theoretician who had criticized Lenin, Trotsky, and other early Soviet leaders for turning the revolutionary cause into a brutalization and bureaucratization of public life (Luxemburg 1961 [1918], 48). Alongside politicians, artists such as Käthe Kollwitz (1867–1945), a committed pacifist and sympathizer of the working class, were also memorialized in the namescape of East Berlin just before the city's official division.

Archetypal cult names on the German road to socialism

After the city's de jure split in 1948 and the founding of the GDR in 1949, "reactionary" ingredients in the namescape were increasingly extirpated and "progressive" symbols added, with "a kind of minor revolution, a 'street-sign revolution,' carried out from above" (Azaryahu 1986, 591). As a 1949 prelude to a flagship socialist construction project, the Stalinist order was manifested by the bestowing of the name *Stalinallee* (until then *Frankfurter Allee* or *Große Frankfurter Straße*)—a new "medal name," to use Gramsci's terminology—for the city's major artery (Colomb 2012, 62).[1] In 1950, another cross-district eastern avenue, *Landsberger Allee*, came to bear the name of Lenin, the brightest of bygone Soviet luminaries. Odonymic reminders of cultural and artistic bonds between the GDR and Soviet Union also proliferated around the turn of the 1950s (Azaryahu 1986, 590). A case in point was a newly renamed cluster of *Ossietzkystraße* (after the pacifist German writer and artist martyr hero Carl von Ossietzky, 1889–1938), *Tschaikowskistraße* (after the Soviet-esteemed classical Russian composer), and *Majakowskiring* (after the legendary Soviet revolutionary poet), located next to one another in an upper-class northern suburb. In its own way, the honoring of the legendary German-Soviet spy Richard Sorge in 1969 also celebrated a cultural brotherhood between the two states. In the early-1970s, *Allee der Kosmonauten* added an internationalist-futurist aspect to the street sign propaganda, by eulogizing the space travelers of the Soviet Union and its allies.

In a more genuinely Marxist spirit, discontinuity with the past was occasionally manifested through names redolent of the socialist ideals of universal peace. One iconic expression of this was *Brunnen der Völkerfreundschaft* ("Fountain of Friendship between Peoples") in Alexanderplatz. Nonetheless, inscriptions honoring leading socialist politicians from particular countries became more common signifiers in the East German capital, reminding us that these naming practices still took place in the territorialized world of nation-states. This "solidarity cult" was made manifest via a "French" *Jacques-Dudas-Sraße*, "Chilean" *Salvador-Allende-Straße*, "Vietnamese" *Ho-Chi-Minh-Straße*, "Indian" *Indira-Gandhi-Straße*, and so forth (Sänger 2006, 175). *Dimitroffstraße*, its name drawn from the head of Comintern in 1934–1943 and Bulgarian Prime Minister of 1946–1949, also carried local connotations. While in exile in Berlin in 1933, Georgi Dimitrov had become a reputed anti-Fascist hero in the Reichstag fire trial for uncovering a Nazi conspiracy. As a variation of internationalist subdiscourse, references to revolutionaries from other eras and political-geographical contexts were also interspersed in the namescape of East Berlin. Names dedicated to Jean-Paul Marat, the late eighteenth-century publisher of *L'Ami du peuple* ("The Friend of the People"), and to Garibaldi, the nineteenth-century hero of the Risorgimento, exemplify this latter trend. Equally traversing boundaries of time and space through an evocation of a popular uprising, the *Straße der Pariser Kommune* marked the centenary of the rebellious Paris Commune.

More broadly speaking, however, the above types of internationalist street names were outnumbered by nationally inward-looking appellations. One facet of the practiced odonymic pedagogy was the domesticization of the Stalinist personality cult model, as late or veteran SED leaders themselves also began to be rewarded, especially in high-profile inner-city locations, with their "own" streets. In one example of the party's self-aggrandizement in this fashion, the GDR's first president Wilhelm Pieck (1876–1960) was elevated onto the street signage of Mitte and Prenzlauer Berg in 1951, on the occasion of his seventy-fifth birthday.

Alongside medal names in the "classic" Stalinist cult model (Murray 2000, 17), there existed numerous other nuances in the "German road to socialism," a doctrine inaugurated by the KPD leader Anton Ackermann in the mid-1940s (Azaryahu 1986, 584–585). As the years passed, this policy developed into a veritable reverse image of "an abrupt post-Second World War suppression of nationalism and ethnic regionalism" (Czepczyński 2008, 4; cf. Ashworth and Tunbridge 1999, 105–106). To use the words of Benedict Anderson (1991, 2), the GDR was grounded "in a territorial and social space inherited from the pre-revolutionary past." One emphasis in the domestic rooting of communism was to co-opt the towering figures of Marx and Engels, the founders of communist theory, both of German origin. Equally significant for the indigenization of the new socialist rule were more lately bygone intellectual-political figures, who were still part of the living collective memory of older-generation East Germans, such as Rosa Luxemburg and Karl Liebknecht, whom Pieck extolled in 1950 as the "true defenders of the national interests of the German people" (cited in Weitz 2001, 61). By the same token, the regal *Doretheenstraße* made way for a street carrying the name of Clara Zetkin (1857–1933), an early figurehead of the women's movement in Germany and beyond, who united socialism and feminism. Continuity-seeking and spirit-enhancing pedagogic thrusts worked in tandem behind the profusion of such names:

> The most difficult hurdle facing the KPD and SED was how to project this counter-memory onto the wider German population in a way that might cultivate a new sense of historical consciousness. Thus, the KPD/SED set out to educate the masses about these events and propagate a specific politicized interpretation in an attempt to gain loyalty and win over supporters for their cause.
>
> (Olsen 2015, 21)

The GDR's endeavors to underline its organic links with the communist hero martyrs and the German workers' historical struggles evidently mirrored a prominent reciprocal relationship between the rulers and the ruled in the state-controlled politics of memory, and in street naming discourses in particular. Intriguingly, at no stage were East Berlin's street signs reserved only for the highest-ranking SED dignitaries (Azaryahu 1986, 1991).

Evoking folk heroes and intra-national bonds

Broadening the historical scope of the state narrative was quintessential for the interlinked goals of indigenization and legitimatization of communist ideology in East Germany (Sänger 2006; Olsen 2015). Indeed, many honorific street names in East Berlin would perhaps be better described as "encyclopedia-drawn" commemorations of distinguished Germans from various vocational fields. For whatever particular reasons,[2] from the advent of the GDR until its eventual demise, name-givers occasionally chose names such as *Steinbachstraße* (after the architect Erwin von Steinbach, c. 1244–1318), *Dörpfeldstraße* (after the archaeologist Wilhelm Dörpfeld, 1853–1940), *Nipkowstraße* (after the inventor Paul Gottlieb Nipkow, 1860–1940), *Max-Herman-Straße* (after a twentieth-century drama scholar), or *Lea-Grundig-Straße* (after a twentieth-century designer). The honoring of artists and creative practitioners was especially favored, with exaltations of non-communist modernists such as *Corinthstraße*, after the painter Lovis Corinth, and *Alfred-Döblin-Straße* after the author of *Berlin Alexanderplatz* (1929). Older generations of German artists were similarly commemorated, provided that their oeuvres entailed traces of anti-militarism, or even better, sympathy for the poor. As if to guarantee a broad "organic" representation of the national past in the street nomenclature, East Berlin's city-text exploited evocations of figures that were part of the living memory of East Berliners as well as name paragons of older origin.

Most commonly by far, however, this expedient historical repository for enhancement of national spirit was tailored by commemorating rebellions of the lower classes at various moments in German history. Almost as a plea for ordinary citizens to acknowledge the GDR's status as the legitimate heir of a long national trajectory of struggles against feudal, capitalist, and Fascist oppressors, there was a strong tendency to honor courageous revolutionaries, resisters, and victims of oppression. In this vein, Käthe Niederkirchner, a female resistance fighter tortured and murdered by the Nazis, was doubly commemorated, first in Mitte in 1951, then in Prenzlauer Berg in 1974 (De Soto 1996, 38). A homage to Joseph Moll, one of the first acknowledged urban revolutionary proletarians active in the mid-nineteenth century tumults across Central Europe, contributed to the co-presence of multiple temporalities in Mitte's "egalitarian" neotoponymy (De Soto 1996). The revolutionary actions of radicalized folk heroes and trade-unionists in 1848 were one source of inspiration, as was the German Peasants' War of the mid-1520s. Even if the quantitative emphasis in (re)naming practices was on more readily recalled anti-Fascist struggles, different episodes in "the people's history" were utilized as odonymic raw material to underscore the GDR's self-image as the culmination of the German people's "national emancipation" (Mevius 2013, 3).

The overt and covert forms of namescape propaganda were not restricted only to high-profile historical areas. In extreme cases, as with the "new town" Fennpfuhl, in the Lichtenberg district, nearly all coinages (eighteen out of twenty) conjured up somewhat lesser-known communist anti-Nazi freedom fighters in the style of *Ernst-Reinke-Straße*, *Paul-Junius-Straße*, and *Judith-Auer-Straße* (Sandvoß 1998). In most suburbs, the re-forging of pre-existing street toponymy took place in a more modest and diversified manner. In Adlershof, in the Treptow district, eighteen street name alterations (one-sixth of all local streets) were carried out between 1948 and 1984, two-thirds of these in 1951 in line with the East Berlin Magistrate's stipulation that "monarchical," "military," and "Fascist" names were to be axed. At this point, *Argonnenweg* (after a First World War battlefield in France), *Metzestraße* (a reference to the French city of Metz, annexed to Germany in 1871–1918), and *Bismarckstraße* (one of several evocations of the "Iron Chancellor" across the districts of Berlin) vanished and were replaced by evocations of meritorious workers, professionals, and resistance fighters from different historical eras (e.g., *Florian-Geyer-Straße*, after a knight who led a rebellious peasant army in the German Peasants' War). As for commemorations of deserving citizens who had ended up living in the neighborhood, streets were dedicated to Peter Kast (a metal worker, editor of the KPD party organ *Die Rote Fahne*, and a Spanish Civil War veteran, 1894–1959) and Anna Seghers (a pacifist novelist and the founder of an anti-Fascist Heinrich-Heine-Klub for German exiles in Mexico, 1900–1983).

Overall, the balance in naming practices in East German cities moved from the representation of power towards a motivation through *Heimat*-based education (Sänger 2006). This shift can be seen in suburbs built later in the GDR period, which were equipped with seemingly more "apolitical" street names in comparison to the East Berlin norm. Cases in point are Marzahn and Hellersdorf, two adjacent high-rise estates on the city's eastern outskirts urbanized in the 1970s and 1980s. Out of a handful of KPD or SED politicians honored in them, there are *Karl-Maron-Straße*, *Martha-Arendsee-Straße*, and *Waldemar-Schmidt-Straße*. Even so, protagonists of resistance movements figured more abundantly in the street signage of the suburbs, such as *Stephan-Born-Straße*, paying homage to a working people's spokesperson in the 1848 uprisings. However, even these archetypal GDR-era "rebel names" were dwarfed by a thematic naming convention inherited from the area's pre-urban and pre-socialist past, with references to "ordinary" towns, municipalities, neighborhoods, and even mountains in the surrounding Brandenburg region and elsewhere in the East German territory dominating the naming of the mega-suburbs, as if reflecting the socialist nation in microcosm. Whereas the Nazi era had seen a westward expansion of local street name references to the Rhineland-Palatinate, the place identities of Marzahn and Hellersdorf were now developed in a more limited territorial sense, with genuine domestic underpinnings. A very conventional tool of homeland-making—the symbolic socialization of an urban population towards "spatial identification with the territorial state as home" (Kaiser 2009; see also Paasi 1996)—was thus employed here for odonymic-pedagogic purposes.

Un-renamed streets and other ambiguities

The above vignettes testify that the political system of the GDR and its local cultural intermediaries across East Berlin (potentially organic intellectuals in the Gramscian sense) did not only issue "medal names" in the strict Stalinist pattern. Much more commonly, name-givers harkened back to earlier periods and civic uprisings in the national past. Although posterity has often portrayed the socialist era as a demise of nationalism, this view rang true in the namescape of East Berlin only in a narrow sense. The city's political-odonymic identity was diffused and ambiguous, notwithstanding occasional large-scale renaming waves (Azaryahu 1986, 601). Socialist name-givers also left a range of conventional naming models and national symbols intact (see similar observations from other contexts: Foote et al. 2000; Saparov 2003). Even in the historical inner-city areas, Prussian dynastic commemorations such as *Friedrichstraße* persisted in the streetscape throughout the existence of the GDR. Given that the GDR had proclaimed itself "the legitimate heir of everything which is progressive in history" (Schmidt 1978, cited in Azaryahu 1997, 483), why were these and other ideologically non-representative street names tolerated in the East German capital?

We are inclined to give a "Gramscian" answer: one key undercurrent in East Berlin's odonymic script mirrored a will to guarantee popular consent for the threatened regime at stake. Essentially, a Soviet-style indigenization policy (Murray 2000; Saparov 2003) was abundantly applied in the first communist state on German soil (Mevius 2013). For another "external" factor behind the prominence of a consent-seeking stance in street naming practices, the dual-state city of Berlin was the epicenter of Cold War propaganda (Colomb 2012). GDR rulers sought to show citizens the state's independence from Moscow through an array of recognizably German historical and cultural symbols (Olsen 2015). Both the Federal Republic and the GDR sought for historical continuity based on national heritage, while making a break with its Nazi-tarnished, undemocratic variations. Just as "West Germany laid claim to the democratic traditions of 1848 and the Weimar Republic" (Olsen 2015, 10), East German politics of memory relied on Marxist interpretations of these and other episodes in the national past.

Compared to its Eastern European allies, the GDR faced an extra challenge to the legitimacy of communist rule, due to the close geographical proximity of the economically prosperous West (Colomb 2012, 50–70). In East Berlin, in particular, people's perceptions of their fellow (West) Berliners, with more economic and individual liberties, were a constant dimension of everyday life. Both explicit and implicit traces of the ideological struggle between the rival political systems emerged in the street toponymy on both sides of the new intra-urban state boundary, indicating that a veritable "toponymic Cold War" was at stake. A poignant example in West Berlin was the renaming in 1953 of the prestigious *Charlottenburger Chaussee* as *Straße des 17. Juni*, a reminder of the brutal crushing of the construction workers' uprising by Soviet tanks on *Stalinallee* in that same year. After the construction of the Berlin Wall in 1960, the GDR authorities sought to win round the East Berliners by renaming three streets in memory of police officers who had died on duty when guarding the "anti-Fascist protection fence" (Marjomäki 1993, 87). It may also be that a comparatively high presence of female freedom fighters in East Berlin's street signage—especially since the 1970s—was partly motivated by the propagandist competition with the West.

All in all, evocations of recent and time-honored struggles between the powerful and the suppressed played a pivotal role in the party-state's attempted construction of legitimacy. Remarkably, from the standpoint of Gramscian hegemony theory, street names drawn from heroes and martyrs of liberation struggles (proletarian or otherwise), more or less "bi-directionally" bestowed with an eye to popular sensibilities, were the archetype of GDR-era street naming. Nevertheless, the believability of the GDR counter-narrative gradually weakened as the state-socialist experiment proved incapable of redeeming its emancipatory and economic promises in the eyes of increasingly disillusioned East Germans. Symptomatic of Berliners' talent for dark humor even under forced consensus, the monumental *Karl-Marx-Allee* (in 1949–1961 *Stalinallee*) was nicknamed *Stalins Badezimmer* ("Stalin's Bathroom") in the late-GDR ("Das längste Baudenkmal Europas" 2011). More crucially for the subsequent march of events, the GDR name paragon Rosa Luxemburg's rebellious dictum, namely that "freedom is always and exclusively freedom for the one who thinks differently," was brought into sharp relief as the unifying slogan of the opposition movement that conquered public spaces with increasing frequency in East Berlin and other East German cities in 1988–1989 (Philipsen 1993; Saunders 2011, 38, 42).

The afterlife of socialist street names in post-socialist (East) Berlin

In the terminology of Henri Lefebvre (1991 [1974], 54), the GDR regime managed to alter "ideological superstructures, institutions or political apparatuses"—and consequently a substantial portion of Berlin's former street toponymy. Even so, the state-socialist system remained a silently questioned "minimal" hegemony for very many East Berliners throughout its existence, or at least degenerated into a "decadent" hegemony over the decades. Eventually, latent popular discontent towards the regime culminated in the *Wende* of 1989–1990. Seen through a Gramscian lens, at stake was an extreme, revolutionary expression of a reciprocal power relationship in which the ruled ultimately overthrew their rulers. Henceforth, the reciprocity of power relations in the capital of unified Germany has pluralized into an ideologically polyvalent field between multiple political parties, the federal-, metropolitan-, and district-level tiers of governance, and different groups of Berliners. In this section, we will consider the more recent fate of different GDR-era street naming discourses— from Stalinist cult names and odonymic internationalism to street names resonant with the indigenization of socialism—in post-socialist East Berlin.

The initial wave of eradication and local protests

A considerable number of socialist-era street names were axed within a few years of Berlin's (re)unification. In the mid-1990s, it even seemed that "the last residues of the GDR past" might soon be effaced from street signs in the historical center of Berlin (Azaryahu 1997, 492). By 1993, however, the volume of de- and re-commemorations had remained deplorably moderate in the eyes of many right-wing advocates of a new "purified" Germany (Eick 2013 [1995], 37). A key reason behind the slow pace of change was that the former East Berlin districts were in charge of making the odonymic transition. In the two years that followed the election of district assemblies in December 1990, only sixty streets were renamed (Azaryahu 1997, 484-7). In this phase, it was mainly glorifications of functionaries and collaborators of the socialist state that were expunged. For instance, *Otto-Nuschke-Straße* was purged (regaining its pre-socialist name *Jägerstraße*), the Red Army-associated *Bersarinstraße* became *Petersburger Straße* (a re-adopted reverence to the newly renamed Saint Petersburg), *Karl-Maron-Straße* became *Poelchaustraße* (a post-socialist commemoration of an anti-Nazi freedom fighter and socialist prison chaplain), *Peter-Kast-Straße* became *Radickestraße* (after a nineteenth-century spirits manufacturer), and the street names dedicated to killed GDR border guards were also changed (Ladd 1997, 212). The eight districts of East Berlin were largely inclined to ideological compromises, mainly limiting themselves to replacing SED-aggrandizing or otherwise explicit tokens of the GDR regime itself, and the district authorities "were careful not to de-commemorate the mainly communist martyrs of anti-Nazi resistance movements who were prominent heroes of the anti-fascist mythology of the GDR" (Azaryahu 1997, 487).

However, the Berlin Senate, run by the Christian Democratic Union (*Christlich Demokratische Union Deutschlands*, CDU), was dissatisfied with the pace of renaming. On the one hand, right-wing hard-liners drew parallels between the GDR and the Third Reich as two successive dictatorships, holding that the whole anti-democratic inheritance of the GDR was to be anathematized (De Soto 1996, 44–45). On the other hand, the district mayors and councils with an electoral mandate generally believed that decisions on the replacement of street names should be "discussed with the citizens of each district" (Flierl 1991, quoted in De Soto 1996, 34). In 1993, the Senate nominated an Independent Commission for Street Name Changes, tasked with seeking compromise and arriving at scholarly and prudent renaming proposals, rather than merely politically motivated ones (Azaryahu 1997; Ladd 1997). Once the Commission's list of recommendations was made public in 1994, neither the anti-communist conservatives nor the leftists complied (De Soto 1996). Tensions between the Senate and the lower tier of government were further exacerbated after the 1995 district elections, when the negative repercussions of privatization, high unemployment, and escalating living costs in the eastern jurisdictions resulted in growing support for the Party of Democratic Socialism (*Partei des Demokratischen Sozialismus*, PDS), the SED's successor party (Azaryahu 1997, 490). It was at this point that the CDU's Herwig Haase, the sitting Senator of Traffic and Public Works, resorted to the Capital Contract of 1993 to enforce renaming a number of streets in the old inner-city neighborhoods. During this "anti-communist street name offensive," Haase overruled the democratically chosen district councils' will and altered the

Independent Commission's renaming suggestions in several cases (De Soto 1996, 43; Ladd 1997, 212–214). In an essentially coerced way, he decreed the changes such as reverting the "socialist-feminist" *Clara-Zetkin-Straße* to *Dorotheenstraße*, changing *Artur-Becker-Straße* to *Kniprodestraße* (returning from a martyr of the Spanish Civil War to a fourteenth-century Teutonic knight), and *Dimitroffstraße* to *Danzigerstraße* (a re-adopted reference to a formerly Prussian city now in Polish territory), despite outbursts of dissatisfaction in the media and on the streets. Haase also intended to abolish *Bersarinplatz*, yet the CDU Mayor Eberhard Diepgen vetoed this particular change in the face of opposition from the Russian Embassy and angry Berliners (Ladd 1997).

Azaryahu (1997, 490–491) largely dismisses the local protests as "a ritual of resistance" by PDS district politicians, if not a case in which dissonant voices were "artificially multiplied" by local newspapers such as the *Berliner Zeitung*, in a way described by Gramsci as typical for generating popular consent in the exercise of hegemony (Gramsci 2007, 1638). Other researchers have placed more emphasis on the protests as a genuine civic matter (De Soto 1996; Ladd 1997; Huyssen 2003; Lisiak 2010). In any case, a multi-front opposition emerged in the face of the conservative hard-liners' coercive renaming campaign, as the policy would not only have rendered the whole symbolic inheritance of GDR-era socialism and its hero(in)es as "non-presentable" in the official collective memory; to rephrase Huyssen (2003, 54), the strict anti-communist policy would also have marginalized a whole range of domains of experience among "an East German population that felt increasingly deprived of its life history and of its memories of four decades of separate development." Seen from this perspective, there was an intriguing mismatch between what historians of memory politics have conceptualized as *national collective memory* versus *mass personal memory* (Snyder 2002).

De Soto's (1996) account of the afterlife of East Berlin's socialist street names further illuminates civic and feminist aspects of the controversy over the CDU-led street naming purification policy. Through her implicitly Gramscian framework, De Soto underscores the embeddedness of post-socialist street naming practices in a wider "politics of culture," including, alongside the institutional political sphere, "processes of conflict and manoeuvring that go on ... internal to communities" (Verdery 1991, 12; cited in De Soto 1996, 30). One example was the street named after Clara Zetkin, in which case the emotional intensity of popular resistance against a single renaming proposal escalated to proportions rarely witnessed in European urban history. A group of women from East and West Berlin founded an Independent Women's Commission for Street Names to oppose the projected rescinding of *Clara-Zetkin-Straße* and the overall under-representation of women in Berlin's odonymy with at that time only 130 out of the approximately 10,000 streets in Berlin named after women (De Soto 1996, 42). Even though the battle over *Clara-Zetkin-Straße* was lost by Haase's decision in November 1995, the commemoration of distinguished women has increased considerably, not least in the former East Berlin (Hobrack 2007), as part of a salient civil society-influenced turn in the design of post-socialist street nomenclature. In light of the tendency to try to rectify gender inequalities in the male-dominated odonymic pantheon, it is also symptomatic that even Clara Zetkin herself made a swift return to Berlin's namescape around the turn of the millennium, when a park and adjacent road were named after her in Hellersdorf.

"Ostalgic" traces in the pluralized namescape

A close look at the city map reveals that most GDR-era street names have survived unchanged, notwithstanding the eradication of several communist "medal names" in the 1990s (Sänger 2006, 10). It can be confidently argued that the overwhelming bulk of these surviving names belong to the "popular" rather than "elite" side of the preceding regime's odonymic pantheon. Most East Berliners have silently accepted the presence of socialist symbols in the streetscape (Schulz zur Wiesch 2007; also, see Colomb 2012, 279). Consequently, many of the city's contemporary street names may strike an average Western visitor as "out of place" (Olsen 2015, 1), as "ideological leftovers" (cf. Czepczyński 2008; Light and Young 2014), or as perplexing mnemonic curiosities. The most blatant cases in this regard are the commemorations of Marx, Engels, Bebel, Luxemburg, Liebknecht, and Thälmann (even though some public references to these figures have been removed) in the touristic inner-city areas of Mitte, Prenzlauer Berg, and Friedrichshain. As a whole, however, the former East Berlin embraces many other odonymic vestiges less often highlighted by city guidebooks as socialist relics. Names commemorating artists and writers with sympathies for the poor, such as *Heinrich-Heine-Platz*, *Käthe-Kollwitz-Straße*, *Majakowskiring*, *Anna-Seghers-Straße*, and *Alfred-Döblin-Straße*, have stood the test of time with hardly any casualties. A chapter of its own is the resilience of names drawn from insurgent folk heroes and anti-Nazi martyrs, once the odonymic archetype of the indigenization of socialism in the GDR. Imparting "ostalgic" overtones to almost every single neighborhood of contemporary East Berlin, the folk heroes of socialism have only rarely been purged from the post-socialist toponymy. In very many ex-GDR suburbs the pervasiveness of rebel and martyr names is clear for anyone with a decent encyclopedic source to hand. In Friedrichshain, for instance, various top-down efforts to gentrify and westernize the city's image into a "colourless and tasteless cosmopolis" (cf. Gramsci 1982, 184) have also more generally nurtured oppositional stances towards further de-commemoration of the socialist past (Huyssen 2003; Colomb 2012). Other naming instances elude easy categorization along the dichotomy of communism versus anti-communism, such as *Silvio-Meier-Straße*, commemorating a squatter of the late-GDR period who was the victim of a neo-Nazi stabbing in 1992 (Merrill 2015).

Hence, in lieu of the early-1990s zeal "to defeat Communism anew every day" (Ladd 1997, 214), and to the continuing astonishment of external right-wing observers (e.g., *Unzensuriert.at*, 2012; Wieliński 2012), the preservation of remaining GDR street names seems to be broadly accepted, even by many of those locals who have no nostalgia for the GDR as such (Schulz zur Wiesch 2007; Colomb 2012). In Gramscian terms, it appears that the surviving socialist discourses in the street toponymy have been increasingly re-interpreted as vestiges from an "organically representative" phase in the history of the city and its inhabitants, along with multiple other pasts that contemporarily figure in the memoryscape of Berlin.

Conclusion

The overarching aim of this chapter's explorations of East Berlin has been to use Gramsci's specific and relatively unknown writings about street naming, together with his more general writings on hegemony, to make sense of the tendencies and ambiguities of socialist and post-socialist street naming. As such, this study has brought into sharp relief a number of populist and resilient aspects of odonymy. In the socialist period, an ideological-pedagogic perennial in street naming was to equate communist rule with the rule of the people, in an attempt to fuel popular belief in the GDR as the culmination of national emancipation and the German road to socialism. Most archetypically, this took place through the evocation of mainly communist anti-Nazi martyrs as well as insurgent folk heroes from different historical eras, and much less frequently through the toponymic self-aggrandizement of the SED and its leaders. Despite the lip-service paid to egalitarianism and popular empowerment through street toponymy and other cultural media, the believability of this rhetorical counter-narrative weakened towards the regime's final demise. As for the post-socialist period, we noted the initial escalation of tensions over the meanings of "democracy" in street naming matters between the metropolitan government (then led by right-wing politicians who saw the entire communist legacy as antithetical to democracy) and East Berlin districts (in which democracy was cherished as autonomous local decision-making). Beyond this dichotomy are civic and authority initiatives to fight the under-representation of female figures in the city's honorific landscape, as well as a somewhat unexpected mutation of GDR-era and GDR-style "rebel" street names into symbols for post-socialist identity discourses among disillusioned East Berliners. As a kind of Gramscian reverse image of a top-down repudiation of the entire socialist past, attitudes towards which historical eras, ideological worldviews, and vernacular symbols are entitled to be publicly commemorated have been considerably pluralized in (East) Berlin.

In distilling more general lessons based on our findings, we must acknowledge the specificity of (East) Berlin both as a socialist and post-socialist city. Local idiosyncrasies such as those related to the proximity of the West during the socialist period, Berlin's reputation as a city whose population is "more politically invested in the vexed issues of city space and planning than elsewhere" (McRobbie 2013, 995), and not the least the relative autonomy of its boroughs in street naming matters (Gill 2005), are likely to have produced street naming practices in the city that are pronouncedly more "reciprocal" in nature than in, for example, an average East-Central European city. Nonetheless, East Berlin has definitely not been the only urban landscape in which ideological continuities, populist rather than elitist overtones, and other ambiguities have been at least fleetingly observed by street naming scholars (see findings parallel to this study: e.g., Azaryahu 1986; Gill

2005; Therborn 2006; Bodnar 2009; Šakaja and Stanić 2011; Stiperski et al. 2011; Marin 2012; Light and Young 2014).

As a noteworthy commonality between the fundamentally different political and societal circumstances under scrutiny, distinctive attempts to ground naming practices in existing socio-cultural forms and popular mindsets—and hence efforts to seek a balance between coercion and consent—surfaced again and again in our material. In both periods analyzed, a whole "encyclopedic" array of commemorations of vocations other than politicians emerged, albeit with varying emphases, with "organic" local and national traditions as well as folk heroes from different historical periods gaining increasing salience in street signage. Conversely, the tempo of overtly elitist honorific naming decelerated as the political systems matured. Neither the socialist nor post-socialist name-givers entirely revoked the street toponymy inherited from previous regimes. Seen from a Gramscian angle, this all indicates that legitimacy-seeking and persuasive attitudes towards civil society have tacitly guided street naming practices from the immediate post-war context up to the post-socialist present.

This chapter's investigations point towards the importance of acknowledging the complexity of toponymic power relations by looking beyond the oversimplifying dichotomy that often steers scholars to assume that top-down (official) and bottom-up (popular) naming are somehow totally separate processes or phenomena. In addition to more general prospects that Gramsci's thinking can open up for theorizations of toponymic power, we contend that two Gramscian notions in particular—those of organicity and reciprocity—ought to play more pronounced roles in the understanding of the power of street naming. Very significantly, the notion of the organicity of a political culture (or lack thereof) directs analytical attention to socio-cultural inequalities of power in terms of the presence or absence of diverse forms of the popular in the toponymic city-text. Given that Gramsci (1982 [1917]) himself called for more sensitive, considered, and authentic street naming, we believe it is instructive for any contemporary toponymic analysis to reflect upon the representation of different social (especially subaltern) groups in the odonymic canon, and indeed in any realm of naming or related language practices. En route, critical questions as to which segments of the local population and which social histories are symbolically privileged and marginalized enter the research design as a matter of course. In this way, a Gramscian approach to organicity can sensitize research with a nuanced understanding of multiple temporalities at play in naming practices, as the analytical-historical interest no longer concerns only elite interpretations of the national past (national collective memory), but also pasts lived and remembered by various groups of "ordinary" people (mass personal memory). In our study of Berlin, the methodological focus on organicity highlighted gender imbalances and associated political intricacies—a power issue rarely addressed rigorously in politicized street naming research until recently (yet see exceptions: e.g., De Soto 1996; Dwyer 2000; Rose-Redwood 2008; Niculescu-Mizil 2014).

We believe that a Gramscian approach underlines the importance and relevance of critical place name scholarship, while fulfilling the aim set out by Gramsci himself to "inculcate the habit of assessing the forces of agency in society with greater caution and precision" (Gramsci 2007, 333; translation in Gramsci 1996, 53). While "official" street naming is by definition a prerogative of nominated authorities (cf. Azaryahu 1997, 481), our Gramscian-inspired explorations have accentuated how naming practices simultaneously mirror often covert cultural strategies to win popular consent for the prevailing political order. We would even go so far as to argue that entirely neglecting this aspect of toponymic power borders on a view that people are mere pawns in the conceptions of power apparatuses "out there." Even elitist projections of ideological worldviews hardly ever develop in a socio-cultural vacuum. This is exactly why there is an urgent need for culturally enriched (Gramscian-inspired or otherwise) understandings of street naming in a variety of political and societal settings, together with similar studies examining other kinds of naming or related language practices. Neither rulers nor street name scholars should ignore the impact of civil society, or take for granted people's reactions to the hegemonic operations of power over language and space.

Notes

1 *Stalinallee* was again renamed *Karl-Marx-Allee* during the subsequent de-Stalinization process in 1961.
2 Street name encyclopedias on German cities typically provide scarce information on the grounds on which "politically neutral" street names were given (Sänger 2011, personal communication).

References

Anderson, B. (1991). *Imagined Communities: Reflections on the Origin and Spread of Nationalism.* London: Verso.
Ashworth, G. J., and Tunbridge, J. E. (1999). "Old Cities, New Pasts: Heritage Planning in Selected Cities of Central Europe." *GeoJournal,* 49(1): 105–116.
Azaryahu, M. (1986). "Street Names and Political Identity: The Case of East Berlin." *Journal of Contemporary History,* 21(4): 581–604.
Azaryahu, M. (1991). *Von Wilhelmplatz zu Thälmannplatz: Politische Symbole im öffentlichen Leben der DDR 1945–1985.* Gerlingen: Bleicher Verlag.
Azaryahu, M. (1996). "The Power of Commemorative Street Names." *Environment and Planning D: Society and Space,* 14(3): 311–330.
Azaryahu, M. (1997). "German Reunification and the Politics of Street Names: The Case of East Berlin." *Political Geography,* 16(6): 479–493.
Azaryahu, M. (2009). "Naming the Past: The Significance of Commemorative Street Names." In L. D. Berg and J. Vuolteenaho (Eds.), *Critical Toponymies: The Contested Politics of Place-Naming* (pp. 53–70). Farnham: Ashgate.
Azaryahu, M. (2011a). "The Critical Turn and Beyond: The Case of Commemorative Street Naming." *ACME: An International E-Journal for Critical Geographies,* 10(1): 28–33.
Azaryahu, M. (2011b). "The Politics of Commemorative Street Renaming: Berlin, 1945–1948." *Journal of Historical Geography* 37(4): 483–492.
Beevor, A. (2003). *Berlin: The Downfall 1945.* London: Penguin.
Berg, L. D. (2011). "Banal Naming, Neoliberalism, and Landscapes of Dispossession." *ACME: An International E-Journal for Critical Geographies,* 10(1): 13–22.

Berg, L. D. and Vuolteenaho, J. (Eds.) (2009). *Critical Toponymies: The Contested Politics of Place Naming*. Farnham: Ashgate.

Bodnar, E. (2009). "'I Have Often Walked Down This Street Before … But What Was It Called?': Changes to Street Names in Budapest from the End of Turkish Rule to the Present." *Past Imperfect*, 15: 115–153.

Carlucci, A. (2013). *Gramsci and Languages: Unification, Diversity, Hegemony*. London: Brill.

Colomb, C. (2012). *Staging the New Berlin: Place Marketing and the Politics of Urban Reinvention Post-1989*. London: Routledge.

Coutinho, C. N. (2012). *Gramsci's Political Thought*. Trans. by P. Sette-Câmara. Leiden: Brill.

Crețan, R. and Matthews, P. W. (2016). "Popular Responses to City-Text Changes: Street Naming and the Politics of Practicality in a Post-Socialist Martyr City." *Area*, 48(1): 92–102.

Czepczyński, M. (2008). *Cultural Landscapes of Post-Socialist Cities*. Aldershot: Ashgate.

"Das längste Baudenkmal Europas" (2011). *Berliner Morgenpost*, March 1.

De Soto, H. G. (1996). "(Re)Inventing Berlin: Dialectics of Power, Symbols and Pasts, 1990–1995." *City & Society*, 8(1): 29–49.

Dwyer, O. J. (2000). "Interpreting the Civil Rights Movement: Place, Memory, and Conflict." *Professional Geographer*, 52(4): 660–671.

Eick, V. (2013 [1995]). "Berlin Is Becoming the Capital—Surely and Securely." In M. Bernt, B. Grell, and A. Holm (Eds.), *The Berlin Reader: A Compendium on Urban Change and Activism* (pp. 33–45). Bielefeld: Transcript Verlag.

Femia, J. V. (1981). *Gramsci's Political Thought: Hegemony, Consciousness and the Revolutionary Process*. Oxford: Clarendon Press.

Foote, K. E., Tóth, A., and Árvay, A. (2000). "Hungary after 1989: Inscribing a New Past on Place." *Geographical Review*, 90(3): 301–334.

Fuchshuber-Weiß, E. (1994). "Straßennamen: Deutsch." In E. Eichler, G. Hilty, H. Löffler, H. Steger, and L. Zgusta (Eds.), *Namenforschung/Name Studies/Les Noms Propres*, vol. 2 (pp. 1468–1475). Berlin: Walter de Gruyter.

Gill, G. (2005). "Changing Symbols: The Renovation of Moscow Place Names." *Russian Review*, 64(3): 480–503.

Giraut, F. and Houssay-Holzschuch, M. (2008). "Au nom des territoires! Enjeux géographiques de la toponymie." *L'Espace géographique*, 37(2): 97–105.

Giraut, F. and Houssay-Holzschuch, M. (2016). "Place Naming as *Dispositif*: Toward a Theoretical Framework." *Geopolitics*, 21(1), 1–21.

Gramsci, A. (1971). *Selections from the Prison Notebooks*. Ed. and trans. by Q. Hoare and G. Nowell-Smith. London: Lawrence & Wishart.

Gramsci, A. (1982 [1917–1918]). *La città futura: 1917–1918*. Turin: Einaudi.

Gramsci, A. (1996). *Prison Notebooks*, vol. 2. Ed. and trans. by J. A. Buttigieg. New York: Columbia University Press.

Gramsci, A. (2007 [1929–1935]). *Quaderni del carcere*, 4 vols. Ed. by V. Gerratana. Turin: Einaudi.

Hobrack, V. (2007). *Frauen in Berlins Mitte: Frauenstrassennamen*. Berlin: Berlin Story Verlag.

Huyssen, A. (2003). *Present Pasts: Urban Palimpsests and the Politics of Memory*. Stanford, CA: Stanford University Press.

Ives, P. (2004). *Language and Hegemony in Gramsci*. London: Pluto Press.

Johnson, R. (2007). "Post-Hegemony? I Don't Think So." *Theory, Culture & Society*, 24(3): 95–110.

Kaiser, R. (2009). "Fatherland/Homeland." In R. Kitchin and N. Thrift (Eds.), *International Encyclopedia of Human Geography*, vol. 4 (pp. 21–28). Amsterdam: Elsevier.

Laclau, E. (2005). *On Populist Reason.* London: Verso.

Laclau, E., and Mouffe, C. (1985). *Hegemony and Socialist Strategy: Towards a Radical Democratic Politics.* London: Verso.

Ladd, B. (1997). *The Ghosts of Berlin: Confronting German History in the Urban Landscape.* Chicago: Chicago University Press.

Lefebvre, H. (1991 [1974]). *The Production of Space.* Trans. by D. Nicholson-Smith. Oxford: Blackwell.

Light, D. (2004). "Street Names in Bucharest, 1990–1997: Exploring the Modern Historical Geographies of Post-Socialist Change." *Journal of Historical Geography,* 30(1): 154–172.

Light, D., and Young, C. (2014). "Habit, Memory, and the Persistence of Socialist-Era Street Names in Postsocialist Bucharest, Romania." *Annals of the Association of American Geographers,* 104(3): 668–685.

Lisiak, A. A. (2010). *Urban Cultures in (Post)colonial Central Europe.* West Lafayette, IN: Purdue University Press.

Lo Piparo, F. (1979). *Lingua intellettuali egemonia in Gramsci.* Roma–Bari: Laterza.

Luxemburg, R. (1961 [1918]). "The Russian Revolution." In B. D. Wolfe (Ed.), *The Russian Revolution, and Leninism and Marxism* (pp. 25–80). Ann Arbor: University of Michigan Press.

Marin, A. (2012). "Bordering Time in the Cityscape. Toponymic Changes as Temporal Boundary-Making: Street Renaming in Leningrad/St. Petersburg." *Geopolitics,* 17(1): 192–216.

Marjomäki, H. (1993). "Saksan kommunistisen puolueen historia Berliinin (Hauptstadt der DDR) katujen nimissä." In H. Nyyssönen (Ed.), *Nimet poliittisessa symboliikassa* (pp. 73–91). Jyväskylä: Jyväskylän yliopisto.

McRobbie, A. (2013). "Fashion Matters Berlin: City-Spaces, Women's Working Lives, New Social Enterprise?" *Cultural Studies,* 27(6): 982–1010.

Merrill, S. (2015). "Identities in Transit: The (Re)connections and (Re)brandings of Berlin's Municipal Railway Infrastructure after 1989." *Journal of Historical Geography,* 50: 76–91.

Mevius, M. (Ed.) (2013). *The Communist Quest for National Legitimacy in Europe, 1918–1989.* Abingdon: Routledge.

Murray, J. (2000). *Politics and Place-Names: Changing Names in the Late Soviet Period.* Birmingham: University of Birmingham Press.

Niculescu-Mizil, A-M. (2014). "(Re)Naming Streets in Contemporary Bucharest: From Power Distribution to Subjective Biography." *Analize: Journal of Gender and Feminist Studies,* 3: 69–94.

Nikitenko, G. Y. (n.d.). "Toponymy of St. Petersburg." *Saint Petersburg Encyclopedia:* www.encspb.ru/object/2804017552.

Olsen, J. B. (2015). *Tailoring Truth: Politicizing the Past and Negotiating Memory in East Germany, 1945–1990.* Oxford: Berghahn.

Paasi, A. (1996). *Territories, Boundaries and Consciousness.* Chichester: Wiley.

Palonen, E. (2015). "The Politics of Street Names: Local, National, Transnational Budapest." In M. Beyenand and B. Deseure (Eds.), *Local Memories in a Nationalizing and Globalizing World* (pp. 51–71). Basingstoke: Palgrave Macmillan.

Philipsen, D. (1993). *We Were the People: Voices from East Germany's Revolutionary Autumn of 1989.* Durham, NC: Duke University Press.

Puzey, G. (2011). "Wars of Position: Language Policy, Counter-Hegemonies and Cultural Cleavages in Italy and Norway." PhD thesis, University of Edinburgh.

Puzey, G. (2016). "Renaming as Counter-Hegemony: The Cases of *Noreg* and *Padania.*" In G. Puzey and L. Kostanski (Eds.), *Names: People, Places, Perceptions and Power* (pp. 165–184). Bristol: Multilingual Matters.

Puzey, G. and Vuolteenaho, J. (2016). "Developing a Gramscian Approach to Toponymy." In C. Hough and D. Izdebska (Eds.), *Names and Their Environment: Proceedings of the 25th International Congress of Onomastic Sciences*, vol. 2 (pp. 66–77). Glasgow: University of Glasgow.

Rose-Redwood, R. (2008). "From Number to Name: Symbolic Capital, Places of Memory and the Politics of Street Renaming in New York City." *Social & Cultural Geography*, 9(4): 431–452.

Rose-Redwood, R., Alderman, D., and Azaryahu, M. (2010). "Geographies of Toponymic Inscription: New Directions in Critical Place-Name Studies." *Progress in Human Geography* 34(4), 453–470.

Šakaja, L. and Stanić, J. (2011). "Other(ing), Self(portraying), Negotiating: The Spatial Codification of Values in Zagreb's City-Text." *Cultural Geographies*, 18(4): 495–516.

Sandvoß, H.-R. (1998). *Widerstand 1933–1945. Widerstand in Friedrichshain und Lichtenberg.* Berlin: Gedenkstätte Deutscher Widerstand.

Sänger, J. (2006). *Heldenkult und Heimatliebe. Strassen- und Ehrennamen im Offiziellen Gedächtnis der DDR.* Berlin: Christoph Links Verlag.

Sänger, J. (2011). Email correspondence with J. Vuolteenaho. March 29.

Saparov, A. (2003). "The Alteration of Place Names and Construction of National Identity in Soviet Armenia." *Cahiers du Monde Russe*, 41(1): 179–198.

Saunders, A. (2011). "The Luxemburg Legacy: Concretizing the Remembrance of a Controversial Heroine?" *German History*, 29(1): 36–56.

Schulz zur Wiesch, L. (2007). "Zum Umgang mit bauliche-Symbolischen Relikten der DDR in Ostberlin." In R. Jaworski and P. Stachel (Eds.), *Die Besetzung des öffentlichen Raumes: Politische Plätze, Denkmäler und Straßennamen im europäischen Vergleich* (pp. 231–258). Berlin: Frank & Timme.

Snyder, T. (2002). "Memory: Poland, Lithuania and Ukraine, 1939–1999." In J-W. Müller (Ed.), *Memory and Power in Post-War Europe: Studies in the Presence of the Past* (pp. 39–58). Cambridge: Cambridge University Press.

Stiperski, Z., Lorber, L., Heršak, E., Ptaček, P., Górka, Z., Kołoś, A., Lončar, J., Faričić, J., Miličević, M., Vujaković, A., and Hruška, A. (2011). "Identity through Urban Nomenclature: Eight Central European Cities." *Geografisk Tidsskrift—Danish Journal of Geography*, 111(2): 181–194.

Therborn, G. (2006). "Eastern Drama. Capitals of Eastern Europe, 1830s–2006: An Introductory Overview." *International Review of Sociology*, 16(2): 209–242.

Thomas, P. D. (2009). *The Gramscian Moment: Philosophy, Hegemony and Marxism.* Leiden: Brill.

Unzensuriert.at (2012). "Kommunismus in ehemaliger DDR noch omnipräsent." January 18: www.unzensuriert.at/content/006662-Kommunismus-ehemaliger-DDR-noch-omnipr-sent.

Verdery, K. (1991). *National Ideology under Socialism.* Berkeley: University of California Press.

Vuolteenaho, J. and Ainiala, T. (2009). "Planning and Revamping Urban Toponymy: Ideological Alterations in the Linguistic Landscaping of Vuosaari Suburb, Eastern Helsinki." In L. D. Berg and J. Vuolteenaho (Eds.), *Critical Toponymies: The Contested Politics of Place Naming* (pp. 227–251). Farnham: Ashgate.

Vuolteenaho, J., and Berg, L.D. (2009). "Towards Critical Toponymies." In L. D. Berg and J. Vuolteenaho (Eds.), *Critical Toponymies: The Contested Politics of Place Naming* (pp. 1–18). Farnham: Ashgate.

Weitz, E. D. (2001). "'Rosa Luxemburg Belongs to Us': German Communism and the Luxemburg Legacy." *Central European History*, 27(1): 27–64.

Wieliński, B. T. (2012). "Germany: Still Living in Lenin Street." *VOXEurop*, January 4: www.voxeurop.eu/en/content/article/1355581-still-living-lenin-street.

Williams, R. (1980). *Problems in Materialism and Culture*. London: Verso.

Williams, R. (1983) *Keywords: A Vocabulary of Culture and Society*, 2nd edn. London: Fontana Press.

6 Building a new city through a new discourse

Street naming revolutions in Budapest

Emilia Palonen

Introduction

Street names establish a particular discursive universe for those strolling through the city, locating themselves simultaneously in urban space and in local discourses. This chapter challenges existing research on urban toponymy through a discourse-theoretical reading that explores the discursive and interconnected character of street names. Viewing street naming regimes as constituting a "discursive universe" draws attention to the fluid and contradictory qualities of street names as a "discursive set." The chapter builds upon the discourse theory of Ernesto Laclau and Chantal Mouffe (1985) to examine street names as discursive nodal points, or "guards," and street renaming as an act of "changing the guards." Changing this set of nodal points is essentially a political operation. Here "political" is understood in terms of relationality and (dis)association, the contingency of the decision on an undecidable terrain (c.f. Norval 2005), generating a common basis and/or a political frontier through the naming process, and an ontological connection or ethical investment in the name (Laclau 2005).

Beyond theory, the chapter discusses the changing city-text in Budapest from the nineteenth century to the present. This implies looking at the renaming of streets as transforming *sets of discursive elements*, where the identity of the names is entangled with the rest of the set, and marked by the past. In some street naming cultures, change in the street names takes place in an evolutionary manner through the vicissitudes of daily usage. In others, street naming is embedded in traditions of revolution, producing what we might call "street naming revolutions." In Budapest, we witness a symbolic "changing of the guard," when the new power-holders decide what aspects of the past deserve to be articulated in the new discursive universe of the city's streetscape. This is enhanced by a feature of the city: a municipality composed of districts, where the same set of names repeat as nodal points of the street naming discourse. This occurred most recently in the 2010s, when, after two electoral periods in opposition, the right-wing parties had a landslide election victory with a two-thirds parliamentary majority, which offered possibilities for both law-making and changing street names.

Behind the discursive approach adopted here is an attempt to read the *city-text*—that is, examine the discursive act of street naming as constituting the landscape as a text. City-texts interweave meaning into the urban landscape and also offer a point of identification and contestation. As Azaryahu (2009, 66) argues, "the city-text does not provide its readers with a chronological narrative, but rather with an authorized index of putative narrative, notwithstanding the lack of historical villains." Commemorative street naming seeks to inscribe a particular vision of the past into the streetscape, thereby transforming "history into local geography" (Azaryahu 2009, 67). Naming arrests the potentially continuous interpretation of the past by offering a political reading of it that aims to establish this interpretive framing as a dominant and durable one.

Public memory-work is a political operation, a value-laden task that seeks to establish a hegemonic viewpoint. In other words, although street names are inherently part of cultural memory (Ferguson 1988; Alderman 2002), dealing with commemorative street names involves actually engaging in a street politics of the present, not just with the past (e.g., Foote and Azaryahu 2007). As Alderman (2002) maintains, street names can be seen as "arenas" for the politics of memory. As the metaphor "arena" entails battle, it follows Gillis's (1994) observation that physical symbols of power offer an opportunity to identify oneself as being against the status quo: openness to contestation and rearticulation is the democratic asset of the city-text (c.f. von Henneberg 2004).

Street names speak to the past as a means of generating a vision for the future, captured in the moment when the mundane is transformed into something more historical and ideological. The understanding of time in this context can be kairological rather than chronological: street names talk about the "now," the simultaneous presence of the past, present, and future, in a Benjaminian way (c.f. Lindroos 1998), attempting, in other words, to regulate their multi-layeredness for envisioning a future.

The poststructuralist discourse-theoretical perspective indicates how street names are relational and acquire their meanings through associations with neighboring elements and the urban milieux more generally. Street names may resonate with us and our beliefs, grow on us, or irritate us. The meanings of new names, introduced at a given moment, are shaped by the entire set of street names. The discarded names also gain their meaning from the other names and substitutes. Street names are important pointers in the cityscape but they also are a discursive set. Often we grow to know them without realizing we are subjected to a particular discourse, whether we endorse or reject it. As Levinson contends:

> organizers of the new regime must decide which, if any, of the heroes of the old regime deserve to continue occupying public space. And the new regime will always be concerned if these heroes might serve as potential symbols of resistance for adherents among the population who must, at least from the perspective of the newcomers, ultimately acquiesce to the new order.
>
> (1998, 10–11)

Levinson shows how these commemorative figures have potential to remain accessible as political symbols of the past or the opposition. Officials decide what is changed, where, and why. Reading street names, we are indeed reading the political (K. Palonen 1993; also, see K. Palonen, this volume). Naming involves political choices in the public domain. However, the institutional processes and struggles are not the only political aspects of street naming. As Rose-Redwood, Alderman, and Azaryahu (2010, 466) point out, "we must broaden our analysis by considering how the 'political' is related to other relatively unexplored questions in place-name studies." In this chapter, I am concerned with how the political is related to the generation of discursive sets, nodal points, and frontiers, marking urban space with new decisions in the moments of (re)naming as well as all the paradoxes which encompass the process of fixing meaning into an uneven discursive space. We will see below how, in the moment of renaming, not all the names will be changed and the new names do not necessarily constitute a harmonious set. They can be read differently and their meanings may change over time. Their existence or disappearance from the map enables public discussion regarding their values, which often draws attention to the contested politics of urban space.

Street names can be regarded as indicators of political changes or tools for sedimenting particular meanings and ideologies—or contesting them. Street names indicate a larger *discursive political change*, but also mark continuity and unevenness in the face of that change. The exclusion or inclusion of new commemorative elements to the list of street names may have crucial effects on the way in which meanings are made and sedimented more generally. Thus, the act of rewriting offers potential for a wider change and *discursive production of meaning*, even as the name changes signal a material transformation in the daily lives and landscapes of people (Alderman 2002).

The making of a discursive universe and the naming of the guards

This study explores particular moments of street naming in the political history of Budapest. In particular, I consider street naming not only as indicative of the ideological transformations in that period (Azaryahu 1992, 1996) but also as generating a discursive universe. It is important to talk about discourse in the context of a universe. Past studies of street naming frequently treat revolutionary change in naming regimes as hard and fast breaks and transitions in power and discourse, and, of course, in a general way this is correct; however, as Yeoh (1996, 304) reminds us, revolutionary change in nation-building is "more akin to an uneven, negotiated process of constant mediations rather than a static consensual once-and-for-all translation of a monolithic ideology into material form." Approaching the urban streetscape as a discursive universe does not discount the revolutionary quality of writing the city-text through renaming, but it does recognize that this renaming happens within broad, and ever expanding sets of multiple, sometimes contradictory, and sometimes allied, discursive meanings.

Alderman (2002) draws upon discourse analysis to study the production of meaning in the context of commemorative street naming. Specifically, he explores the engagement with particular street naming struggles and analyzes public dialogues associated with renaming. The approach I take here is slightly different although it shares the same premise of the relevance of discourses. For Laclau (1996), discourse is not reducible to public speech or writing. It is an articulated set of elements on a discursive field that is conflictual, fluid, and heterogeneous, and where discourses emerge to offer structure. The production of meaning takes place relationally through connections in space. Laclau and Mouffe (1985) see hegemony as the fixing of meaning on an undecidable, uneven terrain. In this process, particular understandings, relations, and contrasts are made commonplace. Street naming is precisely such an operation.

From this poststructuralist perspective, identities do not pre-exist the moment of articulation: the way in which we tie the name to a field of references lends to the identity of the name. Laclau (2005, 2014) has particularly explored the rhetorical dimension that he considers ontological: naming constitutes the named as an object. Names can work as "empty signifiers" that provide a reference point for many ideas and groups so that they become overburdened and emptied out of particular meanings at the same time. This takes our attention to the process of naming, the contextual references of the name, and what identity or range of references is generated by (re)naming.

Street naming emerges as a hegemonic practice: an attempt to establish particular relations and orders of meaning. Hegemonic operations seek to provide fixation of a discursive field that is always in flux. For example, a naming process repoliticizes a seemingly smooth space, and reorganizes it, introduces new relations and meanings. Those naming streets also seek to establish closure and permanence in the names—perhaps to articulate the people or the nation. When there are numerous names to be introduced into a streetscape, we can try to trace the specificity of the particular discourses introduced into the city-text. The multiplicity of names also shows an attempt to regulate the whole terrain: to establish a new hegemony.

Following discourse-theoretical thinking, street names constitute a discursive set, and to be a set, there is always something outside it that for its part defines the set. Each street name constitutes one or multiple elements—as they may be carrying different and potentially contested meanings to the set of meanings or names attributed to the streets. Naming processes, and "the *re*naming of the guard" in particular, make visible the "in" and "out" of the set, calling forth the political frontiers dividing "us" and "them." The set is also internally structured through nodal points that play the role of providing cognitive-historical references, or pointers. The psychoanalytical theorist Jacques Lacan considered that these *points de capiton* had a privileged role in the fixing of meaning (e.g., Stavrakakis 1999, 263–265). A set of new "guards" on the street names would offer pointers that would be subsumed to the everyday. Particular nodal points of the city-text are used in the discursive play of street naming politics. Some streets have particularly celebratory, politicized, or commemorative names, which give a specific flavor to the city-text of the municipality or neighborhood. Key street names or themes introduced in the city-text also highlight a given historical era of the past as well as the ideological orientation of those making decisions in the present.

Reflecting on urban space, we could consider how "street names designate locations and pronounce certain thoroughfares as distinct urban units" (Azaryahu 2009, 53), and how those major streets or boulevards, central squares, metro stations, or other nodes of transport hold a privileged position in the city-text. As such, a city's street names can indeed work as a set of elements, or as interconnected and overlapping sets. Typically, in the layered linguistic landscape of a city these would be sets according to the naming moment—often coinciding with the moment of (re)constructing an area. We could also explore which wider and potentially contradictory or conflictual discursive elements make up the discourse(s) in the city-text at a given time (e.g., Kearns and Berg 2002). When they are contested between political groups, we can view the act of street naming as producing a "political frontier" through processes of spatial and temporal Othering. Over time, multiple discourses often come to inhabit a city-text, and the agonistic politics (Mouffe 2000) of naming is rendered visible through the streetscape itself.

Street naming revolutions as a tradition in Hungary

In postcommunist countries such as Hungary, commemoration and public symbols have proved an important means of politicking, making ideological distinctions and constructing new identities, thereby repositioning Hungary after the fall of the Iron Curtain (Foote, Tóth, and Árvay 2000; Bodnár 2009). Attempts to build a new community by de/recanonization differ from one period to another. The contestation itself can be seen as constituting community and space (Massey 2005). These communities can also be multiple. Naming can be a conflictual process at different levels of governance (E. Palonen 2008). In the postcommunist era, as during other crucial historical moments, the transition from the old to the new was made tangible in the changing of street names: guards of the past and newly celebrated heroes. In Hungary, the "us" and "them" were symbolized in a deeply political process. Indeed, generating two opposing political camps, this oppositional framing of the political terrain became the dominant trend in Hungarian politics. Lately, however, the situation has fragmented somewhat but the governing political forces aim to produce a strong sense of national unity.

Foote, Tóth, and Árvay (2000, 329) maintain that Hungary was a forerunner in the matters of dealing with the past:

> The causes and consequences of World War II and the Holocaust have been discussed for decades, but debate has hardly begun over the war's legacy of Communist rule in Central and Eastern Europe. The Hungarian landscape records the first steps in coming to terms with the postwar period.

Nevertheless, by the turn of the twenty-first century, the past was again in its place—at least in the street names. More recently, it has become clear that dealing with the past as a political operation was only beginning. A new phase could be added to the classification of eras of street naming. And it brought with it both new and recycled discourses.

Layering political discourses upon the Hungarian landscape is done by powerful social actors and groups with relational ties to past and future eras. I propose here that we try to discern the discourses over the whole history of street naming in Budapest, where renaming is more a reoccurring trend than a truly extraordinary event. The renaming process involves both aporias and nuances, since discursive operations always take place on an uneven terrain and discourses have incompatible elements.

Researchers are able to transform a seemingly smooth, yet layered, city-text into periodized classifications. Bodnár (2009), for instance, explores the history of street naming in Budapest. Similarly, Ráday (1998, 2003, 2013) has compiled a comprehensive encyclopedia of Budapest's street names, which I draw upon in the current chapter. Others have considered postcommunist transformations thematically (E. Palonen 2008). In this chapter, I take a periodized perspective through the moments of major changes: from nineteenth-century Budapest under the Habsburg empire and during the formation of the Hungarian Kingdom as an automous area; the interwar period that included the brief Soviet Republic and authoritarian era as well as the postwar state socialist period with its changes particularly around Stalin's death, the 1956 revolution, and its aftermath; and the postcommunist period that witnessed changes in both the early-1990s and 2010s.

In countries like Hungary, where the city-text transforms in a major way, street naming revolutions are, paradoxically, part of an established tradition (E. Palonen 2011). One thing that becomes tangible in the changing street names is the manifestation of a new, particular era. Given the way in which, in Hungary, names have often changed in the past, always in accordance with political trends, street name politics offers prospective salvation to those who do not identify with recent changes. They may think that one day these street names will change again. People do not simply identify with the street names and adopt them mundanely: we can see that the names offer a point of contestation from which to build an oppositional identity.

The Hungarian nineteenth-century metropolis

The early street names and statues in Budapest were locative rather than commemorative. They were also more spontaneously named. Later, they gained political, celebrative, commemorative, and institutional value from the perspective of the power-holders. Budapest was a multicultural city with a German-speaking administration, and the urban toponyms on official maps showed German names irrespective of the usage. The locals in Budapest, however, used a number of different languages in their daily activities (Bodnár 2009).

Metropolitan growth was accompanied by nation-building, culminating in the failed revolution of 1848/49. In the 1840s, some 37 names were translated from German into Hungarian and 20 additional streets renamed. Still, the physical street signs posted in German under Maria Theresa and Joseph II were not transformed overnight into Hungarian ones. The city constructed the Chain Bridge, the first permanent bridge between Buda and Pest in 1849, its corresponding tunnel under the Castle Hill, and an expanded railway network, turning Budapest into one of the most important points in Europe's trade network. It was also the fastest-growing city on the continent in the late-nineteenth century, with the total population doubling between 1869 and 1896 (Gerő and Poór, 1997; Bácskai, Gyáni, and Kubinyi 2000). This rapid transformation and modernization swept away much of the old Pest-Buda. Budapest became the third centrally planned European capital, after Vienna and Paris (Nagy 1998), and the street naming authorities had not only to pay attention to translation but also needed to name a significant number of new streets. After the Compromise of 1867, Budapest became the official capital of the Hungarian Kingdom.

The independence fight (1848–49) brought with it revolutionary street names; already in 1846, officials in Pest named the first square after Szechényi, a moderate Hungarian revolutionary leader and the initiator of the Chain Bridge. During the revolution of 1848, streets in the Castle Hill gained names after St. Stephen and two of the revolutionary leaders (Batthyány and Kossuth), and Pest got its Free Press Street (*Szabadsajtó utca*), Freedom Square (*Szabadság tér*), and March 15 Square (*Március 15. tér*) was named in honor of the Hungarian revolution. Additionally, the terms "Fraternity," "Justice," "National," and "Unity" were included in the city-text, although the exact location of these streets remains unclear (Bodnár 2009).

When the revolution was crushed, pre-revolutionary names were restored and two more squares were named after the Habsburg rulers Franz Joseph and Elisabeth ("Sisi") in 1858. Furthermore, city districts gained Habsburg names such as Leopold, Theresa, Joseph, and Franz, later also Elisabeth. When the dual monarchy was restored in the Compromise of 1867, the Hungarian reformer Ferenc Deák was unofficially commemorated in the streetscape, and the name was officialized ten years later posthumously (Ráday 1998).

Street names were introduced in Budapest as sets (Habsburg, anti-Habsburg/ revolutionary) to generate a basis for the new discursive universe and the establishment of the "guards." Even today these names are present in the map of Budapest, as the late-nineteenth century was the set that was restored in the 1990s. They are the discursive and structuring nodal points of the city-text in Budapest, "floating signifiers" being replaced and restored time and again.

Interwar: from the Soviet Republic to "Berlinization"

The next political conflict that contributed to transforming street names took place in the aftermath of the First World War. During the short-lived Hungarian People's Republic led by Béla Kun in 1919, old statues were wrapped and gypsum statues erected but street names were easier to change to a socialist vocabulary: Queen Elizabeth was replaced with Ilona Zrínyi (1643–1703), the mother of Ferenc Rákóczy II, an anti-Habsburg national hero, already commemorated in the 16th district's street names in the 1910s. Commemorative street names celebrated local and national history (e.g., the Hungarian Jacobins), while the statues and memorials embraced internationalism (E. Palonen 2014).

One of the key traumas of the interwar period was the reduction of Hungarian territory by two-thirds in the Trianon treaty of Versailles in 1921. There was another influx of immigrants to Budapest from the lost territories: now predominantly peasantry and unskilled workers to the overcrowded working-class areas or the suburbs. Political populism was emerging as a strong source of hope. During the interwar period, irredentist names began to appear on the streets of Budapest (Bodnár 2009). Irredentism here refers to the calls for returning the lost lands, as this was the ethos behind commemorative naming. This era of street naming was marked by former right-wing politicians like István Tisza—named once in 1920 and again in 1999 on different streets. The power-holding admiral Miklós Horthy also became a veritable nodal point in the interwar city-text, getting 23 mentions on the street map in 1929.

Commemorative street naming was *geo*political: like much of Central and Eastern Europe, Hungary was tied to the German economy, and the cultural links to the German-speaking world were strong. Characteristically, the square in front of Nyugati (Western) Railway station had been called *Berlini tér* since 1913, until it was renamed *Marx tér* in 1945 (a name which it retained until 1992). During the interwar period, the political direction was south-west: *Mussolini tér* was first proposed in 1928; the renaming took place only after Mussolini's speech on November 6, 1936, in Milano, where he expressed a need to solve Hungary's territorial claims. Afterwards, two more squares and two streets were named after Mussolini (Ráday 2003). Finally, the squares of Andrássy witnessed changes: *Oktogon* was named after Mussolini (1936), and *Körönd* (Circus, today *Kodály körönd*), the next central square on the same Boulevard towards the Heroes' Square, became *Hitler tér* (1938). In contrast to the plethora of places named after Horthy, only one street throughout Budapest was named after Adolf Hitler. Interwar naming sought to produce a new hegemonic order in the discursive universe through the establishment of discursive nodal points.

Socialism

During the socialist period, both street names and other memorials witnessed a series of transformations. Pótó (2001) divides the socialist period into three eras: the destruction of the irredentist memorials, the removal of the aristocracy and the Habsburgs, and socialist commemoration. After the Second World War, the irredentist statues and fascist, royalist, and aristocratic street names were replaced by new anti-fascist and later socialist ones. It started with the geographical-ideological nodal points in the city-text. The central squares commemorating the Habsburgs were renamed after the victors of the Second World War—adding the same vocabulary as elsewhere in Eastern Europe and even beyond. Budapest got its first Stalin square as early as 1946 when, in the heart of Budapest, *Erzsébet tér* (after the Habsburg Queen Elizabeth, "Sisi") was renamed *Sztálin tér*, while *Frankfurter Allee* in East Berlin was renamed *Stalinallee* in 1949 (Azaryahu 1986). Roosevelt's square also took over Franz Joseph in 1946, where the US president was commemorated until recently. Churchill, the British war leader, lost his post as the Prime Minister during the naming process, and was never commemorated in Budapest (Nyyssönen 1992).

In the political center of Budapest, *Grof. Tisza István utca* (Count István Tisza Street, 1925) became *József Attila utca* in 1945. Heroes of the 1848 revolution were considered progressive and took key positions in the socialist Hungarian canon, which was reflected in the street names. The poet Miklos Rádnoti was a suitable example as a victim of the fascists, as was Maxim Gorky. Martyrs of the Second World War, left-wing, anti-fascist resistance also became prominent. *Szabó Ervin tér* was named in 1948 after the nineteenth-century Hungarian socialist/social democrat intellectual. In most cases, these anti-fascists stayed on the map after 1949 when the Soviet-style administration was established. For example, Raoul Wallenberg's street in the former Swedish quarter remains, while Wallenberg himself perished in Soviet Russia.

After the establishment of the Soviet-style system in 1949, the russification of names intensified (for a similar discussion in the context of East Berlin, see Azaryahu 1986). The aristocratic *Eszterházy utca* was renamed *Puskin utca* in 1949, and *Király utca* (King St.) gained a name after another Russian writer, Mayakovski, in 1950. Of this Russian culture, Pushkin still remains. Lenin replaced the female Habsburgs Theresa and Elizabeth on the *Nagykörút* (Great Circular Boulevard), but the male rulers *Ferenc* and *József* were allowed to remain. The Soviet military leader Molotov was commemorated on one street. The new "guards" were adapted well, as by the 1980s, 75 percent of Hungarians were able to identify by name one or more members of the Hungarian resistance in a survey (Csepeli 1997).

The new elements came to define each other. Russian literature and social democrats were politicized. The postwar names were taken as one set, and this also contributed to the removals. As discussed below, between 1945 and 1989, the myriad renamings resulted in a city-text composed of a heterogeneous set. Following Stalin's death in 1953, *Sztalin tér* was renamed *Engels tér*. The failed Hungarian revolution of 1956, led by Imre Nagy, demanded more national sovereignty and more Western socialism. The protests in front of the Parliament, and reversing the statue of Stalin, were crucial nodal points for the discourse of independence for the Hungarian state and communism. *Andrássy* was again renamed twice during and after. Although the revolution was brutally crushed with Soviet tanks, the military leader Molotov's name was removed, and the original name *Vigadó* was returned in 1957.

The "counter-revolution's martyrs" who supported the status quo were subsequently elevated in the city-text. In 1968, Ferenc Münnich, the post-1956 era's first Minister of the Interior was also poshumously commemorated both in statues and street names as a symbol of the post-1956 era. He became a nodal point among the "guard": the revolutionaries in 1989 reversed his statue and in 1990 renamed his street. Some reconciliation can be seen in the commemoration of other left-wingers in the street names. The communist László Rajk, rehabilitated and reburied in 1956 during the failed revolution, was again rehabilitated and commemorated on the streets in 1969 by the Kadarist regime. Both the Marxist philosopher György (Georg) Lukács (1979), who took part in the 1956 revolution but remained communist, and perhaps surprisingly interwar "populist" writer László Németh (1978), were posthumously commemorated in the streets of Budapest during the late-1970s.

Eventually, socialist internationalism replaced Hungarian-Soviet friendship: *Hanoi park* (1968) was named during the Vietnam War, where Hungarian troops also took part (Hajdú 2005; Lóderer 2008), although few know about it. Budapest got its *Allende park* in Kelenföld (1973) and *Nehru park* in 1987, during the visit of the Prime Minister Indira Gandhi, to "validate the domestic credibility of the guiding political ideology" (Bodnár 2009, 145). The Goulash communism of János Kádár focused on the economy rather than nationalism.

In the 1980s, the discursive universe of street names in Budapest started to move in a different direction. With the return of one of the nodal points, the Habsburg Queen Elisabeth, Hungarians' favorite "Sisi," appeared again in Budapest's city-text in 1986. Her statue was also returned to the city in the 1980s, similarly to the rehabilitation of the "national" monarchy that occurred in Berlin when Frederick the Great was commemorated in 1983 (Nyyssönen 1992). Naming Elisabeth in the streets during the mid-1980s was a sign of a transition that had already begun before 1989. The guard on the street names was changing slowly through adding and removing some nodal points from the discursive universe. Despite the popular events and reversal of statues, there was no violent overthrow, sudden revolt, or revolution but a negotiated transformation of the regime. The revolutionary character and the changing hegemony was nevertheless established by changing street names.

Postcommunist street naming in Budapest

The Hungarian tradition of street naming is intensive: bringing in a new "set" of discursive elements at a given time. The transition to democracy from a one-party system started in roundtable talks where the power-holding state socialist party met the opposition. This led to the articulation of the new system with a constitutional court, electoral laws, parliamentary elections, and so on. The local term for the revolution is "system change" (*rendszerváltás*).

Since discourse refers not to textuality alone but also to practices, there were also discursive differences between the political forces in the ways in which the guards have been treated. The streets were changing in Budapest already before the parliamentary and local elections in 1990. On January 23, 1990, the street in the heart of Budapest named after Ferenc Münnich, was renamed *Nándor utca* (Palatine St.). It was important to make the change visible. Still, it was not a homogeneous and smooth process. The Hungarian government and the Municipal Council of Budapest represented different political forces, and their actions generated further dispute.

In April 1990, the City Soviet (the municipality still in the Soviet-style institution) called for the citizens to be patient with the statues, which it regarded as "innocent." It decided to change 38 street names in Budapest and urged those districts that were willing to change names to make their decisions about street renamings by the deadline of June 30, 1990. The subsequent two years witnessed a constant modification of the street names and ten moments of putsch, when the city council decided to change a great number of names at once. These did not remove all commemorative street names introduced during the years of state socialism. Many of the removed names were contested: defining the communist canon was not straightforward. "Ultra-left" as well as broadly speaking leftist or anti-fascist names were decanonized and the changes were largely completed by 1993.

Hungarians were also divided over the preferred course of action towards the city-text (Foote, Tóth, and Árvay 2000). In 1988–89, three points of view emerged (Pótó 2003). The *radical position* of the minority consisted of socio-political critique. The *"preservationist" or "phlegmatic" position*, expressed in the surveys as the majority position, claimed that a change of statues would be too expensive and too complicated. The *museum position* was adopted by those who wanted to remove the statues but place them in a statue park. In short, there were (a) those who wanted to get rid of all the statues, (b) those who did not want to bother dealing with them, and finally (c) those who wanted to preserve statues in a museum of sorts (Boros 1998). Opinions on street names followed a similar pattern: removing all the communist-era street names; supporting minimal, if any, removals; or saving some of them by way of a layer of memory in the city-text.

The new power-holders could not simply remove unwanted names, they also needed an immediate substitute for them. The new names were marked by victimhood, commemorating the 1956 uprising, and the Holocaust—even though the underlying issues were not universally neutral. The late-nineteenth century was appropriated as the golden era (e.g., Pribersky 2003) as a way to avoid dealing with the present, since this was seen as the most neutral period in the Hungarian past with which to return, yet, at the same time, one both raising national feelings and a return to Europe (E. Palonen 2008).

The compromise, amnesia, and unwillingness to build a particular new era were visible in the return of the Habsburgs to the main boulevards of the city. After the pragmatically chosen golden era of the late-nineteenth century, the Hungarian right turned to the celebration of the interwar period. Commemorating Admiral Horthy or Trianon were perhaps demands beyond the mainstream on the right. The postcommunist revolution was a negotiated one in Hungary, and the renaming of streets articulated a return to the nineteenth century as a commemorable past, even though there had been calls for returning to the era that had ended when the Second World War had begun.

The first postcommunist government and city council were strongly involved with renaming. This renaming effort was led by the Hungarian Democratic Forum (MDF), the umbrella party of the national opposition forces. They were eager to change the street names. During the mid-1990s and 2000s, the left-liberal governments and Budapest Municipal Council did not carry out many political renamings. The next elections in 1994 were won by the Socialists, who joined government with the liberal Alliance of Free Democrats (SzDSz). In 1998, the elections were won by the national right, Fidesz, focused on architecture and urban space (E. Palonen 2014). In 2002, Fidesz narrowly lost to the Socialists who again formed government with SzDSz. Politics was marked by polarization and the government changed at each election, from one side of the political spectrum to the other—until 2006, when the Socialists won but riots broke out when the PM admitted to lying. Under the new right-wing government, renamings began again in 2010.

A new revolution against communism

In 2010, the population was dissatisfied with the previous Socialist-led governments and the right-wing government won in a landslide. The party leader of Fidesz, Viktor Orbán, a young rebel politician of the 1989/90 generation and later a fan of Berlusconi, called for a "revolution at the polls." It was enacted in the Hungarian fashion when in power: the symbolic "guard" on the streets was changed. On November 19, 2012, parliament passed law CLXVII, which decreed that the names referring to the "20th century dictatorships" must be changed. Indeed, not all street names related to the Workers' Movement and not all the personalities who were celebrated during the period of 1948–1989 had been removed in the early-1990s. The Academy of Science introduced a list of names to be removed. Heroes such as Endre Ságvári and Anna Koltói, who had become part of the socialist canon of street names, were now to be replaced.

Nevertheless, well-established names may continue to persist through the inertia of habit (Light and Young 2014): in the district of Óbuda, where a citizen consultation was conducted, the locals did not want to remove the former names. Among those to be removed were the Square of the Republic, *Köztársaság tér*, which was renamed after the Polish pope John Paul II. Religion replaced republicanism, it seemed, but in fact "republic" was tied to communist discourse— particularly as the headquarters of the Communist Party was there. This was one of the key locations of the bloody 1956 revolution. Additionally, Hungary's official name was shortened by removing "Republic."

One of the most visible renamings was that of *Moszkva tér*, a major transport hub in Budapest (Hungarian exonym for Moscow). The name of the square and its metro station bore witness to the era of its naming in 1951 and when the Soviet-style metro lines were built in Budapest in the 1960s. Finally, by 2016, the square was refurbished, so the surroundings would also evoke a sense of a new era rather than post-war heritage. It was renamed in 2011, by "returning the guard": the pre-First World War politician Kálmán Széll's name was restored to the square. Széll, a prime minister and minister of finance, became the hero of the Orbán government to the extent that it named the national austerity package after him. The new "guard" in the city-text would be absorbed as a nodal point into the public discourse by becoming a household name. The central transport junction would simultaneously promote the austerity package.

The government has adopted an anti-liberal populist stance. Populism has featured in different forms in the list of new street names (Table 6.1). On the Budapest map, other types of names were also visible. In the Lower Banks of Buda and Pest were personalities active in saving Budapest Jews during the

Table 6.1 "Populist" elements of Budapest's city-text in the 2010s

Commemorated Public Figure	Reputation (Type of Populism)
Bauer, Sándor	Anti-communist martyr, sim. Jan Palach (anti-communism)
Bibó, István	Dissident political theorist (anti-communism)
Dalnoki, Jenő	Hungarian footballer from the 1950s (popular culture)
Domján, Edit	Actress (popular culture)
Görgey, Artúr	Hero of the 1849 revolution (revolutionary)
Illyés, Gyula	Interwar populist writer (literary/political populism)
Kocsis, Sándor	Hungarian football's "Golden Team" of the 1950s
Mansfeld, Peter	Hero of the 1956 revolution (anti-communism)
Nemeth, László	Populist writer
Presley, Elvis	American musician (popular culture)
Romhányi, József	Actor (popular culture)
Zakarias, József	Hungarian football's "Golden Team" of the 1950s
Antal, József (sr.)	Interwar politician small-holder

Second World War and the Nazi occupation, including Carl Lutz, Jane Haining, and Raoul Wallenberg, among others. Another example is that of Count János Eszterházy, a Slovak Hungarian-Polish interwar politician who voted against expelling the Jews and remains a controversial figure in Slovakia. Lacking in the new street names were Jews themselves. This amnesia could be seen in the memorials: the state-funded German Occupation Memorial gained a counter-memorial by active citizens focusing on the victims of the Holocaust in 2014. First on the building site and then in making the now permanently maintained counter-memorial, protesters asserted that the Hungarian Holocaust was not just a consequence of foreign occupation but also a tragedy in which Hungarians themselves were on both sides.

Politicians and religious activists were also commemorated: the first interwar PM József Antall Sr. (an interwar small-holder politician, minister in 1945–46, and father of József Antall, the first post-communist prime minister), and Margit Slachta (the first woman to be elected in the Hungarian diet in 1920 and a strong Protestant activist). The religious-rebellious discourse was strong overall with different nodal points or "guards," including pope John Paul II—a Polish Roman Catholic priest and activist in the Solidarity movement, and the Protestant, Wittenberg-educated reformer and translator of the Hungarian bible, Gáspár Károli.

Other key sites were Hungarianized: the American president Roosevelt had to go in 2011 to be replaced by István Széchenyi, "the Greatest Hungarian," a moderate nineteenth-century reformer and a hero of the power-holding Fidesz, whose heritage is visible in the Chain Bridge, which starts from the square and heads to the tunnel passing through Buda Castle Hill. His life had been made tangible in 2002, in a state-sponsored costume drama.

As always, Fidesz communicated a new era through symbolic politics. They had promised a "revolution at the polls" in 2010. When in office in 1998–2002, Orbán's government focused on memorials and architecture (E. Palonen 2014).

Orbán gained another victory in the elections of 2014. Fidesz, as populist party did not have a clear ideology or vision for the future, but reacted to political strife by generating a counter-discourse. Still, heterogeneous elements and interwar nostalgia have been brought to the fore with the surroundings of the parliament being restored to their pre-1945 condition, including a reproduction of a large statue of Tisza. Orbán has claimed to introduce an "illiberal democracy," and the government has among other things introduced controversial media laws and restricted activities of foreign-sponsored foundations. Immigrants have emerged as the new "Other."

Removing the past was a way to name an enemy, generate the political frontier, and constitute a political "us" of the nation. Nationalism in Hungary has been transforming into a set of subcultures (Feischmidt et al. 2014), and this seems to fit the logic of the city-text, too. Thus far, the Fidesz government has not offered a ready set to implement in every district and town. It has mainly recognized the Other through the set to be removed, those beyond the limit of the government's discourse.

Conclusion

There are multiple overlapping discourses that inhabit the city-text. Rose-Redwood (Rose-Redwood vs. Smith 2016, 372) has recently asked: "what *effects* do our discourses and practices have in constituting the worlds in which we live, and how might we reconstitute them to foster a more equitable co-existence?" Laclau's point about the way in which discourses include disparate elements is concretized in the naming of streets. Treating street names as a set enables us—surprisingly perhaps—to consider them as a fluid, incomplete, transforming, and contradictory set. The "political" in street naming may be about making visible what is past and what is now, or to offer points of contestation, as something ultimately democratic (Mouffe 2000).

In Budapest, there are both ideological and spatial nodal points: for example, the naming of the main squares after the Second World War victors or religious leaders, the main Boulevard Andrássy, sections of the Ring Road, and ultimately the stations and squares became significant focal points of renaming. The renaming of the *Moszkva tér* metro station, and its long-planned refurbishment, demonstrates how certain names and places hold a special value for both citizens and politicians. On the other hand, the names of the banks of the Danube, which are seldom used for postal addresses but can be made visible on the map, offer another angle to the discursive universe of Budapest's street names.

Although the power-holders of a city may have planned to establish a hegemonic reading of the past through the naming of streets, the interpretive act of *reading* the city-text need not abide by the officially sanctioned narrative of the past. In pluralist societies, introducing many different claims and heritages in the streets may very well enable the new set to better resonate with a larger population. Following Laclau (2005), we might say that, in the moment of naming, the inherent multiplicity of the "people" becomes one—if only temporarily.

References

Alderman, D. (2002). "Street Names as Memorial Arenas: The Reputational Politics of Commemorating Martin Luther King Jr. in a Georgia County." *Historical Geography*, 30: 99–120.

Alderman, D. (2003). "Street Names and the Scaling of Memory: The Politics of Commemorating Martin Luther King, Jr. within the African American Community." *Area*, 35(2): 163–173.

Azaryahu, M. (1986). "Street Names and Political Identity." *Journal of Contemporary History*, (21)4, 581–604.

Azaryahu, M. (1992). "The Purge of Bismarck and Saladin: The Renaming of Streets in East Berlin and Haifa, a Comparative Study in Culture-Planning." *Poetics Today*, 13(2): 351–367.

Azaryahu, M. (1996). "The Power of Commemorative Street Names." *Environment and Planning D*, 14(3): 311–330.

Azaryahu, M. (1997). "German Reunification and the Politics of Street Naming: The Case of East Berlin." *Political Geography*, 16(6): 479–493.

Azaryahu, M. (2009). "Naming the Past: The Significance of Commemorative Street Names." In L. Berg and J. Vuolteenaho (Eds.), *Critical Toponymies: The Contested Politics of Place Naming* (pp. 53–70). Farnham: Ashgate.

Bácskai, V., Gyáni, G., and Kubinyi, A. (2000). *Budapest története a kezdetektől 1945-ig*, Budapest: Budapest Archive.

Bodnár, E. (2009). "'I have Often Walked Down This Street Before … But What Was It Called?': Changes to Street Names in Budapest from the End of Turkish Rule to the Present." *Past Imperfect*, 15: 115–152.

Boros, G. (1998). "Budapest's Sculptures and Commemorative Plaques in Public Spaces 1985–1998." In Á. Szöllősy and G. Boros (Eds.), *Budapest köztéri szobrai és emléktáblai 1985–1998* (pp. 7–17). Budapest: Budapest Galéria.

Csepeli, G. (1997). *National Identity in Contemporary Hungary*. New York: Columbia University Press.

Feischmidt, M., Glázer, R., Illyés, Z., Kasznár, V. K., and Zakariás I. (2014). *Nemzet a mindennapokban: Az újnacionalizmus populáris kultúrája*. Budapest: L'Harmattan.

Ferguson, P. (1988). "Reading City Streets." *The French Review*, 61(3): 386–397.

Foote, K. and Azaryahu, M. (2007). "Toward a Geography of Memory: Geographical Dimensions of Public Memory and Commemoration." *Journal of Political and Military Sociology*, (35)1: 125–144.

Foote, K., Tóth, Á., and Árvay, A. (2000). "Hungary after 1989: Inscribing a New Past on Place." *Geographical Review*, 90(3): 301–334.

Gerő, A. and Poór, J. (Eds.). (1997). *Budapest: A History from its Beginnings to 1998*. New York: Columbia University Press.

Gillis, J. (Ed.), (1994). *Commemorations: The Politics of National Identity*, Princeton, NJ: Princeton University Press.

Hajdú T. (2005). "Magyarok a Mekong partján." *Regiment*, 3.

Kearns, R. and Berg, L. (2002). "Proclaiming Place: Towards a Geography of Place Name Pronunciation." *Social & Cultural Geography*, 3(3): 283–302.

Laclau, E. (1996). *Emancipations(s)*. London: Verso.

Laclau, E. (2005). *On Populist Reason.* London: Verso.

Laclau, E. (2014). *Rhetorical Foundations of Society*. London: Verso.

Laclau, E. and Mouffe, C. (1985). *Hegemony and Socialist Strategy*. London: Verso.

Levinson, S. (1998) *Written in Stone: Public Monuments in Changing Societies*. Durham, NC: Duke University Press.

Light, D. and Young, C. (2014). "Habit, Memory, and the Persistence of Socialist-Era Street Names in Postsocialist Bucharest, Romania." *Annals of the Association of American Geographers*, 104(3): 668–685.

Lindroos, K. (1998). *Now-Time, Image-Space*. Jyväskylä: Sophi.

Lóderer, B. (2008). "The Hungarian Peacekeeping Mission in Vietnam." *AARMS*, 7(2): 271–282.

Massey, D. (2005). *For Space*. London: Sage.

Mouffe, C. (2000). *The Democratic Paradox*. London: Verso.

Nagy, L. (1998). *Ces Villes Qui Ont Fait L'Europe: Budapest*. Genéve: Georg.

Norval, A. (2005). "Theorising Hegemony: Between Deconstruction and Psychoanalysis." In L. Tonder and L. Thomassen (Eds.), *Radical Democracy, Politics between Abundance and Lack* (pp. 86–102), Manchester: Manchester University Press.

Nyyssönen, H. (1992). "Vain *kadut* ovat *ikuisia*: Budapestin nimenmuutokset kertovat uusien vallanpitäjien arvoista." *Kulttuurintutkimus*, 9(1): 11–20.

Palonen, E. (2008). "The City-Text in Post-Communist Budapest: Street Names, Memorials and the Politics of Commemoration." *GeoJournal*, 73(3): 219–230.

Palonen, E. (2011). "Rupture and Continuity: Fidesz and the Hungarian Revolutionary Tradition." *La Révolution française [en linge] lrf.revues.org/pdf/353*.

Palonen, E. (2013). "Millennial Politics of Architecture: Reinstating the Nation in Budapest." *Nationalities Papers*, 41(4): 536–551.

Palonen, E. (2014). "The Politics of Street Names: Local, National, Transnational Budapest." In M. Beyen and B. Deseure (Eds.), *Local Memories in a Nationalizing and Globalizing World* (pp. 51–71). Basingstoke: Palgrave Macmillan.

Palonen, K. (1993). "Reading Street Names Politically." In K. Palonen and T. Parvikko (Eds.), *Reading the Political: Exploring the Margins of Politics* (pp. 103–121). Tampere: Finnish Political Science Association.

Pótó, J. (2001). "Rendszerváltások és emlékművek." *Budapesti Negyed*, 32–33: 219–244.

Pótó, J. (2003). *Az emlékeztetés helyei–Emlékművek és politika*, Budapest: Osiris.

Pribersky A. (2003). "Politische Erinnerungskulturen der Habsburger-Monarchie in Ungarn: 'Ein Goldenes Zeitalter'?" In J. Feichtinger, U. Prutsch, and M. Csáky (Eds.), *Habsburg postcolonial. Machstrukturen und kollektives Gedächtnis* (pp. 221–230). Innsbruck: Studien Verlag.

Ráday, M. (1998). *Budapest teljes utcanévlexikona*. Budapest: Dinasztia-Gemini.

Ráday, M. (2003). *Budapest teljes utcanévlexikona*, Budapest: Sprinter.

Ráday, M. (2013). *Budapest utcanevek A–B*. Budapest: Corvina.

Rose-Redwood, R., Alderman, D., and Azaryahu, M. (2010). "Geographies of Toponymic Inscription: New Directions in Critical Place-Name Studies." *Progress in Human Geography*, 34(4): 453–470.

Rose-Redwood, R. vs. Smith, J. (2016). "Strange Encounters: A Dialogue on Cultural Geography Across the Political Divide." *Journal of Cultural Geography*, 33(3): 365–378.

Sinkó K. (1992) "Political Rituals: the Raising and Demolition of Monuments." In P. György and H. Turai (Eds.), *Art and Society in the Age of Stalin* (pp. 73–86). Budapest: Corvina.

Stavrakakis, Y. (1999). *Lacan and the Political*. London: Routledge.

von Henneberg, K. (2004). "Monuments, Public Space, and the Memory of Empire in Modern Italy." *History and Memory*, 16(1): 37–85.

Yeoh, B. (1996). "Street-Naming and Nation-Building: Toponymic Inscriptions of Nationhood in Singapore." *Area*, 28(3): 298–307.

7 Locating the geopolitics of memory in the Polish streetscape

Danielle Drozdzewski

Introduction

In the streets, urban inhabitants encounter semiotic reminders of cultural events, people, and places, whether consciously or unconsciously. Streetscapes are more than just names on a map; in any settlement, one might walk along a street, have coffee in a town square, arrange a meeting, or visit a museum in a historical building. The street, town square, and building could be named after figures of national importance, or commemorate an important event, or serve as a reminder of some traditional (national) ritual. Street names are "ostensibly visible, quintessentially mundane, and seemingly obvious" (Azaryahu 1996, 311). Simultaneously, they are sites for the manipulation of memories. Unlike purpose-built commemorative monuments and memorials, street names "have an immediate practical reality for the populace" as spatial and historical markers (Gill 2005, 481). Street name changes accord with, and give material expression to, a regime's sanctioned versions of history and ideology, weaving narratives of historical longevity into the streetscape. As Azaryahu (1996, 321) has asserted, the potency of street names lies in "their ability to make a version of history an inseparable element of reality as it is constantly constructed, experienced and perceived on a daily basis."

This chapter examines how history has been used as part of the spatial politics of memory of Nazi and Soviet regimes, inculcating their histories and traditions in the Kraków streetscape in Poland. Moreover, and in a parallel process of (de) commemoration, street and place names that did not support their invented histories were erased. Unlike much other research on street naming, this chapter's significance is its temporal analysis of the changes to one bounded area over time. Such analysis is important for political geographers as it exemplifies the street as a site of political contestation, where memory is manipulated and embedded within the ordinary landscape. Furthermore, it shows how representations of identity and history have been (re)inscribed in the landscape in a process of politicizing space. During the twentieth century, street and town square names in the Polish city of Kraków were changed, enacting a critical geopolitics in which territory and space were used as forms of control over an occupied Kraków streetscape. This chapter's example is emblematic of a critical geopolitics that examines the division and marking of space as a contest between "us" and "them," and as crucial in the mitigation of threats to sovereignty and to the security of discourses of political domination (Sharp 2009).

This chapter's key contribution in locating the politics of the urban streetscape is its spotlight on how history and geography are combined in the act of street naming, thereby legitimizing authority over urban space. In tracking the spatialization of geopolitics in the Krakówian streetscape, I undertake a textual and chronologically sequential analysis of historical maps, examining Nazi, Soviet, and Polish governmental uses of the streetscape in Kraków to make evident the purpose for each government's preferred version of history. In undertaking that process it becomes clear that some particulars of the name changes were obfuscated by Poland's history of foreign occupation, and especially the destruction of lives and documents in the wake of the occupations. The chapter's focus, then, is on establishing a narrative that makes clear the sense of purpose in the actual name changes themselves, rather than on the minutiae of specifying who nominated, approved, and instigated changes, or on levels of local resistance to these changes— as interesting as these details may be. In the following sections, I first review the literature on cultural memory and its relation to street naming. I then detail how I have used this scholarship to inform the textual (de)constructions of Kraków's streetscape. Next, I discuss these readings of street name changes in chorological order from WWII through the post-war period to the post-Socialist era.

Geographies of memory in the everyday streetscape

As this volume is dedicated to the political life of urban streetscapes and to the connections between naming, politics, and place, scholarship on toponomy and the politics of memory is a common theme across each of the chapters. Thus, rather than rehearsing this literature here again, I draw out how parallel scholarship on "memory" and the "everyday" critically intersect into the political life of the streetscape. I take this approach to positioning the scholarship informing this chapter because street naming involves the dual process of shaping memory *and* the shared space of everyday life (Hebbert 2005). First, the "everyday" focus is important because streets are basic elements of orientation in, and through, everyday landscapes. The "everyday" takes the form of the "ordinary landscapes in our daily routines," such as streets, shopping centers, parks, and public squares (Winchester, Kong, and Dunn 2003, 35). Second, memory is articulated in public spaces through a variety of media. Sites of memory include, but are not limited to, monuments, memorials, commemorative rituals, and street names. These sites of memory can become "landmarks of a remembered geography and history [which] … form the intersection between official and vernacular cultures" (Johnson 2002, 294). Such remembered geographies and histories in urban spaces have increasingly been the focal point of research on street naming and toponymy (Berg and Vuolteenaho 2009; Rose-Redwood, Alderman, and Azaryahu 2010; Azaryahu 2011, 2012a; Rose-Redwood 2011; Alderman and Inwood 2013).

While memory is routinely imagined as something personally experienced and felt, the urban fabric of the city also holds memory, since "it can act as a witness to the vicissitudes of everyday life—the mundane and the catastrophic" (Drozdzewski 2016, 20). In public spaces, memory is expressed in the built form and layout of the city: in the city's houses, its street names, and curvatures as well as in the commemorative atmospheres permeating postwar cities (cf. Anderson 2009). A city's memories can be personally and collectively remembered, (re)produced, and transmitted—in part—to maintain narratives of (national) identity. Because memories are informed by experiences, events, and stories that are culturally specific, they reveal connections between past and present (Connerton 1989; Assmann 1995), and, thus, the story of a city can be told by reading and moving through its landscapes. Streetscapes are often taken for granted as receptacles of memory because of their mundanity, yet, as this volume attests, they are sites where power is wielded to assert a preference for the depiction of certain memories in place. Consequently, recent scholarship on street and place naming has drawn attention to naming as a "contested spatial practice" (Berg and Vuolteenaho 2009; Rose-Redwood, Alderman, and Azaryahu 2010, 455).

The geopolitics of memory is a complex process determining *"who* gets [representation], in what way and with what political outcomes" (Edkins 2003, 135, italics in original). In the case study considered in this chapter, negotiating the geopolitics of memory in Kraków's streetscape involved different regimes manipulating street names to reference the past with the purpose of reaffirming their existence (and occupation) in that place in the present. As sites of memory in the public sphere, street names are a palpable example of how memory is mobilized to serve political ends (Edkins, 2003) and to inscribe political agendas into the streetscape. Thus, the geopolitics of memory (of the street) relates to whose version of a nation's past is made more visible in the public arena. As a potent force for popularizing political agendas, street names are both visible *and* accessible to large audiences and extensive geographic scales (Alderman, 2003). Building on Alderman's work, I would also contend that its quotidian context means that not only is the street a key focal point for expressing control and power, but its everydayness escalates the frequency by which a populace encounters a new name and memory planted in the streetscape. The power of commemorative choice is therefore tantamount to controlling the consolidation of memory in public spaces. Moreover, control of the street is a more straightforward task for an occupying regime who may instill a fear of reprisal as an instrument for the reinforcement of new names.

Memory's usefulness as a tool for those in power relates, then, to the determination of what is represented materially, how it is portrayed, and where it is positioned. A new regime will seek to assert its version of national identity in public landscapes "through the creation of an urban landscape that demonstrates and affirms the values and ideology of the regime" (Light, Nicolae, and Suditu 2002, 135). The successful transference of ideology to the street involves "signification" using semiotic markers and, as Baker (1992, 4) argues, is associated with a "quest for order," "an assertion of authority," and the projection of "totalisation." In geographical scholarship, attention is readily focused on the (re) production and transmission of public memory discourses in post-war and post-totalitarian states, and on the use of repression, suppression, and power (Argenbright 1999; Till 1999; Foote, Toth, and Arvay 2000; Forest and Johnson 2002; Nagel 2002; Forest, Johnson, and Till 2004; Ward, Silberman, and Till 2012). Interestingly, within this work, less attention has been paid to the role of non-totalitarian governments in changing street names back to their pre-totalitarian names, or the inculcation of new names, democratically selected or otherwise. More often writers have been especially concerned with how memory narratives in post-Soviet states have been (re)defined and publicly articulated following a return to autonomy. These new narratives of identity are drawn from the previously repressed or under-represented personal and experiential narratives of nations' *other* histories. In the next part of this chapter, I discuss the case study of Kraków's streetscape and contextualize its temporal and cultural settings. Following that, I detail my methodological approach.

Memory in the Polish streetscape

Over the past two centuries, the sustained presence of foreign regimes in Poland has created contested memoryscapes. Throughout the twentieth century, the importance of maintaining collective narratives of Polish identity was amplified by three periods of foreign occupation in Poland. From 1793 to 1918, the Tsarist Russian, Prussian, and Austro-Hungarian Empires partitioned Poland. Between 1939 and 1945, the Nazi (National Socialist/Fascist) and Soviet (Socialist) regimes occupied Poland. After WWII, with the initial support of Allied governments, the Soviet regime remained in Poland until 1989. Most recently, the fall of that regime saw the restoration of an autonomous Polish Republic, the current *Rzeczpospolita Polska*. It is in this setting of cultural and political suppression and occupation that Polish identities have been antagonistically positioned in relation to foreign occupation *and* oriented to autonomy (Drozdzewski 2008, 2012). Crucially for my purposes, memory narratives of places, events, and people that are synonymous with Polish identity have been, and remain, important forms of cultural (re) production, providing potent reminders of the nation's quest for freedom. To track how foreign occupation marked the Kraków streetscape, five maps of Kraków, dating from 1934, 1943, 1964, 1985, and 1996, were sourced from Jagiellonian University Library for this analysis. In each map, a section of the *Śródmieście*, the city center, was examined. Suburb boundaries for *Dzielnica I Stare Miasto* (Suburb I, The Old Town) have changed since the 1934 map, so major ring roads around the Old Town and bordering the *Planty* (the former medieval moat) were used as boundaries for the analysis.[1]

In approaching research on a post-war landscape such as Kraków that had undergone not only successive name changes, but sequential periods of war and occupation, it was clear from the outset that the names on maps were only part of that place's wider story of occupation and struggle for autonomy. In Poland, WWII and the Soviet occupation were especially destructive and authoritarian and, in the case of the latter, "without the clear division of responsibility and accountability" (pers. comm., July 23, 2010). In this context, ascertaining who

Table 7.1 Street name changes within the Planty in Kraków, Poland

Polish Name 1934	German Name 1941	Soviet Name 1964/1985	Post-Soviet Name 1996
ul. Basztowa	Werhrmachstr.	ul. Basztowa	
ul. Pijarska	Bastel Str	ul. Pijarska	
ul. Reformacka	Kloks Str.	ul. Reformacka	
ul. Św. Marka	Markus Gasse	ul. Św. Marka	
ul. Dunajweskiego	Westring.	1. Maja	ul. Dunajweskiego
ul. Sławkowska	Hauptstr.	ul. Sławkowska	
ul. Św. Jana	Johannis gasse	ul. Św. Jana	
ul. Floriańska	Floriang.	ul. Floriańska	
ul. Św. Tomasza	Thomas g.	Ludwika Solskiego	ul. Św. Tomasza
ul. Szpitalna	Spitalgasse	ul. Szpitalna	
Pl. Św Ducha	Theater Pl.	Pl. Św Ducha	
ul. Św. Krzyża	Hans von Kulmbach Str.	ul. Św. Krzyża	
Pl. Szeczpańska	Stephan Pl.	Pl. Szeczpańska	
ul. Szeczpańska	Stephang.	ul. Szeczpańska	
Rynek Główny	Adolf Hitler Platz	Rynek Główny	
ul. Andrzeja Potockiego	Ostring.	ul.Westerplatte	
ul. Podwale	Westring.	ul. Podwale	
ul. Mikołajska na Gródku	H Dürerstr.	ul. Mikołajska	
Mały Rynek	Kleiner Markt	Mały Rynek	
Pl. Marjacki	Marien Pl.	Pl. Marjacki	
ul. Szewska	Schusterg.	ul. Szewska	
ul. Jagiellońska	Matheus str.	ul. Jagiellońska	
ul. Św Anny	Annag.	ul. Św Anny	
ul. Sienna	Marketgasse	ul. Sienna	
ul. Stolarska	Tischlerg	ul. Stolarska	
ul. Dominikańska	Dominikanerg.	ul. Dominikańska	
Pl. Wszystkich Świętych	Rathaus Pl.	Pl. Wiosny Ludów	Pl. Wszystkich Świętych
ul. Gołębia	Murner Str.	ul. Gołębia	
ul. Wiśnla	Weichselstr.	ul. Wiśnla	
ul. Bracka	Kasinostr.	ul. Bracka	
ul. Grodzka	Burgstr.	ul. Grodzka	
ul. Franciszańska	Franziskanerg.	ul. Franciszańska	
ul. Straszewskiego	Westring.	ul. Straszewskiego	
ul. Olszewskiego	Celtisgasse.	ul. Olszewskiego	
ul. Poselska	Viet Stoβ str.	ul. Poselska	
ul. Senacka	Wirsingstr.	ul. Senacka	
ul. Kanonicza	Bonerstr.	ul. Kanonicza	
ul. Św Gertrudy	Gertrudenstr.	ul. Ludwika Waryńskiego	ul. Św Gertrudy
ul. Podzamcze	Unter der burg.	ul. Podzamcze	
Pl. Św Magdaleny	JörgHuber	Pl. Św Magdaleny	
Pl. Św Idziego	Burg Pl.	Pl. Św Idziego	
ul. Św Idziego	Agidiusgasse	ul. Św Idziego	

Notes
'g' denotes gasse, which means alley.
'ul.' denotes ulica, which means street.
'str'. denotes strasse, which means street.

Table 7.2 Street name changes on main roads outside the city center of Kraków, Poland.

Polish Name 1934	German Name 1941	Soviet Name 1964/1985	Post-Soviet Name 1996
ul. Zwierzyniecka	Hansestr.	ul. Zwierzyniecka	
ul. Marszałka Józefa Piłsudskiego	Universitetstr.	ul. Manifestu Lipcowego	ul. Marszałka Józefa Piłsudskiego
ul. Karmelicka	Reichstr.	ul. Karmelicka	
ul. Długa	Johann Haller Str.	ul. Długa	
ul. Pawia			
ul. Lubicz	Bahnhofstr.	ul. Lubicz	
ul. Starowiśnla	Alte Weichselstr.	ul. Bohaterów Stalingradu	ul. Starowisnla
ul. Stradomska	Komunandturstr.	ul. Stradomska	

made names changes, who was responsible for the initial research on street names, what were the instances of local resistance, if any, and so on were unobtainable elements of research—in some cases this type of document no longer exists. After substantial archival research and following consultation with Polish academics and a historical curator in Kraków about the likelihood of finding original documents detailing the provenance of street name changes, I made the decision to focus solely on the textual (de)construction of the name changes. Indeed, Gross (1979, 42) has also confirmed that there are "extreme difficulties connected with obtaining reliable data on almost any subject during this [WWII] period" and noted that it is nearly impossible to find materials of "irreproachable veracity" for such research. Nonetheless, I have sought to reference departments or people conceiving of, and authorizing, street renamings where possible though such details are incomplete.

The Kraków street name changes on successive map editions were recorded and synthesized with archival and contemporary secondary sources, and with personal communications about the regimes and their modes of governing in Kraków during the two most recent periods of foreign occupation. In particular, I drew on three Polish chronicles detailing the two periods of foreign occupation in Kraków and two volumes of the comprehensive and encyclopaedic *Dzieje Krakówa* (The History of Kraków, volumes five and six). I also used a publication compiled by the Kraków State Archives that described life in Nazi-occupied Kraków (*Bez Zaciemnienia: Codzienność Okupawnego Krakówa a Materiałach Archiwum Państwowego w Krakówie*), along with secondary sources on Polish history and the foreign occupation of Poland. Other historical sources have strengthened the analysis (Papritz and Sappok 1940; Polish Ministry of Information 1942; Hitler 1953; Krausnick and Broszat 1970; Rich 1973; Garliński 1985; Burleigh 1988; Lukowski and Zawadzki 2001; Davies 2005b; Zamoyski 2009). Tables 7.1 and 7.2 detail all street names in the study area and their names in the pre-WWII Polish republic (1934), the German names in the *Generalgouvernement* (1941), the Soviet names (1964, 1985) and the post-Soviet Polish republic names (1996).

(Re)naming Kraków's streetscape

The following sections of this chapter explore the naming of streets in Kraków, using the 1934 map as a starting point as that year marked the start of national street name standardization and the creation of a "Commission on Establishing the Names of Localities." The commission used the substantial 15 volume *Geographic Dictionary of the Kingdom of Poland and Other Slavic Countries*, published between 1880 and 1902, as its reference point in the standardization of street names (Zych 2011).

WWII and the Generalgouvernement *(Government-General) (1939–1945)*

Following its capture on September 6, 1939, Kraków was established as the capital of *Generalgouvernement* with Hans Frank appointed as the General-Governor on October 26, 1939. The *Generalgouvernement* was not formally incorporated into the Reich but designated as a distinct administrative unit to house the remnants of the Polish and Jewish populations, who had been forcibly displaced from the other territories destined to be solely populated by *Reichsbürger* (Reich citizens) (Rich 1974; Burleigh 1988). Following this mandate, it was important for Kraków to be German in character and outlook, an intention expounded by Hitler (1940, 588) in *Mein Kampf*: "a Germanisation can only be carried out with the soil and never with men" alone. As the capital of the *Generalgouvernement*, Kraków underwent a process of Germanization, where history was used to ensconce ideology and identity in the landscape.

It was the Nazis' intention, and indeed part of a wider Nazi *Geopolitik*, that the persons exiled to the *Generalgouvernement* would form an interim workforce and eventually become an illiterate serfdom. With the ratification of the "final solution," the *Generalgouvernement* would extend the German *lebensraum* and Kraków would "be peopled by Germans" (Hitler 1953, 405). Kraków was "imagined" (cf. Anderson 1991) as "a perfect example of continuity of the German culture and civilisation on the banks of the Vistula river" (Chwalba 2002, 41). In Karl Haushofer's *Geopolitik*, this process of Germanization was termed "earth-boundedness" (Ó Tuathail 1998) and involved the inscription of German character into the land- and streetscape. Nazi propaganda promoted a view of Kraków as primordially German; publicists showed that Kraków was "settled in a location deed based on German law (Magdeburg law)" according to which "Polish people could not become citizens and it was German clans who were encouraged to settle" (Chwalba 2002, 47).

To effect these changes, guidelines on (re)naming streets were issued on August 22, 1940 by Gerhard Sappok, a professor of history, enlisted by Frank to work in a sub-branch of the *Publikationsstelle Berlin-Dahlem* (PuSte) in Kraków (Burleigh, 1988).[2] While this sub-branch produced maps and statistics about Germandom in Kraków, including a German guide to Kraków and "studies of German culture and art in Polish history" (Burleigh 1988, 190–191), Sappok instructed staff in the history department of the *Institut für deutsche Ostarbeit* (IdO) (Institute for German Work in the East) to "work out" and "check" newly proposed street names.[3] Existing Polish street names were checked for references to "anti-German personalities, events [or] Jews"; newly proposed names were mandated to be "closely bound up with the history of Germandom or German cultural achievements"; and, if the new name was a direct translation it "should be as complete and grammatically accurate as possible" (Sappok 1940, cited in Burleigh 1988, 195).[4] The PuSte was responsible for authorizing street name changes, which were proposed by local commissions comprising IdO researchers, local government officials, and local German bourgeoisie.

The 1943 map depicts the outcomes of Sappok's mandate that focused on "fixing" the past in place by elongating and exposing distant or longstanding German historical associations into the present (Figure 7.1). Of the 51 streets and place names examined, only two street names remained unchanged.[5] Name changes can be categorized in four ways, each of which is elaborated below: street names changed to reflect German cityscapes; others directly translated into German; those changed to refer to the ruling Nazi party; and those changed to remember German historical and/or cultural personalities.

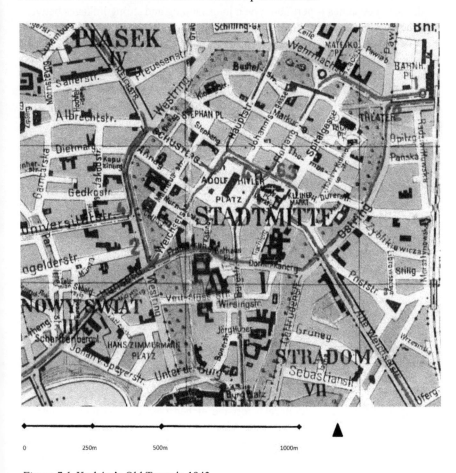

Figure 7.1 Kraków's Old Town in 1943

First, the names of streets and squares were changed to invoke a city structure reminiscent of major German settlements. As such, *Westring* (West Ring) and *Ostring* (East Ring) identified the ring roads around Kraków's Old Town. Similarly, *Pl. Wszystkich Świętych* (All Saints Square) became *Rathaus Platz* (Town Hall Square), and the road adjacent to the Kraków's main train station became *Bahnhofstr* (Station Street). Second, other street names within Kraków's Old Town were kept and the names directly translated to German. For example, *ul. Spzitalna* (Hospital Street) became *Spitelgasse*. Streets named after professions were also Germanized such that *ul. Szewska* (Shoemaker's Street) became *Schusterg*, and *ul. Stolarska* (Joiner's Street) became *Tischlerg*. In the 1943 map, some streets had the reference to "saint" omitted from the new German name, for example, *ul. Św. Marka* (Saint Mark's Street) became *Marcus Gasse* (Marcus Alley), and *ul. Św. Jana* (Saint John's Street) became *Johannis Gasse* (John's Alley). Yet other maps produced during the Nazi occupation have retained the reference "saint" in the same street names. Nonetheless, the decision to keep Catholic street names is pertinent given longstanding and strong linkages between Polish Catholicism and Polish nationalism (Porter 2001). One explanation could be that Frank, knowing that "German officials were thinly spread" in the *Generalgouvernement* and that Poles were employed in lower ranks of the administration, on railways and other utilities, saw this as a conciliatory move (Burleigh 1988, 187; also, see Gross 1979). It could also be the case that Germany's longstanding historical roots in the Holy Roman Empire were as influential as Nazi ideology.

The third category of street name changes instituted more poignant reminders of the presence of the Nazi regime. Azaryahu (1996, 321) has argued that the main virtue of street names is to introduce "history into social communication" to make "a version of history an inseparable element of reality." A striking example was the substitution of "*Rynek Główny*" with "*Adolf Hitler Platz*," which was instituted in 1940 to celebrate one year of victory and occupation in Poland. Further examples of referencing the ruling elite include: *ul. Basztowa* to *Wehrmachstr.* and *ul. Karmelicka* (a major thoroughfare out of the city center) to *Reichstr.* Both *Wehrmachstr.* and *Reichstr.* illustrate overt "statement(s) of the regime's agenda" (Light, Nicolae, and Suditu 2002, 135–136). Moreover, the term "Reich," denoting *kingdom* or *empire* in German, provided connection to the longevity of German rule and power back to the Holy Roman Empire. As Hobsbawm (1972, 3) has pointed out in this regard, "the past is … a permanent dimension of the human consciousness."

The fourth category of street (re)naming was perhaps the most instructive and involved the rewriting of Kraków as a German city and "cultural centre that once exercised a strong and lasting influence" (Sappok 1940, v–vi). Exposing material links to a Germanic past, by referencing Germans who had been active in the development of Kraków's cultural landscape, etched a sense of German entitlement to the city. As Rudolf Pavlu, Starost (Chief Administrator of Kraków, April 1941 to April 1943) stated: "what our ancestors created here as farmers, colonisers, burghers, craftsman and artists should not go down in history as a futile effort" (Pavlu 1942, page unknown, cited in Kluczewski 2009, 33).

The Nazis were shrewd in their choice of which historical periods to represent in Kraków, with name changes primarily emphasizing figures from the Renaissance, regarded in Poland as the Golden Age (c. fifteenth and sixteenth centuries). Then, the ruling Jagiellonian dynasty (1385–1572) controlled the largest ever Polish and multi-ethnic state, and the period is considered one of great wealth, culture, and influence. Some of Kraków's key cultural artifacts date from the Renaissance including the altar in *Kościół Mariacki* (St Mary's Bascilia) and *Wawel* (The King's Castle), which was rebuilt following a fire in Renaissance style by *Zygmunt Stary I* (King Sigismund the Old).

To emphasize the German contribution to Kraków's cultural landscape, well-known German artists, and their works, were named in the streetscape to show that Kraków "was once a pioneer of German art" (Pavlu 1942, cited in Kluczewski 2009, 32). This was a classic illustration of what Alderman (2003, 99) refers to as history being etched "into the geographic fabric of everyday life," with streets named after: Hans von Kulmbach, a German artist who painted three altarpieces for churches in Kraków; Hans and Albrecht Dürer, the former being the court painter of *Zygmunt Stary I*; Jörg Huber, a German sculptor who fashioned a tomb for a Polish King in *Wawel*'s crypt; and Viet Stoss, who was responsible for the most well-known artifact within *Kościół Mariacki*, the triptych altarpiece.

The Nazis were vigilant about the geography of their street naming exercise, renaming streets in close proximity to key cultural symbols, such as the university and *Wawel*. Two streets in close spatial proximity to Jagiellonian University, a key marker of Kraków's cultural development, were renamed after Conrad Celtes and Thomas Murner, two German scholars who studied in Kraków. The placement of these streets adjacent to the university indicates the Nazis' attempts to expose material links to Kraków's intellectual and artistic past. Similarly, two streets closer to *Wawel* were changed to emphasize deliberate associations to *Kazimierz Wielki* (King Casmir III the Great) (1333–1370). *Kazimierz Wielki*—the last king of the Piast Dynasty, preceding the Jagiellonian dynasty—was responsible for the eastward expansion of the Polish state. During his reign, Kraków grew from "a wooden town into a city of brick and stone" (Davies 2005a, 78). Social and cultural infrastructure such as the Gothic Cloth Hall, Jagiellonian University, and numerous churches exemplified the nation building focus of the era. Azaryahu (1996, 322) has argued that historical street naming involves an "artificially fabricated unity between history … and location." As such and near to *Wawel, ul. Senacka* became *Wirsingstr.* to commemorate the German treasurer to *Kazimierz Wielki,* and *ul. Kanonicza* became *Bonerstr.* to honor a member of his court. The sagacity of these changes was cunning; their proximity to *Wawel*—regarded as the cultural center of Kraków where Poland's kings lived and were buried alongside famous Polish writers, actors, and clergyman—flaunted the acquisition of the castle while also seeking to diminish its Polish relevance. Moving past the link between name and location, these changes typify the astuteness of Nazi efforts to emphasize German influence in Kraków. By using historical and national narratives associated with the Polish Renaissance (notably during periods of nation-building under the Piast and Jagiellonian dynasties), the Nazis sought to weaken significant connections to

Polish nationalism by expunging reminders of such narratives and showing that it was Germans who contributed significantly to Kraków's cultural status.

There was but one strong political purpose of name changes during the Fascist occupation of WWII, which was to show that Nazis were reclaiming a city they thought was theirs. The re-inscription of the streets using the German language further emphasized their "identity politics and nationalist policies" (Azaryahu 2012b, 462). Additionally, Burleigh (1988, 194) has argued, the work of German researchers in Kraków showed that "by judicious selection, history could be made to conform with the dictates of … [Nazi] ideology."

Post-WWII: Soviet-led Socialism in Poland (1945–1989)

After WWII, and at the end of Nazi occupation of Kraków, the Soviet regime sought to cement its authority and remove traces of the Nazi regime and Kraków's Polish republican past. Referring to place naming during the Socialist occupation, Domański (1998, 33) maintains that "new names had a double purpose of conveying Socialist ideals and/or eradicating old improper identities—capitalist, religious or non-Polish." During the postwar period, a Committee for Establishing Place Names had the primary aim of renaming western territory from Germany. Name changes would have been instituted by local (town) authorities with penultimate decision-making belonging to the *Polska Zjednoczona Partia Robotnicza* (the ruling Polish United Workers Party) (pers. comm. July 23, 2010). Of note, renaming was completed in Polish; Soviet tactics had a political focus distinct from the cultural preferences shown by the Nazis.

Between 1945 and 1989, seven strategic and compelling name changes occurred in the study area (Figure 7.2). The constitution of a new Soviet-collective history sought to perpetuate certain narratives of class struggle by commemorating Soviet battle sites and individuals, and selecting street names significant in the Soviet calendar. As Young and Light (2001, 944) observe in a similar context, such "re-writing of history sought to emphasise (or invent) long-standing links with the USSR." In Bucharest, Light, Nicolae, and Suditu (2002) found that the Soviet regime generally did not rename streets that already had religious references. In Kraków, however, two streets and a town square named after religious figures (*ul. Św. Gerturdy, ul. Św. Tomasza,* and *Pl. Wszystkich Świętych*) were renamed, presenting a curious anomaly given that the majority of religiously named streets remained unchanged. Two of the three were renamed to commemorate Soviet individuals; the third commemorated a Soviet calendar ritual, indicating that both the previous religious name and the new (Soviet) name played a role in this decision. A Polish Socialist, Ludwik Waryński, was commemorated in place of *ul. Św. Gerturdy*. Waryński was regarded as Poland's first Marxist and founder of Poland's first Socialist magazine. In 1885, he was captured and sentenced by Tsarist authorities and died in prison. The street name change served several purposes: it emphasized Waryński's martyrdom, denounced Tsarist Russians, and accentuated the longstanding existence of Polish Socialism. Furthermore, the Soviets sought to highlight that the "struggles of men like Waryński aroused the hatred of industrialists and other exploiters" (Ferro 2003, 256).

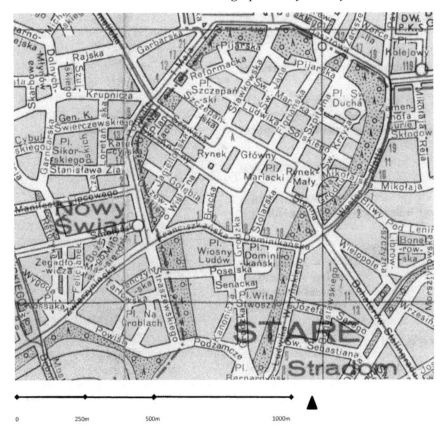

Figure 7.2 Kraków's Old Town in 1964

Then in 1955, the conversion of *Pl. Wszystkich Świętych* (All Saint's Square) to *Pl. Wiosny Ludów* (Spring of Nations) signaled further Soviet attempts to remind the local Polish population of the power and rights of the workers. In the Spring of Nations (1848), Polish insurrectionary forces had planned to face Russia with Prussian forces but they reneged; an ill-fated uprising in Poznań then resulted in the Grand Duchy of Posen being ceded to Prussian forces. Read from a Soviet perspective, the politics of this uprising is symptomatic of Prussian (read German) deceit. *Wiosny Ludów* thus presents as a prudent selection and reinforces the Soviets as a trustworthy collaborator.

After WWII in Soviet-occupied Europe, the commemoration of the war was dominated by a common narrative highlighting the Fascist failure (Judt 1992). This narrative extended to street names, with *ul. Starowiśnla* becoming *Alte Weichselstr.*, then changing to *ul. Bohaterów Stalingradu* (Heroes of the Battle of Stalingrad), a change that emphasized German defeat and Soviet victory. Highlighting German fallibility was also evident in renaming *ul. Andrzeja Potockiego* to *ul. Westerplatte*. Westerplatte is the location where WWII began and pertinent for the maintenance of anti-Nazi narratives. For Poles, Westerplatte is deeply entrenched in cultural memory as a site symbolizing suffering and the struggles of the Polish nation. These examples typify Azaryahu's (1997, 481) assertion that name changes can transform "history into a feature of the natural order of things," concealing its contrived character. There is, however, an additional rationale behind this particular name change. The former name, *ul. Andrzeja Potockiego*, refers to Andrew Potocki, a member of the Polish nobility, and was deeply inconsistent with Socialist ideology to champion the worker.

To visibly bolster ideology in the streetscape, the Soviet regime also used propaganda and were judicious in the choice of locations for name changes. The conversion of *ul. Marszałka Józefa Piłsudskiego* to *Universitetstr.* and then to *ul. Manifestu Lipcowego* (July Manifesto) is an example of propagandist street naming and of purposefully positioning a semiotic marker. Piłsudski was the First Marshall of the Second Polish Republic, formed after WWI and the 123 year partition of Poland. His actions led to the reformation of the Polish State, and he also led Polish forces to victory in the Polish-Soviet War (1919–1921) (Stanisławska-Adamczewska and Adamczewska 2000). He was demonstrably disliked by both Russians and Germans. Thus the Soviets chose neither to keep the Nazi name "*Universitetstr*" because it referenced Jagiellonian University, an anti-communist bastion, nor to revert to the pre-WWII name because it referenced Piłsudski. Rather they chose the July Manifesto, which "according to the official mythology of the Communist regime" signified the beginning of post-war political control of Poland by the Soviet-led Polish Committee of National Liberation (Davies 2005b, 413).[6] It outlined the provisional social, political, and economic reforms to be installed by a Soviet-led government in Poland, in opposition to the London-based Polish government in exile. The aim here was to show that the Polish nation had emerged as a true Socialist entity after WWII without force or a Soviet-led invasion, effectively "turn[ing] the landscape into a world structured by the legitimising myths and symbols of the regime" (Gill 2005, 481). The choice of location for this renaming was decisive. *Ul. Manifestu Lipcowego* runs perpendicular to Jagiellonian University, which remained in defiant intellectual opposition to the Soviet regime. The "construction of any message designed to represent reality" involves decisions about how to locate those realities (Galasiński and Skowronek 2001, 53). By invoking the July Manifesto close to the university, the regime was able to ensure that university academics and students would have contact with that street name.

Post-Socialism: a return to the Rzeczpospolitia Polska

With the return of the *Rzeczpospolitia Polska* in 1989, all but one of the previously renamed streets reverted back to its name on the 1934 map. Polish authorities chose to keep one name from the Socialist era—*ul. Westerplatte*—as a commemoration of WWII. The street name changes "indicated which values were to be recognised as defining the nation and what kind of present and future was envisaged for the country" (Ochman 2013, 32). In the only other Anglophone study on street naming that included Kraków in its analysis of Central European toponyms, Kraków (along with Graz and Prague) had the least number of changes in "city toponymy between 1935 and 1985" (Stiperski et al. 2011, 190).[7] This similar result suggests an overriding importance to revert to the pre-WWII nomenclature. The use of the street to display nationally important cultural memories in the public sphere is not restricted to foreign regimes; the autonomous Polish government also exercised its power to remove references to previous regimes. In Poland more generally, since 2007, the *Instytut Pamięci Narodowej* (IPN) (The Institute of National Remembrance) began a process of de-communizing public space, sending requests to local councils to change street names that "glorified communism" (Ochman 2013, 82). To support this agenda, IPN cited Article 13 of the Polish Constitution and Article 256 of the Polish Penal Code that relate to the prohibition of the propagation of Nazism, Fascism, and Communism.

Conclusion

By means of the sign—a seemingly commonplace, fixed, spatial marker—street names "impose a legitimate vision upon the social world" (Galasiński and Skowronek 2001, 52). While "urban spaces and architecture often give the impression of permanence," this chapter's temporal analysis of street names shows how this component of urban space conveys narratives that are indeed "dynamic, contingent and malleable" (Hagen 2010, 397). Through time, Kraków's street names have provided visible, distinctive, and daily reminders of the historical and socio-political intentions of those governing the city. The names on the street signs are much more than proper nouns. They are expressions of power and politics, each marking the nation-building intentions of the occupier—whether executed in overt or subtle ways. The efficacy of street names as geopolitical tools of memory and contested identities has been demonstrated by the fact that some Polish street names were absent from Kraków for fifty years, from 1939 to 1989, and then reinstated as soon as that became feasible.

Toponymic studies investigate this link between identity and power: thus, much can be ascertained about political and ideological convictions motivating each occupying regime by critically examining its renaming practices. For example, the extent of the name changing in the 1943 map confirms a key tenet of critical geopolitical discourse to lessen the security threat of difference to the Nazi state by making clear divisions between Nazi space and Polish space: German place names in German, in newly conquered German space. A critical geographical approach to examining the geopolitics of memory in this research returns to a key medium of the discipline, the map, to draw attention to how street names augment the relationship between power and identity. The street gives the name a place; it fixes it to a locale in the city, to someone's street of residence, to where someone shops. Foregrounding the spatiality of street names changes as an integral part of a triadic relationship of "where," "whom," and "what" has revealed that purposeful selection extends to the selection of historical events and personalities *and* to the location of the street name changes. Inserting and narrating particular versions of history in strategic locations was, therefore, critically important for both Fascist and Socialist regimes.

A key contribution of this chapter has been to invite more than passing reflection on the ways in which Kraków's urban façade exemplifies wider geopolitical shifts in memory and identity struggles. Given Nietzsche's (2006 [1874], 3) contention that "we wish to use history only insofar as it serves the living," if the past has been effectively layered over by sets of street names both new and paradoxically longstanding though absented, what contemporary purposes do now-silenced names serve? I contend that the Nazi and Soviet regimes used the street to demonstrate power and transcribe that power spatially because street names are easily changed, readily accessible, ubiquitous markers in everyday urban space. Yet this propensity for changeability also imparts impermanence. Returning to the question of contemporary relevance of analyzing historical name changes, I proffer two suggestions that are also agendas for further work. The first is that scholars interested in toponymy engage present day audiences' opinions about living in streets with contested pasts, which have had multiple names. The second is that by investigating how, why, and when names changed in the past, we construct better topographies for understanding the importance of geopolitics to everyday spaces, especially those which are silent witnesses to trauma.

Notes

1 These ring roads are *F.Straszewskiego, Podwale, J.Dunajewskiego, Basztowa, Westerplatte, Św. Gertrudy, Św. Idziego,* and *Podzamcze.*
2 *Publikationsstelle Berlin-Dahlem* (PuSte) was established on December 18, 1939, to conduct research on the territories of the Eastern Front, namely the historical German linkages in these places.
3 The *Institut für deutsche Ostarbeit* (IdO, Institute for German Work in the East) opened in Kraków on April 20, 1940, and had a mandate of pursuing research on ethnic Germandom in Poland.
4 In detailing the PuSte memorandum on street renaming, Burleigh (1988) references the *Bundesarchiv* in Koblenz, Article No R153/951 (*Publikationsstelle Berlin-Dahlem*) G. Sappok, "Richlinen für die Umbenennung von Strassennamen in den Städten dea Generalgouvernments," 22.8.40. The memorandum provides further detail on possible German personalities for street renaming lists of exclusions and references of certain personalities to be removed from the streetscape. It also urges administrators to ensure that those streets with direct translations did not have a suitable German name in the Middle Ages.
5 Two street names remained unchanged over the duration of all three regime changes: *ul. Pawia* and *na Grodku.* Neither represented anything anti-German; nor were the names anti-Socialist. The name *ul. Pawia* dates back to 1878 and possibly relates to a peacock farm ("paw" being the Polish word for peacock); *na grodku* translates as "on the park," as the street is adjacent to the *Planty* parkland (Supranowicz 1995).
6 Manifesto of the Polish Committee of National Liberation issued on July 22, 1944, at Chełm in eastern Poland.
7 This study did not specify the actual streets that were changed or map the area of streets included in the analysis, it only indicated that the streets were in each city's Old Town.

References

Alderman, D. (2003). "Street Names and the Scaling of Memory: The Politics of Commemorating Martin Luther King, Jr. within the African American Community." *Area*, 35(2): 163–173.

Alderman, D. and Inwood, J. (2013). "Street Naming and the Politics of Belonging: Spatial Injustices in the Toponymic Commemoration of Martin Luther King Jr." *Social & Cultural Geography*, 14(2): 211–233.

Anderson, B. (1991). *Imagined Communities: Reflections on the Origin and Spread of Nationalism*. New York: Verso.

Anderson, B. (2009). "Affective Atmospheres." *Emotion, Space and Society*, 2(2): 77–81.

Argenbright, R. (1999). "Remaking Moscow: New Places, New Selves." *Geographical Review*, 89(1): 1–22.

Assmann, J. (1995). "Collective Memory and Cultural Identity." *New German Critique*, 65: 125–133.

Azaryahu, M. (1996). "The Power of Commemorative Street Names." *Environment and Planning D: Society and Space*, 14(3): 311–330.

Azaryahu, M. (1997). "German Reunification and the Politics of Street Names: The Case of East Berlin." *Political Geography*, 16(6): 479–493.

Azaryahu, M. (2011). "The Critical Turn and Beyond: The Case of Commemorative Street Naming." *ACME: An International E-Journal for Critical Geographies*, 10(1): 28–33.

Azaryahu, M. (2012a). "Renaming the Past in Post-Nazi Germany: Insights into the Politics of Street Naming in Mannheim and Potsdam." *Cultural Geographies*, 19(3): 385–400.

Azaryahu, M. (2012b). "Hebrew, Arabic, English: The Politics of Multilingual Street Signs in Israeli Cities." *Social & Cultural Geography*, 13(5): 461–479.

Baker, A. (1992). "Introduction: On Ideology and Landscape." In A. Baker and G. Biger (Eds.), *Ideology and Landscape in Historical Perspective: Essays on the Meanings of Some Places in the Past* (pp. 1–14). Cambridge: Cambridge University Press.

Berg, L. and Vuolteenaho, J. (2009). *Critical Toponymies: The Contested Politics of Place Naming*. Farnham: Ashgate.

Burleigh, M. (1988). *Germany Turns Eastwards: A Study of Ostforschung in the Third Reich*. Cambridge: Cambridge University Press.

Chwalba, A. (2002). *Dzieje Krakówa: Kraków w latach 1939–1945*. Kraków: Wydawnictwo Literackie.

Cole, T. (1999). *Images of the Holocaust: The Myth of the "Shoah Business."* London: Gerald Duckworth & Co.

Connerton, P. (1989). *How Societies Remember*. Cambridge: Cambridge University Press.

Davies, N. (2005a). *God's Playground: A History of Poland*, Vol. 1, Oxford: Oxford University Press.

Davies, N. (2005b) *God's Playground: A History of Poland*, Vol. 2, Oxford: Oxford University Press.

Domański, B. (1998). "The Manifestation of Ideology and Power in the Urban Landscape and in Geographical Teaching: The Case of Poland." In U. Wardenga and W. Wilczynski (Eds.), *Religion, Ideology and Geographical Thought* (pp. 31–44). Kielce: Wyzsza Szkola Pedagogiczna im. Jana Kochanowskiego, Instytut Geografii.

Drozdzewski, D. (2008). "Remembering Polishness: Articulating and Maintaining Identity Through Turbulent Times." Doctoral Dissertation, Department of Geography, University of New South Wales.

Drozdzewski, D. (2012). "Knowing (or Not) about Katyń: The Silencing and Surfacing of Public Memory." *Space and Polity*, 16(3): 303–319.

Drozdzewski, D. (2016). "Encountering Memory in the Everyday City." In D. Drozdzewski, S. De Nardi, and E. Waterton (Eds.), *Memory, Place, Identity: Commemoration and Remembrance of War and Conflict* (pp. 19–37). Abingdon: Routledge.

Edkins, J. (2003). *Trauma and the Memory of Politics*. Cambridge: Cambridge University Press.

Ferro, M. (2003). *The Use and Abuse of History*. Abingdon: Routledge.

Foote, K., Toth, A., and Arvay, A. (2000). "Hungary after 1989: Inscribing a New Past on Place." *Geographical Review*, 90(3): 301–334.

Forest, B. and Johnson, J. (2002). "Unravelling the Threads of History: Soviet-Era Monuments and Post-Soviet National Identity in Moscow." *Annals of the Association of American Geographers*, 92(3): 524–547.

Forest, B., Johnson, J., and Till, K. (2004). "Post-Totalitarian National Identity: Public Memory in Germany and Russia." *Social and Cultural Geography*, 5(3): 357–380.

Galasiński, K. and Skowronek, D. (2001). "Naming the Nation: A Critical Analysis of Names in Polish Political Discourse." *Political Communication*, 18(1): 51–66.

Garliński, J. (1985). *Poland in the Second World War*. Hong Kong: MacMillan Press.

Gill, G. (2005). "Changing Symbols: The Renovation of Moscow Place Names." *The Russian Review*, 64(3): 480–503.

Gross, J. (1979). *Polish Society Under German Occupation*. Princeton, NJ: Princeton University Press.

Hagen, J. (2010). "Architecture, Symbolism and Function: The Nazi Party's 'Forum of the Movement'." *Environment and Planning D: Society and Space*, 28(3): 397–424.

Hebbert, M. (2005). "The Street as Locus of Collective Memory." *Environment and Planning D: Society and Space*, 23(4): 581–596.

Hitler, A. (1940). *Mein Kampf*. London: Hutchinson in assoc. with Hurst & Blackett.

Hitler, A. (1953). *Hitler's Table Talk, 1941–1944*. London: Weidenfeld and Nicolson.

Hobsbawm, E. (1972). "The Social Function of the Past: Some Questions." *Past & Present*, 55: 3–17.

Johnson, N. (2002). "Mapping Monuments: The Shaping of Public Space and Cultural Identities." *Visual Communication*, 1(3): 293–298.

Judt, T. (1992). "The Past is Another Country: Myth and Memory in Postwar Europe." *Daedalus*, 121(4): 83–119.

Kluczewski, M. (2009). *Bez Zaciemnienia: Codzienność Okupowanego Krakówa w Materialach Archiwum Państwowego w Krakówie* (*Without Blackout: Everyday Life of Occupied Kraków in Materials of the State Archive in Kraków*). Kraków: Archiwum Państwowe.

Krausnick, H. and Broszat, M. (1970). *Anatomy of the SS State*. London: Paladin.

Light, D., Nicolae, I., and Suditu, B. (2002). "Toponymy and the Communist City: Street Names in Bucharest, 1948–1965." *GeoJournal*, 56(2): 135–144.

Lukowski, J. and Zawadzki, H. (2001). *A Concise History of Poland*. Cambridge: Cambridge University Press.

Nagel, C. (2002). "Reconstructing Space, Re-creating Memory: Sectarian Politics and Urban Development in Post-War Beirut." *Political Geography*, 21(5): 717–725.

Nietzsche, F. (2006 [1874]). *The Use and Abuse of History*. New York: COSIMO.

Ochman, E. (2013). *Post-Communist Poland: Contested Pasts and Future Identities*. New York: Routledge.

Ó Tuathail, G. (1998). "Introduction to Part 1: Imperalist Geopolitics." In G. Ó Tuathail, S. Dalby, and P. Routledge (Eds.), *The Geopolitics Reader* (p. 20). Glasgow: Routledge.

Papritz, J. and Sappok, G. (1940). *Krakau. Hauptstadt des deutchen Generalgouvernments Polen.* Leipzig: Deutsche Städte-Führer im Osten.

Polish Ministry of Information. (1942). *The German New Order in Poland.* London: Hutchinson & Co.

Porter, B. (2001). "The Catholic Nation: Religion, Identity, and the Narratives of Polish History." *The Slavic and East European Journal,* 45(2): 289–299.

Rich, N. (1973). *Hitler's War Aims: Ideology, the Nazi State, and the Course of Expansion.* London: Andre Deutsch.

Rich, N. (1974). *Hitler's War Aims: The Establishment of the New Order.* London: Andre Deutsch.

Rose-Redwood, R. (2011). "Rethinking the Agenda of Political Toponymy." *ACME: An International E-Journal for Critical Geographies,* 10(1): 34–41.

Rose-Redwood, R., Alderman, D., and Azaryahu, M. (2010). "Geographies of Toponymic Inscription: New Directions in Critical Place-Name Studies." *Progress in Human Geography,* 34(4): 453–470.

Sappok, G. (1940). *Krakau. Hauptstadt des deutschen Generalgouvernments Polen (Kraków: Capital of the German General Government Poland).* Deutsche Städte-Führer im Osten. Leipzig: S. Hirzel.

Sharp, J. (2009). "Critical Geopolitics." In R. Kitchin and N. Thrift (Eds.), *The International Encyclopedia of Human Geography* (pp. 358–362). Amsterdam: Elsevier.

Stanisławska-Adamczewska, T. and Adamczewski, J. (2000). *Kraków, ulica imienia ...* Kraków: Oficyna Wydawnicza "BiK."

Stiperski, A., Lorber, L., Heršak, E., Ptaček, P., Górka, Z, Kołoś, A., Lončar, J., Faričić, J., Miličević, M., Vujaković, A., and Hruška, A. (2011). "Identity Through Urban Nomenclature: Eight Central European Cities. " *Geografisk Tidsskrift,* 111(2): 181–194.

Supranowicz, E. (1995). *Nazwy ulic Kraków a.* Kraków: Instytut Języka Polskiego, Polska Akademia Nauk (PAN).

Till, K. (1999). "Staging the Past: Landscape Designs, Cultural Identity and *Erinnerungspolitik* at Berlin's *Neue Wache.*" *Ecumene,* 6(3): 251–283.

Ward, J., Silberman, M., and Till, K. (2012). *Walls, Borders, Boundaries: Spatial and Cultural Practices in Europe.* New York: Berghahn Books.

Winchester, H., Kong, L., and Dunn, K. (2003). *Landscapes: Ways of Imagining the World.* Harlow: Pearson/Prentice Hall.

Young, C. and Light, D. (2001). "Place, National Identity and Post-Socialist Transformations: An Introduction." *Political Geography,* 20(8): 941–955.

Zamoyski, A. (2009). *Poland: A History.* New York: Hippocrene Books.

Zych, M. (2011). *Standardization of Geographical Names in Poland.* Working Paper No. 25, Commission on Standarisation of Geographical Names Outside of the Republic of Poland. Vienna: United Nations Group of Experts on Geographical Names.

8 Toponymic changes as temporal boundary-making

Street renaming in Leningrad/St. Petersburg

Anaïs Marin

Introduction

Renaming processes discursively demarcate borders between a selected past and a desired future, thereby producing—or destroying—meaningful referentials for self-identification in the present. Paraphrasing Mikhail Bakhtin, who coined the term *chronotopos* to designate the spatio-temporal matrix governing narratives and other linguistic constructions, I suggest that toponymic changes erect "chronotopic" borders in the cityscape.

This will be exemplified in studying place renaming in St. Petersburg, a city that emperor Peter the Great designed to be Russia's "window onto Europe" in 1703, and which subsequently became a beacon of post-Soviet reforms in the early-1990s (Joenniemi 2003). Meanwhile it was renamed twice: in 1914 it became Petrograd—a Russification of its German-connoted name, superstitiously decided by Tsar Nicholas II in the wake of the war. After Lenin's death in 1924, the Soviet regime renamed it Leningrad. Lenin himself was "purged" from the city's name in a popular referendum held on June 12, 1991—the day Russia (then, still the Russian Soviet Federative Socialist Republic, or RSFSR) democratically elected its first president, and St. Petersburg its mayor, Anatoly Sobchak. This was seen as a radical shift in the city's self-identity, one that alienated it from its other founding myth—Leningrad as the "cradle of the October Revolution." In recovering its maiden name, St. Petersburg reconnected its life story to some imagined Golden Age. In artificially putting the Soviet past into parenthesis, however, the 1991 name-change "walled in" part of the heritage constitutive of its identity.

The rival ideologies mobilized at the time have already been widely documented. Most studies insisted on the largely symbolic nature of the rupture between "old" (Soviet) and "new" (post-Soviet, or so it was thought) that renaming Leningrad embodied (Orttung 1995; Hellberg-Hirn 2003; Marin and Morozov 2004). Some romantically interpreted the return to St. Petersburg as a process of identity-recovering that put the city "better in tune with time" upon entering the era of market reforms and "returning" to Europe (Creuzberger, Kaiser, and Mannteufel 2000). According to others, however, renaming did not solve the schizophrenic contradiction implied by the subsequent dichotomization of historical time that returning an *old* name encapsulated. Joenniemi (2003, 606), for example, insists on the paradox of trying to build anew from the old entailed by choosing a renaming prism "burdened by a historical legacy containing powerful expressions of statism, centralism and securitization."

Changing street names, adding commemorative plaques, and tearing down monuments has often accompanied revolutions and regime transition, especially in Eastern Europe (Azaryahu 1997; Bell 1999; Robinson, Engelstoft, and Pobric, 2001; Hrytsak and Susak 2003; Light 2004; Gill 2005). Yet few scholars have analyzed toponymic changes—that is to say, the renaming of a city's districts, streets, and other landmarks of public space—in post-Soviet cities (Murray 2000).

By defining the act of renaming as a *temporal boundary-making practice* that demarcates Soviet and post-Soviet space, this chapter adopts a constructivist viewpoint. It sees borders as *processes* composed of a dynamic set of discourses, symbols, and institutional practices aiming to produce meaning for self-identification (Paasi 1998). Following geographers who imparted a critical shift to place name studies (Berg and Vuolteenaho 2009; Rose-Redwood, Alderman, and Azaryahu 2010), I argue that toponymic changes can be analyzed as an effort to erect *temporal* borders in the shared collective memory to (re)orient the way people situate themselves in the whirl of regime change. Methodologically, the proposed framework implies adding a fourth, *temporal* dimension to the traditional two- or three-dimensional cartographic interpretations of urban toponymies in order to consider the cityscape as a multi-layered chronotopos for selective memory-building (Rose-Redwood 2008a).[1] In drawing *normative* borders to alienate the Soviet past from the "new" St. Petersburg, the ongoing de/re-commemoration of selected historical figures "maps" ideological oppositions (conservative/reformist, autocratic/democratic, collective/individualistic) and geopolitical dichotomies (Us/Them, East/West, Russian/European, etc.) that serve the interests of competing political elites—more than those of ordinary citizens.

Toponymic changes: a theoretical framework

A rather marginal field of research within political geography and even urban studies, onomastics and more specifically the study of toponymy (literarily— place names) and odonymy (street names) is a valuable instrument to understand how a polity memorializes its past and envisages its future.

Deciphering the city-text

Originally, toponymists and cartographers made inventories of place names to study their etymological origins or standardize topographic appellations. Cultural studies and research on the "toponymic silencing" of indigenous cultures in colonial contexts later popularized *textual approaches* of place name changes (Yeoh 1992). This approach proved pertinent to study the waves of renaming that followed the establishment and the demise of the Soviet Union: in most ethnically non-Russian republics, renaming obviously amounted to an ideological (de) colonization of memory (Murray 2000; Saparov 2003; Sereda 2009).

Other case studies showed that in urban contexts the sum of commemorative street names forms a specific "city-text" that can be "read"—hence, the metaphor of the cityscape as a "palimpsest" (Parkhurst-Ferguson 1988, 392). In the footsteps of Walter Benjamin, a *flânerie* type of ethnographic investigation can help decipher the various archaeological layers of meanings superimposed over time in the cityscape. This way the "official memory reservoir" displayed on street signs reveals how the past is selectively constructed as a narrative in which only figures deemed heroic by the acting regime are "canonized"—at least until their names are eventually "purged" by the successor regime or occupant, thus spatially disrupting the linearity of historical time (Azaryahu 1992, 353–354).

Toponyms are signifiers of wider societal trends that mirror the ideological purposes of a dominant culture: odonymic changes can thus be interpreted as a purposeful way of institutionalizing an official narrative legitimizing authority. *Discursive methods* can therefore be mobilized to analyze how place names, like any other textual artifact, effectively appropriate and organize semiotic spaces. Specific to post-communist Europe in this respect is that instead of helping situate people in space, sequences of name changes—in 1918, 1945, and 1989—altogether produced a contradictory "text" that confused dwellers and set generations against one another.

Renaming as temporal boundary-making

Although it touches upon the procedural aspects of renaming, the main focus of this chapter is on the *boundary-making* dimension of renaming. It departs from the Bourdieusian assumption that power struggles are inherent to the very process of naming social reality (Bourdieu 1982). If the performative character of naming is the precondition for any hegemony, place naming is in essence "a political practice of power over space" (Pinchevski and Torgovnik 2002). Place-name-givers struggle to embed cultural signification in the political geographies of *public memory*, manipulating founding myths to produce dominant cultural understandings of cityhood. If, as Bourdieu puts it, "the language of authority never governs without the collaboration of those it governs" (Bourdieu 1991, 113), then social actors ultimately set the border between the acceptable and the unacceptable in terms of memorialization. In other words, new place names must be incorporated and reiterated in popular linguistic practices in order to fulfill their political mission of rooting new ideologies in the mindset of citizens.

The cityscape of St. Petersburg is an interesting "realm of memory" in this respect, because the text inscribed on its physical map in the form of place names catalyzes the space *and* time segments of its multi-layered identity. All through the twentieth century, the city faced implacable contradictions between its self-representations as the (dethroned) European capital of imperial Russia *and* the iconic "cradle of Revolution" of the (now bygone) Soviet Union. In other words, renaming waves made the city's soul sway between the "Northern Venice" myth and the "Leningrad city-hero" myth. Similar to other cities affected by renaming and where contested inscriptions are rearticulated "through the reiterative processes of subsequent performances and counter-performances" (Rose-Redwood 2008b, 882), in St. Petersburg attempts at imposing new hegemonic toponymies face popular resistance. Elderly people who still call themselves "Leningraders" are the most unwilling to use official names in their daily practices: many state their political attachment to the values of the communist past in continuing to call places by their Soviet-era names. In ongoing debates over toponymic changes, the time boundary erected to materialize the latest regime change is therefore still under challenge.

In Russia's second capital, toponymic changes in the 1990s restaged St. Petersburg as the *European* capital of a *new* Russia eager to catch up with the historical time from which it was disconnected in 1917. Hence renaming can be seen here as a *rite of institution* or, using the terminology coined by Maoz Azaryahu for East Berlin, as a *ritual of revolution* (Azaryahu 1997, 479). And as Bourdieu has argued, one of the significant aspects of name changes "is not so much the ritual transition (*rite de passage*) as *the line itself*, because the latter assigns social properties to the categories 'before' and 'after' that it defines and tries to legitimise" (1991, 118, emphasis added). Chronotopic boundary-making is thus inherent to any ritual of toponymic inscription in that renaming also implies legitimizing borders between "Us" and "Them" in time (old/new regime) as well as in space (colonial/indigenous, national/foreign, East/West, etc.).

The following section provides a chronological account of the shifts that affected the discursive construction of normative borders between "old" (conservative/imperialistic—deemed bad) and "new" (reformist/cosmopolitan—i.e., good) in the city's toponymy over the twentieth century. In highlighting the political background of these changes, it illustrates how successive regimes attempted to outcast the founding myths and heroes of the previous regime from official history records. Renaming was therefore a strategy to legitimize the artificial *cordon sanitaire* that each new regime erected to abstract itself from time (the past, be it Tsarist or Soviet) and situate citizens in geopolitical space (Europe/USSR).

Toponymic cleansing in Leningrad

The history of Central and Eastern Europe, with its frequent regime changes and border shifts, is rich in place name changes. The most radical waves of renaming occurred twice in the twentieth century: with the establishment of communist regimes (after 1917 and after WWII) and following their collapse in 1989–1991. Each swing of the pendulum amounted to a normative attempt at reconfiguring people's relations to historically embedded ideologies and geopolitical self-representations. As this section will highlight, waves of toponymic "cleansing"[2] in Russia's second capital followed a rhythm of their own.[3]

The red wave (1918–1924)

In his landmark studies on the politics of street naming, Azaryahu has shown how "in a revolutionary context the renaming of streets … is an act of political propaganda with immense proclamative value and public resonance" (1996, 318). The movement is a dialectic one, he claims: renaming is both "a celebration of triumph and a mechanism for settling scores with the vanquished regime" (Azaryahu 1996, 318). New national histories are constructed, while the achievements of the previous regime are discredited and thrown into the dustbin of history. The re-invention of history was part of the scientific mythology of communism. Rewriting city-texts was but one of the "rituals of revolution" that accompanied and attempted to institutionalize the proclaimed beginning of a new era (Young and Light 2001, 944).

The Soviet regime was particularly good at erasing past names from the toponymic landscape, and it even invented an "anthroponymous Newspeak":[4] by the end of *perestroika* half of the country's pre-1917 place names had been "Sovietized." Although most renamings occurred between 1918 and 1924, Murray (2000) contends that other phases in the construction of communism furthered the "toponomycide": deportations under Stalin (of Caucasian peoples, Crimean Tatars, and ethnic Germans, among others); the "incorporation" and Russification of territories seized during WWII (such as Königsberg/Kaliningrad); and under Khrushchev "rural consolidation" (the amalgamation of collective farms). With de-Stalinization (1953–62) and the end of the cult of personality after Brezhnev's death, a reverse trend at "de-Sovietizing" place names occurred that culminated with *perestroika* (Murray 2000).

St. Petersburg was particularly affected by the name-giving mania of Russian leaders. Built from scratch on an untamed landscape, as goes the legend, in 1703 the city was like a white page, void of socially embedded place names. Two centuries later, its status as the "cradle of three revolutions" predestined it to be a laboratory for the Bolsheviks to implement their materialistic refurbishing of history. By Lenin's death in 1924, at least a third of the city's 1,500 place names had been changed. The city-text was purged of its imperial, aristocratic, and religious toponyms, which were replaced by names commemorating the founding fathers and myths of the Bolshevik Revolution. As elsewhere, the new regime imposed its rhetoric in a multitude of slogan-type toponymies (Socialist, Equality, Proletariat dictatorship, etc.), glorified famous anti-monarchist terrorists (Khalturin, Kalyaev), and communist ideologists (Marx, Bakunin, Kuybyshev). In 1918, the "Field of Mars" (*Marsovoe pole*) was re-baptized as the "Square to the Victims of the Revolution." Several landmarks of the imperial past followed suit, such as "Garden street" *(Sadovaya ul.)* renamed "Third of July Street" in memory of the violent events that took place there in 1917, whereas the "Palace embankment" (*Dvortsovaya nab.*) was renamed "Ninth of January embankment" in memory of the victims of the 1905 uprising.

As Hellberg-Hirn (2003, 125) maintains, such a "fever of renaming was pure word magic, firmly rooted in the belief that a new name would help exorcise the old evil and bring closer the desired radiant future." This holds true as well for the second wave of toponymic changes that affected Leningrad and other "martyr" cities at the height of the Stalinist era.

The catharsis wave (1941–1952)

The Nazi invasion prompted a wide upsurge against individuals and toponyms of German origin throughout the USSR. In Leningrad, place names given in the imperial times after a German home owner, merchant, or scientist were thus "purged" from the city map. The first victims of this de-Prussianization were "Palmenbach square," named after a headmistress of the Smolny institute, and "Rosa Luxemburg street." Russianization later targeted Peterhof (and its derived toponymies), renamed Petrodvorets in 1944. This inaugurated a "catharsis-type" wave of name changes, whereby erasing negatively connoted place names was thought to ward off bad luck, or at least lift up the spirits of the besieged Leningrad population.

On January 13, 1944, almost simultaneously with the launching of the final counter-attack that two weeks later would lead to the full lifting of the Leningrad blockade, the executive committee of the city soviet of workers' deputies decided to remove from the city map 20 toponyms given after 1918. The justification for "restoring previous appellations" was that the pre-Revolution names "were tightly linked with the city's history ... durably rooted in the habits of the population, and, as such, better suited to ensure swift urban circulation."[5] The square named after revolutionary Moisey Uritsky (*Ploshchad' Uritskovo*) thus became "Palace square" (*Dvortsovaya pl.*) again, while other prominent communist figures that had become *personae non grata* in official collective memory (such as Jaures, Vorovsky, Plekhanov, Mussorgsky, and Nakhimson) were de-commemorated. The most symbolically loaded name restitution was that of *Nevsky prospekt*, which Leningraders apparently never got accustomed to calling "October 25th avenue" anyway.

The suffering blockaders endured during the 900 days of siege and bombings may explain why place names remindful of painful events (July 3, January 9) were on this list. Purging Leningrad from "bloodstained" labels resulted in crossing-out many names of high ideological resonance, such as "Proletarian Victory street" or "Square in memory of the Victims of the Revolution." The colour *red* itself suffered from toponymic cleansing: "Red Commanders' avenue" recovered the name "Izmail prospekt" that it had until 1923 (reconnecting it with the nearby Izmail Church) and "Red Square" was renamed "Alexander Nevsky square" in 1952.

This "catharsis-type" wave of name changes can be interpreted along the same lines as Stalin's wartime decision to lift the ban on churches: it helped to galvanize the Soviet people around the war effort, by disavowing some founding landmarks and symbols of Bolshevism. In other words, this war-time wave of name changes, which was the appendage of "martyr-cities" (Leningrad, Stalingrad, Brest), can be seen as a first step towards toponymic *de-Sovietization*. The fact that it occurred in the 1940s explains why Leningrad did not experience as massive a de-Stalinization of place names as other cities did in the Soviet Union following Khrushchev's November 1961 decree and in the rest of the socialist camp already after Stalin's death (Colton 1995, 813; Light, Nicolae, and Suditu 2002).[6] In Leningrad, the next major wave of de-commemoration and name-restitution therefore came only with *perestroika*.

The third wave: popular claims for de-Sovietization (1989–1990)

This wave affected the whole country, especially Union and ethnic republics where name-change claims were presented as a legitimate decolonization ("de-Russification") of public spaces. It all started in 1987 when linguists, editors of literary journals, writers, and academics began to express their anger over the "loss" of Russia's cultural and religious heritage to Sovietized names. In one of the rare monographs dedicated to renaming in the USSR, Murray (2000) details how these activists gained official status in forming the Toponymic Council (1988) and organizing two All-Union Toponymic Conferences (in April 1989 and June 1991) where demands for place name restoration, couched in the official rhetoric of Gorbachev's *new thinking*, were made.

In Leningrad, renaming claims were voiced by the reformist and democratic opposition, which had become dominant in the local political arena. The trend was simultaneous with the awakening of an embryonic civil society ready to defy local authorities to defend St. Petersburg's pre-revolutionary cultural heritage, such as the Hôtel d'Angleterre, the planned destruction of which was prevented in 1987 by the first ever popular mobilization of its kind in the USSR (Orttung 1995, 44–47).

The inhabitants of the Zhdanov district on Vassilievsky Island followed suit and succeeded in having their district recover its original name, *Primorskij rayon* (Maritime district) on February 20, 1989. This was a turning point in the political history of renaming, since it amounted to a victory of the people's will, democratically expressed in petitions relayed by *Leningradskaya Pravda* over the previous weeks. The change was accepted by the executive committee of the city soviet (*Lenispolkom*) and formally endorsed *ex post* by the Supreme Soviet of the USSR on March 30. This precedent actually triggered the third wave of renaming in Leningrad: a week after the symbolic anti-Zhdanov putsch of Primorskij rayon dwellers, the city soviet gave in to popular pressure and issued a decision "On the naming of streets and objects of local subordination" that gave back their historical name to several streets, bridges, and districts of Leningrad.

Leningrad thus started "reconstructing" its toponymy several years before the idea of renaming the city itself was aired. By 1991, the debates were closely intertwined and nourished each other. However, whereas the romantic idea—and Sobchak's winning campaign slogan—of "returning to St. Petersburg its maiden name" was popular mainly among the middle-class intelligentsia close to the spheres of arts, culture, and literature, claims for odonymic changes emerged earlier and from the grassroots on the initiative of inhabitants themselves.

The fourth wave (1991 and onwards): towards a politicization of renaming

Street renaming accelerated from Spring 1990 onwards, following the first democratic election of the municipal soviet of people's deputies. Until 1993, the local legislative assembly was competent for handling popular requests. It issued a number of favorable decisions that substantially "re-peterburganized" the city-text (Table 8.1). In September 1991, the newly elected mayor Anatoly Sobchak appointed a Toponymic Commission to define basic renaming principles and channel propositions submitted by local dwellers, associations defending the local architectural heritage, and district representatives. The task of this consultative body was immense, and many claims could not be satisfied without simultaneously depriving other inhabitants requiring the same place name. In October 1991, the Toponymic Commission positively met popular suggestions brought to its attention via the local press regarding the most urgent cases: de-commemorating the 23 remaining People's Commissars, prioritizing the most cruel of them (Dzerzhinskij, Rakovskij, Tolmachev).

After July 1993, the tempo of renamings slowed down. Out of the 40 name changes that the Commission submitted to the city hall in 1997, only nine were endorsed, and by 2001 this figure was down to only one renaming.[7] According to some critics, the main reason for this deceleration is that issues relating to commemorative renaming became more politicized. Many argue that they were "captured" by Smolny (the headquarters of the municipal administration) after the 1994 institutional crisis that virtually made the local assembly impotent in front of the new executive (the city governor).

Interestingly enough, toponymic changes came back on the agenda in the second half of the 2000s, apparently following the creation, on the initiative of publicist Yurij Bondarenko, of the "Vozvrashchenie" (Restitution) Foundation. Its aim is to lobby the return of historical place names, notably those given after Orthodox churches, throughout the whole country. Out of the 32 proposals that this Foundation submitted to the Toponymic Commission of St. Petersburg in 2007, the authorities endorsed only four. In September 2010, then governor Valentina Matvienko rejected all renaming proposals on the ground that name changes would be too costly (Table 8.2).

Legend for Tables 8.1 and 8.2

TIME OF RENAMING		PLACE RENAMED		
The year in parenthesis in Tables 8.1 and 8.2 refers to these dates of name-changes (when known)		*The abbreviations used in the tables are transcribed and translated as follows*		
1918	October 10, 1918	bul.	*bul'var*	bd.	boulevard
1924	January 22, 1924	lin.	*linija*	la.	lane
1944	January 13, 1944	mo.	*most*	br.	bridge
1952	*unknown*	nab.	*naberezhnaja*	emb.	embankment
1989	February 27, 1989	per.	*pereulok*	imp.	impasse
1991	October 4, 1991	pl.	*ploshchad'*	sq.	square
1993	July 7, 1993	pr.	*prospekt*	ave.	avenue
1994	September 8, 1994	ul.	*ulitsa*	st.	street
2007	August 14, 2007				

In both tables the first column provides a transliteration of the Russian place-name (in italic), and the second its literal translation in English.

Table 8.1 The fourth wave of street renamings in Leningrad/St. Petersburg (1991–onward)

COMMUNIST NAME		IMPERIAL AND POST-SOVIET NAME	
Sad Trudiashchikhsya (1920)	Workers' Garden	*Admiralteyskij sad* (1989)	Admiralty Garden
→ *Sad im. Gor'kogo* (1936)	→ (named after Gorky)	→ *Aleksandrovskij sad* (1997)	→ Alexander Garden
Komissarovskaya ul. (1918)	Commissar st.	*Gorokhovaya ul.* (1991)	Gorokhov st.
→ *Ul. Dzerzhinskovo* (1927)	→ Dzerzhinsky st.		
Krasnaya ul. (1918)	Red st.	*Galernaya ul.* (1991)	Galley st.
Bul. Profsoyuzov (1918)	Trade Unions bd.	*Konnogvardeyskij bul.* (1991)	Horse Guard's bd.
Most Ravenstva (1918)	Equality bridge	*Troitskij most* (1991)	Trinity bridge
→ *Kirovskij most* (1934)	→ Kirov bridge		
Ul. Krasnykh Zor' (1918)	Red Dawns st.	*Kamennoostrovskij pr.* (1991)	Stone Island ave.
→ *Kirovskij pr.* (1934)	→ Kirov ave.		
Pr. Maiorova (1923)	Major's ave.	*Voznesenskij pr.* (1991)	Ascension ave.
Proletarskij per. (1923)	Proletarian's imp.	*Grafskij per.* (1991)	Count imp.
→ *Ul. Marii Ulyanovoy* (1964)	→ Maria Ulyanova st.		
Pr. Ogorodnikova (1923)	Gardener ave.	*Rizhskij pr.* (1991)	Riga ave.
Pl. Revolyutsij (1923)	Revolution sq.	*Troitskaya pl.* (1991)	Trinity sq.
Pr. Karla Marksa (1923)	Karl Marx ave.	*Bol'shoy Sampsonievskij pr.*	Grand Samson ave.
Ul. Krasnoy Konnitsy (1923)	Red Cavalry st.	*Kavalergardskaya ul.* (1991)	Horse Guardsman st.
Pr. Maksima Gor'kovo (1932)	Maxim Gorky ave.	*Kronverkskij pr.* (1991)	Crownwork st.
Pr. Yunogo Proletariya (1923)	Young Proletarian ave.	*Staro-Petergofskij pr.* (1991)	Old Peterhof ave.
→ *Pr. Gaza* (1933)	→ Gaz ave.		
Ul. Brodskovo (1940)	Brodsky st.	*Mikhailovskaya ul.* (1991)	Michael st.
Pl. Mira (1952)	Peace sq.	*Sennaya sq.* (1991)	Hay sq.
Ul. Gogolya (1902)	Gogol st.	*Malaja Morskaja* (1993)	Small Maritime
Ul. Gertsena (1920)	Herzen st.	*Bol'shaya Morskaja* (1993)	Grand Maritime
Nab. Krasnovo Flota (1918)	Red Fleet Emb.	*Admiraltel'skaya nab.* (1994)	Admiralty emb.
Ul. Plekhanova (1923)	Plekhanov st.	*Kazanskaya ul.* (1998)	Kazan st.
Ul. Saltykov-Shchedrina (1932)	Saltykov-Shchedrin st.	*Ul. Kirochnaja* (1998)	Pickaxe st.
Mo. Leytenanta Schmidta (1918)	Lieutenant Schmidt br.	*Blagoveshchenskij most* (2007)	Annunciation bridge
Pl. Dekabristov (1923)	Decembrists' sq.	*Senatskaya pl.* (2008)	Senate sq.

Table 8.2 The wave that was not: un-renamed places with imperial or religious connotations in Leningrad/St. Petersburg

IMPERIAL TIME NAME	SPARED COMMUNIST TIME NAME	(CURRENT NAME)
A. Consensual name		
Kalashnikovskij pr. (1871)	Pr. Bakunina (1918)	Bakunin ave.
Panteleymonovskaya ul. (1777)	Ul. Dekabrista Pestelya (1923)	Decembrist Pestel st.
B. Selected for renaming by the Toponymic Commission (change not endorsed by the City Administration)		
Bol'shaya Dvoryanskaya ul.	ul. Derevenskoy Bednoty (1918) → ul. Kuybysheva (1936)	Poor Peasants' st → Kuybyshev st.
Blagoveshchenskaya pl. (1830)	Pl. Truda (1918)	Labour sq.
Voskresenskaya nab.	Nab. Robesp'era (1923)	Robespierre emb.
Znamenskaya ul. (1845)	Ul. Vosstaniya (1918)	Insurrection st.
1-10aja Rozhdestvenskaya ul.	1-10aja Sovetskaya ul. (1923)	1st-10th Soviet streets
Bol'shaya Spasskaya ul. (1720)	Ul. Krasnogo kursanta (1923)	Red Cadet st.
Preobrazhenskaya ul. (1858)	Ul. Radishcheva (1935)	Radischev st.
Voznesenskij per.	Krasnogradskij per.	Krasnograd (Red city) imp.
Matveevskaya ul.	Ul. Lenina	Lenin st.
Vozdvizhenskaya ul. (1821)	Ul. Tyushina (1923)	Tyuschin st.
Preobrazhenskaya Polkovaya ul. →	Ul. 27ogo Fevralya (1917) → ul. Marata (1918)	27th of February [1917] st. → Marat st.
Nikolaevskaya ul. (1856)		
C. Additional renaming proposals made by the "Restitution Foundation" (suggestion not endorsed by the Toponymic Commission)		
Ofitserskaya ul. (1740s)	Ul. Dekabristov (1918)	Decembrists' st.
Nikolaevskaya nab. (1855)	Nab. Leytenanta Schmidta (1918)	Lieutenant Schmidt emb.
Uspenskaya pl. (1739) →	Pl. Turgenieva (1923)	Turgenev sq.
Pokrovskaya pl. (1822)		
Voskresenskij pr.	Pr. Chernyshevskogo (1923)	Chernyshevskij ave.
10-aya Roty ul. (1770s)	10-aya Krasnoarmeyskie ul. (1923)	10th Red Army st.
Estlyandskij most (1914)	Most Stenka Razina (1923)	Stepan Razin bridge
Tserkovnyj per. (1836)	Per. Radishcheva (1925)	Radischev imp.
Simbirskaya ul. (1858)	Ul. Komsomola (1927)	Communist Youth st.
Lichtenbergskij most (1914)	Krasnooktyabr'skij most (1958)	Red October bridge

Great nobleman st.

Annunciation sq.
Resurrection emb.
[Prophet's] Banner st.
1st-10th Nativity streets
Grand Saviour's st.
Transfiguration st.
Ascension imp.
Matthew st.
Holy Cross Day st.
Transfiguration Regiment st. →
Nicholas st.

Officer's st.
Nicholas emb.
Assumption [Dormition] sq. →
Intercession sq.
Resurrection ave.
10th Squadron st.
Estland bridge
Church imp.
Simbirsk st.
Lichtenberg bridge

Patterns of renaming in post-Soviet St. Petersburg

Building on the findings presented above, the purpose of this section is to examine in which cases the most ideologically loaded place names of St. Petersburg were de-Sovietized, when, and where—and if they were not, to try explaining why a place retained its Soviet-era denomination. Three patterns emerge from this analysis.

A democratic process

Renaming is usually a matter for political elites: a "battleground for control over political space and symbols," the city-text is seldom affected by the preferences of regular citizens (Palonen 2008). This arguably makes toponymic changes in post-*perestroika* St. Petersburg all the more exceptional.

In the 1990s, street renaming unfolded in a bottom-up way: initiatives came from inhabitants and were almost always accepted by the Toponymic Commission which lobbied the name change with city authorities. The fact that changes resulted from a civic mobilization democratically expressed through opinion polls, local referenda, or readers' letters in newspapers is a pattern typical of Leningrad/St. Petersburg. In the second capital, toponymic changes were therefore initially decided more democratically than in Moscow, where most Soviet-era toponyms were changed by the municipal authorities overnight and almost without prior consultations (Gill 2005).

Petersburgans successfully mobilized to also *oppose* changing names given in Soviet times, but which had acquired a positive connotation to their ear. For instance, the legislative assembly and the Toponymic Commission were in favor of giving back their original, eighteenth century appellations to some streets named after Decembrists. Popular protest led to maintaining the names given in 1918 by the Bolsheviks to glorify these early revolution-makers: "Decembrists' square" (*ploshchad' Dekabristov*), called "Senate square" in the imperial times, was therefore spared—at least until 2008 when the above-mentioned Restitution Foundation succeeded in having its name returned.

In suburban areas where new streets were baptized in the 1970s with relatively neutral or positive slogan-type names such as the "Avenue of Enthusiasts" (*Pr. Entuziastov*) or the "Courage square" (*pl. Muzhestva*), inhabitants did not claim any name changes, nor did the municipality impose any. One can therefore assess that toponymic changes, similar in this to the renaming of St. Petersburg city itself, were the result of a fairly democratic decision-making process, at least initially.

Back to the future: the pre-Soviet past as a horizon

In Russian, the term used for name change claims is usually *vozvrashchenie* (restitution) and not *pereimenovanie* (renaming)—the latter qualifying cases when Soviet-era names are replaced by totally new ones, which seldom happened in Leningrad.[8] The use of a term meaning "returning" or "coming back to" has an important psychological and legal sub-text: *vozvrashchenie* also refers to restitution claims of the Orthodox Church, Soviet successor states, and victims of cultural lootings. It implies a notion of rehabilitation to right a past wrong. It also indicates a rather *conservative* stance in relation to the kind of future that claimants want to build.

The question of which restoration point to choose when visiting the past, whom to honor and whom to disgrace, was not a bone of contention in post-Soviet St. Petersburg: most toponymic changes amounted to a "de-Sovietization" and a "re-Petersburganization" of the city-text. Upon "ousting" the remaining red heroes and slogans, name-givers did not display much imagination or desire for innovation. They usually favored a return to traditional, imperial-era designations. In the city center, about half of the contested street names were changed already in October 1991 and almost all recovered their pre-1917 appellation. One of the paradoxical implications of this trend is that even famous figures of St. Petersburg's buoyant nineteenth-century literary life such as Gogol and Herzen were purged from the city-text in 1993, when streets named after them (in 1902 and 1920) were given back their imperial-era names—*Malaya* and *Bol'shaya Morskaya* (Small and Grand Maritime streets), respectively.

One explanation for this dichotomization of debates is that the 1990s wave of toponymic changes was greatly influenced by the *air du temps* of the campaign preceding the 1991 referendum over the city's name. Disputes articulated then around two antagonistic discourses opposing the partisans of Lenin(grad) and Peter(burg), in other words two irreconcilable ideologies incarnated by the rival "fathers" of the city.[9]

For the partisans of renaming, such as mayor Anatoly Sobchak, associating the name "St. Petersburg" with Europeanness was a very useful slogan in support of reforms. It offered an ideal semiotic "packaging" for the city's proclaimed post-Soviet identity at a time when authorities were ambitious to attract foreign investments, Western tourists, and international attention. However, choosing Peter the Great as a "marker" for the city's rebirth, and maintaining the prefix "Saint" that linked it to its patron the Apostle Peter, determined the tracks of time and space within which the "new" St. Petersburg could evolve (Morozov 2002). In limiting the horizon of possibilities, it risked the city becoming "trapped in time" (Joenniemi 2003).[10]

One manifestation of this "entrapment" is the dispute regarding the Marinsky Theater (built in honor of Empress Maria, the wife of Alexander II), which in 1934 had been renamed Kirov Theatre of Ballet and Opera (Joenniemi and Morozov 2003). When in the summer of 1990 prominent representatives of the local cultural scene started calling for the Kirov's renaming, a polemic emerged. Many criticized the choice to return the theater its maiden name, which was eventually officialized in 1992, for furthering the aristocratic elitism of early ballet traditions. The wishes of inhabitants, who advocated honoring the more popular figure of composer Pyotr Tchaikovsky, were also left unsatisfied.

The breach with the Soviet era performed by place name changes after 1991 is thus far from consensual or complete. As Hellberg-Hirn (2003, 140) argues, "the city's toponymy on the whole sways betwixt and between historical periods, thus creating imaginary islands where imprints of a bygone Imperial civilisation amalgamate with remnants of the Soviet past." These different periods coexist and sometimes confusingly overlap on the cityscape, especially when local dwellers keep using the old place name—a conservative "counter-performance" that limits the political scope of renaming.

The wave that was not: un-renamed toponymies

Strangely enough, several ideologically loaded names given during the Soviet era remained in the post-1991 city-text. Although deriving a clear pattern from this would require a more in-depth analysis, some hypotheses as to why these toponymies were not "de-Sovietized" can be proposed.

The first troubling observation is that despite the fact that the Orthodox Church has a growing influence in Russian politics—notably on memory issues—most religious-connoted toponymies were not returned. One notable exception is that "Trinity" (*Troitskaya*) was returned in 1991 to the square and bridge that bore this name before the Revolution. On the contrary, place names referring to the Savior, the Ascension, the Resurrection, the Intercession, Saints, and so on, have not found their way back on the city map—yet their "restitution" is a central issue in the toponymic debates that resumed in 2010.

The issue is far from consensual, as illustrated by the current dispute over returning the adjective *Rozhdestvenskaya* ("Nativity") to the nine consecutive *Sovetskaya* ("Soviet") streets. Most Petersburgans seem attached to this name, possibly because soviets—workers' councils that pre-date Bolshevik rule—play a founding role in the city's self-image as a modern democratic polity.

Another explanation for this non-choice of pre-1917 religious toponyms is that the very building after which the place was named does not exist anymore. Hence *Ploshchad' Vosstaniya* ("Insurrection square") and the adjacent eponymous street retained the names they were given in 1918: the *Znamenskaya* church (Banner of the Prophet Church) after which they had been named was destroyed in the 1930s and never reconstructed. It could also be that many Russian religious terms are difficult to read, pronounce, and remember for foreigners. Since in the early 1990s the city's development strategy relied on attracting Western tourists, this euphonic concern might well explain the disdain for old religious names.

The second category of un-changed toponymies is that of district names. Their resistance to the wind of post-Soviet change actually distinguishes St. Petersburg from Moscow, where all district names with Soviet connotations were wiped out already in the early 1990s (Colton 1995). Out of the 15 districts of St. Petersburg, on the contrary, only five of the ten named after a Soviet hero or slogan were renamed.[11] In superimposing the map of city districts on socio-electoral maps of the 1993, 1995, and 1996 elections, one sees that the un-renamed districts with Soviet ideological resonance actually host the factories that made the fame of Leningrad (e.g., "Kirov," "Bolshevik," "Red Triangle," and "Leningrad Metallurgy"). Knowing that blue collar workers and pensioners were also the most vehemently opposed to de-commemorating Lenin from the city's name itself, the fact that they did not fight for de-Sovietizing the name of their factories or compounds should come as no surprise.

This leads us to the third observation, which concerns the names of metro stations. With the exception of "Peace square" (*pl. Mira*), none of the metro stations was renamed.[12] Regardless of the newly constructed stations, the map of the St. Petersburg metropolitan thus remained almost unchanged: in the central and northern parts of the city, metro stations bear the name of pre-Soviet toponyms (*Nevskij prospekt, Petrogradskaya, Chernaya rechka*). Conversely, in the southern, blue collar outskirts, they retained the original "red slogan" appellations given at the time of their construction after (un-renamed) adjacent streets, places, and factories (*Leninskij prospekt, Prospekt Veteranov, Prospekt Bol'shevikov, Park Pobedy, Kirovskij zavod, Elektrosila, Proletarskaya*, etc.). The conservation of these names with high ideological resonance contrasts, again, with the situation in Moscow, where eight of the ten "Soviet-labeled" metro stations were renamed. This finding converges with the conclusions of Gill (2005, 490–491) about renaming in Moscow that "the closer to the center of the city ... the greater the changes, the further away from the center, the fewer the changes." As for canals, by far the most famous landmarks of the "Northern Venice," it is worth noting that they were left untouched throughout the renaming waves: apart from the Griboedov canal, renamed in 1923, no waterway of St. Petersburg has ever changed name in the past 150 years.

Lastly and quite understandably, very few places were baptized or renamed after the heroes, myths, or slogans of the *perestroika* and the painful reforms that followed. With the exception of Andrey Sakharov, whose name was given to the square facing the Academy of Sciences' Library in 1989, none of the representatives of the reformist wave of the past decades—such as late mayor Anatoly Sobchak— is commemorated in St. Petersburg.

Conclusion

Recurrent in the history of renamings is the logic of opposing and removing the past in order to build a brighter future: in proclaiming new truths, which is a constitutive element of political change, each new regime sets the boundaries of self/other dichotomies *in space* and *in time*. Any place renaming therefore mobilizes the allegories of murder and rebirth. The materialist-communist belief that the course of history could be bent by permanent revolution thus pushed the Bolshevik and later the Soviet authorities to conduct both a physical purge of internal enemies (deportations) and a semiotic cleansing of aristocratic, Orthodox, bourgeois, and ethno-national symbols.

In 1991, when Leningrad gave in to St. Petersburg, discourses favorable to the return of the city's maiden name oftentimes contained an Oedipian subtext: voters deceived by the chimeras of communist propaganda had to symbolically "kill" Lenin, the iconic father of the Revolution, in order for "the city of Peter" to be "born again."[13] Since Petersburg was reborn for the third time on that occasion, although not anymore as the country's capital city, its renaming was also interpreted as a way of closing the 70-year parenthesis of Soviet estrangement incarnated by its traditional rival, Moscow (Spivak 1998; Vendina 2000).

As we have seen, in Leningrad the first wave of toponymic de-Sovietization actually started already in 1944 and amounted to purging several places of negatively connoted names which had failed to penetrate daily linguistic practices. Name changes decided in 1991 were less consensual: they gave way to heated debates among citizens and between the intelligentsia and the bureaucracy. Our archaeological inquiry into the chronotopic layers of the city-text revealed that the choice was oftentimes a dichotomous one, between maintaining the Soviet name and *restoring* its predecessor. In other words, Petersburgans are so attached to the past that a "third way" was very seldom an option: this chilliness somehow led them to reject platforms for entering a *post-modern* age of self-identification, thus leaving St. Petersburg's cityhood nostalgically "trapped" in a lost imperial Age d'Or (Morozov 2002).

The "toponymic" lens indeed provides a fecund frame to analyze ideological changes imposed onto collective memory in times of regime transition as well as the "zigzags" of identity-building that result from such shifts. The naming of places, streets, and other landmarks is probably the most widespread way for political leaders to situate people *in time* during radical political changes: name-givers usually try to construct clearly demarcated identities in selecting toponymic inscriptions that are "associated intertextually with larger cultural narratives and stories" (Rose-Redwood, Alderman, and Azaryahu 2010, 459). In the case of Leningrad/St. Petersburg, the competing narratives mobilized for or against street renaming bear a clear ideological but also a *geopolitical* subtext, one relating to the position of the city, and of post-Soviet Russia more generally, within and towards Western/secular Europe.

This chapter has thus suggested new perspectives for the study of toponymic change as a symbolic boundary-making practice, whereby the shifting of time borders between "past," "present," or even "future" served the political strategy of re-assessing a city's cultural and political identity. The enactment of chronotopic borders in the semiotic cityscape of Leningrad/St. Petersburg was never free of contradictions, however.

In erecting time boundaries and putting whole eras in brackets, toponymic changes in Leningrad/St. Petersburg *destroyed* as much as they produced meaning: the original sin of "purging" the past actually resulted in erasing meaningful landmarks for identification in both time (collective memory) and space (the public arena). As Hellberg-Hirn (2003, 124) observes, in St. Petersburg "the ebb-and-flow of naming activities has mirrored the unfolding of the city in space and time," but the new pattern emerging from the last waves of renaming looks rather "inconsistent and fuzzy," and is usually perceived as such by local dwellers and foreigners alike.

Following the removal of Soviet markers of identity and their replacement with landmarks resuscitated from the imperial past, and illustrative of a conservative type of Europeanity, the temporal boundary-making dynamics inferred by toponymic changes somehow *lost* Petersburgans in translation: trapped in old dichotomies, these "temporal borderlanders" now seem deprived of the symbolic access to post-modern geopolitics that renaming the cityscape anew could have implied.

Notes

1 Maoz Azaryahu was the first to methodologically address the "shift from history to geography" entailed by the "semantic displacements effected by using street names for commemorative purposes," in his study on concurrent Nazi and Prussian memories in post-War Berlin (Azaryahu 2009, 53).
2 The term is borrowed from Rose-Redwood, Alderman, and Azaryahu (2010, 460).
3 This archaeological screening of the city-text was conducted by systematically comparing city maps dating from 1978, 1987, 1993, 2002, and 2008, respectively. For the content analysis of place names and the historical contextualization of name changes, two Petersburgan encyclopaedic dictionaries were consulted (Gorbachevich and Khablo 2002; Sindalovskij 2002) as well as the topography section of the online *Encyclopaedia of St. Petersburg* (www.encspb.ru).
4 This Orwellian metaphor was coined by philologists Vladimir Neroznak and Mikhail Gorbanevsky, who, in 1988, established the Toponymic Council, a body placed under the auspices of the Soviet Fund for Culture chaired by Academic Dmitry Likhachev (Murray 2000, 21, 30).
5 Reshenie "O vosstanovlenii prezhnikh naimenovanij nekotorykh ulits, prospektov, naberezhnykh i ploshchadej goroda Leningrada ot 13/01/1944" [Decision "On the reestablishment of the previous appellations of some streets, avenues, embankments and squares of Leningrad city"]—author's translation.
6 One notable exception was the *Stalinskij rajon* (Stalin district), renamed *Vyborg* district in 1962.
7 *Traditsii i novatsii Peterburgskoy toponomiki* [Traditions and innovations of Petersburgan toponymics], report presented at the eponymous conference held in St. Petersburg on February 14, 2005.
8 The most notable exception is the "square of the Proletarian Dictatorship," renamed "square Rastrelli" in 1991, and not "Laffont" (*Laffonskaya pl.*), as it used to be called until 1952.
9 In its May 25 issue, the local daily *Vechernyj Leningrad* visually summarized this ideological struggle with pictures on facing pages of two famous local statues: the "Bronze Horseman" (Peter the Great) and "Lenin *na bronevike*" (Lenin on an armored car, which stands in front of the Finland Railway Station). Looking in opposite directions, each leader defies the other in pointing an autocratic finger at "his" city.
10 None of the innovative variants discussed in the salons and the press during the campaign—such as Svyato-Peterburg, Leninburg, Nevograd, and Svyato-Petrograd (proposed by Alexander Solzhenytsin)—could compete with the dichotomous choice between Leningrad and St. Petersburg.
11 These were the Stalin, Zhdanov, October, Lenin, and Kuybyshev districts, currently named Vyborg (since 1962), Maritime, Admiralty, Kalinin, and Central district, respectively.
12 *Ploshchad' Mira* metro station was renamed *Sennaya ploshchad'* ("Hay square") following the renaming of the eponymous square situated above.
13 On June 14, 1991, independent local newspaper *Nevskoe Vremya* announced the results of the vote with the following heading: "Happy Rebirth Day, Russia!" followed by three names in bold shrift: "Yeltsin, Sobchak, St. Petersburg."

References

Azaryahu, M. (1992). "The Purge of Bismarck and Saladin: The Renaming of Streets in East Berlin and Haifa, a Comparative Study in Culture-Planning." *Poetics Today*, 13(2): 351–367.
Azaryahu, M. (1996). "The Power of Commemorative Street Names." *Environment and Planning D: Society and Space*, 14(3): 311–330.

Azaryahu, M. (1997). "German Reunification and the Politics of Street Names: The Case of East Berlin." *Political Geography*, 16(6): 479–493.

Azaryahu, M. (2009). "Naming the Past: The Significance of Commemorative Street Names." In L. Berg and J. Vuolteenaho (Eds.), *Critical Toponymies. The Contested Politics of Place Naming* (pp. 53–70). Farnham: Ashgate.

Bell, J. (1999). "Redefining National Identity in Uzbekistan: Symbolic Tensions in Tashkent's Official Public Landscape." *Ecumene*, 6(2): 183–213.

Berg, L. and Vuolteenaho, J. (2009). *Critical Toponymies: The Contested Politics of Place Naming.* Farnham: Ashgate.

Bourdieu, P. (1982). *Ce que parler veut dire. L'économie des échanges linguistiques.* Paris: Fayard.

Bourdieu, P. (1991). *Language and Symbolic Power.* Cambridge: Polity Press.

Colton, T. (1995). *Moscow: Governing the Socialist Metropolis.* Cambridge, MA: Harvard University Press.

Creuzberger, S., Kaiser, M., and Mannteufel, J. (2000). *St. Petersburg, Leningrad, St. Petersburg. Eine Stadt in Spiegel der Zeit.* Stuttgart: Deutsche Verlags Anstalt.

Gill, G. (2005). "Changing Symbols: The Renovation of Moscow Place Names." *The Russian Review*, 64(3): 480–503.

Gorbachevich, K.S. and Khablo, E.P. (2002) *Pochemu tak nazvany? O proiskhozhdenij nazvanij ulits, ploshchadey, ostrovov, rek i mostov Sankt-Peterburga* [Why are they named this way? On the origins of names of streets, squares, islands, rivers and bridges of St. Petersburg]. St. Petersburg: Norint.

Hellberg-Hirn, E. (2003). *Imperial Imprints: Post-Soviet St. Petersburg.* Jyväskylä: SKS.

Hrytsak, Y. and Susak, V. (2003). "Constructing a National City: The Case of L'viv." In J. Czaplicka, B. Ruble, and L. Crabtree (Eds.), *Composing Urban History* (pp. 140–164). Washington, DC: Woodrow Wilson Center Press.

Joenniemi, P. (2003). "The New Saint Petersburg: Trapped in Time?" *Alternatives*, 28(5): 583–609.

Joenniemi, P. and Morozov, V. (2003). "The Politics of Remembering: Saint Petersburg's 300th Anniversary." *Journal of Baltic Studies*, 34(4): 375–398.

Light, D. (2004). "Street Names in Bucharest, 1990–1997: Exploring the Modern Historical Geographies of Post-Socialist Change." *Journal of Historical Geography*, 30(1): 154–172.

Light, D., Nicolae, I., and Suditu, B. (2002). "Toponymy and the Communist City: Street Names in Bucharest, 1948–1965." *GeoJournal*, 56(2): 135–144.

Marin, A. and Morozov, V. (2004). "Iz Leningrada v 'noviy' Sankt-Peterburg: vozvrashchenie imena kak shag v budushchee." [From Leningrad to the 'new' St. Petersburg: name restitution as a step into the future]. In A. Makarychev (Ed.), *Vozvrashchenie imena: identichnost' i kul'turniy kapital pereimenovannykh gorodov Rossii* [Name restitution: identity and cultural capital of Russia's renamed cities] (pp. 83–100). Nizhny-Novgorod: IREX.

Morozov, V. (2002). "The Discourses of St. Petersburg and the Shaping of a Wider Europe: Territory, Space and Post-Sovereign Politics." Paper presented at the 3rd Convent of Central and Eastern European, Nordic and Russian International Studies Associations (CEEISA/NISA/RISA), Moscow: MGIMO, June 20–22, 2002.

Murray, J. (2000). *Politics and Place-Names: Changing Names in the Late Soviet Period.* Birmingham Slavonic Monographs, No. 32. Birmingham, UK: Department of Russian, University of Birmingham.

Orttung, W. (1995). *From Leningrad to St. Petersburg: Democratization in a Russian City.* New York: St. Martin's Press.

Paasi, A. (1998). "Boundaries as Social Processes: Territoriality in the World of Flows." *Geopolitics*, 3(1): 69–88.

Palonen, E. (2008). "The City-Text in Post-Communist Budapest: Street Names, Memorials and the Politics of Commemoration." *GeoJournal*, 73(3): 219–230.

Parkhurst-Ferguson, P. (1988). "Reading City Streets." *The French Review*, 61(3): 386–397.

Pinchevski, A. and Torgovnik, E. (2002). "Signifying Passages: The Signs of Change in Israeli Street Names." *Media, Culture & Society*, 24(3): 365–388.

Robinson, G., Engelstoft, S., and Pobric, A. (2001). "Remaking Sarajevo: Bosnian Nationalism after the Dayton Accord." *Political Geography*, 20(8): 957–980.

Rose-Redwood, R. (2008a). "From Number to Name: Symbolic Capital, Places of Memory and the Politics of Street Renaming in New York City." *Social & Cultural Geography*, 9(4): 431–452.

Rose-Redwood, R. (2008b). "'Sixth Avenue is Now a Memory': Regimes of Spatial Inscription and the Performative Limits of the Official City-Text." *Political Geography*, 27(8): 875–894.

Rose-Redwood, R., Alderman, D., and Azaryahu, M. (2010) "Geographies of Toponymic Inscription: New Directions in Critical Place-Name Studies." *Progress in Human Geography*, 34(4): 453–470.

Saparov, A. (2003). "The Alteration of Place Names and Construction of National Identity in Soviet Armenia." *Cahiers du Monde Russe*, 44(1): 179–198.

Sereda, V. (2009). "Politics of Memory and Urban Landscape: The Case of Lviv after World War II." In S. Dempsey and D. Nichols (Eds.), *Time, Memory, and Cultural Change* (Proceedings of the XXVth IWM Junior Visiting Fellows' Conference). Vienna: Institute for Human Sciences.

Sindalovskij, N.A. (2002). *Slovar' Peterburzhtsa* [The Petersburgan's Dictionary]. St. Petersburg: Norint.

Spivak, D. L. (1998). *Severnaya Stolitsa: Metafizika Peterburga* [The Northern Capital: Metaphysics of Petersburg]. St. Petersburg: Tema.

Vendina, O. (2000). "Moskau und Petersburg. Stadtmythen als Spiegelung ihrer Rivalität." *Osteuropa*, 50(12): 1299–1315.

Yeoh, B. (1992). "Street Names in Colonial Singapore." *Geographical Review*, 82(3): 313–322.

Young, C. and Light, D. (2001). "Place, National Identity and Post-Socialist Transformations: An Introduction." *Political Geography*, 20(8): 941–955.

9 The spatial codification of values in Zagreb's city-text

Laura Šakaja and Jelena Stanić

Introduction

Looked at from the viewpoint of semiotics, a city is a complex semiotic mechanism, a generator of culture that is able to implement that function exclusively due to its "semiotic polyglotism." In that sense, a city represents "a cauldron of texts and codes, variously organized and heterogenic, which belong to diverse languages and diverse levels" (Lotman 1984, 13). Various ethnic, social, and style codes become conjunct in a city, by which they stimulate diverse hybridizations and semiotic translations. The past is given an opportunity in a city landscape to co-exist synchronically with the present. The architecture of a city, its street plan, names of the streets, monuments, and a host of other elements of urban landscape perform "as code programmes that constantly regenerate texts from the historical past" (Lotman 1984, 14).

This chapter explores a part of this complex topo-cultural structure—street toponymy, monuments, and plaques in the urban streetscape. We understand the objects of our inquiry as a "city-text." In the first decade of the twenty-first century, the term *city-text* has become one of the mainstays of works on the geography of street naming and has acquired "almost canonical status" within the literature in the field of urban toponymy (K. Palonen 1993; Azaryahu 1996, 2009; Rose-Redwood 2008; Rose-Redwood, Alderman, and Azaryahu 2010). However, in her account on the politics of landscape in Budapest, Emilia Palonen (2008) used the notion of a "city-text" to refer both to street toponymy and urban statuary. It is in that expanded sense that we use the term in this chapter. We concur with Azaryahu's (1996) viewpoint that the notion of "city-text" is not an analogy or a metaphor, nor does it imply a reduction of the city to a mere text; rather, it emphasizes the manifest and specific semiotic features of the city. In this way, the city-text is a semiotic structure with complex social and communicative functions. It participates in communication between the addresser and addressee of the message, between the public and cultural tradition, between the text and cultural context, and in the communication of the reader with his/herself (Lotman 1981). Text performs the function of collective cultural memory, manifesting the capability of activating certain aspects of history while forgetting others (K. Palonen 1993; Azaryahu 1996, 2009).

Additionally, text performs the role of the mediator that helps the reader to orient his/herself within the cultural constructs. As a spatial inscription, a city-text is enduring but, at the same time, it possesses the ability to re-codify itself in keeping with the situation—in diverse cultural contexts. Therefore, a city-text is a complex mechanism that contains various codes and is able to transform messages and generate new ones (Lotman 1981).

As geographers have argued, the hierarchal status of persons and events is incorporated into the semiotic structure of a city-text. In the ideal configuration of a city-text, urban and historical significance conform. Persons and events of high axiological status are positioned, if possible, in the center, while the lower axiological status is relocated to the periphery or thrown out onto the margins of the text (Azaryahu 1996, 2009; Light 2004; Dwyer and Alderman 2008).

Thus, values are spatially coded within the topo-cultural structure of the city. Reading the cultural landscape as a spatial projection of the axiological system, we use the expression *spatial codification of values* (Užarević 1997). We have tried in this chapter to present the discursive practices that combine the register of values with the register of urban configuration and participate in the translation of messages and meanings from the language of axiology (high–low) to the language of space (center–periphery).

In its theoretical aspects, this chapter relies on the works of the Tartu/Moscow semiotic school, primarily those of Yuri Lotman (1984, 1996, 2001; Lotman and Uspensky 1993 [1971]). According to Lotman's (2000 [1996]) approach, self-description and differentiation from the Other are very important mechanisms of semiotic space. In particular, Lotman introduces the notion of the "semiosphere" to describe a semiotic continuum, or semiotic space, characteristic of any given culture. The semiosphere is the outcome and the condition of cultural development. The semiosphere is heterogeneous and heterofunctional. It assumes a host of connected but diverse code structures and regulates itself by differentiation. All cultures, sub-cultures, and "cultural dialects" commence from division of the world into an internal ("Our") and external ("Their") space. Culture assumes self-description, the creation of its own model. The very fact of description distorts the object of description towards its higher level of organization. Some meanings are canonized and submitted to hierarchical structure, while others are pronounced to be unstructural. Such "irregular" texts are deleted from one's own text and transferred into the space of the "foreign."

As we see, in understanding the importance of the foreign in shaping one's own sense of self, Lotman's semiotic tradition has a lot in common with the poststructuralist/postcolonial conception of relational identity and the Other as a constitutive element in the relation to which identities are measured and constructed (Said 1979; Todorova 1997). One of our objectives in the present chapter is to establish the connection between the alteration of memorial landscapes and the cultural politics of Other(ing) and Self(-defining).

We commence from the stance that each ideological representation assumes, on the one hand, an internal organized quality and the selectivity of self-definition and, on the other hand, separation from the "foreign body." We will try to show that the discursive practices of Othering and Self-referencing (or auto-referencing), as systematic acts of articulation, have been involved in the symbolic representation of the new state in the process of reshaping Zagreb's streetscape in the post-socialist era.

We define Othering as converting into the "Other," relocation from the framework of one's own representation in the process of self-positing and self-defining. It is manifested in sorting out "irregular" parts of the city-text by the demolition (or removal) of certain monuments and plaques, and the erasure of certain street names.

Auto-referencing is the discursive practice of thematicizing characteristics of the self. These are a systematic series of acts inscribing into the landscape references to one's own tradition, ancestry, culture, science, natural features, cities, or regions. These have been manifested in the Zagreb city-text through installing new monuments and plaques, and the allocation of new street names.

Although the notion of the Other is well established in cultural geography (Sibley 1992, 1995; Gregory 1995a, 1995b), there have been few studies on memorial landscapes that adopt such an approach (Myers 1995; Berg and Kearns 1996). By using the concept of Othering, we aim to show in this chapter how names and monuments became tools in refiguring relations to certain groups, nations, and regions as well as their histories in reworking Croatian identity during post-socialist transition.

Another focus of our work highlights "unresolved meanings." We use this term, introduced by Foote (1997), to indicate the condition when different, often opposing, interpretative traditions co-exist and have a chance to struggle for visibility.

Several studies have explored how dual pasts and discursive rivalries over unresolved meanings are configured on the ground (Till 1999; Alderman 2000, 2002, 2010; Azaryahu 2003; Dwyer 2004). Such scholarship considers competing discourses on monuments and street names to show the conflictive nature of remembering the past, the difficulty of recovering long-repressed identities, and the dynamic nature of (re)inscribing memory into urban space. All the foregoing works acknowledge the importance of memorial placement and relative location vis-à-vis the arena's mosaic of identity-based antagonisms (Dwyer and Alderman 2008). In this chapter, we wish to show how the negotiations between conflictive discourses have been transposed and retransposed into the configuration of the symbolic landscape of the Croatian capital.

In recent years, numerous scholars have contributed to monumental landscape studies (Johnson 1995; Foote 1997; Atkinson and Cosgrove 1998; Till 1999; Azaryahu 2003; Dwyer 2004; Hook 2005; Sidaway and Mayell, 2007; Azaryahu and Foote 2008; Alderman 2010) and critical toponymy (Mac Aodha 1989; Yeoh 1992, 1996; Myers 1995; Azaryahu 1996; Berg and Kearns 1996; Alderman 2000, 2002, 2003; Withers 2000; Azaryahu and Kook 2002; Pinchevski and Torgovnik 2002; Rose-Redwood 2008; Vuolteenaho and Berg 2009; Rose-Redwood, Alderman, and Azaryahu 2010). There is a growing body of literature that specifically explores the role of memorial landscapes in affirming and legitimating political identities in post-socialist countries (Azaryahu 1997; Light, Nicolae, and Suditu 2002; Light 2004; Forest, Johnson, and Till 2004; Robinson and Pobrić 2006; Czepczyński 2008; E. Palonen 2008; Light and Young 2010). Our objective is to provide an overview of post-socialist transformations from a different angle. In particular, the current chapter examines the changes in Zagreb statuary and street toponymy, showing how manifestations of three discursive practices—Othering, auto-referencing, and negotiating unresolved meanings—have contributed to the recent transformation of the symbolic landscapes of Croatia's capital city.

Monuments and street names in Zagreb

The installation and removal of public plaques and statuary as well as the renaming of streets in post-socialist Zagreb has been a revealing indicator of political change and an instrument in the recodification of landscape. As the capital of the Republic—in which both the secession from the former Yugoslav state and the war for independence intensified the process of building national identity—Zagreb communicated and mediated a dynamic process of national identity construction. Similarly to other Central and East-European countries (Mach 2006), discussions concerning the meaning of the past dominated public discourse and national politics during Croatia's early post-socialist era. As the national capital, Zagreb is a "point of ideological orientation" (Johnson 1995), which is saturated with messages that indicate official discourses that prescribe new rules for the reading of history.

The mass relocation of monuments, and numerous renamings of streets and squares, became both a reflection and a mechanism of the new politics of landscape. The re-writing of the city primarily pertained to changes in urban toponyms. In the 1990–2007 period, the working body of the Zagreb city assembly for nomination of districts, streets, and squares renamed as many as 474 streets (Stanić, Šakaja, and Slavuj 2009). In regard to monuments, the situation was somewhat different. The removal of monuments, busts, and memorial features in Zagreb was conducted mostly outside the control of authorized institutions. There were only a few officially sanctioned changes in the monument network: that is, in the first decade of transition, only two relocations of statues to less visible places in Zagreb were officially approved by authorized city agencies, and only four busts and eight memorial plaques were removed (moved to museum collections). Nevertheless, according to the data published by the Alliance of Croatian Anti-Fascist Fighters in the period from 1990 to 2000, 73 monuments, 61 memorial-busts, and 164 memorial plaques were demolished, damaged, redesigned, or removed primarily without the official approval of city authorities (Hrženjak 2002).

For the purposes of this chapter, we studied the change in street names and monuments on the basis of analysis of data from the City Office for Cadastre and Geodetic Activities, the City Institute for the Conservation of Cultural and Natural Heritage, the City Office for Building, Housing and Communal Activities, Traffic and Communications, and the City Office for Education, Culture, and Science. We also used public registers of data on memorials of the Revolution (Ugarković and Očak 1979), memorials in the City of Zagreb (Kožarić 2007), and on damaged anti-Fascist monuments in Croatia (Hrženjak 2002). Our sources of information were also city plans from various years and newspaper articles, as well as our own observations.

The "negative Other" as a referent point of identity

Otherness is the characteristic that belongs to the one who (or which) does not fit in with the self-representation of a subject (Burzyńska and Markowski 2009). Otherness is a construct of culture that is subject to an objectifying comprehension. Although it entered into the repertoire of contemporary theory from hermeneutics and psychoanalysis, the notion of the "Other" came to be broadly applied with poststructuralism, and later with postmodernism, postcolonialism, and feminist theory. It would seem that interest in "Otherness" made its way into geography through the influence of postcolonial theory and resulted from the influential research on imaginative geographies (Gregory 1995a, 1995b) and geographies of belonging and exclusion (Sibley 1992, 1995).

We are drawn here to two aspects of the concept. Just as Said documented in his well-known book, *Orientalism* (1979), societies create their feeling of identity to a certain extent through the process of negative definition. Identities on all scales are defined both by what they are and what they are not. Societies are always constructed and understood in terms of difference from others. Therefore, all societies are relational (Crang 1998; Katz 2003). It is precisely that relational stance that we wish to underscore by using the term Othering. The term points to the discursive practice of converting into the Other, proclaiming such Other as a non-member, and by imputing undesirable and negative characteristics to such Other.

The second aspect that interests us relates to borders. All cultures start out from the division of the world into an internal ("Our") space and an external ("Their") space. On this side of the border, one has "our" space, which is confronted with "their space" that is "foreign," "hostile," "dangerous," and "chaotic." That division can be interpreted in diverse ways in various cultural traditions, but the division itself remains universal (Lotman 2000 [1996]). Othering—as pressuring away to the other side of that border, relocation from "one's own" space into "foreign" space—is more than mere forgetting (Legg 2007), since, in its very essence, culture is directed against forgetting. Culture attempts to defeat oblivion, converting it into one of the mechanisms of memory (Lotman and Uspensky 1993 [1971]). Pressured to the margins of a city-text (e.g., demolition of monuments, removal of plaques, renaming streets, etc.), the Other continues to remain a constitutive subject in the unbroken process of self-definition of culture.

So, against whom or against what has Croatia been constructing a border in the post-socialist period? The answer to this question can be clearly read off from the Croatian geopolitical code—from groups of strategic assumptions that determined state foreign policy in the first transition years. Based on statements made by Franjo Tuđman, the first president of independent Croatia, Klemenčić and Topalović (1996) reconstructed the Croatian geopolitical code; that is, the worldview upon which Croatia's foreign policy was based in the mid-1990s. The main assumption in that geopolitical code implied "a division of Europe between the East and the West, in which Croatia had a border position, along the very edge of western civilization" (Klemenčić and Topalović 1996, 27). Within that geopolitical code, Croatia was seen as defending itself from Serbian aggression both in terms of its own territorial integrity and the "value system of western civilization." The renaming of streets in the Croatian capital during the 1990s followed Tuđman's geopolitical code quite consistently. Furthermore, it clearly indicated the "Other" in negative relation to whom the construction of national identity was developed in the first years of the post-socialist period.

Othering the Serbs and Serbia

For Croatia, this "Other" was represented primarily by Serbs and Serbia. Negative stereotyping of the Serbs was fostered by the 1991–1995 war. The war began during the early stage of post-socialism and this fact, naturally, increased the importance of the Serbs as a referential distance factor in relation to whom the Croatian cultural/political self was measured and constructed. In the early-1990s, Serbs and Serbia were erased from the names of Zagreb's streets. Almost all street names in Zagreb referring to Serbian cities (Belgrade, Niš, Zrenjanin, Novi Sad) were changed in the early-1990s. Among the first streets renamed was the one previously named after Vuk Karadžić, a nineteenth-century Serbian ethnographer and reformer of the Serbian language. Due to the fact that Karadžić had advocated the concept of ethnicity based on language, and had considered Croats who spoke the Štokavian dialect to be "Serbs of the Roman Catholic faith" (Karadžić 1982 [1849]), he was perceived in Croatia as a protagonist of Serbian nationalist ideology. Karadžić's study, "Serbs all and everywhere," was politically disputed in the Croatian public sphere on the grounds of its Greater-Serbian concept. The simultaneous elimination of "Karadžić Street" and publication of the *Differential Dictionary of the Serbian and Croatian Language* (Brodnjak 1991) testified to the cultural and national differentiation of Croatia from its south-eastern neighbors.

While the strong national revival in the 1990s was accompanied by a perception of national identity as primordial (ethnic) (Smith 1991; Sekulić 2003), and of national culture as mono-ethnic (Ivančević 1999), during the second decade of transition the primordial understanding of identity, based on the notion of a common ethnic origin, was discarded in the political discourse. Croatia's political aspirations to join the European Union, and its perception of its self-identity as being European, resulted in the affirmation of European multicultural values in Croatia's public sphere. Consequently, this led to acceptance of the view that Croatian (ethnic) Serbs were part of Croatian national culture. A symbol of this shift was the relocation of a magnificent sculpture of the inventor and scientist Nikola Tesla, moved from the poorly exposed courtyard of a scientific institute in a secluded area to the very heart of the city. This kind of semantic upgrade of Tesla, an ethnic Serb born in Croatia, would have been inconceivable in the 1990s.

Othering Yugoslavia

The country from which Croatia had recently seceded was the second negative referential factor in relation to which post-socialist Croatian identity was constructed. Many of the changes in Zagreb's cultural landscape resulted from a reduction in symbols related to Tito's Yugoslavia. By the end of the 1970s, there were over 200 memorial features commemorating the socialist revolution in the urban core of Zagreb (Ugarković and Očak 1979). During the post-socialist period, their number was considerably reduced. All street names recalling events from the history of the Communist Party or Partisan military units were renamed. Names such as "Proletarian Brigade," "8th Party Congress," "Moslavina Detachment," "Bjelovar Detachment," "6th Partisan Division," and "Conference of Zagreb Communists" have vanished. Some of the street names and monuments dedicated to persons who had participated in the Partisan movement and the anti-Fascist struggle were changed as well (Hrženjak 2002).

The key to understanding the current assessment of the communist past is the fact that the Yugoslav anti-Fascist movement was born specifically within the Communist Party and specifically in Croatia. Croatia's anti-Fascist legacy is virtually inseparable from its communist legacy. For this very reason, revolutionary features have not been totally eliminated, either in Zagreb or more generally in Croatia. Many such features are still part of Zagreb's urban landscape (Kožarić 2007). Yet some have been removed and others have been rendered less conspicuous—in accordance with the change in historical importance assigned to the persons whom the monuments commemorate.

A logical question thus arises: in which form is Marshal Tito—the leader of the anti-Fascist movement, the long-term president of Yugoslavia and the Yugoslav Communist Party, and one of the founders and leaders of the Non-Aligned Movement—commemorated? Today, there are no longer numerous plaques on buildings in which he periodically lived, worked, or held meetings. However, the name of one of the largest and most beautiful squares in Zagreb—"Marshal Tito's Square"—has not been changed. Occasional anti-Tito demonstrations and initiatives do occur, but the renaming of the square has never seriously come into question under either right- or left-wing governments, nor has the importance of Tito as a major protagonist in Croatian history.

Othering the Balkans and Russia

For Croatia, as for other Central European countries, the Balkans and Russia represented a negative "constituting Other" in the process of post-socialist identity-building (Todorova 1997). Croatia's ambiguous borders vis-à-vis the Balkans made it an important referential distance factor in the early transitional years. The role of the Balkans as a negative point of reference is more than obvious in the media and the public sphere in general. It is also confirmed by Croatia's continuous refusal to enter into a Balkan association of any kind. Yet one must note that the perception of Zagreb's non-belonging to the Balkans is obviously not exclusively a post-socialist and post-Yugoslav phenomenon—the only street in Zagreb that was named after the Balkans was renamed as early as in the 1960s. By the 1990s, the term Balkan had disappeared from Zagreb's cultural landscape when the name of the largest cinema in Zagreb was changed from *Kino Balkan* to *Kino Europa*, indicating the shift in the geopolitical aspirations of the young country.

The specific political position of former Yugoslavia as a non-aligned country, as well as weaker political and economic relations with Russia, were evident through minor representation of Russia in Zagreb's street toponymy. Those that once existed were renamed after the democratic elections. Thus, in Zagreb today, there are no longer any streets named after Moscow, Leningrad, or Solovlyev. Only "Gagarin Lane"—a narrow pathway without any significance for spatial orientation in the city—survived the wave of renamings.

Othering the international community of communists and revolutionaries

The change in the ruling ideology automatically placed protagonists of Marxism-Leninism, socialist revolutions, and the international communist movement into the category of the negative "Other." Accordingly, shortly after the first democratic elections in 1990, Lenin disappeared from Zagreb's street names and soon fell into oblivion together with many international ideologists, communists, and revolutionaries such as Karl Marx, Georgi Dimitrov, the Spanish fighters, Friedrich Engels, Palmiro Togliatti, Ernesto Che Guevara, Karl Liebknecht, and Wilhelm Pieck. The ladies of the communist movement—Clara Zetkin and Rosa Luxemburg—were the last to symbolically leave Zagreb's streetscape. Along with individuals, symbolic events and dates denoting the class struggle, such as the October Revolution and May Day, would soon disappear as well.

Auto-referencing: inscribing national geography, history, and culture

Auto-referencing is the dimension by which articulation or text draws attention to a situation, context, or subject of its own articulation, composition, structure, code, or belonging—thus, the means by which articulation or text thematicizes certain features of itself (Biti 2000). As Žižek (1993) observes, a nation finds its sense of self-identity by revealing itself as already present in its tradition. By referring to its tradition, descent, culture, science, natural characteristics, settlements, and "friendly countries," Croatia has incorporated its own definition into the Zagreb landscape (Šakaja 2005, 2011).

With change in the political system and geopolitical orientation, national "imaginative geography" also undergoes transformation. Instead of the toponyms from the former Yugoslavia, Croatian geographical nomenclature has been inscribed into the city's street names. Enclosing the territory into a nation-state strengthened the role of Zagreb as a metropolis that was meant to unite the country. The official framework of the term "homeland" now changed and was harmonized with the new state borders. The role of Zagreb as the capital city of independent Croatia was symbolically manifested by an increased number of street toponyms referring to Croatian territory: cities and villages (Našice, Vukovar, Dubrovnik, Čavoglava, Merag, Lubenice, etc.), regions (Slavonia), rivers (Lonja, Drava, etc.), and mountains (the Dinaric Range, Bjelolasica). "Vukovar Avenue" is probably one of the best examples of how defensive nationalism and strong national identification, produced in conditions of aggression and war, were revealed through changes in public memorial features. The name "Vukovar Avenue" was given to one of the main boulevards in the city on November 4, 1991, during the intense battle for the defense of Vukovar.

The new "imaginative geography" excludes the "East" but includes other regions of self-identification. These are states perceived as being part of the common cultural sphere of Central Europe ("Street of the Federal Republic of Germany," "Street of the Republic of Austria") or in common spiritual culture ("Vatican Street"). The new "geographical" streets have also denoted new friendships. The new "Street of Iceland," "Kiev Street," and "Ukrainian Street" were obviously named as an acknowledgment of gratitude owed to the countries that were among the first to recognize Croatia's independence.

The shift in the public discourse towards Croatian history and culture in Zagreb's landscape has resulted in an increased number of streets and squares that now commemorate Croatian kings and dukes. A grand ceremony in October 1990, supported by an artistic and musical program as well as a presidential speech, served as the scene for returning the statue of Josip Jelačić, the viceroy of Croatia in the nineteenth century, to the city's main square. The original name of the square—"Square of Viceroy Jelačić"—was also returned. The statue, originally erected in 1866, was removed by the communist authorities in 1947, when the square was previously renamed. Re-installation of the statue in the initial location—in the most central spot in the urban topography of Croatia's capital—was a symbolic act celebrating accomplishment of the dream of a Croatian state, or the so-called "Croatian dream" (Rihtman-Auguštin 2000, 96). Historians credited Viceroy Jelačić for the unification, at least formally, of all the Croatian lands, after many centuries of fragmentation (Srkulj 1996, Šišić 2004; Goldstein 2008). Thus Jelačić played a mythical role in the Croatian national movement (Rihtman-Auguštin 2000). Both the return of the statue and reclaiming the name of the square were powerful symbolic acts in the context of national integration and aspirations toward a free and independent state.

Although it would be an overstatement to speak of a sacralization of public space, the religious elements, without doubt, have also become much more visible in the post-socialist era. Numerous monuments and new streets have been dedicated to saints and priests. However, streets named after Croatian scientists, musicians, and writers (and even characters from their literary works) undoubtedly represent the most numerous category in the new renamings (Stanić, Šakaja, and Slavuj 2009). The same process of symbolic nationalization of public space has also occurred in the sphere of monuments. During the 1990s, sculptures of numerous Croatian writers, painters, and scientists were placed in Zagreb's central areas. Some of these sculptures have even been subjected to criticism for their grand scale, and they have evoked public discussion on the new spectacular monumental undertakings as political and ideological interventions in the urban landscape, "a splendid memorial to a time of arrogance and violence" and "primeval destruction of the spirit of the city" (Tenžera 1999, 19).

Negotiating unresolved meanings

There are sites "which await the development of interpretative traditions within which they can be assessed" (Foote 1997, 294). They reflect the unresolved state of certain open historical questions with which society has yet to come to terms. Commemoration of "dual pasts" (Azaryahu 2003) involves negotiation and struggle over the placement and relative location of memorials that represent different versions of history. Competition between discourses transposes into space the struggle for visibility in the landscape. The politically contestable nature of place is best expressed under unsettled conditions, when some meanings are still unresolved while no discourse dominates (as yet).

Controversial inclusions and exclusions: communists, anti-fascists, and "the unspoken victims of World War II"

During the period of transition from a totalitarian state to "framed plurality" (Gricanov 2001), a series of sensitive questions were opened up in Croatia. They included the issues of commemoration of World War II and the victims of political oppression under communist rule. When Croatia entered into its post-socialist period, previously silenced discourses on World War II and the post-war period were given access to the public sphere. In 1991, the Commission for Determination of War and Post-war Victims of World War II was established. Since then, authentic secret documents have been published in anthologies under the title, *Partisan and Communist Repression and Crimes in Croatia 1944–1946, Documents* (Dizdar et al. 2005; Geiger 2006). Numerous newly published memoirs also cast new light on the events of that time. Following the reappraisal in the Croatian public sphere of the wartime and the communist past, the association of war veterans' "Croatian Home Guard" and the right-wing Croatian Party of Rights set up new memorials in Croatia to what they called the "unspoken victims" of World War II (Bakša 2006). These new memorials honor members of the regular (or official) army of the pro-Fascist Ustashi state, the NDH (Nezavisna Država Hrvatska, i.e., the Independent State of Croatia) and also civil victims of post-war repressions. While such memorials are numerous in some parts of Croatia, they are quite invisible in Zagreb and appear only on small plaques in non-prominent places. The reason lies, of course, in their controversy. Who were the victims during World War II in the territory of Croatia? Who were the perpetrators? The answers to these questions are neither unequivocal, nor simple. Given the fact that the initiator of the anti-Fascist struggle in Yugoslavia was the Communist Party, both the notion of communism and specifically the Yugoslav communist regime, which is charged today with many crimes, became historically inseparable from the concept of anti-Fascism—which is considered incontestable in Croatia.

On the other hand, the pro-Fascist wartime state, the NDH, formally achieved national freedom and independence, and was opposed both to the idea of unification with Serbs in Yugoslavia and to the communist movement. It is for this reason that the stereotype associating the national, anti-Yugoslav, and anti-communist concept in Croatia during World War II with the Ustashi movement remains so strong. Another important controversy is whether persons recruited forcibly into the regular army under the Ustashi state can be defined as perpetrators, or rather—if they were executed on charges of belonging to the Ustashis—as victims of the war.

The inability to distinguish communists from anti-Fascists has in part encouraged the preservation of the communist legacy. The failure to differentiate Ustashi from anti-communist, anti-Yugoslav, nationally oriented Croats, or simply from apolitical persons recruited into what was the regular Croatian Army at that time, has led to the fact that memories regarding the "unspoken victims of World War II" are still suppressed today. References to the innocent victims of the communist forces in World War II and in the post-war period can always be interpreted as reminiscences of the Ustashi movement. This has made Croatian state authorities extremely cautious when mentioning any World War II national concept, anti-communism, and anti-Yugoslavism, or when referring to communist crimes during the war and in the post-war period. It is indicative that even 60 years after the victory over Fascism, it was felt necessary that the Croatian Parliament distance itself from Fascism and from the Ustashi movement by issuing a Declaration on Anti-Fascism in 2005, in which, inter alia, it "confirmed the anti-Fascist democratic foundation and commitment of the Republic of Croatia and Croatian society" and "confirmed that the fundamental values of anti-Fascism are unequivocally accepted in the Republic of Croatia."

Relocation, resemiotization, and "secondary sacralization" as strategies of competing discourses

A whole series of undefined issues connected with the second half of the twentieth century—primarily World War II (1941–1945, in Croatia) and the Homeland War (1991–1995)—are still waiting for their stabilization in the new official interpretative tradition. Over a decade into the twenty-first century, these issues are still subject to negotiation between opposing discourses. We were able to discern three spatial strategies used by competing discourses in the processes of contestation of previously dominated narratives on Croatian history as well as processes of negotiation on the meanings of historical events.

First, it is a strategy of *relocation*—change of place from central to peripheral areas and vice versa. The above-mentioned Tesla monument was the only case of relocation in the direction from the periphery to the city core. As we have already shown, it reflected the loss of power of primordial ideas of identity, extremely influential in the first decade of Croatian independence. All other cases of relocation in Zagreb relate to "left-overs" (Czepczyński 2008) of the People's Liberation War (PLW) of the time of World War II, which are obviously considered to be still eligible to remain in the city-text, but have been spatially degraded, adjusted to a new place in history and the hierarchy of values. Forms of relocation of "left-overs" that we can see in Zagreb include: a) *moving locations from the center to the periphery*: for example, the sculpture of communist official Moša Pijade, or the street named after the political publicist and revolutionary, Božidar Adžija; b) *transfer from a visible open position to an enclosed area*: for instance, a monument to the prominent communist leader Rade Končar has been moved from the pedestal in front of the factory bearing his name to the factory's yard.

Second, the process of negotiating meanings is also manifested in the *resemiotization of memorials*. Resemiotization of memorials can be attained by appending new elements through the processes of "symbolic accretion" (Foote 1997; Dwyer 2004), and by removal or replacement of some of the elements, on an already existing monument. The most common form of resemiotization in Zagreb was removal of the red star from monuments dedicated to protagonists or victims of the anti-Fascist struggle, which achieved a semiotic separation of anti-Fascism from communism. Resemiotization of the monument to fallen anti-Fascists on Piškor Hill was accomplished not just by replacement of the star with a cross, but also by changing the text on the monument. Namely, a rather long text on the plaque, referring to "great sacrifices for the sake of freedom and socialism" and "lives given for freedom and a better future for new generations" (Hrženjak 2002, 339) was changed to the text commemorating "all those who died for Croatia"—a short statement that belongs to a completely different discourse and at least partially satisfies all the options. Resemiotization of monuments as an act of reconstruction of the symbolic landscape is available to all levels of social agents—from official policy makers to subversive groups, and even individuals. As we have seen from geographical research, examples of resemiotization can be found at various levels of social influence: they vary from modifications of central monuments that set new rules for reading national history (Till 1999; Azaryahu 2003; E. Palonen 2008; Light and Young 2010) to spray-painting on road signs (Rose-Redwood, Alderman, and Azaryahu 2010).

Third, we can also speak about a *secondary sacralization* (Esaulov 2006), or resemiotization of places. We comprehend this term as covering new signs in a place that is already "sacral," which evokes respect because of the already-existing content and possesses a narrative that upgrades the meaning of the place itself. "Sacral nature" and the importance of a place are thus transferred to the importance of the content that is to be incorporated. Resemiotization of places in Zagreb was achieved, for example, by replacing the monument to fighters of the People's Liberation War by sculpture of religious (in Čučerje) or patriotic (in Kustošija) district) meaning. The unsuccessful renaming of the Victims of Fascist Square best reveals the significance of "secondary sacralization." The ruling party's attempt to recode the square into a "sacral" place of Croatian statehood was met with a great public opposition. The change of its name into the Square of Croatian Greats in 1990 transformed the square into a focal point of discussion on the balance between the guilt of the communists and the fascists as well as an assessment of the magnitude of their crimes. Differences of opinion on the approach to World War II were transposed into the urban streetscape. Due to the regular demonstrations against the new name of the square, the square's original name was eventually restored in 2000, a decade after it was renamed as the Square of Croatian Greats.

Where is a place appropriate for the first Croatian president?

Choices for the location of monuments and the renaming of streets, as we have seen in some of the above-mentioned examples, are the result of a process of negotiation and contestation between different social groups and discourses. It is an administrative process through which different interests compete for symbolic control of the public sphere, therefore making the process political (K. Palonen 1993; Azaryahu 1996).

One paradigmatic example of such processes in Zagreb was the decision about the location of a square dedicated to the first president of democratic Croatia. It took more than eight years after the death of Franjo Tuđman before one of the squares in Croatia's capital was named after him. Although the majority of politicians agreed that the first Croatian president deserved a memorial in the form of a street or a square, to agree on the "appropriate" location was a problem. Interpretation of the answer has considerably differed within the public and political spheres. The ruling elites were aware of the fact that the chosen location would determine the position of the former president in the hierarchy of Croatia's pantheon. Right-wing parties proposed locations in the very heart of the city, while left-wing parties, expectedly, were in favor of peripheral areas of the city center. The suggestion that the City Council finally accepted, was the one offered by Zagreb's mayor, a member of the political left. The decision of the City Council provoked strong negative reactions from the right-wing parties. All of them agreed that the selected square was "an inadequate and undefined space," "not worthy enough," "common turf," and "an unarranged park" (Stanić, Šakaja, and Slavuj 2009, 110). The duration of negotiations concerning Tuđman's square and, above all, its ambiguous final location on the very edge of the city's central core, demonstrated that the role of the first president of democratic Croatia has remained undefined, and interpretations of recent history are still confrontational and contested.

With many unresolved problems, and under the weight of the past, Croatia is only now approaching its "point of self-cognition" (Lotman 1992, 30); after the settling of transitional "explosions" one may expect "an activation of the mechanisms of history that must explain what happened [to history itself]."

Conclusion

> The language of proper names moves like a chain of conscious acts of naming and renaming that are strictly separated from each other. A new name corresponds to a new situation. From the mythological viewpoint, the transition from one state towards another is understood through the formula "And I saw a new heaven and a new land ..." and, at the same time, as an act of replacement of proper names.
>
> (Lotman and Uspensky 1992 [1973], 70)

If one were to judge by the renaming of streets, the revelation of "a new heaven and a new land" has occurred often in the history of Croatia. The example that perhaps shows most comprehensively the general tendency is the main street of the town of Vukovar. Through a series of renamings during the twentieth century, Vukovar has changed the name of its main street six times in keeping with states, rulers, and socio-political orders. With the change of states—from the Austro-Hungarian Empire, the Kingdom of Yugoslavia, the Ustashi Independent State of Croatia, socialist Yugoslavia, and the democratic Republic of Croatia—the name of the street has changed, too. In that process, the street was named every time after the then-current highest political authority—the person at the head of the state: from Emperor Franz Joseph, the Yugoslavian kings, Peter and Alexander, to the leader of the Ustashi state, Pavelić, followed by Tito and by Tuđman. The sole constant in all those perpetual changes was the value-spatial code—the ranking of the main city street corresponded exclusively to the ranking of the leading person in the state. Thus, the values were consistently spatially coded, in all the changing systems.

In this chapter, we have tried to show how the social values in post-socialist Zagreb were transposed into the language of space. We hope that we have demonstrated that the symbolic rewriting of Zagreb's city-text was organized and shaped primarily by discursive practices of Othering and Self-referencing, as systematic acts of articulation in the frame of the politics of landscape. We have also discerned acts of relocation, resemiotization, and "secondary sacralization" as spatial strategies used in negotiation of meanings under conditions in which the definition of interpretative tradition is ongoing.

In the refiguring of identity, post-socialist countries turn back to the past, seeking their roots in pre-socialist times. The socialist period in Croatia was preceded by the Independent State of Croatia (the NDH)—a state that was pro-Fascist but, at the same time, realized "the Croatian dream" of independence. The impossibility of merging tradition with such a criminal state, along with the fact that such activation of tradition imposes itself since, from the time of the Middle Ages, Croatia has been independent only twice—then and now—creates a schizophrenic situation with which Croatia is currently obliged to deal. Therefore, World War II is still very much alive in Croatia today, as we have seen in the wavering accents in the spatial rhetoric of memorial landscapes during the post-socialist period. Because of still unsolved historical issues, the recasting of the memorial landscape is obviously still "in progress."

References

Alderman, D. (2000). "A Street Fit for a King: Naming Places and Commemoration in the American South." *Professional Geographer*, 52(4): 672–684.

Alderman, D. (2002). "Street Names as Memorial Arenas: The Reputational Politics of Commemorating Martin Luther King Jr. in a Georgia County." *Historical Geography*, 30: 99–120.

Alderman, D. (2003). "Street Names and the Scaling of Memory: The Politics of Commemorating Martin Luther King, Jr. within the African American Community." *Area*, 35(2): 163–173.

Alderman, D. (2010). "Surrogation and the Politics of Remembering Slavery in Savannah, Georgia (USA)." *Journal of Historical Geography*, 36(1): 90–101.

Atkinson, D. and Cosgrove, D. (1998). "Urban Rhetoric and Embodied Identities: City, Nation and Empire at the Vittorio Emanuele II Monument in Rome, 1870–1945." *Annals of the Association of American Geographers*, 88(1): 28–49.

Azaryahu, M. (1996). "The Power of Commemorative Street Names." *Environment and Planning D*, 14(3): 311–330.

Azaryahu, M. (1997). "German Reunification and the Politics of Street Names: The Case of East Berlin." *Political Geography*, 16(6): 479–493.

Azaryahu, M. (2003) "RePlacing Memory: The Reorientation of Buchenwald." *Cultural Geographies*, 10(1): 1–20.

Azaryahu, M. (2009) "Naming the Past: The Significance of Commemorative Street Names." In L. Berg and J. Vuolteenaho (Eds.), *Critical Toponymies: The Contested Politics of Place Naming* (pp. 53–70). Farnham: Ashgate.

Azaryahu, M. and Kook, R. (2002). "Mapping the Nation: Street Names and Arab-Palestinian Identity: Three Case Studies." *Nations and Nationalism*, 8(2): 195–213.

Azaryahu, M. and Foote, K. (2008). "Historical Space as Narrative Medium: On the Configuration of Spatial Narratives of Time at Historical Sites." *GeoJournal*, 73(3): 179–194.

Bakša, Z. (Ed.) (2006). *Spomen-obilježja*. Zagreb: Hrvatski Domobran—Udruga ratnih veterana.

Berg, L. and Kearns, R. (1996). "Naming as Norming: 'Race,' Gender, and the Identity Politics of Naming Places in Aotearoa/New Zealand." *Environment and Planning D*, 14(1): 99–122.

Biti, V. (2000). *Pojmovnik suvremene književne kulturne teorije*. Zagreb: Matica Hrvatska.

Brodnjak, V. (1991). *Razlikovni rječnik srpskog i hrvatskog jezika*. Zagreb: Školske novine.

Burzyńska, A. and Markowski, M.P. (2009). *Književne teorije XX veka*. Belgrade: Službeni glasnik.

Crang, M. (1998). *Cultural Geography*. London: Routledge.

Czepczyński, M. (2008). *Cultural Landscapes of Post-Socialist Cities. Representation of Powers and Needs*. Farnham: Ashgate.

Deklaracija o antifašižmu (Declaration on Anti-Fascism) (2005). Hrvatski Sabor (Croatian Parliament). March 13.

Dizdar, Z., Geiger, V., Pojić, M., and Rupić, M. (2005). *Partizanska i komunistička represija i zločini u Hrvatskoj 1944–1946: Dokumenti*. Zagreb: Institut za povijest.

Dwyer, O. (2004). "Symbolic Accretion and Commemoration." *Social & Cultural Geography*, 5(3): 419–435.

Dwyer, O. and Alderman, D. (2008) "Memorial Landscapes: Analytic Questions and Metaphors." *GeoJournal,* 73(3): 165–178.

Esaulov, I.A. (2006). "Novye kategorii filologicheskogo analiza dlja ponimanija sushnosti russkoj literetury." Paper presented at the international Symposium Russkaja slovesnost' v mirovom kul'turnom prostranstve. Moscow, December 15.

Foote, K. (1997). *Shadowed Ground: America's Landscapes of Violence and Tragedy*. Austin: University of Texas Press.

Forest, B., Johnson, J., and Till, K. (2004). "Post-totalitarian National Identity: Public Memory in Germany and Russia." *Social & Cultural Geography*, 5(3): 357–380.

Geiger, V. (2006). *Partizanska i komunistička represija i zločini u Hrvatskoj 1944–1946: Dokumenti. Knjiga II: Slavonija, Srijem i Baranja*. Zagreb: Institut za povijest.

Goldstein, I. (2008). *Hrvatska povijest, Knjiga XXI*. Zagreb: Europapress holding.

Gregory, D. (1995a). "Between the Book and the Lamp: Imaginative Geographies of Egypt, 1849–50." *Transactions of the Institute of British Geographers*, 20(1): 29–57.

Gregory, D. (1995b). "Imaginative Geographies." *Progress in Human Geography*, 19(4): 447–485.

Gricanov, A. (2001). "Ideologia." In A. Gricanov and M. Mozheiko (Eds.), *Post-modernizam* (pp. 302–494). Minsk: Interpresservis.

Hook, D. (2005). "Monumental Space and the Uncanny." *Geoforum*, 36(6): 688–704.

Hrženjak, J. (2002). *Rušenje antifašističkih spomenika u Hrvatskoj 1990–2002*. Zagreb: Savez antifasističkih boraca Hrvatske.

Ivančević, R. (1999). "Ruralna i urbana komponenta urbanog identiteta." In J. Cačić-Kumpes (Ed.), *Kultura, etničnost, identitet* (pp. 225–232). Zagreb: Institut za migracije i narodnosti, Naklada Jesenski i Turk and Hrvatsko sociološko društvo.

Johnson, N. (1995). "Cast in Stone: Monuments, Geography and Nationalism." *Environment and Planning D*, 13(1): 51–65.

Johnson, N. (2004). "Public Memory." In J. Duncan, N. Johnson, and R. Schein (Eds.), *Companion to Cultural Geography* (pp. 316–327). Oxford: Blackwell Publishing.

Karadžić, V. (1982 [1849]). "Srbi svi i svuda." In I. Krtalić (Ed.), *Polemike u hrvatskoj književnosti, kolo 1, knjiga 2* (pp. 131–146). Zagreb: Mladost.

Katz, C. (2003). "Social Formations: Thinking about Society, Identity, Power and Resistance." In S. Holloway, S. Rice, and G. Vallentine (Eds.), *Key Concepts in Geography* (pp. 249–265). London: Sage.

Klemenčić, M. and Topalović, D. (1996). "Geopolitički položaj i identitet Hrvatske." In Z. Pepeonik (Ed.), *I. Hrvatski geografski kongres. Geografija u funkciji razvoja* (pp. 21–28). Zagreb: Hrvatsko geografsko društvo.

Kožarić, I. (2007). *Spomenici i fontane u gradu Zagrebu*. Zagreb: HAZU.

Legg, S. (2007). "Reviewing Geographies of Memory/Forgetting." *Environment and Planning A*, 39(2): 456–466.

Light, D. (2004). "Street Names in Bucharest, 1990–1997: Exploring the Modern Historical Geographies of Post-Socialist Change." *Journal of Historical Geography*, 30(1): 154–172.

Light, D. and Young, C. (2010). "Political Identity, Public Memory and Urban Space: A Case Study of Parcul Carol I, Bucharest from 1906 to the Present." *Europe-Asia Studies*, 62(9): 1453–1478.

Light, D., Nicolae, I., and Suditu, B. (2002). "Toponymy and the Communist City: Street Names in Bucharest, 1948–1965." *GeoJournal*, 56(2): 135–144.

Lotman, Y. (1981). "Semiotika kul'tury i poniatie teksta." *Uchenye Zapiski Tartuskogo Gosudarstvennogo Universiteta*, 515: 3–7.

Lotman, Y. (1984). "Simvolika Peterburga i problemy semiotiki goroda." In Y. Lotman, 1992, *Izbrannye stat'i v trekh tomakh, Vol. II* (pp. 9–21). Tallin: Aleksandra.

Lotman, Y. (1992). *Kul'tura i vzryv*. Moscow: Gnozis.

Lotman, Y. (2000 [1996]). "Vnutri mysliashih mirov." In Y. Lotman, *Semiosfera* (pp. 150–390). Sankt-Peterburg: Iskusstvo.

Lotman, Y. (2001). *Universe of the Mind: A Semiotic Theory of Culture*. New York: I. B. Tauris.

Lotman, Y. and Uspensky, B. (1993 [1971]). "O semioticheskom mekhanizme kul'tury." In Y. Lotman, *Izbrannye stat'i v trekh tomakh, Vol. III* (pp. 326–344). Tallin: Aleksandra.

Lotman, Y. (1992 [1973]). "Mif, imya, kul'tura." In Y. Lotman, *Izbrannye stat'i v trekh tomakh, Vol. I* (pp. 58–75). Tallin: Aleksandra.

Mac Aodha, B. (1989). "The History and Nature of Irish Street Names." *Names*, 37(4): 345–365.

Mach, Z. (2006). "Multicultural Heritage, Remembering, Forgetting, and the Construction of Identity." In S. Schröder-Esch and J. Ulbricht (Eds.), *The Politics of Heritage and Regional Development Strategies: Actors, Interests, Conflicts* (pp. 27–31). Weimar: Bauhaus-Universität.

Myers, G. (1995). "Naming and Placing the Other: Power and Urban Landscape in Zanzibar." *Tijdschrift voor Economische en Sociale Geografie*, 87(3): 237–246.

Palonen, E. (2008). "The City Text in Post-Communist Budapest: Street Names, Memorials, and the Politics of Commemoration." *GeoJournal*, 73(3): 219–230.

Palonen, K. (1993). "Reading Street Names Politically." In K. Palonen and T. Parvikko (Eds.), *Reading the Political* (pp. 103–21). Tampere: The Finnish Political Science Association.

Pinchevski, A. and Torgovnik, E. (2002). "Signifying Passages: The Signs of Change in Israeli Street Names." *Media, Culture & Society*, 24(3): 365–388.

Rihtman-Auguštin, D. (2000). *Ulice moga grada*. Beograd: Biblioteka XX vek.

Robinson, G. and Pobrić, A. (2006). "Nationalism and Identity in Post-Dayton Accords: Bosnia-Herzegovina." *Tijdschrift voor Economische en Sociale Geografie*, 97(3): 237–252.

Rose-Redwood, R. (2008). "'Sixth Avenue is Now a Memory': Regimes of Spatial Inscription and the Performative Limits of the Official City-Text." *Political Geography*, 27(8): 875–894.

Rose-Redwood, R., Alderman, D. and Azaryahu, M. (2010). "Geographies of Toponymic Inscription: New Directions in Critical Place-Name Studies." *Progress in Human Geography*, 34(4): 453–470.

Said, E.W. (1978). *Orientalism*. New York: Vintage Books.

Sekulić, D. (2003). "Građanski i etnički identitet: Slučaj Hrvatske." *Politička Misao*, 40(2): 140–166.

Sibley, D. (1992) "Outsiders in Society and Space." In K. Anderson and F. Gale (Eds.), *Inventing Places: Studies in Cultural Geography* (pp. 107–122). Melbourne: Longman Cheshire.

Sibley, D. (1995). *Geographies of Exclusion*. London: Routledge.

Sidaway, J. and Mayell, P. (2007). "Monumental Geographies: Re-situating the State." *Cultural Geographies*, 14(1):148–155.

Smith, A. (1991). *National Identity*. Reno/Las Vegas: University of Nevada Press.

Srkulj, S. (1996). *Hrvatska povijest u devetnaest karata*. Zagreb: AGM.

Stanić, J., Šakaja, L., and Slavuj, L. (2009). "Preimenovanja zagrebačkih ulica i trgova." *Migracijske i etničke teme*, 25(1–2): 89–124.

Šakaja, L. (2005). "From Velebit to Casablanca: (Re)construction of Geography and Identity in the Names of Croatian Enterprises." *Europa Regional*, 13(3): 123–132.

Šakaja, L. (2011). "An Insight into the 'Arbor Mundi': A Reconstruction of Value Models from Catering Establishment Names." In D. Belyaev and Z. Roca (Eds.), *Contemporary Croatia: Development Challenges in a Socio-Cultural Perspective* (pp. 201–234). Lisbon: Edições Universitárias Lusófonas.

Šišić, F. (2004). *Povijest Hrvata. Pregled povijesti hrvatskoga naroda 1526–1918. Knjiga II*. Split: Marjan tisak.

Tenžera, M. (1999). "Agresija na Zelenu potkovu." *Vjesnik*, February 26.

Till, K. (1999). "Staging the Past: Landscape Designs, Cultural Identity and Erinnerungspolitik at Berlin's Neue Wache." *Ecumene*, 6(3): 251–283.

Todorova, M. (1997). *Imagining the Balkans*. New York: Oxford University Press.

Ugarković, S. and Očak, I. (1979). *Zagreb grad heroj: spomen obilježja revoluciji*. Zagreb: August Cesarec.

Užarević, J. (1997). "Prostorno kodiranje vrijednosti. Tijelo i prostor." In M. Medarić (Ed.), *Hijerarhija* (pp. 19–27). Zagreb: ZZK.

Vuolteenaho, J. and Berg, L. (2009). "Towards Critical Toponymies." In L. Berg and J. Vuolteenaho (Eds.), *Critical Toponymies: The Contested Politics of Place Naming* (pp. 1–18). Farnham: Ashgate.

Withers, C.W.J. (2000). "Authorizing Landscape: 'Authority,' Naming and Ordnance Survey's Mapping of the Scottish Highlands in the Nineteenth Century." *Journal of Historical Geography*, 26(4): 532–554.

Yeoh, B. (1992). "Street Names in Colonial Singapore." *Geographical Review*, 82(3): 313–322.
Yeoh, B. (1996). "Street Naming and Nation-Building: Toponymic Inscriptions of Nationhood in Singapore." *Area*, 28(3): 298–307.
Žižek, S. (1993). *Tarrying with the Negative: Kant, Hegel and the Critique of Ideology*. Durham, NC: Duke University Press.

10 Nationalizing the streetscape

The case of street renaming in Mostar, Bosnia and Herzegovina

Monika Palmberger

Introduction

In present-day Bosnia and Herzegovina (BiH), the naming of public places is ascribed great importance and is often the cause of disputes between the three constituent peoples—Bosniaks, Croats, and Serbs—some of which have even resulted in legal battles before the courts.[1] Along with public squares, airports, and other cultural institutions, many streets were renamed during, and after, the 1992–1995 war by the national group that dominated each respective territory. In general, the renaming process has a twofold effect on a city's streetscape; first, it eradicates the old name and thereby aims to "de-commemorate" the event, person, or place that was previously remembered, and, second, the act of renaming establishes a new commemorative space (Azaryahu 1997; Rose-Redwood, Alderman, and Azaryahu 2010). Street naming is a state-wide practice in Bosnia and Herzegovina that has been used to establish areas of influence and assign a certain territory exclusively to only one "nation."[2] The nation's claim for exclusive rights of a certain territory is manifested in the new names, which establish a historic link between a certain place and the nation. In the case of West Mostar, which will be the focus of this chapter, the de-commemoration concerns the socialist past while the new commemorative space is dedicated to Croat national history.

Before the war, many streets in Bosnia and Herzegovina (and across Yugoslavia), honored the socialist era. Tito's self-declared aim to unite the Yugoslav people and to enforce a shared identity was inscribed upon the urban streetscape. Building on the image of the brave Yugoslav partisans, many streets were, for example, named in memory of important Partisans who fought against the Nazis during World War II. During the 1992–1995 war, and after the national division of Bosnia and Herzegovina, streets were renamed in order to emphasize the national division of the territory and to erase the socialist past.

With the Dayton Peace Agreement, signed on December 14, 1995, the 43-month-long war in Bosnia and Herzegovina officially ended. From that day on, Bosnia and Herzegovina became a shared state of the three constituent peoples—Bosniaks, Croats, and Serbs—with Sarajevo as its capital. The country was split into two entities (plus the special district of Brčko): the Serb Republic (which forms 49 percent of its territory) and the Federation of Bosnia and Herzegovina with its 10 cantons (which forms 51 percent). The Washington Agreement that established the Federation of Bosnia and Herzegovina envisaged Mostar as a united Bosniak-Croat city and as the capital of the Herzegovina-Neretva Canton (Canton 7). For Bosnia and Herzegovina's Croats who claimed Mostar to be their "capital city" (in contrast to Bosniak-dominated Sarajevo and Serb-dominated Banja Luka), the renaming of streets on the Croat-dominated west side was an act of inscribing this claim upon the urban landscape.

This chapter first describes the process of street renaming in Croat-dominated West Mostar. It shows how by renaming streets and public places, Croat nationalist elites erased the socialist past in favor of a Croat national history that was etched into West Mostar's cityscape. As will be shown, this process runs parallel to the general rewriting of history. Despite the various efforts at such revisions, the chapter questions the immediate effect that the renaming of streets has had on the population and their historical consciousness (e.g., the attempt to erase positive memories of socialist Yugoslavia). A first effort is made to set up a dialogue between recent literature on street naming, urban memory, and generational memory.

The material presented in this chapter is part of a broader ethnographic study on memory discourses in Mostar that combines research on national as well as personal/generational memory (Palmberger 2016). Extensive fieldwork was conducted between 2005 and 2008 (with short revisits in 2010 and 2014), including participant observation, interviews, memory-guided city walks, informal conversations, and media analysis.

Renaming as a political strategy in times of regime change

The renaming of streets is not unique to Bosnia and Herzegovina; rather, it is a common practice when regime change calls for a new historiography. Often one of the first acts of a new political regime is the renaming of the physical environment. The collapse of the communist regimes in eastern and south-eastern Europe offers a wealth of examples for the transformation of cityscapes, including the renaming of streets, squares, and even entire cities themselves (Azaryahu 1997; Ugrešić 1998; Light 2004; Rihtman-Auguštin 2004; Gill 2005; Palonen 2008). But this process is not restricted to post-socialist Europe and can be found in other cases when regime change or significant changes in power relations have taken place (Kliot and Mansfield 1997; Leitner and Kang 1999; Swart 2008). Taking Cyprus as an example, a radical renaming of public space occurred after the Turkish invasion and occupation of northern Cyprus in 1974. In Cyprus' Greek-dominated south, old street names have largely remained, yet the Turkish-dominated north has seen a rigorous renaming of streets and other places in order to "Turkify" the territory. In the course of this venture, even old Ottoman place names were renamed because the administration did not trust their "Turkishness" (Kliot and Mansfield 1997, 512).

A new political era is often heralded by naming and renaming "captured territory," as has been the case in many modern nation-states:

> For nationalism naming and re-naming—the continuing transformation of the supposedly eternal physical environment—is one of its most powerful and

contentious tools, as well as one of power's most explicit attempts to rewrite the past, literally reinscribing the surface of the world, and changing the name on the map—often while laying claim to something more ancient and authentic than the "old" one.

(Hodgkin and Radstone 2006, 12)

In many parts of the world, street names have served to evince an official version of the national past by commemorating historical figures and events. This is why street names are prone to a process of renaming in times of political change.

Street signs are mundane objects. Accordingly, it may appear that the impact of commemorative street names on the production of a sense of shared past, and in evincing official versions of history, is significantly less than that of historical monuments, historical museums, or memorial ceremonies. However, commemorative street names (like other place names) conflate history and geography and merge the past that they commemorate into ordinary settings of human life. It is precisely due to its mundane character that the act of street naming acquires its ideological force by presenting history as the "natural order of things" (Azaryahu 1997, 481).

The aim of nationalizing territory in Yugoslavia started long before the war in the 1990s. A good example is Belgrade at the end of the nineteenth century, which underwent a process of the renaming of public space (Stojanović 2007). At that time, an elite commission—including well-respected politicians and intellectuals— was authorized to rename Belgrade's streets. Up to that point, streets had been named after trades and professions, important buildings, or simply their outward appearance. In the late-nineteenth century, many streets were renamed after geographical places important in Serbia's national history and major cities in the Slav world. If a virtual map were drawn connecting the places "remembered" in the new street names, the borders of medieval Serbia would come to the forefront. With this project, the nationally conscious intellectuals of the commission hoped to bring Belgrade's population to identify itself with the places remembered in the new street names so that they would accept them as "their own" (Stojanović 2007, 76). As Dubravka Stojanović (2007) vividly shows in her analysis of this process, the new names stood in sharp contrast to those chosen by Belgrade's business owners for their restaurants and inns, which were much more internationally oriented, with businesses preferring names of distant places such as "America," "New York," "Bosporus," "Little-Paris," "Little-Istanbul," and "Monaco." Stojanović's observations on the renaming of Belgrade's public spaces thereby support the interpretation that those behind the official renaming of streets did not necessarily act according to the understanding of the wider society, as will be discussed later in this chapter.

While the marking of public space is a common practice in the nation-building process, what does the renaming of streets tell us other than revealing the wish of new power-holders to promote certain events while neglecting others? What does it tell us about the people who walk and live in those streets? Should we think of historical consciousness as being initiated from the top (by political elites) and passively received by the population? This view has often directed the analysis of transient regimes. As Keith Brown argues:

> Yet in a region of transient regimes, what is emphasized about the inhabitants is their supposed willingness to adopt another national affiliation quickly. In parallel fashion, the new state is presumed to be ready and able to accept them as *tabulae rasae* and to inscribe national identity on them anew. … What one might term "experienced" history drops out of sight as the rhythm of every aspect of life is taken to be determined by the continuities or disjunctures in "top-down" history.
>
> (2003, 129)

Rather than accepting such a top-down approach to history, this chapter builds on the premise that individuals are shaped by the experiences of the different historico-political periods through which they live (Schuman and Scott 1989; Borneman 1992; Rosenthal 2006). These experiences may show continuities and discontinuities and may agree or conflict with each other, but they have an impact on people's perceptions of their society and its past (Palmberger 2016). Although political changes may come about abruptly and radically, it would be inaccurate to assume that a society fully adapts to all of these changes, and even more inaccurate to imagine that such societal changes take place at the same speed at which political elites change. This does not mean that individuals are unaffected by existing canonical national historiographies when orienting themselves anew in society and that they do not take part in reaffirming them. But autobiographical memories, which do not necessarily fit into the official historiography promoted by the ruling elites, need to find a place in the analysis as well (Palmberger 2013a, 2016).

Much research on the renaming of public space leaves the question as to how the wider population receives this process unanswered. In avoiding this question, such studies do not adequately account for the active role that urban residents play in shaping their own historical consciousness as part of their everyday encounters with the city's commemorative streetscape. Light and Young (2014, 683) have made a plea that we need "further investigation into how place names (and place name changes) are embraced, negotiated, or rejected within the everyday lives of the inhabitants of the city." In order to answer this call, this chapter builds on the work of urban scholars who critically investigate place-making as a relational practice that has social dissonance and contestation as an integral part of it (Massey 1994; Alderman 2000; Muzaini and Yeoh 2005; Till 2005; Rose-Redwood 2008) and on works of memory scholars who understand memory as an active process as well as personal and collective-national memories as utterly intertwined (Tonkin 1992; Ricoeur 2006; Passerini 2007).

Remaining divisions manifested in Mostar's cityscape

The Herzegovinian city of Mostar became a fiercely contested territory during the 1992–1995 war and has thereafter remained a divided city, with a

Bosniak-dominated east and a Croat-dominated west. Mostar represents a special post-war situation, as it is the only city of its size in Bosnia and Herzegovina that has been left divided among two national groups almost equal in size. The composition of Mostar's population has changed drastically as a consequence of the war. Before the war, the population was made up of 35 percent Muslims (Bosniaks), 34 percent Croats, 19 percent Serbs, and 12 percent others (including those who identified themselves as Yugoslavs); presently, Mostar is split in half between Croats and Bosniaks, who make up the vast majority of the population.[3] Today, most Mostarci (Mostarians) define themselves as Bošnjaci/Muslimani (Bosniaks/Muslims), Hrvati (Croats), or Srbi (Serbs), unless they are members of one of the minorities or are among the few who continue to call themselves Jugosloveni (Yugoslavs). Although the main line of identification is religion (most Bosniaks are Muslims, most Croats are Catholics, and most Serbs are Orthodox), the divisions are more of a national than a religious kind (Palmberger 2006). Still, the claim of national suppression during Tito's socialist Yugoslavia went hand in hand with the claim of religious suppression.

The lives of most Bosniaks and Croats are widely separated. If they do not actively seek to interact with one another, Bosniaks and Croats actually share little time with their national counterparts: Bosniak and Croat children attend different schools, teenagers go to different universities, adults have separate workplaces, and leisure time is predominantly spent on "one's own" side of the city (Palmberger 2010, 2013b; Hromadžić 2015). Only a small number of people still maintain friendships with pre-war friends of a different nationality and even for them the nature of their relationships has often changed.

Although there are indeed no clear signs marking the exact border between Bosniak- and Croat-dominated Mostar, markers giving hints of the "nationality" of the city's two sections exist. Apart from street names, which will be discussed in more detail later in this chapter, these are primarily religious symbols: Catholic churches on the west side and mosques on the east side.[4] As found throughout Bosnia and Herzegovina, also in and around Mostar these places of worship have significantly grown in number. Many mosques and churches (often foreign-funded) have been built in recent years, and they attempt not only to outnumber one another but also compete in size. Since religion is the main marker of national identity in the country, religious symbols are the most straightforward territorial markers. This does not necessarily mean, however, that Bosnians welcome the massive investment in churches and mosques. Quite to the contrary, many of my interlocutors expressed great displeasure at what they regarded as a waste of money, money they thought would have been better invested in public amenities like schools and hospitals.

One of the most striking religious territorial markers in Mostar is a huge cross overlooking the city, which was erected in 2000 on the summit of Mount Hum. The cross, around 30 meters high, stands out in the landscape and is one of the first things visitors see when driving into the city. The installation of this cross greatly provoked the Bosniak population, especially considering the fact that a great part of the heavy damage to the city was caused by artillery that was positioned on this mountain. The Croat population, on the other hand, presented the cross as a symbol of peace and the Bosniak request to remove it was seen as a sign of Islamic intolerance against Croats and their Catholic religion. After several years, however, the cross has become, if not an accepted part of life, then at least a popular subject for jokes among the Bosniak population. For example, they joke that the cross, if not good for anything else, at least provides much-needed shade during hot summer days. On another mountain on the east side of the city, there is a huge sign laid out in white stones stating in capital letters, "BiH volimo te" (BiH we love you). Peculiarly, before the war it read "Tito volimo te" (Tito we love you) but had to be revised after Tito's death and the breakup of Yugoslavia.

Most supporters of the new state of Bosnia and Herzegovina can be found among Bosniaks, while Croats generally show more patriotic sentiments for Croatia. The Bosnia and Herzegovina flag serves to illustrate this. On public holidays, in West Mostar the flag is only displayed on official governmental buildings (a new practice fostered by the international community) and on the buildings of international organizations, while on the Bosniak-dominated east side the flag can be seen on many buildings, even on small shops. The nationalization of history is promoted through a plurality of channels in Bosnia and Herzegovina (Torsti 2004; Donia 2010). In addition to political speeches and media reports, the nationalization of history is also very actively supported by a considerable number of academic scholars and through public commemorations, the divided education system, and the memorial culture that also manifests itself in new street names. Let us now turn to the political practice of renaming streets in Mostar.

The politics of exclusion: street renaming in Mostar

In terms of street names in Mostar, which will be the focus of the remainder of the chapter, it is necessary to distinguish between East and West Mostar. While in the former, street names for the most part remained the same as they had been before 1992, the streetscape in the latter witnessed considerable renaming. This process started when West Mostar was declared the capital of Herceg-Bosna during the war in the 1990s. Herzegovina with Mostar as its main city has been central to the Croats' drive toward independence, for the Ustasha movement during World War II, and for the HVO (Hrvatsko vijeće obrane, Croat Defense Council) during the war in the early-1990s. Today, street names, newly erected memorials, and religious symbols mark the public space of West Mostar as part of the Croat nation. The claim of Mostar being the city of Bosnia and Herzegovina's Croats leads, in its extreme interpretation, to a denial of Bosniak (and Serb) existence or to a denial of the Bosniak-dominated part of the city. The claim that Mostar is an exclusively Croat city goes so far that the Bosniak east side of the city is simply ignored (e.g., in books on or maps of Mostar, see Augustinović 1999). Interestingly, Pilvi Torsti (2004) shows how Bosniak tourist guides in Mostar continue to present the entire city similarly to before the war, while Croat guides concentrate only on West Mostar and leave the Ottoman heritage, such as the Old Town, unmentioned.

The new street names emphasize a shared history with the motherland of Croatia by recalling Croat historic personalities and important Croat cities. The former include names of members of the Catholic Church and politically influential persons from the medieval Croat Kingdom as well as the so-called "Independent State of Croatia" (Nezavisna Država Hrvatska, NDH).[5] The new street names invoke the national meta-narrative by recalling the past glory of the medieval Croat Kingdom as well as the long period of victimization of Croats on the way to national liberation from the Nazis. This meta-narrative is also common in history textbooks (Torsti 2004) and was taken up in history lectures I attended at the Croat-dominated university in West Mostar. Among local historians, a central discursive strategy was the linking of the recent with the more distant past, even if the latter was not officially the object of study. Numerous connections to the distant past were made in order to reinforce the ancient history of the Croat nation and to point out the animosity that Croats have faced throughout time (Palmberger 2016).

Like the advocates of Croatia's war of independence (1991–1995), nationalist Croats in Bosnia and Herzegovina defined their "true" national identity in sharp contrast to the Yugoslav identity and the socialist past: heroes of Yugoslavia were called criminals and any reminders of them had to be erased from everyday life. Most monuments from the socialist past in West Mostar were razed during and after the war with the exception of an immense Partisan memorial cemetery that is still located there, even if seemingly neglected and heavily contested by the majority of Mostar's Croats. In the case of street names, the socialist past was erased by "Croatianizing" them. For example, the street once called Omladinska (Street of the Youth) was renamed Hrvatske mladeži (Croat Youth). The simple message behind this was that Croats should no longer be reminded of the Union of Pioneers of Yugoslavia (Savez pionira Jugoslavije). Instead of bringing up fond memories of being a member of the multi-ethnic Yugoslav Pioneers, the new street name aims to direct feelings and affection exclusively toward the Croat youth.

A similar example is Trg Rondo, a central roundabout and square in West Mostar that was renamed Trg Hrvatskih Velikana—Trg Mate Bobana (Croat Nobles Square—Mate Boban Square) after the president of Herceg-Bosna, the Croat quasi-republic during the 1992–1995 war. Rondo is also the location of a cultural center formally called Dom kulture (House of Culture). Today, big letters on the top of the building proclaim its new name: Hrvatski dom herceg Stjepan Kosača (Croat House—Duke Stjepan Kosač) (Figure 10.1).

In West Mostar, streets recalling the socialist period and those named after people known for their role in Serb or Bosniak national history were replaced by the names of Croat rulers, such as kings and dukes, or religious leaders, including cardinals and bishops (Figure 10.2). Others were renamed in memory of recent national heroes and victims, or after Croat cities in order to emphasize their affiliation with the mother-country Croatia. In this spirit, JNA (the Jugoslovenska narodna armija, Yugoslav People's Army) street became Kneza Branimira (Duke of Dalmatian Croatia in the ninth century), and Bulevar Narodne Revolucije (Boulevard of the People's Revolution) became Bulevar Hrvatskih Branitelja (Boulevard of the Croat Defenders). Thus the boulevard once named after the

Figure 10.1 The newly renamed House of Culture, *Croat House—Duke Stjepan Kosač*

People's Revolution was renamed in honor of the Croat defenders who half a century later fought for Croat national independence.

The renamed streets clearly show that the heroes of today are no longer the Partisans who established Tito's Yugoslavia but those who fought, both to defend the Croat nation and for its liberation. However, streets are not only dedicated to national heroes but also to victims. For example, one street in West Mostar has been renamed ulica Bleiburskih žrtava (Victims of Bleiburg Street). When the Partisans met the British troops in Bleiburg, an Austrian town, in April 1945, the British handed over more than 18,000 captured members of various anti-Partisan forces (including Croat Ustasha soldiers) who had sought refuge in Allied-controlled Austria. But most of them were massacred when they reached Yugoslavia (Malcolm 2002).

Another street, previously called ulica Jakova Baruha Španca, after a Spanish communist revolutionary, is today called ulica Žrtava komunizma (Victims of Communism Street). Ulica Petra Drapsina, named after a leading Partisan in the liberation of Mostar on February 14, 1945, was renamed ulica Franjevačka (Franciscan Street). The day of Mostar's liberation by the Partisans (still remembered positively by Mostar's elderly population, particularly, although not solely, among Bosniaks) is perceived as a day of mourning by ruling Croats, who remember the execution of several clerics by the Partisans, after each of whom a street has been named. Since the official Croat commemoration of February 14, 1945, is not a day of celebration but one of mourning, the street formerly known as Avenija 14. Februar (Avenue of 14 February) was renamed Avenija Kralja Tomislava.[6] Interestingly, the street in memory of this Croat ruler of the Middle Ages was renamed in Bosniak-dominated Sarajevo.

The renaming of Mostar's streets, however, did not remain unchallenged. When Mostar was under the interim EUAM (European Union Administration)[7] from

Figure 10.2 A street in West Mostar newly named after a Catholic priest born in 1871 and "replacing" a street name honoring the Yugoslav Partisans

July 1994 until January 1997, the goal was to restore it as a multinational city. In this respect, the renamed streets were seen as an obstacle. When, in 2004, the High Representative, Paddy Ashdown, issued a new city statute for Mostar prescribing a unified city council and administration, he also established a commission for revising the names of streets, squares, and other public places.[8] The commission consisted of seven members, of whom three were of Croat, three of Bosniak, and one of Serb national background. The commission's task was to advise the city council, which in turn had been put in charge of changing the names of two-thirds of all streets and institutions. The commission's existence did not become widely known among Mostar's population and only attracted limited media attention. Between 2004 and 2007, there were a number of media reports on the commission's work, mainly criticizing its inefficiency and slowness. While the Bosniak-dominated press expressed interest in a faster and more satisfactory process of changing to the new names, the Croat-dominated press tended to downplay the importance of the commission. In the newspaper Dnevni List (a Croat-leaning daily published in Mostar), for example, the activities of the commission were criticized for diverting attention from Mostar's more pressing problems such as high unemployment, the illegal construction of buildings, and the lack of residential housing.[9]

The preliminary results of the commission were presented to the city council at its session on May 5, 2006.[10] The commission's task was presented as an effort to rename all streets and institutions that had names associated with fascism and totalitarianism. The commission was forced to admit that its members had had difficulties in compromising on the changes and therefore had only been able to agree on the renaming of a very small number of streets, such as those named after ministers of the NDH, including the streets ulica Mile Budaka, ulica Jure Francetića, and ulica Vokića-Lorkovića. After the commission had presented its results and the municipal councilors of the HDZ (Hrvatske demokratska zajednica, Croat Democratic Union, the Croat nationalist party) had suggested that streets associated with Tito's socialism should also be renamed, a fierce debate arose. The argument that the HDZ brought forward was that Tito's Yugoslavia had been a repressive and totalitarian regime just like that of the NDH. Members of the SDA (Stranka demokratska akcije, Party of Democratic Action, the Bosniak nationalist party) as well as the SDP (Socijaldemokratska partija, Social Democratic Party, the successor of the Communist Party) opposed this and denounced the HDZ's claim as being purely tactically motivated in order to divert attention from this uncomfortable subject. Their argument was that communism could not be equated with fascism. Members of the HDZ disagreed and claimed that it was clear who had been oppressed under Tito's rule—namely Croats, as Croats had not been permitted to use their language and practice their culture in Yugoslavia. Finally, the councilor and representative of the Jewish community intervened by saying that his family had also suffered during Tito's rule but that nevertheless one should not lump all the injustices of past regimes together as if they were equal.

In the days following the city council session, press releases by Bosniak-dominated parties such as the SBIH (Stranka za BiH, Party for Bosnia and

Herzegovina) and the SDA, as well as the SDP, printed in local newspapers demanded all changes of street names to be reversed. To them, changing only a few street names would merely be a cosmetic solution. This point of view presented clear opposition to that voiced in the Croat newspaper, Dnevni List, which argued that the public was not interested in street names but rather wanted the city council to focus on more pressing problems.

Bosniak and Croat representatives (or those who claim to represent the Bosniak or Croat nation) clearly follow different interests and hold different opinions about the process of reversing Mostar's new street names, as initiated by the commission. Still, as mentioned above, the new street names did not become a pressing issue discussed by the local media nor was the commission's work much debated among Mostar's citizens. The remainder of this chapter considers the ways in which Mostarians engage with the past and shows how personal memories are not as easily overwritten as street names.

Memory, nostalgia, and everyday urban encounters

In the introduction to the volume, *The Art of Forgetting*, one of the editors suggests: "We cannot take it for granted that artefacts act as the agents of collective memory, nor can they be relied upon to prolong it" (Forty 1999, 7). Memorials and commemoration sites need people to read them, which means first of all they have to notice and pay attention to them. This is also true for street names. During my fieldwork, I observed that Croats in West Mostar were often unaware of the new street names and other urban toponyms. For instance, the majority of urban residents still call the newly named central square, Trg Hrvatskih Velikana—Trg Mate Bobana, by its former and simpler name, Trg Rondo, and many of those who grew up in pre-war Mostar continue to refer to streets by their old names. Generally, the location of public buildings and other sights were described to me in terms of proximity to other known places rather than by providing the street names. Similarly, my informants were often unaware of memorials (or at least their meaning).

Light and Young (2014), who made a similar observation in post-socialist Bucharest, relate this reluctance among the population to switch to the new name to habit (rather than resistance). I would not overstress the point of resistance in the case of West Mostar either, as much points to the fact that the reluctance to change to the new names is grounded in habit. But the lack of knowledge about the new street names at least shows that the majority of Mostar's Croats did not actively engage with the process of renaming streets. The situation was different for the non-Croat population, especially for Bosniak and Serb returnees. For them these territorial markers were a painful reminder of the fact that what they once used to call home had been taken away from them. This suggests that the act of Croatianizing West Mostar's street names first and foremost signals to non-Croats that West Mostar is no longer their home. One of my Bosniak informants who grew up in West Mostar described the feeling of being a stranger in her former home when she said, "I just don't feel at home there [West Mostar] anymore, even if I lived there for almost 30 years [before the war]. Everything has changed there, the people, the buildings and even the street names!

It is important, however, to acknowledge that:

> national places of memory are not simply imposed onto an empty landscape. … Although elites have had more control over the establishment of places of memory in public settings, they cannot control how they are perceived, understood, and interpreted by individuals and various social groups.
>
> (Till 2003, 295 and 297)

This becomes apparent when citizens actively protest against replacing an old name with a new one, as was the case in Sarajevo when a similar commission to that in Mostar suggested renaming Sarajevo's main artery, ulica Maršala Tita (after the Yugoslav statesman Josip Broz Tito), in honor of Alija Izetbegović (a Bosniak activist and first president of Bosnia and Herzegovina). Here it became evident that the decisions of the cultural, academic, and political elites about what should be publicly remembered and what should be silenced did not resonate with the views of a good part of Sarajevo's citizens (Robinson, Engelstoft, and Pobric 2001). People took to the streets in protest because they did not want to erase the memory of their former president. It is likely that even the relocating of street names, inspired by the Partisan movement, from the center to the periphery after the war in the 1990s, was a compromise for Sarajevo's citizens who did not want to see their (former) heroes leaving the city altogether. But it is not only in Sarajevo that nostalgic discourses of Tito's Yugoslavia persist; they are also still vivid in Mostar, not only among Bosniaks but also among Croats.

Nostalgia among Mostarian Croats may be subtler and not articulated in protests. Nevertheless, it is clearly present in personal narratives, thereby indirectly countering the official historical representations of Yugoslavia. I encountered great admiration for Tito not only among Bosniaks, but also among Croats, as, for example, with one of my interlocutors, Danica, born 1926. For Danica, Mostar is closely linked with Tito, whom she will never stop admiring for what he achieved for Yugoslavia. For her, as for several others of her generation, Tito is more like a saint than an ordinary mortal. When I once asked Danica what Tito meant for Mostar, she gave me the following answer:

> Everything, just everything! He was an extraordinary man, everyone thought that! Everyone liked him, everyone! … He did not care who was who but just cared for everyone, helped everyone as much as he could. He really was a great man! And as long as he was alive we lived, how do you say, "ko bubreg u loju" ["like a kidney in lard," meaning they had plenty of everything, similar to the English expression "like a bee in clover"].

Nostalgia, as became clear during the interviews I conducted with Mostarians of different generations, concerns first and foremost memories of socio-economic security and well-being but also the pre-war good-neighborliness (komšiluk) among the different nations. Nostalgic discourses can even be found among those who welcome what is often referred to as "national liberation" and even among those who are today clearly behind the national division of Mostar (Palmberger 2008, 2013a). Even among young Croats who were educated during and after the war, nostalgia for Yugoslavia was not uncommon. Although most young Croats I met supported the "national liberation" of Croats and their language, they still held positive memories of Yugoslavia, personal memories as well as those passed on to them by their parents and grandparents. This was, for example, the case with Sanja, born in 1981. Sanja at times expressed nostalgia for Yugoslavia, such as when recalling childhood memories of her excitement at the prospect of becoming one of Tito's Pioniri (Pioneers), or of the apartment complex where she grew up, which housed families of all national backgrounds:

> I remember we lived at my grandparents', my mother's parents. We lived here and other Croats there and a Serb family over there and next to them another Croat family and downstairs Muslims and one mixed couple—she was Serb and he Muslim. They were all married couples of similar age like my parents, and they all had kids. We used to play together, hanging out, chatting. My parents used to drink coffee each day with our Serbian neighbors and they visited us for Christmas.

Sanja's nostalgia is mainly directed toward the multi-ethnic coexistence she experienced as a child in the apartment complex she grew up in. She recalls this place and its tenants as one big family despite the families' different nationalities. But Sanja is also "remembering" Yugoslavia as a place where people had jobs, compared to the great unemployment people face today. Even if she studied the Croat language (a subject only offered at university after the war) and stressed several times that she appreciated the Croat "national liberation," she was still critical of contemporary developments, such as when she said, "Now we have our own language but no job. What do we need our own language for if we do not have a job!"

Individuals are not only exposed to changing political contexts but are also confronted with their personal past experiences, which is reflected in the ethnographic examples provided above. My findings suggest that individuals' reconstructions of the past remain more flexible and situational than those of "memory makers" (Kansteiner 2002), namely the elites who decide on renaming streets or historians teaching in schools and at universities. While the latter's narrative is strategic and goal-oriented, the former's is characterized by target-seeking tactics. This distinction relates but does not fully correspond to Michel de Certeau's distinction between strategy and tactic. For de Certeau, strategy is linked to institutions and structures of power: "I call a strategy the calculation (or manipulation) of power relationships that becomes possible as soon as a subject with will and power (a business, an army, a city, a scientific institution) can be isolated" (de Certeau 1984, 35–36). Discursive strategies employed by those who claim to represent the nation are used to narrate independent, coherent national histories, to legitimize and objectify them. A tactic, in de Certeau's sense, is utilized by individuals to create space for themselves in a field of power. A tactic is influenced, but not determined, by rules and structures (de Certeau 1980). In positioning themselves in relation to the past, Mostarians are confronted with the political ruptures manifested in their personal lives and in the history of the wider society. Discursive tactics present in their narratives are utilized to deal with these ruptures (Palmberger 2016).[11]

Conclusion

As I have shown in this chapter, West Mostar underwent a severe process of renaming streets and thereby nationalizing the territory. Despite attempts to counteract and reverse some of the new names, most of them remain. While streets can simply be renamed, thereby eradicating certain aspects of a shared past, this does not seem to be possible for the wider population, at least not in the same radical manner. This does not change the fact that Croatianizing streets in West Mostar is a policy of exclusion that unequivocally signals to the non-Croat population that this part of the city is no longer their home.

In this chapter, I have pointed to the importance of taking into account that depending on their age Mostarians have been exposed to different nationality politics (often in conflict with one another) and have experienced in the past different forms of coexistence. I thus have argued that autobiographical memories, which do not necessarily fit into the official historiography promoted by the ruling elites, need to find a place in the analysis of urban memory scholars. Moreover, I have suggested two different kinds of stratagems in the narratives between those who are professionally involved in writing history and those who are not.

In summary, it can be said that no direct link can be simply assumed between a national historiography inscribed in the cityscape by cultural, academic, and political elites and the way people face these national markers in everyday life and relate to the past. It is therefore important to stress the fact that the process of renaming streets tells us first of all about the changes in the dominant public discourse and political orientation and not necessarily about people's understandings of, and positions toward, the past. This does not mean, however, that they do not join in (and thereby also strengthen) nationalist discourses, but it suggests that perceptions and representations of the past are more manifold and overlapping than depicted in the topography of street names.

Notes

1 When the issue of renaming towns in the Serb Republic (Republika Srpska) was brought before the Constitutional Court of Bosnia and Herzegovina, it was decided that this violated the rights of the other two constituent peoples (Croats and Bosniaks) to collective equality and to freedom from discrimination (Feldman 2005).
2 In this chapter I refer to "nation" instead of "ethnicity." In Bosnia and Herzegovina, people employ the terms narod/nacija (people/nation) to describe group identities. Moreover, the term "ethnic" has often been used in a selective and hierarchical way and has been ascribed only to some groups and not to others (Baumann 1996).

3 In 2007, the Federalni Zavod za Statistiku estimated the population of Mostar to be 111,198.
4 Another identity marker, though not visible in the cityscape, is language, even if the languages on the Bosniak-dominated east and the Croat-dominated west side of Mostar are only minimally distinguishable.
5 The NDH was a quasi-puppet state and had been established with the support of Germany and Italy in April 1941.
6 See Slobodna Dalmacija, February 24, 1995.
7 The EUAM was envisaged in the Washington Agreement and was supposed to enforce "a unified police force (led by the West European Union); freedom of movement across the front line and public security for all; the establishment of conditions suitable for the return of refugees and displaced persons to their original homes; the establishment of a democratically elected council for a single unified city; and the reconstruction of the buildings and infrastructure as well as the reactivation of public services" (Yarwood 1999, 7).
8 A similar commission was set up in Sarajevo as one of the post-war cantonal government's first actions (Robinson, Engelstoft, and Pobric 2001). Advised by the commission, streets carrying the names of historic personalities of Serb (and also, but to a lesser degree, Croat) origin in particular were renamed, while signs in Cyrillic script (used by Serbs) were removed. Streets recalling the Serb and Croat presence in the city were renamed.
9 See Slobodna Dalmacija, February 24, 1995.
10 Special thanks to Larissa Vetters, a fellow anthropologist and friend, for sharing her field notes on this with me.
11 Tactic as de Certeau describes it, however, is more closely linked to resistance than the way tactic is used here. Relating tactics closely to resistance would suggest that the narratives of my interlocutors represent "counter-memories" or "alternative histories" and that we can draw a clear line between "official" and "popular" representations of the past, between history and memory. But this is not the case.

References

Alderman, D. (2000). "A Street Fit for a King: Naming Places and Commemoration in the American South." *The Professional Geographer*, 52(4): 672–684.
Augustinović, A. (1999). *Mostar: Ljudi, kultura, civilizacija*. Mostar: Hrvatska kulturna zajednica u Federaciji BiH.
Azaryahu, M. (1997). "German Reunification and the Politics of Street Names: The Case of East Berlin." *Political Geography*, 16(6): 479–493.
Baumann, G. (1996). *Contesting Culture: Discourse of Identity in Multi-Ethnic London*. Cambridge: Cambridge University Press.
Borneman, J. (1992). *Belonging in the Two Berlins: Kin, State, Nation. Cambridge Studies in Social and Cultural Anthropology*. Cambridge: Cambridge University Press.
Brown, K. (2003). *The Past in Question: Modern Macedonia and the Uncertainties of Nation*. Princeton, NJ: Princeton University Press.
de Certeau, M. (1980). "On the Oppositional Practices of Everyday Life." *Social Text*, (3): 3–43.
de Certeau, M. (1984). *The Practice of Everyday Life*. Berkeley: University of California Press.
Donia, R. (2010). "The New Masters of Memory: Libraries, Archives, and Museums in Postcommunist Bosnia-Herzegovina." In F. Blouin, Jr. and W. Rosenberg (Eds.), *Archives, Documentation, and Institutions of Social Memory* (pp. 393–401). Ann Arbor: University of Michigan Press.
Feldman, D. (2005). "Renaming Cities in Bosnia and Herzegovina." *International Journal of Constitutional Law*, 3(4): 649–662.

Forty, A. (1999). "Introduction." In A. Forty and S. Küchler (Eds.), *The Art of Forgetting* (pp. 1–18). Oxford: Berg.

Gill, G. (2005). "Changing Symbols: The Renovation of Moscow Place Names." *The Russian Review*, 64(3): 480–503.

Hodgkin, K. and Radstone, S. (2006). "Introduction: Contested Pasts." In K. Hodgkin and S. Radstone (Eds.), *Memory, History, Nation: Contested Pasts* (pp. 1–21). New York: Routledge.

Hromadžić, A. (2015). *Citizens of an Empty Nation: Youth and State-Making in Postwar Bosnia-Herzegovina.* Philadelphia: University of Pennsylvania Press.

Kansteiner, W. (2002). "Finding Meaning in Memory: A Methodological Critique of Collective Memory Studies." *History and Theory*, 41(2): 179–197.

Kliot, N. and Mansfield, Y. (1997). "The Political Landscape of Partition: The Case of Cyprus." *Political Geography*, 16(6): 495–521.

Leitner, H. and Kang, P. (1999). "Contested Urban Landscapes of Nationalism: The Case of Taipei." *Ecumene*, 6(2): 214–233.

Light, D. (2004). "Street Names in Bucharest, 1990–1997: Exploring the Modern Historical Geographies of Post-Socialist Change." *Journal of Historical Geography*, 30(1): 154–172.

Light, D. and Young, C. (2014). "Habit, Memory, and the Persistence of Socialist-Era Street Names in Postsocialist Bucharest, Romania." *Annals of the Association of American Geographers*, 104(3): 668–685.

Malcolm, N. (2002). *Bosnia: A Short History*. London: Pan.

Massey, D. (1994). *Space, Place, and Gender*. Minneapolis: University of Minnesota Press.

Muzaini, H. and Yeoh, B. (2005). "War Landscapes as 'Battlefields' of Collective Memories: Reading the Reflections at Bukit Chandu, Singapore." *Cultural Geographies*, 12(3): 345–365.

Palmberger, M. (2006). "Making and Breaking Boundaries: Memory Discourses and Memory Politics in Bosnia and Herzegovina." In M. Bufon, A. Gosar, S. Nurković, and A-L. Sanguin (Eds.), *The Western Balkans—A European Challenge: On the Decennial of the Dayton Peace Agreement* (pp. 525–536). Koper: Založba Annales.

Palmberger, M. (2008). "Nostalgia Matters: Nostalgia for Yugoslavia as Potential Vision for a Better Future?" *Sociologija. Časopis za sociologiju, socijalnu psihologiju i socijalnu antropologiju*, 50(4): 355–370.

Palmberger, M. (2010). "Distancing Personal Experiences from the Collective: Discursive Tactics among Youth in Post-War Mostar." *L'Europe en formation*, (357): 107–124.

Palmberger, M. (2013a). "Ruptured Pasts and Captured Futures: Life Narratives in Post-War Mostar." *Focaal—Journal of Global and Historical Anthropology*, 66: 14–24.

Palmberger, M. (2013b). "Acts of Border Crossing in Post-War Bosnia and Herzegovina: The Case of Mostar." *Identities: Global Studies in Culture and Power*, 20(5): 544–560.

Palmberger, M. (2016). *How Generations Remember: Contested Memories in Post-War Bosnia and Herzegovina*. Basingstoke: Palgrave Macmillan.

Palonen, E. (2008). "The City-Text in Post-Communist Budapest: Street Names, Memorials, and the Politics of Commemoration." *GeoJournal*, 73(3): 219–230.

Passerini, L. (2007). *Memory and Utopia: The Primacy of Intersubjectivity, Critical Histories of Subjectivity and Culture*. London: Equinox.

Ricoeur, P. (2006). *Memory, History, Forgetting*. Chicago: University of Chicago Press.

Rihtman-Auguštin, D. (2004). "The Monument in the Main City Square: Constructing and Erasing Memory in Contemporary Croatia." In M. Todorova (Ed.), *Balkan Identities: Nation and Memory* (pp. 180–196). London: Hurst & Company.

Robinson, G., Engelstoft, S. and Pobric, A. (2001). "Remaking Sarajevo: Bosnian Nationalism after the Dayton Accord." *Political Geography*, 20(8): 957–980.

Rosenthal, G. (2006). "The Narrated Life Story: On the Interrelation between Experience, Memory and Narration." In K. Milnes, C. Horrocks, N. Kelly, B. Roberts, and D. Robinson (Eds.), *Narrative, Memory & Knowledge: Representations, Aesthetics, Contexts* (pp. 1–16). Huddersfield: University of Huddersfield Repository.

Rose-Redwood, R. S. (2008). "'Sixth Avenue is Now a Memory': Regimes of Spatial Inscription and the Performative Limits of the Official City-Text." *Political Geography*, 27(8): 875–894.

Rose-Redwood, R. S., Alderman, D. and Azaryahu, M. (2010). "Geographies of Toponymic Inscription: New Directions in Critical Place-Name Studies." *Progress in Human Geography*, 34(4): 453–470.

Schuman, H. and Scott, J. (1989). "Generations and Collective Memories." *American Sociological Review*, 54(3): 359–381.

Stojanović, D. (2007). "Die Straßen Belgrads 1885–1914." In U. Brunnbauer, A. Helmedach, and S. Troebst (Eds.), *Schnittstellen. Gesellschaft, Nation, Konflikt und Erinnerung in Südosteuropa* (pp. 65–79). Munich: R. Oldenbourg.

Swart, M. (2008). "Name Changes as Symbolic Reparation after Transition: The Examples of Germany and South Africa." *German Law Journal*, 9(2): 105–121.

Till, K. (2003). "Places of Memory." In J. Agnew, K. Mitchell, and G. Toal (Eds.), *A Companion to Political Geography* (pp. 289–301). Oxford: Blackwell.

Till, K. (2005). *The New Berlin: Memory, Politics, Place*. Minneapolis: University of Minnesota Press.

Tonkin, E. (1992). *Narrating Our Past: The Social Construction of Oral History*. Cambridge: Cambridge University Press.

Torsti, P. (2004). "History Culture and Banal Nationalism in Post-War Bosnia." *Southeast European Politics*, 5(2–3): 142–157.

Ugrešić, D. (1998). *The Culture of Lies: Antipolitical Essays*. University Park, PA: Penn State University Press.

Yarwood, J. (1999). *Rebuilding Mostar: Urban Reconstruction in a War Zone*. Liverpool: Liverpool University Press.

11 The politics of toponymic continuity

The limits of change and the ongoing lives of street names

Duncan Light and Craig Young

Introduction

One of the tenets of critical place name studies is that urban toponyms are embedded within broader structures of power, authority, and ideology (Vuolteenaho and Berg 2009). Place naming is thus one component of broader political projects concerned with governmentality, state formation, and nation-building (Rose-Redwood, Alderman, and Azaryahu 2010). Urban toponyms act to reify a particular set of political values in the urban landscape and in this way they "are instrumental in substantiating the ruling socio-political order and its particular 'theory of the world' in the cityscape" (Azaryahu 1996, 312). Furthermore, since urban place names are produced in particular political contexts, they are vulnerable to changes in the political order (Azaryahu 1996, 2009), which bring to power new regimes with different sets of political values and aspirations, with the result that names attributed by the former order may become discordant with the new agenda. For this reason, renaming the urban landscape is one of the most familiar acts (or rituals) accompanying revolutionary political change.

This process of "toponymic cleansing" (Rose-Redwood, Alderman, and Azaryahu 2010, 460) constitutes an unambiguous and public statement about the demise of the former regime (Azaryahu 2009, 2012a). Renaming streets is part of broader processes of "landscape cleansing" (Czepczyński 2008) through which the "official public landscape" (Bell 1999, 183) of the old regime is unmade through acts of "symbolic retribution" (Azaryahu 2011, 29), such as pulling down statues. Since shifts in political order produce a reconfiguring of the "known past" (Kligman and Verdery 2011, 9), the new names attributed to streets and landmarks introduce a new political agenda into the cityscape and, in theory, into the practices of everyday life (Azaryahu 2009; Rose-Redwood, Alderman, and Azaryahu 2010). Such renaming draws a clear boundary between a particular past and aspirations for a new future (Marin 2012). The renamings that accompany political change have been a central focus of critical toponymic scholarship (Azaryahu 2012a), particularly in contexts such as post-socialism (Azaryahu 1997, 2012a; Light 2004; Gill 2005; Palonen 2008; Marin 2012; Drozdzewski 2014), the post-colonial (Yeoh 1996; Nash 1999; Whelan 2003), and post-Apartheid South Africa (Guyot and Seethal 2007; Swart 2008).

However, in this chapter we argue that a focus on renaming streets and other urban landmarks in the wake of political change has tended to neglect the issue of *continuity* in the toponymic landscape. Previous scholarship has been predominantly concerned with issues of change (through renaming) but we seek to highlight the importance of recognizing that there are many instances of a significant *lack* of change; that is, where ideologically charged street names from a previous political order persist within the urban landscape. As a number of authors have argued (Azaryahu 2012a, 2012b; Rose-Redwood 2008; Shoval 2013), the renaming of the urban landscape is not always immediate and thorough. Moreover, politically inspired toponymic change can often unfold in a rather incoherent, inconclusive, spatially diverse, and protracted manner, and the actions of key urban actors are less systematic and co-ordinated than might be expected. All this means that it is important to recognize the *limits* of renaming the urban landscape following political change (Rose-Redwood 2008).

Therefore, by considering a range of "left-over" toponymic landscapes we seek to open up an agenda focusing on the politics of continuity in the toponymic landscape and the limits to renaming. To do this, the chapter explores three broad themes: the limits to the political process of renaming; the effects of the actions of those urban managers and employees responsible for implementing the renaming of streets; and the responses among the urban populace to changes in street names. Our theoretical approach is twofold. First, like other critical place name scholars, we make use of political semiotics (Azaryahu 1996; Rose-Redwood, Alderman, and Azaryahu 2010) in that we focus on street names as signs with multiple meanings within the urban landscape. In particular, we focus on the ways in which such signs demonstrate continuity with the past rather than a decisive break with it. Second, we focus on the agency and performances of key urban actors and the ways in which these can thwart official processes of renaming. We illustrate our arguments with a range of examples and case studies from post-socialist contexts. This is partly because our research interests focus on street names in post-socialist countries (particularly Romania) but also because the complex (and sometimes ambiguous) nature of post-socialist political change has produced numerous examples of continuity within the toponymic landscape (and here we seek to build on previous studies that have focused on changes to urban toponyms in post-socialist contexts). The examples which we present are intended to be illustrative rather than paradigmatic (Azaryahu 1996), and we recognize that the situation in other contexts (such as post-colonialism) may be quite different. We conclude the chapter by sketching out a research agenda for the "politics of toponymic continuity."

Street renaming and the limits of "top-down" political power

The renaming of streets following political change might appear to be uncomplicated since the incoming order will usually have control of the necessary administrative and bureaucratic apparatus. However, there are various instances where a new regime has the ability to rename the urban landscape but does not see this process through to completion. This may occur for a range of reasons. In some cases, political change may not be accompanied by a desire to erase the symbolic traces of the former order. While a new regime might portray itself as representing a radical break from the past, it may, in fact, have an ambivalent relationship to its predecessor (rather than simply being hostile to it). In such circumstances, there may be limited concern to mark a decisive break with the past so that the new regime shows more continuity with—rather than difference from—its predecessor. Such a position will be reflected in the approach to renaming the urban landscape created by the former regime.

One such example is post-Soviet Russia. Following the collapse of the Soviet Union in 1990–1991, Russia sought to dismantle the structures of state socialism (single-party rule and a command economy) and replace them with democratic rule and a market economy. However, Gill (2005) argues that many post-communist politicians had deep roots in the power structures of the Soviet regime and were not motivated by a burning desire to disavow the Soviet past (also, see Forest and Johnson 2002). For this reason, there was less concern to erase the symbolic urban landscape created by communism, with the result that many Soviet-era street names remained unchanged. For example, in Moscow many streets named after leading communist revolutionaries and Soviet politicians retained their names such as "Lenin Street" or "Red Army Street" (Gill 2005). Similarly, in St. Petersburg streets named after key events in communist historiography and the institutions of the socialist state have kept their original names such as "Dictatorship of the Proletariat Square," "Communist Youth Street," or "Lenin Square," while the *Oblast* which surrounds the city has retained the name of "Leningrad" (Marin 2012).

Another example is the city of Minsk (Belarus) which also shows considerable continuity in Soviet-era street names. Between 1990 and 1993, only 14 streets and one square were renamed, because early in the 1990s former-Soviet nomenklatura gained positions in the new urban administration and opposed proposals to return streets to their pre-1917 names (Bylina 2013). Although pressure from political groups such as the Belarusian Peoples' Front had achieved some changes, this ended in 1994 when Alexander Lukashenko came to power and forged strong links with the Russian Federation. Interestingly, the limited street name changes that did occur in the early-2000s—such as "Francysk Skaryna Avenue" becoming "Praspekt Nezelazhnasci" (Independence Avenue) and "Masherov Avenue" changing to "Praspekt Peramozhcau" (Victors Avenue)—were linked to attempts to cement Russian-oriented myths about what Russians call the "Great Patriotic War" (WWII) in the Minsk landscape and Belorussian identity (Bylina 2013). Here a realignment of state politics to ally with the Russian Federation (which itself had not pursued an aggressive renaming strategy) underpinned the continuity of Soviet-era street names in Belarus. These two examples thus illustrate the limits of renaming as related to political continuity and a lack of political will for change despite an apparently radical change in political order.

The limits to state power and the resulting lack of comprehensive renaming are also evident in the case of streets in Romania named after Vasile Roaita during the socialist era (1947–1989). Romania's socialist regime lauded Roaita as a teenage proletarian hero who was shot by the police during a strike in Bucharest's railway yards in 1933. Consequently, streets, schools, collective farms, and a seaside resort were named after him: in 1954, there were nine such streets in Bucharest alone (Light, Nicolae, and Suditu 2002). However, this celebration of Roaita changed after Nicolae Ceaușescu assumed power in 1965. As he became the focus of an extravagant personality cult, Ceaușescu was presented as the foremost young activist in Romanian communism. Hence, Roaita swiftly fell from favor and was effectively airbrushed from the historical narrative (Boia 2002). The streets in Bucharest which commemorated Roaita were renamed, and, by 1973, only one remained (located right on the very edge of the city). This was renamed in 1990 after the fall of Ceaușescu's regime.

Yet, in Voluntari and Jilava, two settlements just outside Bucharest, and in two villages in Transylvania, there are streets which have retained the name of Vasile Roaita. All survived both the decommemoration of Roaita after Ceaușescu's rise to power, and the fall of the socialist regime. Moreover, in Voluntari there are a number of other streets which continue to commemorate minor Romanian Communist Party activists. The continued commemoration of Roaita is not an isolated case. For example, there are five streets in Romania named "August 23," a hallowed date in Communist Party historiography which commemorates the 1944 overthrow of Romania's pro-Axis leader, an event for which the communist regime claimed the credit.

Why have these streets retained their names, despite a decree-law of March 1990 that called for the change of names which were no longer in concordance with Romania's new political aspirations? Ilfov County, in which both Voluntari and Jilava are situated, has long been a stronghold of the Social Democratic Party (Gallagher 2005), a party that, in the post-socialist period, has been favored by former members of the Romanian Communist Party. Local politicians in Voluntari and Jilava probably held a more favorable view of Romania's socialist past and were, therefore, less concerned to erase its symbolic legacy. The significance of the case of Vasile Roaita is that it illustrates the limits of state-level political authorities to enforce changes to streets and other urban landmarks. Even if there is an "official" policy on which names are (or are not) ideologically appropriate, there is no certainty that such a policy will be uniformly applied throughout the country. As Verdery argues: "Policies may be *made* at the center, but they are *implemented* in local settings, where those entrusted with them may ignore, corrupt, overexecute, or otherwise adulterate them" (1991, 84). There is a temptation to portray the implementation of street name changes as reflecting the aspirations of a homogeneous political elite, but this may not always be the case. This is probably the explanation for the four streets in Romania that still carry Roaita's name: local administrators responsible for decommemorating Roaita neglected to do so, or did not consider it sufficiently important or urgent.

In other cases, a new political order may have the political will to rename the urban landscape but lack the material or financial resources to implement their policies. Renaming streets is often assumed to be relatively cheap (Azaryahu 2009), but this is not necessarily the case. A single new street name sign may not in itself be expensive, but if multiple signs are needed for an individual street (and multiple streets are to be renamed), the costs quickly mount. Furthermore, following a change in political order, the new regime usually has other more urgent financial commitments, particularly if radical political change is accompanied by major economic restructuring (which was the case in many post-socialist countries). While changing street names may account for a small proportion of city budgets, it may be regarded by urban managers as a low priority at a time of budget constraints (Light 2004; Gill 2005). Another consideration is the costs to citizens that result from changing a street name (in terms of changing addresses on identity documents). Indeed, such costs can be a major point of debate in naming struggles and have a major political effect on the (un)willingness of a government to impose a new name upon and through the landscape (e.g., Alderman and Inwood 2013). The result is that renaming streets can quickly cease to be a priority. In other words, the renaming of streets may be an early declarative and rhetorical act by an incoming regime, but seeing this process through to completion may be much less important (and can be delegated to lower levels of government who, in turn, may not carry it out).

In post-socialist Bucharest, for example, there are over 4,000 streets (many of which were named to reflect the agenda and priorities of state socialism), but less than 300 were renamed in the 1990s (Light 2004). Other studies of street renaming in post-socialist capitals have recorded similar figures (e.g., Azaryahu 1997; Gill 2005; Palonen 2008; Marin 2012). Moreover, in Bucharest the majority of renamings took place in the central part of the city: almost two-thirds of renamed streets were within 4 km of the city center (Light 2004), with similar findings reported in Moscow (Gill 2005). Although it had the opportunity to comprehensively reconfigure Bucharest's toponymic landscape, Bucharest's City Hall opted for a more restrained approach which concentrated on the most ideologically charged names and on the city center. No doubt City Hall was well aware of the costs involved in a more comprehensive purging of socialist-era street names. In 2000, individual new name plates cost USD $4 each (Anon. 2000). Individually such a sum is trivial, but if applied to a comprehensive renaming campaign throughout the city, the costs can quickly become a major burden for local government. Furthermore, City Hall had other priorities, such as renewing the city's infrastructure and assuring the provision of services. Consequently, the street renaming process quickly ran out of steam and many streets outside the city center retain names with distinctly socialist resonances, for example, "Street of the Worker," "Street of Concrete," "Street of Reconstruction," and "Road of the Cooperative Farm" (for similar examples, see Azaryahu 1997; Gill 2005; Marin 2012). Again, the ability of regimes to implement comprehensive change in the toponymic landscape can be limited and may founder on various practicalities. Indeed, regimes may actually play a strategic game and focus on the centers of capital cities.

Finally, elites with the power of renaming are not homogeneous. A variety of state institutions and political elites may have different (or even competing) agendas regarding renaming (Forest and Johnson 2002; Forest, Johnson, and Till

2004). For example, many of Bucharest's metro stations were originally given names reflecting the ideological agenda of the socialist state and many of these survived the changes of 1989, such as "Square of Work," "New Times," "Peace," "May 1," and (until 2009) "Peoples' Army." Although allocated in a particular ideological context, these names are sufficiently ambiguous and can be reinterpreted in a way appropriate for a post-socialist state. Here another key elite actor—the company that owns the metro and its infrastructure—has taken a different approach to renaming from that of other parts of the state. Again, states and urban authorities are not all-powerful and continuities in naming may reflect the actions of other influential actors.

These examples point to the limits of the political process of renaming streets after revolutionary political change. In many instances (and particularly in post-socialist contexts), such renaming is not comprehensive, driven by an ideological imperative to purge the urban landscape of the symbols of the former regime. Instead, the process is more pragmatic and the emphasis is on changing particular names (those that are most ideologically inappropriate) in particular places (the city center). The result is what we could call "leftover" or "residual" toponymies: street names allocated by the former regime which in some way reflect the values and agenda of that regime. More research is required to explore the extent to which there is a consistent geography to such leftover toponymies (for example, a greater likelihood for them to persist in the more peripheral parts of the city). That the new regime is prepared for such street names to remain "in place" indicates that the use of street names as proclamative ideological statements may be less powerful than is assumed.

Street renaming and the actions of lower-level urban actors

While we have identified above how elites with the political power to rename the urban landscape can fail to see the process through to completion, we know practically nothing about the role played by a range of lower-level actors and agents in the city who can, wilfully or unintentionally, subvert the attempts of political elites to introduce new place names. The role of such actors in implementing political decisions about changing street names has been almost completely overlooked in the critical toponymy literature (yet, see Azaryahu 2012c). This suggests a need to focus on the everyday mundane governance of street renaming and the labor required to achieve it, both of which can play a role in the limits of renaming.

For urban managers to implement top-down policies of street renaming requires the allocation of resources for the production of new signage, plus the labor costs of installing it. Following a period of political change, the allocation of funding may be uncertain (or reduced). Furthermore, urban managers may have more urgent priorities in adjusting to the demands of the incoming political order. Consequently, in balancing financial priorities, urban managers may decide that they cannot immediately afford the costs of producing new signage in order to implement street name changes and so may elect to delay the process until appropriate resources are available. They may even ignore central directives about renaming streets in order to focus on more pressing issues.

In post-socialist Bucharest, well over a decade after the collapse of Ceauşescu's regime, there were many streets which retained their socialist names and signage, even though they had been officially renamed in the early-1990s. This can only have caused confusion for the people who lived there, who may now have been uncertain of their exact address. It also meant that taking a taxi to some parts of the city necessitated using a socialist-era street name, and such a simple performative utterance destabilizes official efforts to rename the urban landscape (Kearns and Berg 2002). Such a delay in introducing new signage into the urban environment following an official decision to change the names of streets has also been reported in a range of other contexts (Azaryahu 1992, 2012c; Shoval 2013).

In other cases, new street name plates have been affixed alongside the old ones. For example, in the city of Timişoara in western Romania (birthplace of the 1989 revolution), there are numerous instances where the socialist era street name (and name plate) remained in place (in April 2016) alongside the new names and plates (in a different format) allocated in the post-socialist era (Figure 11.1). This apparently results from a decision by an official in the City Hall to retain the old signage in order to avoid confusion about addresses among the residents of those

Figure 11.1 Old and new street names in Timişoara, Romania (2015). *Strada Turgheniev* commemorates Ivan Turgenev, a nineteenth-century Russian writer. The street was renamed in 1993 to commemorate a senior figure in the Romanian Orthodox Church.

streets and to ease wayfinding within the city.[1] In such instances, the role of a street name as a means of spatial identification and orientation takes priority over its semiotic role as a commemorative marker (Azaryahu 1996). The result is a curious and unresolved form of parallel toponymy which, once again, raises questions about the power and limits of ideologically motivated street name changes.

In Bucharest, there are many similar instances of socialist-era signage remaining in place, but the explanations appear to be different. For example, in the center of the city one of the principle arteries—"Boulevard of the Republic" (named in the first months of the socialist era)—returned to its pre-WWII name of "Queen Elisabeth Boulevard" in 1995. Yet, while many of the name plates with the socialist-era toponym were removed, there were several that remained in place throughout the late-1990s and early-2000s. One survived until late-2006 (when it was removed during the preparations for Romania's accession to the European Union). Other examples of isolated socialist-era name plates can be found in many parts of the city. A similar situation is apparent in Tbilisi, Georgia, where new street names, particularly in the central parts of the city (those most likely to be encountered by tourists), are bilingual in Georgian and English. These have replaced older street name signs in Russian. However, not far from the city center, there are numerous surviving Soviet-era signs in Georgian and Russian, even on renovated buildings. In some cases, workmen have decided to simply spray pebble-dash over the Russian language sign rather than taking it down, leaving a ghostly remnant of the previous regime.

This points to the role of another important group of urban actors: the workers who are responsible for affixing new street name plates and taking down the old ones. The actions of this group play a vital role in implementing broader political decisions about renaming streets: they are responsible for literally putting the new names "in place." However, there is the possibility that they can also thwart the process in a variety of ways. In the case of Bucharest, we can only speculate about why city workers neglected to remove the socialist-era signage. It may be that they did not notice the old signs, or that the old signage is physically difficult to remove due to the way that it is fixed to buildings. Alternatively, workers may have chosen not to remove the old name plates if they were not given explicit instructions to do so. The ideological fervor which drives state-led, top-down renaming strategies may mean little to workers who have to actually physically implement these changes (some of whom may decide that it is more practical not to remove the old names and signs). Indeed, by the time the new names had been chosen and were ready to be installed, many of the workers were probably entirely indifferent to the remnants of the socialist era which remained in the city. Here the mundane practices and attitudes of city workers and the materiality of the old signage combine to underpin the persistence of toponymies in the urban landscape. The materiality and "agency" of old nameplates can thus also play a role in the limits of top-down political renaming projects.

Another important group of urban actors includes those responsible for making the new signage. In the context of a broader confusion about the changing names of streets, they may misunderstand their instructions. This appears to be the only explanation for cases in central Bucharest where new signage was produced and affixed to buildings which still displayed the socialist-era name. For example, *Strada Măndineşti* in the historic center of the city was renamed *Strada Sf. Dimitru* (after a nearby church) in 1993 but signage installed in the 1990s listed its original name with the "changed" name in brackets and some of these signs remained in place in December 2015 (Figure 11.2).

In the case of post-socialist Bucharest, the managers of apartment blocks represent another group of urban actors who operate independently from the city authorities responsible for street naming and whose actions undermined the process. In Bucharest, the address of the block is painted above each entrance and many blocks also display small metal plates indicating particular entrances and the apartments which can be accessed from them. If a street changed its name in the post-socialist period, then it was the role of each block manager to change the signage. However, many block managers (who have found their role diminished in the post-socialist period) were slow to do this or did not even bother. They may have lacked funds to have the address repainted; they may have been unwilling to change a name to which they and the residents were accustomed; they may not have thought it important; or they may have simply forgotten about it. The outcome is that socialist-era names can still be found on blocks, even if the street signage displays the correct name (Figure 11.3).

The sometimes conflicting actions of city governments and the committees responsible for implementing changes in street names can also play a role here. It is well known that urban administrations are complex, and sometimes characterized

Figure 11.2 A street name sign in central Bucharest (2005). *Strada Măndineşti* was renamed *Strada Sf* [Saint] *Dumitru* in 1993. However, the signage gives the former name with the new name in brackets.

Figure 11.3 Old and new street names on an apartment block in Bucharest (2009). During the socialist era the street was named *Strada Furnirului* (Street of the Wood Laminators). It was renamed *Strada Vintila Mihăilescu* (after a Romanian geographer) in 1992. However, the old name remains on a number of the apartment blocks along this street.

by political disagreement or poor communication between departments. This appears to explain a rather confused approach to renaming a metro station in Minsk. In 1992, the former "Lenin Square" was renamed "Independence Square," as was the nearby metro station. However, the toponymic cleansing was far from thorough as the name "Lenin Square" remained on signs within the metro system (in addition to a surviving monument of Lenin) (Bylina 2013). In 2003, the city authorities decided to reintroduce the name "Lenin Square" to the metro station. Public protests followed and the street names commission within the city's Executive Committee proposed to reinstate "Independence Square" as the name for the metro station. This was never implemented with the commission citing public protest against the name change. Thus the Soviet-era toponym "Lenin Square" has reappeared and persists due to disagreements within the city authority.

The toponymic traces of a former regime can thus survive for a wide variety of reasons, including a lack of resources or political will to replace them; misunderstanding of what changes are to be implemented; a possible unwillingness among workers to do anything more than instructed; a lack of interest in the renaming of streets; or simply a failure to recognize it as important. A political decision to change a street name does not necessarily mean that the name will be changed (at least not immediately) or that the material signage which marked the former name will be removed. These examples illustrate how the projects of political elites can be compromised through the mundane actions of a wider range of lower-level urban actors (both within and outside the administrative apparatus of the local state). For these reasons, top-down projects to rename the urban landscape can be much less immediate, visible, and effective than is sometimes supposed. Again, this points to the limits of the process of renaming the urban landscape after a period of political change.

Everyday popular responses to street name changes

Although there has been considerable academic interest in the renaming of streets following political change, most researchers have focused on the top-down, political-administrative process of renaming. However, the responses of the urban population to such renamings have received only scant attention. Indeed, the wider issue of how people use urban place names is an area where more research is required (Azaryahu 2011; Light and Young 2014). Among political elites there seems to be an unstated assumption that renaming the urban landscape for political ends will be *effective*; that new names will be accepted by the inhabitants of the city and will be quickly absorbed into everyday life. However, street name changes do not necessarily enjoy popular support and can be contested or resisted (Azaryahu 1996; Kearns and Berg 2002; Alderman 2008; Rose-Redwood, Alderman, and Azaryahu 2010; Alderman and Inwood 2013; Light and Young 2014), such that new names attributed to the urban landscape can fail to gain widespread popular acceptance (de Soto 1996; Myers 1996; Rose-Redwood 2008; Marin 2012; Shoval 2013; Light and Young 2014).

Urban residents can oppose street name changes for a number of reasons. They may feel an attachment to the old name and this can be especially important following radical political change when residents may look for the reassurance offered by the familiar (Gill 2005). Here it is important to acknowledge that ideologically imposed street names may undergo a process of "semantic displacement" (Azaryahu 1996, 321), through which the name becomes detached from the person or event which it commemorates. To the inhabitants of the city, a name may be understood as just a name (rather than a proclamative ideological statement). Indeed, many urban dwellers may not even know the significance of what or who is commemorated by a street name but still form mundane attachments to it as the place where they live or socialize. Therefore, they may be unsympathetic to top-down attempts to change it.

Alternatively, residents may contest a new name because they do not identify with who or what is commemorated by it. While the incoming regime may seek to impose a new hegemonic narrative of national history, not everyone in the population will necessarily agree with the choice of new names. Furthermore, residents may distrust the motives behind the attribution of a new name. A further reason why residents may oppose street renamings is for the personal inconvenience it causes them. To understand this we only have to think of the number of people, institutions, and organizations that we need to inform if we move house and change our address. Changing the name of a street places a burden on the residents of that street to change their identity papers, and inform employers, banks, utility companies, and friends of their new address. This all involves time and expense and for this reason renamings can be unpopular (particularly if there is a delay between a political change and the subsequent changing of street names).

The actual practices (or "tactics" following De Certeau 1984) of resistance to a new toponym that has been imposed by political elites can take two forms. First, citizens can simply refuse to use a newly allocated name (Yeoh 1992; Myers 1996; Shoval 2013). For example, in Bucharest in 1997 the Christian Democratic National Peasant Party, which controlled the City Hall, elected to change the name of "May 1 Boulevard" to "Ion Mihalache Boulevard" (after a pre-WWII politician who was a member of the party). This renaming was deeply unpopular with many in the city who argued that May 1 represented an international day of worker's solidarity that did not have exclusively socialist associations. The renaming was also interpreted as a rather clumsy attempt by the ruling party to foreground one of its "own" people (Light and Young 2014). Consequently, many Bucharesters deliberately do not use the "official" name (preferring to continue to use "May 1 Boulevard"), and a group of residents of the boulevard submitted a formal request for it to return to its original name (Anon. 2002). Shops and businesses located on the boulevard frequently use both names in their publicity in acknowledgment that there are many who do not know the boulevard by its official name. Thus toponyms can continue in everyday practice even if officially removed, further illustrating the limits of renaming practices.

A second way to oppose a change of street name is to seek to intervene in the administrative process, either to prevent a new name being attributed, or to seek to reverse a previous renaming. The rationale for this is often a mixture of the ideologically laden nature of street names with more mundane and prosaic considerations, such as confusion among urban residents, concerns with the cost and inconvenience associated with having the street where they live renamed, or popular attachment to long-established names. For example, in Moscow in the early-1990s, the Presidium of Moscow City Council began a renaming process during which it changed about 70 street names. However, public opposition to this process grew, particularly linked to the confusion caused in everyday life by the renamings, with the result that the City Council halted the renaming process, ensuring the survival of names which were due for removal (Vakhrusheva 1993). In one particular case, that of renaming "Ulitsa Pushkinskaya" to "Bolshaya Dmitrovka," Muscovites opposed renaming on grounds of the cost to local government at a time when it had other priorities and the fact that Pushkin's name was strongly associated in their minds with that location.

A further example from Moscow illustrating this complex mix of political opposition and more mundane considerations is that of what is now "Alexander Solzhenitsyn Street," which was renamed in 2008 from "Big Communist Street" (Harding 2008). This name change was the subject of political opposition by the communist Left Front youth organization which mounted a legal challenge. However, residents also opposed the change because of the cost and inconvenience of altering essential documents. Here Muscovites signed a petition by the hundreds and residents of the street took more direct action, physically tearing street signs from buildings (Harding 2008). In the Siberian city of Irkutsk, architects and historians petitioned the city to halt renaming proposals on the grounds of protecting the historical value represented by the toponymic landscape and fears that residents would become confused (Goble 2013). However, counter-examples can be found. Bylina (2013), for example, reports that the public, mass media, and intellectuals in Minsk express discomfort with the continuity of Soviet-era street names in the post-Soviet period, illustrating that public responses to renaming processes will be highly varied in different contexts.

However, it is possible to expand the terms of the debate here by recognizing that the use of old toponyms can persist even when officially and materially they have been changed, simply because of everyday practices and habit. Geographers, and those studying the politics of toponymic change, have perhaps been too keen to focus on resistance. While the contestation of new street names is important, we also have to recognize that it is not the only popular process which subverts the imposition of the new names. We also need to consider a range of unreflexive practices and habits among urban residents that are often overlooked (though see De Soto 1996; Rose-Redwood 2008; Light and Young 2014). Elsewhere, for example, we consider the case of "Moghioroş Market" in Bucharest, a socialist-era toponym that commemorates Alexandru Moghioroş (1911–1969), who was a senior member of the Romanian Communist Party (Light and Young 2014). After 1989, Bucharest's City Hall changed the name to "Drumul Taberei Market," reflecting the name of the neighborhood in which it is located. However, the name "Moghioroş" remains in daily use, sometimes instead of the new name and sometimes in parallel to it. The name is largely devoid of its original meaning (few people remember who it commemorates). Local people continue to use the original name because they have always done so, or they hear others use it, rather than because they are resisting the de-Communization strategies of the post-socialist Romanian state. Businesses also use the old name so that people understand where they are located. In this case, it is simply mundane, habitual practices that keep the old toponym in current use.

This section has explored a little understood aspect of the politics of toponymic continuity and the limits to political power when it comes to renaming strategies, namely public responses to renaming. For a variety of reasons, reflecting a complex mix of the political and the practical, residents may actively oppose renamings, seek to reverse them, or choose to ignore official renaming practices. These can be political actions but can also be due to habit or even apathy. These points also raise the question of the extent to which people in their everyday lives pay attention to, or connect with, street names and changes. Publics may not share the importance attached by political elites to new names, which highlights the performative limits of street names as political statements.

Conclusion

The study of toponymic cleansing has rightly established itself as a prominent and popular theme within the critical toponymy literature. Such studies will continue to be important, not least because they reveal the significant role of street renaming in the interplay between ideology, power, identity, urban governance, and landscape change. However, in this chapter, we have argued that critical toponymic studies should go beyond examining the issue of street renaming as part of regime change to also consider the "politics of toponymic continuity." To conclude this chapter, we identify three areas which we consider central to developing this research agenda.

First, more research could address continuities in ideologically charged toponyms, from the scale of individual streets to the toponymic landscape of entire cities. Previous studies have tended to focus on which streets are renamed and why, but more investigation is required of why some streets are not renamed. This is not so much about a quantitative evaluation of how many streets retain their names—after all, it is unrealistic to think that an urban administration would seek to change all street names—but about the politics of which are deemed to not require eradication. Such a choice is value-laden and inherently political and may involve retaining (or ignoring) street names which may, from external perspectives, seem appropriate for changing. However, historical figures and events are ambiguous and are always socially and politically constructed. Hence, while it might seem obvious that a new regime would want to remove ideologically inappropriate names, implementing this process may be considerably less straightforward and people can have all kinds of complex relationships to place names. The politics of such relationships and choices—by states, urban authorities, and urban populations—require much more thorough investigation. This needs to be done in the context of carrying out more nuanced analyses of the comprehensiveness of renaming, which considers the more complex geographies of renaming and continuity as part of the same process. The issue of geographical complexity in the thoroughness of renaming, from the intra-urban scale to looking across the urban hierarchy outside capital cities, requires much more consideration, and such studies could also be more sensitive to any temporal dynamics.

Second, a focus on the politics of continuity also demands a greater appreciation of both the messy politics of renaming and the potentially incoherent strategizing and implementation that follows. Previous research has perhaps tended to draw too neat a link between regime change and street renaming, implying a straightforward political process. However, political tensions and in-fighting (not just between political viewpoints and parties, but within urban administrations or between state- and urban-scale administrations) require greater attention (e.g., Palonen 2008). Further down the line, what is really lacking is an understanding of how lower-level actors within and outside of urban administrations (committees, urban managers, block managers, work units, and workers) influence this process. In particular, it may be the case that the fate of particular street names rests on mundane decisions around budgets and resources, or the approaches of the workers detailed to actually take down old nameplates and put up new ones.

Last, a major research lacuna is the ways in which various publics form different relationships to street names, beginning with the question of the extent to which street names (and changes) actually do resonate in any way within people's everyday lives. The assumption that changing the toponymic landscape actually has an impact on urban residents requires much more critical investigation. Clearly in some places people do react to changes to street names, but this may not necessarily constitute political opposition, and may be informed by much more mundane and prosaic considerations (like cost and inconvenience). Alternatively, urban residents may be happy to continue living with street names which incoming regimes might consider ideologically inappropriate because they have developed long-term personal and even emotional relationships with those names. Engaging with the issue of residents' emotional and everyday lived geographies of street names, and how they impact upon continuity and change, is a major challenge for our proposed "politics of toponymic continuity," which itself suggests a new direction for critical toponymies.

Note

1 We are grateful to Remus Creţan for this observation.

References

Alderman, D. (2008). "Place, Naming and the Interpretation of Cultural Landscapes." In P. Howard and B. Graham (Eds.), *The Ashgate Companion to Heritage and Identity* (pp. 195–213). Aldershot: Ashgate.

Alderman, D. and Inwood, J. (2013). "Street Naming and the Politics of Belonging: Spatial Injustices in the Toponymic Commemoration of Martin Luther King Jr." *Social and Cultural Geography*, 14(2): 211–233.

Anon. (2000). "200 de Străzi fără Plăcuţe de Identificare." *Romania Libera*, December 4: 25.

Anon. (2002). "Bulevardul Ion Mihalache s-ar Putea Numi Din Nou 1 Mai." *România Liberă (Bucureşti* Supplement), November 22: I.

Azaryahu, M. (1992). "The Purge of Bismarck and Saladin: The Renaming of Streets in East Berlin and Haifa, a Comparative Study in Culture Planning." *Poetics Today*, 13(2): 351–367.

Azaryahu, M. (1996). "The Power of Commemorative Street Names." *Environment and Planning D: Society and Space,* 14(3): 311–330.

Azaryahu, M. (1997). "German Reunification and the Politics of Street Names: The Case of East Berlin." *Political Geography*, 16(6): 479–493.

Azaryahu, M. (2009). "Naming the Past: The Significance of Commemorative Street Names." In L. Berg and J. Vuolteenaho (Eds.), *Critical Toponymies: The Contested Politics of Place Naming* (pp. 53–67). Farnham: Ashgate.

Azaryahu, M. (2011). "The Critical Turn and Beyond: The Case of Commemorative Street Naming." *ACME: An International E-Journal for Critical Geographies*, 10(1): 28–33.

Azaryahu, M. (2012a). "Renaming the Past in Post-Nazi Germany: Insights into the Politics of Street Naming in Mannheim and Potsdam." *Cultural Geographies*, 19(3): 385–400.

Azaryahu, M. (2012b). "Rabin's Road: The Politics of Toponymic Commemoration of Yitzhak Rabin in Israel." *Political Geography*, 31(2): 73–82.

Azaryahu, M. (2012c). "Hebrew, Arabic, English: The Politics of Multilingual Street Signs in Israeli Cities." *Social and Cultural Geography*, 13(5): 461–479.

Bell, J. (1999). "Redefining National Identity in Uzbekistan: Symbolic Tensions in Tashkent's Official Public Landscape." *Ecumene*, 6(2): 183–213.

Boia, L. (2002). *Istorie şi Mit în Conştiinţa Românească* (Third Edition). Bucharest: Humanitas.

Bylina, V. (2013). "Minsk Toponymics: Communist Street Names in a Medieval City." *BelarusDigest*, January 11, http://belarusdigest.com/story/minsk-toponymics-communist-street-names-medieval-city-12722.

Czepczyński, M. (2008). *Cultural Landscapes of Post-Socialist Cities: Representations of Powers and Needs*. Aldershot: Ashgate.

De Certeau, M. (1984). *The Practice of Everyday Life*. Berkeley: University of California Press.

De Soto, H.G. (1996). "(Re)inventing Berlin: Dialectics of Power, Symbols and Pasts, 1990–1996." *City and Society*, 8(1): 29–49.

Drozdzewski, D. (2014). "Using History in the Streetscape to Affirm Geopolitics of Memory." *Political Geography*, 42: 66–78.

Forest, B. and Johnson, J. (2002). "Unraveling the Threads of History: Soviet-Era Monuments and Post-Soviet National Identity in Moscow." *Annals of the Association of American Geographers*, 92(3): 524–547.

Forest, B., Johnson, J., and Till, K. (2004). "Post-Totalitarian National Identity: Public Memory in Germany and Russia." *Social and Cultural Geography*, 5(3): 357–380.

Gallagher, T. (2005). *Theft of a Nation: Romania since Communism*. London: Hurst.

Gill, G. (2005). "Changing Symbols: The Renovation of Moscow Place Names." *The Russian Review*, 64(3): 480–503.

Goble, P. (2013). "Renaming Craze in Russia Extends from Stalingrad to Street Level." *Window on Eurasia*, February 10: http://windowoneurasia2.blogspot.co.uk/2013/02/window-on-eurasia-renaming-craze-in.html

Guyot, S., and Seethal, C. (2007). "Identity of Place, Places of Identities: Change of Place Names in Post-Apartheid South Africa." *South African Geographical Journal*, 89(1): 55–63.

Harding, L. (2008). "Signs of Dispute on Moscow's Solzhenitsyn Street." *The Guardian*, December 12: www.theguardian.com/world/2008/dec/12/russia

Kearns, R. and Berg, L. (2002). "Proclaiming Place: Towards a Geography of Place Name Pronunciation." *Social and Cultural Geography*, 3(3): 283–302.

Kligman, G. and Verdery, K. (2011). *Peasants under Siege: The Collectivization of Romanian Agriculture, 1949–1962*. Princeton, NJ: Princeton University Press.

Light, D. (2004). "Street Names in Bucharest 1990–1997: Exploring the Modern Historical Geographies of Post-Socialist Change." *Journal of Historical Geography*, 30(1): 154–172.

Light, D., Nicolae, I., and Suditu, B. (2002). "Toponymy and the Communist City: Street Names in Bucharest 1947–1965." *GeoJournal*, 56(2): 135–144.

Light, D. and Young, C. (2014). "Habit, Memory and the Persistence of Socialist-Era Street Names in Post-Socialist Bucharest, Romania." *Annals of the Association of American Geographers*, 104(3): 668–685.

Marin, A. (2012). "Bordering Time in the Cityscape: Toponymic Changes as Temporal Boundary-Making: Street Renaming in Leningrad/St Petersburg." *Geopolitics*, 17(1): 192–216.

Myers, G. (1996). "Naming and Placing the Other: Power and the Urban Landscape in Zanzibar." *Tijdschrift voor Economische en Sociale Geografie*, 87(3): 237–246.

Nash, C. (1999). "Irish Placenames: Post-Colonial Locations." *Transactions of the Institute of British Geographers*, 24(4): 457–480.

Palonen, E. (2008). "The City-Text in Post-Communist Budapest: Street Names, Memorials and the Politics of Commemoration." *GeoJournal*, 73(3): 219–230.

Rose-Redwood, R. (2008). "'Sixth Avenue is Now a Memory': Regimes of Spatial Inscription and the Performative Limits of the Official City-Text." *Political Geography*, 27(8): 875–894.

Rose-Redwood, R., Alderman, D., and Azaryahu, M. (2010). "Geographies of Toponymic Inscription: New Directions in Critical Place-Name Studies." *Progress in Human Geography*, 34(4): 453–470.

Shoval, N. (2013). "Street-Naming, Tourism Development and Cultural Conflict: The Case of the Old City of Acre/Akko/Akka." *Transactions of the Institute of British Geographers*, 38(4): 612–626.

Swart, M. (2008). "Name Changes as Symbolic Reparation after Transition: The Examples of Germany and South Africa." *German Law Journal*, 9(2): 105–20.

Vakhrusheva, A. (1993). "Lost? City Weights End to Street Renaming." *Moscow Times*, July 14.

Verdery, K. (1991). *National Ideology under Socialism: Identity and Cultural Politics in Ceauşescu's Romania*. Berkeley: University of California Press.

Vuolteenaho, J., and Berg, L. (2009). "Towards Critical Toponymies." In L. Berg and J. Vuolteenaho (Eds.), *Critical Toponymies: The Contested Politics of Place Naming* (pp. 1–18). Farnham: Ashgate.

Whelan, Y. (2003). *Reinventing Modern Dublin: Streetscape, Iconography and the Politics of Identity*. Dublin: University College Dublin Press.

Yeoh, B. (1992). "Street Names in Colonial Singapore." *Geographical Review*, 82(3): 313–322.

Yeoh, B. (1996). "Street-Naming and Nation-Building: Toponymic Inscriptions of Nationhood in Singapore." *Area*, 28(3): 298–307.

12 Toponymic complexities in Sub-Saharan African cities

Informative and symbolic aspects from past to present

Liora Bigon and Ambe J. Njoh

Introduction

> The linguist Pièrre Alexander noticed that on the official map of Cameroun made before independence a certain "Ambababoum" is shown as an important village on the road from Yaoundé to Bafia. However, it does not exist and has never existed within living memory.
>
> (Baesjou 1988, 1)

Rather than relating to any reality, the above quotation is a colonialist fictional toponymic construct of a rural, not urban, environment. Risking criticism for exposing the colonized spatiality in Sub-Saharan Africa to ridicule, we use this quotation as an opening for discussing the reverse. Our interest is not in existing names for non-existing places, but in non-existing names for existing places. In short, we are interested in the problem of toponymic ambiguity in urban Sub-Saharan Africa.

Toponymic inscription—that is, place naming generally and street naming in particular—as well as physical addressing systems, are critical components of an effective and efficient urban management system.[1] It is central to the orderly, systematic, and semiotic construction of the city. By designating locations and pronouncing certain thoroughfares as distinct urban units, it also conflates urban space and the symbolic realm of cultural signification (Azaryahu 2009). In this chapter, both the informative and symbolic dimensions of toponymic inscription are analyzed in light of three interrelated spatial problems in contemporary Africa. The first is the failure by municipal authorities to prioritize toponymic inscription. Municipal authorities in Sub-Saharan Africa have seldom prioritized the need to identify places, produce meaningful maps, codify streets, or generate comprehensible and unambiguous addressing systems for their cities (Njoh 2010). The second concerns the colonial roots or origins of the toponymic ambiguity problematic in Africa. Particularly, we discuss generic and specific names in the colonial urban vocabularies of both French and British regimes, the main colonizing powers on the continent. In the process, we expose the dualistic nature of the relevant nomenclature in the colonial period. Here, we hasten to note that street naming was a consequence of residential segregation on a hierarchicalized racial basis (Bigon 2012). The third concerns power struggles in built space, particularly critical during the colonial period. We use this period as a point of departure for a more intense focus on the nuances and complexities of urban toponymy in the postcolonial era.

Despite its indisputable importance in urban management in Sub-Saharan Africa, toponymic inscription has been accorded only scant attention in the relevant literature. Njoh has expressed dismay at the tendency to ignore this problem. He contends that with the exception of a few (Farvacque-Vitkovic, Godin, Leroux, and Chavez 2005; Coetzee and Cooper 2007; Njoh 2010; Bawumia 2012), most analysts have ignored this area of study. Consequently, several gaps remain in knowledge of its implications for socio-economic development in Africa. In recent critical toponymic scholarship, street names are recognized as products of cultural, social, and political struggles over spatial and cognate toponymic practices (Rose-Redwood, Alderman, and Azaryahu 2010). However, the manner in which these struggles are resolved, and the resultant street name, constitute a function of several factors, including the historical, socio-cultural, geographical, and political contexts. Thus, knowledge of the implications of toponymic inscription is best fostered by contextualizing the variables of interest.

By examining the toponymic inscription problematic in Sub-Saharan Africa, we go beyond "simply reflecting the impress of the state or elite ideologies" (Myers 1996, 237). This chapter seeks to unearth the impact of toponyms on spatial policies and everyday practices—be they of the "top-down" or "bottom-up" variety. We draw on specific examples from a variety of cities throughout Sub-Saharan Africa, with a focus on Cameroon and Senegal where we conducted field work, for illustrative purposes.

Urban vocabularies, toponymic inscription, and implications

Clearing his throat to overcome his nerves, he began by criticizing the countries of Europe, who dazzled us with the sun of independence, when in fact we're still dependent on them, since we still have avenues named after General de Gaulle and General Leclerc and President Coti and President Pompidou, but in Europe there are no avenues named after Sese Seko, or Idi Amin Dada, or Jean-Bedel Bokassa or any of the other fine men known personally to him, and valued for their loyalty, humanity, and respect of the rights of man.

(Mabanckou 2010, 14–15)

The above words were once uttered by the Cameroonian-born writer Alain Mabanckou. The words highlight, though in an ironic way, the inherent tension between African states and their former European métropoles in postcolonial times. The words also draw attention to a more worrisome problem, which arises from the tendency to adopt appellations from Eurocentric lexicons as toponyms in Sub-Saharan Africa. While content-related aspects of such names are not our main concern, we remark that unambiguous addresses of the genre indicated by Mabanckou—intended for commemorative or other purposes—are relatively rare in Africa. Where they exist, their origin can be traced to the colonial era and their spatiality is relatively limited.

Postcolonial authorities have rarely considered the task of developing a precise address and property identification system a priority. A precise address is one that includes unambiguous details on the permanent or temporary location of a person, event, place, or thing: addresses of this genre are rarely found in African cities. However, we would be remiss if we failed to mention recent developments that have included, if only peripheral, attention from politico-administrative authorities in the region. For instance, according to the Ghanaian administrator Mahamudu Bawumia, a well-designed system of street, place, and property identification is a prerequisite for the transformation of Ghana's economy into a modern and globally competitive one. Such a system, Bawumia (2012) insists, is necessary to facilitate the navigation of built space, thereby facilitating commercial and related activities.

Perhaps most importantly, precise and unambiguous addresses are necessary for the proper functioning of modern navigation-facilitating gadgets that depend on Geographic Positioning Systems (GPS). The need for precise street, place, and property identification systems has been amplified in recent years by the processes of globalization. Globalization has resulted in rapidly integrating all regions, including Africa. Africa can neither develop nor derive any benefits from this process without redressing its toponymic inscription problem (Anson 2007; UN-DESA 2008). Regimes of urban management are gravely compromised by the inability of service delivery and other devices to function in Sub-Saharan Africa. At the micro-economic level, for example, while throughout the Global North a variety of goods and services can now be ordered and paid for online through smart phones from the comfort of one's home, online transactions in Africa remain a luxury in a few cases, and non-existent in most. The region is replete with cities characterized by nondescript spatial structures. A paramount feature of these cities is that they contain numberless buildings, nameless streets, or streets that bear names that are not sign-posted (Njoh 2003).

Like the modern spatial structures with which they are associated, the sign-posting of street names, and other toponyms, in Sub-Saharan Africa is a colonial legacy. It is therefore paradoxical to associate the problem of nondescript spatial structures in the region with colonialism. Yet, this is indeed the case. During the colonial era, urban Africa reposed on a dual platform. Within the framework of this dualistic urban system, colonial towns were divided into two main districts (Njoh 1999, 2007; Bigon 2009). One district, the Native District (or *la ville des indigènes*), was exclusively for members of the "native" population. The other section, the European District (or *la ville des européenes*), was, as the name suggests, an exclusively European enclave. While several "in-between" spaces existed, we hasten to note that, in general, the native districts covered a much larger geographic area than their European counterparts throughout Sub-Saharan Africa. Unsurprisingly, the native districts were disproportionately underserved, if at all, when it came to basic service and infrastructure provisioning.

Colonial authorities were determined to establish European spatial and environmental standards in the colonies. However, they were significantly constrained by their shoestring budgets. This severely limited the extent to which they could transform their wishes into real and implementable policies. In the spatial development arena, this meant a substantial scaling-down of the orbit of certain policies. In the case of toponymic inscription, the orbit was limited to the European districts. Thus, while streets and places were christened and their names sign-posted in these districts, no commensurate initiatives were undertaken in the native districts. Over time, the native areas, complete with their nondescript structures, expanded to usurp the European districts. Thus, toponymic ambiguity in urban Sub-Saharan Africa can be seen as rooted in the colonial policies that encouraged the growth of native districts in urban areas.

It is important to appreciate the basis and *raison d'être* for selecting street names and other toponyms in colonial Sub-Saharan Africa. For colonial authorities, the opportunity to christen a place or street there was often considered an occasion to embellish the power of their native countries in a foreign land. Our observation thus is in line with Brenda Yeoh's (1992) assertion that, more often than not, the traditions of toponymic inscription sought to express the power of the "namer" over the object being named. In British colonial Singapore as in colonial Sub-Saharan Africa, place names were drawn from a Eurocentric spatial and environmental design lexicon. Ignoring the interest of indigenes of the colonized territories, urban toponyms as well as the built space of which they are a part, reflect the European vision of what a human settlement should be in terms of its form and function. As to their functioning, colonial built space and commensurate features were designed to benefit members of the expatriate population. In line with the thinking that emerged in concert with the Age of Enlightenment, the establishment of a network of official street names introduced a sense of order into what was otherwise nondescript urban space. In contrast—and the very existence of a contrast played a vital role in the formation of colonial imageries—the spatial structure of the indigenous districts was nondescript.

The dualistic urban structure that was created by colonial authorities is not only of historical significance. Rather, it has far-reaching implications for contemporary development efforts. After all, this is the structure that colonial authorities bequeathed to their indigenous heirs. Thus, it follows that it is the structure comprising the nucleus around which contemporary urban growth has been occurring throughout the continent. With the demise of colonialism and the concomitant departure of the Europeans, one would have expected an end to the dualistic urban structure. This was certainly not the case. Instead, no sooner had the Europeans departed than they were replaced by elite members of the emerging bureaucracy. Accordingly, what used to be a dual urban structure characterized by a European and a native district became one containing an exclusive enclave for the socio-economic elite and a district for the rest of society.

With considerable success, the indigenous leadership has jealously guarded the privileged enclaves of their European predecessors. Currently, these enclaves, complete with carefully written and conspicuously posted street names, exist as islands of spatial orderliness in an ocean of spatial chaos.[2] Figure 12.1, a photograph of a major intersection in Cameroon's commercial city, Douala,

Figure 12.1 Clearly written, conspicuously posted, and well-positioned street signs at an intersection in the formal area of Akwa, the erstwhile colonial district, of Douala, Cameroon (photograph by Ambe Njoh)

vividly captures this situation. Yet it would be an exaggeration if not sheer fabrication to say that complete spatial order is the order of the day in any part of urban Sub-Saharan Africa. This is because even in the most ideal situations one finds streets that go by two or more names (Njoh 2010). Usually, one of these names, the more popular one, is the one known to the urban residents while the other, the less popular one, appears in official records.

Toponymic inscription in British and French colonial Sub-Saharan Africa

> It was a gardened city. A great number of the inhabitants spent their lives on the gardens, and the fountains and parks … around that city, just like all the cities we know, like Johannesburg for instance, grew up a shadow poverty and beastliness. A shanty town. Around that marvellous ordered city, another one of hungry and dirty and short-lived people. And one day the people of the outer city overran the inner one, and destroyed it.
>
> (Lessing 1972, 151)

The above words belong to a renowned novelist from segregated Zimbabwe (formerly Southern Rhodesia). They suggest that toponymic constructs in that country were a consequence of both actual and conceptual spatial divisions. Conceptual spatial divisions determined actual spatial divisions, and vice versa. Zimbabwe was not unique in this regard. Rather, such spatial divisions, binary oppositions, and contradictions constituted a ubiquitous feature of colonial Africa as a whole. We focus more intensely on the urban centers as opposed to peripheries in order to expose their bipartite and imaginative character as well as related associations and inherent ironies. Our empirical referents are the territories that came under the colonial orbit of Britain and France, the dominant colonial powers in the region.

An Anglophone glimpse

Embracing an anthropological qualitative insight, the generic language of British colonial urbanism has been analyzed in some detail by Anthony King (1976). By dwelling on key notions such as the "cantonment," "hill station," "mall," and "bungalow-compound complex," King illuminated the reliable connections between classifying terminological systems and colonial space, conceived as a social, cultural, behavioral, and perceptual space. However, when trying to move away from the colonial urban "heart"/"center" (in India) towards its colonized "fringe"/"periphery," an equivalent account is lacking from King's pioneering study, especially from the indigenous viewpoint. Another prominent account of indisputable historiographic value that sheds light on colonial urban space and toponymy is the 1922 work of Lord Lugard.[3] Yet Lugard's work not only lacks critical perspective, it also fails to include indigenous urban forms or the perceptions of indigenous people of their settlements. In his comprehensive account, Lugard actually sought to establish the British colonial vision regarding political doctrines and economies, including the structure and terminologies of the colonial urban forms.

British colonial urbanism was mainly characterized by racial segregation. The resultant spatial structure segregated Europeans from Africans by creating separate residential areas for the expatriate minority on elevated terrain. Officially, this dual spatial structure which accompanied the policy of "indirect rule" was designed to promote public health—the latter also served as a pretext for planning-law codification. For example, Lugard's Township Ordinance of 1917 contained a health provision whose functioning, it was claimed, depended on racial segregation. The concept of "township" as defined by the ordinance meant an enclave outside of the native administration and jurisdiction, separately governed and reserved for Europeans and non-Europeans. The township was further sub-divided into smaller residential units, and served like the hub as opposed to the periphery of human settlements (Lugard 1922, 150–152; Home 1983). In apartheid South Africa, however, the concept of "township" usually referred to urban enclaves that were built on the periphery of towns and cities, usually set aside for non-whites. Apart from the fact that the non-white areas were poorly equipped, they were sometimes turgid with large informal settlements (Mabin 1992). Moreover, in the local parlance, the term "township" connotes "suburb."

An essential physical component of the Lugardian township was the "greenbelt" or "sanitary cordon." This was typically an open space of at least 440 yards that served to separate European from African residential areas. This minimum distance was based on the belief that such a distance was too great for malaria-causing mosquitoes to traverse (it was clear that mosquitoes could actually be carried by the wind much farther) (Lugard 1922, 148–149; Home 1997, 148). We shall only stress here a striking irony in the Lugardian scheme, which was the conspicuous absence of the indigenous town from urban development plans. Yet, rather early during the colonial era the indigenous town throughout Sub-Saharan Africa had expanded and was encroaching upon the "center" of the colonial administrative, business, and residential hub. Failure to include such towns on colonial city maps constitutes a manifestation of this problem.[4] Thus, within the colonial mindset, the "indigenous urbanite" was not conceptually an integral part of the "city." It was especially in the case of Sub-Saharan Africa that the "other" (part of the) city was also an object apart from the world. The *ville réelle*, in contrast to the *ville officielle*, was essentially marginalized and peripheralized. Representing the "otherness" that stood in binary opposition to "our" civilized spatial model, the African indigenous town was considered—if we may borrow Achille Mbembe's words—"the intractable, the mute, the abject, a failed and incomplete example of something else" (2001, 1–4).

Its vociferous silence is noticeable in the colonial documentation, and if a reference or description was given to this seemingly constant and ultimate periphery, it was usually negative. In British Zanzibar, the British architect and town planner Henry Vaughan Lanchester suggested, in the 1920s, a blueprint for a layout of what he called the "hutting grounds to the east" (Myers and Muhajir 2014, 99–101). This area was segregated from new European suburbs. At about the same time authorities were also launching sporadic attacks on the "hutting" phenomenon in British colonial Lagos. And, in the discourse of toponymic inscription, Lagos gained notoriety in colonial circles for the many, albeit pejorative, names by which it was known. Some referred to it as "a rubbish heap," "a rabbit warren of shanties and rickety wooden 'upstairs', awash with mud and garbage," and so on (Wren 1952 [1924], 10; Leith-Ross 1983, 85). In 1946, a report by the Lagos Town Planning Commission characterized the outlook of indigenous Yoruba cities as "disgraceful," concluding that even Lagos, which had grown increasingly cosmopolitan, "remains a Yoruba village with a village mentality" (*Report* 1946, 17). However, the generic terms "slums" and "squatters," problematic and relational in themselves, dominated the colonial planning vocabulary after the Second World War.

A Francophone glimpse

A remarkable attribute of contemporary toponymic inscriptions in urban "centers" as opposed to "peripheries" in French colonial urbanism is their striking similarities to their British counterparts. This revelation is surprising considering the overt differences in colonial doctrines and administrative organization between both regimes in Sub-Saharan Africa (Bigon 2014). The idea of a socio-spatial and racial division through residential segregation prevailed in the French-speaking territories (including Belgian Congo). But unlike the English-speaking colonies (including South Africa), racial residential segregation was enforced there rather informally. Within this framework the urban "center" was the only part that was considered the "real" and "civilized" city. It was meant for the white population, while the urban "periphery" was designated as the non-European zone.

In the French colonial cities such as Abidjan (Côte d'Ivoire), Brazzaville (Congo, PRC), Kayes (French Sudan, present-day Mali), and Dakar (Senegal), the neighborhood of the expatriate population was called *Plateau*. The "Plateaux" prototypes were designated and configured as the European administrative and residential districts. Originally implying higher ground, this term, a key notion in the French colonial urban discourse, represented the ideals and the elitist dimension of the French presence in West Africa. Geographically, the Plateau as a preferred zone that was intended for the expatriate population was associated with public health considerations and with the tradition of military camps of the European colonial powers. These camps, especially overseas, were generally placed at a distance from the local population, as the cases of the British "cantonment" (and "Hill Station") in India or Sierra Leone show (King 1976; Goerg 1997). In the French case, topography was employed to symbolize the unequal distribution of socio-political power between the Europeans and the locals. The symbolic meaning of *Plateau* was particularly conspicuous in Niamey (Niger), where the European quarter that was so-named was in fact not established on higher ground at all. In Kayes, a few structures and the presence of only a small number of military and civilian French servicemen was enough to justify this name.[5] Subsequent to the demise of colonialism, these previously exclusive European enclaves became privileged urban spaces for the indigenous socio-economic and politico-administrative elite.

In the French colonial urban discourse, the Plateau was often regarded as the "European city" (*ville europèenne*) or "white city" (*ville blanche*). Its African counterpart was branded the "African city" (*ville africaine*), "indigenous village" (*village indigène*), "village of the blacks" (*village des noirs*), or "indigenous quarter/neighborhood" (*quartier indigène*). In North Africa, it was also called the "new city" (*ville nouvelle*), in order to distinguish it from the "old city," or the "traditional city," of the indigenous population.[6] The Plateau was also occasionally referred to as the "urban zone" (*zone urbaine*), while its African counterpart was called "semi-urban zone" (*zone semi-urbaine*). In many places the European part of the city was called the "residential zone" (*zone résidentielle*), even where it did not actually serve residential purposes. This contrasted with the "African quarters/neighborhoods" (*quartiers africains*). In some cases the term "*cite*" was used in reference to the African district. This is quite ironic because it bears medieval connotations in French, as opposed to the term "*ville*" (city) (Topalov 2012).

Through the usage of this terminology, the narrative of the colonizer, his urban practices, values, and building standards were promoted as the ultimate and absolute ones. The "periphery" of the colonized was crystallized as an antagonist, considered only partly urbanized or as an essentially rural sphere in relation to the white area. Official toponymic inscriptions such as street names were almost exclusively identified with the Plateaux. In early colonial Dakar, for instance, these consisted of commemorative names reflecting the imagery of the French sector alone (Faure 1914, 148–154). If nothing else, this served to alienate the indigenous population from the city center. Outside of Dakar's Plateau, only the two streets that linked it to the surrounding area bore any official and sign-posted names. The names in this particular case are noteworthy for one reason. They were outside the norm of French colonial toponymic practices because they commemorated Africans. However, those so commemorated were two Senegalese leaders who had cooperated with the French regime during their territorial conquest initiatives. The Médina, a neighboring quarter spartanly planned by the colonial administration in the 1910s to house the Dakarois, comprised numbered street names, which were not clearly sign-posted (Figure 12.2). Moreover, Dakar's Médina and certain areas of its Plateau were referred to by another informal set of names that resulted from a bottom-up naming process. These names were used by the autochthones (Bigon 2008).

Similar to their British counterparts, colonial authorities in Dakar also conceptually and administratively excluded indigenous areas from the municipal borders. Also, as was the case in the British colonies, French colonial authorities sought to eliminate huts from urban areas and their vicinities. Here, authorities tolerated nothing but buildings of permanent materials or what they referred to as *"en dur."* Perishable materials, or anything that was not considered as *"en dur"* (mud, cloth, straw, cardboard, tarred carton, and lattice-work) were illegal in the

Figure 12.2 A house at the corner of Streets No. 5 and No. 8 in Dakar's Médina. The resident has sign-posted it by hand, indicating his occupation (photograph by Liora Bigon).

colonial urban centers. Outside of their official borders, in what gradually became *villages* (or *quartiers*) *indigènes*, regulations were less strict, and non-permanent building materials were allowed.[7] By establishing two sets of laws for different regions sharing the same urban space, the development of the whole of the municipal area seemed unnecessary. Yet despite all the efforts on the part of the colonial authorities, the straw-hut-landscape never entirely disappeared from these colonial towns. Considered as "organic," "spontaneous," and "random," these sometimes improvised, but nevertheless contextually relevant structures, became the ultimate image of these towns.

By the period of decolonization, the ever-growing gap between the European *beaux quartiers* and the African *bidonvilles* became stark. The term "bidonville," that is, a "shanty-town" or "slum," referred to the temporary building materials that were used for traditional construction. The term is derived literally from the French *bidon*, meaning "tin can." It was originally associated with the empty oil containers that were abundant, and served as roofing material especially in North Africa during the Second World War (Abu-Lughod 1980, 330). This derogatory French term is also used nowadays for corrugated iron roofing sheets that are used extensively in Sub-Saharan Africa.

In place of the greenbelt employed by British colonial authorities, the French used the *cordon sanitaire*. Here, the purpose was to separate European from African districts. In the French colonial urban lexicon, the *cordon sanitaire* also goes under other appellations, including *zone interdite* or *zone non edificandi*. In practice, these zones actually assumed a variety of forms, such as a stadium (as in Dakar, Senegal), public parks (as in Rabat, Morocco), a dry creek (e.g., Niamey, Niger), lagoons (as in Abidjan, Côte d'Ivoire), river channels (as in Brazzaville, Congo, PRC), or some other geological barrier (as was the case in Moroccan cities such as Fez, Marrakesh, and Meknes). Since the demise of colonialism, many such parochial terminologies have been replaced by global and more technical ones, as part of a general ideological change.

Postcolonial toponymic ambiguity: the case of Cameroon

In major cities and towns throughout the continent, the dualistic urban centers created by colonial authorities have evolved. This evolution has not helped the toponymic inscription problematic. While street signage exists in some gated communities and very few other zones, the nondescript areas have now grown, proliferated, and usurped the small planned districts or the formerly European enclaves. Thus, privileged urban spaces complete with well-aligned, named, and conspicuously signed streets are now an exceeding rarity throughout the region. Yet it is difficult to miss the stark contrast between these privileged spaces and the "unplanned" areas engulfing them. To the visitor, these areas appear "nondescript," "chaotic," and "disorderly." The residents of these cities see things differently. For them, getting around is never the problem a visitor may imagine. The resident sees names for streets and places where the visitor sees none. These names are engraved in the residents' shared mental imageries of their cities. The keyword here is "shared," for it is only because these imageries are shared that a taxi- or cab-driver is able to know with certitude his passengers' destinations. Also, were these imageries not of the shared variety, it would be difficult to describe venues for business transactions or other social interaction.

While the importance of formalized toponyms cannot be discounted, at the same time, it is difficult to trivialize the socio-psychological implications of names commemorating non-Africans on African soil. These implications go beyond the more simplistic colonizer–colonized power relations. To be sure, some of the colonial commemorative street names were removed after independence, though their colonial name is actually still preferred by many of the urban inhabitants.[8] This has created another barrage of problems of its own, not least of which is the phenomenon of a street or place going by multiple names. Typically, a street or place would be known by two names. The one is often official while the other is may be unofficial but more popular.

Our fieldwork in Cameroon provides further support to this assertion. In town after town we noticed streets with multiple names whether sign-posted or not. In the country's national capital, Yaoundé, a major street such as Avenue John Ngu Foncha is more popularly known as Nkom Nkana. In the same city, the street shown on the official urban plan and sign-posted as Rue 1.750 is known by locals as Nouvelle Route Bastos. In Douala, the country's chief commercial city, a major street was officially changed from Rue Njoh Njoh to Rue Soppo Priso in the 1990s. However, locals continue to refer to it by its former name despite the fact that the street sign-post and official records have, since the 1990s, referred to it as Rue Soppo Priso. In some older parts of Douala, the toponymic-inscription problem is borne of sheer neglect. For instance, in New Bell, which was established by German colonial authorities as a residential district for native-foreigners, the street signs are faded and barely visible. The metal posts bearing them appear to have taken more than their fair share of abuse. In almost every case, the post is twisted and either lying on, or barely sustained at an irregular angle to, the ground.

In Limbé, one of the country's oldest cities along the Atlantic Ocean, the toponymic problematic is of a different genre. Based on Eurocentric accounts, Limbé was founded in 1858 by Alfred Saker, a British Baptist missionary. The town was named Victoria in honor of Queen Victoria of England. The town went under that name from its founding to 1982. In fact, despite its colonial roots, some Anglophone Cameroonians of the older generation prefer to refer to the town as Victoria. This bolsters the assertion that place names create and maintain emotional attachments to places (Kadmon 2004; Rose-Redwood, Alderman, and Azaryahu 2010). Despite the town's neatly configured orthogonal street pattern, few streets have sign-posted names. Yet, from a bottom-up perspective, there are hardly any nameless streets throughout the city.

Some 16 kilometers from Limbé on the way to Douala is a major junction town with an estimated population of 70,000 known as Mutengene. This town's morphology and fabric are particularly interesting for their toponymic implications. The town boasts neither a neatly configured street pattern nor paved streets. The buildings have barely visible hand-scribbled letters and numbers (Figure 12.3). These have been inscribed by the local electrical power provider for billing

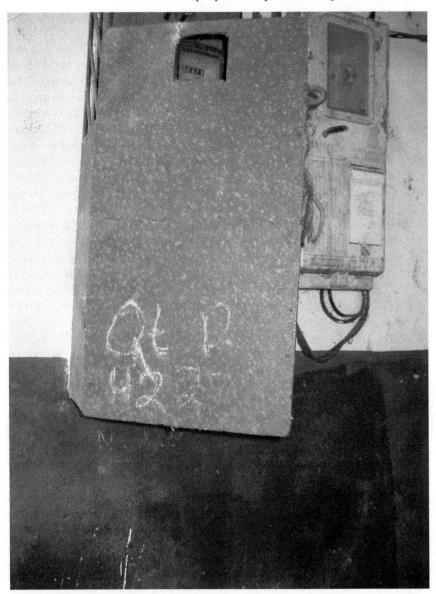

Figure 12.3 An example of the signage system of Mutengene, as inscribed in white chalk by authorities of the Société Nationale de l'Electricité du Cameroun (SONEL), the quasi-national electricity corporation in Cameroon (photograph by Liora Bigon)

record-keeping purposes. Mutengene is a veritable testament to our earlier observation that where a visitor may see chaos and disorder, the locals see an unmistakably well-defined space. The town has six major streets—Buea Road, Tiko Road, and Limbé Road (all highways), and Electric Line Buea Road, Electric

Line Tiko Road, and Electric Line Limbé Road—and several minor streets, none of which are sign-posted.

Anyone used to an unambiguous built space is likely to ponder how one ever navigates the nondescript built space characteristic of urban centers in Cameroon and other African countries. In such places, knowledge of the popular as opposed to the official name of streets and places is necessary. In Yaoundé, for instance, an individual wishing to travel by taxicab from one part of the city to the street officially known as Avenue John Ngu Foncha would do well to tell the cab-driver to take him or her to Nkom Nkana (between la SNEC and Carrefour Madagascar) in Tsinga. Here, as implied above, the cab-driver is likely unaware that Avenue John Ngu Foncha is the official name of rue Nkom Nkana. Yet, the problem is not only with streets going by multiple names. In some cases, the problem is with multiple streets going by the same name. The case of Ndamukong Street is illustrative (Njoh 2010). A main paved thoroughfare and several minor ones on both sides of this street in Bamenda, Cameroon's third largest city, are known as Ndamukong Street.

Cameroon's toponymic-inscription problem is not limited to the absence of street/place names. Rather, it possesses a linguistic dimension. The country is officially bilingual, with French and English—a legacy of its colonial heritage—as its official languages. However, the country's bilingual status is largely symbolic alone, since most official business is conducted solely in French. Similarly, signs throughout the Francophone zone (i.e., four-fifths) of the country are solely in French. In addition, highway signs throughout most of the country, including the Anglophone zone, are also solely in French. This renders the navigation of built space difficult for most of the country's population, especially Anglophones without knowledge of written French.

In all fairness to authorities in Cameroon, they have taken some steps to ameliorate the country's toponymic problematic. The earliest recorded initiative in this regard includes the 1971 Circular establishing street/place naming criteria throughout the country. The Circular effectively charged municipal authorities with the task of christening places and streets (Farvacque-Vitkovic et al. 2005; Njoh 2010). A second initiative in this regard concerns the designation of a special governmental agency in charge of toponymic inscription in the nation's urban centers. The 1990s witnessed the entry of international development agencies in the country's toponymic inscription arena. Noteworthy in this connection was the World Bank's targeting of physical addressing and property identification problems as part of its broader country-specific development program of 1992 (Njoh 2010; Goerg 2012).

Conclusion

In this chapter, we have examined a variety of problems related to toponymic inscription in contemporary urban Africa in terms of their nature and extent in an era of globalization. By tracing the direct relation of some of these problems to the British and French colonial legacies, and their dualistic urban legacies, we have shown that urban space throughout Africa is a product of the continent's rich and complex history. In spite of the overt difference between the two dominant colonizing powers in terms of administration, ideologies, and political doctrines, as well as their different linguistic backgrounds, the British and French toponymic systems shared similar semantic motifs regarding colonial urban space. These motifs reflected an imaginative process of "othering" and "peripherializing" the colonized populations and their settlement perceptions and organization.

Presently, it is the formerly colonial "periphery," that is, the constantly growing informal part of the city, that is home to a cross-section of the population, including members of the middle-class. In contrast to the privileged space of the elite, this part of the city is typically nondescript—replete with named but "sign-less" streets. Many areas in this part of the city have street lights that are hardly lit and signs that are more often leaning at awkward angles to the ground than vertically erect. In the midst of what a stranger may consider chaos and disorder, people appear to be going about their business with facility. Yet the need for an unambiguous system of street/place and property identification in this era of globalization cannot be overstated.

Notes

1 While the practical meaning of the concept urban management is generally agreed upon by urbanists, its definition remains in controversy (Stern 1993; Mattingly 1994).
2 We are aware of the fact that postcolonial urban mapping gradually incorporates toponyms of quarters beyond the European residential zones, central business districts and the African quarters that were planned by the colonizers in their proximity (such as Poto-Poto in Brazzaville, Cocody in Abidjan, New Bell in Douala, and Dakar's Médina). These were traditionally mapped by the colonizers by the 1930s. Yet still, because of the fact that slum and squatter settlements can reach up to 80 percent of the total urban areas under question, only the names of the main roads are normally indicated in current mapping.
3 Lugard was the first High Commissioner of the Protectorate of Northern Nigeria (1900–1906), Governor of Hong Kong (1907–1912), and Governor-General of colonial Northern and Southern Nigeria (1912–1919). See also Lugard (1922).
4 See, for instance, relevant maps from the 1910s of Nigerian cities: National Archives of Nigeria (Ibadan): SCO 26, 14623, Classification of townships under the Township Ordinance, 1917; The British Archives (London): CO 1047/659, Plan of the Town of Forcados, Southern Nigeria, 1910; Rhodes House (Oxford): Papers about the removal of the capital of the Northern Province, 1914–1916. MSS. Brit. Emp. S. 99, 1: 1914–1916.
5 Royal Commonwealth Society Collection, Cambridge UK, CASE A59, *Senegambie-Niger reports: reports to the Governor General from local officials*, vol. 4 (5 vols.): Cercle de Kayes.
6 For the difference between the North African "old city" (*casbah, médina*) and the "traditional city" in relation to the European "new city," see Hamadeh (1992).
7 Archives Nationales du Sénégal, Dakar, NS H22, l'Hygiène à Dakar, 1919–1920 (inside: Rapport sur l'hygiène à Dakar de 1899–1920, pp. 354–355). Also, see Seck (1970).
8 We noticed this regarding Avenue Roume in Dakar (after one of the early Governor-Generals of French West Africa), in popular use instead of Avenue Senghor (after the first Senegalese president upon independence).

References

Abu-Lughod, J. (1980). *Rabat: Urban Apartheid in Morocco*. Princeton, NJ: Princeton University Press.

Anson, J. (2007). *Connecting the "Unconnected" in Sub-Saharan Africa: Postal Networks Can Leverage Access to Infrastructure.* Bern: United Nations Universal Postal Union.

Azaryahu, M. (2009). "Street Names and Iconography." In R. Kitchin and N. Thrift (Eds.), *International Encyclopedia of Human Geography* (pp. 460–466). Oxford: Elsevier.

Baesjou, R. (1988). "The Historical Evidence in Old Maps and Charts of Africa with Special Reference to West Africa." *History in Africa,* 15: 1–83.

Bawumia, M. (2012). "Formalizing the Ghanaian Economy is a Key to Economic Transformation." *Politics of Friday,* July 27.

Bigon, L. (2008). "Names, Norms and Forms: French and Indigenous Toponyms in Early Colonial Dakar, Senegal." *Planning Perspectives,* 23(4): 479–501.

Bigon, L. (2009). *A History of Urban Planning in Two West African Colonial Capitals.* Lewiston, NY: Mellen Press.

Bigon, L. (2012). "Between 'Centers' and 'Peripheries': On the Ironies of Colonial Urban Terminology in Africa." Unpublished paper delivered at the specialist session, "What's in a Name? How We Label Peripheral Places," European Association of Urban History (EAUH) 11th International Conference, Prague, August 29–September 1.

Bigon, L. (2014). "Transnational Networks of Administrating Disease and Urban Planning in West Africa: The Inter-Colonial Conference on Yellow Fever, Dakar, 1928." *GeoJournal,* 79(1): 103–111.

Coetzee S. and Cooper, A. (2007). "The Value of Addresses to the Economy, Society and Governance: A South African Perspective." Paper for the 45th Annual Conference of the Urban and Regional Information System Association (URISA), Washington DC, August 20–23.

Farvacque-Vitkovic, C., Godin, L., Leroux, H., and Chavez, R. (2005). *Street Addressing and the Management of Cities.* Washington, DC: The World Bank.

Faure, C. (1914). *Histoire de la presqu'île du Cap Vert et des origines de Dakar.* Paris: Larose.

Goerg, O. (1997). *Pouvoir colonial, municipalités et espaces urbains: Conakry Freetown des années 1880–1914.* Paris: l'Harmattan.

Goerg, O. (2012). "Conakry." In S. Bekker and Th. Göran (Eds.), *Capital Cities in Africa* (pp. 8–31). Cape Town: HSRC.

Hamadeh, Sh. (1992). "Creating the Traditional City: A French Project." In N. AlSayyad (Ed.), *Forms of Dominance* (pp. 241–260). Brookfield, VT: Avebury.

Home, R. (1983). "Town Planning, Segregation and Indirect Rule in Colonial Nigeria." *Third World Planning Review,* 5(2): 165–175.

Home, R. (1997). *Of Planting and Planning: The Making of British Colonial Cities.* London: Spon.

Kadmon, N. (2004). "Toponymy and Geopolitics: The Political Use—and Misuse—of Geographical Names." *The Cartographic Journal,* 41(2): 85–87.

King, A. (1976). *Colonial Urban Development: Culture, Social Power and Environment.* Boston, MA: Routledge, Kegan Paul.

Leith-Ross, S. (1983). *Stepping Stones: Memories of Colonial Nigeria, 1907–1960.* M. Crowder (Ed.). London: Peter Owen.

Lessing, D. (1972). *The Four-Gated City.* Frogmore: Granada.

Lugard, F. D. (1922). *The Dual Mandate in British Tropical Africa.* Edinburgh: William Blackwood.

Mabanckou, A. (2010). *Broken Glass,* translated by H. Stevenson. New York: Soft Skull.

Mabin, A. (1992). "Comprehensive Segregation: The Origins of the Group Areas Act and its Planning Apparatuses." *Journal of Southern African Studies,* 18(2): 405–429.

Mattingly, M. (1994). "Meaning of Urban Management." *Cities,* 11(3): 201–205.

Mbembe, A. (2001). *On the Postcolony*. Berkeley: University of California Press.

Myers, G. (1996). "Naming and Placing the Other: Power and the Urban Landscape in Zanzibar." *Tijdschrift voor Economische en Sociale Geografie*, 87(3): 237–246.

Myers, G. and Muhajir A. (2014). "Zanzibar as the Garden City of Tomorrow." In L. Bigon and Y. Katz (Eds.), *Garden Cities and Colonial Planning* (pp. 99–101). Manchester: Manchester University Press.

Njoh, A. J. (1999). *Urban Planning, Housing and Spatial Structures in Sub-Saharan Africa.* Aldershot: Ashgate.

Njoh, A. J. (2003). *Planning in Contemporary Africa: The State, Town Planning and Society in Cameroon.* Aldershot: Ashgate.

Njoh, A. J. (2007). *Planning Power: Town Planning and Social Control in Colonial Africa.* London: University College London.

Njoh, A. J. (2010). "Toponymic Inscription, Physical Addressing and the Challenge of Urban Management in an Era of Globalization in Cameroon." *Habitat International*, 34: 427–435.

Report of the Lagos Town Planning Commission (1946). Lagos: Government Printer.

Rose-Redwood, R., Alderman D., and Azaryahu, M. (2010). "Geographies of Toponymic Inscription: New Directions in Critical Place-Name Studies." *Progress in Human Geography*, 34(4): 453–470.

Seck, A. (1970). *Dakar: métropole ouest africaine.* Dakar: IFAN.

Stern, R. (1993). "Urban Management in Development Assistance: An Elusive Concept." *Cities*, 10(2): 125–138.

Topalov, Ch. (2012). "The Urban Vocabulary of Social Stigma in Late 20th c. France." Paper for the European Association of Urban History (EAUH) International Conference, Prague, August 28–September 1.

UN-DESA (2008). *World Urbanization Prospects: The 2007 Revision.* New York: United Nations Department of Economic and Social Affairs (UNDESA), Population Division.

Wren, Ch. (1952 [1924]). *Beau Geste*. London: John Murray.

Yeoh, B. (1992). "Street Names in Colonial Singapore." *Geographical Review*, 82(3): 313–322.

13 Coloring "Rainbow" streets

The struggle for toponymic multiracialism in urban post-apartheid South Africa

Wale Adebanwi

Introduction: going down "problem road"

Some of the challenges associated with street renaming in a post-conflict, multiracial society such as South Africa are illustrated in the renaming of Cowey Road, one of the most upscale streets in Durban. It was renamed in 2008 after Problem Mkhize, a black South African trade unionist and anti-apartheid activist who was forced to go into exile during apartheid. While the renaming honors one of those who made sacrifices to ensure the building of a multiracial society, many entrepreneurs on the street felt that the new name could *harm* their businesses. These business owners were not concerned with the symbolic implications of honoring one of the heroes of their freedom. Rather, they focused on the potential economic implications of the renaming. One property owner said that he had a prospective tenant who decided not to rent the property because of the new street name. "He looked at everything and was happy but said he did not want his business on a street named Problem" (Goldstone 2008). In this case, "revolutionary" renaming clashes with "commodification" as renaming threatens, or is assumed to threaten, the financial or symbolic profit derived from the existing name (Giraut and Houssay-Holzschuch 2016, 8; cf. Rose-Redwood 2008b, 444).

As South Africans continue to struggle with the legacies of apartheid and respond to the challenges of the creation of an inclusive multiracial society, place renamings have constituted some of the most visible signs of the social and political (re)configurations of this "post-racial" society. As A.J. Christopher argues, the "momentous social engineering projects from colonialism and segregationism to apartheid and, currently, the democratic transformation" have all had "profound spatial implications and left significant legacies in the geography of the country" (1994, 1). Therefore, in the attempts to re-order the socio-political space between the majority black population and the minority white population so as to remove what Achille Mbembe (2007, 161) describes as "the marks of the Beast in the landscape," there is an enormous investment in the symbolic value of street renaming as a potential instrument of de-racialization (which some see as re-racialization) in the context of the arduous struggle to build a multiracial society. No doubt, this process of de-racialization is tied to a decolonization paradigm. However, because the colonial experience in South Africa was not merely racial, but institutionally and officially racist, renaming has been approached more as de-racialization by its protagonists (and as re-racialization by its antagonists) than as decolonization per se.

This chapter explores a series of South African case studies of street renaming that illustrate the interconnectedness of toponymy and the politics of racialization as post-apartheid cities are "confronted with a daunting array of challenges" (Nel, Hill, and Maharaj 2003, 223). As Khadija Patel (2012) states, "[f]ew issues raise the national temperature quite like the prospect of new signage in the streets" in South Africa. This is so because renaming is not merely an aspect of the transformation witnessed in South Africa, but a spatial practice "which more than many others forces people to recognize that a far-reaching process is under way" (Koopman and Deane 2005, 85). Generally, "[a]t the heart of the matter ... [is] a debate on the harm that the new or old names would cause to people" in post-apartheid South Africa, as the *Mail & Guardian* (2016) concludes.

While a majority of the black population insist on "restorative justice" through the renaming of streets from apartheid-era names to older or newer names, a critical section of the minority white population claims that this process, if unchecked, would lead to the erasure of an important part of the nation's past, their own imprint on that past, and their present. In identifying "the general logics underlying a specific naming process," Giraut and Houssay-Holzschuch (2016, 7) encourage us to distinguish, relate, and compare the different elements that are critical for interpreting renaming. These include geopolitical contexts, technologies, and actors. Building on their important argument about the "who" and "why" of place renaming and the overlapping of contextual logics, actors' motivations, and the technologies employed, this chapter examines the cultural politics of street (re)naming in post-apartheid South Africa as (1) a vehicle for the critique of power relations in the urban setting of a post-conflict society; (2) a form of ideological debate on the (in)visibility of history in the construction of a shareable present and a common future; (3) an attempt to harness, manipulate, and/or transform historical spatial relations, and therefore racial, political, and socio-economic relations; and (4) a practical political deliberation on the role of time, space, and language in the building of a multiracial society.

This chapter argues that the celebration of, and strong opposition to, street signs that the gale of street renaming has attracted, show that street renaming is not merely a symbolic act; rather, it is integral, if not central, to the idea and ideal of South Africa as a "Rainbow nation." Thus, street renaming is a crucial process of affirming and contesting what it means to be a (post-apartheid) multiracial society. The chapter interprets street renaming in the country's four important cities, Pretoria, Johannesburg, Cape Town, and Durban, as ways of confronting and assuaging the country's harmful past as well as negotiating its present and constructing its future.

Race, power, subjectivity, and street (re)naming

Recent works on the "contested politics of place naming" have provided innovative ways of analyzing nationalism, (post)colonialism, identity politics, and collective memory (Rose-Redwood, Alderman, and Azaryahu 2010; Rose-Redwood and

Alderman 2011). Much of this critical toponymic scholarship has underscored the crucial role that street (re)naming plays in the social production of urban space (e.g., Azaryahu 1996; Myers 1996; Yeoh 1996; Carlos, Faraco, and Murphy 1997; Alderman 2000, 2002, 2003; Light 2004; Rose-Redwood 2008a, 2008b; Swart 2008; Adebanwi 2012; Bigon 2016).

Giraut and Houssay-Holzschuch (2016) contend that Foucauldian perspectives robustly illuminate the different dimensions of the issues at stake in street (re) naming. I have argued elsewhere that in analyzing street renaming, governmentality can be recast as "the conduct of (mis)conduct," going beyond the conventional Althusserian position in which interpellation is presented as an "ideological *disposifit*" (Adebanwi 2012, 648). I found the Gramscian argument about articulation more persuasive in that it transcends Althusser's understanding of interpellation as demonstrative only of the ideology of the dominant class, while connecting it to Foucauldian governmentality as a form of interpellation "produced and reproduced by the tensions between subjectivity and power" (Adebanwi 2012, 646). Thus, we can transcend Althusser's focus on dominant classes given that the dominated can also mobilize interpellation. In this chapter, I examine street naming by building upon Foucault's conception of governmentality in the narrow sense of the conduct of conduct as "an *assemblage* of practices, techniques and rationalities for the shaping of the behaviour of others and of oneself" (Dean 1999, 250, emphasis added). However, I contend that the practice of street renaming, as a response to an "injurious" action, can be used as a strategy for the conduct of (mis)conduct (Adebanwi 2012, 647).

By focusing on the Foucauldian notion of *dispositif*, rather than Althusser's formulation, and going beyond the "general meaning" of governmentality, Giraut and Houssay-Holzschuch (2016, 6) make a persuasive argument for viewing a *dispositif* as "opening up promising theorising prospects" in understanding street naming. Against this backdrop, in examining the struggle for toponymic multiracialism in urban post-apartheid South Africa, I suggest that street renaming constitutes not only the conduct of conduct, but a more elaborate *dispositif* which refers to "a thoroughly heterogeneous *ensemble* consisting of discourses, institutions, architectural forms, regulatory decisions … laws, administrative measures …. The apparatus itself is the system of relations that can be established between these elements" (Foucault 1990, 194, cited in Giraut and Houssay-Holzschuch 2016, 6, emphasis added).

I think the emphasis on "assemblage" in Foucault's articulation of the conduct of conduct and "ensemble" in his analysis of *dispositif* are both useful in understanding the South African case for several reasons. First, assemblage denotes *accumulation*, while ensemble denotes *bringing together*. Therefore, on the one hand, street renaming in the post-apartheid era constitutes an attempt by the ascendant order—that is, the post-apartheid regimes, cultural groups, civil society groups, and so on—at righting the wrongs accumulated over three centuries through the present *conduct* of past *misconduct* at the national and municipal levels; on the other hand, the reasons provoking the specific renaming and the targeted results of such renaming bring together or combine different contexts, technologies, and actors (illustrated below), as brilliantly argued by Giraut and Houssay-Holzschuch (2016). Second, approached as both the conduct of conduct and as *dispositif*, the cases examined in this chapter help to critically illustrate Foucault's (1986) argument about how '"history unfolds' in its inherent spatiality" (Soja 1989, 17). Foucault argues that the heterogeneous spaces of sites and relations—which he calls "heterotopias"—can be constituted in every society, but they take different forms and change over time in the context of the unfolding of history as enfolded in spatiality.

This Foucauldian perspective (Foucault 1971) has three important implications in the South African case. The first issue is the heterogeneity of sources for the country's pre-colonial, apartheid-era, and post-apartheid toponyms, which has led to the current challenges of renaming. The second issue involves the different layers of meanings that these toponyms have had historically for the different races/ethnicities/cultural groups and the different asymmetric relationships that these toponyms provoke or invoke. Finally, there is also the question of utopia on which Foucault focuses in examining the concept of heterotopia, which is also crucial in the South African case. Despite the manifold dystopias of racial tension, bad governance, violence, and crime, there is consensus on imagining the country as a Rainbow nation and a multicultural melting-pot.

Consequently, even though Foucault does not identify the street as one of the many sites in which history unfolds spatially, I suggest that it is sufficient that he identifies heterotopia as "capable of juxtaposing in a single real place several spaces [and] several sites" which are "in themselves incompatible" (Foucault 1986, 25). In the South African example, the attempts at ensuring such compatibility provoke the struggle for and against street renaming in the making of a Rainbow nation.

Street fighting

Until his release from prison on February 11, 1990, the name of Nelson Mandela was taboo in official quarters of apartheid South Africa, largely because he was branded a "terrorist." It was not until 1994 when he was elected president in representative democratic elections that his name became literally a toponymic target within South Africa. As a way of producing and allocating "symbolic capital in the form of recognition and prestige within the public sphere" (Azaryahu 2012, 74), naming places after Mandela sought to enfold Mandela—as *the* representation of the victory over apartheid—"into everyday life contexts that seem to be detached from political and ideological contexts." A decade later, the country's leading newspaper, *Mail & Guardian* (April 2, 2004), reported a "spree to baptize roads, bridges, public places and universities after Mandela," thus pointing to what the *Telegraph* of London describes as an "insatiable appetite for a piece of the icon" (Laing 2011).

The renaming of places after Mandela, who was described by *Newsweek*'s Arlene Getz (2008) as "the first truly unifying national symbol in a country that had no common anthem or flag," embodies the movement toward a post-racial society in South Africa. As the embodiment of the creation, legitimation, and sustenance of a new political order (Giraut and Houssay-Holzschuch 2016), Mandela's name is unsurprisingly central in the renaming processes. Consequently, it can be argued that in South Africa, the naming of places generally, and the renaming of places after Mandela in particular, are used to intervene in the post-apartheid conversation among multiple races in the struggle to build what has been called a "Rainbow nation." Renaming, therefore, involves a spatially and temporally constituted debate about the basis and rationale—and perhaps functionality—of a utopia; that is, post-racial nationhood in South Africa.

However, the legitimation of a post-apartheid nation and society is challenged by those who regard this re-ordering of the socio-political space as one that is not leading to a "post-racial" nation and society as assumedly desired by most South Africans. In many ways, the dimensions of this controversy are enfolded in the perennial questions of time and space and the manner in which, as Foucault (1982, 22) argues, "certain ideological conflicts animating present-day polemics oppose the pious descendants of time and the determined inhabitants of space." In the South African case, the ideological conflicts that manifest in the struggles for and against renaming are complicated by the fact that the polemists on both sides have different attitudes toward (historical and present) *time* even though they are all inhabitants of the same space.

Indeed, the renaming of places is not an innocent act. Given that street names are cognitive maps, the spatial cognition raised by street names can not only be structured by historical experiences and events but also configured around ideological standpoints, identities, and (re)determined through political intervention. Against this backdrop, place naming can become a critical part of contested racial politics, because "place names provide a rich source of discussion on space and power through varied strategies for contestation embedded in their use" (Myers 1996, 237). The toponymic practices as examined here point to the tensions inherent in the social order as represented by the power to name places and the capacity of others, both legal and extra-legal, to challenge the power of (re)naming. These are done based on different conceptions of subjectivity which either affirm the power of some groups and/or challenge the power of others.

Coloring Rainbow streets: toponymic politics in post-apartheid South Africa

The history of place naming in South Africa since the second half of the fifteenth century when the Europeans started giving names to places in their languages is a most telling, even if grave, testimony to the ways in which the "symbolic politics of naming are imbricated in the very material politics of accumulation by dispossession" (Berg 2011, 13). The domination of the indigenous groups and space by Europeans led to the alteration, adaptation, translation, and supplanting of existing names (Raper 1989). As South Africa began to *adapt* to what E.R. Jenkins euphemistically describes as "demographic changes," place names reflecting the nature of power and the emergent forms of subjectivity began to "tell the story of waves of European settlements, of the extinction of indigenous peoples, flora and fauna, of successive political dispensations, of urbanization and Balkanization, [and] of changes in the fortunes of the languages" (1990, 60). By the late-nineteenth and throughout the twentieth century, the country and its large cities became "so redolent of colonialism" (Wines 2007) and white domination that they turned out to be targets of material and ideological struggles in the post-apartheid era. It is understandable, therefore, that place renaming became a major national project in the post-apartheid era, constituting an attempt by the dispossessed to repossess, including the need for appropriated things, both material and symbolic—including linguistic—to be re-appropriated. However, it is significant that even though the struggle for and against renaming has often raised the political temperature in the country in the post-Mandela era, in the period between 2000 and 2014, of all the geographical names registered by the South African Geographical Names Council, only 20% involved renaming.

In spite of the lower proportion of actual changes in the post-apartheid era, renaming has been enlisted as a principle of minimizing the racialism imprinted into the landscape by apartheid and maximizing the inclusiveness of the imagined post-racial society. Given the cultural and "linguistic hegemony" that results from place naming by dominant groups, when there is "a radical change in the political order" (Giraut and Houssay-Holzschuch 2016, 6)—such as the end of apartheid—attempts at massive renaming are not uncommon (Azaryahu 1990, 1992; Coetser 2004; Swart 2008; Guyot and Seethal 2007; Palonen 2008; Giraut, Guyot, and Houssay-Holzschuch 2008; Orgeret 2010). In the light of the struggles and controversies that mark the politics of street renaming in the post-apartheid era, this phenomenon is beginning to attract the necessary attention in the scholarly literature (Jenkins et al. 1996; Jenkins 2007; Swart 2008; Palonen 2008; Ndletyana 2012; Duminy 2014).

Indeed, the wave of street renaming in South Africa, which *The Guardian* of London succinctly describes as "signs of the times" (Smith 2012), has become one of the most visible means of affirming the termination of apartheid as well as confirming (black) majority rule. However, since the end of apartheid, there have been marked changes in the attitude of the leaders of the country to renaming. Though President Mandela encouraged limited renaming, he insisted that the whole ethos of a Rainbow nation involved sustaining the names of even some of those who built and sustained the racist order. For instance, Mandela cautioned against the renaming of Hendrik Verwoerd Dam after Albert Luthuli, the Nobel Peace Prize winning former ANC leader (Ndletyana 2012, 92). But President Mbeki's attitude was different. After succeeding Mandela in 1999, Mbeki supported and mobilized the people for greater toponymic changes. He was very vocal about his disappointment with existing apartheid-era names. Under his leadership, there was an explosion of actual and attempted renaming. Nine years later, Mbeki's successor, President Zuma, inherited such a contentious atmosphere regarding renaming that he called for a conciliatory approach. Even though his rhetoric was geared more towards empowerment of black South Africans before and after he took power, in his reaction to the "war" over renaming in the country, he had to embrace the Rainbow nation ethos. In his State of the Nation address in 2009, Zuma pledged to take a "common national approach to the changing of geographic and place names," which would "involve all South Africans in forging an inclusive national identity" (Brown 2010).

Despite the conciliatory tone of the leadership of the country and the ANC, the planned and actual changes are opposed by those whose identities, ideological position, and/or histories have been erased and marginalized in the strong wind of renaming. Yet supporters of massive renaming dismissed the conciliatory attitude captured by President Zuma's statement about "Government efforts to mollify slighted whites while making a break with the past" as "pandering." For example, the Tshwane Royal House issued a statement on the proposal to change the name of Pretoria to Tshwane, stating that: "It seems government is so eager to pander to the tantrums of a tiny white Afrikaner minority, at the expense of the black majority who fought so hard for liberation" (Brown 2010).

The African National Congress-led South African Government formalized the popular desire for toponymic transformation in the country with the Road Name Change Act in 2007. The Act seeks to rename streets "which have links to pre-1994 colonialism." Despite opposition, after many changes of street names and other toponyms that marked the immediate triumph of majority rule in May 1994, there seems to have been a renewed enthusiasm in the last seven years for more changes. The majority party, the ANC, and its majority black supporters, have been behind most of the recent calls for toponymic changes (Jenkins et al. 1996; Jenkins 2007). Much racial—and class-based—tension has been raised by the changing urban geography in post-apartheid South Africa, because "the legacy of apartheid's spatial and social design continues to dominate the urban scene despite policy efforts" (Lemanski 2006, 564). This relates to many areas of local and national life from issues of desegregation, assimilation, identity crisis, and inter-racial relations to urban governance, environment politics, and social planning, including issues of housing and poverty.

Many of these issues are mirrored by the struggle over street renaming. From the move to change the name of the administrative capital city from Pretoria to Tshwane, to the proposed changes of many street names in the country's four key cities (Cape Town, Durban, Johannesburg, and Pretoria), South Africa seems to be in an era of toponymic revolution. The four cities are unsurprisingly typical in the acrimonious struggle over renaming, because as Smith (1992, 2) notes, "the doctrine of apartheid" was "inextricably bound up with urbanization" as the free movement of the African majority population was largely constrained by "pass laws" which controlled access to the cities at "levels consistent with demands for labor" (also, see Beavon 1992). Against this backdrop, in the transformation of these cities from "inequitable and racially divided cit[ies] in a pariah state to … cosmopolitan metropole[s]" focused on creating "a socially just, democratic and sustainable urban future" (Beall, Crankshaw, and Parnell 2002, 4–5), street renaming has emerged as one of the symbolic ways of ensuring transformation.

In understanding the context of the toponymic revolution, as pointed out by Giraut and Houssay-Holzschuch (2016, 7–8), it is important to note that the "radical change in the political order" that produced this occurred against the backdrop of an earlier conquest, "the subjugation, or control of a territory through force," which produced the initial renaming in the pre-liberation era. Therefore, the post-apartheid era renaming is a context in which "conquest" is being righted by "revolution." The technologies being used in the contexts examined here are four-fold, depending on the particular situation: *cleansing*, which involves erasing the existing (apartheid-era) street names; *restoring*, which involves not only putting the imprint of the "original" owners of the country on the street but also "reinstituting dominated memories and cultures"; *founding*, involving the use of street renaming to "create, legitimize, and ultimately, sustain a new political and cultural order" both at the local and national levels; and *challenging*, which in relation to founding actively contests extant "history" and the existing cultural tapestry imposed by old street names while presenting and defending alternative ideological (liberationist) and cultural (multiculturalist) histories of the present. Examples of these are discussed below. The actors in these processes of renaming, with coalescing and often times contradictory and clashing objectives, include the national, local, and municipal states and office holders at these levels as well as civil society, which is dominated by racial, ethnic, and cultural groups.

Even though criticisms and protests have forced relevant municipal and national authorities to submit the practice of name changes to a more democratic process— or, at least, what appears so—in most cases, the authorities are going ahead with the changes. One major compromise reached over the struggle for changes of city names was the 1999 division of the country into municipalities as a third tier of government (Koopman 2012). In many cases, the municipalities took the African language names of the cities or towns. Thus, the city of Pretoria is in the Municipality of Tshwane, while the city of Durban is run by the eThekwini Municipality. In the next section, I will examine the politics of renaming in four key South African cities in the post-apartheid era.

Durban: "red-tape" renaming

Durban, a major coastal city in the eastern part of South Africa, was first renamed by the Portuguese as *Rio de Natal* in the fifteenth century and then renamed Port Natal by the British in the nineteenth century. This name was officially replaced by *D'Urban* in honor of the colonial Governor of Cape. It was later simply called Durban (Koopman 2012).

Red tape has become the most common element in the attempt to erase the unjust past in Durban's streets signs. To prevent disorientation because of the renaming of most of the major streets downtown, and in the central suburban areas of the city, the old names are crossed over by red tape, while the new street names are posted above them. There have been many proposed and actual street name changes in Durban, signifying what Wines (2007) describes as a "political brouhaha of the first order" and "an object lesson in the pitfalls of building South African democracy."

On May 1, 2007, a 6,000-strong group of protesters marched through the city's downtown protesting the planned renaming of 180 streets and public buildings.

They complained that some of the names were chosen "not to honor modern South African heroes, but to heap glory on the African National Congress." Also, they insisted that supporters of the minority Democratic Alliance party were offended by the plan to rename streets after Fidel Castro, Che Guevara, and Yasir Arafat, "ANC heroes who, they argued, were hardly democrats, and hardly in the anti-apartheid forefront" (Wines 2007). They were incensed that Andrew Zondo, the ANC guerrilla who killed five white civilians in a 1985 bombing, was to be honored with a street name in the neighborhood where he killed his victims. Evidently, the ANC "freedom fighter" was the protesters' "terrorist." Mary de Haas, an anthropologist and expert on political and racial violence in KwaZulu-Natal, told the *New York Times*, "The whole thing has been provocative .... People want reconciliation, decent-minded people. They don't want to reopen old wounds" (Wines 2007). Between July and September 2008 alone, 99 street name changes were adopted and implemented by the eThekwini Council in Durban (Orgeret 2010, 298). In erecting the new names, the municipality kept the old names which were crossed over with a thin strip of red tape. This was in itself a powerful symbol of the cancellation of the (apartheid) past and the inauguration of a multiracial present.

In 2003, President Thabo Mbeki, who was partly responsible for the scope and pace of renaming, said:

> I am embarrassed by the temerity with which the subject of name-changing is approached. There are probably only a handful of places in South Africa named after a white person who wasn't a land-grabbing murderer. The fact that *Grahamstown, Harrismith* and, say, *Durban*, are still named after John Graham, Harry Smith and Benjamin d'Urban is appalling.
>
> (Jenkins 2007, 104)

Changes in street names in Durban have included names of heroes, ANC stalwarts, and martyrs of the liberation struggle such as Steve Biko Road, Biko being an ANC martyr, General Joseph Nduli Street, named after a Commander of *uMkhonto we Sizwe* (Zulu for "Spear of the Nation"), the armed wing of the ANC, and Chris Hani Road, named after the assassinated ANC leader (Koopman 2012). Others changes include Argyle and Brickhill Roads which were renamed after Sandile Thusi and Sylvester Ntuli, respectively (Figure 13.1). In 1988, Thusi, then a researcher in the University of Natal, was detained under the state-of-emergency regulation for his anti-apartheid activities. Ntuli was at the forefront of the 1961 "One Pound a Day" strike and was shot twice in the lower abdomen by the apartheid police but survived.

Apart from mass protests, resistance to such name changes have also included court challenges, extensive letters of protest published in the local press, spray-painting, and other physical desecration of the new street signs (Orgeret 2010; Koopman 2012). Some of the protesters have accused the ANC-dominated Durban City Council of the "destruction of our heritage" (Koopman 2012, 147) and using name changes to "salute those whose extremist vitriol demanded

Figure 13.1 Taking anti-apartheid activism to the streets in Durban, South Africa (photograph reprinted with permission from Kyle G. Brown)

imposition of a Soviet-style one-party autocracy on this country rather than multiparty democracy" (Turner 2009, 128). Mangosuthu Buthelezi, the leader of the Inkatha Freedom Party, accused the ANC of a "rush to rewrite the history" of the province, adding that "[r]enaming must not be conducted in a manner befitting Mao's Cultural Revolution, in which names and events that do not fit the ruling party's liberation narrative are disdainfully ejected" (Wines 2007). The mayor of the city, Obed Mlaba, responded to these criticisms by stating that "the spoils of democracy include ensuring that the towns and cities, the roads and streets reflect the people and history, the collective culture of ALL South Africans. Universal franchise alone will not undo decades of oppression and racism" (Turner 2009, 129). He was echoed by Vusa Khoza, an ANC ward councillor, who wrote that the renaming constituted an attempt at writing a "proper" history of KwaZulu-Natal, thus "making history and giving our people a sense of belonging, relevance and ownership of their environment" (Orgeret 2010, 298).

Cape Town: limited renaming

Cape Town, like the rest of the Western Cape, has experienced limited renaming because the majority of the city's population are not black. However, after the public outcry that followed the attempt to change Adderley Street to Nelson Mandela Avenue and Wale Street to FW de Klerk Street, honoring South Africa's two Nobel Prize recipients and "architects of the political transition" (Ndletyana 2012, 94), the mayor of Cape Town, Gerals Morkel, announced that the city would not follow the examples elsewhere in South Africa. He noted that "the wholesale altering of names" in other parts of South Africa "has left in its wake divisions and sectoral bitterness."

Subsequently, where the city has embarked on renaming, the process has been consultative, elaborate, and rigorous. The Western Cape (Province) government set up a committee in 2003 which identified 11,000 place names to be considered for change. For many years, nothing changed. In 2007, the City of Cape Town commenced a public process for naming and renaming streets and other public places. A Panel of Experts assessed the proposals received from the public. The Panel recommended 31 naming proposals for approval by the Council. The Council subsequently embarked on public consultation. Out of this, the City implemented four name changes. Oswald Pirow Street, named after the late Nazi-sympathizer and former Justice Minister, was changed to Chris Barnard Street, Eastern Boulevard became Nelson Mandela Street, and the concourse between the Artscape theater and the Civic Centre was renamed after Albert Luthuli. Additionally, Castle Street was renamed after a matriarch of Khoisan, Krotoa, who served in the seventeenth century as an interpreter for the Dutch, while Western Boulevard also changed to Helen Suzman Boulevard.

The proposal for changes has therefore followed a more inclusive process in Cape Town than in Durban. The proposed renaming of 27 streets included calls on residents to submit comments to the mayoral committee, particularly regarding the seven streets named after such racial segregationists as Jan Smuts, the late Afrikaner prime minister of the Union of South Africa, and Hendrik Verwoerd, the man who conceived and implemented apartheid.

Despite attempts to ensure that street renaming is more inclusive in Cape Town, in 2012, a blogger, Stroob, exclaimed, "Leave Cape Town the F&*K Alone," while adding on a more sober tone:

> We should never deny our past, but there seems to be an increasing vendetta to erase any fragment of white heritage, and no matter how hard certain people try, I am not ashamed of who I am. I am South African and the future lies in building something together, not taking from one person and palming it off to another.
>
> (Stroob 2012)

Given the surviving leverage of the heirs of the old order, two different and contrasting attitudes toward cleansing, restoration, and founding as technologies of ideology are evident here. While most black South Africans (who now constitute about 39% of the city's population) see renaming as a way to *cleanse* the racist past, *restore* pre-colonial ownership of the space, as well as emphasize the founding of a new political order, most Afrikaners (and the colored who mostly speak Afrikaans) support *preserving* the existing names, which are reminders of the *founding* of a new order by their own progenitors, the Boers. Therefore, *conquest* (the past) refuses to be erased or cleansed by *revolution* (the present) in the struggle for multiculturalism.

Johannesburg: liberation and renaming

Perhaps more than any other major city, the City of Johannesburg adopted a very inclusive process in its renaming exercises, even while paying attention to the historic struggle against racial domination and hatred. As a "divided city" and a "multilingual, religiously diverse and polycultural city," the political authorities in the city recognize that "negotiating difference is a crucial aspect of combating social exclusion and managing social cohesion" (Beall, Crankshaw, and Parnell 2002, 8). The city has a clear Policy on the Naming and Renaming of Streets and Public Places which is geared towards celebrating "Joburg's shared past and future" (City of Johannesburg 2014).

In "a fitting tribute to the memory of youth leaders who changed the face of South Africa and made an immense contribution to the liberation of our country," the city announced the renaming of four streets in honor of Tsietsi Mashini, Lekgau Mathabathe, Wycliff Tobo, and Danny Kekana as part of commemorating the thirtieth anniversary of the uprising that started in June 16, 1976, popularly called the "Soweto uprising" (City of Johannesburg 2006). The uprising was a black student-organized protest in the township of Soweto near Johannesburg against apartheid-era Bantu education.

The renaming of the streets after the four black South Africans who took part in the uprising involved "a thorough consultation process with family members and the running of advertisements in newspapers inviting the community to participate in the process" (City of Johannesburg 2007). In 2014, the city also renamed some of the busiest streets in the Central Business District after well-known heroes in the struggle for liberation to commemorate the twentieth anniversary of the country's democratic transition. The renaming followed an extensive consultation process starting a year earlier. Four activists who played prominent roles in the anti-apartheid movement, and led the famous Women's March to the Union Buildings in Pretoria involving 20,000 women of all races in 1956, had streets renamed in their honor. The four are representative of the "City's demographics and all have strong historical ties with Johannesburg and its place in the transformation of South Africa" (City of Johannesburg 2014). Sauer Street was renamed Pixley ka Isaka Seme Street after one of the founders of the African National Congress; Bree Street was renamed Lilian Ngoyi Street after the former Secretary General of the ANC Women's League and National Chairman of the Federation of South African Women; Jeppe Street was renamed Rahima Moosa after a "formidable woman" who "led the initiatives to unite the liberation movement" (City of Johannesburg 2014); President Street was renamed Helen Joseph Street after a founding member of the Congress of Democrats; and Noord Street was renamed Sophie de Bruyn Street after the youngest and only surviving leader of the Women's March. Furthermore, two student activists who played prominent roles in the Soweto uprising were also honored. Japie Vilankulu Crescent replaced Lion Crescent while Thabeta Street was renamed Hastings Ndlovu Street.

However, among other changes of apartheid-era street names, perhaps the most crucial changes for black South Africans in Johannesburg were the renamings of D.F. Malan Drive, Hendrik Verwoerd Drive, and Hans Strijdom Road. The first was changed in 2001, while the other two were renamed in 2007. The street named after Malan, who, as prime minister in the National Party government started the implementation of the policy of apartheid in 1948, was replaced with Bevert Naudé Drive. Naudé, also an Afrikaner, was a cleric and theologian who opposed apartheid. Verwoerd Drive was changed to Bram Fischer Drive. Verwoerd, also a former prime minister, is regarded as the mastermind behind the racial policy of apartheid. *BuaNews* reports that by replacing Verwoerd's name with that of Fischer, an Afrikaner lawyer and activist who was jailed for defending Mandela and other anti-apartheid activists, Johannesburg "has rejected the architect of apartheid for a gentle, caring advocate who despised the oppressive system" (Davie 2008). Strijdom Road, named after another former prime minister, an Afrikaner nationalist and a strong proponent of segregationist ideas that led to the implementation of apartheid, was renamed Malibongwe Drive. Translated as "praise the women," the Johannesburg Development Agency announced that renaming the latter was to commemorate the 1956 Women's March against the official policy of non-white women carrying passes. Because the name changes included both black South Africans and Afrikaners who participated in the struggle for freedom, Johannesburg's street renaming pointedly showed how past conquest was *righted* by the revolutionary changes brought about by the collapse of apartheid leading to the cleansing of street names inherited from the unjust past. The new names signify the founding of a new multicultural political order while challenging the leftovers of the racist heritage.

Pretoria: contesting the center of the nation

The case of Pretoria is very interesting for its peculiarity. As the administrative capital of the country, or what Azaryahu (1988, 241) describes as "the center of political life of the nation," Pretoria's "street names … have a particularly representative importance when compared with those of other towns and cities" in the country. This is also true for the name of the capital city itself. Pretoria is named after the Voortrekker leader, Andries Wilhelmus Jacobus Pretorius. Voortrekker (Afrikaans and Dutch for pioneers) are the Dutch who, in what was called the Great Trek, moved en masse from the British-controlled Cape Colony in the 1830s and 1840s into the interior. They are the direct ancestors of the present-day Afrikaners. Pretorius was a leader of the Boers instrumental in the creation of *Zuid-Afrikaansche Republiek* (South African Republic). He is famous among the Afrikaners and infamous among black Africans for leading the

Voortrekker battles against the indigenous people including the "Battle of Blood River" in which the Zulu soldiers suffered 3,000 casualties. Memories of this battle and others led by Pretorius, through which large areas were lost by the indigenous people and subsequently renamed by the Voortrekker and their progeny, remain fresh in the minds of black South Africans. Hence the struggle to cleanse the city of his name and memory.

Thus, in 2005, the hundred-and-fiftieth anniversary of the founding of Pretoria was used by the ANC-led City of Tshwane Metropolitan Council in an attempt to officially change the city's name from Pretoria to the indigenous name, Tshwane. This was resisted by the white population. One group hoisted a placard which provided a divisive meaning for the words in the proposed renaming:

Taking
Stealing
Hijacking
White's
Assets
Names
Equities

(cited in Ndletyana 2012, 94)

For the group, the attempt to change the city's name was a form of anti-white (specifically anti-Afrikaner) re-racialization. A compromise was eventually reached in which the greater city is called the metropolitan municipality of Tshwane, while the core city is called Pretoria.

In the immediate post-apartheid era, few African names replaced Afrikaner and European street names in Pretoria. However, a public hearing for more name changes in 2008 ended in chaos (Brown 2010). Proposals for renaming were "met with howls of derision from members of the Afrikaner community" with some of them erupting "into racist songs" while preventing people from speaking. Freedom Front Plus councilor and member of Tshwane's Public Place and Street Names Committee, Conrad Beyers, stated that "local governments are targeting Afrikaner heroes and replacing them with the names of ANC party stalwarts," while adding "[t]hey're changing the heroes of one community to the names of the heroes of another community. We say that is not a solution." On the contrary, Khorombi Dau, member of the Mayoral Committee for Sport, Recreation, Arts, and Culture in the municipality of Tshwane insisted that Afrikaner and European names should be removed. Dau stated that "[t]hose names should be removed. They belong to a dark part of our history" (Brown 2010).

Despite the opposition and in line with the wishes of the black population, in 2011 the Tshwane Metropolitan Mayor Kgosientso Ramokgopa announced plans for "massive street" renaming in Pretoria. The process, he added, was to be "conducted to accommodate the names of those who fought for the liberation of this country." After Prince Edward Street was renamed for Nelson Mandela, for some time Pretoria did not witness many other street renamings in honor of the heroes of the anti-apartheid struggle. After 18 years of the ANC's dominance in power, its supporters expressed surprise, even anger, at the fact that Pretoria's "streets still bear the names of leading figures from South Africa's white-dominated past, making it impossible to cross Pretoria without passing a mention of the fathers of apartheid" (*News24* 2012a). Even though the population of Pretoria has become diverse in the post-apartheid era, the city is still dominated by the Afrikaners. The new effort to change the names of major streets, according to Ramokgopa, is "about *striking a balance* between the memory of the country's former masters and their successors" (*News24* 2012a, emphasis added). After a series of court cases to halt the changes, about 30 streets in downtown Pretoria had new street signs, with a red line striking out the old Afrikaner names. The changes do not exactly "strike a balance" for some members of the Afrikaner community.

The renaming of the apartheid-era Hans Strijdom Drive as Solomon Mahlangu Drive, and D.F. Malan Drive, named after an apartheid-era prime minister, as Beyers Naudé Drive were particularly offensive to the Afrikaner community. The Afrikaners dismissed Mahlangu as a "terrorist." In June 2015, the court ruled that the City of Tshwane was wrong in removing the names of Strijdom, Malan, and others, because the court had issued an order in 2013 that the old street names should be retained alongside the new names. Earlier in 2013, the municipality removed the old street names which had appeared temporarily with the new names, while AfriForum was still challenging the changes in court. AfriForum's lawyer, Werner Human, described the group's latest victory as one for everyone "opposed to the cultural vandalism by the Tshwane Metro Council" (Skelton 2015a). Human added that the City had targeted street names "with exceptional cultural value for Afrikaners and other minorities."

The City promised to appeal the June 2015 judgment at the Supreme Court of Appeal. Its spokesperson, Blessing Manale, stated that the court directive that the dual name plate signage must be maintained was only to satisfy the "colonialist egos and apartheid nostalgia of the AfriForum" (Skelton 2015b). In August 2015, for the fourth time, AfriForum won the court battle to retain the old street names, and the group's lawyer, Willie Spies, told the media, "Our endeavors for the promotion of mutual respect for the heritage of cultural minorities in South Africa have not been in vain" (Ngozo 2015).

But AfriForum and Spies's joy came to an end recently. On July 7, 2016, the Constitutional Court sitting in Johannesburg set aside the High Court interdict preventing the City of Tshwane from renaming certain streets. Chief Justice Mogoeng rejected as "mind-boggling" Afriforum's argument "that looking at names linked to other race groups would cause 'harm and toxicity' to white Afrikaners." The majority judgment concluded: "This leaves very little room for the acceptance of black people as fellow human beings deserving of human dignity and equality, talk less of honoring them for their pursuit of justice and freedom in South Africa." Afriforum's position that the renaming of streets "would cause emotional hurt or suffering to those who cherish them," added Mogoeng, was "highly insensitive" to other cultural or racial groups:

It is divisive, somewhat selfish and does not seem to have much regard for the centuries-old deprivation of "a sense of place and a sense of belonging" that black people have had to endure. As a result, the victims of colonialism and apartheid were entitled to orders directing authorities to remove names that perpetuated the colonial and apartheid legacy.

(Areff 2016)

Before this judgment, some whites in Pretoria had expressed worries "about losing their cultural identity in the South African capital" because of the name changes. However, Mayor Ramokgopa responded that "Afrikaners are not hated or the object of contempt, but it is a fact that all the streets in the city are named after Afrikaners. It will never be argued that Afrikaners did not play a role, but the city must represent everyone's past." The Democratic Alliance (DA) leader Helen Zille disagreed with the actual practices of the ANC-led government, yet approved of the rhetoric of Ramokgopa on the need for toponymic inclusivity. She pleaded that South Africans "must acknowledge our discriminatory and unjust past, and genuinely seek to develop inclusive cities, where all feel welcome" (*News24* 2012a).

The changes in Pretoria even had reverberating effects in The Netherlands. A Dutch right-wing political party, *De Partij voor de Vrijheid* (the Party for Freedom), PVV, issued a statement at The Hague demanding action from the Dutch cabinet in support of the retention of Afrikaans street names in Pretoria. "The Netherlands Embassy situated in Queen Wilhelmina Avenue should refuse to accept a new name," said the PVV, adding that renaming the street after a black South African would constitute a "slap in the face of the Dutch royal family" (*News24* 2012b).

Respected cleric, Archbishop Desmond Tutu, also intervened. He told the people of Pretoria: "Don't let it be a divisive exercise—as happened in KwaZulu-Natal. We should be magnanimous. Let's not rub people's noses in the dust, don't fill people with resentment" (Smith 2012).

Conclusion

Place renamings have become some of the most important symbols of political change in South Africa since 1994. In their number, size, and impact, the renaming of streets in South Africa is only comparable in contemporary history to post-communist societies in the 1990s, which Azaryahu (2011, 29) describes as "toponymic cleansing." In the South African context, some argue that street name changes reflect majority black rule and the ANC's domination of the political space rather than some sort of utopian post-racial nation. For many whites and opponents of the ANC, what is being witnessed in the country's four most important cities is not the writing of the Rainbow into street signs but attempts to metaphorically change the color of the street signs into black-only. These toponymic conflicts are not only reflections of the "contested versions of South Africa's history" (Swart 2008, 119); more importantly, they are struggles over how to remember the past in the liberatory present as part of the construction of a democratic and inclusive society. As Khumalo (2006) contends, street renaming can help to show "whose story is history."

Two recurrent themes in much of the opposition to the regime of renaming include the argument or perception that the process is not fully democratic (or, that it is outright undemocratic) and that it tends to silence a version of history while over-emphasizing, even over-glorifying, a particular political-ideological narrative. The two central themes of the challenges of place renaming in post-apartheid South Africa therefore raise the question of whether this flurry of renaming constitutes "symbolic reparation" for those who suffered under white minority rule (majority black South Africans, in particular) or "symbolic retribution" against those who benefitted from apartheid (minority white South Africans). While Azaryahu (2011, 29) argues that such renaming in South Africa constitutes a form of "symbolic retribution," Swart (2008) contends that it should be understood as "symbolic reparation." In fact, the Truth and Reconciliation Commission (TRC) recommended that the renaming of geographical features would constitute a form of "symbolic reparations to address South Africa's unjust past" (Patel 2012). However, what Azaryahu and Swart emphasize differently is that, as a vehicle of commemoration, street naming is potentially compensatory and/or potentially punitive.

Against this backdrop, the fate and future of the South African multiracial society is imagined as contingent upon the reconstitution of the cultural and political landscape through the renaming of streets. As technologies of historical *correction* (compensatory or/and punitive), involving, in different ways, toponymic cleansing, founding, restoring, and/or challenging, this process often privileges majoritarian interpretations of inclusion read strictly through the prism of anti-apartheid struggle over and above technologies of *transformation* which accept elements of the harmful historical past as part of the uneasy process of living together in the present. The latter was Mandela's position, which has been and is being contested under the leadership of his successors. Mandela asked that the process of renaming "should not be the terrain of 'petty revenge' or defensiveness." Mandela's plea is critical because, as Swart (2008, 113) rightly argues, "[i]t is dangerous to represent a country's history as only consisting of a certain selective, sanitized portion of history."

As the examples of street renaming in Johannesburg remind us, when street name changes focusing specifically on cleansing, restoring, challenging, and/ or founding are predicated on the overarching goal of transformation, that is, *transforming* memory rather than merely *preserving* it, renaming is less controversial and more inclusive. In most cases, the renaming of streets after heroes of the anti-apartheid struggle and other anti-colonial activists in the four cities point to this. While some of the protagonists and most of the antagonists of renaming would want to *preserve* memory rather than *transform* it, I suggest that the idea and ideal of a multiracial society, the Rainbow nation, is essentially about transformation. Transformation, which I argue is more in the spirit of the negotiated process that ended apartheid, implies that the past cannot be totally toponymically cleansed, erased, or fully restored. The past in

South Africa, like every national past, includes uncomfortable and uneasy heritage. Therefore, the present remains a transformational process in the building of a common future.

As a technique and rationality of governing people and space, the struggle for street (re)naming in South Africa exemplifies what Foucault (1988, 19) calls a "strategic game between liberties." The conception of liberty by black South Africans and heirs to the liberation clash with that of many Afrikaners, heirs of the old order. In the fight for and against renaming, we see what Dean (1999, 245) describes as "the nature of politics as a struggle or competition between competing forces, groups or individuals attempting to influence, appropriate or otherwise control the exercise of authority." Against this backdrop, I suggest that street renaming in South Africa constitutes a form of governmentality as evident in the cases examined. The struggle represents both the conduct of conduct and *dispositif.* As technologies of ensuring transformation through projecting historical restitution, ensuring cultural restitution, and/or symbolic reparation, street renaming is not only mobilized to shape the behavior of both the protagonists and antagonists of street name changes (conduct of conduct) in the actually existing (racially, political, socially, and economically) divided society. It also constitutes propositions about the system of relations among the races, cultural and interest groups, and political parties (*dispositif*) in the post-apartheid urban contexts that can lead to the creation of a truly multicultural nation. The first captures the past and present dystopia, while the other points to the imagined utopia. In this way, new signage on the streets, emerging from heterogeneous sites and relations, reflects the accumulation of historical experiences while gesturing at the eventual unfolding of these experiences in a democratic and multicultural present and future.

References

Adebanwi, W. (2012). "Glocal Naming and Shaming: Toponymic (Inter)National Relations on Lagos and New York Streets." *African Affairs,* 111 (445): 640–661.

Alderman, D. (2000). "A Street Fit for a King: Naming Places and Commemoration in the American South." *Professional Geographer,* 52(4): 672–684.

Alderman, D. (2002). "Street Names as Memorial Arenas: The Reputational Politics of Commemorating Martin Luther King Jr. in a Georgia County." *Historical Geography,* 30: 99–120.

Alderman, D. (2003). "Street Names and the Scaling of Memory: The Politics of Commemorating Martin Luther King, Jr. within the African-American Community." *Area,* 35(2): 163–173.

Areff, A. (2016). "New Tshwane Street Names Can Go Up—ConCourt," *News24,* July 21: www.news24.com/SouthAfrica/News/new-tshwane-street-names-can-go-up-concourt-20160721

Azaryahu, M. (1988). "What is to be Remembered: The Struggle over Street Names in Berlin, 1921–1930." *Telaviver Jahrbuch fur deutsche Geschichte,* 17: 241–258.

Azaryahu, M. (1990). "Renaming the Past: Changes in 'City Text' in Germany and Austria, 1945–1947," *History and Memory,* 2(2): 32–53.

Azaryahu, M. (1992). "The Purge of Bismarck and Saladin: The Renaming of Streets in East Berlin and Haifa, a Comparative Study in Culture-Planning," *Poetics Today*, 13(2): 351–367.

Azaryahu, M. (1996). "The Power of Commemorative Street Names." *Environment and Planning D: Society and Space*, 14(3): 311–330.

Azaryahu, M. (2011). "The Critical Turn and Beyond: The Case of Commemorative Street Naming." *ACME: An International E-Journal for Critical Geographies*, 10(1): 28–33.

Azaryahu, M. (2012). "Rabin's Road: The Politics of Toponymic Commemoration of Yitzhak Rabin in Israel." *Political Geography*, 31(2): 73–82.

Beall, J., Crankshaw, O., and Parnell, S. (2002). *Uniting a Divided City: Governance and Social Exclusion in Johannesburg*. Abingdon, UK: Earthscan.

Beavon K. (1992). "The Post-Apartheid City: Hope, Possibilities, and Harsh Realities." In D. Smith (Ed.), *The Apartheid City and Beyond* (pp. 231–242). London: Routledge.

Berg, L. D. (2011). "Banal Naming, Neoliberalism, and Landscapes of Dispossession." *ACME: An International E-Journal for Critical Geographies*, 10(1): 13–22.

Bigon, L. (2016). Introduction: "Place Names in Africa: Colonial Urban Legacy, Entangled History." In L. Bigon (ed.) *Place Names in Africa: Colonial Urban Legacies, Entangled Histories* (pp. 1–26). Cham, Switzerland: Springer.

Brenner, N. (2009). "What is Critical Urban Theory?" *City*, 13(2–3): 198–207.

Brown, K. (2010). "South Africa's Street Signs, Place Names Lead to More Struggle." *Toronto Star*, May 28: www.thestar.com/news/world/2010/05/28/south_africas_street_signs_place_names_lead_to_more_struggle.html

Carlos, J., Faraco, G., and Murphy, M. (1997). "Street Names and Political Regimes in an Andalusian Town." *Ethnology*, 36(2):123–148.

Christopher, A. (1994). *The Atlas of Apartheid*. London: Routledge.

City of Johannesburg. (2006). "City to Rename Streets after Student Heroes." Official Website of the City of Johannesburg, June 15: www.joburg.org.za/index.php?option=com_content&task=view&id=798&Itemid=168

City of Johannesburg. (2007). "City to Rename Streets After Student Heroes." Official Website of the City of Johannesburg, May 22: http://joburg.org.za/index.php?option=com_content&task=view&id=798&Itemid=159

City of Johannesburg. (2014). "New Street Names Celebrate Joburg's Shared Past ... and Future." Official Website of the City of Johannesburg, September 16: www.joburg.org.za/index.php?option=com_content&id=9175:new-street-names-celebrate-joburgs-shared-past-and-future&Itemid=266

Coetser, A. (2004). "Echelons of Power and Naming Practices: A Case Study." *Nomina Africana*, 18(1&2): 45–59.

Davie, L. (2008). "Apartheid Street Names Replaced." *BuaNews*. June 2: http://allafrica.com/stories/printable/200806021225.html

Dean, M. (1999). *Governmentality: Power and Rule in Modern Society*. London: Sage.

Duminy, J. (2014). "Street Renaming, Symbolic Capital, and Resistance in Durban, South Africa." *Environment and Planning D: Society and Space*, 32(2): 310– 328.

Elden, S. and Crampton, J. (2007). "Space, Knowledge and Power: Foucault and Geography." In S. Elden and J. Crampton (Eds.), *Space, Knowledge and Power: Foucault and Geography* (pp. 1–16). Aldershot, UK: Ashgate.

Ferguson, P. (1988). "Reading City Streets." *The French Review*, 61(3): 386–397.

Foucault, M. (1971). *The Order of Things*. New York: Vintage Books.

Foucault, M. (1986). "Of Other Spaces." *Diacritics*, 16(1): 22–27.

Foucault, M. (1988). "The Ethic of Care for the Self as a Practice of Freedom." In J. Bernauer and D. Rasmussen (Eds.), *The Final Foucault* (pp. 1–20). Boston, MA: MIT Press.

Foucault, M. (1990). *Power/Knowledge: Selected Interviews and Other Writings, 1972–1977*. Colin Gordon (Ed.). New York: Pantheon Books.

Foucault, M. (1991). "Governmentality." In G. Burchell, C. Gordon, and P. Miller (Eds.), *The Foucault Effect: Studies in Governmentality* (pp. 87–104). Chicago: University of Chicago Press.

Foucault, M. (2002 [1982]). "Space, Knowledge, Power." In J. Faubion (Ed.), *Power: Essential Works of Foucault*, Volume 3 (pp. 239–256). London: Penguin.

Foucault, M. (2006). *Psychiatric Power: Lectures at the College De France, 1973–1974*. New York: Palgrave Macmillan.

Getz, A. (2008). "Mandela at 90: How He Shaped a Nation," *Newsweek*, July 16: www.newsweek.com/mandela-90-how-he-shaped-nation-93223

Gill, G. (2005). "Changing Symbols: The Renovation of Moscow Place Names." *The Russian Review*, 64(3): 480–503.

Giraut F., Guyot, S., and Houssay-Holzschuch, M. (2008). "Enjeux de mots: les changements toponymiques sud-africains, Espace géographique." *Espace Géographique*, 2(37): 131–150.

Giraut, F. and Houssay-Holzschuch, M. (2016), "Place Naming as *Dispositif:* Towards a Theoretical Framework." *Geopolitics*, 21(1): 1–21.

Goldstone, C. (2008). "Goin' On Down to Problem Street." *IOL News*, August 30: www.iol.co.za/news/politics/goin-on-down-to-problem-street-414444#.Vg1-unpViko

Guyot, S. and Seethal, C. (2007). "Identity of Place, Places of Identities: Change of Place Names in Post-apartheid South Africa." *South African Geographical Journal*, 89(1): 55–63.

Jenkins, E. (1990). "From Leliefontein to Megawatt Park: Some Trends in the Naming of South African Places." *English Academy Review*, 7(1): 60–67.

Jenkins, E. (2007). *Falling Into Place*. Claremont, South Africa: David Philip.

Jenkins, E., Raper, P., and Möller, L. (1996). *Changing Place Names*. Durban: Indicator Press.

Katznelson, I. (1993). *Marxism and the City*. New York: Oxford University Press.

Khumalo, F. 2006. "Deciding Whose Story is History." *Sunday Times*, July 23.

Koopman, A. (2012). "The Postcolonial Identity of Durban." *Names and Identity*, 4(2): 133–159.

Koopman, A. and Deane, J. (2005). "New Names for Old: Transformation in the Streets of Pietermaritzburg." *Natalia*, 35: 85–90.

Laing, A. (2011). "Nelson Mandela Analysis: 'Madiba's Magic' is Evoked by Virtually Every Politician in South Africa." *Telegraph*, January 28: www.telegraph.co.uk/news/worldnews/nelson-mandela/8287160/Nelson-Mandela-analysis-Madibas-Magic-is-evoked-by-virtually-every-politician-in-South-Africa.html

Leach, N. (2002). "Erasing the Traces: The 'Denazification' of Post-apartheid Johannesburg and Pretoria." In N. Leach (Ed.), *The Hieroglyphics of Space: Reading and Experiencing the Modern Metropolis* (pp. 92–100). London: Routledge.

Lemanski, C. (2006). "Desegregation and Integration as Linked or Distinct? Evidence from a Previously 'White' Suburb in Post-apartheid Cape Town." *International Journal of Urban and Regional Research*, 30(3): 564–586.

Light, D. (2004). "Street Names in Bucharest, 1990–1997: Exploring the Modern Historical Geographies of Post-socialist Change." *Journal of Historical Geography*, 30(1): 154–172.

Magome, M. (2011). "Madiba's Name Replaced with that of Killer." *Pretoria News*, July 19.

Mail & Guardian. (2004). "The Politics of Madiba Magic." April 2: http://mg.co.za/article/2004-04-02-the-politics-of-madiba-magic

Mail & Guardian. (2016). "Street Names Should Recognize all Heroes, Concourt Hears." May 19: http://mg.co.za/article/2016-05-19-street-names-should-recognise-all-heroes-concourt-hears

Mbembe, A. (2007). "Why am I Here?" In L. McGregor and S. Nuttal (Eds.), *At Risk: Writings On and Over the Edge of South Africa* (pp. 144–170). Johannesburg: Jonathan Ball Publishers.

Merrifield, A. (2002). *Metro-Marxism.* New York: Routledge.

Myers, G. (1996). "Naming and Placing the Other: Power and the Urban Landscape in Zanzibar." *Tijdschrift voor Economsche en Sociale Goegrafie*, 87(3): 237–246.

Ndletyana, M. (2012). "Changing Place Names in Post-Apartheid South Africa: Accounting for the Unevenness." *Social Dynamics: A Journal of African Studies*, 38(1): 87–103.

Nel, E., Hill, T., and Maharaj, B. (2003). "Durban's Pursuit of Economic Development in the Post-Apartheid Era." *Urban Forum*, 14(2–3): 223–243.

News24. (2012a). "Mandela Drive 'Renaming' Case Dropped." February 21.

News24. (2012b). "Pretoria Name Changes Upset Dutch Party." March 29: www.news24.com/SouthAfrica/Politics/Pretoria-name-changes-upset-Dutch-party-20120328

Ngozo, A. (2015). "City Loses Battle over Street Names." *Pretoria East Record*, August 12: http://rekordeast.co.za/60333/city-loses-battle-over-street-names

Oldfield, S. (2005). "Urban Transition in South Africa: Negotiating Segregation." In P. Gervais-Lambony, F. Landy, and S. Oldfield (Eds.), *Reconfiguring Identities and Building Territory in India and South Africa* (pp. 325–342). New Delhi: Manohar.

O'Neil, M. (1991). "Evaluation of a Conceptual Model of Architectural Legibility." *Environment and Behaviour*, 23(3): 259–284.

Orgeret, K. (2010). "The Road to Renaming—What's in a Name? The Changing of Durban Street Names and its Coverage in *The Mercury*." *Journal of African Media Studies*, 2(3): 297–320.

Palonen, E. (2008). "The City-Text in Post-Communist Budapest: Street Names, Memorials, and the Politics of Commemoration." *GeoJournal*, 73(3): 219–230.

Patel, K. (2012). "The Return of Name-Changing Cliffhanger." *Daily Maverick*, March 29: www.dailymaverick.co.za/article/2012-03-29-south-africa-the-return-of-the-name-changing-cliffhanger

Raper, P. (1989). *Dictionary of Southern African Names.* Johannesburg: Lowry Publishers.

Republic of South Africa. (1989). "Debates in Parliament." Cape Town: Government Printer.

Roberts, S. (1988). "Metro Matters; Battle to Block the Re-naming of Fifth Avenue." *New York Times*, February 15: www.nytimes.com/1988/02/15/nyregion/metro-matters-battle-to-block-the-re-naming-of-fifth-avenue.html

Rose-Redwood, R. (2008a). "'Sixth Avenue is Now a Memory': Regimes of Spatial Inscription and the Performative Limits of the Official City-Text." *Political Geography*, 27(8): 875–894.

Rose-Redwood, R. (2008b). "From Number to Name: Symbolic Capital, Places of Memory and the Politics of Street Renaming in New York City." *Social and Cultural Geography*, 9(4): 431–452.

Rose-Redwood, R. 2011. "Rethinking the Agenda of Political Toponymy." *ACME: An International E-Journal for Critical Geographies*, 10(1): 34–41.

Rose-Redwood, R. and Alderman, D. (2011). "Critical Interventions in Political Toponymy." *ACME: An International E-Journal for Critical Geographies*, 10(1): 1–6.

Rose-Redwood, R. S., Alderman, D. and Azaryahu, M. (2010). "Geographies of Toponymic Inscription: New Directions in Critical Place-Name Studies." *Progress in Human Geography*, 34(4): 453–470.

Skelton, D. (2015a). "Tshwane Must Put Old Street Names Back Up." *Times*, June 2: www.timeslive.co.za/local/2015/06/02/Tshwane-must-put-old-street-names-back-up

Skelton, D. (2015b). "Pretoria: Where the Streets Have Two Names." *Times*, June 3: www.timeslive.co.za/thetimes/2015/06/03/Pretoria-Where-the-streets-have-two-names

Smith, D. (1992). "Introduction." In D. Smith (Ed.), *The Apartheid City and Beyond: Urbanization and Social Change in South Africa* (pp. 1–10). London: Routledge.

Smith, D. (2012). "Signs of the Times: Street Names Debate Rages in Pretoria." *The Guardian* (London). March 23: www.guardian.co.uk/world/2012/mar/23/street-names-debate-pretoria

Soja, E. (1989). *Postmodern Geographies: The Reassertion of Space in Critical Social Theory*. London: Verso.

Soja, E. (1993) "History: Geography: Modernity." In S. During (Ed.), *The Cultural Studies Reader* (pp. 113–125). London: Routledge.

Stroob. (2012). "Leave Cape Town the F&*k Alone." *MyCityByNight*, July 19: www.mycitybynight.co.za/leave-cape-town-the-fk-alone

Swart, M. (2008). "Name Changes as Symbolic Reparation after Transition: The Examples of Germany and South Africa." *German Law Journal*, 9(2): 105–120.

Tolsi, N. (2008). "The Spray-paint Revolution." *Mail & Guardian*, September 24: http://mg.co.za/article/2008-09-24-the-spraypaint-revolution

Turner, N. (2009). "Odonymic Warfare: The Process of Renaming Streets in Durban, South Africa." *Nomina Africana*, 23(1): 118–133.

Wines, M. (2007). "Where the Road to Renaming Does Not Run Smooth." *New York Times*, May 5, A4: www.nytimes.com/2007/05/25/world/africa/25durban.html?_r=1&pagewanted=print

Yeoh, B. (1996). "Street-Naming and Nation-Building: Toponymic Inscriptions of Nationhood in Singapore." *Area*, 28(3): 298–307.

14 Street renaming, symbolic capital, and resistance in Durban, South Africa

James Duminy

Introduction

Early on a humid South African summer morning in mid-January 2009, in the affluent suburb of Durban North, the Mayor of Durban, Obed Mlaba, wearing casual clothes, climbed a short ladder, gripped a detergent-soaked brush, and began to clean the crude spray-paint from the obscured sign of Dr. Kenneth Kaunda Road. Little over five months previously the new metallic sign, then gleaming proudly in commemoration of Zambia's famous independence leader and long-time president, had been erected to mark the official renaming of Northway Road. Present with the mayor to launch eThekwini Municipality's hands-on "clean-up campaign" of defaced signs—part of "an ongoing process" designed to "rid the city of negative sentiments from citizens who are not embracing change"—was City Manager Michael Sutcliffe, as well as an illustrious collection of influential local African National Congress (ANC) members and councillors (*eThekwini Online* 2009a). The extent of street sign vandalism in Durban, especially in middle-income suburban areas, had been alarming since the erection of new signs for 99 renamed roads in August 2008. Mlaba explained:

> What we are seeing [the defacing of the new street names] is precisely the effects of the fact that South Africans have not been made to integrate and reconcile properly—and have not begun to understand their continent and its leaders, including the role the African continent played in our freedom.
>
> (*eThekwini Online* 2009b, additions in original)

The mayor proceeded to issue various punitive threats at the anonymous, nocturnal spray painters: "If the culprits are caught, they will be forced to face the law and they will be prosecuted accordingly. I do not understand why people cannot accept change" (*Daily News* 2009).

Some passersby indicated their support for the mayor's effort; others reportedly "showed signs of disapproval" (*eThekwini Online* 2009b). A local resident, present at the event, described sign vandalism as "disgusting" and "costly"—the expressions of obscure individuals bent on "fighting change." Nevertheless, she suggested that the "street names will be vandalized again overnight" (*Daily News* 2009). A local representative of the Democratic Alliance (DA), the ANC's main political opposition in Durban, rejected the campaign launch as a "cheap publicity stunt," stating that "the ANC should know that you can never force unpopular changes and decisions on communities which have rejected them" (*Daily News* 2009).

The public performance of what the street renaming process officially meant, in contrast to the actual utterances of public opponents, signals some of the salient aspects of the furiously confrontational discourse that came to surround the Durban street renaming project, which took place from 2007 to 2008—albeit with plans stretching back at least to 1999. Those for and against the process contested questions of who or what is worthy of commemoration in Durban; of whose vision of and for post-apartheid South African society is "correct"; of the "real" meanings or intentions hidden in the official process and its associated acts of resistance; and of who or what has legitimate authority over the production of the urban symbolic environment, amongst a multitude of other historical, economic, logistical, and aesthetic issues.

Street renaming in post-apartheid Durban must be seen within the city's wider history of enforced race-based segregation and post-apartheid symbolic transformation. In the early-twentieth century, the city pioneered the application of segregationist policy through the so-called "Durban System" of racial administration. Apartheid policy attempted to institutionalize the general ideological conviction that "the urban" was the permanent domain of white citizens, with other race groups viewed as temporary sojourners to the city. With the passing of national legislation such as the Group Areas Act of 1950, Durban's central business and residential districts were reserved for Whites, whilst African and Indian people residing in relatively central locations such as Cato Manor were forcibly removed (in the late 1950s) to newly constructed townships on the city's outlying periphery.

With this history of enforced racial segregation, following the end of apartheid Durban has faced acute challenges in terms of municipal restructuring and socio-spatial integration. Despite concerted efforts to develop municipal capacity for "integrated development planning," to some extent the city's basic pattern of race-based segregation has persisted, largely through market mechanisms reproducing spatial inequalities based on class. However, the city's central business district has experienced an influx of black residents and businesses from the late-1980s, just as white business and residential property interests have relocated to nearby centers such as Umhlanga and Ballito, and sprawling upmarket developments reaching northward from the city (Todes 2008). Middle-income to upper-income suburbs surrounding the city center have experienced less radical transformations, although gradually their racial profile has shifted in conjunction with the rise of a black South African urban middle-class. It was in these central and mostly affluent precincts that the renaming project and its discontents materialized.

In the context of persistent patterns of socio-spatial fragmentation in many South African cities, renaming has become a means of "symbolic transformation."

Since the first national democratic elections in 1994, the ruling ANC party has renamed numerous municipalities and urban features throughout the country. Renaming has provided a platform for the redress of painful memories of racial exclusion as well as the enactment of new territorial imaginaries and visions of South African history and culture, often framed within the image of a young but reconciled and multicultural African nation (Guyot and Seethal 2007).

Occasionally, renaming projects have been met with resistance from local residents and political opponents wary of their high financial cost, or sensitive to the possibility that such efforts may constitute a hegemonic attempt by the ANC to "obliterate the past." In Durban, the perceived radicalness of the historical vision projected by the ANC exacerbated these tensions, leading to an unprecedented degree of local public interest and opposition. Although public concern and antagonism emanated from a variety of sources, for different reasons, and across racial and class lines, local state representatives responded by casting all in terms of "counter-transformation," identifying and confronting their opponents as conservative elements opposed to "positive change" at the local and national scales, but generally without an explicitly racialized politics.

Whilst the motivations and controversies surrounding the street renaming project were grafted onto South Africa's and Durban's wider histories of enforced exclusion and post-apartheid symbolic transformation, the event itself gave rise to a more localized and contemporary terrain of conflicts, scalar politics, and political subjectivities. These local dynamics are the substance of this chapter, which examines the case of street renaming in Durban with a critical analytical perspective of place naming as "text," "arena," and "performance" (Dwyer and Alderman 2008). Emphasis is placed on the coproductive material and symbolic dynamics underpinning these acts of symbolic transformation and resistance. I argue that theorizations of "naming as symbolic resistance" (Alderman 2008) need to take account of at least two dynamics, as evident in the Durban case: firstly, the differences between actors who disagree with certain name–place associations, yet agree with the principle of renaming, and those who reject or contest the projected symbolic authority of the "namer." Secondly, authorities may act to confront and "name" their critics as part of an overall, iterative process of toponymic resistance and legitimation, which includes—but extends beyond—the "formal" disagreements or dissent raised within civil society. I argue that such a "performative" conception of symbolic capital and resistance may aid understanding of renaming processes, especially those carried out in contested memorial landscapes.

The following section examines the Durban renaming in terms of the hierarchies of symbolic prestige and distinction produced and reified by the process. The third section considers acts of contestation and resistance, highlighting the diversity of discourses and practices that expressed some form of opposition to the process. This leads into a discussion of how key local political actors confronted this opposition, and actively legitimated the basis for the symbolic project of street renaming. Concluding reflections on the implications of this research for critical place name scholarship follow.

The Durban street renaming process

Local government interest in renaming the streets of Durban preceded the turn of the twenty-first century, when the municipal council devised a policy framework for the necessary participatory and administrative procedures to be followed. Mayor Mlaba, of the ANC, first publicized the idea of renaming streets, monuments, buildings, parks, and stadiums across the municipality in 1999, yet apart from several low-profile name changes with little or no political relevance, the street renaming policy remained largely unimplemented (*The Mercury* 2003). Public proposals gathered dust as councillors directed their energies towards achieving election success. Political interest in street naming only reemerged in January 2007, with the local ANC leadership of (now renamed) eThekwini Municipality determined to pursue a national party resolution to "honour the heroes" of the post-apartheid era. Mlaba announced the ANC's intention to rename eight of the city's major roads and streets at a full council meeting, stating that the renamings were "in line with the creation of a united, non-sexist South Africa" (*Ezasegagasini Metro* 2007). As some ANC councillors noted at the time, this was to be "Phase One" of an overall process.

Representatives of opposition parties, particularly the Inkatha Freedom Party (IFP) and DA, reacted to the sudden announcement with trepidation. The matter was raised in connection with the renaming of Durban airport in honor of the anti-apartheid struggle icon Moses Mabhida and seemed to have entered the council agenda without their prior knowledge (eThekwini Council 2007).

Despite opposition concerns (discussed in greater detail below), the ANC majority in the council ensured that Phase One was approved and implemented, with an official renaming ceremony held on March 23, 2007. Prior to this, on March 9, advertisements calling for further public nominations of street name changes ran in local newspapers, marking the beginning of Phase Two, which would culminate in the renaming of 99 streets, predominantly located in the city center and affluent surrounding suburbs of Durban (Figure 14.1).

The names of most of Durban's central and suburban roadways reflect an obvious bias towards the city's British colonial history. In the case of Durban North, a suburb forged according to British town planning principles in the Garden City tradition, the Durban North Estates Company named a majority of the new streets after places in London (McIntyre 1956). Similarly, David Dick's popular history *Who Was Who in Durban Street Names* (2008) recognizes that a considerable proportion of street names in the central business district and surrounding suburbs were borrowed from places in the United Kingdom and Ireland; many others from colonial authorities in the Cape, Natal, and post-unification South Africa. Colonial military commanders and engagements, including British conflicts with Indian, Zulu, Boer, German, and Italian forces, provided over 120 names. A typical example was Aliwal Street, now Samora Machel Road, originally named in honor of Sir Harry Smith's 1849 victory "over a large force of Sikhs" near the village of Aliwal in Punjab, India (*Sunday Tribune* 2008a). The version of history represented by these names is neatly

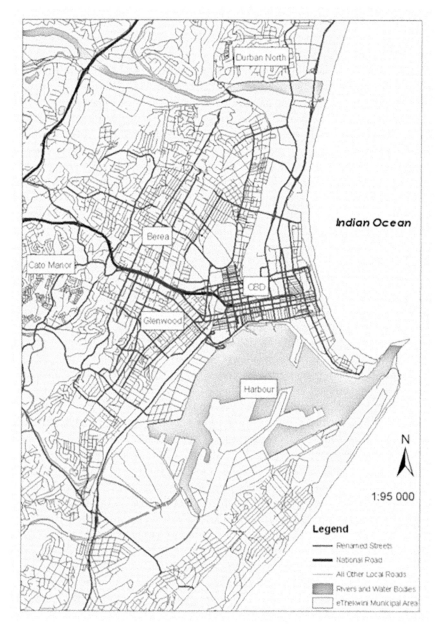

Figure 14.1 Map of renamed streets in Durban, South Africa circa 2008 (cartography by James Duminy)

captured by John McIntyre in the introduction to his *Origin of Durban Street Names*, first published in 1956:

> The names which mark the streets we tread every day—names which are household words but which have no significance for most of us—frequently enshrine and commemorate some historical fact or preserve the name of some historical personage or of some worthy citizen who has served the community in one sphere or another. Many of them bear the names of courageous pioneers and early settlers who played their parts in establishing the flourishing and prosperous city we know to-day.
>
> (1956, i)

Durban's original street names were thus commemorative of a European history, of a European pioneering effort on subtropical African soil. Over time, their persistence in the city-text evidently irked local political actors. Half a decade before the final completion of the street renaming process, ANC member Nigel Gumede, chair of the Municipal Infrastructure Committee, explained the ANC's general objection: "We believe those old names were given in terms of skewed considerations because they were simply entrenching the old order that was cherished by the minority" (*The Mercury* 2003).

Such opinions constituted the starting point for the local ANC leadership's decision to conduct its symbolic transformation of the urban landscape. In 2007, eThekwini Municipality published a list of all the approved name changes for Phases One and Two, including a short justification for the selection of each proposed name.[1] Of the 107 names bestowed post-2007, 11 were apolitical, referring to local economic activity, local educational or cultural benefactors, musicians, or significant figures of nineteenth-century Zulu history. The overwhelming majority honored individuals specifically for their involvement in either anti-apartheid or international revolutionary, usually anti-colonial movements. In general, two trends are discernable: firstly, women constituted roughly one-fifth of all the incoming names—a proportion that contrasts noticeably with the male-dominated symbolism of Durban's street name system as a whole. Secondly, whilst the list included activists from a wide variety of interest groups, including youth clubs, student organizations, and trade unions, approximately two-thirds were explicitly motivated in terms of their previously active membership in the ANC or one of its institutional allies.

The official motivations given by eThekwini Municipality were generally short, providing brief biographies of the people or things concerned, usually describing a significant event in the life of a local figure. The renaming of Edwin Swales VC Drive to Solomon Mahlangu Drive, for example, was motivated by the latter's heroics on behalf of uMkhonto we Sizwe, the disbanded military wing of the ANC: "On March 2, 1977, Solomon was sentenced to death by hanging. On April 6, 1979, 23 year old Solomon Mahlangu faced the gallows, raised his hand in the ANC salute, and met his death at the hands of a racist regime." Mahlangu's commemoration is justified by his unfailing opposition to the apartheid government. The blurb from an official local state poster put it clearly:

> The street renaming is indeed an ultimate step forward towards honouring all the heroes and heroines who fought a good fight for a good cause. Chief among these, are those whom in pursuit of freedom ventured their way through the troubled bridges of apartheid. Therefore as eThekwini council we feel honoured to be part of such an historic process of ensuring that the names of these great men and women of the struggle remain known even to the generations to come.[2]

The "official" view is that participation in the anti-apartheid struggle is a legitimate source of heroic status, distinction, and prestige (that is, symbolic capital). In fact, it is not only the legitimate, but the *predominant* source. Steve Biko, despite not having been a member of the ANC, therefore warranted commemoration. International anti-colonial and revolutionary leaders such as Che Guevara, Kenneth Kaunda, and Julius Nyerere also fall within the definition of having "fought a good fight for a good cause," and for this reason deserved commemoration alongside those with more obviously local or national significance. The composition of the new street names thus lent the anti-apartheid struggle a degree of ideological and historical continuity by linking it with legitimate revolutionary movements internationally, including the Tanganyika African National Union (in the case of Nyerere) and Movimiento 26 de Julio.

With some exceptions, the renamed streets themselves were "prominent" thoroughfares—that is, when prominence is defined in terms of their geographical linking effect. Those chosen as commemorative places were predominantly highways, arterial linking routes, and important inter-neighborhood and intra-neighborhood thoroughfares (Figure 14.1). The most prominent roads were invariably renamed after influential and revered anti-apartheid activists or ANC leaders. Inkosi Albert Luthuli's immense symbolic status (as long-time ANC president and Nobel Peace Prize winner) afforded him the privilege of association with one of the most important roads in the entire municipal area, the M4 Southern Freeway. Other roads with similar functional capacity were invariably and similarly renamed after military or political veterans of organizations related to the ANC. The city manager showed a keen awareness of the need to balance a street's scale and a name's symbolic value, stating: "you can't have a little street named after a hugely prominent individual. There might be some good suggestions, but for the wrong road ... In these cases we might mix and match" (*The Mercury* 2007a).

Evidently, a perceived relationship between the commemorated agent's symbolic status and the street's size and functionality underlay the renaming process. Individual name changes were deemed "appropriate" when there was a correspondence between symbolic and functional hierarchies. Therefore, the spatial "prominence" deliberately afforded to key ANC members within the city-text was a reflection of their preferential ranking within an underlying hierarchy of symbolic importance.

This section has shown that the Durban street renaming project was, on one level, a demonstration of socio-political change, deriving its meaning from the ANC's refusal to forget painful memories of segregation and subjugation (Legg 2005) as well as a negation of the city's colonial and apartheid history. Furthermore,

Figure 14.2 Renamed street sign in Glenwood, Durban, South Africa, 2014. New signs
had identical structures and the same "DIN A Text" official typeface. Old
signs were left atop the new, crossed out with red tape (photograph by
Andrew Duminy).

this demonstration depended upon material practices, including the physical
process of changing street signage and the allocation of material urban space to
produce and reify symbolic hierarchies of distinction (Figure 14.2). This does not
suggest that expressions of symbolic power such as official naming procedures are

simply reflective of pre-existing and well-defined divisions operating within the symbolic field. In fact, it is through official interventions that such divisions are produced, reiterated, and institutionalized, or indeed "materialized" (Butler 1993), in the public domain. That is precisely the reason that post-independence organizations such as the ANC carry out grand projects of symbolic transformation—it allows the fixing of certain meanings and categories of perception in conditions of political and ideological uncertainty. This raises the question of popular recognition and legitimacy. The technique of allocating symbolic capital according to an individual's opposition to apartheid is legitimate—that is, it can confer a symbolic effect—only if "the struggle" is popularly recognized as a "good fight for a good cause." That people will have different interpretations of symbolic prominence is inevitable, especially in places with histories of racial and ideological conflict such as Durban. Indeed, the following section discusses cases in which residents of the city advanced very different notions of historical representation and symbolic distinction.

Contestation and resistance

The Durban street renaming process generated an unprecedented degree of antagonistic public debate. Although Phase One was not met with significant public opposition, the ANC's political opponents in the eThekwini Council, in the form of the Democratic Alliance (DA), Inkatha Freedom Party (IFP), and Minority Front (MF), were concerned from the outset that the process lacked (their) participation, and that it projected a highly partisan image of anti-apartheid struggle history. It was the sudden commencement of Phase Two, in quick succession to Phase One's controversies, that catalyzed the greatest public and political outrage. Advertisements calling for public name change proposals as part of Phase Two ran in local newspapers on March 9, 2007. On April 21, a total of 181 proposals were published in local newspapers, asking for public comments and objections. By May 21, the municipality had received 12,000 written public objections (*The Mercury* 2007b).

The local media became a particularly active site of public debate and discursive contestation. Local daily newspapers, especially independent morning publications aimed at English readers, such as *The Mercury*, bulged with indignant letters from concerned residents or visitors of all races. As with the arguments delivered by political parties, many questioned the legitimacy of the official participatory process leading to the renamings, and they reacted to the perceived insult and "political triumphalism" of the ANC's project. More significantly, however, public concern arose in response to specific name changes, where the renaming created associations between spatial, material, and symbolic characteristics that were perceived as inappropriate. A professor at the University of KwaZulu-Natal captured a recurrent theme of middle-class opinion by suggesting, "if somebody wants to change a name, change it to something that makes sense. Name it after a person or something significant that happened in the area" (*The Mercury* 2008a).

In this view, the relevance of a name change is determined by the extent to which the commemorated individual acted within and directly influenced the locality concerned. Indeed, judgments about whether a commemorated individual had exemplified some form of local historical agency became a primary point of contestation. Occasionally this was framed in terms of the particularities of local identity (*with whom do locals identify?*). So, Brendon Pillay of the Bayview Tenants and Ratepayers Association objected to the proposed renaming of Higginson Highway, Chatsworth, in honor of Yasser Arafat, because the Palestinian figurehead "has no relevance to Chatsworth." The local Indian community would "more readily identify with struggle stalwarts such as Fatima Meer, Ismail Meer, Yusuf Dadoo and Chris Hani" (*Sunday Tribune* 2007).

Other challenges to the renaming process did not necessarily demand a close, palpable geographical correspondence between historical action and commemorated actor. Rather, they sought an appropriate balance between the material and symbolic statuses of the commemorated agent and the commemorative place. An illustrative example is the renaming of Point Road as Mahatma Gandhi Road, intended to commemorate the time Gandhi spent living in Durban (from 1893 to 1914) and his contributions to the development of the civil rights movement in South Africa, including his role in founding the Natal Indian Congress in 1894. Point Road, in a material sense, is a formerly prosperous inner-city area now in a state of economic decline (and currently the target of significant inner-city regeneration efforts); symbolically, it is Durban's red light district, the "capital" of the city's illicit drug and prostitution industry. The stark contrast between Point Road's "sleaziness" and the global eminence of Gandhi led some in Durban's Indian communities to see the association, and the "symbolic dissonance" it involved, as an insult to Gandhi's reputation and family. Others were less perturbed, but regretted that an alternative, "more appropriate" road had not been chosen to befit his status. As his granddaughter and Durban resident Ela explained, "Gandhi would have settled in Point Road to change people's immoral ways ... My only concern is that he should have been given one of the more important roads, given his contribution to the non-violent movement in South Africa" (*The Mercury* 2005).

Here the source of concern is a dissonance between the "prominence" of individuals, in this case measured primarily in terms of their local actions and accomplishments, and the functional and symbolic significance of commemorative places. These and other concerns meant that general public discourse became increasingly organized around the question of "relevant spatiality," in terms of deciding who was appropriate for commemoration (that is, whether their material legacy included a specifically *local* impact and hence warranted commemoration within Durban specifically), but also in terms of the appropriate scale at which people thought Durban's new heroes should be remembered.

Those concerned with the naming of Mahatma Gandhi Road perceived that the "importance" of the road did not befit his status. How they judged this importance is not clear, but the criteria without doubt included perceptions of material or functional "prominence." In this sense, a road can be more or less appropriate as a commemorative place depending on its geographical linking effect, local property values, and the extent and character of local economic activity. In the association of certain names with certain streets, it was precisely when expectations of symbolic and material value were not met ("Gandhi deserves a more important street") or when there was a certain "dissonance" between the distinctiveness of the agent and the street concerned ("Point Road's sleazy image undermines Gandhi's legacy and reputation") that public interest and debate were sparked. In these circumstances, people such as Ela Gandhi generally accepted the right of the local state to grant names, the "need" for renaming and symbolic transformation, as well as the legitimacy of the anti-apartheid struggle as a source of symbolic distinction or prestige. They took issue with particular name–place associations, and, therefore, their activities had less to do with resistance of the symbolic imposition than with contestation of its content.

While these discursive games, primarily associated with concerns and questions over symbolic dissonance or local relevance, played out in the local media, the renaming process also emerged as a prime arena for the "infrapolitics" of symbolic subordination, a contestation largely performed in material urban space, attracting a range of less formalistic, occasionally illegal, modes of opposition. The continued use of the original street names, for example, is one area of "low-profile resistance" (Scott 1990). Other demonstrations of reluctance to adopt the new names were more overt, as with cases of street sign vandalism. Within a week of their installation in late August 2008, several signs along Albert Dlomo and Lina Arense Roads in the suburb of Glenwood had been obscured with black spray paint or "destroyed" (*Sunday Tribune* 2008b). Signs commemorating Esther Roberts, a founder of the South African Institute of Race Relations, had been removed. Deputy Mayor of Durban Logie Naidoo blamed local DA councillors for the acts, as well as various "right-wingers," for whom he promised sting-style prosecution traps would be set.

A less destructive mode of anonymous protest emerged in the form of an unofficial "civil renaming," performed on a minor street in the residential area of Berea in September 2008. Here the name of Kinnord Place was neatly crossed out with red tape, in the manner of all officially renamed streets, and a look-alike sign bearing the "new name" of Mike Sutcliffe Boulevard fixed atop it (*The Mercury* 2008b). The road chosen to honor the city manager, who had previously claimed, "You can't have a little street named after a hugely prominent individual," was an unimposing cul-de-sac. Sutcliffe himself reacted with good humor towards the informal renaming, which brought into focus a plethora of public concerns with the street renaming, including its perception as an autocratic imposition, the self-flattering tendencies of the local ANC as well as the intimate role played by the city manager in the process. Nevertheless the carnivalesque act, through the satirical inversion of symbolic authority, actively problematized the recognized legitimacy of the "official" renaming process (Darnton 1984).

In light of these findings, it is worth revisiting the concept of "symbolic resistance" and the tendency to include a broad range of acts, including formal political contests and the employment of competing, informal place names, under this label (Alderman 2008). The Durban renaming process indeed emerged as an "arena" for a wide variety of contesting acts and utterances by various sections of the public. The extent to which this variety of activities can be described as "resistance" is limited, however, for the Durban case provided numerous examples of people accepting the local state's "right" to act as the holder of the monopoly of legitimate symbolic violence—their concerns lay primarily with the participatory deficiency of the renaming process, and the symbolic "dissonance" produced through specific name–place associations. On the other hand, a willingness to embrace the legitimate symbolic authority of the state was not present with symbolic gestures such as street sign defacing and acts of informal renaming. Such acts, generally undertaken anonymously and occasionally involving the material inversion of symbolic authority, implied a challenge to the local state's right to determine the meanings of the urban symbolic environment, in addition to the "legitimate" categories of perception and appreciation implied by the renaming project.

The diversity of these acts and practices complicates any conceptualization of "symbolic resistance," and we shall return to the theoretical implications of these findings in the conclusion. Before this, however, we must consider the ways in which local state or ANC party representatives responded to their critics and justified the renaming project, in order to see the meanings of the renaming event as defined, over time, by interacting forces within a wider "perlocutionary field" (Rose-Redwood 2008).

The prose of counter-insubordination

As the acts described in the previous section unfolded in public discourse and urban space, representatives of the ANC or local state reacted to their challengers emphatically, casting all in the terms of "anti-transformation." In this section, I focus on the discursive practices of certain key actors and delegates of the ANC, the municipal government, or both, as they confronted, named, and attempted to discredit their opponents.

With the publicly fought contest gaining intensity by late April 2007, excited by the initiation and publication of Phase Two, the response from the municipality, or more precisely the city manager, involved lengthy rationalizing texts and public statements, of which the following extract from the online *City Manager's Newsletter*, published on May 2, is an example:

> Adverts ran on March 9, 2007 in major local newspapers calling on the public to put forward proposals for the renaming of roads, streets, freeways, municipal buildings, community halls, parks and other public places within the municipal region. Posters were also placed in different Sizakala centres and libraries. The public was encouraged to email, fax, post or even hand-deliver to these centres. The closing date for submissions was the 30th March 2007, giving the public 21 days to engage with the municipality. And even after this closing date, a few submissions were also considered. A total of 245 proposals were received.
>
> (*City Manager's Newsletter* 2007a)

In contrast to the claims of the political opposition (see section 2), the representation of the street renaming process provided by the newsletter implies that all relevant public participatory requirements were unequivocally fulfilled. The city manager points out the municipality's accommodative stance towards late submissions. He is also careful to mention the Sizakala (the isiZulu word for "get help") centers, many of which are located in eThekwini's townships, and the possible option of hand delivery. The verisimilitude of the account is enhanced by the use of a measured, pragmatic vocabulary and the inclusion of objects and processes relating to responsible democratic governance (advertisement, submission, consideration, and so on).

However, the question of whether or not the process had been procedurally and legally correct was not all that was at stake. Project proponents needed a reason for undertaking the costly business of renaming in the first place; the story of the renaming needed to fit within a larger narrative of symbolic transformation. On April 21, 2007, the latest list of name change proposals for Phase Two was published in local newspapers, with the explicit purpose of securing "public comment." The city manager received thousands of objections. The following response was authored approximately a fortnight later:

> The unfortunate part of the street renaming process is that no matter how much our (1) country has changed, there remains a core of people (2) who simply do not want to accept that change. We (3) all know that of the more than 30 000 street names in our (4) city, over 99% were named during the colonial or apartheid eras. However, when the council unanimously agrees to a process to allow for public participation ... we (5) find elements (6) miscommunicating the process itself and creating mayhem and confusion.
>
> *(City Manager's Newsletter* 2007b)[3]

In the first line of this passage, South Africa is referred to as "our country" and in the following sentence, Durban as "our city." The author appears to speak on behalf of a certain group, one that has a degree of "belonging" within both the nation and the city. Exactly who or what constitutes this group is not entirely clear. It can be assumed from the text's source—an official municipal publication that specifically addresses the rate-paying citizens of eThekwini Municipality—that the city manager writes as a delegated agent of the street renaming committee, which he led, and the municipality as a whole, of which he was the highest-ranking civil servant. Yet, he also reveals an implicit claim to represent the interests of some sort of a public majority, which is evident in the use of the collective "we." By claiming that "we all know ... ," he projects his personal understanding of the context for street renaming as "common knowledge," as something that should be shared by every resident of Durban. He speaks as a "simple symbolic substitute of the people" (Bourdieu 1991, 212–213), performing "a symbolic takeover by force," which, as Bourdieu argues, appears as a "takeover of form." This is most commonly exhibited by the spokesperson's permanent shift from the use of "I" to that of "we" (Bourdieu 1991, 213). In doing so, the city manager commits an act of symbolic violence on all those whom he claims to represent, according to the "oracle effect," which "is what enables the authorized spokesperson to take his authority from the group ... in order to exercise recognized constraint, symbolic violence, on each of the isolated members of the group" (Bourdieu 1991, 212). In other words, references to the collective "we" enable the production of the interests of the group, and thereby the definition of boundaries of acceptable action.

If the city manager claims to speak as "the people," who lies beyond the boundaries of this group? Impersonal linguistic forms are used to reference a "core of people" that is opposed to "change," as well as "elements" that act to disrupt the renaming process. Apparently, the division between "us" and "them" is determined by a corresponding set of interests pertaining to both a general process of "change" and the renaming project. The author and the other constituents of the collective "we" feel favorably towards both. "They," on the other hand, resist or "refuse to accept" both.

These references to "change" deserve greater attention. We see that in the first sentence South Africa is represented as being in a state of change. No mention is made of what constitutes such change, and no explanation given as to why it might be desirable. The author merely states that localized opposition to the street renaming process is representative of the more general opposition to "change" on a national scale. In doing so, he depicts a correspondence between the interests and objectives surrounding either process. This style of language, involving repeated reference to the desirability of "change," is characteristic of the ANC's political discourse of "transformation." Giliomee, Myburgh, and Schlemmer (2001) describe transformation as a "term without content," and an "indefinable moral end" making possible a political mode of vanguardism, and its meaning is basically derived from the ANC's strong ideological connection with the past (Saunders 2008). Essentially, transformation refers to a continuation of the anti-apartheid movement—an ongoing, far-reaching process of change within South African political and socio-economic fields. The starting point for this process is the objective socio-political structures of apartheid; the final cause or end result is possibly when all forms of capital (such as political, economic, cultural, and symbolic capital) in South African society are allocated in direct proportion to its racial structure.

Since the late-1990s, transformation—understood as a progressive and entirely morally justifiable process with a resolute teleological structure—has emerged as a central ideological theme and discursive strategy of the ANC. Yet the vagueness of the concept allows some "flexibility" in terms of how it is employed by representatives of the ANC party or state. It is precisely this degree of conceptual flexibility that allowed City Manager Sutcliffe to represent the Durban street renaming as nationwide transformation writ small. Two key effects are produced by creating this relationship. Firstly, it implies that Durban's local state acted in consonance with the central state authority and its ANC leadership, which is responsible for delivering transformation on a larger scale. Thus, the interests and activities of the local state are tied to those of an institutional apparatus with a far greater capacity to confer political and symbolic capital upon a delegated agent (himself, in this case). The city manager is not a delegate of the ANC or national state in actuality, yet his rhetorical style allows him to defend the actions of himself and eThekwini Municipality with all the symbolic power and popular recognition of the political discourse of transformation. He thus implicitly draws upon this popular recognition, these stocks of capital, in order to frame the street renaming process as being, in principle, legitimate and desirable.

Secondly, the linkage between street renaming and transformation enables the categorization of any local dissenting agency, such as an objector, within a much broader group. This was explicitly demonstrated by an ANC member of the eThekwini Council, Vusi Khoza, who stated: "Those people who are opposing the road name changes are really saying they don't want change and transformation in South Africa" (*The Independent on Saturday* 2007). In this view, acting against the renaming is tantamount to acting against transformation. As the latter is entirely moral and desirable, it follows that opposition to the renaming is morally and ideologically backward and irrelevant. Thus, in casting these relations, the city manager and others with similar institutional support from the state or ANC created the opportunity to categorize and discredit the intentions and opinions of any dissenting agency, without resorting to an explicitly racialized language of accusation.

In this section, I have argued that for local ANC actors to deploy the language of "transformation" as a counter-oppositional discourse during the Durban renaming debate, the street renaming had to be represented as a constitutive part of a desirable and wide-reaching process of change unfolding on a national scale. By consistently referring to agents and events in the language and rhetorical style of "transformation," ANC-affiliated actors categorized the entire project (including themselves and the new names) within a grand teleological narrative of progressive social change. Legitimacy was conferred by association. At the same time, those opposed to some aspect of the renaming project could then be categorized as anti-transformative, and subjected to all the symbolic violence that municipal or ANC representatives could muster, most acutely expressed in accusations of being "pro-apartheid."

Conclusion

This chapter has analyzed post-apartheid street renaming in the city of Durban with a conceptual approach based on the metaphors of "text," "arena," and "performance" (Dwyer and Alderman 2008). Each of these notions provides insights into the complexity of this process, and so the study generally affirms their utility as sensitizing analytical concepts for studying memorial landscapes. Firstly, through the metaphor of "text," we have seen that the meanings and norms surrounding the renaming were produced through the "interweaving" of symbols and objects in the production of the city-text through, for example, the hierarchical allocation of particular names (seen as more or less prestigious) to streets of different size and prominence. We have also seen that the renaming project was "defined, contextualized, and configured" (Rose 2002, 391) in relation to historical and political discourses active on a wider geographical scale, as a way of lending the initiative some legitimacy in the face of bitter public dissent. In so doing, the renaming event was drawn and rescaled into a political discourse, usually reserved for the national scale, based on the projected symbolic authority of the ANC as the vanguard of post-apartheid transformation.

Secondly, the Durban case confirms the importance of understanding public memorializations as "arenas" for the emergence and performance of diverse, competing claims surrounding historical memory as well as contemporary political and symbolic legitimacy. This case is remarkable for its diversity of modes and acts of contestation and resistance, which varied significantly in terms of attitude towards the state and the principle of renaming. Some disagreed with aspects of the project, such as particular name–place associations that were perceived as offensive, through rationalized arguments delivered in the media or in court; others challenged the legitimacy of the projected symbolic authority and its implied norms through everyday language and practice, or anonymous transgressions performed in public space. These acts were met, and no doubt spurred on, by a vigorous counter-politics carried out by key local political actors.

With these findings in mind, this chapter has sought to address the potential limitations of a conceptual framework based on "naming as symbolic resistance," with a view to developing the utility of "symbolic resistance" as a theoretical category for studying the politics of place naming. Firstly, the ambiguity of the term—does "symbolic resistance" refer to resistance "to the symbolic" (that is, actions in opposition to a symbolic imposition), to resistance that is performed through symbolic means, or to both? By keeping the definition of "symbolic resistance" flexible enough to encompass the full range of acts and relations attending renaming projects, the question of what may be termed an act of "resistance" is greatly complicated, with the risk that it could signify nothing more than a "reaction," or simply carrying a strong opinion on a contested matter of public discourse without necessarily disagreeing with the basic rationale of political and symbolic transformation. Secondly, an analytical focus on "resistance" (defined as a conscious reaction to an already existing entity or power) may detract attention from describing and explaining the various political subjectivities and practices that can flourish between the projected poles of dominator/subordinate, producing the coherent appearance of this binary as an effect of their relations, or possibly even creating "alternative spatialities" that extend beyond any interests and desires defined in opposition to an ostensibly hegemonic power (Rose 2002).

Therefore, either a more rigorous definition of "symbolic resistance" or some theoretical refinement is necessary to improve the concept's potential for studying the politics of place naming. Against an ontological reading of symbolic resistance as a distinct category of intentional practices, I have argued that a key area for further conceptual development lies with a performative understanding of resistance as the "discursive occasion" (Butler 1993) for the "disruption" of projected norms or social categories or, put differently, as a "subversion" that is a "consequence of the slippages inherent in citation" (Gregson and Rose 2000, 437). Here resistance is viewed as a "potential" generated within the citation or act of naming, made possible through the incompleteness and "self-subversion" of the official discourse, and undefined by the intention or choice of an "anterior active human agent" (2000, 438). In examining "symbolic resistance," then, what matters are the acts and spaces that give existence to this potential and associated "arenas of resistance" through the disruption of projected norms. Performing place renaming unsettles the meanings attached to these places, revealing the arbitrariness of the official city-text as a historical discourse, and thereby enables the emergence of a variety of overlapping and sometimes conflicting arenas of resistance. In these temporary spaces, actors project and contest different conceptions of "legitimate" history through various modes and scales of discursive performance. They can appropriate symbols or artifacts (including street signs) associated with "dominant" actors as ways of contesting or disrupting the legitimacy of those very symbols (Rose-Redwood, Alderman, and Azaryahu 2010), but they do not *necessarily* do so. Furthermore, arenas of resistance and the "symbolic resistance" they entertain include not only the practices of "subordinate" groups, but also those of powerful actors, which disrupt or subvert the meanings of oppositional acts. An analytical frame drawing upon this approach demands that we take into account the diversity, specificity, and relationality of all performances and counter-performances resisting and reconstituting the "perlocutionary field" of the naming process (Rose-Redwood 2008). It would further seek to explain the more or less coherent dominator/subordinate binary as a projected after-effect of these interactions.

Finally, this study confirms the value of conceiving of naming as a performative practice, in which symbolic power and capital are seen as reproducible yet unstable, as emergent from the relations cast between creative acts of iteration and destabilization, rather than as a property deduced from a presupposed hegemony. Arguably, this perspective is especially important for studying official symbolic acts in urban settings with intense local cultural diversity and histories of ideological and political conflict, such as Durban, because in these cases it is likely that the "performative limits of the official city-text" (Rose-Redwood 2008) will be more overt, that the projected geopolitical or ideological imaginaries will be more contentious, and that the process will be met with a greater diversity and urgency of performative contestations. With these findings and conclusions, I hope that this study will prompt further critical investigation into the discursive performativity of contested street naming procedures.

Notes

1 Downloaded from the official website of eThekwini Municipality: www.durban.gov.za/durban/government/renaming/Final%20List-%20Street%20Naming2.xls
2 Downloaded from the official website of eThekwini Municipality: www.durban.gov.za/durban/government/renaming/Street%20Renaming%20Poster%20A4.pdf
3 For ease of reference to the text, instances where the author refers to various agencies in either impersonal or personal terms were identified with a numeric label.

References

Alderman, D. (2008). "Place, Naming and the Interpretation of Cultural Landscapes." In B. Graham and P. Howard (Eds.), *The Ashgate Research Companion to Heritage and Identity* (pp. 195–213). Aldershot: Ashgate.

Bourdieu, P. (1991). *Language and Symbolic Power*. Cambridge, MA: Harvard University Press.

Butler, J. (1993). *Bodies That Matter: On the Discursive Limits of "Sex."* London: Routledge.

City Manager's Newsletter (2007a). May 2: www.durban.gov.za/durban/government/renaming/news-articles/the-process

City Manager's Newsletter (2007b). May 6: www.durban.gov.za/durban/government/media/cmn/cmnitem.2007-05-06.2303123121/view

Daily News (2009). "Council Issues Warning to Street Name Vandals." January 16: 3.

Darnton, R. (1984). "Workers Revolt: The Great Cat Massacre of the Rue Saint-Severin." In R. Darnton (Ed.), *The Great Cat Massacre and Other Episodes in French Cultural History* (pp. 75–106). New York: Basic Books.

Dick, D. (2008). *Who Was Who in Durban Street Names*. Durban: Clerkington.

Dwyer, O. and Alderman, D. (2008). "Memorial Landscapes: Analytic Questions and Metaphors." *GeoJournal*, 73(3): 165–178.

eThekwini Council (2007). "Minutes of Council Meeting, Folweni." January 31: www.durban.gov.za/Online_Tools/Pages/Minutes_Agendas.aspx

eThekwini Online (2009a). "Replacement of Defaced Street Signs." January 14: www.durban.gov.za/durban/government/media/press/pressitem.2009-01-14.9353917816

eThekwini Online (2009b). "Council's Clean-Up Campaign Ongoing." January 23: www.durban.gov.za/durban/services/services_news/council2019s-clean-up-campaignongoing

Ezasegagasini Metro (2007). "Mayor Obed Mlaba Tables a List of Eight Streets to Be Renamed at Full Council Seating, Folweni." February 8: www.durban.gov.za/durban/government/renaming/news-articles/row-over-street-renaming

Giliomee, H., Myburgh, J. and Schlemmer, L. (2001). "Dominant Party Rule, Opposition Parties and Minorities in South Africa." *Democratization*, 8(1): 161–182.

Gregson, N. and Rose, G. (2000). "Taking Butler Elsewhere: Performativities, Spatialities and Subjectivities." *Environment and Planning D: Society and Space*, 18(4): 433–452.

Guyot, S. and Seethal, C. (2007). "Identity of Place, Places of Identities: Change of Place Names in Post-Apartheid South Africa." *South African Geographical Journal*, 89(1): 55–63.

Legg, S. (2005). "Sites of Counter-Memory: The Refusal to Forget and the Nationalist Struggle in Colonial Delhi." *Historical Geography*, 33: 180–201.

McIntyre, J. (1956). *Origin of Durban Street Names*. Durban: W.E. Robertson.

Rose, M. (2002). "The Seductions of Resistance: Power, Politics, and a Performative Style of Systems." *Environment and Planning D: Society and Space*, 20(4): 383–400.

Rose-Redwood, R. (2008). "'Sixth Avenue is Now a Memory': Regimes of Spatial Inscription and the Performative Limits of the Official City-Text." *Political Geography*, 27(8): 875–894.

Rose-Redwood, R., Alderman, D. and Azaryahu, M. (2010). "Geographies of Toponymic Inscription: New Directions in Critical Place-Name Studies." *Progress in Human Geography*, 34(4): 453–470.

Saunders, C. (2008). "Memorializing Freedom Struggles." *Safundi*, 9(3): 335–342.

Scott, J. (1990). *Domination and the Arts of Resistance: Hidden Transcripts*. New Haven, CT: Yale University Press.

Sunday Tribune (2007). "Arafat Proposal a 'Slap in the Face'." April 8: www.iol.co.za/news/politics/arafat-proposal-a-slap-in-the-face-1.322154#.Uw7sH3kmbfM

Sunday Tribune (2008a). "Street Names Confusion Set to Continue." August 31: www.iol.co.za/news/politics/street-names-confusion-set-to-continue-1.414517#.Uw7sXnkmbfM

Sunday Tribune (2008b). "Durban's New Street Names Vandalised." August 24: www.iol. co.za/news/politics/durban-s-new-street-names-vandalised-1.413625#.Uw7ssnkmbfM

The Independent on Saturday (2007). "Renaming at Crossroads." April 28: www.iol.co.za/ news/politics/renaming-at-crossroads-1.350559#.Uw7s2nkmbfM

The Mercury (2003). "Plan to Rename Durban's Streets Revived." June 10: www.iol.co.za/ news/politics/plan-to-rename-durban-s-streets-revived-1.72667#.Uw7tHnkmbfM

The Mercury (2005). "Unsung Heroes Find a Place on Durban Streets." March 8: www.iol. co.za/news/politics/unsung-heroes-find-a-place-on-durban-streets-1.235725#. Uw7tTHkmbfM

The Mercury (2007a). "Durban Name-Change Process Re-Opened." July 11: www.iol.co.za/ news/politics/durban-name-change-process-re-opened-1.361459#.Uw7tf3kmbfM

The Mercury (2007b). "About-Turn on Name Changes." May 23: www.iol.co.za/news/ politics/about-turn-on-name-changes-1.354225#.Uw7tq3kmbfM

The Mercury (2008a). "Street Names Must Reflect Durban's History." October 8: www.iol. co.za/news/south-africa/street-names-must-reflect-durban-s-history-1.419295#. Uw7uD3kmbfM

The Mercury (2008b). "Taking the Mickey out of the Renaming Process." September 16: www.iol.co.za/news/south-africa/taking-the-mickey-out-of-the-renaming-process-1.416566#.Uw7uOnkmbfM

Todes, A. (2008). "Reintegrating the Apartheid City? Urban Policy and Urban Restructuring in Durban." In G. Bridge and S. Watson (Eds.), *A Companion to the City* (pp. 617–629). Oxford: Blackwell.

15 Street naming and the politics of belonging

Spatial injustices in the toponymic commemoration of Martin Luther King, Jr.

Derek Alderman and Joshua Inwood

Introduction

In outlining a new agenda for geographical research on place naming, Rose-Redwood (2011) stresses the importance of naming rights. He notes how the right to name a place—including parks, schools, and streets—is increasingly controlled and commodified in today's society, thus limiting the ability of communities to claim and use those public spaces and their names as sites of social life and expression (Rose-Redwood et al. 2010). Meanwhile, a growing number of members of historically marginalized groups—especially racial and ethnic minorities—are turning to place naming, and commemorative street naming in particular, as a political strategy for addressing their exclusion and misrepresentation within traditional, white-dominated constructions of local and national heritage. We are interested in the central and contradictory place that street naming holds in people's lives and their struggles over racial identities and rights, understood here not only as the legal authority to name a place but also the broader rights of people of color to participate in the production of place and to have their histories recognized publicly within cities and towns (Berg and Kearns 1996).

Toponyms are expressive and constitutive of the politics of citizenship, conferring a greater degree of belonging to certain groups over others while also serving as sites for battles to widen the "distribution of citizenship" and the use of space (Dunn 2003). Naming practices work, ideologically, to disenfranchise or empower historically marginalized groups as they make claims for urban space, political legitimacy, and the "politics of belonging," which defines membership to a group and ownership of a place. Schein (2009, 811) points to the importance of exploring the "oppositional politics of belonging" that undergird the production of landscape, drawing particular attention to how African Americans have traditionally been "written out" of prevailing notions of belonging. As he argues, such an oppositional politics of belonging focuses not only on moments of exclusion but also points of intervention, where marginalized groups might claim citizenship and struggle to create a more racially inclusive landscape.

Our objective in this chapter is to identify and discuss the kind of oppositional politics of belonging that animates debates over street naming, thus elucidating broader political struggles over the right to the city. A case study of (re)naming streets for slain civil rights leader Martin Luther King, Jr. offers an opportunity to explore African American struggles to reshape the identity of urban streetscapes, the contours of social memory, and the larger sense of political membership and social inclusion. Streets named for King are more than just monuments to the U.S. Civil Rights Movement. They are the materialization of ongoing African American claims for civil rights, racial equality, and civic fairness in historical representation. Many proponents see King street naming as an anti-racist spatial practice, a way of inscribing a new vision of race relations into the American landscape. Yet King streets are actively shaped by racism, white privilege and supremacy, and locational discrimination that threaten to reinforce, rather than challenge, the spatial and social boundaries that have traditionally constrained black power and identity within cities—a bitterly ironic memorial to a man famous for battling segregation.

The politics of remembering Dr. King serves as an effective way to think, more broadly, about *street naming as a mechanism of spatial (in)justice*. Spatial justice stresses the spatiality of belonging, recognizing that social (in)justice does not simply have geographical outcomes; rather, space plays a more fundamental role in constituting and structuring the broader processes of discrimination or equality (Soja 2010). The spatiality of ongoing efforts to recognize historically silenced racial and ethnic groups through street naming is critical to their potential to transform the politics of belonging. Where we remember the past matters along with what (and who) we remember. Indeed, the contested politics of naming streets for King is not simply a matter of determining whether the civil rights leader will be honored but also debating where that name is best situated within public space. As African American activists have long and stubbornly asserted, it is not enough to name just any street for King. In fact, some of them have refused to rename a road for the civil rights leader when they believe the street does not occupy a sufficiently prominent or visible place in cities or does not transgress longstanding racial and economic divides. The ultimate location of a named street affects the social meaning and political efficacy of King's commemoration while also symbolizing the degree of cultural power and rights held by black citizens. Confining where King can be remembered publicly, especially in relation to the aforementioned social divides, places limits on recognizing and recovering the civil rights leader's historical identity as a challenger of the liberal-democratic-capitalist order.

In this chapter, we focus on street naming in terms of the "right to participate" and "right to appropriate," and identify some of the barriers that hinder the full realization of these rights for African Americans and the creation of a streetscape that truly reflects the teachings of King. Two brief case studies from the southeastern United States (Statesboro, Georgia and Greenville, North Carolina) illustrate how opponents, sometimes with the (un)witting cooperation of black activists, impose scalar limits on the rights of African Americans to participate in the street naming process and appropriate the spatial identity of streets outside of their neighborhoods, thus creating procedural and distributive injustices in the toponymic commemoration of King.

A street fit for a King?

While many victims of oppression and discrimination in the United States have pursued the renaming of public spaces to reclaim dignity and identity, African Americans have been especially vocal in calling for these changes. In arguing for a greater recognition of their experiences and struggles, black activists, community leaders, and elected officials have carried out a campaign of renaming places to celebrate black historical figures—particularly from the Civil Rights Movement. Street names have proven to be a popular battleground for these struggles for legitimacy because of the way they permeate our daily vocabulary—both visual and verbal (Kearns and Berg 2002).

(Re)naming roads for Martin Luther King, Jr. is especially important in African American efforts to rewrite the U.S. commemorative toponymic landscape. Although the Civil Rights Movement was carried out by many leaders and workers, King is perhaps the most widely identified national icon associated with the struggle for racial justice, often to the exclusion of the many women, young people, and local activists who also drove the Movement (Dwyer and Alderman 2008). By 2014, well over 900 cities and towns in the United States had named a street for King. Although these named streets are found in forty states and the District of Columbia, over 70 percent of them are clustered in the southeastern region among both large cities and small towns. It is in the Southeast where the earliest Civil Rights Movement battles were fought and this is the current home of a majority of the country's African American population.

On the surface, the widespread presence of King streets belies their contested nature, seeming to signal a victory for African Americans and progressive whites when, in reality, the naming process and the ultimate location of these streets tell a different story. Street name commemoration of King evokes highly public protests and debates because of its potential to touch and connect disparate groups—some of which may not identify with King (Alderman 2000). Yet, the controversy over honoring King with a street name is not only about the civil rights leader's social and historical contributions but also about people contesting the racial (re)signification of space and the (re)negotiation of individual and collective identity (Caliendo 2011). African Americans face the prevailing assumption among the conservative white establishment and other opponents that King's name should be confined spatially to the black community rather than cutting across traditional racial boundaries in cities. For many activists, naming a major thoroughfare that stretches beyond minority neighborhoods is essential to educating the broader white public about the importance of King and all African Americans. These debates about where (and where not) to locate King's name and memory take place between blacks and whites, but they also occur within the African American community and thus prompt us not to essentialize black identities and political goals. Naming activists articulate different spatial strategies, which include naming streets only in black neighborhoods (Alderman 2003). Some naming proponents are more interested in inspiring and mobilizing their fellow African Americans—rather than challenging the historical consciousness of whites—while others fear losing ownership of the civil rights leader's image in light of the vagaries of white-controlled place naming decisions.

Some opposing whites believe that naming a street for King will stigmatize the identity of their neighborhood: "As a direct result of racial (mis)representations in public memory, King streets ... signify Blackness, poor Black people, and even a dangerous neighborhood whereby commemoration recalls not social achievements by African Americans but a socioeconomic decay of Black neighborhoods" (Caliendo 2011, 1157). There are King streets that defy that image (Mitchelson et al. 2007), but public opposition frequently leads to the naming of side streets or portions of roads located within economically struggling, African American areas of cities and towns. As some activists argue, to marginalize the commemoration of King on blighted streets within the black community, particularly in the face of African American requests not to do so, is to perpetuate the same force of segregation that the civil rights leader battled against (Alderman 2000). Tilove (2003, 122) perhaps put it best when he wrote: "To name any street for King is to invite an accounting of how the street makes good on King's promise or mocks it."

While the politics of naming streets involves struggles to define King's historical reputation and his cross-racial resonance (Alderman 2002), the process also speaks to the obstacles that face African Americans as they struggle to challenge the control historically exercised by whites over racial/ethnic minorities in the United States. These struggles prompt us to consider how the Civil Rights Movement, both in terms of how it has changed society and how it is remembered, is an evolving and unfinished project. Rather than a simply symbolic gesture, street naming for many African American activists is about gauging society's relative progress in fulfilling the goals of the Movement, to ground truth contemporary race relations and to gauge, materially, public attitudes about equality and justice. Martin Luther King Streets are where ideology hits asphalt for the communities who debate and determine which street is fit for a King.

Street naming and spatial justice

It is important to reflect on how the geography of place names—where they are located and, even more importantly, where they are not—can advance or obstruct the realization of the political goals of historically marginalized social groups. Political struggles over naming streets for King often revolve around the issue of location, with proponents and opponents putting forth competing ideas about where best to emplace King's memory within the cultural landscape and who, in effect, has a right to certain public spaces in the city. At the same time, citizenship can be spatially managed through the structure of decision-making (Dunn 2003). One's physical and socio-economic location within a city, particularly in relation to the potentially renamed street, is frequently used by government authorities and naming opponents to define and limit the place naming rights of African Americans.

Spatial (in)justice is a useful concept for understanding how King street naming proponents view and mobilize their cause in spatial terms and how the opposition responds by actively using geography to contest these claims to the city. The concept of spatial justice has gained increasing attention across the humanities, social sciences, and planning circles (Bromberg et al. 2007; Soja 2010). Spatial justice recognizes that social, economic, and political injustices are frequently based on, and perpetuated through, the ways in which we organize, use, and control places and spatial processes. Social life is inherently territorialized and any meaningful effort to create social justice must address the geographical order that constitutes and shapes social inequalities and unfair decision-making (Bromberg et al. 2007).

Using spatial justice framework, we analyze the politics of naming American roads after Martin Luther King Jr. in terms of the "right to appropriate" and the "right to participate." Although these rights have been examined previously in the context of Lefebvre's right to the city (Purcell 2003), they have saliency beyond the specific way that the French thinker critiqued capitalism and the state and conceived the claiming of space by inhabitants. Inwood (2012) has noted the marginalized position that African American spatial claims and struggles hold in the traditional right to the city literature. He has argued for a broader and more inclusive notion of rights that address the legacies of racial segregation and exclusion and the history of uneven access to urban spaces by people of color. Our analysis of street naming examines the right to participate and appropriate within the broader context of African American opposition to the legacies of racism and white privilege, allowing us to identify some of the distributive and procedural injustices that characterize the naming process and the central role that space, especially scale, play.

The right to appropriate and the distributive injustices of street naming

When African Americans use street naming to exercise their right to appropriate urban space in the name of King, they employ a strategic mapping of the city, figuratively and sometimes literally, to find a street that best fits their political and commemorative agenda. According to Purcell (2002, 103), the right to appropriate means "not only the right of [marginalized social groups] to occupy already-produced urban space" but also "the right to produce urban space so that it meets the needs of inhabitants." In other words, to rework the spatial and social relations that have historically reproduced racially segregated urban space, street naming proponents pay close attention to and try to achieve a distributive justice in which King and the African American community are recognized publicly. Distributive justice has long been a foundational concept in social justice studies (Rawls 1971), and it continues to be important (Boone et al. 2009). Distributive justice is traditionally concerned with ensuring a fair allocation of goods and opportunities among social groups, but it can be defined in spatial terms (Harvey 1973) and thus include a focus on public access to certain place-based resources or services as well as the geographical distribution of social groups relative to certain opportunities and hazards (Bullard and Johnson 1997; Walker and Day 2012).

In applying a spatial justice framework to street naming, it is important to consider the intra-urban location of the toponym and how the appropriation and production of urban space through naming is situated in relation to wider geographical distributions of people, wealth, and transportation within cities. The distributive reach of named streets affects who will have direct contact with the name (and conversely, who will not) as well as the general landscape prominence of the name—all of which impact a minority group's power to reshape the city so that they are seen and heard. The ability of street names to (re)distribute certain meanings and identities across the city does not simply raise the visibility of King and the black community, but signals an important widening of the "distribution of citizenship" (Dunn 2003) and broader messages about who matters and belongs.

Larger questions of geographical distribution and access to urban space are important in shaping the meaning and efficacy of naming streets after King. Assessing whether the streets achieve a distributive justice requires asking questions such as: Where are King's namesakes located in relation to the spatial distribution of race and class distinctions within cities? To what extent do streets named for King occupy central civic spaces and are they geographically accessible to the larger community, especially whites? To what extent do King streets, because of their location, operate as a bridge or boundary between different social and economic areas of cities? Martin Luther King streets—depending upon their place relative to wider distributions of people and resources—could work to marginalize or raise the visibility and public importance of African Americans. As Raento and Watson (2000, 728) contended: "Naming and re-naming are strategies of power, and location matters, because this power is only truly exercised when it is 'seen' in the appropriate place."

The theme of distributive justice appears in the comments of many African Americans who push to have a street named. Important to their vision of appropriating and producing a legitimate place for King is making sure that, relationally, the named road transcends traditional racial boundaries and occupies a location situated within a social geography that embodies integration and inclusiveness rather than marginalization and segregation. Facing public opposition to such proposals, municipal authorities tend to pursue a distributional tactic that does the exact opposite. They agree to rename only part of a major street that aligns with the geographical boundaries of the African American community, not allowing the name change to encroach on white, often wealthier parts of the same street. While officials believe this spatial confinement strategy effective in minimizing (white) controversy and appeasing the black community, vocal street naming proponents have frequently interpreted it as racist and have called to have King's name extended spatially down the entire length of road.

The social construction of scale lies at the heart of controlling the distributive justice of street naming and the right of African Americans to appropriate the production of space beyond their neighborhoods (Alderman 2003). Scale plays an important, but often under-theorized role, in the politics of place naming (Hagen 2011). Toponymic disputes do not simply happen at different fixed scales. Rather, proponents and opponents compete to determine the geographical scale at which King and African Americans will be recognized and, in turn, the scale at which associations or linkages would (or would not) be created between the wider white community and its black citizens. Maintaining racial segregation requires a policing of scale. Certain activities by African Americans are allowed in certain places as long as they are not scaled beyond the black community and disrupt segregated space. In fighting to maintain or redefine this scale of racial power relations, proponents and opponents deploy different scalar configurations of identity and citizenship through street naming. Proponents of achieving a distributive justice through King street naming advocate for a "toponymic rescaling," hoping to reframe the spatial identities of places in new ways that make more room for African American belonging (Rose-Redwood 2011, 38). In contrast, opponents to this rescaling rely on, and publicly perform, a traditional urban scalar narrative that uses racial fear, residential segregation, and the rhetoric of neighborhood invasion to justify keeping the black community and King in their place.

A street naming dispute in Greenville, North Carolina, exposes how opponents impose scalar limits on the right of African Americans to appropriate the identity of urban space and how African Americans react to this distributive injustice in different, conflicting ways. Greenville is located in eastern North Carolina approximately 85 miles from the state capitol of Raleigh. Greenville's West Fifth Street became Martin Luther King, Jr. Drive in 1998. Originally, the African American leaders who brought forward the request wanted all of Fifth Street renamed—not just part of it—but residents and business owners on the eastern end strongly opposed the proposal. King's namesake marks a downtown area that is predominantly African American whereas East Fifth is mostly white (Batchelor 2006a). Moreover, a clear difference in wealth and development exists between the east and west segments of the street. This racial and economic boundary has long been in place and some older Greenville African Americans have spoken about how East Fifth Street was "forbidden territory" for them historically (Namaz 2006, A12).

Proposals to extend King's name down the rest of Fifth Street were made by local African Americans in subsequent years. However, these efforts failed to win approval of the Greenville City Council, leading to deep frustration within the African American community. One prominent black leader, Michael Garrett, was quoted as saying: "Having a street that runs straight through town with a different name in the black section is a throwback to the old Jim Crow Days" (Batchelor 2006b, B1). Of course, Jim Crow was not simply about separating the races, but also about normalizing unequal power between the races. One proponent for extending King down all of Fifth Street, Rufus Huggins (2006, D2), sought to challenge the taken-for-granted nature of white privilege at work through the street name controversy:

> Greenville citizens do not realize [that] most streets in the predominantly black community are named after someone white … our white brothers and sisters have a problem with just having one street [in the white community] … being named after someone black.

In January 2006, the local chapter of the SCLC led a boycott of the Martin Luther King Prayer Breakfast in protest of the city's failure to rename all of Fifth Street. This action sparked several months of public debate, with many residents along

East Fifth continuing their adamant opposition to the renaming. King supporters held marches down Fifth Street, including the eastern section. One of these marches drew resistance from a group of young white men who taunted the marchers, yelled "Fifth Street Rules," and displayed the Confederate Battle Flag, long a symbol of white racist resistance in the region (White 2006). While proponents for renaming the entire length of Fifth sought to rescale the identity of the street and to assert their right to appropriate a previously forbidden portion of urban space, opponents clearly placed boundaries around King's meaning and the legitimacy of local black citizenship. Many East Fifth Street residents claimed that their street name had historical value and was part of their heritage (Spell 2006), angering some African Americans who thought King was more historically important than a numeral. Others suggested that King's name would bring down property values and invite crime, gangs, and illegal drugs into their neighborhoods and that limiting the scale of the street naming was essential to the social preservation of the East Fifth neighborhood (Gabbard 2006). Critics pointed to the depressed condition of the existing King Drive. African Americans were, in effect, blamed for being the victims of broader processes of inequality, discrimination, and segregation, and opponents called into question their identity as responsible citizens and whether they had the right to appropriate other urban spaces when they supposedly could not take care of their own.

Seeking to settle what they saw as a contentious issue and unwilling to force East Fifth Street to undergo an address change, municipal leaders voted along racial lines in late 2006 to place King's name on the then-undeveloped U.S. 264 Bypass that partially encircled Greenville. The bypass had been identified as a possible alternative to Fifth Street by an ad hoc committee organized by East Carolina University, who claimed neutrality even though it owned property on East Fifth. Believing that there was a state rule against roads having duplicate names, the council also voted to have the existing Martin Luther King Jr. Drive revert back to West Fifth Street (Batchelor 2006c). Even after discovering that such a rule did not exist, white municipal leaders approved the removal of King's name, prompting some African Americans to argue that the name change was part of a larger plan of redevelopment and black dispossession planned for the area (Batchelor 2007).

Not all whites opposed renaming all of Fifth Street and several outspoken white citizens protested the decision to move King's name to the bypass. African Americans also held different views about how (and where) best to honor King. Indeed, three prominent black leaders who had initially called for the renaming of East Fifth Street later reversed themselves and supported the bypass option, much to the shock and anger of other African Americans, including two city council members. White city council members took advantage of the situation, asserting that the dissenting African American leaders represented the "real" views of the black community and that the presence of ideological differences among African Americans somehow made the campaign to name all of Fifth Street less legitimate. These assertions drew upon a longstanding racist supposition that African Americans form a monolithic community with a single voice. The leaders who now advocated for naming the bypass were motivated by personal rivalries with other black leaders and the belief that renaming East Fifth was increasingly out of reach and naming a new road was better than King's name remaining segregated. Also important to them were arguments from white citizens that the street name debate was unnecessarily dividing the local community along racial lines and thus a peaceful compromise was needed (Johnson 2006). But what kind of peace was produced? To use King's own words, by moving the civil rights leader's name to the bypass, white city council members constructed a "negative peace" or an absence of tension (for whites) rather than constructing a "positive peace," which King characterized as a presence of justice for African Americans (King 1986 [1963], 295).

Positive peace-building practices, on the other hand, are "practices that encourage the growth of social, political and legal solutions that address the underlying causes" of inequality and often focus on supporting institutions and processes that try to break cycles of discrimination (Inwood and Tyner 2011, 448). By engaging in the process to rename only portions of Fifth Street, the political leadership in Greenville was promoting a process that recognized King, but failed to address the underlying histories of discrimination, segregation, and uneven access to resources that have characterized the separate and unequal geographies of Jim Crow segregation. As a consequence, the fundamental questions of who belongs where, and on whose terms, are obscured from the debate (Schein 2009). Thus the decision by the white political leadership to rename only part of Fifth Street was a none-to-subtle reinforcement of historical geographies of exclusion and discrimination, which while conforming to negative peace-building practices, ultimately obfuscated the larger question of resources that is at the heart of struggles around belonging. Street naming matters because it is often the first step in broader struggles over social, political, and economic capital that may fundamentally alter historical patterns of exclusion and discrimination.

Accordingly, even though some opponents to renaming East Fifth, and even some black leaders, saw the naming of the bypass as a legitimate appropriation of urban space in the name of King and African Americans, it ultimately was a production of space that never really achieved the distributive justice and the rescaling of urban spatial identity and race relations that was originally intended. In fact, Greenville's naming dispute speaks, more forcefully, to the power of the white community to access and reshape urban space through street naming and indicates potential limitations to the politics of belonging that do not outline and connect to broader struggles over economic and political resources. African Americans living along King, now West Fifth Street, had to bear the expense and inconvenience of changing their address, to ensure, in effect, that white property owners on East Fifth Street would not have to do so. Tragically, one might argue that African Americans lost the right to appropriate and produce space in their own neighborhood, especially in light of the many Martin Luther King birthday celebrations and marches historically held on the once named road and the impossibility of holding those same activities on a busy four lane bypass. Moreover, the controversial decision to move King out of downtown ensured that the geography of the civil rights leader's commemoration would not violate the territorial limits and sense of divided racial order of the white community on East Fifth Street. Because proponents sought to use the re-scaling of the street's identity as a way of testing as well as creating racial integration, the city's decision represented a bypassing of King's proverbial dream.

The right to participate and the procedural injustices of street naming

Interestingly, the politics of belonging also stresses the importance of the "right to participate," which gives "inhabitants the right to take a central role in decision-making surrounding the production of urban space" (Purcell 2003, 578). Exercising the right of participation (along with appropriation), citizens can assert their use-rights and directly challenge the hegemony of property rights and the valuing of urban space as a commodity to exchange (Purcell 2002). Rose-Redwood and colleagues (2010) have called for a greater consideration and protection of the use value of place names in the face of growing efforts to commercialize the toponymic process. While the actual selling and buying of naming rights is an important infringement on the right of ordinary people to participate in the production of space, the socially exclusionary nature of toponymic decision-making is felt across cities beyond merely financial transactions, especially when public authorities view place naming rights as a natural extension of property rights. This is particularly evident when examining the procedural injustices that hinder African American participation in the renaming of streets outside of their neighborhoods.

Procedural justice, like distributive justice, has an established history in social science (Boone et al. 2009). Scholars recognize that a lack of fairness in how public disputes and decisions are made and legally resolved can impact one's right to participate as well as produce and sustain unequal distributive outcomes and access. Naming and renaming places involve decision-making procedures and policies. A procedural or participatory justice perspective would address the factors that limit the full participation of African Americans in local government decisions about whether to name a street for King and which specific street to rename. Even when a street is renamed for the civil rights leader, it can still work to exclude African Americans if they have no actual voice in the naming process. This can happen when municipal leaders reject initial requests to rename major thoroughfares and elect instead to attach King's name to smaller streets, sometimes overriding the protests of the activists who brought the original proposal to city leaders.

There is frequently a spatial context to the procedural injustices of naming streets for King. Local governments increasingly enforce a rather narrow geographical as well as social scaling of cultural citizenship when renaming a street. One's citizenship or right to the street is defined by where one is located in relation to the street and the economic conditions underlying that locational relationship. In many street name debates, those who own property along potentially renamed streets often play a deciding role in name changes, even though the street (and by extension, its name) is theoretically a public space rather than a private good. Indeed, some cities have responded to controversy over selecting a street to rename for King by establishing ordinances that require a majority (and sometimes even a supermajority) share of property owners located on a particular street to approve a proposed name change. The interests and opinions of a road's property owners are considered over those who rent or simply work or travel on the road in question. Placing such clear territorial and class limits on cultural citizenship and whose voice matters in the street naming process has seriously limited the ability of African Americans to honor King on roads upon which they are not the majority of property owners.

These restrictive street naming ordinances work to frame African Americans as "outside agitators" within their own cities, continuing a tactic begun during the Movement to discredit the African American struggle for equality as non-local and thus ignoring what King (1986 [1963]) referred to as the mutuality and interrelatedness of all communities. Even when these procedural hurdles are not used in direct opposition to King street naming, they nevertheless affect the process. Recognizing the difficulty in getting approval from the many white property owners on a major road, some African Americans will propose renaming a smaller or a less racially diverse road segment that appears winnable even if it is not their first choice. In this respect, even when black activists are leading the toponymic process, these ordinances rescale the structure of political membership and democratic participation in regressive ways that reproduce a segregated geography of street naming, prompting us to consider yet another way that scale is strategically manipulated to control and limit the right to (name) the city.

The impact that procedural injustices can play in shaping the location and racially distributive scale of the street eventually named for King was especially apparent in Statesboro, Georgia. Statesboro, which is the county seat of Bulloch County, lies between the two population centers of Macon, in central Georgia, and Savannah, on the coast. In February of 1997, African American leaders from the NAACP and the Bulloch County Ministerial Alliance proposed to have Northside Drive renamed for Martin Luther King Jr. (Hackle 1997). Northside Drive, one of the longest and busiest commercial arteries in Statesboro, is part of U.S. Highway 80 and passes by the city's mall and nearly 200 businesses. Donnie Simmons, one of the local NAACP leaders behind the proposal, expressed it best when he said:

> Dr. King lived a highly visible life and should have a highly visible place named ... I can never agree to renaming a street restricted to the black community. This would bury Dr. King in the black community and say that Dr. King was only for blacks. ... King was against injustice for every man [sic].
> (Simmons 1997)

Not unlike similar struggles across the country, the proposal to rename Northside drew significant resistance from the street's white property and business owners, many of whom signed a petition against the name change and complained about the financial burden of changing their address. Opponents downplayed the use-value of the road's name to African Americans as a public symbol and stressed the exchange value of maintaining the name for customers, suppliers, and their bottom line (Rogers 1997). While this argument was represented to the public simply as a matter of cost and convenience, it actually masked a deeper anxiety about white discomfort and protecting racial boundaries for the sake of commercialism. The owner of a business on Northside argued: "When someone calls me up asking for directions to the store and I say 'We're located on MLK road,' those people might think I'm located on the black side of town. Now, I'm not a racist but that fact may keep people from coming to my store" (Henry 1997).

Arguments made by property interests on Northside Drive proved influential, prompting the Statesboro City Council in May of 1997 to unanimously pass an ordinance that required 75 percent of property owners on a street to approve a proposed name change before it could be formally voted on by council members. The ordinance also required the petitioners of a street name change to pay half the cost for new street signage, a policy that spoke to: (1) how much the city sought to discourage renaming, especially for major roads; and (2) the extent to which street name rights were clearly defined in terms of exchange value and revenue (Gross 1997). Even though the King street debate began before the passage of the ordinance, supporters of renaming Northside were required to follow the newly created decision-making rules, which led some black leaders to claim that the ordinance targeted their request. NAACP leader Donnie Simmons argued that the ordinance thwarted the efforts of African Americans. He contended: "They [the city council] know good and well we're not going to get 75 percent of the whites to name a street for King" (quoted in Gross 1997, 1A). Moreover, because Northside Drive was a major highway, the estimated cost of the renaming would be $8,000–10,000 (USD), a sizable sum for the local NAACP or any minority organization.

The situation was further complicated by the approval of the new ordinance by African American city councilman David Shumake, who argued that the ordinance provided blacks a mechanism for demonstrating public support for renaming to the city council. In fact, he argued that the ordinance would actually protect black interests by preventing city leaders from later removing King's name from Northside once it was changed. In contrast to Simmons, Shumake suggested that "Blacks can get Northside renamed if they organize, shake bushes, and mobilize," although this was difficult to envision given the level of vitriolic opposition expressed by Northside's businesses and property owners. Shumake expressed hesitancy about "forcing a street address change down the throat of the [white] community" (Shumake 1997). As this situation illustrates, even when it appears that African Americans have a place in the decision-making process, such as having a seat on the city council, this does not guarantee that procedural or participatory justice is achieved. The ordinance, by putting the power to initiate a name change in the hands of those on Northside rather than the city council, worked not only to limit the place naming rights and participatory power of the broader Statesboro African American community but also Shumake himself.

Ultimately, Statesboro's street renaming ordinance facilitated the renaming of a street for King, but it was not Northside Drive. In December 2002, the city council voted to rename two connecting roads (Blitch and Institute) after receiving a proposal from African American city councilman Gary Lewis. Following ordinance guidelines, Lewis spent six months going door to door to collect signatures from property owners along the two streets (Martin 2002). Blitch and Institute Streets were smaller, poorer, and more African American than Northside. Some opponents, including members of the NAACP, questioned the extent to which the chosen streets were prominent enough to bear King's name. Statesboro's ordinance not only made the renaming of a major road difficult, it also forced black leaders to limit their commemorative agenda to streets that could be renamed in light of the property owner and signage cost requirements, specifically roads largely limited to the confines of the black community. While the ordinance gave proponents such as Lewis a means of ensuring that King's memory would be emplaced in the landscape, it nevertheless territorialized street naming and the right to participate, legally sanctioned the privatization of public space, and contributed to the growing power of property owners and commercial interests to define the limits of urban citizenship and belonging.

Conclusion

The critical place name literature has not widely examined street naming in terms of the struggle for equality and civil rights from the standpoint of spatial justice and struggles over belonging. The naming of streets for King provides a glimpse into where we in the USA are in terms of race relations, casting doubt on conservative declarations that we have moved into a post-racial or post-civil rights era. Recognizing King within the official streetscape is not simply a dry retelling of important histories. Rather, for African American activists, place naming can be an emotion-laden and politically charged spatial tool for redefining the scale at which they belong in the American city and the right to claim urban space and memory.

More than that, however, the struggle to (re)name streets for King and its connection to broader scholarly work on the politics of belonging illuminates the contradictory and sometimes incommensurate goals of activists who seek to claim urban space. On the one hand, the struggle over King streets illustrates the way portions of the African American community are attempting to assert themselves symbolically and materially. However, as African Americans pursue street naming as part of the right to belong, they encounter obstacles—both outside of and within their own communities—that limit their ability to redistribute the resources of the city and to rescale naming rights in ways that achieve King's vision of positive peace-building practices that address racism, citizenship, and justice.

References

Alderman, D. (2000). "A Street Fit for a King: Naming Places and Commemoration in the American South." *Professional Geographer*, 52(4): 672–684.

Alderman, D. (2002). "Street Names as Memorial Arenas: The Reputational Politics of Commemorating Martin Luther King, Jr. in a Georgia County." *Historical Geography*, 30: 99–120.

Alderman, D. (2003). "Street Names and the Scaling of Memory: The Politics of Commemorating Martin Luther King, Jr. within the African-American Community." *Area*, 35(2): 163–173.

Azaryahu, M. (1996). "The Power of Commemorative Street Names." *Environment and Planning D: Society and Space*, 14(3): 311–330.

Batchelor, S. (2006a). "Debate over MLK Street Name Goes Back 17 Years." *The Daily Reflector*, August 26: A1.

Batchelor, S. (2006b). "Downtown Business Owners Differ on Moving MLK Name." *The Daily Reflector*, November 5: B1.

Batchelor, S. (2006c). "Council Split 4–2 on King Naming." *The Daily Reflector*, December 15: A1.

Batchelor, S. (2007). "Council Meeting Racially Charged." *The Daily Reflector*, March 9: A1.

Berg, L. and Kearns, R. (1996). "Naming as Norming: 'Race,' Gender, and the Identity Politics of Naming Places in Aotearoa/New Zealand." *Environment and Planning D: Society and Space*, 14(1): 99–122.

Boone, C., Buckley, G., Grove, J., and Sister, C. (2009). "Parks and People: An Environmental Justice Inquiry in Baltimore, Maryland." *Annals of the Association of American Geographers*, 99(4): 1–21.

Bromberg, A., Morrow, G., and Pfeiffer, D. (2007). "Why Spatial Justice?" *Critical Planning*, 14: 1–4.

Bullard, R. and Johnson, G. (Eds.) (1997). *Just Transportation: Dismantling Race and Class Barriers to Mobility*. Stony Creek, CT: New Society Publishers.

Caliendo, G. (2011). "MLK Boulevard: Material Forms of Memory and the Social Contestation of Racial Signification." *Journal of Black Studies*, 42(7): 1148–1170.

Dunn, K. (2003). "Using Cultural Geography to Engage Contested Constructions of Ethnicity and Citizenship in Sydney." *Social & Cultural Geography*, 4(2): 153–165.

Dwyer, O. and Alderman, D. (2008). *Civil Rights Memorials and the Geography of Memory*. Athens: University of Georgia Press.

Gabbard, D. (2006). "Arguments Against Street Renaming Flawed." *The Daily Reflector*, July 9: D1.

Gross, D. (1997). "Statesboro Ordinance May Thwart MLK Tribute." *Savannah Morning News*, May 21: 1A.

Hackle, A. (1997). "Renaming Northside MLK Jr. Pushed." *Statesboro Herald*, February 19: 1.

Hagen, J. (2011). "Theorizing Scale in Critical Place-Name Studies." *ACME: An International E-Journal for Critical Geographies*, 10(1): 23–27.

Harvey, D. (1973). *Social Justice and the City*. Baltimore, MD: Johns Hopkins Press.

Henry, D. [pseudonym] (1997). Interview with author, September 5. Owner of business on Northside Drive, Statesboro, Georgia.

Huggins, R. (2006). "Many White Names, Why Not a Black One?" *The Daily Reflector*, August 6: D2.

Inwood, J. (2012). "The Politics of Being Sorry: The Greensboro Truth Process and Efforts at Restorative Justice." *Social & Cultural Geography*, 13(6): 607–624.

Inwood, J. and Tyner, J. (2011). "Geography's Pro-Peace Agenda: An Unfinished Project." *ACME: An International E-Journal for Critical Geographies,* 10(3): 442–457.

Johnson, C. (2006). "Black Leaders React to Vote to Rename Bypass for King." *The Daily Reflector*, August 12: A1.

Kearns, R. and Berg, L. (2002). "Proclaiming Place: Towards a Geography of Place Name Pronunciation." *Social & Cultural Geography*, 3(3): 283–302.

King, M.L. Jr. (1986 [1963]). "Letter from Birmingham Jail." In J. Washington (Ed.), *The Essential Writings and Speeches of Martin Luther King Jr.* (pp. 289–302). San Francisco, CA: Harpercollins.

Martin, L. (2002). "City Approves Martin Luther King Jr. Drive." *Statesboro Herald*, December 5: 1.

Mitchelson, M., Alderman, D. and Popke, J. (2007). "Branded: The Economic Geographies of MLK Streets." *Social Science Quarterly*, 88(1): 120–145.

Namaz, N. (2006). "Fifth the Fitting Venue to Honor King." *The Daily Reflector*, August 16: A12.

Purcell, M. (2002). "Excavating Lefebvre: The Right to the City and its Urban Politics of the Inhabitant." *GeoJournal*, 58(2): 99–108.

Purcell, M. (2003) "Citizenship and the Right to the Global City: Reimagining the Capitalist World Order." *International Journal of Urban and Regional Research*, 27(3): 564–590.

Raento, P. and Watson, C. (2000). "Gernika, Guernica, *Guernica*? Contested Meanings of a Basque Place." *Political Geography*, 19(6): 707–736.

Rawls, J. (1971). *A Theory of Justice*. Cambridge, MA: Belknap Press.

Rogers, D. (1997). "Northside Change Concerns Businesses." *Statesboro Herald*, February 27: 1 & 9.

Rose-Redwood, R. (2011). "Rethinking the Agenda of Political Toponymy." *ACME: An International E-Journal for Critical Geographies*, 10(1): 34–41.

Rose-Redwood, R., Alderman, D., and Azaryahu, M. (2010). "Geographies of Toponymic Inscription: New Directions in Critical Place-Name Studies." *Progress in Human Geography*, 34(4): 453–470.

Schein, R. (2009). "Belonging Through Land/Scape." *Environment and Planning A*, 41(4): 811–826.

Shumake, D. (1997). Interview with author, May 21. Member of Statesboro City Council.

Simmons, D. (1997). Interview with author, May 21. Member of Bulloch County NAACP leadership.

Soja, E. (2010). *Seeking Spatial Justice*. Minneapolis: University of Minnesota Press.

Spell, L. (2006). "Councilman Offers Solution to King Debate." *The Daily Reflector*, June 15: A12.

Tilove, J. (2003) *Along Martin Luther King: Travels along Black America's Main Street*. New York: Random House.

Walker, G. and Day, R. (2012). "Fuel Poverty as Injustice: Integrating Distribution, Recognition and Procedure in the Struggle for Affordable Warmth." *Energy Policy*, 49: 69–75.

White, J. (2006). "Marcher Wants Flag Incident Probed." *The Daily Reflector*, August 3: A1.

16 From number to name

Symbolic capital, places of memory, and the politics of street renaming in New York City

Reuben Rose-Redwood

Introduction

Places of memory are sites where the symbolic imaginings of the past interweave with the materialities of the present. The production of place is generally part of a socio-spatial project "to institute horizons, to establish boundaries, to secure the identity of places," but as Massey (1994, 5) argues, "such attempts at the stabilization of meaning are constantly the site of social contest." Places should be viewed, therefore, less as clearly delineated "objects" with distinct spatial identities and more as always-unfinished products of social relations (Massey 2005). Each place of memory is constructed *in relation* to other places, and it is this relationality of place that requires critical analysis. A relational conception of place and space thus provides a useful starting point for examining urban street naming systems as sites of symbolic struggle over the politics of public remembrance.

In his analysis of symbolic power, Pierre Bourdieu emphasizes the important role that naming practices play in the mobilization of symbolic capital:

> In the symbolic struggle for the production of common sense or, more precisely, for the monopoly of legitimate *naming* as the official—i.e. explicit and public—imposition of the legitimate vision of the social world, agents bring into play the symbolic capital that they have acquired in previous struggles.
>
> (1991, 239, italics in original)

For Bourdieu, the notion of "symbolic capital" refers to the various forms of distinction and prestige acquired through cultural recognition. He maintains that the accumulation of symbolic capital can serve different ends, being converted into economic capital in some instances and used to establish social solidarities (social capital) or consolidate cultural status (cultural capital) in other circumstances (Bourdieu 1986; Painter 2000). A number of scholars have suggested that Bourdieu's theory of symbolic capital is directly applicable to understanding the politics of place naming. In particular, Alderman (2008) provides a conceptual framework that examines place naming as both a form of "symbolic capital" and "symbolic resistance," where the former emphasizes the role of place naming as a marker of prestige and the latter focuses on the various ways in which marginalized groups resist the imposition of elite naming practices. While it is important to examine the symbolic struggles over commemoration between groups, there are also tensions *within* both elite and marginalized groups that deserve attention (Forest, Johnson, and Till 2004). Consequently, the binary opposition between "elite" dominance and the symbolic resistance of the "marginalized" has a tendency to oversimplify the multiple layers of contestation over social recognition among myriad groups.

This chapter argues that an exclusionary politics of symbolic erasure can be found in both elite attempts to rename streets as a means of converting symbolic capital into economic capital as well as among historically marginalized groups that seek cultural recognition yet in the process privilege one subset of the group over another. The exclusionary dimension of street renaming is most evident not at the scale of the individual street name change but in relation to the "city-text" as a whole (Azaryahu 1996). The cultural meaning of a toponym differs greatly depending upon the socio-spatial context within which it is placed. Naming a small street in a predominantly African American neighborhood after Martin Luther King Jr., for example, will have a very different commemorative effect than renaming a major thoroughfare that traverses an entire city in honor of King (Alderman 2003). Similarly, if a street naming system has historically been dominated by the commemoration of men, then the naming of a street after a woman may take on additional symbolic importance (Dwyer 2000). It is for these reasons that street names can best be understood intertextually as part of a relational theory of place.

If the streetscape can indeed be seen as a "memorial arena" (Alderman 2002), it is also a space in which "public forgetting" is inscribed into the very texture of the landscape itself (Hoelscher and Alderman 2004, 347). Understanding the relation between spatial designation and discursive-material erasure requires a critical analysis of the very notion of commemorative place naming. Traditionally, scholars have made a distinction between commemorative and non-commemorative toponyms, following the influential work of George Stewart (1954, 1958). From this perspective, a place or street name is seen as "commemorative" if it honors the memory of a specific individual, group, prior settlement, or abstract ideal. While acknowledging that there are "border-line cases," Stewart (1954, 2) nevertheless contrasts commemorative names with other classes of toponyms, such as descriptive, possessive, and euphemistic place names, among others. Such a toponymic classification system certainly has its practical uses, yet it underestimates the commemorative dimension of *all* naming practices and thereby elides the inseparable relation between memory and place naming. A descriptive toponym may appear to simply describe the geographic features of a place (Stewart 1954), whereas possessive place naming privileges the owners of property and is a central strategy of land appropriation (Carter 1988). However, I argue in this chapter that the very act of place naming is an attempt to discursively reconfigure a given space as a place *to be remembered*. Naming a place, therefore, is itself a commemorative practice, whether those names are descriptive, possessive, or otherwise.

Take the example of a street in Manhattan named Minetta Lane (Moscow 1978). When the Dutch settled New Amsterdam in the seventeenth century, they named a small brook in the area Mintje Kill (or "little stream"). After the British took control of Manhattan Island, this descriptive name was then Anglicized, becoming Minetta Brook, and the street that later covered the brook was named Minetta Lane. There are several different levels of memory-production at work here. First, the original act of naming the stream brought it into the sphere of language as an "object" to be remembered by a given name. After being translated from one toponymic lexicon to another, the brook was then commemorated by the street name. From this simple example, we can see how even descriptive toponyms are commemorative in that they bring geographic features within the realm of public remembrance. The same argument can be made with respect to possessive place names that commemorate the owners of property in a given locale. If all place names are commemorative, the key question then is precisely what is to be remembered or forgotten at a particular place of memory? Should the memory of geographic features, prior owners of property, or national heroes be toponymically associated with a specific site? It is clear that different place names come with their own associations of memory, ontological priorities, and cultural politics, but they all take part in constructing places of selective remembrance and oblivion.

In this chapter, I examine New York's streetscape as a "memorial arena" in which multiple layers of socio-spatial exclusion are at work in the production of commemorative landscapes. Drawing upon Pierre Bourdieu's theory of symbolic capital, I maintain that street naming is a strategic element of an "economy of practices" for marking geographical space as both a place of memory and erasure. The practice of symbolic erasure is most evident in the act of street *re*naming, where one name is officially replaced by another. However, places of memory do not exist in isolation but as part of broader networks of commemorative spaces. To understand the spatial politics of memory and forgetting, therefore, it is necessary to consider the intertextuality of spatial inscription as well as the relationality of place-making more generally.

After providing a brief overview of the history of street naming in New York, the remainder of the chapter is divided into two case studies that both involve the renaming of Manhattan's numbered streets and avenues. The first example focuses on the project to rename the numbered avenues on the Upper West Side during the latter-nineteenth century, while the second case explores the history of renaming Harlem's streets to commemorate civil rights leaders a century later. By juxtaposing these two street renaming projects side by side, I emphasize how the complex interplay between different forms of capital (symbolic, cultural, social, and economic) and the dialectic of memory/erasure have historically resulted from different social configurations and may produce divergent outcomes. Both cases consider attempts to rename formerly numbered streets and avenues, and the benefit of considering them together is that they illustrate the multiple interests— as well as the exclusionary politics of race, class, and gender—involved in such shifts from "number" to "name." In doing so, this chapter extends the current literature on street naming as a commemorative practice by linking it to a broader relational view of place-making, memory, and symbolic capital.

Naming and numbering the streets of New York: a historical overview

As the city of New York grew from the small Dutch trading post of New Amsterdam in the seventeenth century to the expansive metropolis of today, its cultural landscape witnessed dramatic material and symbolic transformations. Prior to European settlement, the Munsee-speaking Lenape referred to the area as "Lenapehoking," which translates as "The Land of the People," and the name Manhattan itself is believed to have come from the Lenape word for "Island of Hills" (Burrows and Wallace 1999). The Lenape established numerous paths and trails throughout the region, including a portion of what is now Broadway in Manhattan. Much of the Lenape presence was both physically and symbolically erased from the landscape as the Dutch and British took possession of the area. Just as most historical narratives have traditionally begun at the moment of European arrival, street names have primarily commemorated the city's European heritage. The Dutch began formally naming streets in New Amsterdam under the regime of Peter Stuyvesant, who ruled from 1647 to 1664, and many of the Dutch street names were later Anglicized by the British. Streets were often named after landowners, or members of landowning families, and were thus markers of property ownership. During the eighteenth and nineteenth centuries, streets in lower Manhattan were also named in honor of merchants, war heroes, philanthropists, surveyors, politicians, inventors, religious leaders, publishers, writers, urban institutions, and topographical features (Raulin 1984).

Although many streets were named during the colonial period, few street signs were actually posted at the corners of intersections prior to the Revolutionary War. The issue of constructing a comprehensive system of street signs proved to be a significant challenge to municipal authorities well into the nineteenth century. As Henkin (1998, 41) remarks, "what is most striking about the street signs of antebellum New York is that their coverage of the city was so inadequate, incomplete, and even, at times, contested." As the city expanded northward, municipal officials adopted a state-authorized street plan, known as the Commissioners' Plan of 1811, which consisted of a grid of streets and avenues that were numbered rather than named (Spann 1988). On Manhattan's East Side, two additional north–south thoroughfares—Lexington and Madison Avenues— were added to the original plan in the 1830s, and part of Fourth Avenue was later renamed Park Avenue in 1888 (Feirstein 2001).

Just as the "anonymous" numbered streets and avenues of the original grid plan were beginning to be laid out in the 1820s, spatial designations such as "Place" and "Square" became fashionable as a mark of social distinction among property owners, who in some cases rechristened streets as "places" without the approval of city officials. The publisher of the local city directory, Thomas Longworth, criticized such "places of exclusiveness" by arguing that they bestowed special privileges on a select few to the detriment and "confusion" of the many (1833, 685). Longworth eventually agreed to include the informal names of "places" in his directory. However, he nevertheless could not help but disparage such attempts at acquiring prestige by the propertied classes. As he rather sarcastically put it:

if there be any honour or dignity resulting from the adoption of the tag *Place*, it ought to be enjoyed by the citizens at large … it is therefore to be hoped that … [the Common Council] will cause the subject to be investigated, expunge the word *street*, and substitute the word *place* throughout the city—let us all have a *place*.

(1841, 813, emphasis in original)

Certainly, we should not take Longworth at his word here, but he does draw our attention to the way in which the construction of "place" was a means of obtaining symbolic capital in nineteenth-century New York. He also raises the important question, albeit in jest, of the equitable distribution of recognized "places" in the city.

Given its symbolic import, the renaming of streets has become a major political issue in New York and has ignited social tensions over the politics of memory. While most street renaming bills pass without much debate, there have been a number of cases involving considerable controversy (e.g., Ranzal 1976; Roberts 1988; Edozien 2007). The City Council has often been criticized for devoting too much time to the renaming of streets, since it was not uncommon for more than 40 percent of all local laws passed annually in New York City to consist of street name changes (Gargan 1981; Feeney 1990; Garcilazo 1992; Siegel 1993; Lee 2001; Haberman 2002). Critics often charge that the city should devote its time to more "serious" matters, while proponents insist that street naming is an important component of public recognition in a multicultural society.

Drawing upon archival materials, the remainder of this chapter demonstrates the important role that street naming has played throughout the city's history. By examining the meeting minutes of the West Side Association, among other sources, I demonstrate how the renaming of the West Side avenues in the nineteenth century was part of a deliberate strategy among property owners to reshape the material and symbolic landscape of the Upper West Side. I then compare the renaming of the avenues on the West Side with the commemorative street renamings in Harlem during the second half of the twentieth century to illustrate the multiple layers of exclusion involved in the accumulation of symbolic capital and the construction of places of memory.

"Freedom from shanties" and the renaming of the West Side avenues

The cultural politics of "appropriate" socio-spatial signification

Between 1880 and 1890, the numbered avenues west of Central Park in Manhattan were renamed as Central Park West, Columbus, Amsterdam, and West End Avenues in an attempt by property owners to garner symbolic capital and thereby facilitate the development of the West Side (Table 16.1). For several decades, the West Side was home to German, Irish, and Dutch working-class immigrants who rented plots of land from property owners and constructed make-shift wooden houses and cultivated gardens in what came to be known in the popular press as "Shantytown." According to some estimates, there were as many as 10,000 shanty

Table 16.1 The renaming of the West Side avenues, 1880–1890

New Street Name	Previous Street Name	Year of Street Name Change
West End Avenue	Eleventh Avenue	1880
Central Park West	Eighth Avenue	1883
Columbus Avenue	Ninth Avenue	1890
Amsterdam Avenue	Tenth Avenue	1890

dwellers on the West Side by 1880, with ground-rents ranging from $20 to $100 per year (Stern, Mellins, and Fishman 1999; Neuwirth 2005). The renaming of the West Side avenues occurred at precisely the moment when property owners sought to evict the shanty dwellers from the West Side, and I shall explore the interconnections between these processes of material and symbolic erasure below.

In 1866, a group of influential landowners founded the West Side Association, which lobbied the city for the extension of public works projects on the West Side to enhance property values (Burrows and Wallace 1999; Stern, Mellins, and Fishman 1999; Scobey 2002; Neuwirth 2005). As Scobey (2002, 34–35) points out, the Executive Committee of the Association consisted of "every large commercial interest in New York" at the time. While they may have disagreed on other matters, the members of the West Side Association were all deeply concerned that the shanty dwellers would scare off more affluent tenants and permanently make their mark upon the cultural landscape through the common use of place names that might eventually become codified after continuous usage. That fear was, I argue, one of the major impetuses that led the West Side Association to lobby for the renaming of the avenues on the West Side.

The project to rename the West Side avenues was first conceived in the early 1870s. In 1871, A. W. Colgate read a paper before the West Side Association on the subject of "Appropriate names for the new avenues and public places on the West Side." "We all know how it is," Colgate explained to his audience, "that any name, good or bad, once fastened to a locality is pretty sure to stick." He went on to note that:

> It passes readily into conversation, appears in print, and soon finds its way, not only into literature, but also into titles, mortgages, and other instruments pertaining to the transfer of real estate. ... We should also remember that good names cost no more than bad ones, and that the only way to avoid the bad, is to be beforehand with the good. The present inhabitants [read: shanty dwellers], such as they are of the West Side, are not likely to give any names that property owners would care to see adopted, and yet they may unconsciously christen many of the main streets, with names not easily got rid of. Witness in London—Rotten row, Hog lane, Crab-tree street, Peacock street, Shoe lane, and others equally as absurd, which had there [*sic*] origin in this way, and which generally retain their homely names, even though their neighborhoods become aristocratic.
>
> (Colgate 1871, 22)

Right from the very beginning, Colgate insisted on the necessity of fixing "good" street names before the shanty tenants could do so, and he hoped to ensure that the names given by property owners, not tenants, would be "sure to stick" to the cultural landscape of the West Side. Colgate's call for "appropriate" street names was based upon a recognition that such spatial designations readily circulated as symbolic markers of distinction through the various "instruments pertaining to the transfer of real estate." The symbolic capital associated with a "good" street name, Colgate argued, might translate into economic capital, whereas a "bad" name could have the opposite effect.

For landowners to maximize the symbolic capital of their property, Colgate suggested that three categories of street names were generally appropriate: historical (i.e., "the names of famous men"), geographical (i.e., "names suggested by the topography of the place"), and proprietary names (i.e., "names of the original holders of large parcels of real estate through or near which the streets run"). Unsurprisingly, he favored proprietary names, at least in principle, since "[t]he names of the original landholders afford the largest and perhaps the best selection of all, and precedent is largely in favor of their adoption, especially as many of these old families were distinguished in the early history of the city" (Colgate 1871, 25). Colgate's preference for proprietary street names was more than a mere aesthetic preference but should rather be situated within the context of struggles between landowners and shanty inhabitants on the West Side. Calling for the West Side's numbered avenues to be rechristened to commemorate the "original holders" of real estate in the area was a clear sign that Colgate sought to remake the cultural landscape as a symbolic marker of property and propriety, thereby excluding the shanty-dwelling immigrant population from the realm of legitimate socio-spatial signification.

Colgate concluded that the early adoption of at least some type of nomenclature, before the colloquialisms of Shantytown gained legitimacy, "would aid in bringing the adjacent property into notice and would give it a locality and even a value which it does not now possess" (1871, 26). He was confident that whatever the West Side Association recommended would "no doubt be favorably received by the Department of Public Parks, and thus soon find its way into the maps, and so become part and parcel of the city" (Colgate 1871, 27). After Colgate's speech, the president of the West Side Association, William Martin, concurred with his assessment, and, according to the *Proceedings*, Martin reiterated that:

> it was important to consider the subject maturely, and in advance, lest names not well selected, should attach to these new names and places, which it would not be easy to get rid of. ... We must take care lest names not so appropriate ... become started and adhere to these new and unnamed places.
>
> (see Colgate 1871, 28–29)

The new streets and avenues being laid out on the West Side already had names— the numerical designations from the Plan of 1811—yet West Side property owners, such as Colgate and Martin, thought that a numbered street did not have the same distinguishing qualities and symbolic power as a "proper" street name.

Symbolic erasure, forced eviction, and "warfare" on the West Side

By the end of the 1870s and beginning of the 1880s, the West Side Association began lobbying the municipal authorities to legally rename the West Side avenues. The Association's decision to lobby for street names was inseparable from its desire to displace—both figuratively and literally—the inhabitants of the shanties. At a West Side Association subcommittee meeting on September 27, 1879, the Committee on Streets and Avenues was called on to report again at the following meeting on the "proper course to pursue to legalize" the names chosen by the Association. On the very same page of the meeting minutes, the Committee on Buildings was asked to consider the dilemma of "what action is necessary in order to ensure *freedom from Shanties* and other Nuisances on the West Side" (West Side Association 1879–1885, 62, emphasis added). The renaming of the avenues and the eviction of the shanty inhabitants were both part of the same struggle to market the West Side as a site of social exclusivity.

In 1880, the West Side Association lobbied the city to rename Eleventh Avenue as "West End Avenue," given its associations with the elite section of London

Figure 16.1 "Freedom from Shanties" (*Harper's New Monthly Magazine* 1880)

bearing the same name (Raulin 1984). The matter was considered by the city's Committee on Streets and Street Pavements, and the resolution was later approved by the Board of Alderman (*Proceedings of the Board of Alderman* 1880). The West Side Association then petitioned city officials to rename Eighth Avenue, which was formally rechristened as "Central Park West" in 1883. New designations for Ninth and Tenth Avenues were eventually adopted in April of 1890, being changed to Columbus and Amsterdam Avenues, respectively, which have "stuck" into the present. The renaming of avenues on the West Side occurred at the same time that a boom in property development opened the prospects of increasing profits for West Side landowners and speculators (Scobey 2002). All the incentives were now in place to render the tenants of Shantytown superfluous, at least from the perspective of their landlords. "Freedom from Shanties" was the rallying cry among property owners, yet the residents of Shantytown were not willing to be displaced so easily. In 1880, the same year that the West End Avenue was christened, West Side landowners began what the *New York Times* (1880) referred to as all-out "warfare" against their shanty tenants. Landowners generally went to the courts to get official eviction notices and then attempted to physically force their tenants off the land and demolish their wooden dwellings (Figure 16.1). The tensions ran high when the eviction notices were delivered to the tenants. Dogs were often unleashed on the deputy marshals and bailiffs who brought the notices, and most landowners "never visit[ed] the locality without being well armed" (*New York Times* 1880, 8). By 1890, however, the West Side property owners had successfully removed the vast majority of the shanties and all of the numbered avenues on the West Side had been renamed.

Taking history to the streets: Harlem and the spatial politics of collective memory

Cultural recognition and commemorative street naming in Harlem

A century after the renaming of the West Side avenues, many of Harlem's streets, avenues, and parks were renamed to commemorate African American civil rights leaders (Table 16.2). The renaming of streets in Harlem was part of a nationwide movement calling for the cultural recognition of African Americans and other historically marginalized social groups (Rhea 1997; Alderman 2000). The city's streetscape was seen as a potential site where African American achievements could be recognized through the construction of places of memory. The primary aim was less the conversion of symbolic capital into economic capital, as we saw with the renaming of the West Side avenues, but rather the creation of a commemorative space in which the symbolic capital of a street name could provide a "place" for acknowledging the important contributions of African Americans to the city and the nation. While Harlem's streetscape became a space of recognition, it was also a site of symbolic erasure, with the exclusion of African American women from places of memory throughout the 1970s and 1980s. The subsequent effort to create a "place" for African American women among

Table 16.2 A select list of commemorative place names in Harlem, 1925–2007

New Place Name	Previous Place Name (or Co-Name)	Year of Name Change
Dorrence Brooks Square	—	1925
A. Philip Randolph Square	Admiral George Dewey Park	1964
Marcus Garvey Park	Mount Morris Park	1973
Adam Clayton Powell Jr. Blvd.	Seventh Avenue	1974
Frederick Douglass Blvd.	Eighth Avenue	1977
Jackie Robinson Park	Colonial Park	1978
Langston Hughes Place	—	1982
African Square	—	1983
Dr. Martin Luther King Jr. Blvd.	125th Street	1984
Malcolm X Blvd.	Lenox Avenue/Sixth Avenue	1987
Sugar Ray Robinson Corner	—	1989
Mary McLeod Bethune Place	—	1993
Fredrica L. Teer Square	—	1994
Duke Ellington Circle	—	1995
Harriet Tubman Avenue	St. Nicholas Avenue	2002
The Honorable Percy E. Sutton Avenue	Fifth Avenue	2007

Harlem's street names during the 1990s illustrates how street naming provides a "memorial arena" within which different commemorative strategies are contested.

Harlem holds a special place in the public imagination as the "capital of black America" (Jackson 2001, 19). Yet during the latter-nineteenth and early-twentieth centuries, white property owners used restrictive covenants in order to prevent African Americans from buying, or even renting, property in Harlem. It was only after a steep decline in the real estate market in 1905 that property owners began renting to African Americans, and both white and black realty companies sold properties in Harlem to blacks (Taylor 2002). The fear of a so-called "Negro invasion" led many whites to leave the area in an early instance of "white flight." Unlike the eventual displacement of the inhabitants of Shantytown, however, Harlem remained a predominantly black community throughout the twentieth century (Osofsky 1996 [1966]; Boyd 2003).

During the 1920s, the black population in Harlem increased dramatically to over 200,000, and the number of white residents continued to sharply decline. Between 1925 and the Great Depression, Harlem was the site of considerable cultural and artistic experimentation, with black writers, artists, and musicians taking part in what came to be known as the "Harlem Renaissance" (Wintz and Finkelman 2004; Carroll 2005). This period has, in many respects, become a sort of "golden age" to which historical representations of Harlem continue to harken back. By the mid-1920s, the African American presence in Harlem was beginning to make its cultural mark on the city's symbolic landscape. In 1925, one of the first public squares to honor an African American in New York City was dedicated as Dorrence Brooks Square at 136th Street and Edgecombe Avenue, named after a black soldier who had fought and died in World War I. It was not until the 1970s, however, that the commemoration of African Americans would completely reshape Harlem's streetscape.

One of the earliest of such renamings occurred when the African Nationalist Pioneer Movement successfully lobbied to rechristen Harlem's Mount Morris Park as Marcus Garvey Park in 1973, as a way to honor the Jamaican-born Pan-African nationalist. Over the course of the next two decades, Harlem witnessed a proliferation of street renamings to honor slain civil rights leaders as well as black artists, musicians, and athletes. New York City Councilman Frederick Samuel sponsored many of these street renaming bills and explained their purpose by remarking that "[w]e're trying to say, particularly to our young people, that more happened to black folks than slavery to welfare" (as quoted in Quindlen 1983, 27). Renaming Harlem's streets, then, was a strategy of reshaping collective memories *within* the African American community as much as it was a demand for recognition by society at large.

The majority of the street renaming bills sailed through the City Council without much debate, most likely because they were generally confined to Harlem. The one exception was the unsuccessful proposal to rename Fifth Avenue as "Marcus Garvey Boulevard," which sparked one of the most significant street naming conflicts within Harlem's recent history. The African Nationalist Pioneer Movement lobbied for the street name change in part because it was the centennial year of Garvey's birth. When two community boards approved the new name, a number of politicians—including US Congressman Charles Rangel—initially came out in favor of the change (Browne 1988). However, many of the middle-class black residents of Riverbend Co-op and the Riverton Houses, near 139th Street and Fifth Avenue, bitterly opposed the name change. Gloria Harrison, a resident of the Riverbend Co-op and a professional accountant, led a petition drive in opposition to Marcus Garvey Boulevard. The vice chairwoman of Riverbend likewise ridiculed the Garvey designation by exclaiming, "Imagine, 'Saks Marcus Garvey'" (as quoted in Roberts 1988, B1), implying that Saks Fifth Avenue had a more prestigious ring.

The president of the Uptown Chamber of Commerce went so far as to argue that "if there's one avenue we would like to maintain its name, its Fifth, for everything it connotes to the country and for the continuity between Harlem and the rest of the city" (as quoted in Roberts 1988, B1). Fifth Avenue may be a numerical designation, but over the years it has accumulated a considerable amount of symbolic capital with many proclaiming it "an international symbol of fashion and wealth" (Patterson 1998, 216). When the president of the Uptown Chamber of Commerce enlisted the prestigious connotations of Fifth Avenue as a means of shooting down the Marcus Garvey name change, therefore, he was tapping into a politics of cultural recognition of a very different sort—one that privileged the image of wealth and economic status associated with Fifth Avenue. While some opponents may very well have been critical of Garvey's political philosophy, it is worth noting that they framed all of their arguments against the street name change largely in terms of its impact on the symbolic capital of a Fifth Avenue address. Eventually the critics prevailed, yet after all the controversy surrounding the renaming of Fifth Avenue in the 1980s, it is remarkable that the city renamed upper Fifth Avenue as The Honorable Percy E. Sutton Avenue in 2007, commemorating one of Harlem's prominent African American leaders, and challenging the symbolic power of Fifth Avenue.

A *"rightful place" for African American women in Harlem's streetscape*

What is striking about the commemorative street names in Harlem dating from the 1970s and 1980s is that they are all named in honor of African American men. The first street in Harlem to be named after an African American woman was Mary McLeod Bethune Place, also known as 134th Street, which was renamed in 1993. The proposal to rename one of Harlem's streets for an African American woman was the work of a class of second-grade students at P.S. 92 (also known as Mary McLeod Bethune School). In the Fall of 1992, elementary school teacher Syma Solovitch was giving a history lesson on the famous African American men honored with commemorative street names in Harlem when one of her seven-year-old students, Rondu Gantt, asked a simple yet perplexing question: "Why isn't there any street in Harlem named after an African-American woman?" (as quoted in Allen 1993, 33). Gantt's question led to a year-long class project not only to study the matter but also to lobby for such a commemoration (Allen 1993; Bernstein 1993; Solovitch 1993). Solovitch and her students began by studying the achievements of African American women and eventually decided to choose Bethune because of her distinguished career and support of education (Hanson 2003). The fact that their school was already named in her honor was, no doubt, also a consideration.

The measure was supported by the local community board as well as the City Council's Committee on Parks, Recreation, and Cultural Affairs. The bill was officially sponsored by C. Virginia Fields and various other council members, unanimously approved by the Council, and signed by the Mayor in 1993 (Allen 1993; Bernstein 1993). During the public hearing, one of the supporters of the bill, council member Stanley Michels, was very explicit in his condemnation of the exclusion of women in general, and African American women in particular, from the writing of American history. Michels explained that he, along with various other council members, was "very enthusiastic" to co-sponsor the bill, because "those of us who have studied American history, know her [i.e., Bethune's] rightful place and the fact that she has not been recognized for many years, her rightful place in American history" (*Public Hearing on Local Laws* 1993, 10). "Too often in American history," he observed:

> we find lack of women because the historians were men, I think, and therefore they didn't give them their rightful place. ... But Mary McLeod Bethune, I hope and pray, when the history books are rewritten to really start to be fair, they will give her her rightful place in American history, certainly rightful place in the history of our time, because she did so much.
>
> (*Public Hearing on Local Laws* 1993, 11)

There are several significant points worth making with respect to Michels' comments. First, he emphasized the phrase "rightful place" a total of five times and in some cases twice within the same sentence. His insistence that Bethune deserved a "place" had a double meaning, both historical and geographic. On the one hand, Michels hoped that Bethune and other women would be acknowledged, and therefore have a "place," within history textbooks in order to recognize their achievements. Yet he also saw the renaming of 134th Street as a way to quite literally give Bethune a "place" within the cultural landscape of New York City. The commemoration of Bethune laid the groundwork for subsequent commemorative street names in honor of African American women, such as Fredrica Teer and Harriet Tubman, and it will likely inspire additional commemorative practices in the future.

Conclusion

In the present chapter, I have argued that the renaming of streets opens a space in which the symbolic struggles over remembrance and erasure are anchored in specific sites that serve as places of memory. The attempt to legally rename a street has historically been adopted by myriad groups as an important strategy for acquiring legitimacy, prestige, and cultural recognition in the form of symbolic capital. This chapter has highlighted two key moments in the history of renaming New York's streets to demonstrate how the symbolic capital associated with street naming may be linked to an elite project of symbolic erasure and forced eviction, on the one hand, and the cultural recognition of a historically marginalized group, on the other. These two case studies confirm Alderman's (2000, 672) claim that street naming can be "used for resisting the hegemonic order as well as reproducing it." Yet, it is both theoretically and politically important not to reduce the symbolic struggle over street naming to a binary opposition between the "elite" and the "marginalized," because such a characterization obscures the multiple axes of exclusion at stake in the production of commemorative spaces. The case of gender exclusion in the renaming of Harlem's streets is instructive in this regard, and it is hoped that future studies of the politics of street naming will explore the different layers of exclusion and erasure in struggles over commemoration and place-making.

I have also argued that the relation between street naming and memory is more complex than most traditional accounts of commemorative street names would suggest. The distinction between commemorative and non-commemorative street names limits our understanding of the symbolic power of toponymy in constructing places of memory and oblivion. As the renaming of the West Side avenues illustrates, the designation of descriptive street names such as "Central Park West" and "West End Avenue" was a means of bringing the West Side into the realm of public memory as a site of social exclusivity, which was linked not only to the symbolic erasure but also to the physical removal of the working-class immigrant population that resided in that section of the city. Similarly, the renaming of Ninth Avenue to commemorate Christopher Columbus reveals more about the perception of prestige among property owners in nineteenth-century New York than it does about Columbus himself. While Columbus Avenue is "commemorative" in the traditional sense of a street name honoring a famous individual, we must also explore the commemorative dimensions of descriptive, possessive, and other street names as well.

Although this chapter has focused primarily on the shift from "number" to "name," it is worth noting that numbered streets make up commemorative spaces despite their seemingly strict utilitarian function for spatial orientation. The symbolic capital of a Fifth Avenue address should remind us that numerical inscriptions also have a "place" in the landscape of public memory. This line of argument leads to a much broader conception of commemorative space, which moves beyond the traditional view that confines commemorative street naming primarily to those designations that honor specific individuals. Since commemoration takes numerous different forms in the streetscape, future critical place-name studies should explore the multiple ways in which memory and erasure are implicated in the production of place.

References

Alderman, D. (2000). "A Street Fit for a King: Naming Places and Commemoration in the American South." *Professional Geographer*, 52(4): 672–684.

Alderman, D. (2002). "Street Names as Memorial Arenas: The Reputational Politics of Commemorating Martin Luther King Jr. in a Georgia County." *Historical Geography*, 30: 99–120.

Alderman, D. (2003). "Street Names and the Scaling of Memory: The Politics of Commemorating Martin Luther King, Jr. within the African American Community." *Area*, 35(2): 163–173.

Alderman, D. (2008). "Place, Naming, and the Interpretation of Cultural Landscapes." In B. Graham and P. Howard (Eds.), *The Ashgate Research Companion to Heritage and Identity* (pp. 195–213). Aldershot, UK: Ashgate.

Allen, M. (1993). "Boy's Takin' it to the Street: Crusade for Black Woman." *New York Daily News*, October 24: 33.

Azaryahu, M. (1996). "The Power of Commemorative Street Names." *Environment and Planning D*, 14(3): 311–330.

Bernstein, E. (1993). "Second Graders Write Own Page in Civic Book." *New York Times*, November 7: 6.

Bourdieu, P. (1986). "The Forms of Capital." In J. Richardson (Ed.), *Handbook of Theory and Research for the Sociology of Education* (pp. 241–258). New York: Greenwood Press.

Bourdieu, P. (1991). *Language and Symbolic Power*. Cambridge, MA: Harvard University Press.

Boyd, H. (Ed.). (2003). *The Harlem Reader*. New York: Three Rivers Press.

Browne, J. (1988). "Group Opposes Renaming Street for Garvey." *Amsterdam News*, February 27.

Burrows, E. and Wallace, M. (1999). *Gotham: A History of New York City to 1898*. New York: Oxford University Press.

Carroll, A. (2005). *Word, Image, and the New Negro: Representation and Identity in the Harlem Renaissance*. Bloomington: Indiana University Press.

Carter, P. (1988). *The Road to Botany Bay: An Exploration of Landscape and History*. New York: Alfred A. Knopf.

Colgate, A. (1871). "On the Subject of Appropriate Names for the New Avenues and Public Places on the West Side." In *Proceedings of Second Public Meeting, Held on the 11th January, 1871, West Side Association, New-York, 1870–1871* (pp. 21–29). New York: J. Adnah Sackett.

Dwyer, O. (2000). "Interpreting the Civil Rights Movement: Place, Memory, and Conflict." *Professional Geographer*, 52(4): 660–671.

Edozien, F. (2007). "Sonny Carson Loses Street Fight." *New York Post*, May 31: www.nypost.com/seven/05312007/news/regionalnews/sonny_carson_loses_street_fight_regionalnews_frankie_edozien.htm

Feeney, S. (1990). "A Corner Named Confusion." *Daily News*, March 16: 61.

Feirstein, S. (2001). *Naming New York: Manhattan Places & How They Got Their Names.* New York: New York University Press.

Forest, B., Johnson, J. and Till, K. (2004). "Post-Totalitarian National Identity: Public Memory in Germany and Russia." *Social & Cultural Geography*, 5(3): 357–380.

Garcilazo, M. (1992). "Council's Back Playing 'Name Game' with City's Streets." *New York Post*, December 26: 3.

Gargan, E. (1981). "More and More Streets Get a Change but in Name Only." *New York Times*, September 1: B5–B6.

Haberman, C. (2002). "Carving out a Corner for Everyone." *New York Times*, February 2: B1.

Hanson, J. (2003). *Mary McLeod Bethune & Black Women's Political Activism.* Columbia: University of Missouri Press.

Harper's New Monthly Magazine (1880). "Squatter Life in New York." September: 562–569.

Henkin, D. (1998). *City Reading: Written Words and Public Spaces in Antebellum New York.* New York: Columbia University Press.

Hoelscher, S. and Alderman, D. (2004). "Memory and Place: Geographies of a Critical Relationship." *Social & Cultural Geography*, 5(3): 347–355.

Jackson, J. (2001). *Harlemworld: Doing Race and Class in Contemporary Black America.* Chicago: University of Chicago Press.

Johnson, N. (2004). "Public Memory." In J. Duncan, N. Johnson, and R. Schein (Eds.), *Companion to Cultural Geography* (pp. 316–327). Oxford: Blackwell Publishing.

Lee, D. (2001). "The Street is Familiar, but Can't Remember the Nickname." *New York Times*, April 29, Sec. 14: 5.

Longworth, T. (1833). *Longworth's American Almanac, New-York Register and City Directory.* New York: Thomas Longworth.

Longworth, T. (1841). *Longworth's American Almanac, New-York Register and City Directory.* New York: Thomas Longworth.

Marcuse, P. (1987). "The Grid as City Plan: New York City and Laissez-Faire Planning in the Nineteenth Century." *Planning Perspectives*, 2(3): 287–310.

Massey, D. (1994). *Space, Place, and Gender.* Minneapolis: University of Minnesota Press.

Massey, D. (2005). *For Space.* London: Sage Publications.

Moscow, H. (1978). *The Street Book: An Encyclopedia of Manhattan's Street Names and Their Origins.* New York: Fordham University Press.

Neuwirth, R. (2005). *Shadow Cities: A Billion Squatters, A New Urban World.* New York: Routledge.

New York Times (1880). "Ten Thousand Squatters: A Warfare Begun by West Side Landowners." April 20: 8.

Osofsky, G. (1996 [1966]). *Harlem, the Making of a Ghetto: Negro New York, 1890–1930.* Chicago: Ivan R. Dee.

Painter, J. (2000). "Pierre Bourdieu." In M. Crang and N. Thrift (Eds.), *Thinking Space* (pp. 239–259). London: Routledge.

Patterson, J. (1998). *Fifth Avenue: The Best Address*. New York: Rizzoli.

Proceedings of the Board of Alderman of the City of New York, from January 5 to March 30. 1880. Volume CLVII: 76, 249. New York: Martin B. Brown.

Public Hearing on Local Laws. 1993. *Intro. 796*, New York City: Ellen P. Reach Stenographic Reporting Services. November 12.

Quindlen, A. (1983). "About New York: A Day for Renaming Places." *New York Times*, April 23: 27.

Ranzal, E. (1976). "Beame Upheld in Council on Street Name Change." *New York Times*, June 9: 40.

Raulin, A. (1984). "The Naming of Urban Space: A Study of Manhattan Place Names." PhD dissertation, Graduate Faculty of Political and Social Science, The New School for Social Research.

Rhea, J. (1997). *Race Pride and the American Identity*. Cambridge, MA: Harvard University Press.

Roberts, S. (1988). "Battle to Block the Re-naming of Fifth Avenue." *New York Times*, February 15: B1.

Scobey, D. (2002). *Empire City: The Making and Meaning of the New York City Landscape*. Philadelphia, PA: Temple University Press.

Siegel, J. (1993). "Full Circle in Street Name Game." *Daily News*, May 2: 30.

Solovitch, S. (1993). "The Story Behind the Official Unveiling of Mary McLeod Bethune Place," unpublished manuscript.

Spann, E. (1988). "The Greatest Grid: The New York Plan of 1811." In D. Schaffer (Ed.), *Two Centuries of American Planning* (pp. 11–39). Baltimore, MD: Johns Hopkins University Press.

Stern, R., Mellins, T., and Fishman, D. (1999). *New York 1880: Architecture and Urbanism in the Gilded Age*. New York: Monacelli Press.

Stewart, G. (1954). "A Classification of Place Names." *Names*, 2(1): 1–13.

Stewart, G. (1958). *Names on the Land: A Historical Account of Place-naming in the United States*. Boston, MA: Houghton Mifflin.

Taylor, M. (2002). *Harlem Between Heaven and Hell*. Minneapolis: University of Minnesota Press.

West Side Association. (1879–1885). *Minute Book*. New-York Historical Society, MssColl, New York: West Side Association.

Wintz, C. and Finkelman, P. (Eds.) (2004). *Encyclopedia of the Harlem Renaissance*. New York: Routledge.

17 Toponymic checksum or flotsam?

Recalculating Dubai's grid with Makani, "the smartest map in the world"

Maral Sotoudehnia

Introduction

> Makani is the new geo-address system for the city of Dubai. It consists of 10 digits. Each Makani number gives you the location of the entrance of a building.
>
> (Makani 2015)

> The spatial practices of street addressing—the naming of streets, numbering of buildings, and construction of street signage systems—have a larger political significance, because they have historically played an important role in the social production of calculable spaces that make up the "geo-coded world."
>
> (Rose-Redwood 2012, 297)

> Software challenges us to re-inscribe what we comprehend as inscription.
>
> (Thrift and French 2002, 331)

The Government of Dubai is currently phasing in Makani, a "first-of-its-kind smart system for geographic addresses" ("Hamdan Launches" 2015). Designed by the municipal branch of Dubai's Government, Dubai Municipality, Makani uses ten digit codes to "identify locations and intended destinations instead of having to determine the areas [*sic*] name, street number and building number" (Dubai Smart Gov. 2015, 5). Arabic for "my place" or "my location," Makani provides users equipped with smartphones and internet access with an accurate wayfinding tool to navigate the Emirate (Dubai Smart Gov. 2015; Makani 2015). The application relies on satellites to digitally codify urban space, which can then be accessed haptically via smart devices or desktop computers. These Makani numbers are also etched onto each entrance of every building (Makani 2015). The application enhances existing geo-location services by offering voice navigation to destinations, allegedly improving emergency response times and providing real-time traffic information.

The promise of an effective wayfinding system for a rapidly expanding city like Dubai offers local residents and visitors an undeniable civic service, but what interests me, here, is how applications like Makani function as spatial inscription technologies that encode urban space (Zook and Graham 2007; Kitchin and Dodge 2011). Through Makani's code, the application reformats Dubai as a "text" with a "coherent 'page layout'" (Rose-Redwood 2009, 201). This new typography of the city-text enables smart users to "touch the ontic" of the city's newly re-ordered grid (Spivak 1993, 30; cf. Thrift and French 2002, 312). Makani opens up Dubai's map by bringing every spatial object online, regardless of any previous toponyms or identifiers. The application offers a singular case to illuminate how power operates through digital addressing to enact another "'theory of the world' ... contingent on the ruling social and moral order" (cf. Azaryahu 1992, 351; Light, Nicolae, Suditu 2002). Much like toponyms and other spatial nomenclature, Makani numbers are "more than a means of facilitating spatial orientation" (Azaryahu 1992, 351). In Dubai's case, the application transforms street names into ornamental signposts and offers evidence of the increasing role smart geo-addressing conventions play in the cultural production of "calculable spaces" and behavioral data (Rose-Redwood 2012, 297; Zegras et al. 2015).

The aim of this chapter is to present an initial investigation of Dubai's smart geo-addressing application, Makani, as a new line of inquiry for critical toponymy and the study of spatial inscription practices more generally. I examine Makani, and offer a preliminary analysis of digital geo-coding systems as "key technologies" that automatically produce urban space (Thrift and French 2002). Following Zegras et al. (2015, 125), I am interested in examining the role that code, through smart geo-addressing practices, plays in place-making and "how smart geo-spatial inscription technologies are developed, targeted, disseminated for 'public' use, and interpreted by consumers." Despite an emerging interest in the geo-web or Web 2.0 applications, there continues to be a significant lack of recent research investigating the spatial and cultural politics associated with GIS technologies (Kingsbury and Jones 2009; Rose-Redwood 2012; Lin 2013). Very little research currently examines smart GIS applications and their related discourses from non-Western perspectives (Lin 2013). While many studies look to Dubai as an urban "mecca of conspicuous consumption" (Bagaeen 2007; Davis 2007; cf. Acuto 2010, 272; Kanna 2011, 2013), few geographers examine the political role that smart spatial technology plays in the Emirate's "hyper-entrepreneurialism" and continued expansion (Acuto 2010, 272).

In the present chapter, I begin by reviewing key ideas about the spatiality of code and how they have been enlisted by dominant smart city narratives (Hollands 2008, 2015; Kitchin and Dodge 2011). I bring both in dialogue with contemporary debates about the critical study of place naming, numbering, and inscription more generally (Rose-Redwood, 2006, 2009, 2012; Alderman 2009; Azaryahu 2011). Next, I offer an initial analysis of Dubai's Makani application. In particular, I interrogate Dubai's smart "spatial regime of inscriptions" and query how the application alters existing place-identities associated with concurrent commemorative street naming practices (Rose-Redwood 2009, 201, italics omitted). I pay close attention to the vagaries of Makani's code, how geo-addressing might lead to misdirection and produce new spaces of exclusion or inclusion made possible through the smart application's implementation (Graham 2002). Finally, I cast my attention to Makani's proprietary framework, focusing on some of the challenges associated with government-designed smart applications and policies that encourage the uncritical creep of code into daily life through the information that users give up, often unknowingly. Makani, I argue, serves as a unique example of the "toponym-as-commodity" (Rose-Redwood and Alderman 2011, 3), since the app's proprietary limits facilitate the commodification of space through its identifiers and associated user data (Thrift and French 2002; Dalton and Thatcher 2015).

From number to name ... to number? Code/spaces and the production of Dubai's smart city-text

Geographers are beginning to examine software and how it affects material life (Thrift and French 2002; Graham 2005; Zook and Graham 2007; Kitchin, Dodge and Zook 2009; Graham and Zook 2011; Kitchin and Dodge 2011; Townsend 2013; Kitchin 2014, 2015). Most investigations of the spatiality of code attend to the mounting "cultural hold" (Thrift and French 2002, 310) that software, information and communication technologies (ICTs), and other "coded worlds" (Graham 2005, 563) have over daily urban experiences. Thrift and French's (2002, 311) now seminal study on the *automatic production of space* emphasizes code's growing significance to urban dwellers: "Software is more like a kind of traffic between beings, wherein one sees, so to speak, the *effects* of the relationship. What transpires becomes reified in actions, body stances, general anticipations." Although invisible, code enacts lasting effects. Kitchin and Dodge's (2011, 16) concept of *code/space* similarly acknowledges the ineluctable relationship between code and space by positioning the two as co-constitutive, while Graham's (2005, 563) study of *software-sorted geographies* attends to the ways by which neoliberal and Keynesian practices are "continuously brought into being through code." Graham and Zook (2011, 116) further draw our attention to the matter of digital mapping practices by stating that, "digital and online palimpsests now undoubtedly have become an important shaper of many people's mental maps." Much of the critical research on the topic focuses on the rising ubiquity of code and what it means for urban space, the activities that animate it, and the "digital traces" left behind (Elwood 2010, 353).

Recent critical urban scholarship on software-enhanced spaces often concerns itself with technological innovations that render the city computable, intelligent, or smart (Komninos 2002; Hollands 2008, 2015; Angelidou 2014, 2015; Kitchin 2014). As with any neologism, many investigations attempt to flesh out what constitutes a "smart city" (Angelidou 2014, 2015; Hollands 2015; Luque-Ayala and Marvin 2015). A number of authors tackle the "definitional impreciseness" surrounding smart cities that exhibit "some kind of positive urban-based technological change via ICTs" (Hollands 2008, 302; see also Angelidou 2014, 2015; Kitchin 2015; Zegras et al. 2015). Luque-Ayala and Marvin (2015, 2107) point out that present studies on urban smartness "lack a critical perspective compounded by an undue emphasis on technological solutions that disregard the social and political domains" in which they operate. The authors call for research to focus on specific smart "political rationalities and governmental techniques" (Luque-Ayala and Marvin 2015, 2108). Shelton, Zook, and Wiig (2015) similarly suggest that future work should attempt to move beyond essentializing constructions of exceptional or paradigmatic smart cities and focus instead on *actually existing* examples of smart urbanism.

Given that code has become a ubiquitous and often unseen presence in many cities, critical and empirical examinations of smart urbanism would equip researchers to begin uncovering how, as Lin (2013, 902) points out, "GIS embodies, and is embedded in, complex social relations with wide-ranging societal implications." Researchers could consider the context-specificity of space and the various and inconsistent ways it is "beckoned into existence by code" (Thrift and French 2002, 311). One way forward is to bring discussions about code/space in conversation with geographical ideas about place, its construction, performance, and politics. Current debates in critical toponymy can help fill this gap.

Recent investigations in critical toponymy acknowledge that place names, numbers, and spatial objects produce, contest, and reconfigure social space as well as privilege specific and "official" histories (Azaryahu 1996; Light, Nicolae, and Suditu 2002; Rose-Redwood 2008a). As Light, Nicolae, and Suditu (2002, 143) explain, "[s]treet names can be 'read' as the micro-scale or local level outcome of much broader structures of power and authority." What is commemorated and decommemorated reifies a certain politics or ideology and determines who or what gets remembered, forgotten, and omitted. Alderman (2009, 178), for instance, explains that place names can "become embroiled in the politics of defining what (or who) is historically significant or worthy of public remembrance." Although a street name can recognize local events or histories, it can also enable "active" or "public forgetting" (Hoelscher and Alderman 2004, 347; Rose-Redwood 2008a). But, as Azaryahu (2011, 29–30) suggests, critical place name studies should not only consider *how* a street name functions as a legible "text of memory" but should also take into account "the possibility of ostensible incoherence, polysemy and heterogeneity ... to explain the contradictions and inconsistencies that reflect the history of the 'text' itself."

And yet, little scholarship has explored the interconnections between spatial ordering strategies, the inscription of "memorial arenas" into the urban landscape, and smart geo-addressing practices (though, see Rose-Redwood 2006, 2009, 2012; Alderman 2009). Rose-Redwood's (2009, 201) study of early U.S. house-numbering practices illustrates how the numerical identification of houses rationalized urban space and helped imagine "the city as a 'text'." Rose-Redwood (2009, 220) concludes by arguing that future research should probe spatial inscription conventions that depend upon GIS to organize the city (see also Curry, Phillips, and Regan 2004; Elwood 2010). In a more recent article on rural re-addressing practices in West Virginia, he restates the need for a greater understanding of *all* geo-coding applications, be they analog or "machine-readable," in order to better illuminate how "spatial representations, ontologies, and the world" intersect (Rose-Redwood 2012, 298–299). Alderman's (2009, 268) examination of domain names and the politics of misdirection makes the pointed case to interrogate the "virtual equivalent of place names."[1] Few researchers have followed Rose-Redwood's (2008a, 433) call to interrogate the processes and effects of digital spatial ordering and erasure through various, "if not all, acts of spatial designation" (also, see Rose-Redwood 2012). Meanwhile, critical geo-web studies interested in the political rationalities of smart or digital spatial inscription technologies seldom investigate "the imaginations and discourses that motivate spatial technology development" (Wilson 2014, 538; see also Leszczynski and Wilson 2013; Wilson and Graham 2013; yet Thatcher 2013 offers a compelling counter-example to the studies cited here). Minimal research has considered how software, namely through smart technologies designed, trademarked, and rolled-out by governments as a public service, produces or transforms space, and to what effects (Vanolo 2013). With this in mind, I turn my attention to geo-addressing technologies in Dubai.

Geo-addressing in Dubai

Dubai's basic road infrastructure was initially built during the 1970s and 1980s and has included a variety of naming conventions (Wippel et al. 2014). Following the city's astronomical development throughout the last forty years, it is no secret that Dubai's grid has changed dramatically and quickly (Pacione 2005; Bagaeen 2007; Elsheshtawy 2008; Acuto 2014; Buckley 2013). As a result, spatial nomenclature in Dubai currently involves a combination of numeric, descriptive, and commemorative identifiers to provide users with a variety of ways to understand and navigate the grid. Dubai's highways and major roads, for instance, rely on a codified letter and number system. Roads containing the prefix E followed by two or three numbers connect Dubai to other Emirates (e.g., the E11 highway), whereas intra-Emirati roads use a D prefix instead (e.g., the road D94). Many such identifiers, however, exist alongside descriptive or commemorative toponyms. Highway E11, for instance, also refers to the famous Sheikh Zayed Road, while highway D94 is also commonly known as Jumeirah Road. In short, although Dubai does indeed have a designated naming convention, it is one complicated by rapid construction that expands and re-configures the grid. Multiple conventions often cause confusion as streets are simultaneously named according to a hybrid letter–number system *and* commemorative or denotative toponym.

These polysemic toponymic conventions result, in part, from the city's unmatched and unrelenting urban development. Called everything from the "instant city" (Bagaeen 2007) to the "superlative city" (Kanna 2013), Dubai's rapid expansion has often been linked to entrepreneurial logics that seek to position the city as an example of urban exceptionalism (Acuto 2010, 2014; Kanna 2011, 2013; Buckley 2013).

Dubai would certainly benefit from the implementation of a coherent spatial identification system that enables people to get from point A to point B easily. With rapid growth and expansion, navigation has become difficult and frustrating for many (Lala 2012; "New Street Names" 2012). Various governmental ministries have worked continuously over the past two decades to create spatial nomenclature, including thematic place names and numeric signifiers, to alleviate the Emirate's incongruent and often confusing grid (Lala 2012). One recent news article sums up the issue by stating that "[m]any residents don't know the official name or number of their street. It is common for people to use landmarks or unofficial street descriptions for reference" (Masudi 2015). Spatial inscription has become so inconsistent that even cab drivers often struggle to locate addresses, many of which are often duplicated across the city ("New Street Names" 2012). Makani, a smart geo-addressing application, promises a solution to improve wayfinding in Dubai.

Smart geo-addressing in Dubai: Makani

In 2012, the Government of Dubai announced that it would partner with Garmin, the navigation products and services company, in order to introduce a digital map for the Emirate ("Dubai Addresses" 2012). Intended as a civic service to improve record keeping, reduce emergency response times, and navigational frustration, Makani, which is currently being introduced across Dubai, uses a Military Grid Reference System (MGRS) in order to identify locations in Dubai with undeniable accuracy and precision ("Dubai Addresses" 2012).

Makani is officially under the purview of Dubai Municipality's GIS Department, who, under the auspices of Emirati Law "is considered to be the only official body which allows producing geographical data in the Emirate" (Dubai Municipality 2015). In addition, Makani's "logo and the concept of geographic addressing system and the content of this application are owned by Dubai Municipality and protected by intellectual property laws" (Makani 2015). Both points are important to unpack, as they point to significant propriety restrictions coded into Makani and the user data associated with the application.

It is in this underexplored conceptual space that I make the following intervention. My primary interest lies in demonstrating how smart geo-addressing applications are spatial ordering technologies that produce new and varied spaces of the *city-text* (Rose-Redwood 2008a, 2012; Azaryahu 2011). In what follows, I consider some of the possible challenges and complications surrounding smart geo-addressing inscription practices through a close reading of Makani. Makani offers an initial glimpse into the spatial politics of smart geo-addressing applications and how they have the capacity to produce code/space.

Code/space and the politics of Makani

Makani and misdirection

Makani functions much like other geo-addressing platforms: it presents a satellite map, which is framed by a search bar equipped with a drop-down menu for advanced searches, an address book icon near the top of the screen, and a toolbar near the bottom left. Despite promotional messages de-emphasizing the need to cite any specific place names (Dubai Municipality 2015), the application's search function offers a series of alternative inputs to Makani numbers (Figure 17.1). Chief among these substitutes is a header that reads "search by place name" (Makani 2015). The application still allows for the input of existing place names in English and Arabic to identify spatial objects, but the spelling and specific categorization of typed-in toponyms can complicate navigation. Spelling errors in Makani slow down and impede the identification of a particular place, thus bounding what can be accessed, and how. Various places on the famous Palm Jumeirah, for instance, are misspelled, or express "Jumeirah" as "Jumeriah," "Jumeria," or "Jumaira" (Figure 17.2).[2] Locating specific sites with the word "Jumeirah" becomes an onerous task as the user can only use the geo-coded grid through its encoded orthography, which is inconsistent (Makani 2015). Makani's orthographical errors do not involve domain names, but they nonetheless bring to mind what Alderman (2009, 273) calls "typo squatting," a practice whereby slightly misspelled popular domain names are purposefully purchased to capture any user-error and misdirection. It is unlikely that typographical errors in Makani's smart map are consciously guided by competitors, interest groups, or the Government, yet such miscalculations undermine Makani's professed efficacy (Zaske 2015).

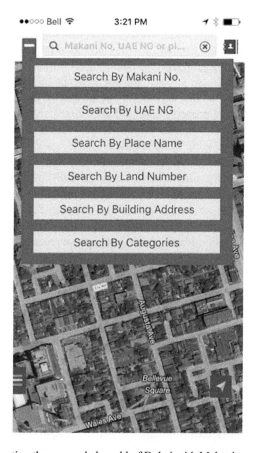

Figure 17.1 Navigating the geo-coded world of Dubai with Makani

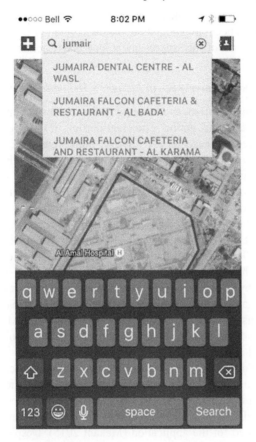

Figure 17.2 Miscalculating encoded orthography with Makani

Spatial inscription blunders also illustrate how easy intended misdirection could be, whether by government, or by future corporations with partial or full control of Makani's code. As Zook and Graham explain of the internet, it is:

> not some purely randomized network in which all nodes have a relatively equal position. Instead it is best described as a scale-free network in which a small proportion of nodes function as highly connected hubs while the much larger group of remaining nodes have a relatively low degree of integration into and influence over the network.
>
> (2007, 1323)

While I am inspired, like Elwood (2010, 354) and Kingsbury and Jones (2009), by the notion that the "transformative potential of technologies lies in their indeterminacy," smart geo-addressing applications like Makani are often considered low-hanging fruit for cities seeking to maximize entrepreneurial logic and monetize urban space (Hollands 2015). Although it is imperative to avoid uncritically adopting fatalistic interpretations of digital geo-addressing applications, it is also fruitful to begin thinking about the digitization of urban space, and what the possible enclosure of such spaces might look like (Zook and Graham 2007).

Looking for answers: code/space in Makani's Help and FAQ

Makani's Help button offers another entry point to consider smart software as a technology of spatial inscription. The Help portion of the application is further organized by three sub-headers: FAQ, Quick Tutorial, and the user guide. I will focus on the FAQ and user guide sections. The majority of the FAQs are standard questions one can expect from any navigation application, such as "What is Makani?" or "What is geo-address?," but other inclusions highlight some of the politics associated with smart technologies that encode the very spaces they bring into existence. The answer listed for the question, "Can I search for shops or other points of interest POI in Makani?," signals an active attempt to promote what Elsheshtawy (2008) refers to as the *Dubai spectacle*, exemplified by a "culture of consumption." The response that Makani provides reads: "Yes you can search for point of interest by inputting its name. You can also search more than 25000 shops by inputting its name in the general search field" (Makani 2015). By emphasizing toponyms of consumption, or "shops," the Government uses Makani numbers to promote investment through user consumption and thus memorializes economic growth above all else.

The user guide walks individuals through annotated screenshots of the application's coordinate inputs and provides basic information about Makani connectivity and interoperability. The first page shows the user the Apple Store, Google Play, and Blackberry icons, the only compatible smart phone operating systems (OS) listed for the application (Makani 2015). Despite any attempt by Dubai Municipality to "Provide integrated Geospatial information of the Emirate of Dubai and enable everyone to utilize it" (Makani 2015), Makani only targets users with access to exclusive smart devices and reliable wireless internet connections (though, the Makani website can be accessed via wired connections as well). By design, Makani shuts out anyone using a non-dominant smartphone or OS (e.g., Windows Phone), "dumb" mobile technology, or unconnected users without internet, computers, or a mobile device. The version of Dubai on offer by Makani becomes a luxury only available to the hyper-wealthy and hyper-connected, or what Vanolo (2013, 5) calls "smart people." Instead of improving wayfinding, Makani has the capacity to further stratify a city already divided by wealth, class, and status. This brings to mind Azaryahu's (1996) concern that place-identifying practices may legitimize particular ideologies, function as a hegemonic tool of governance, or be used as a calculative technology (also, see Rose-Redwood 2006). Makani, a smart geo-addressing app promoted as a "public" navigational aid further limits access to an already segregated city (Davis 2007; Kanna 2011; Buckley 2013; Thatcher 2013).

The text in Makani's user guide makes visible how "data are always expressions of power ... that are never ontologically prior to their interpretation" (Dalton and

Thatcher 2015, 3), since use of the app volunteers individual data for the Government to collect, commodify, monitor, and interpret for whatever uses it deems suitable. By recoding Dubai's toponymic landscape with apps like Makani and collecting user information about how the apps and the spaces they physically calculate are being used, the Government can access greater and richer information about its population. The Government can use data collection and transformation techniques to convert the individual into a commodity and "produce social relations and geographic spaces of consumption" (Dalton and Thatcher 2015, 5; Zook and Graham 2007).

Makani's proprietary framework also precludes, "through a royal decree (Law No. 6, 2001)," any other body from "producing geographical data in the Emirate" ("Makani" 2015). This proprietary condition takes entrepreneurial governance to unforeseen levels, where government-designed smart applications can be transformed into commodities to be trademarked, copyrighted, sold, and manipulated by governments who produce them exclusively.

Smart geo-coding and Dubai's commemorative toponyms

> The new Makani e-map application has many benefits, and will provide new names for streets, simplify the address system and coordinate location databases for government and private bodies.
>
> ("Dubai's E-Address" 2015)

For many navigating Dubai's grid day-to-day, Makani's ten-digit identifiers simplify navigation throughout the city. Yet the application renders current commemorative place names ornamental, as users "have no need to mention street or area names" anymore (Dubai Municipality 2015). By replacing the need to read, enunciate, or interpret toponyms with a simple finger-tap or swipe, the production of place can take on an extreme form of what Berg and Kearns (2009) call "norming." The "'linguistic settlement' that *produces* place through simple enunciation" continues to operate through the "code/space" made possible by geo-addressing applications like Makani, but how that settlement occurs and what it memorializes becomes opaque (Berg and Kearns 2009, 19, italics in original; Kitchin and Dodge 2011, 16).

Makani's de-commemorative capacity becomes all the more apparent as one scrutinizes its implementation alongside other wayfinding projects underway. The Government of Dubai's municipal branch, Dubai Municipality, and its Roads and Transport Authority, have committed to an Emirate-wide toponymic overhaul by introducing a commemorative naming project. The campaign intends to inject a sense of nationalism "inspired by Emirati culture" through the renaming of the city's streets (Jacotine 2015). As the Director-General of Dubai Municipality explains in a press interview, the project considers "the entire element of Dubai's history, culture and traditions with the aim at introducing Dubai's heritage to the generations to come in all ways possible" (Sambidge 2014). Central to the renaming campaign is an active attempt to imbue over 22,000 streets across the city with toponyms that pay homage to "the history and culture of the area to reflect Dubai's heritage" (Jacotine 2015).

In addition to celebrating Dubai's history, culture, and natural features, the commemorative renaming project promises to, like Makani, ease navigation. Throughout the project's implementation, Government officials have stressed the navigational benefits of an "easier and simpler" toponymic landscape ("430 Streets" 2013). In a statement about the initiative, the CEO of the Traffic and Roads Agency expressed the locational advantages of themed, commemorative street names:

> Under the theme system areas in the vicinity of the sea ... will have street names reflecting the marine environment like the names of fish, traditional boats and ships as well as other elements of the sea. Similarly, street names in the Financial District will reflect various traditional currencies. This will help locate the streets easily.
>
> ("430 Streets" 2013)

Such statements call into question the logic and practicality underpinning a simultaneous commemorative and numeric-GPS geo-addressing system, especially one that aims to create "a language understood by everyone" through satellite-generated ten-digit codes that otherwise hold no semantic value for users (Dubai Municipality 2015). Whereas toponyms can function as commemorative tools (Azaryahu 1996), Makani numbers accrete symbolic value through the very act of digital and physical spatial encoding. Makani's ten-digit codes follow Rose-Redwood's (2009, 201) argument that the "encoding of geographic space often entails the creation of a spatial regime of inscriptions that is literally inscribed on the spaces it thereby constructs." The Government nonetheless acknowledges that a commemorative "naming convention will help motorists and road users identify locations easily compared with the earlier system which uses street numbers" while also promoting Makani's smart geo-locational abilities (Jacotine 2015). Makani, according to one government-sponsored ad, universalizes the grid so that "no place in Dubai is difficult to find anymore" (Dubai Municipality 2015). The ad further lauds Makani's unmatched ability to help users "get a location in seconds" by stating that "future business cards will only have Makani numbers for its location" (Dubai Municipality 2015). Although both projects claim to achieve the same goal—that is, rendering the grid navigable and improving locational services—the simultaneous implementation of both technologies appears at the very least confused, if not contradictory altogether, as both spatial ordering systems use opposing spatial identification methods.

Through the commemorative renaming project, the Government of Dubai actively recognizes, as Berg and Kearns (2009, 44) do, that "place names are important signifiers of meaning, providing symbolic identity to people, place and landscape." The renaming initiative, after all, attempts to construct and celebrate a national identity. Yet the very governmental department involved in a nation-building toponymic exercise is also promoting a "universal" navigational tool that strips away any need to utter local names at all (Dubai Municipality 2015; Makani 2015). The histories and existing place-identities associated with street names and landmarks become even more difficult to access for a variety of user groups. Makani may increase the efficiency and utility of nomenclature across the city, but it also undercuts any attempt to commemorate local histories, events, or people.

Both the app and commemorative naming project exemplify entrepreneurial logic and focus on creating an easy-to-navigate grid for a "global" population. As Dubai Municipality's GIS Director emphasizes, Makani will make traveling through the Emirate "fast, easy and accurate" so that "[t]here will be no problems with addresses" (Masudi 2014). For instance, the response listed for "Why Makani system uses only numbers?," under the application's FAQ page, caters entirely to the construction of an ethnically diverse and global userbase: "Everyone can read numbers easily … For example the word Beirut could be difficult for a Chinese [*sic*] to pronounce but 1234 is very easy." The professed efficacy of a universally legible city-text is redolent of other entrepreneurial tactics that seek to eradicate established "lucrative niches" (cf. Acuto 2010, 275) and exploit any resulting locational and comparative advantages. During an inaugural installation of a Makani plaque at the base of the famed Emirates Towers, Sheikh Hamdan, the ruler overseeing Makani, proclaimed that the application "would help transform Dubai 'into the smartest city in the world, and consequently, offer a model for all others to follow suit'" (Zaske 2015). Persistent world-making rhetoric employed by Dubai's ruling class illustrates, as Acuto (2010, 274) points out, the Emirate's continued commitment "to diversify and rapidly reinvent its function to external needs." Such superlative aspirations illustrate the political purchase of constructing smart cities as paradigmatic, exceptional, or models for other governments to follow (Hollands 2015; Kitchin 2015; Luque-Ayala and Marvin 2015). By pitching two very different wayfinding conventions to a "global" population, Dubai's Government is drawing upon a narrative of unparalleled innovation and modernity in the hopes of attracting the world's attention (Acuto 2010).

As Makani's adoption increases, individuals unfamiliar with Dubai's grid will have decreasing exposure to symbolically relevant toponyms. This may result in multiple and competing spatial texts, accessible only to a select few. Both Makani codes and commemorative place names could, as Rose-Redwood (2008b) suggests, be read differently by different local and supranational populations. As he notes, "Local communities … are generally far from homogeneous and competing factions may define the 'local' in very different ways" (Rose-Redwood 2008b, 878). Locals or residents with historical knowledge of the city's grid may, for instance, be aware of memorial arenas or historically important place names whereas tourists or migrants new to the city may never even invoke them. Dumbphone users or those lacking mobile technologies of any kind, conversely, may only get exposure to Makani and, by extension, the city's grid, through its physical inscription at every geo-codable location. Those excluded from the augmented realities of smart-mapping technologies may be denied symbolic admittance to the code/spaces Makani numbers designate (Kitchin and Dodge 2011; Masudi 2014). Although dumbphone users can still relay Makani numbers to friends or emergency service providers via text, or over the phone (which still presumes mobile access), those without smart capabilities will likely navigate the grid much differently (and perhaps with greater difficulty) than *smart* users (Vanolo 2013; Al Serkal 2014). This disparity not only highlights the inherent polarization of urban spheres enhanced by smart applications, but it also illuminates one way by which urban space is rationalized into different, exclusionary strata: individuals who can access all spaces, including newly enhanced, digitally mediated locations, those who may have partial admittance to the city's smart grid, and users who are relegated to using an analog version of the city.

Finding "locatable addresses" with Makani

> Soon it will be nearly impossible to get lost in Dubai.
>
> (Zaske 2015)

In addition to diminishing the symbolic value of commemorative place names, Makani identifies spatial objects.[3] Like other geo-addressing systems, Makani transforms difficult-to-identify-or-find places into "locatable addresses" (Rose-Redwood 2012, 299). In particular, Makani makes visible and navigable a number of migrant worker camps, which Kanna (2011, 69) describes as "[i]mprovised or illegitimate dwellings" that "exist in a sort of interstitial space developed neither by the state nor by its allied merchants." Labor camps in Al Muhaisnah, Al Naboodah, and the Lamprell camp in Sonapur, are all encoded with Makani's ten-digit identifiers, thus making them easier than ever to locate. While transforming these camps into codified spatial objects could be read as yet another extension of Makani's efficient civic service, their presence on a government-designed and controlled smart-map can also lead to more advanced and refined forms of technologically led discrimination (Curry, Phillips, and Regan 2004; Rose-Redwood 2012). Dubai's new smart map can thus "open up new areas of the city, previously unknown or effectively unreachable to residents" (Zegras et al. 2015, 125). Zegras et al. (2015, 125) suggest that making these "new areas" could empower local residents to comprehend a city's "spatial potential," but it remains to be seen whether or not Dubai's Makani coordinates will function to include or exclude marginalized populations.[4] Makani's new spatial references might, as Rose-Redwood (2012, 314) suggests, "be mobilized within the centres of calculation to enhance the security mechanisms of the modern state" or succeed in their professed goal of improving in-city navigation.

Makani nevertheless exposes some of the uneven development of ICTs. Graham (2002, 35) suggests that innovations in ICT can lead to the "'disembedding' of dominant economic, social, and cultural activities, and the social and technological distancing of the powerful from the less powerful." "Urban societies," he explains, "become separated into the 'on-line' and the 'offline' in complex tapestries of inclusion and exclusion which work simultaneously at multiple geographical scales" (Graham 2002, 37). This polarization cannot be reduced to a simple connected/disconnected duality; rather, connectivity to ICTs is variegated, shifting, and fraught with contradictions. The world is thus not stratified into those who are plugged in and those who are not, but to what degree people can be plugged in, and in what ways they can access ICTs or, by extension, the city. This re-contouring of the digital divide calls into question previous interpretations of ICTs and connectivity by advancing, instead, the idea that communication through technology occurs horizontally *and* vertically (Graham 2002).

Regardless of Makani's ability to clarify Dubai's confusing grid, the app demonstrates that "the technical itself has a politics which opens the possibility of viewing the realm of the technical as a potential site of democratic struggle and contestation" (Rose-Redwood 2006, 482). Dubai is not a democratic city-state, but Makani is nonetheless promoted to would-be users as a wayfinding tool to improve daily life that also rationalizes urban space into calculable places that become easy to govern, control, and monitor.

Black-boxed worlds: closed-source code, Makani, and the proprietary smart city

Makani uses closed-source software, which means that nobody but its creator (the Government of Dubai) can see or change its underlying code. This may appear banal to most readers, but as source-code for civic apps continues to move towards open data and collaborative platforms, such as government-sponsored app contests (Townsend 2013), Makani's proprietary architecture makes it impossible for users to integrate with or derive any information from the code/spaces in question without having to rely on the app's (extremely limited) interaction model. From the perspective of an end-user (or any well-meaning programmer hoping to extend Makani's underlying system), the only thing to be done with a Makani code is to type it into the Makani app. By comparison, freely available and well-documented geo-locating interfaces like GPS allow users to freely transform, embed, recalculate, and reconfigure navigational data to serve any number of use cases. While Makani's FAQ includes text about the app's interoperability with other mapping platforms (e.g., Google Maps), Dubai's smart visitors and residents have little choice about how navigation will be delivered, and how the technology will order their experiences (Thatcher 2013). As the Director of Dubai Municipality's GIS division explains, "Makani is ... getting great feedback and everyone will be forced—in a positive sense of the word—to use it" (Masudi 2015). Such comments suggest that users will be "forced" to use a world-class government mapping service, but they also expose the political risks of closed-source code. Mandatory use of a spatial identification system facilitates the collection of data from all users, who have little to no detail of the spaces encoded, how Makani codes are designated, what personal information can be read, by whom, who it may be shared with, or (possibly) sold to (Kitchin 2014).

Makani can also facilitate the commodification of urban space. Since Dubai Municipality holds proprietary rights over the application, the Government could ostensibly sell behavioral or personal information collected through the application to a third party if it ever decides to monetize user information. While it is currently impossible to determine what information Dubai Municipality may be collecting through the application, data for sale could range from personal information accessed and stored through the application (such as details from one's address book, or frequently "tapped" Makani numbers) to aggregate data such as transit network usage and real-time traffic information. Though not toponyms, Makani and similar apps redefine Rose-Redwood and Alderman's (2011, 3, italics omitted) notion of the "toponym-as-commodity," wherein data collected through smart geo-addressing software could become commodities for sale in and of themselves. In other words, the code itself, through its outsourcing to third parties, has the capacity to monetize space.

Conclusion

Makani illustrates the growing political role that smart, spatial technology plays in the production and ordering of urban space and how it has the capacity to be enlisted by hyper-entrepreneurial rhetoric now widely discussed by most critical scholars studying Dubai and the Middle East more generally. In Makani's case, spatial identification takes on new entrepreneurial meaning as code produces new instantiations of the "toponym-as-commodity." The identifier itself, based on closed-source and proprietary code produced by the state, could easily be manipulated, rented, or sold for monetary gain should the Government of Dubai choose to do so. Moreover, smart geo-addressing systems like Makani enact new worlds by bringing anything that can be identified as a spatial object online while effacing symbolic values not coded into the application. This striates the city by augmenting realities for "smart" citizens, while reconfiguring or omitting "dumb" users from new, code-produced spaces.

Makani exposes ethical issues pertaining to smart governance and how it facilitates the collection and manipulation of user-generated information. Despite rising interest from scholars on the topic, most governments approach smart technologies with awe and interest (Townsend 2013). Part of the attraction of smart governance is that it can furnish governments with the information necessary to determine which services are being appropriately delivered and how best to increase or improve user access to civic services. Tied to any perceptible benefits of code-led governance are a suite of unanticipated pitfalls that threaten to reconfigure what services *all* residents and visitors can access, how smart technologies change daily practices in the city, and to what effects. This, despite the fact that most governments continue to court smart policy measures in the name of progress, transparency, and improved civic experience (Townsend 2013).

In addition to the Government of Dubai's decision to rename local streets to showcase Dubai's cultural and geographical histories, Makani adds a digital layer to Dubai's existing grid in order to simplify navigation and eradicate the eventual need to utter any place names (Dubai Municipality 2015). While this may appear to offer a much needed solution to a city that has undergone rapid development (Bagaeen 2007), the implementation of a geo-addressing system that relies on smart technology and users to function brings with it some serious questions about urban life, the grid, and how code can alter place-identities, amplify existing disparity, and function as an insidious tool of surveillance for a government already in control (Vanolo 2013). Both Makani and Dubai's commemorative renaming project have yet to be fully phased in and *used* by residents and visitors alike, so it is impossible to draw any conclusions about the effects of two very different uses of spatial identification conventions. The preliminary account offered above, though, identifies the need to bring such discussions about the spatial politics of inscription practices in dialogue with emerging debates about "code/space" and how both can be enlisted by governments hoping to create a "smart" or "intelligent city" (Kitchin and Dodge 2011, 16; also, see Komninos 2002; Townsend 2013). In particular, this chapter has highlighted the growing need to investigate Emirati and Middle Eastern smart geo-addressing practices in order to shed much needed light on how spatial technologies produce, order, and calculate space in non-Western cities. As Dubai, its neighboring Emirates, and cities around the world continue to enlist "smart" tools to rationalize urban space (e.g., what3words), geographers should question the growing role that code plays in the production of a *city-text*. Software, after all, has the capacity to change life and enact new, smart, geo-coded worlds.

Notes

1 Although Alderman (2009, 268) frames internet domain names as the "virtual equivalent of place names" in order to expose the spatial injustices made possible through the manipulation of Internet Domain Names, his study also illustrates a broader need to engage with digital place-naming practices that rationalize space anew.
2 This is the only fully operational terraformed island in Dubai, which is shaped like a palm tree.
3 Not all Makani codes are online yet, but government officials have stated that each "building in Dubai will have a plate with its 10-digit number inscribed on it" (Zaske 2015).
4 In Zegras et al.'s (2015) study, the authors examine paper maps in Dhaka, Bhangladesh.

References

"430 Street Names Renamed in Dubai." (2013). *UAE Interact*, October 21: www.uaeinteract.com/docs/430_streets_renamed_in_Dubai/57766.htm

Acuto, M. (2010). "High-rise Dubai Urban Entrepreneurialism and the Technology of Symbolic Power." *Cities*, 27(4): 272–284.

Acuto, M. (2014). "Dubai in the 'Middle'." *International Journal of Urban and Regional Research*, 38(5): 1732–1748.

Alderman, D. (2009). "Virtual Place Naming, Internet Domains, and the Politics of Misdirection: The Case of www.martinlutherking.org." In L. Berg and J. Vuolteenaho (Eds.), *Critical Toponymies: The Contested Politics of Place Naming* (pp. 267–284), Farnham: Ashgate.

Al Serkal, M. (2014). "Dubai Municipality to Apply New Address System 'Makani' Soon." *GulfNews*, July 22: http://m.gulfnews.com/news/uae/general/duba-municipality-to-apply-new-address-system-makani-soon-1.1362717

Angelidou, M. (2014). "Smart City Policies: A Spatial Approach." *Cities*, 41(S1): S3–S11.

Angelidou, M. (2015). "Smart Cities: A Conjuncture of Four Forces." *Cities*, 47: 95–106.

Azaryahu, M. (1992). "The Purge of Bismarck and Saladin: The Renaming of Streets in East Berlin and Haifa, a Comparative Study in Culture-Planning." *Poetics Today*, 13(2): 351–367.

Azaryahu, M. (1996). "The Power of Commemorative Street Names." *Environment and Planning D*, 14(3): 311–330.

Azaryahu, M. (2011). "The Critical Turn and Beyond: The Case of Commemorative Street Naming." *ACME: An International E-Journal for Critical Geographies*, 10(1): 28–33.

Bagaeen, S. (2007). "Brand Dubai: The Instant City; or the Instantly Recognizable City." *International Planning Studies*, 12(2): 173–197.

Berg, L. and Kearns, R. (2009). "Naming as Norming: 'Race', Gender, and the Identity Politics of Naming Places in Aotearoa/New Zealand." In L. Berg and J. Vuolteenaho (Eds.), *Critical Toponymies: The Contested Politics of Place Naming* (pp. 19–52), Farnham: Ashgate.

Buckley, M. (2013). "Locating Neoliberalism in Dubai: Migrant Workers and Class Struggle in the Autocratic City." *Antipode*, 45(2): 256–274.

Crampton, J., Graham, M., Poorthuis, A., Shelton, T., Stephens, M., Wilson, M., and Zook, M. (2013). "Beyond the Geotag: Situating 'Big Data' and Leveraging the Potential of the Geoweb." *Cartography and Geographic Information Science*, 40(2): 130–139.

Curry, M., Phillips, D., and Regan, P. (2004). "Emergency Response Systems and the Creeping Legibility of People and Places." *The Information Society*, 20(5): 357–369.

Dalton, C. and Thatcher, J. (2015). "Inflated Granulated: Spatial 'Big Data' and Geodemographics." *Big Data & Society*, 2(2): 1–15.

Davis, M. (2007). "Sand, Money and Fear in Dubai." In M. Davis and D. Monk (Eds.), *Evil Paradises: Dreamworlds of Neoliberalism* (pp. 48–68). New York: W.W. Norton.

Dodge, M., Kitchin, R., and Zook, M. (2009). "How Does Software Make Space? Exploring Some Geographical Dimensions of Pervasive Computing and Software Studies." *Environment and Planning A*, 41(6): 1283–1293.

"Dubai Addresses its Need for Directions with Navigation System." (2012). *The National*, December 6: www.thenational.ae/news/uae-news/dubai-addresses-its-need-for-directions-with-navigation-system

Dubai Municipality. (2015) *How to Use Makani App?—English*. [Video file]. May 7: www.youtube.com/watch?v=J1N8N76-R1M

Dubai Smart Gov. (2015). "Dubai Municipality Launches 'Makani' Geographical Location System for Dubai." *Government of Dubai*, April: www.dsg.gov.ae/SiteCollectionImages/Content/DeG%20Documents/April-2015-en.pdf

"Dubai's E-Address System Begins in October" (2015). *WAM*, August 25: www.emirates247.com/news/emirates/dubai-s-e-address-system-begins-in-october-2015-08-25-1.601364

Elsheshtawy, Y. (2008). "Navigating the Spectacle: Landscapes of Consumption in Dubai." *Architectural Theory Review*, 13(2): 164–187.

Elwood, S. (2010). "Geographic Information Science: Emerging Research on the Societal Implications of the Geospatial Web." *Progress in Human Geography*, 34(3): 349–357.

Graham, M. and Zook, M. (2011). "Visualizing Global Cyberscapes: Mapping User-Generated Placemarks." *Journal of Urban Technology*, 18(1): 115–132.

Graham, S. (2002). "Bridging Urban Digital Divides? Urban Polarisation and ICTs." *Urban Studies*, 39(1): 33–56.

Graham, S. (2005). "Software-sorted Geographies." *Progress in Human Geography*, 29(5): 562–580.

"Hamdan Launches Dubai's 'Makani' Location App." (2015). *Wam*, July 5: www.arabiansupplychain.com/article-11276-dubai-streets-renaming-project-continues/

Hoelscher, S. and Alderman, D.H. (2004). "Memory and Place: Geographies of a Critical Relationship." *Social & Cultural Geography*, 5(3): 347–355.

Hollands, R.G. (2008). "Will the Real Smart City Please Stand Up?" *City*, 12(3): 303–320.

Hollands, R.G. (2015). "Critical Interventions into the Corporate Smart City." *Cambridge Journal of Regions, Economy and Society*, 8(1): 61–77.

Jacotine, S. (2015). "Dubai Streets Renaming Project Continues." *ITP Business Publishing Ltd.*,May 8:www.arabiansupplychain.com/article-11276-dubai-streets-renaming-project-continues

Kanna, A. (2011). *Dubai: the City as Corporation*. Minneapolis: University of Minnesota Press.

Kanna, A. (ed.) (2013). *The Superlative City*. Cambridge, MA: Harvard University Press.

Kingsbury, P. and Jones, J.P. (2009). "Walter Benjamin's Dionysian Adventures on Google Earth." *Geoforum*, 40(4): 502–513.

Kitchin, R. and Dodge, M. (2011). *Code/Space*. Cambridge, MA: MIT Press.

Kitchin, R. and Dodge, M. (2014). "The Real-Time City? Big Data and Smart Urbanism." *GeoJournal*, 79(1): 1–14.

Kitchin, R. and Dodge, M. (2015). "Making Sense of Smart Cities: Addressing Present Shortcomings." *Cambridge Journal of Regions, Economy and Society*, 8(1): 131–136.

Komninos, N. (2002). *Intelligent Cities: Innovation*. New York: Routledge.

Lala, A. (2012). "Address System with Street Names Would Help Us—DHL." *ITP Business Publishing Ltd.*, July 12: www.arabiansupplychain.com/article-7756-address-system-with-street-names-would-help-us--dhl/

Leszczynski, A., Wilson, M. (2013). "Theorizing the Geoweb." *GeoJournal*, 78(6): 915–919.

Light, D., Nicolae, I., and Suditu, B. (2002). "Toponymy and the Communist City: Street Names in Bucharest 1948–1965." *GeoJournal*, 56(2): 135–144.

Lin, W. (2013). "Digitizing the Dragon Head, Geo-coding the Urban Landscape: GIS and the Transformation of China's Urban Governance." *Urban Geography*, 34(7): 901–922.

Luque-Ayala, A. and Marvin, S. (2015). "Developing a Critical Understanding of Smart Urbanism?" *Urban Studies*, 52(12): 2105–2116.

Makani. (2015). *Dubai Municipality*. Accessed at: www.makani.ae/desktop/?lang=E

Masudi, F. (2014). "Dubai Buildings to Enable Coordinate Tracking." *Gulf News General*, September 4: http://gulfnews.com/news/uae/general/dubai-buildings-to-enable-coordinate-tracking-1.1380619

Masudi, F. (2015). "Project to Replace Street Numbers with Names Shelved in Dubai." *Al Nisr Publishing, LLC*, May 5: http://gulfnews.com/news/uae/general/project-to-replace-street-numbers-with-names-shelved-in-dubai-1.1505600

"New Street Names to be Phased in for Dubai's Roads." (2012). *InternetCont Ltd.*, November 6: http://dubaimetro.eu/featured/11808/new-street-names-to-be-phased-in-for-dubais-roads

Pacione, M. (2005). "Dubai." *Cities*, 22(3): 255–265.

Rose-Redwood, R. (2006). "Governmentality, Geography, and the Geo-coded World." *Progress in Human Geography*, 30(4): 469–86.

Rose-Redwood, R. (2008a). "From Number to Name: Symbolic Capital, Places of Memory, and the Politics of Street Renaming in New York City." *Social & Cultural Geography*, 9(4): 432–452.

Rose-Redwood, R. (2008b). "'Sixth Avenue is Now a Memory': Regimes of Spatial Inscription and the Performative Limits of the Official City-Text." *Political Geography*, 27(8): 875–894.

Rose-Redwood, R. (2009). "Indexing the Great Ledger of the Community: Urban House Numbering, City Directories, and the Production of Spatial Legibility." In L. Berg and J. Vuolteenaho (Eds.), *Critical Toponymies: The Contested Politics of Place Naming* (pp. 199–225), Fartham: Ashgate.

Rose-Redwood, R. (2012). "With Numbers in Place: Security, Territory, and the Production of Calculable Space." *Annals of the Association of American Geographers*, 102(2): 295–319.

Rose-Redwood, R., and Alderman, D. (2011). "Critical Interventions in Political Toponymy." *ACME: An International E-Journal for Critical Geographies*, 10(1): 1–6.

Sambidge, A. (2014). "Dubai Says Renaming of all Main Streets Completed." *Arabian Business Publishing Ltd.* August 9: www.arabianbusiness.com/dubai-says-renaming-of-all-main-streets-completed-560498.html?service=printer&page=

Shelton, T., Zook, M., and Wiig, A. (2015). "The 'Actually Existing Smart City'." *Cambridge Journal of Regions, Economy and Society*, 8(1): 13–25.

Spivak, G.C. (1993). *Outside in the Teaching Machine.* New York: Routledge.

Thatcher, J. (2013). "Avoiding the Ghetto through Hope and Fear." *GeoJournal*, 78(6): 967–980.

Thrift, N. and French, S. (2002). "The Automatic Production of Space." *Transactions of the Institute of British Geographers*, 27(3): 309–335.

Townsend, A.M. (2013). *Smart Cities: Big Data, Civic Hackers, and the Quest for a New Utopia.* New York: W.W. Norton.

Vanolo, A. (2013). "Smartmentality: The Smart City as Disciplinary Strategy." *Urban Studies*, 51(5): 883–898.

Wilson, M. W. (2014). "Continuous Connectivity, Handheld Computers, and Mobile Spatial Knowledge." *Environment and Planning D: Society and Space*, 32(3): 535–555.

Wilson, M.W., Graham, M. (2013). "Situating Neogeography." *Environment and Planning A*, 45(1): 3–9.

Wippel, S., Bromber, K., Steiner, C., and Krawietz, B. (Eds.) (2016). *Under Construction: Logics of Urbanism in the Gulf Region.* New York: Routledge.

Zaske, S. (2015). "EMEA: Dubai Lays Claim to World's Smartest Map System." *RCR Wireless News*, April 28: www.rcrwireless.com/20150428/europe/emea-dubai-claims-to-have-worlds-smartest-map-system-tag7

Zegras, P.C., Eros, E., Butts, K., Resor, E., Kennedy, S., Ching, A., and Mamun, M. (2015). "Tracing a Path to Knowledge? Indicative User Impacts of Introducing a Public Transport Map in Dhaka, Bangladesh." *Cambridge Journal of Regions, Economy and Society*, 8: 113–129.

Zook, M. and Graham, M. (2007). "The Creative Reconstruction of the Internet: Google and the Privatization of Cyberspace and Digiplace." *Geoforum*, 38(6): 1322–1343.

18 Contemporary issues and future horizons of critical urban toponymy

Reuben Rose-Redwood, Derek Alderman, and Maoz Azaryahu

Critical urban toponymy and the spaces of polyvocality

The naming of streets is a political act, but it is much more than this as well. As the contributions to this book illustrate, street naming is an act of signification that produces a city-text, a form of public commemoration that constitutes places of memory, a medium through which struggles for social justice are materialized, and a performative enactment of sovereign authority over the spatial organization of cities. It is both a political technology of governmentality as well as a taken-for-granted practice of everyday urban life. A seemingly mundane aspect of urban administration, street naming systems also make up the very foundations of urban spatial imaginaries. Naming streets therefore plays an important role in the making of "urban worlds," and the act of street naming is one of the primary means of historicizing space and spatializing history. It is little wonder, then, that political regimes have sought to employ street naming to naturalize their own authority and that the renaming of streets is one of the first acts to accompany political revolutions. Although the agents of sovereign power seek to establish and maintain the urban streetscape as a well-ordered "cosmos," the temporal succession of political regimes often produces urban toponymic spaces that are defined as much by "incoherence, polysemy and heterogeneity" as by any semblance of coherent ideological order (Azaryahu 2011, 30).

Just as the urban streetscape is a heteroglossia of many voices juxtaposed in a common space, so too is the present book a collection of diverse perspectives on a common field of inquiry. This applies just as much to the editorial collective as it does to the chapter contributors. Although the introductory chapter to this book is presented to the reader in a singular voice, its polyvocality shines through when one considers that each of the editors has approached their own scholarship on the politics of street naming from a different viewpoint. Maoz was one of the earliest scholars to examine the politics of street naming during the 1980s, and he has devoted much of his career to exploring the political semiotics of the city-text. Derek came to the field of street naming studies in the 1990s, and his work has been instrumental in calling attention to the urban streetscape as a cultural arena of social justice. Inspired by the work of both Maoz and Derek, Reuben entered the field toward the end of the first decade of the twenty-first century, and he has drawn upon theories of performativity to rethink the power of street naming as a spatial practice. While there are certainly conceptual differences among such approaches, we view these as creative tensions that have the potential to spark synergies across theoretical divides.

Given the polyvocal nature of our collective editorial endeavor, we decided to conclude this book by giving each of the editors a chance to share their own thoughts on the field of critical urban toponymy and what opportunities and challenges lie ahead for future scholarship. In the sections that follow, each of us has selected a recent example of the politics of street naming to provoke critical reflection on the political life of urban streetscapes as an opening to consider contemporary issues and future horizons of urban toponymic scholarship.

Banal commemoration, the written word, and beyond

Maoz Azaryahu

During the summer of 2015, Israeli media widely and almost excessively reported a juicy story involving the name of a small alley in a city at the outskirts of the metropolitan area of Tel Aviv (Hovel 2015). The print and electronic media were busy reporting the revelations about the scandalous activities of the city's mayor, which came to light following a police investigation. Charged with dozens of counts of sexual harassment and corruption, the story that attracted the most media attention was about how the mayor had named an alley after his lover not by her name but by a moniker known to the two lovers only. As it transpired, City Hall approved the name put forward by the mayor without any deliberation or explanation. Public indignation was laced with ridicule. Soon enough the offensive street signs were removed. A year later, in August 2016, the vacancy was filled with the name of Golda Meir, the first woman to serve as Israel's prime minister between 1969 and 1974. With the new street signs, an explicit commemoration replaced an implicit and illicit one, and the moral order reflected in the street signs of a small alley in an Israeli city was seemingly restored.

The source of indignation was the sense that the clandestine naming of an alleyway after the mayor's lover was not a legitimate honorific gesture since it violated the understanding that the commemorative naming of streets should be reserved as a measure of public faming for those who deserve it. The cultural norm in modern democratic societies is that public commemoration is a mechanism for converting reputation into fame. Unwarranted fame, especially when coupled with abuse of power, provokes resentment.

Inscribed on name plates, street signs are trivial in the original sense of the Latin word, *triviālis*, which translates as that which "may be met with anywhere; common, commonplace, ordinary, everyday, familiar, trite" (*Oxford English Dictionary* 2016). Street signs are found everywhere and hence are commonplace. Since they belong to the language of urban space, they are mostly used in ordinary situations and when invested with remembrance, they perform as banal commemorations. Interestingly, academics were slow to realize what officials, activists, and lobbyists of different ideological persuasions and orientations had been amply aware of without any attempt at theoretical grounding—namely, that a street name is also a political resource. Behind the veneer of the trivial and the banal associated with street names as signifiers of location, there is often the possibly contentious politics of symbolic allocation of prestige and glory. Media coverage of street names, and recent academic attention to street naming evinced in publications in prestigious venues, expresses contemporary interest in identity-politics. Concurrently, they also articulate fascination with unmasking the politics woven into the everyday, a fascination which is a by-product of a contemporary Western concern with the ostensible omnipresence of Power.

As an expression of human curiosity, etiological stories about how place names come into existence and what they "really" mean pervade ancient mythologies. The linguistic orientation underlying toponymic studies has focused on the philological analysis of older names. The lack of credible historical records rendered etiological concerns with the reasons behind place naming speculative. Street names, on the other hand, are a feature of urban modernity, and their origin and genealogy are largely well documented. As this edited volume clearly shows, the availability of documentation offers exciting possibilities for a rigorous and fruitful analysis of how, and to what extent, street names are contingent on power relations. It is noteworthy that focusing on (re)naming streets effectively integrates ostensibly old-fashioned etiological concerns into contemporary, theoretically-based and critically-oriented interpretations of urban toponymies.

The politics of urban streetscapes extends beyond street names and naming to also include street signs. Street signs communicate a plethora of additional political messages. Significantly, the authority of official street names is conveyed and communicated by means of "the intense visuality of the written word" in the public domain (Gade 2003, 430). A related issue is the politics of language in multi-lingual societies, evident not only in the choice of toponymic language(s) but also in the hierarchy signified by the geometric arrangement of names on a street sign: "above" and "below" are an expression of power. Graphic design also belongs to the politics of signification. The colors chosen are one thing. In Tel Aviv and Jerusalem, name plates are blue and white to accord with the colors of Israel's national flag. Notwithstanding the seemingly identical form of the street signs in East and West Berlin, the different fonts used in respective parts of the formerly divided city indicated partition; the proliferation of the thicker "western" font in the former East Berlin after reunification implied western hegemony. The design form of a street sign also merits critical consideration. The fact that street signs in Romania's capital city of Bucharest emulate in their design and color the distinct street signs in Paris is a powerful statement about identity and cultural orientation.

When aimed at rewriting the historical narrative inscribed on street signs, renaming streets is an unequivocal expression of power. However, when considering the political life of urban streetscapes, attention should also be accorded to the possible survival of former street names in the names of shops. Such traces of former periods bear witness to the limits of official *damantaio memoriae*. A case in point is the former *Belle-Alliance-Platz* in Kreuzberg, Berlin (Ryan, Foote, and Azaryahu 2016, 151–152). The name was given in 1814 by the

Prussian state to commemorate the victory over Napoleon. In 1886, it also became the name of a pharmacy located there. In 1946, the square was renamed after Franz Mehring, a prominent left-wing historian of the German workers' movement. However, the pharmacy was not renamed, thereby preserving the former name and its Prussian connotations in the streetscape.

The understanding that commemorative street names belong to the symbolic foundations of identity has yielded many useful insights into processes of social formation and the geopolitics of public memory. However, the lure of critical analysis should not divert our attention from some fundamental issues regarding streets and their names that transcend power politics per se. One such issue concerns how place names in general, and street names in particular, partake in the social and individual dynamic of place-making (Foote and Azaryahu 2009). Names are enmeshed in a web of signification that both distinguishes and constitutes places in the geography of culture. As this edited collection demonstrates, naming involves politics. Yet naming is the necessary condition for transforming space into place only. The political economy of place-making transcends place naming.

Street naming, violence, and memory-work

Derek Alderman

On July 13, 2015, Sandra Bland, an African American woman, was found hung to death in a Waller County, Texas, jail cell. She had been arrested after a minor traffic violation (switching lanes with no turn signal) erupted into an argument with the police officer who had stopped her and the subsequent use of excessive force by that officer. Although the death of Bland was ruled a suicide, jail authorities eventually settled a wrongful death lawsuit with her family (Bacon 2016). Coming in the immediate wake of the Charleston, South Carolina, massacre at the Emanuel AME Church and numerous highly publicized instances of police brutality against African Americans, the case of Sandra Bland was a lightning rod for national media attention and the outrage of the Black Lives Matter movement. Protesters argued that the arrest, motivated by racism, should never have happened in the first place and that Bland might still be alive if not for the negligence of her jailers and a law enforcement system long criticized for the disproportionate incarceration of people of color (Alexander 2012).

Street renaming later became an important chapter in the Sandra Bland story. Little more than a month after her tragic death and at the request of demonstrators, the City Council of Prairie View, Texas, voted to rename University Drive as Sandy Bland Parkway. University Drive was the road where Bland had been pulled over and assaulted by police. As a memorial and political statement, the proposed name change became the center of emotionally charged calls for greater racial justice in America, with hundreds of Prairie View A&M University alumni and students marching from the campus down to the site of Bland's arrest and then on to city hall. There were even calls for Chicago—Bland's hometown and a city with its own legacy of racialized police violence—to rename a street for the fallen woman (Solomon 2016). Prairie View Council members said they hoped the street naming would remind "law enforcement to always follow best practices when making [traffic] stops" on the road (Chapin 2016). For some, the renaming had even broader meaning and symbolic power as a means of keeping Bland's name in the public's view and memory. The street renaming became connected to the wider #SayHerName campaign, which highlights the frequently forgotten experiences of black female victims of police brutality.

The making of Sandy Bland Parkway reflects what many contributors to this book recognize. Street naming, as a social and spatial practice, is not an empty gesture; rather, it reflects and projects broader struggles over material relations, political rights, and social power. Prairie View's new street moniker not only memorializes the name and death of one woman, it also locates the roadside victimization that many African Americans fear and face at the hands of the state. Moreover, the Bland Parkway reaffirms a central theme in this volume: street naming has consequences for the distribution of recognition within urban communities and who is remembered in those communities. In an American landscape traditionally consumed with valorizing histories of white male privilege and supremacy, Sandy Bland Parkway represented a corrective to that racialization and gendering of the streetscape—if only temporarily. The renaming will remain in effect for only up to five years without another city council vote. Given recent presidential election politics and the resurgence of hate speech and groups in the United States, one may fear that Bland's namesake will be white-washed away in the not-too-distant future.

It is difficult to know if affixing Bland's name on a road will do all that proponents hope for, partly because of the nation's current racial politics and partly because of the inherent narrative and political limits of street naming as a form of resistance and counter-memory (Alderman 2015). Yet the case of Sandra Bland and the growing number of cases that employ naming as a form of reparation prompt a question not yet fully addressed in critical toponymic studies, both inside and outside the confines of this book. What is the exact relationship between street naming and violence? In other words, what role have urban streetscapes played in marking and even perpetuating histories of injury, trauma, and discrimination? And, conversely, what is the potential for street naming to participate in what Karen Till (2012) calls the "memory-work" of remembering and recovering from past structures of violence and exclusion as well as imagining and materializing more just urban futures?

Analyzing street naming in terms of its complicity in reproducing, and hopefully overcoming, the legacies of violence might put some readers on their heels, but such a perspective is meant to capture the important impact that urban streetscapes have on the psychosocial well-being of people as well as the still under-theorized material and symbolic connections between the "right to name" and the "right to the city." In other words, what exactly is the involvement of street naming in the struggles of subaltern groups not only as they claim, use, and identify with urban spaces but also as they carry out the biopolitics of inhabiting, surviving, and overcoming unequal life chances in the city? Asking such questions is essential to addressing Azaryahu's (2011) important criticism that scholars have failed to fully understand the place-making practices, memory-work, and the accumulated lived experiences and meanings that surround street naming.

Given the violence inherent in settlement and urbanization—from the displacing and genocidal effects of colonialism and imperialism to the more contemporary destructiveness of neoliberal accumulation (Berg 2011)—the naming and claiming of space has always had a close and intimate relationship with violence. While seemingly new to some scholars, this naming–violence nexus has never been lost on those marginalized groups who are the recipients, victims, and sometimes the challengers of these meanings and materialities. Because these unjust patterns of street naming have existed for so many generations, they have taken on the power of becoming an unquestioned norm or habit. While streetscapes inflict trauma in immediate and direct ways, the power of place naming also comes from producing a "slow" or "attritional" violence that wounds how we see and define ourselves to the point that many people, even some members of marginalized groups, are not aware of these effects (Nixon 2011). This violence is especially insidious since it skews how we narrate the past and undermines our ability to root modern inequalities within their historical contexts.

In closing, as critical street naming scholars call for more investigation into the reception of naming among urban residents in their everyday lives, one should not lose sight of those groups with a history of being violently written out of streetscapes. The last thing our scholarship should do is reproduce these injurious silences. Indeed, in developing a socially responsible research agenda for the future, critical toponymic scholars will need to reflect further on the role of their own practices within the politics of street naming and possibly identify opportunities for engaging and assisting public debates and struggles over memory-work.

Envisioning urban toponymic activism beyond the politics of recognition

Reuben Rose-Redwood

On September 15, 2016, a number of prominent street signs in Toronto were officially changed as part of a project to reclaim the indigenous names for places in the city. Although the streets were not formally renamed, honorary signs listing the Anishinaabe name for each place were affixed above the official English settler-colonial street signs. Several years earlier, when the Idle No More movement was in full swing, two Anishinaabe scholar-activists, Susan Blight and Hayden King, posted stickers with the "Indigenous translations of Toronto street names, plastering them over the English signs" (*CBC News* 2016). They started by renaming a section of Queen Street as Ogimaa Mikana, which translates as "Leader's Trail," in honor of "all the strong women leaders of the Idle No More Movement" (Ogimaa Mikana Project 2016). This caught the attention of the local Business Improvement Area, which subsequently led the effort to install officially sanctioned street signs in 2016. In an editorial published in the *Globe and Mail* a month after the street signs were put in place, Blight and King (2016) acknowledged that these "efforts contribute to reinserting indigenous peoples into a landscape historically intent on their erasure." However, they also cautioned that "[t]here is a danger that these gestures become mere performance rather than actively helping to repatriate indigenous land and life."

This example of street name changes brings together a number of important issues that have been raised throughout this book. As Maoz Azaryahu notes above, the political life of urban streetscapes extends not only to the renaming of streets but also to the very design of, and hierarchical ordering of different languages on, systems of street signs. Yet if we focus our attention upon the production and reception of street signs alone, we run the risk of losing sight of how particular histories and peoples have been "violently written out of streetscapes," as Derek Alderman reminds us. It is therefore crucial not to fetishize processes of signification *or* habits of speech in an uncritical fashion but rather to critically interrogate the ways in which the practices of street naming are implicated in the *naturalization* of urban space through the material and symbolic erasure of subjugated knowledges and place-based ontologies.

In this respect, the field of critical toponymy has much to learn from contemporary indigenous resurgence movements and the efforts to reclaim indigenous toponymies. Why so? Because they can help us better understand the limits to the politics of recognition that underpin most discussions of street naming as a form of memory-work. When urban streetscapes are rightly critiqued as spaces of white masculinity, this often leads to a call for more public recognition of racialized groups and women through the naming of streets. I fully acknowledge the importance of these political struggles for recognition within contexts of white supremacist and patriarchical domination. Yet it is important to point out that while such struggles for recognition aim to construct more inclusionary street naming systems, they generally leave the sovereign authority of the state to maintain a monopoly over legitimate naming unquestioned. In other words, we have yet to cut off the king's head in critical toponymic theory. This issue is not merely a philosophical matter but has a pressing sense of political urgency within the context of indigenous struggles for self-determination, because indigenous peoples are increasingly not asking for recognition *from* the settler-colonial authority but are instead affirming their *own* authority to name places following their own customary traditions (Rose-Redwood 2016). This political move takes such struggles beyond the politics of recognition by revalorizing the practices of self-affirmation (Coulthard 2014).

This is precisely what we saw with the Ogimaa Mikana Project discussed above, where stickers with indigenous place names were initially posted on street signs without the approval of city officials. It is tempting to dismiss this as a temporary symbolic gesture and to instead place more emphasis on how these names were eventually granted legitimacy by appearing on official street signs. Yet this narrative plays right into the hands of the settler-colonial state, because it presupposes that the latter possesses the authority to name as a *fait accompli*. However, if we take theories of political performativity seriously, it becomes clear that the power to name does not precede the act of naming itself, just as sovereign power does not pre-exist the performative enactment of sovereignty but rather depends upon the repetitious assertion of political authority (Rose-Redwood and Glass 2014). This has implications not only for studies of indigenous toponymies but for the politics of place naming more generally, because it leads us to question the taken-for-grantedness of the monopoly powers over naming that sovereigns claim to possess. This is particularly important to consider in contexts where there are competing claims to sovereign authority, but it also encourages us to critically re-examine the prosaic assertions of sovereignty over naming that we encounter in our daily lives. And if the sovereign power to name depends upon the reiterative enactment of toponymic practices to sustain its authority, this suggests that the naturalized norms it seeks to legitimate are far more fragile than is often supposed.

How we approach the study of street naming says a lot about our own political persuasions, yet it is surprisingly rare to find self-reflexive accounts of the social and political positionality of scholars themselves within critical toponymic studies. Most accounts of the politics of place naming appear to narrate the struggles over toponymy from seemingly Olympic heights. Yet surely there can be a place for scholar-activism within the field of critical toponymy, since the claim to neutrality in toponymic conflicts has the effect of maintaining existing power assymmetries. The question then becomes: shall we seek to *conserve* existing toponymic regimes, advocate for *reformist* naming policies, or support *insurrectionary* toponymic movements?

The case of the Ogimaa Mikana Project emerged as an insurrectionary reclamation of indigenous toponymies by a pair of scholar-activists but was subsequently transformed into a reformist initiative by the Business Improvement Area. While the greater visibility of indigenous place names in Toronto's streetscape has indeed enhanced the recognition of indigenous toponymies in the city, it has also reinforced the legitimacy of the settler-colonial state, under the auspices of the business community, to authorize the "official" naming of places. All of which leads to the question: how might we envision the political life of urban streetscapes beyond the politics of recognition? Or, put differently: how might we re-imagine the spatial practices of public memory as part of an affirmative politics of urban space that moves beyond the dependency which accompanies the quest for recognition by the sovereign gaze?

Future horizons of critical urban toponymy

The publication of this edited collection marks a significant milestone for the field of critical urban toponymy, since it is the first edited book to focus specifically on the politics of street naming as a subject of interdisciplinary scholarly inquiry. It has been a decade since we first considered the publication of such a book, and, during this time, street naming studies has matured as a field of critical urban scholarship. No longer the purview of onomastic specialists alone, the present volume demonstrates that studies of street naming have much to contribute to historical and contemporary scholarship in the fields of urban politics, cultural landscape studies, and memory studies. Although considerable ground has already been covered over the past three decades, there are new interdisciplinary connections that have yet to be fully explored, and we are hopeful that this book will inspire future studies of the political life of urban streetscapes that extend the horizons of urban toponymic scholarship in new directions.

The field of critical toponymy is currently witnessing a period of theoretical innovation and experimentation. We view the theoretical pluralism of this field as one of its key strengths, but it is also important for such theoretical differences and disagreements to be examined and debated. Given that the prospect of a singular paradigm of critical toponymy achieving hegemonic status will not likely materialize anytime soon, embracing the agonistic ethos of dissensus will surely be more productive than seeking to impose a forced consensus on the field. That being said, there are a number of theoretical avenues and thematic areas that we hope future scholarship will pursue, including: the political economy of urban place naming as a neoliberal strategy of city branding; the use of street naming as a form of urban place-making; emotional and affective geographies of urban toponymy and the reception of place names in everyday life; the role of place naming in the racialization and gendering of urban space; the relation between toponymic erasure, material dispossession, and violence; the reclamation of indigenous toponymies; and the virtual life of street naming in online digital environments, among other themes.

In methodological terms, archival and cartographic research methods have long been indispensable to urban toponymic scholarship and will likely remain essential resources well into the future. However, the methodological toolkit of critical toponymy has now expanded to include an assortment of qualitative methods, from semi-structured interviews to ethnographic techniques, and there is even potential for recent developments in critical quantitative geography to make important contributions to the field as well. The in-depth case study approach has proven to be a particularly fruitful method for teasing out the nuances of toponymic politics, and while broader meta-level typologies and general frameworks are important as efforts of synthesis, the empirical richness of the case study approach will necessarily continue to be a mainstay of critical toponymic research. One methodological area which we have barely scratched the surface of is how the politics of place naming is playing out in the virtual spaces of social media, which are now just as much a part of the archival record as conventional governmental archives. Such new virtual arenas of social and political life provide a treasure trove of multi-media materials for future toponymic studies, including video recordings of official street naming ceremonies, personal commentaries, and even comedy sketches related to place name changes.

The theoretical and methodological developments in critical toponymy over the past three decades have greatly enhanced our understanding of the political life of urban streetscapes. Yet pressing questions must continuously be raised anew if the field of critical toponymy is to have any relevance in the world of contemporary urban politics. Most importantly, what is the "political life" of critical toponymic scholarship itself? How is toponymic scholarship being employed in public discourse, and what political interventions ought we to make in current political struggles over place naming? The answers to these questions will differ from one scholar to the next, but if the critical turn in toponymic studies has taught us anything, it is surely that we can't afford to remain neutral as the "life" of spatial politics is unfolding in the streets all around us.

References

Alderman, D. (2015). "Naming Streets, Doing Justice? Politics of Remembering, Forgetting, and Finding Surrogates for African American Slave Heritage." In S. Choo (Ed.), *Geographical Names as Cultural Heritage* (pp. 193–228). Seoul: Kyung Hee University Press.

Alexander, M. (2012). *The New Jim Crow: Mass Incarceration in the Age of Colorblindness.* New York: The New Press.

Azaryahu, M. (2011). "The Critical Turn and Beyond: The Case of Commemorative Street Naming." *ACME: An International E-Journal for Critical Geographies*, 10(1): 28–33.

Bacon. J. (2016). "Sandra Bland's Family Settles Wrongful Death Case for $1.9M." *USA Today*, September 15: www.usatoday.com/story/news/nation/2016/09/15/sandra-blands-family-reportedly-settles-wrongful-death-case-19m/90400160/

Berg, L. (2011). "Banal Naming, Neoliberalism, and Landscapes of Dispossession." *ACME: An International E-Journal for Critical Geographies*, 10(1): 13–22.

Blight, S. and King, H. (2016). "Naming is a Good Start—But We Need to Do More for Reconciliation." *Globe and Mail*, October 17: www.theglobeandmail.com/opinion/naming-is-a-good-start-but-we-need-to-do-more-for-reconciliation/article32373624

CBC News. (2016). "New Street Signs Put Toronto's Indigenous History Front and Centre." September 20: www.cbc.ca/news/canada/toronto/new-street-signs-put-toronto-s-indigenous-history-front-and-centre-1.3771548

Chapin, J. (2016). "Texas City Names Road after Sandra Bland." *USA Today*, August 26: www.usatoday.com/story/news/nation/2015/08/26/sandra-bland-boulevard-texas/32409847/

Coulthard, G. (2014). *Red Skin, White Masks: Rejecting the Colonial Politics of Recognition.* Minneapolis: University of Minnesota Press.

Gade, D. (2003). "Language, Identity and the Scriptorial Landscape in Quebec and Catalonia." *Geographical Review*, 93(4): 428–448.

Foote, K. and Azaryahu, M. (2009). "Sense of Place." In R. Kitchin and N. Thrift (Eds.), *International Encyclopedia of Human Geography* (10: pp. 96–100). Oxford: Elsevier.

Hovel, R. (2015). "Former Or Yehuda Mayor Who Named a Street After a Lover Indicted." *Haaretz*, July 15: www.haaretz.com/israel-news/.premium-1.666073

Nixon, R. (2011). *Slow Violence and the Environmentalism of the Poor*. Cambridge, MA: Harvard University Press.

Ogimaa Mikana Project. (2016). "Ogimaa Mikana: Reclaiming/Renaming": http://ogimaamikana.tumblr.com

Oxford English Dictionary. (2016). "Trivial." Oxford: Oxford University Press.

Rose-Redwood, R. (2016). "'Reclaim, Rename, Reoccupy': Decolonizing Place and the Reclaiming of PKOLS." *ACME: An International E-Journal for Critical Geographies*, 15(1): 187–206.

Rose-Redwood, R. and Glass, M. (2014). "Geographies of Performativity." In M. Glass and R. Rose-Redwood (Eds.), *Performativity, Politics, and the Production of Social Space* (pp. 1–34). New York: Routledge.

Ryan, M., Foote, K., and Azaryahu, M. (2016). *Narrating Space/Spatializing Narrative: Where Narrative Theory and Geography Meet.* Columbus: Ohio State University Press.

Solomon, D. (2016). "The Street Where Sandra Bland Was Pulled Over Has Been Renamed After Her." *Texas Monthly*, August 26: www.texasmonthly.com/the-daily-post/the-street-sandra-bland-was-pulled-over-has-been-renamed-sandra-bland-blvd/

Till, K. (2012). "Wounded Cities: Memory-work and a Place-Based Ethics of Care." *Political Geography*, 31(1): 3–14.

Author name index

Abu-Lughod, J. 211
Acuto, M. 291, 294, 301
Adamczewski, J. 126
Adebanwi, W. 15–6, 17, 18, 220
Ainiala, T. 75
Alderman, D. 1, 2, 3, 5, 6–7, 11, 12, 17, 18, 42, 79, 99, 100, 100–1, 115, 116, 133, 146, 147n2, 150, 151, 152, 161, 168, 171, 185, 189, 195, 203, 212, 219–20, 242, 254, 256, 261, 262, 264, 274, 275, 282, 286, 291, 292, 293, 296, 304, 305n1, 309, 313, 315
Alexander, M. 312
Allen, M. 285
Al Serkal, M. 302
Anderson, B. 83, 116
Angelidou, M. 292
Anson, J. 204
Areff, A. 233
Arendt, H. 28
Argenbright, R. 117
Aristotle 38
Árvay, A. 102, 117
Ashworth, G. J. 83
Assmann, J. 116
Atkinson, D. 152
Austin, J.L. 15, 25–6
Azaryahu, M. 1, 2, 5, 6, 7, 8, 9–10, 10, 11, 17, 18, 28, 58, 70, 72, 74, 76, 79, 80, 81, 82, 84, 86, 88, 89, 91, 93, 99, 100, 102, 105, 106, 114, 115, 116, 122, 123, 124, 126, 133, 134, 135, 135–6, 146, 147n1, 147n2, 150, 151, 152, 159, 161, 162, 168, 169, 170, 185, 186, 188, 189, 190, 191, 192, 195, 202, 203, 212, 219, 220, 221, 223, 230, 233, 234, 256, 275, 291, 293, 295, 298, 300, 309, 312, 314, 315

Bácskai, V. 104
Baesjou, R. 202

Bagaeen, S. 291, 294, 304
Baker, A. 116
Bakša, Z. 159
Bar-Gal, Y. 4
Batchelor, S. 265, 266
Bawumia, M. 203, 204
Beall, J. 224, 229
Beavon K. 224
Beevor, A. 81
Bell, J. 133, 185
Benjamin, W. 19, 28
Berg, L. 1, 3, 6, 7, 10, 13, 15, 42, 75, 78, 79, 115, 116, 133, 152, 185, 191, 195, 222, 259, 261, 299, 300, 314
Bernstein, E. 285
Bigon, L. 10, 11, 17, 18, 41, 202, 204, 209, 210, 220
Biti, V. 157
Black, K. 12
Bodnár, E. 92, 102, 103, 104, 105, 107
Boia, L. 188
Boone, C. 263, 268
Borneman, J. 171
Boros, G. 108
Bourdieu, P. 18–9, 134, 135, 252–3, 274, 276
Boyd, H. 283
Brandt, Willy 58
Brodnjak, V. 155
Bromberg, A. 263
Broszat, M. 119
Browne, J. 284
Brown, K. 171, 224, 231
Buckley, C. 43, 46, 47
Buckley, M. 294, 298
Bullard, R. 263
Burleigh, M. 119, 120, 121, 122, 124
Burrows, E. 277, 279
Burzyńska, A. 154
Butler, J. 1, 15, 248, 255

Bylina, V. 187, 194, 197
Byrnes, G. 42

Caliendo, G. 261, 262
Carlos, J. 220
Carroll, A. 283
Çelik, Z. 1
Chapin, J. 313
Chavez, R. 203
Christopher, A.J. 218
Chwalba, A. 120
Coetser, A. 223
Coetzee S. 203
Cohen, A. 48
Cohen, B. 41
Colgate, A. W. 279–80
Colomb, C. 86, 90
Colton, T. 137
Connerton, P. 116
Cooper, A. 203
Cosgrove, D. 4, 152
Coulthard, G. 315
Cousin, J. 9, 10
Coutinho, C. N. 76
Crang, M. 154
Crankshaw, O. 224, 229
Creţan, R. 3, 16, 80, 199
Creuzberger, S. 132
Csepeli, G. 106
Curry, M. 293, 302
Czepczyński, M. 83, 90, 152, 160, 185

Dahamshe, A. 10, 41
Dalmacija, S. 182n6, 182n9
Dalton, C. 292, 298–9
Darnton, R. 250
Davie, L. 230
Davies, N. 119, 123, 126
Davis, M. 291, 298
Day, R. 263
Deane, J. 219
Dean, M. 220, 235
de Certeau, Michel 180–1, 182n11, 196
de Haas, Mary 226
Derrida, J. 15
De Soto, H. G. 75, 84, 88, 89, 92, 195, 197
Dizdar, Z. 159
Dodge, M. 291, 292, 299, 301, 305
Domański, B. 124
Donia, R. 173
Drozdzewski, D. 17, 18, 116, 117, 185
Duminy, J. 14, 16, 17, 18, 42, 223
Duncan, J. 2–3, 4

Duncan, N. 2–3
Dunn, K. 115, 259, 262, 263–4
Dwyer, O. J. 3, 8, 11, 92, 151, 152, 242, 254, 261, 275

Ebert, F. 60–1, 61
Edkins, J. 116
Edozien, F. 278
Eick, V. 88
Elsheshtawy, Y. 294, 298
Elwood, S. 293, 297
Emmerson, D. 42
Engelstoft, S. 133, 179, 182n8
Entrikin, J.N. 15
Enzensberger, H.M. 30
Esaulov, I.A. 161

Faraco, G. 220
Faraco, J. 5
Farvacque-Vitkovic, C. 203, 214
Favro, D. 1
Feeney, S. 278
Feirstein, S. 277
Feischmidt, M. 110
Femia, Joseph 77
Ferguson, P. 5, 8, 19, 99
Ferro, M. 124
Finkelman, P. 283
Firmstone, H.W. 44–5, 45, 47, 48, 49, 52
Fishman, D. 279
Flierl, T. 27, 29
Foote, K. 8, 86, 99, 102, 108, 117, 152, 159, 312
Forest, B. 117, 152, 187, 189, 275
Forty, A. 178
Foucault, M. 220–1, 222, 235
French, S. 290, 291, 292, 293

Gabbard, D. 266
Gade, D. 311
Galasiński, K. 119, 126, 127
Garcilazo, M. 278
Gargan, E. 278
Geiger, V. 159
Gerõ, A. 104
Getz, A. 221
Giliomee, H. 253
Gill, G. 10, 91, 114, 126, 133, 142, 145, 169, 185, 187, 189, 195
Gillis, J. 99
Giraut, F. 2, 7, 11, 13, 80, 218, 219, 220, 221, 222, 223, 224
Glass, M. 14, 316
Goble, P. 197

Godin, L. 203
Goerg, O. 209
Goldstein, I. 158
Goldstone, C. 218
Gorbachevich, K.S. 147n3
Goren, T. 59
Graham, M. 291, 292, 297, 298, 299
Graham, S. 291, 294, 302–3
Gramsci, A. 18, 75, 76–80, 82, 86, 89, 90,
    90–1, 91, 92–3
Gregory, D. 152, 154
Gregson, N. 255
Gricanov, A. 159
Gross, D. 270
Gross, J. 122
Guyot, S. 185, 223, 242
Gyáni, G. 104

Haberman, C. 278
Hackle, A. 269
Hagen, J. 127, 264
Hajdú T. 107
Halbwachs, M. 4
Hamadeh, Sh. 215n6
Harding, L. 196, 197
Harvey, D. 4
Harwood, J. 43
Haughton, H. 49, 51, 52
Haushofer, Karl 120
Hebbert, M. 1, 115
Hellberg-Hirn, E. 132, 136, 143, 146
Henkin, D. 277
Henry, D. 270
Hercus 12
Hill, T. 219
Hitler, A. 120
Hobrack, V. 89
Hobsbawm, E. 122
Hodgkin, K. 169–70
Hoelscher, S. 275, 293
Hollands, R.G. 291, 292, 297, 301
Home, R. 207, 208
Honecker, E. 65
Hook, D. 152
Houssay-Holzschuch, M. 2, 4, 7, 11, 13,
    80, 218, 219, 220, 221, 222, 223, 224
Hovel, R. 310
Hromadžić, A. 172
Hrytsak, Y. 133
Hrženjak, J. 153, 156, 161
Huggins, R. 265
Huyssen, A. 89, 90

Ingersoll, R. 1

Inwood, J. 3, 7, 12, 17, 18, 79, 115, 189,
    195, 263, 267

Jackson, J. 283
Jacotine, S. 299, 300
Jaffe 13
Jenkins, E. 222–3, 223, 224, 226
Joenniemi, P. 132–3, 143
Johnson, G. 263, 267
Johnson, J. 117, 152, 153, 187, 189, 275
Johnson, N. 115
Johnson, R. 76
Jones, J.P. 291, 297
Jones, R. 10
Judt, T. 125

Kaiser, M. 132
Kaiser, R. 85
Kang, P. 169
Kanna, A. 291, 294, 298, 302
Kansteiner, W. 180
Karadžić, V. 155
Katz, C. 154
Kearns, R. 3, 6, 15, 42, 152, 191, 195, 259,
    261, 299, 300
Khablo, E.P. 147n3
Khumalo, F. 234
King, A. 207, 209
King, M.L. Jr. 267, 269
Kingsbury, P 291, 297
Kitchin, R. 291, 292, 299, 301, 303, 305
Klemenèić, M. 154–5
Kligman, G. 185
Kliot, N. 41, 169
Kluczewski, M. 122, 123
Komninos, N. 292, 305
Kong, L. 115
Kook, R. 152
Koopman, A. 219, 225, 226
Koselleck, R. 25
Kožarić, I. 153, 156
Krausnick, H. 119
Kubinyi, A. 104
Kundera, M. 56–7

Lacan, J. 101
Laclau, E. 18, 76, 98, 101, 110
Lacombe, P. 4, 9, 10
Ladd, B. 81, 88, 89, 90
Laing, A. 221
Lala, A. 294, 295
Lanchester, H.V. 208
Lee, D. 278
Lee, K. 46

Lefebvre, H. 87
Legg, S. 154
Leith-Ross, S. 208
Leitner, H. 169
Lemanski, C. 224
Leroux, H. 203
Lessing, D. 206
Leszczynski, A. 294
Levinson, S. 99–100
Light, D. 1, 2, 3, 6, 7, 8, 10, 11, 14, 16, 17,
    18, 80, 90, 92, 109, 122, 124, 133, 136,
    137, 151, 152, 161, 169, 171, 179, 185,
    188, 189, 195, 196, 197, 220, 291, 293
Lindroos, K. 99
Lin, W. 291, 293
Lóderer, B. 107
Longworth, T. 277–8
Lotman, Y. 150, 151, 154, 162
Lowenthal, D. 4
Lugard, F. D. 207–8, 215n3
Lukowski, J. 119
Luque-Ayala, A. 292, 293, 301

Mabanckou, A. 203
Mabin, A. 207
Mac Aodha, B. 152
Mach, Z. 153
McIntyre, J. 243, 245
McRobbie, A. 91
Maharaj, B. 219
Makepeace, W. 51
Mak, L. 48
Malcolm, N. 176
Mannteufel, J. 132
Mansfield, Y. 169
Marin, A. 17, 18, 80, 92, 132, 185, 187,
    189, 195
Marjomäki, H. 87
Markowski, M.P. 154
Martin, L. 271
Marvin, S. 292, 293, 301
Massey, D. 1, 11, 19, 171, 274
Masudi, F. 295, 300–1, 301, 303
Matsubara, K. 11
Matthews, P. 3, 16, 80
Mattingly, M. 215n1
Mayell, P. 152
Mbembe, A. 208, 218
Mellins, T. 279
Mencken, H.L. 4
Merrill, S. 90
Merriman, P. 10
Mevius, M. 84, 86
Miles, J.C. 9

Milo, D. 4–5, 27, 32
Moníková, L. 28
Monmonier, M. 12
Morin, K. 13
Morozov, V. 132, 143, 146
Moscow, H. 275–6
Mouffe, C. 18, 76, 98, 101, 102
Muhajir A. 208
Murphyao, A. 12
Murphy, M. 5, 220
Murray, J. 80, 83, 86, 133, 136, 138,
    147n4
Muzaini, H. 171
Myburgh, J. 253
Myers, G. 5, 15, 19, 152, 195, 196, 203,
    208, 220, 222

Nada, S. 7
Nagy, L. 104
Namaz, N. 265
Närhi, E.M. 28
Nash, C. 11, 185
Ndletyana, M. 223, 228, 231
Nel, E. 219
Neuwirth, R. 279
Ngozo, A. 232
Nicolae, I. 3, 122, 124, 137, 152, 188, 291,
    293
Niculescu-Mizil, A-M. 92
Nietzsche, F. 128
Nikitenko, G. Y. 80
Nixon, R. 314
Njoh, A. J. 17, 41, 202, 203, 204, 206, 214
Nora, P. 4
Norval, A. 98
Nyyssönen, H. 106, 107

Ochman, E. 126
Oèak, I. 153, 156
Olsen, J. B. 83, 84, 86, 90
Orgeret, K. 223, 226, 227
Orttung, W. 132, 138
Osofsky, G. 283
Ó Tuathail, G. 120

Paasi, A. 85, 133
Pacione, M. 294
Palmberger, M. 17, 18, 169, 171, 172, 174,
    180, 181
Palonen, E. 3, 10, 11, 17, 18, 102, 103,
    104, 108, 110, 142, 150, 152, 161, 162,
    169, 185, 189, 198, 223
Palonen, K. 1, 5, 15, 17, 18, 19, 25, 26, 27,
    100, 150

Papritz, J. 119
Parkhurst-Ferguson, P. 134
Parnell, S. 224, 229
Passerini, L. 171
Patel, K. 219, 234
Pavlu, R. 122, 123
Pekonen, O. 35
Peteet, J. 12
Philipsen, D. 87
Phillips, D. 293, 302
Pinchevski, A. 3, 134, 152
Pirie, G. 44
Pobrić, A. 152
Pobric, A. 133, 179, 182n8
Poon, L. 13
Poór, J. 104
Porter, B. 122
Pótó, J. 105
Pred, A. 5, 9
Pribersky A. 108
Purcell, M. 263, 268
Pusch, L.F. 32
Puzey, G. 17, 18, 78, 80

Quindlen, A. 284

Ráday, M. 103, 104, 105
Radstone, S. 169–70
Raento, P. 264
Raja-Singam, S. 45, 51
Ranzal, E. 278
Raper, P. 222
Raulin, A. 277, 282
Rawls, J. 263
Regan, P. 293, 302
Regier, A. 19
Rhea, J. 282
Rich, N. 119, 120
Ricoeur, P. 171
Rihtman-Auguštin, D. 158, 169
Roberts, S. 278, 284
Robinson, D. 41
Robinson, G. 133, 152, 179, 182n8
Rogers, D. 269
Rose, G. 254, 255
Rosenthal, G. 171
Rose-Redwood, R. 1, 2, 3, 7, 8, 9, 11, 12,
   13, 14, 17, 18, 19, 42, 75, 79, 80, 92,
   100, 110, 115, 116, 133, 135, 146,
   147n2, 150, 152, 161, 168, 171, 185,
   186, 195, 197, 203, 212, 218, 219–20,
   220, 251, 256, 259, 265, 268, 290, 291,
   292, 293, 294, 295, 298, 300, 301, 302,
   302–3, 304, 309, 315, 316

Said, E.W. 151, 154
Šakaja, L. 3, 7, 11, 17, 18, 92, 153, 157,
   162
Sambidge, A. 299
Sänger, J. 82, 84, 85, 90, 93n2
Saparov, A. 86, 133
Sappok, G. 119, 120–1, 122
Sauer, C. 4
Saunders, A. 87
Saunders, C. 253
Schechner, R. 1
Schein, R. 259, 267
Schlemmer, L. 253
Schulz zur Wiesch, L. 90
Schuman, H. 171
Scobey, D. 279, 282
Scott, J. 171, 250
Seethal, C. 185, 223, 242
Sekulić, D. 155
Sereda, V. 133
Sharp, J. 115
Shelton, T. 293
Shortridge, J.R. 4
Shoval, N. 16, 186, 191, 195, 196
Shumake, D. 270
Sibley, D. 152, 154
Sidaway, J. 152
Siegel, J. 278
Silberman, M. 117
Simmons, D. 269, 270
Sindalovskij, N.A. 147n3
Šišić, F. 158
Skelton, D. 232
Skinner, Q. 25, 27
Skowronek, D. 126, 127
Slavuj, L. 153, 162
Smith, A. 155
Smith, D. 223
Smith, J. 110
Snyder, T. 89
Soja, E. 221, 260, 263
Song, O. 51
Spann, E 277
Spell, L. 266
Spivak, D. L. 145
Spivak, G.C. 291
Srkulj, S. 158
Stanić, J. 3, 7, 11, 17, 18, 92, 153, 162
Stanisława-Adamczewska, T. 126
Stavrakakis, Y. 101
Stern, R. 215n1, 279
Stewart, George 4, 275
Stiperski, A. 127
Stiperski, Z. 92

Stojanović, D. 170
Suditu, B. 3, 122, 124, 137, 152, 188, 291, 293
Susak, V. 133
Swart, M. 12, 169, 185, 220, 223, 233, 234

Tantner, A. 9
Tassin, J. 47
Taylor, M. 283
Tenžera, M. 158
Terho, O. 28
Thale, C. 9
Thatcher, J. 292, 294, 298, 299, 303
Therborn, G. 92
Thomas, P. D. 76
Thrift, N. 290, 291, 292, 293
Till, K. 117, 152, 161, 171, 179, 189, 275, 313
Tilove, J. 262
Todes, A. 241
Todorova, M. 151, 156
Tonkin, E. 171
Topalov, Ch. 209
Topalović, D. 154–5
Torgovnik, E. 3, 134, 152
Torsti, P. 173, 174
Tóth, Á. 102, 108, 117
Townsend, A.M. 292, 303, 304, 305
Tucker, B. 3, 7
Tunbridge, J. E. 83
Turner, N. 227
Tyner, J. 267

Ugarković, S. 153, 156
Ugrešić, D. 169
Uspensky, B. 151, 154, 162
Užarević, J. 151

Vakhrusheva, A. 196
Vanolo, A. 294, 298, 302, 305
Vendina, O. 145
Verdery, K. 1, 75, 89, 185, 188

Vetters, L. 182n10
von Henneberg, K. 99
Vuolteenaho, J. 1, 2, 3, 7, 10, 17, 18, 42, 75, 78, 79, 80, 115, 116, 133, 152, 185

Walker, G. 263
Wallace, M. 277, 279
Wanjiru, M.W. 11
Ward, J. 117
Watson, C. 264
Weber, M. 18, 26, 28
Weitz, E. D. 83
Whelan, Y. 185
White, J. 266
Wieliński, B. T. 90
Wiig, A. 293
Williams, R. 76
Wilson, M. 294
Winchester, H. 115
Wines, M. 223, 225, 226, 227
Wintz, C. 283
Wippel, S. 294
Withers, C.W.J. 152
Woodman, P. 12
Wren, Ch. 208
Wright, J. 4

Yarwood, J. 182n7
Yeoh, B. 5, 17, 18, 52, 100, 152, 171, 185, 196, 205, 220
Young, C. 1, 2, 7, 8, 11, 14, 16, 17, 18, 80, 90, 92, 109, 124, 136, 161, 171, 179, 195, 196, 197

Zamoyski, A. 119
Zaske, S. 296, 301, 302, 305n3
Zawadzki, H. 119
Zegras, P.C. 291, 302, 305n4
Zeidel, R. 12
Zelinsky, W. 4
Žižek, S. 157
Zook, M. 291, 292, 293, 297, 298, 299

Subject index

Page numbers in **bold** refer to figures, page numbers in *italic* refer to tables.

African Americans 6–7, 12–3, 18, 259–71, 282–6, 312–3; women 282–3
African National Congress 224, 226, 240, 242, 243, 245, 248, 253, 254
AfriForum 232
Alexander I, Czar 33, **33**–4
Alexander the Great 9
Alexandria 9
Alliance of Croatian Anti-Fascist Fighters 153
Anglophone hegemony 4
Antioch 9
Aotearoa 6, 42
Art of Forgetting, The (Forty) 179
Ashdown, Paddy 177
authority, legitimization 8–9, 115
autobiographical memory 171, 181
automatic production of space 292
auto-referencing 151, 152, 157–8
Avanti! 77–8, 108
Azaryahu 2–3
Aztecs 41

Balkans, the 156–7
Belarus 187
Belgian Congo 209
Belgrade 170
belonging 252; and identity 261; politics of 259–71; right to appropriate 263, 263–8; right to participate 260, 263, 268–71; spatiality of 260; spatial strategies 261–2
Berkeley School 4
Berlin 29, 74; 1945–1948 58; *Belle-Alliance-Platz* 311–2; division of 59, 60, **60**, 80; German Empire (Kaiserreich) 57; Gramscian approach 90–1; Independent Commission for

Street Name Changes 88–9; liberation of 81; pluralized namescape 90–1; post-socialist 87–93; reunification 72; Third Reich 58, 60, 63–4, 81; Weimar Republic 57; *see also* East Berlin; West Berlin
Berlin Wall 87
biopolitics 313
Black Lives Matter movement 12, 312
Bland, Sandra 312–3
Blight, Susan 314–5
borders 154–5
Bosnia and Herzegovina, renaming policy 168–81, 181n1
Bosniaks 172–3, 173, 177, 178, 179–80
boundary-making 5, 18, 132–46, 154; temporal 132–3
Bucharest 16, 124, 179, 188, 189, 190, 191, 192, 193, **193**, **194**, 196, 197, 311
Budapest 18, 98–111, 150; commemorative street names 105, 109–10, *110*; German Occupation Memorial 109; Interwar period 104–5; metropolitan growth 103–4; postcommunist 107–11, *110*; renaming 98, 103, 106, 107–11; socialist period 105–7; street naming revolutions 98, 103

Caesarea 9
Cameroon 203, 205–6, **206**, 211–4, **213**
Cape Town 224, 227–9
captured territory, renaming 169–70
catharsis-type renaming 137
Ceaușescu, Nicolae 188
challenging 225
circulatory flows 1
cities, naming 9

citizenship: cultural 268; distibution of 264; politics of 259
city-text 2–3, 19, 29, 133–5, 256, 309; definition 150; ideal configuration 151; rewriting 136; role 150–1; smart 292–5; spatial codification 150–63
city-text analysis 7–11; Budapest 98–111; narrative structure 8
city workers 192
civil renaming 250
Civil Rights Movement (US) 260, 261, 262
civil society 76
class power 17–8
cleansing 225, 228
clerical names 30, 31
coded worlds 292
Cold War 86
collective memory 219–20
colonialism 5, 10, 218, 314
colonial urban order 17, 41–54; commemorative street names 45; counter-toponymics 50–3, 53–4; municipal street names 49–50; public health 44, 52; and race 46–8; street naming policies 42–3, 43–4; street naming process 44, 51; street naming rationales 44–6; surveillance 52
Columbus, C. 41
commemorations, lifespan of 59–60
commemorative choice 116
commemorative rehabilitation 70
commemorative spaces 287
commemorative street names 5, 6, 8–9, 9–10, 18, 28, 31, 32, 99, 170, 276, 311–2; African American women 285–6; Budapest 105, 109–10, *110*; choice 116; colonial 45; contestation and resistance 248–51; Dubai 299–302; explicit 310; Haifa **68**; Helsinki 34, 36, 36–7; location 260; Martin Luther King, Jr. 259–71; Mostar 175–6; New York 282–5, *283*, 285–6, 286–7; politics of 260; renaming 56, 57, 68–9; Singapore 49; spatial injustices 259–71; symbolic prestige 245–8
commercialization 268
compensatory naming 29
Confederate States of America 14
contemporaneous plurality 1
contestation 195–7, 248–51, 255
contested spatial practice 116
contingency 98
continuity, toponymic 185–99

control 76
counter-insubordination 251–4
counter-toponymics 19, 50–3, 53–4
critical urban toponymy, future of 316–8
Croatia 174; anti-Fascist legacy 156; auto-referencing 157–8; geopolitical code 154–5; othering 155–7; unresolved meanings 159–62; Vukovar 162–3; World War II heritage 159–60
Croats 172–3, 173–4, 178, 179–81
cult names 82–4
cultural arena 3, 11, 16, 19
cultural capital 274
cultural citizenship 268
cultural geography 4, 9
cultural hegemony 76
cultural indicators 4
cultural landscape studies 4
cultural mediators 76
cultural memory 115, 115–7
cultural power 260
cultural signification 202
Cyprus 169

Dakar 210, **210**
Dayton Peace Agreement 168
decanonization 31
decolonization 211
decommemoration 10, 57, 61, 66–7, 74, 78, 137, 139, 168, 299–302
digital mapping 292
discourse theory 98, 99, 100–1
discrimination 260, 261, 267
discursive elements 98
discursive methods 134
discursive political change 100
discursive sets 101
discursive strategies 180
discursive tactics 181
discursive universe 100–2
dispositif 220, 235
distributive injustices, right to appropriate 263–8
distributive justice 263
Dubai 19; commemorative street names 299–302; Dubai Municipality 290; geo-addressing 294–5; hyper-entrepreneurialism 291, 304; labor camps 302; Makani geo-address system 290–305; Makani numbers 290, 291, 300–2, 304; renaming 300–1, 304; smart city-text 292–5; spatial nomenclature 294; spatial regime of inscriptions 291

Durban 16, 42, 218, 224, 225–7, **227**;
approved name changes 245–6; civil
renaming 250; clean-up campaign 240;
colonial history 243, 245; contestation
and resistance 248–51, 255–6;
counter-insubordination 251–4; Group
Areas Act of 1950 241; renaming 218,
224, 225–7, **227**, 240–56, **244**, **247**;
renaming process 243, 245–8, 251–2;
segregation 241; transformation
discourse 253–4; vandalism 240–1, 250
Durban City Council 226–7

East Berlin 5, 18, 57, 74–5, 106; Cold War
86; commemorative rehabilitation 70;
creation of 59, **60**; cult names 82–4;
decommemoration 61, 66–7; division of
86–7; Festival of Youth and Students,
1951 64–5; folk heroes 84–5; Gramscian
approach 75, 86, 87, 91; historical
background 57–8; intra-national bonds
84–5; Nazi names purged 63–4, 81;
objectives 71; political-odonymic
identity 86; post-socialist 87–93;
pressures and incentives 63–5;
propaganda 85, 86; Prussian names
commemorative rehabilitation 70;
recommemoration 67; renaming 60–2,
63–5, 69–70, 71–2, 80–91, 135;
renaming of the monarchic past 64, 67;
renaming patterns 66–7; street naming
policy 29, 63–4, 80–91; street signs 311;
un-renamed streets 86–7; *see also* Berlin
Ehrenström, J.A. 33, 34
Elwood 292
empowerment 302
empty signifiers 101
Engel, C.L 33, 34
equality 260
Eurocentric lexicons 203–6, 205
European Union 155
European Union Administration, Mostar
176–7
everyday life 185; performative space
14–6, 18; and toponymic continuity
195–7, 199
everyday, the 115
exclusion 37; politics of 173–8; spaces of
291
exercitives 25–6

Farrer, R.J. 53
female names 13, 285–6
feminism 13

feminist naming culture 32
Finland 32–8, 39
folk heroes 84–5
forenames, use of 34
founding 225, 229
France 4–5; colonial urbanism 208–11,
210; street naming policy 27, 29
Frank, Hans 120
French Revolution 10, 56

Gandhi, Mahatma 249–50
Gaza 41
gender exclusion 282–3, 285–6, 286
gender politics 13, 17
geo-address system 290–305;
closed-source code 303–4;
de-commemorative capacity 299–302;
ethical issues 304; Help and FAQ
298–9; key technologies 291; locatable
addresses 302–3; misdirection 295–8,
297; search function 295–6, **296**; smart
city-text 292–5
Geographic Positioning Systems (GPS)
204
geography 4
geopolitical transformations 17
geopolitics 15–6, 56, 146; definition 116;
Kraków 117, *118*, 119–27, *119*, **121**, **125**;
of memory 115–7; spatialization of 115
Georgia 192
geo-web studies 294
Germany: 1945–1948 58; feminist naming
culture 32; German Empire
(Kaiserreich) 57; Independent
Commission for Street Name Changes
88–9; post-socialist 87–93; reunification
72, 87; Soviet Zone of Occupation 61,
64; street naming policy 29; Third Reich
58, 63–4, 81; Weimar Republic 57
Ghana 204
globalization 204
Golan 41
governmentality 220
graphic design 311
Graz 127
Great Britain, colonial urbanism 207
Great Depression, the 283
Greenville, North Carolina, street naming
dispute 265–8

Haase, Herwig 88–9
habit 14, 16
Haifa 18, 57; Arab names purged 66, 69,
71; becomes part of Israel 60;

commemorative street names 68–9, **68**; historical background 58–9; Municipal Council elections 65–6; objectives 71; population 62; pressures and incentives 65–6; renaming 62–3, 70, 71–2; renaming patterns 68–9, **68**; Street Names Committee 66, 68–9, 71
Hammarskjöld, Dag 29
Harlem, New York 278, 282–6, *283*
Harlem Renaissance 283
Hayti 13
hegemony 18, 76, 76–7, 78–9, 87, 101, 134, 255
Helsinki 5, 25, 27, 32–8, 39
Henri IV, King of France 9
historical consciousness 170–1
historical memory 255
history: control of 56; nationalization of 173; re-invention of 136
Holocaust, the 102, 108, 109
honorific street naming, politics of 74
Hungarian Democratic Forum 108–9
Hungary, street naming revolutions 102–3

identity 261; national 116, 116–7, 155, 172; and power 127; recognition of 11–4; relational 151, 154–5; scalar configurations 265
identity-based antagonisms 152
identity markers 182n4
identity politics 124, 219–20
ideological fervor 192
imaginative geography 157–8
India 207
indigenous place names, reclaiming 314–6
information and communication technologies (ICTs) 292, 302–3
infrastructural power 1
Institut für deutsche Ostarbeit 120, 128n3
Instytut Pamiêci Narodowej 127
internet domain names 305n1
intra-national bonds 84–5
Irkutsk 197
Israel 41–2, 60, 68–9, 72, 310, 311

Jerusalem 311
Johannesburg 224, 229–30, 234

Kennedy, John F. 29
King, Hayden 314–5
King, Martin Luther, Jr. 6–7, 18; cross-racial resonance 262; toponymic commemoration 259–71

King streets 6–7, 261–2, 275; and distributive justice 263–8; Greenville street naming dispute 265–8; procedural injustices 268–71; and spatial justice 262–3; Statesboro street naming dispute 269–71; visibility 264, 269
Kraków 18, 114; Commission on Establishing the Names of Localities 120; Committee for Establishing Place Names 124; cultural artifacts 123; cultural landscape 122–3; the *Generalgouvernement* 120; geopolitics of memory 116; *Institut für deutsche Ostarbeit* 120; memory narratives 117; Nazi regime 120–4, **121**; post-socialist 126–7; propaganda 126; *Publikationsstelle Berlin-Dahlem* 120–1, 128n2, 128n4; renaming 117, *118*, 119–27, *119*, **121**, **125**, 128n4, 128n5; *Rzeczpospolitia Polska* 126; sources 119; under Soviet-led Socialism 124–6, **125**

Lagos 15–6, 208
landscape-as-text 2–3
landscape cleansing 185
landscape symbolism, politics of 4
language: politics of 311; representationalism 14–5; and street signs 10
leftover toponymies 190
legitimacy 248, 254, 254–5
Leningrad 18, 134, 145; catharsis wave (1941–1952) 137; decommemoration 139; de-Prussianization 137; de-Sovietization (1989–1990) 137, 138, 146; founding myth 132; geopolitical subtext 146; politicization of renaming 138–9; red wave (1918–1924) 135–6; renaming 132, 135–9, *139–41*, 147; temporal boundary-making 132–3; toponymic cleansing 135–9, *139–41*; Toponymic Commission 138–9; Toponymic Council 147n3; *see also* St. Petersburg
Limbé, Cameroon 212
linguistic landscape 102
linguistic orientation 311
linguistic settlement 299
linguistic textuality 15
locational discrimination 260
Lodz 30

Makani geo-address system 290–305; adoption 301; closed-source code

303–4; de-commemorative capacity
299–302; ethical issues 304; Help and
FAQ 298–9, 301; key technologies 291;
locatable addresses 302–3; misdirection
295–8, **297**; numbers 290, 291, 300–2,
304; politics of 295–9; proprietary
framework 291–2, 299, 303–4; satellites
290; search function 295–6, **296**; spatial
regime of inscriptions 291; text 291
Mandela, Nelson 221–2, 223, 234
marginalized groups 259–71
mass personal memory 89, 92
meaning, discursive production of 100
memorial arenas 293
memorial landscapes 16, 152
memorials: Mostar 179–80;
resemiotization of 161, 163
memory 12, 56–7, 178–9; autobiographical
171, 181; collective 219–20; cultural
115, 115–7; and the everyday 115;
expression of 116; geopolitics of
114–28; historical 255; manipulation of
114; mass personal 89, 92; national
collective 89, 92; places of 274, 276,
282; politics of 99, 115; public 10, 99,
134, 287; sites of 4–5, 115, 116;
transforming 234–5; usefulness 116–7
memory-building 133
memory makers 180
memory narratives 117
memory-production 276
memoryscapes, contested 117
memory-work 313–4
mental maps 292
methodology 317
metro stations 194
Mexico 41
Michels, Stanley 285–6
Military Grid Reference System (MGRS)
295
military names 30, 31
Minsk 187, 194, 197
monarchic names 30, 31, 64, 67
monuments 8–9, 152, 153, 158, 160–1,
162
Moonshi, Dr H.S. 53
Moscow 145, 187, 196–7
Mostar 18, 169; city council 177–8;
commemorative street names 175–6;
divisions 171–3; East 173; European
Union Administration 176–7, 182n7;
House of Culture 174, **175**; memorials
179–80; nostalgia 179–81; population
172, 182n2; religious territorial markers

172–3; renaming 168, 173–81, **175**, **176**;
street naming commission 177–8; West
173, 174–6, 179, 181
Mutengene, Cameroon 212–4, **213**

NAACP 269–71
name–place associations 249–50
name regime 30
naming polity 30, 38–9
naming rights 259, 268, 270, 313, 316
Napoleon 10
narrative structure 8
national collective memory 89, 92
national heroes 35
national identity 116, 116–7, 155, 172
nationalism 17, 169–70
nation-building 10–1, 33, 103, 170–1
Native Americans 13
naturalization 315
negative Other, the 154–5, 156
neoliberalism 314
Netherlands, The 233
New York 15, 19; appropriate street names
279–80; commemorative street names
282–5, *283*, 285–6, 286–7; Committee
on Parks, Recreation, and Cultural
Affairs 285; Fifth Avenue 284–5, 287;
"Freedom from Shanties" 281–2, **281**;
Harlem 278, 282–6, *283*; Harlem
Renaissance 283; the Great Depression
283; historical background 277–8;
Minetta Lane 275–6; Negro invasion
283; numbered streets 277, 280, 284–5,
286–7; proprietary names 280; renaming
275–87, *279*; street renaming bills 284,
285; symbolic erasure 279, 281–2, **281**,
282–3; Uptown Chamber of Commerce
284; West Side Association 278,
279–80, 281–2; West Side avenues
278–82, *279*, **281**, 286–7; white flight
283
New Zealand 6, 42
Niger 209
norming 299
nostalgia 179–81
numbered streets 9, 277, 280, 284–5,
286–7

official public landscape 185
Ogimaa Mikana Project 314–6
oppression 261
organic intellectuals 76
Orientalism (Said) 154
Osez le Féminisme 13

Othering and Otherness 5, 18, 102, 151, 208; definition 152; Zagreb 154–7

Paris 5, 9, 10, 13, 29, 311
parliamentary debates 27
past, the: reconstructions of 180; renaming 56–7, 59–60, 63, 72
perestroika 136, 137
performative practice 256
performative space 3; everyday life 14–6, 18
performativity 16
personality cult model 83
Petrograd 132; *see also* St. Petersburg
place: construction of 277–8, 282; and race 46–8; sense of 12; symbolic erasure 282–3
place-making 312, 317
Poland 117, 126, 127
political control 56
political cosmos 1
political semiotics 186
political society 76
politicization 26–7, 31–2, 38–9
politicking 26–7, 28, 30, 33, 34, 38
politics 25–7
polity 27
polyvocality 309–10
possession, taking 41–2
post-colonialism 11, 185, 219–20
postcolonial toponymic ambiguity 211–4, 213
post-conflict societies 12
post-socialism 185
poststructuralist perspective 101
power 311; achieving 11; cultural 260; cultural arena 11; Gramsci's analysis 75, 76–7; and identity 127; and social justice 11; of street naming 41–2, 54; symbolic 247–8, 256
power relations 92, 211, 219
Prague 28, 127
Pretoria 224, 230–3
procedural injustices 268–71
procedural justice 268
propaganda 85, 86, 126
property ownership 17–8
proprietary names 280
public commemoration 56
public forgetting 275, 293
public health 44, 52, 207, 208
public memory 10, 134
public memory-work 99
public space 10, 56, 158, 170–1

Publikationsstelle Berlin-Dahlem 120–1, 128n2, 128n4

race and racism 6–7, 12–3, 14, 17, 19, 46–8, 260
racialization 17, 219
racial (re)signification 261
Raffles, Stamford 43
recognition 248; political struggles for 314–6; politics of 3
recommemoration 10, 57, 67, 74, 78
regime change 18, 28, 42, 56, 57, 186–90; and city-text analysis 7–11; and de-commemoration 10; and renaming 134–5, 169–71; toponymic cleansing 185
regulations 30
relational identity 151, 154–5
relevant spatiality 249–50
relocation 160–1, 163
remembering, politics of 260
renaming 1, 2, 10–1, 19, 25, 56–71, 101, 311, 312–3; aftermath 69–70; Bosnia and Herzegovina 168–81, 181n1; and boundary-making 132–46; Budapest 98, 103, 106, 107–11; Cape Town 224, 227–9; captured territory 169–70; catharsis-type 137; civil 250; commemorative street names 56, 57, 68–9; conditions for 59–60, **60**; contestation and resistance 248–51, 255–6; cost 188–9, 190–1, 252, 270; counter-insubordination 251–4; decommemoration 61; Dubai 300–1, 304; Durban 218, 224, 225–7, **227**, 240–56, **244**, **247**; East Berlin 60–2, 63–5, 66–7, 71–2, 80–91, 135; effectiveness 195–7; everyday popular responses to 195–7; exclusionary dimension 275; geopolitical subtext 146; Haifa 62–3, 65–6, 68–9, **68**, 70, 71–2; Helsinki 36; implementation 192–4; indigenous names 314–6; Johannesburg 224, 229–30, 234; justification 29; Kraków 117, *118*, 119–27, *119*, **121**, **125**, 128n4, 128n5; Leningrad 135–9, *139–41*, 147; limits of 185–99, 186–90; lower-level urban actors 190–5; Moscow 145; Mostar 168, 173–81, **175**, **176**; motivations 242; museum position 108; New York 275–87; objectives 56–7, 71; opposition to 195–7; patterns 66–9; perceptions of 80; politicization 138–9; politics of 173–8, 198;

preservationist position 108; pressures and incentives 63–6; Pretoria 224, 230–3; procedural injustices 268–71; public performance 240–1; radical position 108; and regime change 134–5, 169–71; relevance 248–9; research 198–9; resistance 242; as a rite of institution 135; St. Petersburg 132, 136, 138, *139–41*, 142–5, 147n13, 187; and social justice 12–3; South Africa 218–35; Soviet Union 135–9, 138, *139–41*; symbolic acts 60; temporal boundary-making 132–3, 134–5, 135–9, *139–41*, 142–6; theoretical framework 133–5; transformation discourse 253–4; Vukovar 162–3; Zagreb 153, 154–7, 155
representationalism 14–5
reputational politics 17–8
resemiotization of memorials 161, 163
resilience 90
resistance 13, 16, 248–51, 255–6
restorative justice 219
restoring 225, 228
revolutionary change 100
right to appropriate 263, 263–8
right to participate 260, 263, 268–71
Romania 6, 187–8, 191–2, **191**, 311
Russia 135, 187; All-Union Toponymic Conferences 138; de-Sovietization 143, 146; othering 156–7; Toponymic Council 138
Russia, Imperial 32–8
Rzeczpospolitia Polska 126

sacralization, public space 158
St. Petersburg 18, 145; de-Sovietization 143; geopolitical subtext 146; metro stations 145; multi-layered identity 134–5; renaming 132, 134–5, 136, 138, *139–41*, 142–5, 147n13, 187; semiotic packaging 143; temporal boundary-making 132–3, 136, 142–5; Toponymic Commission 139, 142; un-renamed toponymies 144–5; *see also* Leningrad
saints 33
Sarajevo 168, 169, 179, 182n8
scale, social construction of 264–5
scholarship 1–2; critical turn 3–7
secondary sacralization 161, 163
segregation 202, 204, 207, 209, 218, 241, 267
self-identification 157–8
self-referencing 151

semantic displacement 8
semiosphere, the 151
semiotic markers 116
semiotic packaging 143
semiotics 2–3, 15, 186
Senegal 203
Serbia 155, 170
Serbs 155, 172
signifying system 4, 5, 116
Singapore 5, 18, 42; Asian communities 46–8, 50; Asian street naming practices 48–50, 51–3, 53–4; Chinatown 51; commemorative street names 49; counter-toponymics 50–3, 53–4; municipal street names 49–50, 52–3; naming process 44, 51; street naming policies 42–3, 43–4; street naming rationales 44–6
smart city-text 292–5
social communication 122
socialist internationalism 107
socialist street naming discourses 80
social justice 3, 11–4, 17, 18, 263, 309
socio-spatial signification 278–82, *279*, **281**
software-sorted geographies 292
South Africa 10, 16, 17, 18, 185, 207, 209; anti-white re-racialization 231–3; Cape Town 224, 227–9; challenging 225; cleansing 225, 228; Durban 218, 224, 225–7, **227**, 240–56, **244**, **247**; European settlements 222–3; founding 225, 229; Geographical Names Council 223; ideological conflicts 221–2; Johannesburg 224, 229–30, 234; legacies of apartheid 218–9; legitimation 222; and Mandela 221–2, 223, 234; municipalities 225; Policy on the Naming and Renaming of Streets and Public Places, Johannesburg 229; Pretoria 224, 230–3; renaming 218–35; restorative justice 219; restoring 225, 228; Road Name Change Act 224; Soweto uprising 229; state of change 253; toponymic cleansing 233; toponymic multiracialism 218–35; toponymic politics 222–5; transformation discourse 253–4; Truth and Reconciliation Commission 234; Western Cape (Province) 228
sovereign monopoly 16, 316
Soviet Union 10, 80, 133, 134, 187; de-Prussianization 137; *perestroika* 136, 137; renaming 135–9, 138, *139–41*

space: automatic production of 292; commodification of 292; contested 114; racial (re)signification 261; taming 11

Spain 5

spatial codification: auto-referencing 157–8; monuments and street names 153; and othering 154–7; unresolved meanings 159–62; values 151; Zagreb 150–63

spatial cognition 222

spatial injustices: commemorative street names 259–71; mechanism of 260

spatial inscription practices 291

spatial justice 17, 260, 262–3, 263–4

spatial narratives 5

spatial ordering 9

spatial politics 114

speech acts 15, 18

stability principle 28

Stalin, Josef 61–2, 80, 83, 106, 136

Statesboro, Georgia, street naming dispute 269–71

state, the 26

Steinheil, Fabian 33

Stockholm 9

street naming 1, 114, 198; appropriate 279–80; Asian practices 48–50, 51–3, 53–4; colonial policies 42–3, 43–4; colonial process 44, 51; colonial rationales 44–6; counter-toponymics 50–3; critical turn 2–3, 3–7; descriptive 49; discursive elements 98; East Berlin policy 29, 63–4, 80–91; economic activities 49; Gramscian approach 75, 76–80; Helsinki 32–8, 39; naming polity 30, 38–9; normative criteria 28; policy 27, 27–8, 29, 32–8; politicization 27, 31–2, 38–9; politicking 28–9, 30, 33, 34, 38; politics of 3, 5, 11, 12, 25–39, 74–5, 222–5, 310–2; polyvocality 309; power of 41–2, 54; procedural injustices 268–71; proprietary names 280; and race 46–8; regulations 30; rhetoric 38–9; right to appropriate 263–8; right to participate 260, 268–71; socialist discourses 80; spatial injustices 259–71; and spatial justice 262–3, 263–4; Sub-Saharan Africa 205; Turin 77–80; unofficial 27–8

street naming revolutions 98, 102–3

streetscapes 2, 3, 114, 116

street signs 9, 127, 134, 170, 188–9, 190–3, **191**, **193**, **194**, 240–1, 250, 256, 310–2: East Berlin 311; language 10;

Sub-Saharan Africa 204, 210, **210**, 211, 212; West Berlin 311

street, the 1

Sub-Saharan Africa 41, 202–15; Cameroon 203, 211–4, **213**; colonial authorities 204–5; colonial roots 202; decolonization 211; postcolonial authorities 204; postcolonial toponymic ambiguity 211–4, 213; postcolonial urban mapping 215n2; Senegal 203; street naming policy 205; street signs 204, 210, **210**, 211, 212; toponymic ambiguity 205; toponymic inscription, Anglophone 207–8, 214–5; toponymic inscription, Francophone 208–11, **210**, 214–5; toponymic-inscription problem 202–3, 212–4, **213**; townships 207–8; urban vocabularies 203–6, **206**; Zimbabwe 206–7

surveillance 52

Sweden 9

symbolic accretion 8

symbolic acts 60

symbolic capital 16, 17–8, 19, 62, 274–87; accumulation 284–5; appropriate street names 280; definition 274–5; New York 277–87

symbolic erasure 275, 276, 279, 281–2, **281**, 282–3, 286

symbolic infrastructure 1

symbolic power 247–8, 256

symbolic prestige 242, 245–8

symbolic reparation 10, 234

symbolic resistance 250–1, 255–6, 274–5

symbolic retribution 10, 185, 234

symbolic subordination 250

Tbilisi 192

Tel Aviv 310, 311

temporal boundary-making 132–46; Leningrad 132–3, 135–9, *139–41*; practice 133; and renaming 132–3, 134–5, 135–9, *139–41*, 142–6; St. Petersburg 132–3, 136, 142–5; theoretical framework 133–5

territorial claims 12

textual approaches 133–4

themantic displacement 195

theoretical pluralism 317

Timişoara 191–2, **191**

toponymic ambiguity, Sub-Saharan Africa 202–15

toponymic cleansing 185–99, 233; Leningrad 135–9, *139–41*; limits of 186, 186–90

toponymic continuity 185–99; and
    everyday popular responses 195–7, 199;
    limits of political power 187–90;
    lower-level urban actors 190–5, 198;
    post-socialism 186–99
toponymic inscription: Anglophone
    Sub-Saharan Africa 207–8, 214–5;
    Francophone Sub-Saharan Africa
    208–11, **210**, 214–5
toponymic multiracialism 218–35; Cape
    Town 224, 227–9; Durban 224, 225–7,
    227; ideological conflicts 221–2;
    Johannesburg 224, 229–30, 234;
    Pretoria 224, 230–3
toponymic rescaling 265
toponymic silencing 133
toponymic studies: critical turn 2, 3–7;
    traditional approach 3–4
Toronto 314–6
townships 207–8
transformation discourse 253–4
transient regimes 171
Turin 75, 77, 77–80
typography 9

United States of America 4; Black Lives
    Matter movement 312; Civil Rights
    Movement 260, 261, 262; Greenville
    street naming dispute 265–8; heritage
    protection laws 14; King street presence
    260, 261–71; numbers as street names 9;
    renaming 12–3; Revolutionary War 277;
    social justice 12, 14, 18; Statesboro
    street naming dispute 269–71
unresolved meanings 152, 159–62
urban management 202, 203, 215n1
urban space: access to 264;
    commodification of 303–4; digitally
    codified 290; digitization 298; gendering
    3; naturalization of 315; social
    production of 2, 220
urban toponymic activism 314–6
urban vocabularies, Sub-Saharan Africa
    203–6, **206**
Ustashi movement 159–60

values, spatial codification 151
vandalism 240–1, 250
victimization 174
Vietnam War 107
violence, legacies of 312–4, 315
voting 26
Vukovar 162–3

Washington Agreement 168–9
West Bank 41
West Berlin 37, 70–1, 72; street naming
    policy 27, 29; street signs 311; *see also*
    Berlin
white flight 283
white privilege 260
white supremacy 17
women: African Americans 285–6;
    symbolic erasure 282–3
World Bank 214
world-making 19
World War II 102, 105, 110, 120–4, **121**,
    159–60

Yaoundé, Cameroon 214
Yugoslavia 155–6, 168, 170, 174, 177,
    180

Zagreb 18; auto-referencing 157–8;
    geopolitical code 154–5; imaginative
    geography 157–8; monuments and
    street names 153, 158, 160–1, 162;
    Othering 154–7; Othering the Balkans
    and Russia 156–7; Othering the
    international communist movement
    157; Othering the Serbs and Serbia 155;
    Othering Yugoslavia 155–6; relocations
    160–1, 163; renaming 153, 154–7, 155;
    resemiotization of memorials 161, 163;
    secondary sacralization 161, 163;
    sources 153; spatial codification
    150–63; status 153; unresolved
    meanings 159–62; World War II
    heritage 159–60
Zanzibar 5, 208
Zimbabwe 206–7